PRICE

an intermediate text

THEORY

DAVID D. FRIEDMAN

University of Chicago

second edition

HC65BA
PUBLISHED BY
SOUTH-WESTERN PUBLISHING CO.
CINCINNATI, OH   WEST CHICAGO, IL   DALLAS, TX   LIVERMORE, CA

by SOUTH-WESTERN PUBLISHING CO.
Cincinnati, Ohio

Library of Congress Cataloging-in-Publication Data

Friedman, David D.
   Price theory: an intermediate text / David D. Friedman. — 2nd ed.
     p. cm.
   Includes bibliographies and index.
   ISBN 0-538-80564-1
   1. Microeconomics. 2. Prices. I. Title.
HB172.F75 1990
338.5′2—dc20
                                              88-93052
                                                     CIP

1 2 3 4 5 6 7 8 9 0 D 8 7 6 5 4 3 2 1 0 9
Printed in the United States of America

FOREWORD

Modern economics is above all a way of thinking about social behavior. When a person decides to engage in any activity, the economist instinctively looks for benefits to that person that exceed his costs; conversely, if he decides not to engage in an activity, the economist looks for costs that exceed the benefits. Moreover, if two persons voluntarily engage in a transaction or trade, the economist looks for gains to *both* participants, not gains to one and losses to the other.

Recent decades have seen growing confidence that this economic way of thinking provides important insights into human behavior under quite different economic systems and institutions. It has been used to help understand primitive societies studied by anthropologists as well as advanced economies of the modern day; capitalist countries like the United States as well as Communist countries like China and Cuba; personal interactions that do not use explicit markets, like marriage and gift giving, as well as transactions in organized markets, like the stock market; decisions to engage in crime as well as decisions to study economics; and decisions by college graduates with high IQ's as well as decisions by illiterates with low IQ's.

Although the range of behavior analyzed with the economic way of thinking has been greatly extended during the past several decades, textbooks on economic principles generally have taken a much narrower view of the scope of economics. This is not surprising since recent developments in a scientific field usually do not find their way into textbooks for many years. Fortunately, several economics texts in recent years have begun to take a broader view, and this text by David Friedman does so in the most thoroughgoing and satisfactory manner of any that I have seen. Every chapter shows evidence of a skilled and imaginative economist applying his tools to the world around him. Perhaps I can whet the reader's appetite for the book with a few examples culled from different chapters.

Plea bargaining occurs when prosecutors agree to lighter sentences in return for guilty pleas by defendants. Plea bargaining has been frequently criticized for permitting guilty criminals to escape with excessively light sentences, but Friedman shows in Chapter 18 that the system of plea bargaining indirectly may raise the punishments to defendants who bar-gain! Plea bargaining avoids costly trials for some defendants and thereby enables prosecutors to spend more of their limited budgets on trials of defendants without plea bargains. By spending more on each trial, the prosecutor raises the likelihood of getting a conviction with a stiffer sentence.

The crucial point is that these stiffer sentences also *raise* the sentences of defendants who plea bargain. Prosecutors can now refuse to plea bargain unless a defendant accepts a relatively stiff sentence because defendants who refuse to bargain can expect a stiffer sentence. This is a good example of the so-called "Prisoner's Dilemma," or of the conflict between individual and group incentives. By bargaining *alone*, defendants are forced to accept less favorable terms than they could extract by bargaining *together*.

Since radio and television programs are costly to produce but are "free" to viewers, each station must find indirect ways to cover the cost of producing programs. The most common way is to advertise products of companies that pay for commercials. A less common way, mainly used by "educational" radio and television, is to ask viewers for contributions. However, efforts to raise contributions encounter the same conflict between group and individual incentives found in plea bargaining. Viewers could get better programming by contributing together, but each one separately has an incentive to view without contributing.

Religious programming can provide proper incentives by claiming that contributions to support a religion or preacher improve the standing of the contributor with his God. Therefore, each viewer cannot free-ride by shifting the burden of support to others because he then fails in his duty to God, who is aware of the behavior of everyone. Friedman advances this argument to explain why religious preaching on radio appears to be more common than religious preaching through written media.

As a final example, consider tariffs, quotas, and other protection against imports. Almost 200 years ago, Alexander Hamilton argued that "infant" industries in the United States should be protected by tariffs so that the growth of these industries would not be stifled by competition from imports. Yet the evidence is clear that import protection is mainly given not to growing infant industries but to what Friedman calls "senile" industries, like steel and shoes (see Chapter 19). He shows how competition for political influence among special interest groups provides political support for tariffs and other trade restrictions that mainly benefit old declining industries. This is an excellent example of how the economic way of thinking is used to explain political behavior.

Economic theory is a powerful engine that permits a more rapid and deeper application of the economic way of thinking to behavior. Concepts like utility, cost, production functions, investment, equilibrium, and strategic behavior are useful in building this engine. Since the economic way of thinking is quite foreign to ordinary ways of thinking about behavior, command of economic theory requires dedication and systematic study to master its logic and structure. These are developed in the first 16 chapters of this text, although applications are also liberally sprinkled throughout these chapters. Friedman relies on geometry and verbal reasoning and generally avoids mathematics. Nevertheless, the discussion is sufficiently rigorous and also considers various weaknesses as well as strengths of economic theory.

I highly recommend this text to students and others with curiosity about our economic and social world. David Friedman obviously enjoys his work, for his enthusiasm is manifest on practically every page. You may find his enthusiasm contagious and also have fun as you use your new way of thinking to understand, and perhaps improve, the world around you.

Gary S. Becker
University Professor of Economics and Sociology
University of Chicago

PREFACE

Many students have been persuaded, by their experience in high school and college, that taking a course consists of memorizing a set of conclusions. Reading a textbook then becomes an exercise in creative highlighting, designed to extract from five hundred pages of verbiage the thirty or forty pages containing the answers to the questions that will appear on the final exam.

Such a collection of answers is about as easy to remember as a collection of random numbers, and not much more useful. Students who take such courses generally forget shortly after the final most of what they have learned.

This book is based on a different idea of how economics (and most other things) should be taught—the idea that since answers are hard to remember and easy to look up, one should instead concentrate on learning ways of thinking. The book has two central purposes. The first is to introduce you to what one of my competitors has called "the economic way of thinking." Economists—even economists with widely differing political views—have in common an approach to understanding human behavior that seems natural to them and very odd indeed to most non-economists. This book is designed to introduce you to that way of thinking, in the hope that many of you will find it interesting and at least some may find it irresistible. I am in that sense a missionary.

The second central purpose of the book is to teach you the analytical core of economics as it now exists. One of the features of economics that distinguishes it from most of the other social sciences is that it has such a core—a set of well worked out and closely related ideas that underlie almost everything done in the field. That core is price theory—the analysis of why things cost what they do and of how prices function to coordinate economic activity.

This book is organized into six sections. Section I is a general introduction to what economics is and why it is worth learning. Section II shows how the prices at which goods and services are sold and the quantities produced and consumed are determined in a simple economy. It is the most important part of the book. If you completely understand it you will know economics, in the same sense that a French six-year-old knows French. You may still be missing many details and complications, but you will understand the essential logic of how an economy works. Section III adds the most important of the complications omitted in the previous section, including firms, monopoly, change, and uncertainty. Section IV introduces the idea of economic efficiency and shows how it can be used to evaluate the outcome of different economic arrangements. Section V presents a number of real-world applications of the ideas of the previous sections, some of them conventional, most not. The final chapter of the book discusses what economics is good for and what economists do.

Some chapters have special sections at the end identified by a colored bar running down the margin. These sections contain material that, while interesting in itself and perhaps useful in later courses, is not essential to understanding the rest of the text. They are intended for students who find the ideas of the chapter sufficiently interesting to want to pursue them further.

One thing I hope you will pay attention to as you go through the book is the importance of understanding things rather than merely remembering them. You should try to develop (if you have not already developed) a built-in alarm that goes off whenever I say "it follows that" and you see no particular reason why it follows or whenever I say that the answer is a particular point on a graph and you see no good reason why it should be that point instead of some other point. Whenever the alarm goes off, go back over the argument to see if you have missed something. If what I am saying still does not make sense, ask your instructor, or another student, or someone. It is all supposed to make sense, and if it does not, one of us is making a mistake. You may eventually conclude that the mistake is mine (or the typesetter's) but you should start by assuming that it is yours.

DEDICATION

This book is dedicated to

A.S.,
D.R.,
A.M.,
and M.F.,

from whom I learned economics and to

Linda,
Ruben,

and all of the others who have made the value of teaching it greater than the cost.

I would also like to thank the people who helped me write this book—the creators of the computers (LNW for the first edition, Macintosh for the second), word processors (LeScript and WriteNow), and graphics software (MacPaint and MacDraw) with which it was written. Thanks are also due to David Besanko, Jerry Fusselman, James Graves, and Lawrence Lynch for useful comments and suggestions, and special thanks to Wolfgang Mayer for assistance in finding and correcting defects above and beyond what an author may reasonably expect from a reviewer.

ADDITIONAL MATERIALS

In addition to the textbook itself, there are an instructor's manual (which provides suggested test questions) and a set of computer programs. The programs are intended for student use; they are designed to teach a few concepts that I believe can be taught better by a computer than by a book. Within the text, discussions which have corresponding programs are marked in the margins by a colored icon of a computer diskette. The programs are self-documenting. Instructors who wish to make them available to their students should request diskettes from South-Western Publishing Company, specifying Macintosh or MSDos. The diskettes are not copy protected; any student taking a course for which this book is a required text is entitled to copy and use them.

TABLE OF CONTENTS

ECONOMICS FOR

section I

PLEASURE AND PROFIT

chapter 1

WHAT IS ECONOMICS?

Economics is often thought of either as the answers to a particular set of questions (How do you prevent unemployment? Why are prices rising? How does the banking system work? Will the stock market go up?) or as the method by which such answers are found. Neither description adequately defines economics, both because there are other ways to answer such questions (astrology, for example, might give answers to some of the questions given above, although not necessarily the right answers) and because economists use economics to answer many questions that are not usually considered "economic" (What determines how many children people have? How can crime be controlled? How will governments act?).

I prefer to define economics as a particular way of understanding behavior; what are commonly thought of as economic questions are simply questions for which this way of understanding behavior has proved particularly useful in the past:

Economics is that way of understanding behavior that starts from the assumption that people have objectives and tend to choose the correct way to achieve them.

The second half of the assumption, that people tend to find the correct way to achieve their objectives, is called **rationality**. This term is somewhat deceptive, since it suggests that the way in which people find the correct way to achieve their objectives is by rational analysis—analyzing evidence, using formal logic to deduce conclusions from assumptions, and so forth. No such assumption about how people find the correct means to achieve their ends is necessary.

One can imagine a variety of other explanations for rational behavior. To take a trivial example, most of our objectives require that we eat occasionally, so as not to die of hunger (exception—if my objective is to be fertilizer). Whether or not people have deduced this fact by logical analysis, those who do not choose to eat are not around to have their behavior analyzed by economists. More generally, evolution may produce people (and other animals) who behave rationally without knowing why. The same result may be produced by a process of trial and error; if you walk to work every day, you may by experiment find the shortest route even if you do not know enough geometry to calculate it. Rationality in this sense does not necessarily require thought. In the final section of this chapter, I give two examples of things that have no minds and yet exhibit rationality.

Half of the assumption in my definition of economics was rationality; the other half was that people have objectives. In order to do much with economics, one must strengthen this part of the assumption somewhat by assuming that people have *reasonably simple objectives*; with no idea at all about what people's objectives are, it is impossible to make any prediction about what people will do. Any behavior, however peculiar, can be explained by assuming that the behavior itself was the person's objective. (Why did I stand on my head on the table while holding a burning $1,000 bill between my toes? I *wanted* to stand on my head on the table while holding a burning $1,000 bill between my toes.)

To take a more plausible example of how a somewhat complicated objective can lead to apparently irrational behavior, consider someone who has a choice between two identical products at different prices. It seems that for almost any objective we can think of, he would prefer to buy the less expensive item. If his objective is to help the poor, he can give the money he saves to the poor. If his objective is to help his children, he can spend the money he saves on them. If his objective is to live a life of pleasure and luxury, he can spend the money on Caribbean cruises and caviar.

But suppose you are taking a date to a movie. You know you are going to want a candy bar, which costs $1.00 in the theater and $0.50 in the Seven-Eleven grocery you pass on your way there. Do you stop at the store and buy a candy bar? Do you want your date to think you are a tightwad? You buy the candy bar at the theater, impressing your date (you hope) with the fact that you are the sort of person who does not have to worry about money.

One could get out of this problem by claiming that the two candy bars are not really identical; the candy bar at the theater includes the additional characteristic of impressing your date. But if you follow this line of argument, no two items are identical and the statement that you prefer the lower priced of two identical items has no content. I would prefer to say that the two items are identical enough for our purposes but that in this particular case your objective is sufficiently odd so that our prediction (based on the assumption of reasonably simple objectives) turns out to be wrong.

WHY ECONOMICS MIGHT WORK

Economics is based on the assumption that people have reasonably simple objectives and choose the correct means to achieve them. Both halves of the assumption are false; people sometimes have very complicated objectives and they sometimes make mistakes. Why then is the assumption useful?

Suppose we know someone's objective and also know that half the time that person correctly figures out how to achieve it and half the time acts at random. Since there is generally only one right way of doing things (or perhaps a few) but very many wrong ways, the "rational" behavior can be predicted but the "irrational" behavior cannot. If we predict this person's behavior on the assumption that he is rational, we will be right half the time. If we assume he is irrational, we will almost never be right, since we still have to guess *which* irrational thing he will do. We are better off assuming he is rational and recognizing that we will sometimes be wrong. To put the argument more generally, the tendency to be rational is the consistent (and hence predictable) element in human behavior. The only alternative to assuming rationality (other than giving up and concluding that human behavior cannot be understood and predicted) would be a *theory* of irrational behavior—a theory that told us not only that someone would not always do the rational thing but also *which particular irrational thing* he would do. So far as I know, no satisfactory theory of that sort exists.

There are a number of reasons why the assumption of rationality may work better than one would at first think. One is that we are often concerned not with the behavior of a single individual but with the aggregate effect of the behavior of many people. Insofar as the irrational part of their behavior is random, its effects are likely to average out in the aggregate.

Suppose, for example, that the rational thing to do is to buy more hamburger the lower its price. People actually decide how much to buy by first making the rational decision then flipping a coin. If the coin comes up heads, they buy a pound more than they were planning to; if it comes up tails, they buy a pound less. The behavior of each individual will be rather unpredictable, but the total demand for hamburger will be almost exactly the same as without the coin flipping, since on average about half the coins will come up heads and half tails.

A second reason why the assumption works better than one might expect is that we are often dealing not with a random set of people but with people who have been selected for the particular role they are playing. Consider the heads of companies. If you selected people at random for the job, the assumption that they want to maximize the company's profits and know how to do so would not be a very plausible one. But people who do not want to maximize profits, or do not know how to, are unlikely to be chosen for the job; if they are, they are unlikely to keep it; if they do, their companies are likely to become increasingly unimportant in the economy, until eventually the companies go out of business. So the simple assumption of profit maximization plus rationality turns out to be a good way to predict how firms will behave.

A similar argument applies to the stock market. We may reasonably expect that the average investment is made by someone with an accurate idea of what companies are worth—even though the average American, and even the average investor, may be poorly informed about such things. Investors who consistently bet wrong on the stock market soon have very little to bet with. Investors who consistently bet right have an increasing amount of their own money to risk—and often other people's money as well. Hence the well-informed investors have an influence on the market out of proportion to their numbers as a fraction of the population. If we analyze the workings of the market on the assumption that all investors are well informed, we may come up with fairly accurate predictions in spite of the inaccuracy of the assumption. In this as in all other cases, the ultimate test of the method is whether its predictions turn out to describe reality correctly. Whether something is an economic question is not something we know in advance. It is something we discover by trying to use economics to answer it.

SOME SIMPLE EXAMPLES OF ECONOMIC THINKING

So far, I have talked of economics in the abstract; it is now time for some concrete examples. I have chosen examples involving issues not usually considered economic in order to show that economics is not a particular set of questions to be answered but a particular way of answering questions. I will begin with two very simple examples and then go on to some slightly more complicated ones.

You are laying out a college campus as a rectangular pattern of concrete sidewalks with grass between them. You know that one of the objectives of many people, including many students, is to get where they are going with as little effort as possible; you suspect most of them realize that a straight line is the shortest distance between two points. You would be well advised to take precautions against students cutting across the lawn. Possible precautions would be constructing fences or diagonal walkways, adding tough ground cover, or replacing the grass with cement and painting it green.

One point to note. It may be that everyone will be better off if no one cuts across the lawn (assuming the students like to look at green lawns without brown paths across them). Rationality is an assumption about individual behavior, not group behavior. The question of under what circumstances individual rationality does or does not lead to the best results for the group is one of the most interesting questions economics investigates. Even if a student is in favor of green grass, he may correctly argue that his decision to cut across provides more benefit (time saved) than cost (slight damage to the grass) *to him*. The fact that his decision provides additional costs, but no additional benefits, to other people who also dislike having the grass damaged is irrelevant unless making those other people happy happens to be one of his objectives. The total costs of his action may be greater than the total benefits; but as long as the costs to him are less than the benefits to him, he takes the action. This point will be examined at much greater length in Chapter 18, when we discuss public goods and externalities.

A second simple example of economic thinking is Friedman's Law for Finding Men's Washrooms—"Men's rooms are adjacent, in one of the three dimensions, to ladies' rooms." One of the builder's objectives is to minimize construction costs; it costs more to build two small plumbing stacks (the set of pipes needed for a washroom) than one big one. So it is cheaper to put washrooms close to each other in order to get them on the same stack. That does not imply that two men's rooms on the same floor will be next to each other (although men's rooms on different floors are usually in the same position, making them adjacent vertically). Putting them next to each other reduces the cost, but separating them gets them close to more users. But there is no advantage to having men's and ladies' rooms far apart, since they are used by different people, so they are almost always put on the same stack. The law does not hold for buildings constructed on government contracts at cost plus 10 percent.

As a third example, consider someone making two decisions—what car to buy and what politician to vote for. In either case, the person can improve his decision (make it more likely that he acts in his own interest) by investing time and effort in studying the alternatives. In the case of the car, his decision determines with certainty which car he gets. In the case of the politician, his decision (whom to vote for) changes by one ten-millionth the probability that the candidate he votes for will win. If the candidate would be elected without his vote, he is wasting his time; if the candidate would lose even with his vote, he is also wasting his time. He will rationally choose to invest much more time in the decision of which car to buy—the payoff to him is enormously greater. We expect voting to be characterized by **rational ignorance**; it is rational to be ignorant when the information costs more than it is worth.

This is much less of a problem for a concentrated interest than for a dispersed one. If you, or your company, receives almost all of the benefit from some proposed law, you may well be willing to invest enough resources in supporting that law (and the politician who wrote it) to have a significant effect on the probability that the law will pass. If the cost of the law is spread among many people, no one of them will find it in his interest to discover what is being done to him and oppose it. Some of the implications of that will be seen in Chapter 19, where we explore the economics of politics.

In the course of this example, I have subtly changed my definition of rationality. Before, it meant making the right decision about *what to do*—voting for the right politician, for example. Now it means making the right decision about *how to decide what to do*—collecting information on whom to vote for only if the information is worth more than the cost of collecting it. For many purposes, the first definition is sufficient. The second is necessary where an essential part of the problem is the cost of getting and using information.

A final, and interesting, example is the problem of winning a battle. In modern warfare, many soldiers do not fire their guns in battle, and many of those who fire do not aim. This is not irrational behavior—on the contrary. In many situations, the soldier correctly believes that nothing he can do is very likely to determine who wins the battle; if he shoots, especially if he takes time to aim, he is more likely to get shot himself. The general and the soldier have two objectives in common. Both want their army to win. Both also want the soldier to survive the battle. But the relative importance of the second objective is much greater for the soldier than for the general. Hence the soldier rationally does not do what the general rationally wants him to do.

Interestingly enough, studies of U.S. soldiers in World War II revealed that the soldier most likely to shoot was the member of a squad who was carrying the Browning Automatic Rifle. He was in a situation analogous to that of the concentrated interest; since his weapon was much more powerful than an ordinary rifle (an automatic rifle, like a machine gun, keeps firing as long as you keep the trigger pulled), his actions were much more likely to determine who won—and hence whether he got killed—than the actions of an ordinary rifleman.

The problem is not limited to modern war. The old form of the problem (which still exists in modern armies) is the decision whether to stand and fight or to run away. If you all stand, you will probably win the battle. If everyone else stands and you run, your side may still win the battle and you are less likely to get killed (unless your own side notices what you did and shoots you) than if you fought. If everyone runs, you lose the battle and are quite likely to be killed—but less likely the sooner you start running.

One proverbial solution to this problem is to burn your bridges behind you. You march your army over a bridge, line up on the far side of the river, and burn the bridge. You then point out to your soldiers that if your side loses the battle you will all be killed, so there is no point in running away. Since your troops do not run and the enemy troops (hopefully) do, you win the battle. Of course, if you lose the battle, a lot more people get killed than if you had not burned the bridge.

We all learn in high school history how, during the Revolutionary War, the foolish British dressed their troops in bright scarlet uniforms and marched them around in neat geometric formations, providing easy targets for the heroic Americans. My own guess is that the British knew what they were doing. It was, after all, the same British Army that less than 40 years later defeated the greatest general of the age at Waterloo. I suspect the mistake in the high school history texts is not realizing that what the British were worried about was controlling their own troops. Neat geometric formations make it hard for a soldier to advance to the rear unobtrusively; bright uniforms make it hard for soldiers to hide after their army has been defeated, which lowers the benefit of running away.

The problem of the conflict of interest between the soldier as an individual and the soldiers as a group is nicely illustrated by the story of the battle of Clontarf, as given in *Njal Saga*. Clontarf was an eleventh century battle between an Irish army on one side and a mixed Irish-Viking army on the other side. The Vikings were led by Sigurd, the Jarl of the Orkney Islands. Sigurd had a battle flag, a raven banner, of which it was said that as long as the flag flew, his army would always go forward, but whoever carried the flag would die.

Sigurd's army was advancing; two men had been killed carrying the banner. The Jarl told a third man to take the banner; the third man refused. After trying unsuccessfully to find someone else to do it, Sigurd remarked, "It is fitting the beggar should bear the bag," cut the banner off the staff, tied it around his own waist, and led the army forward. He was killed and his army defeated. The story illustrates nicely the essential conflict of interest in an army, and the way in which individually rational behavior can prevent victory. If one or two more men had been willing to carry the banner, Sigurd's army might have won the battle—but the banner carriers would not have survived to benefit from the victory.

And you thought economics was about stocks and bonds and the unemployment rate.

PUZZLE

You are a hero with a broken sword (Conan, Boromir, or your favorite Dungeons and Dragons character) being chased by a troop of bad guys (bandits, orcs, . . .). Fortunately you are on a horse and they are not. Unfortunately your horse is tired and they will eventually run you down. Fortunately you have a bow. Unfortunately you have only ten arrows. Fortunately, being a hero, you never miss. Unfortunately there are 40 bad guys. The bad guys are strung out behind you, as shown.

Problem: Use economics to get away.

Note: You cannot talk to the bad guys. They are willing to take a substantial chance of being killed in order to get you—after all, they know you are a hero and are still coming. They know approximately how many arrows you have.

Section I   Economics for Pleasure and Profit

SOME HARDER EXAMPLES— ECONOMIC EQUILIBRIA

So far, the examples of economic reasoning have not involved any real interaction among the rational acts of different people. We dealt either with a single rational individual—the architect deciding where in the building to put washrooms—or with a group of rational individuals all doing more or less the same thing. Very little in economics is this simple. Before we start developing the framework of price theory in the next chapter, you may find it of interest to think through some more difficult examples of economic reasoning, examples in which the outcome is an equilibrium produced by the interaction of a number of rational individuals.

I will use economics to analyze two familiar situations (supermarket lines and crowded expressways), showing how economics can produce useful and nonobvious results and how the argument can be expanded to deal with successively higher levels of complexity. The logical patterns that appear in these examples reappear again and again in economic analysis. Once you clearly understand when and why supermarket lines are all the same length and lanes in the expressway equally fast, and why and under what circumstances they are not, you will have added to your mental tool kit one of the most useful concepts in economics.

Supermarket Lines

You are standing in a supermarket at the far end of a row of checkout counters with your arms full of groceries. The line at your end blocks your view of the other lines; you know your line is long, but you do not know if the others are any shorter. Should you stagger from line to line looking for the shortest line, or should you get in the nearest one?

The first and simplest answer is that all the lines will be about the same length, so you should get into the one next to you; it is not worth the cost of searching for a shorter one. Why?

Consider any two adjacent lines in Figure 1-1, say Lines 4 and 5. Some shoppers will approach the checkout area not from one end, as you did, but from the aisle that lies between those two lines. Since those shoppers can easily see both lines, they will go to whichever one appears shorter. By doing so, they will lengthen that line and shorten the other; the process continues until both lines are the same length. The same argument holds for every other pair of adjacent lines, so all lines will be the same length. It is not worth it for you to make a costly search for the shortest line.

There are a number of implicit assumptions in this argument. When these assumptions are false the argument may break down. Suppose, for

Figure 1-1

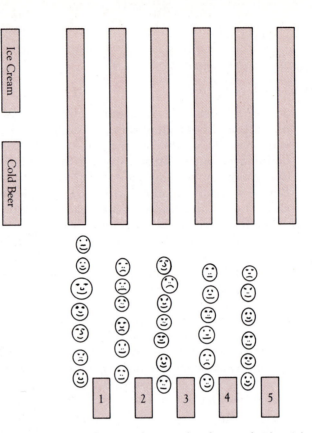

Supermarket, viewed from above. Lines tend to be equal; Line 1 is a special case because many customers get ice cream and cold beer last.

example, that you are at the far end of the row of checkout counters because that is where the ice cream freezer and the refrigerator with the cold beer are located. Many other customers also choose to get these things last and so enter the checkout area from that end. Even if everyone who comes in between Lines 1 and 2 goes to Line 2, there are not enough such people to make Line 2 as long as Line 1. If everyone understands the argument of the previous paragraph and acts accordingly, Line 1 will be longer than Line 2 (and probably much longer than the other lines), and the conclusion of the argument will be wrong.

Imagine that you program a computer to assign customers to lines in a way that equalizes the length of the two lines, as described above, and tell it that 10 people per minute are entering the checkout area at one end (where they can only see Line 1) and 6 per minute are entering between the two lines. The computer informs you that of the 6 customers coming in between the two lines, 8 must go to Line 2 and −2 to Line 1. Since 10 customers are going to Line 1 from the end, the total number going to Line 1 is 10 plus −2, which equals 8—the number going to Line 2. The computer, having solved the problem you gave it, sits there with a satisfied expression on its screen.

You then reprogram it, pointing out that fewer than zero customers cannot go anywhere. Mathematically speaking, you are asking the computer to solve the problem subject to the condition that a certain number (the number of customers coming in between the two lines and going to one of them) cannot be negative. The computer replies that in that case, the best it can do is to send all 6 customers to Line 2—leaving the lines still unequal.

This sort of result is called a **corner solution** because it corresponds to the mathematical situation where the maximum of a function is not at the top of its graph but instead at a corner where the graph ends, as shown in Figure 1-2a. In such a situation, the normal conclusion (in the supermarket case, that all the lines must be the same length) may no longer hold. The corresponding result in Figure 1-2a is that the graph is not horizontal at its maximum—as it would be if the maximum were at an **interior solution**, as it is in Figure 1-2b. In economics—especially mathematical economics—the usual role of corner solutions is to provide annoying exceptions to general theorems.

Are there other situations in which the conclusion—that all lines will be the same length—does not hold? Yes.

So far, I have assumed that for people coming in between two lines, it is costless to see which line is shorter. This is not always true. The relevant length, after all, is not in space but in time; you would rather enter a line of 10 customers with only a few items each than a line of 8 customers with full carts. Estimating which line is shorter requires a

Figure 1-2

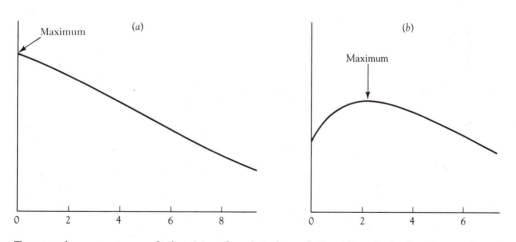

Two maxima—a corner solution (*a*) and an interior solution (*b*). At the interior maximum, the slope of the curve is zero; at the corner maximum, it need not be.

certain amount of mental effort. If the system works so well that all lines are exactly the same length (in time), then it will never be worth that effort. Hence no one will make it; hence there will be nothing keeping the lines the same length. In equilibrium the length of lines must differ by just enough to repay (on average) the effort of figuring out which line is shorter. If it differed by more than that, everyone would look for the shortest line, making all lines the same length (assuming no corner solution). If it differed by less than that, nobody would.

It may have occurred to you that I am assuming all customers have the same ability to estimate how long a line will take. Suppose a few customers know that the checker on Line 3 is twice as fast as the others. The experts go to Line 3. Line 3 appears to be longer than the other lines (to nonexperts, that is; allowing for the fast checker, the line is actually shorter, in time although not in length). Nonexperts avoid Line 3 until it shrinks back to the same length as the others. The experts (and some lucky nonexperts—the ones who are still in Line 3) get out twice as fast as everyone else.

Word spreads; the number of experts increases. As long as, with all the experts going through Line 3, Line 3 can still be as short (in appearance) as the other lines, the increasing number of experts does not reduce the payoff to being an expert. Every time one more expert enters the line (making it appear slightly longer than the others), one more nonexpert decides not to enter it.

Eventually the number of experts becomes large enough to crowd out all the nonexperts from that line. As the number of experts increases further, Line 3 begins to lengthen. It cannot be brought back to the same length as the other lines by the defection of nonexperts (who mistakenly believe that it is longer in waiting time as well as length) because there are none of them going to it and the experts know better. Eventually the number of experts becomes so great that Line 3 is twice as long as the other lines and takes the same length of time as they do; the gain from being an expert has now vanished.

To put the same argument in more conventional economic language, rational behavior (in the sense of "making the right decision") requires information. If that information is itself costly, rational behavior consists of acquiring information (paying information costs) only as long as the return from additional information is at least as great as the cost of getting it. If certain minimal information is required to equalize the time-length of lines, then the time-length of lines must be sufficiently unequal so that the saving from knowing which line is shorter just pays the cost of acquiring that information. That principle applies to both the cost of looking at lines to see which is shortest and the cost of studying checkers to learn which ones are faster. The initial argument was given in an approximation in which information was costless; such an approximation greatly simplifies many economic arguments but should be used with care.

　　　　　　　　Section I　Economics for Pleasure and Profit

There is at least one more hidden assumption in the argument as given. I have assumed that everyone in the grocery store wants to get out as quickly as possible. Suppose the grocery store (Westwood Singles Market) is actually the local social center; people come to stand in long lines gossiping with and about their friends and trying to make new ones. Since they do not want to get out as fast as possible, they do not try to go to the shortest line; so the whole argument breaks down.

Rush Hour Blues

A similar analysis can be applied to lanes on the freeway. When you are driving on a crowded highway, it always seems that some other lane is going faster than yours; the obvious strategy is to switch to the faster lane. If you actually try to follow such a strategy, however, you discover to your amazement that a few minutes after you switch lanes, the battered blue pickup that was behind you in the lane you left is now in front of you.

To understand why it is so difficult to follow a successful strategy of lane changing, consider that by moving into a lane you slow it down. If there is a faster lane then people will move into it, equalizing its speed with that of the other lanes, just as people moving into a short line lengthen it. So a lane remains fast only as long as drivers do not realize it is.

Here again, a more sophisticated analysis would allow for the costs (in frayed nerves and dented fenders) of continual lane changes. On average, if everyone is rational, there must be a small gain in speed from changing lanes—if there were not, nobody would do it and the mechanism described above would not work. The payoff must equal the cost for the *marginal* lane changer—the least well qualified of those following the lane-changing strategy. If the payoff were less than that, he would not be a lane changer; if it were more, someone else would. In principle, if you knew how much a strategy of lane changing cost each driver (in dents and nerves—less for those with strong nerves and old cars) and how many lane changers it took to reduce the benefit from lane changing by any given amount, you could figure out who would be the marginal lane changer and how much the gain from lane changing would be. By the end of the course, you should see how to do this. If you see it now, you are already an economist—whether or not you have studied economics.

Even More Important Applications to Think About

Doctors make a lot of money. Doctors also spend many years as medical students and interns. The two facts are not unrelated. Different wages in different professions are set by a process similar to that described above. If one profession is, on net, more attractive than another (taking account of wages, risks, costs of learning the profession, and so on), more people go into the more attractive profession and by so doing drive down the wages. All professions are in some sense equally attractive—to the marginal person. In deciding what profession you want to enter, it is not enough to ask what profession pays the highest wage. Not only are there other factors, there is also reason to expect that the other factors will be worst where the wage is best. What you should ask instead is what profession you are particularly suited for in comparison to other people making similar choices. This is like deciding whether to follow a lane-switching strategy by considering how old your car is compared to others, or deciding whether to look for a shorter line in the grocery store according to how much you are carrying.

A similar argument applies to the stock market. It is often said that if a company is doing very well, you should buy its stock. But if everyone else knows that the company is doing well, then the price of its stock already reflects that information. If buying it were really such a good deal, who would sell? The company you should buy stock in is one that you know is doing better than most other investors think it is—even if in some absolute sense it is not doing very well.

A friend of mine has been investing successfully for several years by following almost the opposite of the conventional wisdom. He looks for companies that are doing very badly and calculates how much their assets would be worth if they went out of business. Occasionally he finds one whose assets are worth more than its stock. He buys stock in such companies, figuring that if they do well their stock will go up and if they do badly they will go out of business, sell off their assets—and the stock will again go up.

If all of this is obvious to you the first time you read it (or even the second), then in your choice of careers you should give serious consideration to becoming an economist.

NEGATIVE FEEDBACK

Several of the situations described in this chapter involved a principle called **negative feedback**. A familiar example of negative feedback is driving a car. If the car is going to the right of where you want it, you turn the wheel a little to the left; if it is going to the left of where you want, you turn it a little to the right. This is called feedback because an error in the direction you are going "feeds back" into the mechanism that controls your direction (through you to the steering wheel). It is negative feedback because an error in one direction (right) causes a correction in the other direction (left). An example of positive feedback is the shriek when the amplifier attached to a microphone is turned up too high. A small noise comes into the mike, is amplified by the amplifier, comes out of the speaker, and feeds back into the mike. If the amplification is high enough, the noise becomes louder each time around, eventually overloading the system.

In the supermarket line example, the lines are kept at about the same length by negative feedback: If a line gets too long compared to other lines, people stop going to it, which makes it get shorter. Similarly, when a lane on the expressway speeds up, cars move into it, slowing it down. In each case, what we are mostly interested in are not the details of the feedback process but rather the nature of the stable equilibrium—the situation such that deviations from it cause correcting feedback.

RATIONALITY WITHOUT MIND

In defending the assumption of rationality, I pointed out that it is not the same as the assumption that people reason logically. Logical reasoning is not the only, or even the most common, way of getting a correct answer. I will demonstrate this with two extreme examples—cases in which we observe rationality in something that cannot reason, since it has no mind to reason with. In the first case, I will show how a mindless object—a collection of matchboxes filled with marbles—can learn to play a game rationally. In the second, I will show how the rational pursuit of objectives by genes—mindless chains of atoms inside your cells—explains a striking fact about the real world, something so fundamental that it never occurs to most of us to find it surprising.

Computers That Learn

Suppose you want to build a computer to play some simple game, such as tic-tac-toe. One way is to build in the correct move for every situation. Another, and in some ways more interesting, approach is to let the computer teach itself how to play. Such a learning computer starts out moving randomly. Each time a game ends, the computer is told whether it won or lost and adjusts its strategy accordingly, lowering the probability of moves that led to losses and increasing the probability of moves that led to wins. After enough games, the computer may become a fairly good player.

The computer does not think. Its "mind" is simply a device that identifies the present situation of the game, chooses a move by some random mechanism, and later adjusts the probabilities according to whether it won or lost. A simple version consists of a bunch of matchboxes filled with black and white marbles, laid out on a diagram of the game. Moves are chosen by picking a marble at random, with the color of the marble determining the move. The mix of marbles in each matchbox is adjusted at the end of the game to make moves that led to a win more likely and moves that led to a loss less likely. A matchbox computer, or its more sophisticated electronic descendants, does not think, yet it is rational. Its objective is to win the game and, after it has played long enough to "learn" how to win, it tends to choose the correct way of achieving that objective. We can understand and predict its behavior in the same way that we understand and predict the behavior of humans. "Rationality" is simply the ability to get the right answer; it may be the result of many things other than rational thinking.

Economics and Evolution

There is a close historical connection between economics and evolution. Both of the discoverers of the theory of evolution (Darwin and Wallace) said they got the idea from Thomas Malthus, an economist who was also one of the originators of the so-called Ricardian Theory of Rent (named after David Ricardo, who used it but did not invent it), one of the basic building blocks of modern economics.

There is also a close similarity in the logical structure of the two fields. The economist expects people to choose correctly how to achieve their objectives but is not very much concerned with the psychological question of how they do so. The evolutionary biologist expects genes—the fundamental units of heredity that control the construction of our bodies—to construct animals whose structure and behavior are such as to maximize their reproductive success (roughly speaking, the number of their descendants), since the animals that presently exist are descended from those that were reproductively successful in the past and carry the genes that made them successful. The biologist need not be concerned very much with the detailed biochemical mechanisms by which the genes control the organism. Many of the same patterns appear in both economics and evolutionary biology; the conflict between individual interest and group interest that I mentioned earlier reappears in the conflict between the interest of the gene and the interest of the species.

A nice example is Sir R.A. Fisher's explanation of observed sex ratios. In many species, including ours, male and female offspring are produced in roughly equal numbers. There is no obvious reason why this is in the interest of the species; one male suffices to fertilize many females. Yet the

Figure 1-3

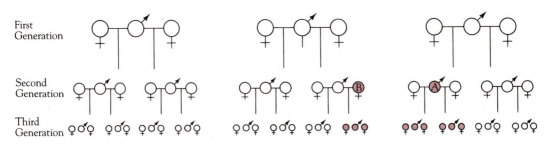

Three generations of a population with a male:female ratio of 1:2. Members of the first generation who have a son produce twice as many grandchildren as those who have a daughter, so genes for having sons increase in the population, swinging the sex ratio back toward 1:1.

Section I   Economics for Pleasure and Profit

sex ratio remains about 1:1, even in some species in which only a small fraction of the males succeed in reproducing. Why?

Fisher's answer is as follows. Imagine that two thirds of offspring are female, as shown in Figure 1-3. Consider three generations. Each individual in the third generation has both a father and a mother, so if there are twice as many females as males in the second generation, the average male must have twice as many children as the average female. This means that an individual in the first generation who produces a son will, on average, have twice as many grandchildren as one who produces a daughter. Individual A on Figure 1-3, for example, has six children, while Individual B only has three. A's parents got twice as great a return in grandchildren for producing A as B's parents did for producing B.

If there are more females than males in the population, couples who produce sons have more descendants, on average, than those who produce daughters. Since couples who produce sons have more descendants, more of the population is descended from them and has their genes—including the gene for having sons. Genes for producing male offspring increase in the population.

The initial situation, in which two thirds of the population in each generation was female, is unstable. As long as more than half of the children are female, genes for having male children spread faster than genes for having female children; so the percentage of female children falls. Similarly, if more than half the children were male, genes for having female children would have the advantage and spread. Either way, the situation must swing back towards an even sex ratio.

In making this argument, I implicitly assumed equal cost for producing male and female offspring. In a species with substantial sexual dimorphism (male and female babies of different size), the argument implies that the total weight of female offspring (weight per offspring times number of offspring) will be about the same as that for male offspring. One could add further complications by considering differences in the costs of raising male and female offspring to maturity. Yet even the simple argument is strikingly successful in explaining one of the observed regularities of the world around us by the "rational" behavior of microscopic entities. Genes cannot think—yet in this case and many others, they behave as if they had carefully calculated how to maximize their own survival in future generations.

PROBLEMS

1. In defending the rationality assumption, I argued that while people sometimes make mistakes, their correct decisions are predictable and their mistakes are not. Can you think of any alternative approaches

to understanding human behavior that claim to predict the mistakes? Discuss.

2. Give examples (other than buying candy for your date—the example discussed in the text) of apparently irrational behavior that consists of choosing the correct means to achieve an odd or complicated end.

3. In this chapter and throughout the book I treat individual preferences as givens—I neither judge whether people have the "right" preferences nor consider the possibility that something might change individual preferences.

   a. Do you think some preferences are better than others? Give examples. Discuss.

   b. Describe activities that you believe can only be understood as attempts to change people's preferences. How would you try to analyze such activities in economic terms?

4. Friedman's Law for Finding Men's Washrooms could be described as fossilized rationality—whether the architect lives or dies, his rationality remains set in concrete in the building he designed.

   a. Can you think of other examples? Discuss.

   b. Can you describe any cases where instead of deducing the shape of something from the rationality of its maker, we deduce the rationality of its maker from its shape? Discuss.

5. What devices (other than those discussed in the text) are used by generals, ancient and modern, to prevent soldiers from concluding that it is in their interest to run away, not aim, or in some other way act against the interest of the army of which they are a part?

6. The problem I have discussed exists not only in your army but in the enemy's army as well. Discuss ways in which a general might take advantage of that fact, giving real-world examples if possible.

7. In a recent conversation with one of our deans, I commented that I was rather absent-minded—I had missed two or three faculty meetings that year—and wished I could get him to make a point of reminding me when I was supposed to be somewhere. He replied that he had already solved that problem, so far as the (luncheon) meetings he was responsible for. He made sure I would not forget them by always arranging to have a scrumptious chocolate dessert.

   a. Is this an economic solution to the problem of getting me to remember things? Discuss.

   b. In what sense does or does not the success of this method indicate that I "choose" to forget to go to meetings? Discuss.

8. This chapter discusses situations where rational behavior by each individual leads to results that are undesirable for all. Give an example of such a situation in your own experience; it should not be one discussed in the chapter.

9. Many voters are rationally ignorant of the names of their congressmen. List some things you are rationally ignorant of. Explain why your ignorance is rational. Extra credit if they are things that many people would say you ought to know.

10. The analyses of supermarket lines, freeway lanes, and the stock market all had the same form. In each case, the argument could be summarized as "The outcome has a particular pattern because if it did not, it would be in the interest of people to change their behavior in a way that would push the outcome closer to fitting the pattern." Such a situation is called a stable equilibrium. Can you think of any examples not discussed in the text?

11. Analyze express lanes in supermarkets. Is the express lane always faster? If not, when is it and when is it not?

12. In the supermarket example, I started by assuming that you had your arms full of groceries. Why? How does that assumption simplify the argument?

13. The friend whose investment strategy I described is a very talented accountant. When I met him, he was in his early twenties and was making a good income teaching accounting to people who wanted to pass the CPA exam. Does this have anything to do with his investment strategy?

14. Is there any reason why my accountant friend should prefer that this book, or at least this chapter, not be published?

15. Give some examples of negative and positive feedback in your own experience.

16. Certain professions are very attractive to their members and very badly paid. Consider the stereotype of the starving artist—or a friend of mine who is working part-time as a store clerk while trying to make a career as a professional lutenist. Is the association between job attractiveness and low pay accidental, or is there a logical connection? Discuss.

17. You have been collecting data on the behavior of a particular stock over many years. You notice that every Friday the 13th the stock drops substantially, only to come back up over the next few weeks; your conclusion is that superstitious stockholders sell their stock in anticipation of bad luck. What can you do to make use of this information? What effect does your action have? Suppose more people notice the behavior of the stock and react accordingly; what is the effect?

18. Generalize your answer to the previous question to cover other situations where a stock price changes in a predictable way. What does this suggest about schemes to make money by charting stock movements and using the result to predict when the market will go up?

19. Suppose that in Floritania the total cost of bringing up a son is three times the cost of bringing up a daughter, since Floritanians do not believe in educating women. Floritanians simply love grandchildren; every couple wants to have as many as possible. Due to a combination of modern science and ancient witchcraft, Floritanian parents can

control the gender of their offspring. What is the male/female ratio in the Floritanian population?

20. The principal foods of the Floritanians are green eggs and ham. It costs exactly twice as much to produce a pound of green eggs as a pound of ham. The more green eggs that are produced, the lower the price they sell for, and similarly with ham.
    a. You are producing both green eggs and ham. Green eggs sell for $3/pound; so does ham. How could you increase your revenue without changing your production cost?
    b. What will be the result on the prices of green eggs and ham?
    c. If everyone acts rationally, what can you say about the eventual prices of green eggs and ham in Floritania?

FOR FURTHER READING

For a good introduction to the economics of genes, I recommend Richard Dawkins's *The Selfish Gene* (New York: Oxford University Press, 1976).

A more extensive discussion of the economics of warfare can be found in my essay, "The Economics of War," in J.E. Pournelle (ed.), *Blood and Iron* (New York: Tom Doherty Associates, 1984).

For a very different application of economic analysis to warfare, I recommend Donald W. Engels's *Alexander the Great and the Logistics of the Macedonian Army* (Berkeley: University of California Press, 1978). The author analyzes Alexander's campaigns while omitting all of the battles. His central interest is in the problem of preventing a large army from dying of hunger or thirst and the way in which that problem determined much of Alexander's strategy. Consider, as a very simple example, the fact that you cannot draw water from a well, or 5 wells, or 20 wells, fast enough to keep an army of 100,000 people from dying of thirst.

The relationship between individual rationality and group behavior is analyzed in Thomas Schelling's *Micromotives and Macrobehavior* (New York: W.W. Norton and Co., 1978).

chapter 2

HOW ECONOMISTS THINK

This chapter consists of three parts. The first describes and defends some of the fundamental assumptions and definitions used in economics. The second attempts to demonstrate the importance of price theory, in part by giving examples of economic problems where the obvious answer is wrong and the mistake comes from not having a consistent theory of how prices are determined. The third part briefly describes how, in the next few chapters, we are going to create such a theory.

PART I—ASSUMPTIONS AND DEFINITIONS

There are a number of features of the economic way of analyzing human behavior that many people find odd or even disturbing. One such feature is the assumption that the different things a person values can all be measured on a single scale, so that even if one thing is much more valuable than another, a sufficiently small amount of the more valuable good is equivalent to some amount of the less valuable. A car, for example, is probably worth much more to you than a bicycle, but a sufficiently small "amount of car" (not a bumper or a headlight but rather the use of a car one day a month, or one chance in a hundred of getting a car) has the same value to you as a whole bicycle—given the choice, you would not care which of them you got.

This sounds plausible enough when we are talking about cars and bicycles, but what about really important things? Does it make sense to say that a human life—as embodied in access to a kidney dialysis machine or the chance to have an essential heart operation—is to be weighed in the same scale as the pleasure of eating a candy bar or watching a television program?

Strange as it may seem, the answer is yes. If we observe how people behave with regard to their own lives, we find that they are willing to make trade-offs between life and quite minor values. One obvious example is someone who smokes even though he believes that smoking reduces life expectancy. Another is the overweight person who is willing to accept an increased chance of a heart attack in exchange for some number of chocolate sundaes.

Even if you neither smoke nor overeat, you still trade off life against other values. Whenever you cross the street, you are (slightly) increasing your chance of being run over. Every time you spend part of your limited income on something that has no effect on your life expectancy, instead of using it for a medical checkup or to add safety equipment to your car, and every time you choose what to eat on any basis other than what food comes closest to the ideal diet a nutritionist would prescribe, you are choosing to give up, in a probabilistic sense, a little life in exchange for something else.

Those who deny that this is how we do and should behave assume implicitly that there is such a thing as enough medical care, that people should (and wise people do) first buy enough medical care and then devote the rest of their resources to other and infinitely less valuable goals. The economist replies that since additional expenditures on medical care produce benefits well past the point at which one's entire income is spent on it, the concept of "enough" as some absolute amount determined by medical science is meaningless. The proper economic concept of enough medical care is that amount such that the improvement in your health from buying more would be worth less to you than the things you would have to give up to pay for it. You are buying too much medical care if you would be better off (as judged by your own preferences) buying less medical care and spending the money on something else.

I have defined *enough* in terms of money only because the choice you face with regard to the goods and services you buy is whether to give up a dollar's worth of one in exchange for getting another dollar's worth of something else. But market goods and services are only a special case of the general problem of choice. You are buying enough safety when the pleasure you get from running across the street to talk to a friend just balances the value to you of the resulting increase in the chance of getting run over.

So far, I have considered the trade-off between small amounts of life and ordinary amounts of other goods. Perhaps it has occurred to you that we would reach a different conclusion if we considered trading a large amount of life for a (very) large amount of some other good. My argument seems to imply that there should be some price for which you would be willing to let someone kill you!

There is a good reason why most people would be unwilling to sell their entire life for any amount of money or other goods—they would have no way of collecting. Once they are dead, they cannot spend the money. This is evidence not that life is infinitely valuable but that money has no value to a corpse.

Suppose, however, we offer someone a large sum of money in exchange for his agreeing to be killed in a week. It still seems likely he would refuse. One reason (seen from the economist's standpoint) is that as we increase the amount we consume in a given length of time, the value to us of additional amounts decreases. I am very fond of Baskin-Robbins ice cream cones, but if I were consuming them at a rate of a hundred a week, an additional cone would be worth very little to me. I weigh life and the pleasure of eating ice cream on the same scale, yet no quantity of ice cream I can consume in a week is worth as much to me as the rest of my life. That is why, when I initially defined the idea that everything can be measured on a single scale, I put the definition in terms of a comparison between the value of a given amount of the less valuable good and a sufficiently small amount of the more valuable, instead of comparing a given amount of the more valuable to a sufficiently large amount of the less valuable.

Wants or Needs?

The economist's assumption that all (valued) goods are in this sense comparable shows itself in the use of the term **wants** rather than *needs*. The word *needs* suggests things that are infinitely valuable. You need a certain amount of food, clothing, medical care, or whatever. How much you need could presumably be determined by the appropriate expert and has nothing to do with what such things cost or what your particular values are. This is the typical attitude of the noneconomist, and it is why the economist's way of looking at things often seems unrealistic and even ugly. The economist replies that how much of each of these things you will, and should, choose to have depends on how much you value them, how much you value other things you must give up to get them, and how much of such other things you must give up to get a given amount of clothing, medical care, or whatever. Your choices depend, in other words, on your tastes and on the costs to you of the alternative things that you desire.

One reply the noneconomist (perhaps I mean the antieconomist) might make is that we ought to have enough of everything. If you have enough movies and enough ice cream cones and enough of everything else you desire, you no longer have any reason to choose less medical care or nutrition in order to get more of something else (although combining good nutrition with enough ice cream cones could be a problem for some of us). Perhaps our objective should be a society where everybody has enough. Perhaps, it is sometimes argued, the marvels of modern technology, combined with the right economic system, could bring such a society within our reach, making the problems of choosing among different values obsolete.

This particular argument was more popular 20 years ago than it is now. Currently the fashion has changed and we are being told that limitations in natural resources (and in the ability of the environment to absorb our wastes) impose stringent limitations on how much of everything we can have. Yet even if that is not true, even if (as I suspect) resource limits are no more binding now than in the past, "enough of everything" is still not a reasonable goal. Why?

It is often assumed that if we could only produce somewhat more than we do, we would have everything we want. In order to consume still more, we would each have to drive three cars and eat six meals a day. This argument confuses increasing the value of what you consume with increasing the amount you consume. A modern stereo is no bigger and consumes no more power than its predecessor of 30 years ago, yet moving from one to the other represents an increase in consumption. I have no use for three cars, but I would like a car three times as good as the one I now have. There are many ways in which my life could be improved if I consumed things that are more costly to create but no larger than those I now have. My desire for pounds of food is already satiated and my desire for number of cars could be satiated with a moderate increase in my income, but my desire for quality of food or quality of car would remain even at a much higher income, and my desire for more of *something* would remain unsatiated as long as I remained alive and conscious under any circumstances I can imagine.

From both introspection and conversation, I have formulated a general law on this subject. Everyone feels that there is a level of income above which all consumption is frivolous. For everyone, that level is about twice his own. An Indian peasant living on $500/year believes that if only he had $1,000/year, he would have everything he could want with a little left over. An American physician living on $50,000/year (after taxes) doubts that anyone has any real use for more than $100,000/year.

Both the peasant and the physician are wrong, but both opinions are the result of rational behavior by those who hold them. Whether you are living on $500/year or $50,000/year, the consumption decisions you make, the goods you consider buying, are those appropriate to such an income. Heaven would be a place where you had all the things you have considered buying and decided not to. There is little point wasting your time learning or thinking about consumption goods that cost ten times your yearly income, so the possession of such goods is not part of your picture of the good life.

Value

So far I have discussed, and tried to defend, two of the assumptions that go into economics: **comparability,** the assumption that the different things we value are comparable, and **nonsatiation,** the assumption that in any plausible society, present or future, we cannot all have everything we want and must give up some things we desire in order to have others. In talking about value, I have also implicitly introduced an important definition—that **value** (of things) means how much we value them and that how much we value them is properly estimated not by our words but by our actions. In discussing the trade-off between the value of life and the value of the pleasure of smoking, my evidence that the two are comparable was that people choose to smoke, even though they believe doing so lowers their life expectancy. This definition is called the **principle of revealed preference**—meaning that your preferences are revealed by your actions.

The first part of the definition of value embodied in the principle of revealed preference might be questioned by those who prefer to base value on some external criterion—what we should want or what is good for us. The second might be questioned by those who believe that their values are not fairly reflected in their actions, that they value health and life but just cannot resist one more cigarette. But economics is supposed to describe how people act, and we are therefore concerned with value as it relates to action. A smoker's statement that he puts infinite value on his own life may help to explain what he believes, but it is less useful for understanding what he will do than is the kind of value expressed when he takes a cigarette out and lights it.

Even if revealed preference is a useful concept for our purpose, should we call what it reveals value? Does not the word carry with it an implication of something beyond mere individual preference? That is a philosophical question that goes beyond the subject of this book. If using the word *value* to refer equally to a crust of bread in the hands of a starving man and a syringe of heroin in the hands of an addict makes you uncomfortable, then substitute *economic value* instead. But remember that the addition of "economic" does not mean "having monetary value," "being material," "capable of producing profit for someone," or anything similar. Economic value is simply value to individuals as judged by them and revealed in their actions.

> Economics Joke #1: *Two economists walked past a Porsche showroom.*
> *One of them pointed at a shiny car in the window and said, "I want that."*
> *"Obviously not," the other replied.*

Choice or Necessity?

The difference between the approaches to human behavior taken by economists and by noneconomists comes in part from the economist's assumptions of comparability and insatiability, in part from the definition of value in terms of revealed preference, and in part from the fundamental assumption of rationality that I made and defended in the previous chapter. One form in which the difference often appears is the economist's insistence that virtually all human behavior should be described in terms of choices. To many noneconomists, this seems deceptive. What, after all, is the point of saying that you choose not to buy something you cannot afford?

When you say that you cannot afford something, you usually mean only that there are other things you would rather spend the money on. Most of us would say that we could not afford a $1,000 shirt. Yet most of us could save up $1,000 in a year if it were sufficiently important—important enough that you were willing to spend only a dollar a day on food (roughly the cost of the least expensive full-nutrition diet—powdered milk, soy beans, and the like), share a one-room apartment with two roommates, and buy your clothing from Goodwill.

Consider an even more extreme case, in which you have assets of only a few hundred dollars and there is something enormously valuable to you that costs $100,000 and will only be available for the next month. In a month, you surely cannot earn that much money. It seems reasonable, in this case at least, to say that you cannot afford it. Yet even here, there is a legitimate sense in which what you really mean is that you do not want it.

Suppose the object were so valuable that getting it made your life wonderful forever after and failing to get it meant instant death. If you could not earn, borrow, or steal $100,000, the sensible thing to do would be to get as much money as possible, go to Reno or Las Vegas, work out a series of bets that would maximize your chance of converting what you had into exactly $100,000, and make them. If you are not prepared to do that, then the reason you do not buy the object is not that you cannot afford its $100,000 price. It is that you do not want it—enough.

In part, the claim that people do not really have any choice confuses the lack of alternatives with the lack of attractive or desirable ones. Having chosen the best alternative, you may say that you had little choice; in a sense you are correct. There may be only one *best* alternative.

One example of this confusion that I find particularly disturbing is the argument that the poor should be "given" essential services by government even if (as is often the case) they end up having to pay for the services themselves through increased taxes. Poor people, it is said, do not really choose not to go to doctors—they simply cannot afford to. Therefore, a benevolent government should take money from the poor and use it to provide the medical services they need.

If this argument seems convincing, try translating it into the language of choice. Poor people choose not to go to doctors because to do so they would have to give up things still more important to them—food, perhaps, or heat. It may sound heartless to say that someone chooses not to go to a doctor when he can do so only at the cost of starving to death, but putting it that way at least reminds us that if you "help" him by forcing him to spend his money on doctors, you are compelling him to make a choice—starvation—that he rejected because it was even worse than the alternative—no medical care—that he chose.

The question of how much choice individuals really have reappears on a larger scale in discussions of how flexible the economy as a whole is—to what extent it can vary the amount of the different resources it uses. Our tendency is to look at the way things are now being done and assume that that way is the only possible one. But the way things are now done is the solution to a particular problem—producing goods as cheaply as possible given the present cost of various inputs. If some input—unskilled labor, say, or energy or some raw material—were much more or less expensive, the optimal way of producing would change.

A familiar example is the consumption of gasoline. If you suggest to someone that if gasoline were more expensive he would use less of it, his initial response is that using less gasoline would mean giving up the job he commutes to or walking two miles each way to do his shopping. Indeed, when oil prices shot up in the early 1970s, many people argued that Americans would continue to use as much gasoline as before at virtually any price, unless the government forced them to do otherwise.

There are many ways to save gasoline. Car pooling and driving more slowly are obvious ones. Buying lighter cars is less obvious. Workers choosing to live closer to their jobs or employers choosing to locate factories nearer to their workers are still less obvious. Petroleum is used to produce both gasoline and heating oil; the refiners can, to a considerable degree, control how much of each is produced. One way of "saving" gasoline is to use less heating oil and make a larger fraction of the petroleum into gasoline instead. Insulation, smaller houses, and moving south are all ways of saving gasoline.

PART 2—PRICE THEORY—WHY IT MATTERS

This book has two purposes—to teach you to think like an economist and to teach you the set of ideas that lie at the core of economic theory as it now exists. That set of ideas is **price theory**—the explanation of how relative prices are determined and how prices function to coordinate economic activity.

There are at least two reasons to want to understand price theory (aside from passing this course). The first is to make some sense out of the world you live in. You are in the middle of a very highly organized system with nobody organizing it. The items you use and see, even very simple objects such as a pen or pencil, were each produced by the coordinated activity of millions of people. Someone had to cut down the tree to make the pencil. Someone had to season the wood and cut it to shape. Someone had to make the tools to cut down the trees and the tools to make the tools and the fuel for the tools and the refineries to make the fuel. While small parts of this immense enterprise are under centralized control (one firm organizes the cutting and seasoning of the wood, another actually assembles the pencil), nobody coordinates the overall enterprise.

Someone who had visited China told me about a conversation with an official in the ministry of materials supply. The official was planning to visit the United States in order to see how things were done there. He wanted, naturally enough, to meet and speak with his opposite number—

whoever was in charge of seeing that U.S. producers got the materials they needed in order to produce. He had difficulty understanding the answer—that no such person exists.

A market economy is coordinated through the price system. Costs of production—ultimately, the cost to a worker of working instead of taking a vacation or of working at one job instead of at another, or the cost of using land or some other resource for one purpose and so being unable to use it for another—are reflected in the prices for which goods are sold. The value of goods to those who ultimately consume them is reflected in the prices purchasers are willing to pay. If a good is worth more to a consumer than it costs to produce, it gets produced; if not, it does not.

If new uses for copper increase demand, that bids up the price, so existing users find it in their interest to use less. If supply decreases—a mine runs out or a harvest fails—the same thing happens. Prices provide an intricate system of signals and incentives to coordinate the activities of several million firms and several billion individuals. How this is done you will learn in the next few months.

Four Wrong Answers

The first reason to understand price theory is to understand how the society around you works. The second reason is that an understanding of how prices are determined is essential to an understanding of most controversial economic issues while a misunderstanding of how prices are determined is at the root of many, if not most, economic errors. Consider the following four examples of cases where the obvious answer is wrong and where the error is an implicit (wrong) assumption about price theory. I shall not prove what the right answer is, although I shall give you some hints about where the counterintuitive result comes from.

Rental Contracts. Tenants rent apartments from landlords. Cities often have laws restricting what lease agreements are legal. For example, the law may require the landlord to give the tenant three months' notice before evicting him, even if the lease provides for a shorter term.

It seems obvious that the effect of such a law is to benefit tenants and hurt landlords. That may be true for those tenants who have already signed leases when the law goes into effect. For most other tenants, it is false. The law either has no effect or it injures both tenants and landlords (on average; there may be particular tenants, or particular landlords, who benefit).

The reason most people expect such a law to benefit tenants is that they have, without realizing it, assumed that the law does not affect how much rent the tenant must pay. If you are paying the same rent and have a more favorable lease, you are better off. But this assumption is implausible. Although the law says nothing about rents, it indirectly affects both the operating costs of landlords (they are higher, since it is harder to get rid of bad tenants) and the attractiveness of the lease to tenants (who are now guaranteed three months' notice). With both supply and demand conditions for rental housing changed, you can hardly expect the market rent to remain the same—any more than you would expect the market price of cars to be unaffected by a law that forced the manufacturers to produce cars that were more costly to build and more desirable to buy. It turns out that either the law has no effect at all (the landlords would have chosen to offer the guarantee anyway in order to attract tenants and so be able to get more rent) or it injures both parties (the advantage of greater security does not compensate the average tenant for the resulting increase in his rent). I am asserting this, not proving it; the argument will be worked out in detail in Chapter 7.

Popcorn Prices.   The second counterintuitive result concerns popcorn. Movie theaters normally sell popcorn (and candy and sodas) for substantially higher prices than they are sold for elsewhere. There is an obvious explanation—the movie theater has a captive audience. While it is obvious, it is also wrong. Assuming that both customers and theater owners are rational, a straightforward economic argument can be constructed to show that selling food at above-cost prices lowers the net income of the theater owner. Explaining the observed prices requires a more complicated argument.

Here again, the error is in assuming that a price—this time the price the theater can get for a ticket—is fixed, when it will in fact depend on the characteristics of what is being sold, including, in this case, how much the theater charges for food. If that does not seem plausible to you, imagine that instead of exploiting its captive market with high food prices, the theater exploits it by charging an additional dollar per customer for seat rental. Just as the customers have nowhere else to buy their popcorn, so they have nowhere else to rent seats in the movie theater. If the price the theater can sell tickets for is unaffected by the price of popcorn, why should it be affected by the availability or price of other amenities—such as seats?

Obviously the conclusion is absurd. The theater charges the ticket price it does because any increase costs it more in lost customers than it gains from the higher price per ticket. Since an additional fee for seats is equivalent to raising the ticket price (unless customers are willing to watch the movie while standing), it will lower, not raise, the theater's profits.

The effect of raising popcorn prices is more complicated than the effect of renting seats, since it is easier to vary the amount of popcorn you eat according to its price than to vary the number of seats you sit in; we will return to the question of why popcorn in theaters is expensive in later chapters. But the error in the obvious explanation of expensive popcorn—assuming the price at which tickets can be sold is unaffected by changes in the quality of the product—is the same.

Why Price Control Makes Gasoline More Expensive. A third counter-intuitive result is that although price control on gasoline lowers the price consumers pay for gasoline in dollars per gallon, it raises the cost to consumers of getting gasoline, where the cost includes both the price and nonmonetary costs such as time spent waiting in line.

To see why this is true, imagine that the uncontrolled price is $1/gallon. At that price, producers produce exactly as much gasoline as consumers want to consume (which is why it is the market price). The government imposes a maximum price of $0.80/gallon. As a first step in the argument, assume producers continue producing the same quantity as before. At the lower price, consumers want to consume more. But you cannot consume gasoline that is not produced, so stations start running out. Consumers start coming to the stations earlier in the day, just after the stations have received their consignments of gasoline. Although this may enable one driver to get gasoline instead of another, it still does not allow drivers as a group to consume more than is produced, so the stations still run out. As everyone tries to be first, lines start to form. The cost of gasoline is now a cost in money plus a nonmonetary cost—waiting time (plus getting up early to go to the gas station); you can think of the latter as equivalent, from the consumer's standpoint, to an additional sum of money. As long as the money equivalent of the nonmonetary cost is less than $0.20, the total cost per gallon (waiting time plus money) is less than $1/ gallon. Consumers still want to consume more than is being produced (remember that $1 /gallon was the market price at which quantity demanded and quantity supplied were equal), and the lines continue to grow. Only when the cost—time plus money—reaches the old price are we back in a situation where the amount of gasoline that consumers want to buy is equal to the amount being produced.

So far, we have assumed that the producers produce the same amount of gasoline when they are receiving $0.80/gallon as when they are receiving $1/gallon. That is unlikely. At the lower price, producers produce less—marginal oil wells close down, older and more inefficient refineries go out of use, and so on. Since less is being produced than at a price of $1/gallon, consumers are still trying to consume more than is being produced even when the cost to them (price plus time) reaches $1/gallon; the lines have to grow still longer, making the cost even higher, before quantity demanded is reduced to quantity supplied. So price control raises the cost of gasoline. In Chapter 17, this analysis will be applied in more detail to price control under a variety of arrangements.

Improved Light Bulbs. The final example concerns light bulbs. It is sometimes argued that if a company with a monopoly of light bulbs invents a new bulb that lasts ten times as long as the old kind, the company will be better off suppressing the invention. After all, it is said, if the new bulb is introduced, the company can only sell one tenth as many bulbs as before, so its revenue and profit will be one tenth as great.

The mistake in this reasoning is the assumption that the company will sell the new bulb, if introduced, at the same price as the old. If consumers were willing to buy the old light bulbs for $1 each, they should be willing to buy the new ones for about $10 each. What they are really buying, after all, are light bulb hours, which are at the same price as before. If the company sells one tenth as many bulbs at ten times the price, its revenue is the same as before. Unless the new bulb costs at least ten times as much to produce as the old, costs are less than before and profits therefore are higher. It is worth introducing the new bulb.

In all of these cases, when I say something is true on average, what I mean is that it is strictly true if all consumers are identical to each other and all producers are identical to each other. This is often a useful approximation if you wish to distinguish distributional effects within a group from distributional effects between groups.

Naive Price Theory

All of these examples have one element in common. In each case, the mistake is in assuming that one part of a system will stay the same when another part is changed. In three of the four cases, what is assumed to stay the same is a price. I like to describe this mistake as naive price theory—the theory that the only thing determining tomorrow's price is today's price. Naive price theory is a perfectly natural way of dealing with prices—if you do not understand what determines them. In each of the three cases—theater tickets, light bulbs, and apartments—we were considering a change in something other than price. In each case, a reader unfamiliar with economics might argue that since I said nothing about the price changing when the problem was stated, he assumed it stayed the same.

If that seems like a reasonable defense of naive price theory, consider the following analogy. I visit a friend whose month-old baby is sleeping in a small crib. I ask him whether he plans to buy a larger crib or a bed when the child gets older. He looks puzzled and asks me what is wrong with the crib the child is sleeping in now. I point out that when the child gets a little bigger, the crib will be too small for him. My friend replies that I had asked what he planned to do when the child got older—not bigger.

It makes very little sense to assume that as a baby grows older he remains the same size. It makes no more sense to assume that the market price of a good remains the same when you change its cost of production, its value to potential purchasers, or both. In each case, the assumption "if you did not say it was going to change, it probably stays the same" ceases to make sense once you understand the causal relations involved. That is what is wrong with naive price theory.

Why, you may ask, do I dignify this error by calling it a price theory? I do so in order to point out that in each of these cases, and many more, the alternative to correct economic theory is not doing without theory (sometimes referred to as just using common sense). The alternative to correct theory is incorrect theory. In order to analyze the effect of introducing longer lasting light bulbs (or the other cases I have just discussed), you must, explicitly or implicitly, assume something about the effect on the price; you do not avoid doing so by assuming that there is no effect.

PART 3—THE BIG PICTURE, OR HOW TO SOLVE A HARD PROBLEM

In order to understand how prices are determined, we must somehow untangle a complicated, intricately interrelated problem. How much of a good a consumer chooses to consume depends both on the total resources available to him—his income—and, as the earlier discussion suggested, on how much of other things he must give up to get that good—in other words, on how much it costs. How much it costs depends, among other things, on how much he consumes, since his demand affects what producers can sell it for. How much producers sell and at what price will affect how much labor (and other productive resources) they choose to buy, and at what price. Since consumers get their income by selling their labor (and other productive resources they own), this will in turn affect the income of the consumers, bringing us full circle. It seems as though we cannot solve any one part of the problem until we have first solved the rest.

The solution is to break the problem into smaller pieces, solve each piece in a way sufficiently general that it can be combined with whatever the solutions of the other pieces turn out to be, then reassemble the whole in such a way that all of the solutions are consistent with each other. First, in Chapters 3 and 4, we consider a consumer with either a given income or a given endowment of goods, confronted with a market and a set of prices, and analyze his behavior. Next, in Chapter 5, we consider a producer producing either for his own consumption or for sale; the producer can transform his labor into goods and either consume them or sell them on the market. In Chapter 6, we consider trade among individuals, mostly in the context of a two-person (or two-country) world. In Chapter 7, we put together the material of Chapters 3, 4, and 5, showing how the interaction of (many) consumers who wish to buy goods and (many) producers who wish to sell them produces market prices. Finally, in Chapter 8, we close the circle, combining the results of the previous five chapters to recreate the whole interacting system.

What we will be analyzing, in this section of the book, is a very simple economy. Production and consumption are by and for individuals; there are no firms. The world is predictable and static; complications of change and uncertainty are assumed away. Once we understand the logic of that simple economy, we will be ready to put back into it, one after another, the complications initially left out.

PROBLEMS

1. Give examples of ways in which you yourself make trade-offs between your life and relatively minor values; they should not be examples given in the chapter.
2. Suppose we were talking not about what people *do* value but about what they *should* value. Do you think comparability would still hold? Discuss. If your answer is no, give examples of incomparable values.
3. State the principle of revealed preference in your own words. Give an example, in your own or your friends' behavior, where stated values are different from the values deduced from revealed preference.
4. Life is not the only thing that is said to be beyond price. Other examples are health, love, salvation, and the welfare of our country. Give examples, for yourself and others, of ways in which (small amounts of) such "priceless" things are routinely given up in exchange for minor values.
5. Figure 2-1 shows how the total pleasure I get from eating ice cream cones varies with the number of ice cream cones I eat each week.

Figure 2-1

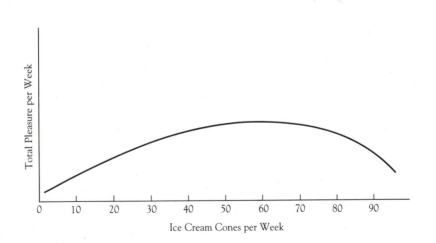

Total pleasure per week from eating ice cream cones, as a function of the rate at which they are eaten.

Figure 2-2

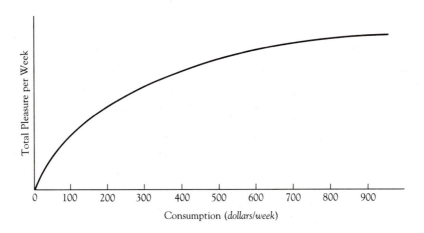

Total pleasure per week from all consumption, as a function of weekly expenditure.

Figure 2-2 shows how the total pleasure I get from all the goods I buy varies with the number of dollars worth of goods I buy each week. Discuss and explain the similarities and the differences in the two figures.

6. Describe some likely short-run and long-run adjustments that people would make to each of the following changes. Assume in each case that the change is permanent, reflecting some underlying change in technology, resource cost, or the like.
   a. Land prices go up tenfold.
   b. Electricity prices go up tenfold.
   c. All heating costs triple.
   d. The government imposes a $20,000 baby tax for every baby born in the United States.
   e. Electricity prices go down by a factor of 100.
   f. Due to extensive immigration, hard-working (but unskilled) workers are readily available for a dollar/hour.

7. You are an economist, you have a child, and you decide to make him wash out his mouth with soap whenever he uses a bad word or phrase. The first forbidden word on your list is "need." What would other words or phrases be? If possible, give examples that have not been discussed in the chapter.

8. The chapter describes how millions of people cooperate to produce a pencil. Describe how you or someone you know is involved in producing a pencil. A computer. An atomic bomb. The examples should be real ones.

9. Which of the principles discussed in the chapter did the Porsche joke illustrate? Explain.

10. It is part of American folklore that from time to time some genius invents a razor blade that lasts forever or a car engine that runs on water, only to have his invention bought up and suppressed by companies that want to continue making money selling razor blades or gasoline. Does this seem plausible? Discuss.

11. I recently received a letter from a credit card company (call it ACCCo.) urging me to support a law that would make it illegal for merchants to charge a higher price to customers who use credit cards. Such a law currently exists but is about to expire. The letter argues as follows:

> To begin with, present law already permits merchants to offer discounts to customers who choose to pay with cash. Such discounts can benefit customers—and we have long been for them. They allow you to either pay the regular price and have the convenience of using your credit card, or pay cash and receive a discount.
>
> We think you and all consumers should have this freedom of choice. It is a choice with no penalty and numerous benefits.
>
> *A credit card surcharge, however, is entirely different. It would penalize you whether you used cash or a credit card. If you paid cash, you would be charged the full price. If you wanted—or needed—to use your credit card, you would be charged a penalty over and above the regular price.*

   a. Is the distinction made by ACCCo. between permitting cash discounts and permitting a surcharge for use of a credit card a legitimate one? Discuss.

   b. ACCCo. apparently believes that it is in its interest to have credit card surcharges prohibited (how do I know that?). Is it obvious that it is right? From the standpoint of credit card companies, what are the *advantages* of permitting such surcharges?

12. While negotiating with a firm that wished to publish this book, I got into a conversation on the subject of the secondhand market for textbooks. The editor I was talking with complained that sales of a textbook typically drop sharply in the second year because students buy secondhand copies from other students who bought the books new the year before. While she had no suggestions for eliminating the secondhand market, she clearly regarded it as a bad thing.

   I put the following question to her and her colleagues. Suppose an inventor walks in your door with a new product—timed ink. Print your books in timed ink and activate it when the books leave the warehouse. At the end of the school year, the pages will go blank. Students can no longer buy secondhand textbooks. Do your profits go up—or down?

To make the problem more specific, assume that presently textbooks are sold for $30 each, that students resell them to other students for $15, and that each textbook costs the publisher $20 to produce and lasts exactly two years. Discuss.

13. "We should require every barber to have a year of training and to pass an exam. The barbers would be a little worse off, since they would have to be trained, but the rest of us would obviously be better off, since our hair would be cut better."

Discuss. Is this last sentence of the quote true?

PRICE = VALUE = COST:

section II

COMPETITIVE EQUILIBRIUM
IN A SIMPLE ECONOMY

chapter 3

THE CONSUMER: CHOICE AND INDIFFERENCE CURVES

PRICE, COST, AND VALUE

A very old puzzle in economics is the relation between price, value to the consumer, and cost of production. It is tempting to say that the price of a good is determined by its value to the user. Why, after all, would anyone buy a good for more or sell it for less? But if this is so, why are diamonds, which are relatively unimportant (most of us could get along quite well if they did not exist), worth so much more per pound than water, which is essential for life? If the answer is that diamonds are rare and that it is rarity rather than usefulness that determines price, I reply that signatures of mine written in yellow ink are even rarer than original autographs of Abraham Lincoln but bring a (much) lower price.

Perhaps it is cost of production that determines price. When I was very young, I used to amuse myself by shooting stalks of grass with a BB gun. That is a costly way of mowing the lawn, even considering that the cost per hour of a nine-year-old's time is not very high. I think it unlikely that anyone would pay a correspondingly high price to have his lawn mowed in that fashion.

This puzzle—the relation between value to the consumer, cost of production, and price—was solved a little over 100 years ago. The answer is that price equals both cost of production and value to the user, both of which must therefore be equal to each other. How market mechanisms arrange that triple equality will be discussed in the next few chapters. In this chapter and the next, we shall analyze the behavior of a consumer who must decide what to buy with his limited resources; among the things we shall learn in the process is why, as a consequence of rational behavior by the consumer, price equals (marginal) value.

LANGUAGES

There are several different languages in which the problem of consumer behavior—and many other problems in economics—can be analyzed.

Each of these languages has advantages and disadvantages. One may use the language of calculus, making assumptions about the form of the "utility function" that describes the individual's preferences among different goods and deducing the characteristics of the bundle of goods that maximizes it. This has the advantage of allowing compact and rigorous mathematical arguments and of producing very general results, applicable to a wide range of possible situations. It has the disadvantage that even if you know calculus, you probably do not know it in the same sense in which you know English. Unless you are very good at intuiting mathematics, you can follow a proof step by step from assumptions to conclusions and still not know why the result is true. For these reasons, calculus and utility functions will be used only in some of the optional sections of this text. The ordinary sections will not assume any knowledge of either, although a few concepts borrowed from calculus will be explained in simple terms and used where necessary.

Another possible language is geometry. Most of us can understand abstract relations better as pictures than as equations; hence geometric arguments are easier to intuit. One disadvantage of geometry is that it limits us to situations that can be drawn in two dimensions—typically, for example, to choices involving only two different goods. A second disadvantage is that we may, in drawing the picture, inadvertently build into it assumptions about the problem—possibly false ones.

The third language is English. While not as good as mathematical languages for expressing precise quantitative relations, English has the advantage of being, for most of us, our native tongue. Insofar as we think in words at all, it is the language we are used to thinking in. Unless we have very good mathematical intuition, all mathematical arguments eventually get translated, in our heads, into words, and it is only then that we really understand them. Alfred Marshall, possibly the most important economist of the past century, wrote that economic ideas should be worked out and proved in mathematical form and then translated into words; if you find that you cannot put your analysis into words, you should burn your mathematics. Since it is often hard to keep track of quantitative relations in a verbal argument, explanations given in English will frequently be supplemented by tables.

This chapter presents the logic of a consumer, first in verbal form, then in a simple geometrical form suitable for describing the choice between two different goods. The analysis is continued in the next chapter, which uses a somewhat more complicated geometric argument, designed to produce calculus results without actually using calculus. Among the results are the answers to three interesting questions: How does the amount you buy depend on price? How much do you benefit by being able to buy something at a particular price? What is the relation between price and value?

THE CONSUMER I: ENGLISH VERSION

Your problem as a consumer is to choose among the various bundles of goods and services you could purchase or produce with your limited resources of time and money. There are two elements to the problem—your preferences and your opportunity set. Your preferences could be represented by a gigantic table showing all possible **bundles**—collections of goods and services that you could conceivably consume—and showing for every pair of bundles which one you prefer. We assume that your preferences are consistent; if you prefer A to B and B to C, you also prefer A to C. Your **opportunity set** can be thought of as a list containing every bundle that you have enough money to buy. Your problem as a consumer is to decide which of the bundles in your opportunity set you prefer.

I will simplify the problem in most of this chapter by considering only two goods at a time—in this part of the chapter, apples and oranges. We may imagine either that these are the only goods that exist or else that you have already decided how much of everything else to consume. We assume that both apples and oranges are **goods**, meaning that you prefer more to less. Things that are not goods are either **neutral** (you do not care how much you have) or **bads** (you prefer less to more: garbage, strawberry ice cream, acid rock). As these examples suggest, whether something is a good or a bad for you depends on your preferences; some people like strawberry ice cream.

Preferences: Patterns on a Table

Table 3-1 is a a list of bundles of apples and oranges. For each bundle, the table shows its name (A–L), how many apples and oranges it contains, and its **utility**—an abstract measure of how much you value the bundle. The statement "Bundle A and bundle C have the same utility" is equivalent to the statement "Given a choice between A and C, you would not care which you got." The statement "Bundle G has greater utility than bundle B" is equivalent to "Given a choice between B and G, you would choose G." Listing a utility for each bundle is a simple way of describing your preferences; by comparing the utilities of two bundles, we can see which you prefer.

Table 3-1

Bundle	Apples	Oranges	Utility	Bundle	Apples	Oranges	Utility
A	10	0	5	F	2	8	5
B	7	1	5	G	10	1	6
C	5	2	5	H	8	2	6
D	4	3	5	J	7	3	6
E	3	5	5	K	9	1	?
				L	7	5	?

Section II   Price = Value = Cost

Utility is being used here as an **ordinal** measure—the order matters (bundle G has more utility than bundle F, so you prefer G to F) but the amount does not. In Chapter 13, we will expand the idea of utility in a way that converts it into a **cardinal** measure—one for which both order (bundle G has more utility than bundle F) and size (bundle G has 1 *utile* more utility than bundle F) matter. Since in this chapter utility describes the choices of one individual, we need not worry about **interpersonal utility comparisons**—questions such as "Does an orange have more utility to me or to you?" We will say a little more about that question in Chapter 15, when we are trying to evaluate changes that make some people better off and some worse off.

Since bundles A–F have the same utility (5), you are indifferent among them. If you started with 4 apples and 3 oranges (D) and somehow gained an apple and lost an orange, moving from D to C, you would be neither better nor worse off. We will say that in such a situation an apple and an orange have the same value to you, or alternatively, that the value of an apple is 1 orange; the value of an orange is 1 apple.

It is important to note that the statement "The value of an apple is 1 orange" is true only between C and D. As we move up or down the table, values change. If you start with 5 apples and 2 oranges, you must receive not 1 but 2 apples to make up for losing 1 orange; in this situation (between B and C), the value of an orange is equal to that of 2 apples. An orange is worth 2 apples; an apple is worth half an orange.

The numbers in bundles A–F follow a pattern—as you move up the table, it takes more and more apples to equal 1 orange; as you move down, it takes more and more oranges to equal 1 apple. The numbers are set up this way because, as a rule, the more you are consuming of something, the less you value consuming one more. If you have very few oranges, you will be willing to give up a good deal to have one more (assuming you like oranges). If you are already consuming 12 oranges per day, you will be willing to give up very little to have 13 instead. As we move up the column, each successive bundle has fewer oranges and more apples, so in each successive case oranges are worth more to you and apples less, making each orange worth more apples. This general pattern is referred to as a declining **marginal rate of substitution**—the rate at which additional apples substitute for additional oranges declines with increases in the number of apples or decreases in the number of oranges.

Another way of seeing the pattern is to ask how many oranges it takes to raise your utility by 1. If you start at A, the answer is that it takes 1 orange; adding 1 orange to your bundle puts you at G, with a utility of 6, up 1 from 5. If you start at B, it takes 2 extra oranges to move you to J, increasing your utility by 1. At B you already have 1 orange, so the extra utility you get from an additional orange (the **marginal utility** of an orange) is less than at A, where you start with no oranges at all.

The name for this pattern is the **principle of declining marginal utility**—marginal utility because what is declining as you have more and more oranges is the additional utility to you of having one more orange. It is the same principle that was introduced in the previous chapter when I discussed why I would not trade my life for any quantity of Baskin-Robbins ice cream cones. Figure 2-1 showed that as the rate at which I consumed ice cream cones increased, the additional utility from each additional cone became less and less. Eventually I reached a rate of consumption at which increased consumption resulted in decreased utility—the additional utility from additional ice cream cones was negative.

Trading toward an Optimal Bundle

Suppose you start with bundle A on Table 3-1, and someone offers to trade oranges for your apples at a rate of 1 for 1. You accept the offer, and trade 1 apple for 1 orange. That gives you bundle K. Since K has more apples than B and as many oranges, you prefer K to B; since B is equivalent to A, you prefer K to A. We do not know what K's utility is, but it must be more than 5 (and less than 6. Why?).

To figure out how many apples you would be willing to exchange for oranges at a rate of 1 for 1, we would need to add many more bundles to the table. That problem is more easily solved using the geometric approach, which will be introduced in the next part of the chapter. There are, however, a number of lessons that can be drawn from this rather simple analysis of consumer choice.

The first is that the value of something is whatever we are (just) willing to give up for it. Two things have the same value if gaining one and losing the other leaves us neither better nor worse off—meaning that we are indifferent between the situation before the exchange and the situation after the exchange. This is an application of the principle of revealed preference discussed in the previous chapter—our values are defined by the choices we make.

A second lesson is that the value of goods (to you) depends not only on the nature of the goods and your preferences but also on how much of those goods you have. If you have 1 apple and 12 oranges, an orange will be worth very little (in apples). If you have 10 apples and no oranges, an orange is worth quite a lot of apples—3, according to Table 3-1.

The third lesson is that the price (or cost) of a good is the amount of something else you must give up to get it. In our example, where someone is willing to trade oranges for apples at a rate of 1 for 1, the price of an apple is 1 orange and the price of an orange is 1 apple. This is called **opportunity cost**—the cost of getting one thing, whether by buying it or producing it, is what you have to give up in order to get it. The cost of an A on a midterm, for example, may turn out to be three parties, two football games, and a night's sleep. The cost of living in a house that you already own is not, as you might think, limited to expenditures on taxes, maintenance, and the like; it also includes the interest you could collect on the money you would have if you sold the house to someone else instead of living in it yourself.

Opportunity cost is not a particular kind of cost but rather the correct way of looking at all costs. The money you spend to buy something is a cost only because there are other things you would like to spend the money on instead; by buying A, you give up the opportunity to buy B. Not getting the most valuable of the B's that you could have bought with the money—the one you would have bought if A had not been available— is then the cost to you of buying A. That is why, if you were certain that the world was going to end at midnight today, money would become almost worthless to you. Its only use would be to be spent today—so you would "spend as if there were no tomorrow."

The final lesson is that you buy something if and only if its cost is less than its value. In the example we gave, the cost of an orange was 1 apple. The value of an orange, between bundles A and B, was 3 apples. So you bought it. That put you at bundle K. If, starting from there, the value of an orange was still more than 1 apple, you would have bought another. As you trade apples for oranges, the number of apples you have decreases and the number of oranges increases. Because of the principle of declining marginal utility, additional oranges become less valuable and apples become more valuable, so the value of (one more) orange measured in apples falls. When, as a result of trading, you reach a bundle for which the value of yet another orange is no more than its price, you stop trading; you have reached the best possible bundle, given your initial situation (bundle A) and the price at which you can trade apples for oranges.

So far, I have only considered trading (and valuing) whole apples and oranges. As long as we limit ourselves in this way, concepts such as the value of an apple are somewhat ambiguous. If you have 4 apples and 3 oranges, is the value of an apple the number of oranges you would give up in order to get 1 more apple (1 orange) or the number of oranges you would accept in exchange for having 1 fewer apple (2 oranges)? This ambiguity disappears if we consider trading very small amounts of the two goods.

If this sounds messy with apples and oranges, substitute apple juice and orange juice. If we move from four quarts of apple juice either up or down by, say, a teaspoon, the value to us of apple juice changes only very slightly, and similarly with the value of orange juice, so the rate at which we are just willing to exchange apple juice for orange juice should be almost exactly the same whether we are giving up a little apple juice in exchange for a little orange juice or giving up a little orange juice in exchange for a little apple juice. This is the sort of relation that is hard to put into words. It should become a little clearer in the next section, where the same argument is repeated in a geometric form, and clearer still to those of you familiar with calculus.

THE CONSUMER II: GEOMETRY AND INDIFFERENCE CURVES

Figure 3-1 shows another way of describing the preferences shown in Table 3-1. The horizontal axis represents apples; the vertical axis represents oranges. Instead of showing utility, we show **indifference curves** U_a, U_b, and U_c. Each indifference curve connects a set of bundles that have the same utility—bundles among which the consumer is indifferent. Higher indifference curves represent preferred bundles. Note, for instance, that point H on U_b is a bundle containing more apples and more oranges than point B on U_a. Since we have assumed that apples and oranges are both goods (you would rather have more than less), you prefer H to B. Since all bundles on U_a are equivalent to B (by the definition of an indifference curve) and all bundles on U_b are equivalent to H (ditto), any bundle on U_b is preferred to any bundle on U_a. Similarly any bundle on U_c is preferred to any bundle on either of the other two indifference curves. This conclusion depends only on assuming that apples and oranges are goods; it does not require us to know the actual utilities of the different bundles.

Figure 3-1

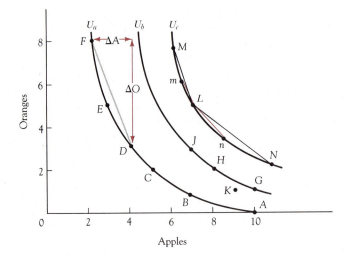

Indifference curves showing your preferences among different bundles of apples and oranges. The slope of an indifference curve shows the value of one good measured in terms of the other. $\Delta O/\Delta A$ is the average slope of indifference curve U_a between F and D. The slopes of mL and Ln are almost equal, indicating that it does not matter whether you measure value in terms of a little more of a good or a little less, provided you consider only very small changes.

A table such as Table 3-1 can show only a finite number of bundles; one of the advantages of the geometric approach is that one indifference curve contains an infinite number of points, representing an infinite number of different bundles. Another advantage is that looking at the blank space between the indifference curves shown on a figure such as Figure 3-1 reminds us that the indifference curves we draw, or the bundles on a table such as Table 3-1, are only a tiny selection from an infinite set. Any point on the figure, such as $J, K,$ or $L,$ is a bundle of goods—so many apples, so many oranges—a bundle you prefer to those on the indifference curves below it and to which you prefer those on the indifference curves above it. Through any such point, you could draw a new indifference curve containing all the bundles you regard as equivalent to it.

Preferences: The Shape of Indifference Curves

All of the indifference curves I have drawn have a similar shape—they slope down and to the right, and the slope becomes less steep the farther right you go (this shape is sometimes described as *convex* or as *convex to the origin*). Why?

The curves slope down to the right because both apples and oranges are goods. If one bundle (J) has more of both apples and oranges than another (C), so that a line through them would slope up and to the right, both points cannot be on the same indifference curve. You would obviously prefer $J,$ which has more of both goods, to $C.$ But an indifference curve connects bundles among which you are indifferent. So if a bundle (C) has more apples than another on the same indifference curve (D), putting it farther right, it must have fewer oranges—putting it lower. So indifference curves must slope down to the right, up to the left. If, for some (large) quantity of apples, apples became a bad (you had so many that you would prefer fewer to more), the indifference curve would start to slope up; in order to keep you on the same indifference curve, additional apples (a bad) would have to be balanced by additional oranges (a good).

Two different indifference curves cannot intersect. If they did, the point of intersection would represent a bundle that was on both curves, and therefore had two different utilities. A different way of saying the same thing is to point out that if two indifference curves do intersect, they must have the same utility (the utility of the bundle that is in both of them) and are therefore really one indifference curve.

What can we say about the shape of the curve? As you move from point F to point D along $U_a,$ the number of apples increases by ΔA and the number of oranges decreases by $\Delta O.$ Since F and D are on the same indifference curve (U_a), you are indifferent between them. That implies that ΔA apples have the same value to you as ΔO oranges; one apple is worth $\Delta O/\Delta A$ oranges.

$\Delta O/\Delta A$ is the value of an apple measured in oranges. It is also (minus) the slope of the line FD—which is approximately equal to the slope of U_a between F and D (more nearly equal the smaller ΔO and ΔA are). The slope gets less steep as you move down and to the right along the indifference curve because the value of apples measured in oranges becomes less as you have more apples (farther right) and fewer oranges (lower). This is the same pattern we already saw in Table 3-1.

Figure 3-1 also allows us to see geometrically why the meaning of the value of apples becomes less ambiguous the smaller the changes (in quantity of apples and oranges) we consider. Suppose we start at point L on indifference curve U_c. For large changes in both directions, the two ways of calculating the value of an apple (how many oranges would you have to get to make up for losing one apple versus how many oranges would you be willing to lose in exchange for getting one apple) correspond to finding the slopes of the lines LM and LN, which are substantially different. For small changes, they correspond to finding the slopes of the shorter lines Lm and Ln, which are almost equal. As the change approaches zero, the two slopes approach equality with each other and with the slope of the indifference curve at L.

The indifference curves on one figure in a textbook are usually very similar; sometimes they are simply the same curve shifted to different positions. In part that is because it is easier to draw them that way; in part, because for many utility functions indifference curves that are close to each other have similar shapes.

Numerical Example

In Figure 3-1, point D is a bundle of 4 apples and 3 oranges, and point F is a bundle of 2 apples and 8 oranges. ΔA is 2 apples and ΔO is 5 oranges. The slope of the line connecting D and F is (minus) $5/2$. $5/2$ is also the value of an apple—2 apples are worth 5 oranges, so an apple is worth $5/2$ of an orange.

Finding the Optimal Bundle

In the previous section, we considered an individual who started with a particular bundle of apples and oranges (A) and could trade apples for oranges at a rate of 1 for 1. In this section, we will analyze essentially the same situation, starting out in a slightly different way. We begin by assuming that you have an income (I), which you can use to buy apples and oranges; the price of apples is P_a and the price of oranges is P_o. If you spend your entire income of $100 on apples at $0.50 apiece, you can buy I/P_a ($100/$0.50 = 200) apples and no oranges, putting you at point K on Figure 3-2a. If you spend your entire income on oranges at $1 apiece, you can buy I/P_o ($100/$1 = 100) oranges and no apples, putting you at point L. You should be able to convince yourself, by either algebra or trial and error, that the line B connecting L and K (called the

budget line) represents all of the different combinations of apples and oranges that you could buy—assuming you are going to spend your entire income. Its equation is $I = a(P_a) + o(P_o)$ where a is the quantity of apples you buy and o is the quantity of oranges. Put in words, that says that the amount you spend on apples and oranges equals quantity of apples times price of apples plus quantity of oranges times price of oranges—equals your entire income. Remember that at this point, apples and oranges are the only goods that exist.

Numerical Example

Suppose your income is $100/month; P_a = $0.50/apple; P_o = $1/orange. Table 3-2 shows some of the different bundles that you could buy with your $100 income. Figure 3-2a shows the corresponding budget line.

Indifference curves, such as those of Figure 3-1, show a consumer's preferences. The budget line plus the region below it (bundles that cost less than his income) show the alternatives available to him—his opportunity set. Figure 3-2a shows both.

The bundles on indifference curve U_5 are preferred to those of the other two curves; unfortunately there is no point that is both on U_5 and on (or below) the budget line—no bundle on U_5 that the consumer can buy with his income. There are two points on U_1 that are also on the budget line (M and N), representing two bundles that the consumer could buy; in addition, the portion of U_1 between the two points is below the budget line and therefore represents bundles that the consumer could buy and still have some money left over. Should the consumer choose one such point? No. Points O and P are on both the budget line and U_2; since U_2 is above (hence preferred to) U_1, the consumer prefers O or P to M or N or any other bundle on U_1.

Should the consumer choose a bundle represented by O, P, or one of the points in between, such as Q? Again the answer is no. Remember that the three indifference curves are merely the three I have chosen to draw out of the infinite number needed to describe the consumer's preferences. Consider point R. It represents a bundle containing more of both goods than Q; hence it is preferable to Q. Since all points on U_2

Table 3-2

Apples	Oranges	Expenditure
200	0	200 apples × $0.50 + 0 oranges × $1 = $100
160	20	160 apples × $0.50 + 20 oranges × $1 = $100
120	40	120 apples × $0.50 + 40 oranges × $1 = $100
100	50	100 apples × $0.50 + 50 oranges × $1 = $100
60	70	60 apples × $0.50 + 70 oranges × $1 = $100
20	90	20 apples × $0.50 + 90 oranges × $1 = $100
0	100	0 apples × $0.50 + 100 oranges × $1 = $100

Figure 3-2

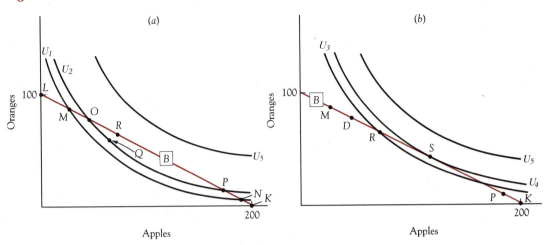

The solution to the consumer-choice problem for a world of only two goods. *B* is the budget line for a consumer who has $100 and can buy oranges at $1 each or apples at $0.50 each. The optimal bundle is *S*, where the budget line is tangent to an indifference curve, since there is no point on *B* that is on a higher indifference curve than U_4.

are equivalent, *R* must also be superior to *O* and *P*. To find out whether it is the best possible bundle, we draw the indifference curve on which it lies—U_3 on Figure 3-2*b*. As I have drawn it, there is another point, *S*, that lies on a still higher indifference curve and is also on the budget line.

Should the consumer choose *S*? Yes. Its indifference curve, U_4, just touches the budget line. Since any higher indifference curve must be above U_4, it cannot intersect the budget line. *S* is the optimal bundle.

It appears that the highest indifference curve consistent with the consumer's income is the one that is just tangent to the budget line, and the optimal bundle is at the point of tangency. This is the usual solution; Figures 3-3*a* and 3-3*b* show two exceptions. In each case, the budget line is the same as in Figure 3-2 but the indifference curves are different; the figures represent the same income and prices as Figure 3-2 but different preferences.

On Figure 3-3*a*, the consumer's optimal point is *X* on indifference curve U_2. He could move to a still higher indifference curve by moving down and to the right along the budget line—except that to do so, he would have to consume a negative quantity of oranges! Similarly, in Figure 3-2*b*, in order to do better than point *Y*, he would have to consume a negative quantity of apples. These are both corner solutions. In the normal case (interior solution), where the optimal bundle contains both apples and oranges, the result of the previous paragraph holds—the optimal bundle is at the point of tangency.

Section II   Price = Value = Cost

Figure 3-3

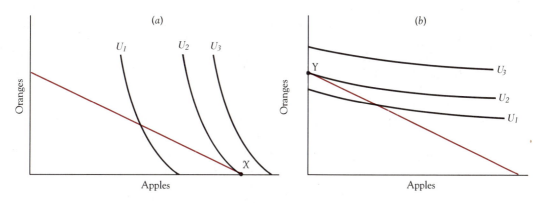

Corner solutions on an indifference curve diagram. X shows a situation in which the consumer's preferred bundle contains only apples; Y shows a situation in which it contains only oranges.

Price = Value

If two lines are tangent, that means that they are touching and their slopes are the same. The budget line runs from the point $(0, I/P_o)$ to the point $(I/P_a, 0)$, so its slope is $-(I/P_o)/(I/P_a) = -P_a/P_o$. The rate at which you can trade apples for oranges (while keeping your total expenditure fixed) is simply the ratio of the price of an apple to the price of an orange. That is the same thing as the price of an apple measured in oranges; if apples cost \$0.50 and oranges \$1, then in order to get one more apple you must give up half an orange. The price of an apple (measured in oranges) is half an orange. So the slope of the budget line is minus the price of an apple measured in oranges.

The slope of the indifference curve, as I showed earlier in this chapter, is minus the value of an apple measured in oranges. So, in equilibrium, the price of an apple measured in oranges (the rate at which you can transform oranges into apples by selling one and buying the other) is equal to the value of an apple measured in oranges (the **marginal rate of substitution**—the rate at which oranges substitute for apples as consumption goods, the number of oranges you are willing to give up in exchange for an apple). This is the same result that I sketched verbally at the end of the first part of the chapter, when I said that you would keep trading until you reached a point where the value of an additional orange (in apples) was equal to its cost (also in apples).

One possible reaction to this result is "that's obvious; of course the value of something is the same as its price." Another is "this is a bunch of meaningless gobbledygook." Both are wrong.

To see why the first reaction is wrong, consider what we mean by price and value. Price is what you *have* to give up in order to get something. Value is what you *are just barely willing* to give up to get something. Nothing in those two concepts makes it obvious that they are the same.

The second reaction is much more defensible. You have just been bombarded with a considerable junkpile of abstractions; it may take a while to dig yourself out. You may find it useful to go through the argument in each of the four ways it is presented (two so far, two in the next chapter) until you find one that makes sense to your intuition. Once you have done that, you should be able to go back over the other three and make sense out of them too. One of the reasons for using several different languages is that different people learn in different ways.

This equality between relative prices and relative values is one example of a very general pattern that we will see again and again. I will refer to it as the **equimarginal principle**—marginal because the values being compared are values for one more apple, orange, or whatever. It is a statement not about our tastes but about equilibrium—where we are when we stop trading. The same pattern has already appeared several times, in a very different context, in the optional sections of Chapter 1, where we saw that in equilibrium all lines in a supermarket and all lanes on a freeway are equally attractive—provided that the cost of getting to them is the same.

The Invisible World—A Brief Digression

Another response you may have at this point is "Where do all these tables and indifference curves come from, anyway? How can you possibly know what my preferences are? How, for that matter, can I know exactly how many apples I would give for an orange? Are economists people who go around asking people what bundles they are indifferent among—and are they fools enough to believe the answers?"

I shall answer the five questions in order. The tables and figures all came out of my head—I made them up, subject to the requirement that the numbers in the table have a certain pattern and the curves a certain shape. I cannot tell what your preferences are. You do not know exactly what your preferences are. No. No.

If we cannot find out what indifference curves are, what good are they? The answer is that indifference curves—like much of the rest of economics—are tools used to help us think clearly about human behavior. By using them, we can show that if people have preferences and rationally pursue them (the assumptions that I made and defended in Chapter 1), certain consequences follow. So far in this chapter, I have concentrated on one particular consequence—the equality between relative values and relative prices. I will show others later. Indifference curves and the like are useful as analytical tools; it is a serious error to think of them as things we actually expect to go out and measure.

Income and Substitution Effects

Now that we know what indifference curves are, we shall use them to show how the amount you consume of a good varies with your income and with the price of the good. Figure 3-4 shows what happens as income rises, with price held constant. B_1 is the same budget line we have seen before, corresponding to an income of $100 and prices of $1/orange and $0.50/apple. B_2 is the budget line for the same prices but for an income of $125, B_3 for an income of $150. Since relative prices are the same in all three cases, all three budget lines have the same slope, making them parallel to each other. In each case, I have drawn in the indifference curve that is just tangent to the budget line. As income rises, the consumption bundle shifts from X to Y to Z; in the case illustrated, consumption of both apples and oranges rises with income—they are **normal goods.** The line *IEP* is the **income expansion path** showing how consumption of apples and oranges changes as the consumer's income increases.

Figure 3-5 shows the same pattern of income and prices but a different set of indifference curves, corresponding to an individual with different preferences. This time, as income increases, the consumption of oranges increases but the consumption of apples decreases! In such

Figure 3-4

Optimal bundles for 3 different incomes—2 normal goods. X is the optimal bundle for an income of $100, Y for an income of $125, and Z for an income of $150—as shown by B_1, B_2, and B_3. Consumption of both apples and oranges increases with increasing income.

Figure 3-5

Optimal bundles for three different incomes—a normal good and an inferior good. As income increases, consumption of oranges increases but consumption of apples decreases; so apples are an inferior good. *IEP* is the income expansion path.

a situation, apples are an **inferior good**—a good of which we consume less the richer we are. Hamburger and beans are both plausible examples of inferior goods, for some ranges of income. As a very poor person becomes less poor, he eats hamburger instead of beans; his consumption of beans goes down as his income goes up, so for that range of incomes beans are an inferior good. As his income becomes still higher, he starts eating steak instead of hamburger. His consumption of hamburger goes down as his income goes up, so for that range of incomes, hamburger is an inferior good.

In describing the budget lines B_1, B_2, and B_3, I gave specific values for income and prices. I could just as easily have told you that income was $200, $250, and $300 and that prices were $2/orange and $1/apple; that would have produced exactly the same budget lines. The reason is obvious: If you double your income and simultaneously double the price of everything you buy, your real situation is unchanged—you can buy exactly the same goods as before.

I could also have told you that income was $100 for all three budget lines and that the price of an orange was $1 for B_1, $0.80 for B_2, and $0.66 2/3 for B_3, with corresponding prices ($0.50, $0.40, $0.33 1/3) for apples. A drop in the price of everything you consume has the same effect on what you can buy as an increase in income.

Section II   Price = Value = Cost

It is not obvious when we should describe changes on an indifference curve diagram—or changes in the situations that such diagrams represent—as changes in prices and when we should describe them as changes in income. That is not because there is something wrong with indifference curves but because the distinction between a change in income and a change in price is less clear than it at first seems. We are used to thinking of prices and incomes in terms of money, but money is important only for what it can buy; if all prices go down and my income stays the same, my **real income**—my ability to buy things—has risen in exactly the same way as if prices had stayed the same and my money income had gone up.

If income and prices all change at once, how can we say whether my real income has gone up, gone down, or stayed the same? Income is useful for what it can buy; the value to me of the bundle of goods that I buy is indicated, on an indifference curve diagram, by what indifference curve it is on. It therefore seems natural to say that a change in money income and prices that leaves me on the same indifference curve as before has left my real income unchanged. A change that leaves me on a higher indifference curve has increased my real income; a change that leaves me on a lower indifference curve has lowered my real income.

The prices that are important are **relative prices**—how much of one good I must give up to get another. As I showed earlier, the price of one good in terms of another corresponds to (minus) the slope of the budget line. So a change in money income and money prices that alters the slope of the budget line while leaving me on the same indifference curve is a pure change in prices—prices have changed and (real) income has not. A change that leaves the slope of the budget line the same but moves it so that it is tangent to a different indifference curve is a pure change in income—real income has changed but (relative) prices have not. An example of the former is shown on Figure 3-6a; an example of the latter, on Figure 3-6b.

Figure 3-7 shows the effect of a decrease in the price of apples. B_1 is the same budget line as before; A is the optimal bundle on B_1. B_2 is a budget line for the same income (\$100) and the same price of oranges (\$1/orange), but for a new and lower price of apples (\$0.33 $\frac{1}{3}$ per apple). C is the optimal point on that budget line. We can decompose the movement from point A to point C into two parts, as shown in Figure 3-7. A pure change in price with real income fixed would leave us on the same indifference curve, changing the budget line from B_1 to B' and the optimal bundle from A to B. A pure change in income would keep relative prices (the slope of the budget line) unchanged, while moving us to a different indifference curve. That is the movement from bundle B on budget line B' to bundle C on budget line B_2; note that B' and B_2 are parallel to each other. The change in our consumption as we move from A to B is called the **substitution effect** (we substitute apples for oranges because they have become relatively cheaper); the change as we move from B to C is called the **income effect**.

Figure 3-6

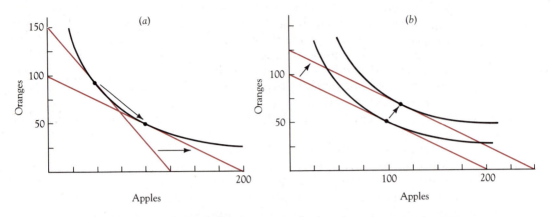

(a)   (b)

A pure change in price (*a*) and a pure change in income (*b*). On Figure 3-6*a*, relative prices change, but real income does not, since the individual ends up on the same indifference curve after the change. On Figure 3-6*b*, relative prices stay the same but real income increases.

Figure 3-7

The effect of a fall in the price of apples. When the price of apples falls, the optimal bundle changes from *A* to *C*. The movement from *A* to *B* is a substitution effect—relative prices change; real income does not. The movement from *B* to *C* is an income effect; real income changes, relative prices do not. A further price drop moves the optimal bundle to *D*. The line *PEP*, running from *A* to *C* to *D*, is the price expansion path.

      Section II   Price = Value = Cost

A pure substitution effect always increases the consumption of the good that has become relatively cheaper. You can see that by looking at the shape of the indifference curve and imagining what happens as the budget line rolls along it (as it does from B_1 to B'). This corresponds to lowering the price of one good while at the same time cancelling out the gain to the consumer by either raising the price of the other good or lowering income. On net, the consumer is neither better off nor worse off. The result is to increase the consumption of the good that has become cheaper. The pure income effect from a decrease in the price of a good (an increase in real income), on the other hand, may either increase or decrease its consumption, according to whether it is a normal or an inferior good.

A drop in the price of one good without any compensating change in income or other prices produces both a substitution effect and an income effect, as shown on Figure 3-7; apples are cheaper than before relative to oranges, and the lower price of apples makes the consumer better off than before. The substitution effect always increases the consumption of the good whose price has fallen; the income effect may increase or decrease it. You can see the net effect by looking at the **price expansion path** (*PEP* on Figure 3-7), which shows how consumption of both goods changes (from *A* to *C* to *D*) with changes in the price of one good.

This suggests the possibility of a good so strongly inferior that the income effect more than cancels the substitution effect—as its price falls, its consumption goes down. Imagine, for example, that you are spending most of your income on hamburger. If the price of hamburger falls by 50 percent while your income and all other prices remain the same, your real income has almost doubled. Since you are now much richer than before, you may decide to buy some steak and reduce your consumption of hamburger. The substitution effect tends to make you consume more hamburger; at the lower price of hamburger, the money required to buy an ounce of steak would buy twice as much hamburger as before the price change; so steak is more expensive in terms of hamburger than before. But you are now much richer—so you may choose to eat more steak in spite of its higher relative cost.

A good whose consumption goes down instead of up when its price goes down is called a **Giffen good**. It is not clear whether any such goods actually exist. The reason is that most of us consume many different goods, spending only a small part of our income on any one. A drop in the price of one good has a large effect on its relative price (hence a large substitution effect) but only a small effect on our real income. A Giffen good must either consume a large fraction of income or be so strongly inferior that the effect of a small change in income outweighs that of a large change in relative price.

Students frequently confuse the idea of an inferior good with the idea of a Giffen good. An inferior good is a good that you buy less of when *your income* goes up. There are many examples—for some of you,

Figure 3-8

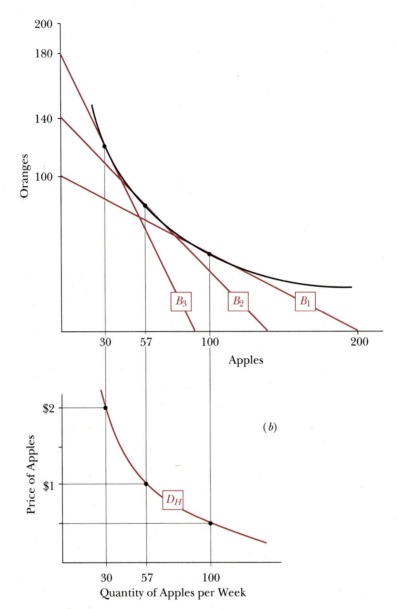

The derivation of an income-compensated demand curve. Budget lines B_1, B_2, and B_3 show different combinations of prices and income corresponding to the same real income. D_H is the resulting income-compensated (Hicksian) demand curve.

Table 3-3

Budget Line	Price of Apples	Price of Oranges	Income ($/week)	Quantity of Apples Purchased per Week
B_1	$0.50	$1.00	100	100
B_2	$1.00	$1.00	140	57
B_3	$2.00	$1.00	180	30

McDonald's hamburgers or bicycles. A Giffen good is a good that you buy less of when *its price* goes down. A Giffen good must be an inferior good, but most inferior goods are not Giffen goods.

If Giffen goods are rare or nonexistent, why have I spent time discussing them? The main reason is that in much of economic analysis (including a good deal of this book), we assume that demand curves slope down—that the higher the price of something is, the less of it you buy. If I am going to use that assumption over and over again, it is only fair to give you some idea of how solid it is—by describing the circumstances in which it would be false.

Demand Curves

Figure 3-6*a* showed the effect on consumption of a pure change in price. Figures 3-8*a* and *b* and Table 3-3 show how the same analysis can be used to derive an **income-compensated demand curve** (also known as a **Hicksian demand curve** after economist John Hicks). The budget lines on Figure 3-8*a* correspond to a series of different prices for apples, from $0.50/apple to $2/apple. The price of oranges is held constant at $1/orange. Table 3-3 shows prices, quantities, and income for each budget line. Figure 3-8*b* is the resulting demand curve. It shows the relation between price of apples and quantity purchased for the consumer whose preferences are represented on Figure 3-8*a*. It is an income-compensated demand curve because, as we increase the price of apples, we also increase income by just enough to keep the consumer on the same indifference curve. We thus eliminate the income effect; the change in the quantity purchased is due to the substitution effect alone.

Figures 3-9*a* and *b* and Table 3-4 show the similar derivation of an **ordinary demand curve** (called a **Marshallian demand curve** after economist Alfred Marshall). This time, just as on Figure 3-7, the price of

Table 3-4

Budget Line	Price of Apples	Price of Oranges	Income ($/week)	Quantity of Apples Purchased per Week
B_1	$0.50	$1.00	150	120
B_2	$1.00	$1.00	150	65
B_3	$2.00	$1.00	150	20

apples is changed while both the price of oranges and income are held constant. The higher the price of apples, the worse off the consumer; his dollar income is the same but, since his dollars will buy fewer apples, his real income is lower. So the higher the price of an apple on Figure 3-9a, the lower the indifference curve to which the corresponding budget line is tangent. This time the change in quantity purchased includes both an income and a substitution effect.

For most economic problems, the relevant demand curve is the Marshallian one, since there is generally no reason to expect a change in the

Figure 3-9

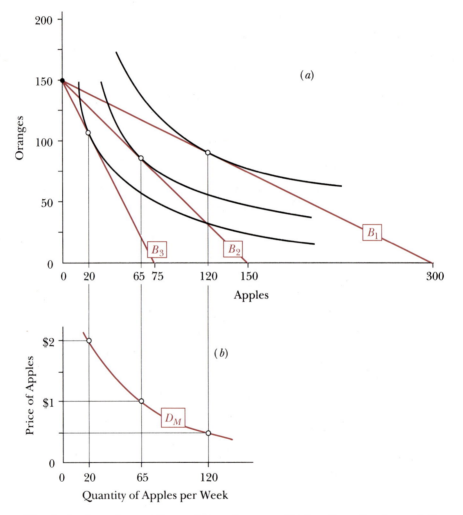

The derivation of an ordinary demand curve. Budget lines B_1, B_2, and B_3 show different prices of apples but the same income and price of oranges. D_M is the ordinary (Marshallian) demand curve.

Section II   Price = Value = Cost

Figure 3-10

Quantity of Apples per Week

Ordinary and income-compensated demand curves for the same individual. D_M is the ordinary (Marshallian) demand curve; D_H is the income-compensated (Hicksian) demand curve.

price of one good to cause a compensating change in income or other prices. Some parts of economic theory, however, including consumer surplus, which will be explained in Chapter 4, can be derived rigorously only by using income-compensated demand curves.

The Marshallian demand curve D_M on Figure 3-9*b* and the Hicksian demand curve D_H on Figure 3-8*b* are significantly different, as you can see on Figure 3-10. That is because we are considering a world with only two goods. Since raising the price of one of them makes the consumer significantly worse off, his behavior (the amount of the good he buys) is substantially different according to whether we do or do not compensate him for the change.

But in the real world, as I pointed out earlier, we divide our expenditure among many goods. If I spend only a small fraction of my income on a particular good, a change in its price has only a small effect on my real income. In such a case, the difference between the two demand curves is likely to be very small. For this reason, we will generally ignore the distinction between ordinary and income-compensated demand curves in what follows.

Application: Housing Prices—A Paradox

You have just bought a house. A month after you have concluded the deal, the price of houses goes up. Are you better off (your house is worth more) or worse off (prices are higher) as a result of the price change? Most people will reply that you are better off; you own a house and houses are now more valuable.

You have just bought a house. A month after you have concluded the deal, the price of houses goes down. Are you worse off (your house is worth less) or better off (prices are lower)? Most people, in my experience, reply that you are worse off. The answers seem consistent, even to those who are not sure what the right answer is. It appears obvious that if a rise in the price of housing makes you better off, then a fall must make you worse off, and if a rise makes you worse off, then a fall must make you better off.

Although it appears obvious, it is wrong. The correct answer is that either a rise or a fall in the price of housing makes you better off!

Before proving this, I will first describe the situation a little more precisely. I am assuming that you have an income (I), part of which went to buy the house. One may imagine either that your income is from a portfolio of stocks and bonds, part of which you sold in order to buy the house, or that you have a salary, part of which must now go for interest on the mortgage. In either case, you have bought housing and, as a result, have less to spend on other goods.

I am also assuming that none of the circumstances determining how much housing you want are ever going to change, except for the price of housing; if the price of housing stayed the same, so would the amount of housing you want. You are not, in other words, planning to have children and move to a bigger house or planning to retire, sell your house, and move to Florida. To simplify the argument, I will ignore all costs of buying, selling, or owning housing other than the price—sales taxes, realtor's commissions, and the like. Finally, I will assume that the change in price was unexpected; when you bought the house you were assuming that the price of housing, like everything else, was going to stay the same forever.

Now that I have described the situation more precisely, you may want to stop and try to figure out how my answer—that a change in either direction benefits you—can be true.

The situation is shown in Figure 3-11. The vertical axis represents housing; the horizontal axis represents expenditure on all other goods. The budget line B_1 shows the different combinations of quantity of housing and quantity of other expenditure you could have chosen at the initial price of housing ($50/square foot). Point A_1 is the optimal bundle–the amount of housing you bought. It is on indifference curve U_1.

Line B_2 shows the situation after the price of housing has risen to $75/square foot. B_2, your new budget line, must have a slope of (minus) 1 square foot of housing/$75, since that is the new price of housing—the rate at which you can exchange dollars spent on all other goods for housing, or vice versa. The new budget line must go through point A_1, since one of the alternatives available to you is to do nothing—to keep the bundle that you had before the price change. You can choose to move away from point A_1 along the budget line either up (buy more housing, trading dollars for housing at a rate of $75/square foot) or down (sell your house and move to a smaller one—sell some of your housing for money at $75/square foot). So your new budget line, B_2, is simply a line with slope $-1/75$ drawn through point A_1.

Figure 3-11

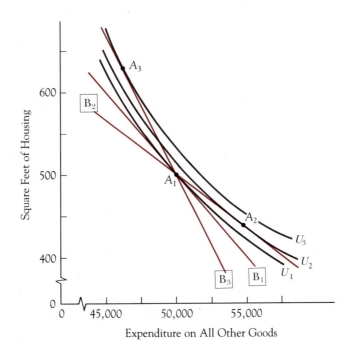

The effect on a homeowner of a change in the price of housing. B_1 shows the alternatives available at the original price of housing; B_2 shows those available if the price of housing rises after the house is bought; B_3 shows the alternatives available if the price falls. A_1 shows the homeowner's bundle of housing and all other consumption after the house is built and before there is any change in housing prices.

The figure shows what you choose to do; your new optimal point is at A_2. Since housing is now more expensive than before, you have chosen to sell your house and buy a smaller one—the gain in income is worth more to you than the reduction in the amount of housing you consume. You are now on indifference curve U_2, which is above (preferred to) U_1.

Line B_3 shows the situation if the price of housing goes down rather than up after you buy your house—to \$30/square foot. It is drawn in exactly the same way except that the price ratio is now $1/30$. Again, you have the choice of keeping your original house, so the line has to go through A_1. Your new optimal point is A_3; you have adjusted to the lower price of housing by selling your house and buying a bigger one. You are now on U_3—which is above U_1! The drop in the price of housing has made you better off.

By looking at the figures, you should be able to convince yourself that the result is a general one; whether housing prices go up or down after you buy your house, you are better off than if they had stayed the same. The same argument can be put in words as follows:

> What matters to you is what you consume—how much housing and how much of everything else. Before the price change, the bundle you had chosen—your house plus whatever you were buying with the rest of your income—was the best bundle of those available to you. If prices had not changed, you would have continued to consume that bundle. After prices change, you can still choose to consume the same bundle. The house belongs to you, so as long as you choose to keep it, the amount of money you have to spend on other things is unaffected by the price of the house.
>
> You cannot be worse off as a result of the price change—at worst you continue to consume the same bundle (of housing and other goods) as before. But since the optimal combination of housing and other goods depends, among other things, on the price of housing, it is unlikely that the old bundle is still optimal. If it is not, that means there is now some more attractive alternative, so you are now better off; a new alternative exists that you prefer to the best alternative (the old bundle) that you had before.

This seemingly paradoxical result is interesting in part for what it shows us about the relative virtues of our different languages. In solving the problem geometrically, the drawing tells us the answer. All we have to do is look at Figure 3-11 in order to see that any budget line that goes through A_1 with a different slope than B_1 has to intersect some indifference curve higher than U_1—whether the slope is steeper (lower price of housing) or shallower (higher price of housing). What the drawing does not tell us is *why* it is true. When we solve the problem verbally, we are likely to get the wrong answer (as at the beginning of this section, where I concluded that a fall in the price should make you worse off). But once we do get the right answer (possibly with some help from the figures), we not only know what is true, we also understand why.

I have ignored the transaction costs associated with buying and selling houses—realtor's commissions, sales taxes, the time spent finding a satisfactory house, and so on. If such costs are included, the result is that small changes in housing prices have no effect at all on you—it is not worth paying the transaction costs necessary to increase or decrease your consumption of housing. Large changes in either direction benefit you.

If you still find the result puzzling, the reason may be that you are confusing two quite different questions—whether a change in price makes you better off, given that you have bought a house, and whether having bought a house made you better off, given that the price is going to change. I have been discussing the first question. I asked whether, given that you had bought a house, a subsequent change in price made you better or worse off. The conclusion was that it made you better off, whether the price went up or down. That does not mean that buying the house was a good idea; if the price is going to go down, you would have been still better off if you had waited until it did so before you bought. The alternatives we have been comparing are "buy a house and have the price go down (or up)" versus "buy a house and have the price stay the same," not "buy a house and have the price go down (or up)" versus "have the price go down (or up) and *then* buy a house."

Application: Subsidies

Figure 3-12 shows your preferences between potatoes and expenditure on all other goods. You have an income of $150/week; the price of potatoes is $3/pound. If you spend all your income on potatoes, you can consume 50 pounds per week of potatoes and nothing else. If you spend nothing on potatoes, you have $150/week left to spend on all other goods. Line *B* is your budget line; point D is the bundle you choose.

Figure 3-12

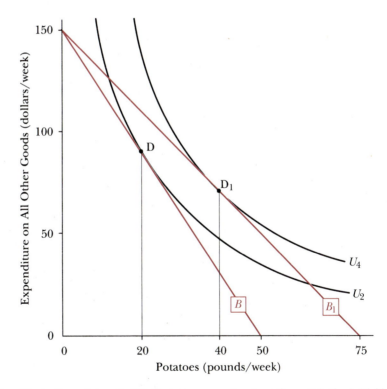

The effect of a potato subsidy that someone else pays for. *B* is the initial budget line, B_1 is the budget line after the government announces that it will pay one third of the cost of the potatoes you buy.

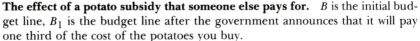

Chapter 3   The Consumer: Choice and Indifference Curves   **63**

The potato lobby convinces the government that potatoes are good for you and should therefore be subsidized. For every $3 you spend on potatoes, the government gives you $1. So for each pound of potatoes you buy, you have $2 less (instead of $3 less) to spend on other goods—the cost of potatoes to you is now only $2/pound instead of $3/pound.

If you choose to buy no potatoes, you are unaffected by the subsidy and can spend your entire income of $150/week on other goods. If you choose to spend your entire income on potatoes, you can now buy 75 pounds per week. B_1 is your new budget line. Your optimal bundle is D_1. Your consumption of potatoes has risen. Since you are on a higher indifference curve than before—U_4 instead of U_2—you are better off than before. You are happier (and, if the potato farmers are right, healthier); the potato farmers are selling more potatoes; all is well with the world.

There is one problem. At point D_1 you are consuming 40 pounds per week of potatoes (if that seems unreasonable, you may assume that some of the potatoes are converted into vodka before you consume them). Each pound costs $3, of which you pay only $2; the other dollar is provided by the subsidy. So the total subsidy is $40/week. Some taxpayers somewhere are paying for that subsidy. Before we conclude that the potato subsidy is a complete success, we should include their costs in our calculations.

To do so, I will assume that consumers and taxpayers are the same people. For simplicity I will also assume that everyone has the same income and the same preferences, as shown on Figures 3-12 and 3-13. Each individual has a pretax income of $I = \$150$/week and an aftertax income of $I - T$, where T is the amount of tax paid. To find T on the figure, note that a consumer who buys no potatoes has $I - T$ (income minus tax) available to spend on everything else, so $I - T$ is the vertical intercept of the budget line. While we do not yet know what T is, we do know that the total amount collected in taxes must be the same as the amount paid out in subsidy (we ignore the cost of collecting taxes and administering the subsidy).

For the population as a whole, tax collected equals subsidy paid, and the amount of subsidy paid depends on how many pounds of potatoes people buy. But from the standpoint of each individual in a large population, the quantity of potatoes he buys has a negligible effect on the total subsidy and hence on his taxes. So each individual takes T as given and finds his optimal bundle, as shown on Figure 3-13. Since the effective price of potatoes is still $2/pound (pay $3 and get $1 back as subsidy), the corresponding budget line (B') has the same slope as B_1 on Figure 3-12.

How do we know that the budget line is B', instead of some other line with the same slope? B' is the only budget line for which the tax collected from each taxpayer ($T = I - (I - T) = \$150$/week $- \$120$/week $= \$30$/week) is exactly equal to the subsidy paid to each taxpayer ($\$1$/lb $\times$ 30 lb/week at point D')—as it must be, since everyone is identical and total taxes paid must equal total subsidy received.

Figure 3-13

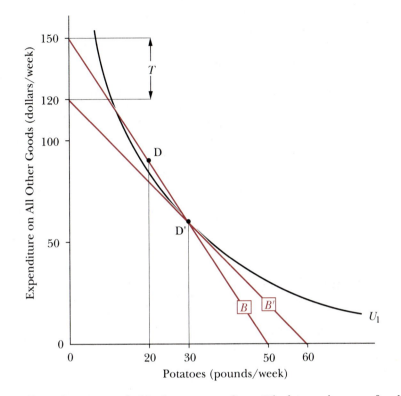

The effect of a potato subsidy that you pay for. *T* is the tax that pays for the subsidy; *B'* is the budget line for a consumer who pays the tax and can receive the subsidy. At D', the optimal point on *B'*, the consumer pays exactly as much in tax as he receives in subsidy—and is worse off than he would be, at D, if neither tax nor subsidy existed.

When Is a Wash Not a Wash? D', the bundle you choose to consume, lies on both *B'*, your budget line given the tax and subsidy, and *B*, your original budget line. This is not an accident. In the simple case I have described, everyone buys the same amount of potatoes, receives the same amount of subsidy, and pays the same amount of taxes; so taxes and subsidy must be equal not only for the population as a whole but for each individual separately. If you pay as much in taxes as you receive in subsidy, tax and subsidy cancel; the bundle (potatoes plus expenditure on all other goods) that you purchase is one you could have purchased from your original income if there had been neither tax nor subsidy. So it must be on *B*, your initial budget line.

That, in fact, is how I found *B'* in the first place. I knew that *B'* had to be parallel to B_1. I also knew that its optimal point, where it was tangent to an indifference curve, had to occur where it intersected *B*. *B'* was the only line that met both conditions.

D' is on a lower indifference curve than D—the combination of tax and subsidy makes you worse off. This is not accidental. Since D' is on your original budget line, it is a bundle that you could have chosen to consume if there had been no subsidy and no tax. In that situation, you chose D instead, so you must prefer D to D'. So the combination of a subsidy and a tax that just pays for the subsidy must make you worse off.

In accounting, a transaction that results in two terms that just cancel—a $1,000 gain balanced by a $1,000 loss—is referred to as a wash. Your first reaction on reading the previous few paragraphs may be that the sort of tax/subsidy combination I have described is a wash; since you are getting back just as much as you are paying, there is no net effect at all.

In one sense, that is true; in another and more important sense, it is not. The total dollar value of your consumption bundle is the same with or without the tax/subsidy combination; in that sense, there is no effect. But, as you can see on Figure 3-13, the bundle you choose is different in the two cases; with the tax and subsidy, you end up choosing a less attractive consumption bundle—one on a lower indifference curve—than without it.

The reason for the difference goes back to a point I made earlier—that although the amount of the tax is determined for the population as a whole by how many pounds of potatoes are consumed, each individual will and should treat the amount of the tax as a given when deciding how many potatoes to buy. Given what everyone else is doing, your budget line (with the tax and subsidy) is *B'*, not *B*. Since *B'* does not include D, you do not have the option of choosing that bundle. All of us, acting together, could choose D; each of us, rationally responding to the subsidy and the rational behavior of everyone else, chooses D'. This seemingly paradoxical result—that in some situations, rational behavior by every individual leaves each individual worse off—is not new. We encountered it before when we were explaining why armies run away and traffic jams.

Where You Are Going, Not How You Get There.   Students faced with something like the potato subsidy problem often make the mistake of trying to solve it in stages. First, they draw the budget line representing the subsidy (B_1). From that they calculate how many potatoes the consumer buys, then from that they calculate the tax necessary to pay for the subsidy. The problem with this approach is that imposing the tax shifts the budget line, which changes the number of potatoes consumed, which changes the amount of subsidy paid out, which changes the amount of tax needed to pay for the subsidy! You are caught in an infinite loop; each time you solve one part of the problem another part changes.

The solution is to ignore the series of successive approximations by which someone trying to find the tax that just paid for the subsidy would grope his way towards the solution, and simply ask what the solution must look like when he has finally reached it. That is what we did on Figure 3-13. A subsidy of \$1/lb implies a budget line parallel to B_1. A tax that just pays for the subsidy implies a budget line whose optimal point (where it is tangent to an indifference curve) occurs where it intersects B—meaning that consumers with that budget line buy a quantity of potatoes such that the tax just pays for the subsidy. B' is the only budget line you can draw on Figure 3-13 that meets both of those conditions, so it must be the solution.

Fine Point. One assumption implicit throughout this discussion is that the tax/subsidy does not affect the market price of potatoes; that was always assumed to be \$3/pound. The assumption is a reasonable one if we imagine that the subsidy and tax apply to only a small part of the population—say, a single town. Changes in the potato consumption of Podunk are unlikely to have much effect on the world market price of potatoes. It is less reasonable if we consider a program applying to the entire population of the United States. One effect of the subsidy is to increase the demand for potatoes, which should produce an increase in their price. That is one of the reasons why the potato farmers are in favor of the subsidy.

This raises a second question. So far, in analyzing the problem, we have only considered the interests of the consumers and the taxpayers; what about the producers? Is it possible that if we take them into account as well, the net effect of the subsidy is positive?

Insofar as we can answer that question—insofar, in other words, as we have a way of adding up different people's gains and losses—the answer is no. Even including the effect on the producers, the net effect of the subsidy is negative. You will have to wait until Chapter 17 to learn why.

Other Constraints

The same techniques that we have been using to analyze the constraint imposed upon a consumer by his limited income could just as easily be used to analyze other sorts of constraints. Consider, for example, someone on a thousand calorie/day diet. He faces a calorie constraint. Each food has a price in calories per ounce; he must choose a bundle of foods whose total cost is no more than a thousand calories. If he is considering only two alternative foods the thousand calorie bundles will lie along a budget line; his optimal bundle will be where that budget line is tangent to an indifference curve.

There is another constraint that applies to everyone, even those fortunate enough not to have to diet. Most things we do, including earning money and spending it, require time. Each of us must allocate his limited budget of 24 hours a day among a variety of uses—work, play, consumption, rest. If we consider only two alternatives, holding the rest fixed, we again have a choice that can be represented by an indifference curve diagram.

OPTIONAL SECTION

UTILITY FUNCTIONS
Utility

Utility and the utility function were important ideas in the development of economics and remain useful as tools for thinking about rational behavior. The idea of utility grows out of the attempt to understand all of an individual's choices in terms of a single thing he is trying to maximize—happiness, pleasure, or something similar. We call this his utility. Utility is observed only in choices. The statement "The utility to you of a Hawaiian vacation is greater than the utility to you of a moped" is equivalent to the statement "Given the choice between a Hawaiian vacation and a moped, you would choose the vacation." It does not mean "A vacation is more useful to you than a moped." Used as a technical term in economics, utility does not have the same meaning as in other contexts.

A **utility function** is a way of describing your preferences among different bundles of goods. Suppose we consider only two goods—apples and pears. The statement "Your utility function is 3 × (number of pounds of apples) + 2 × (number of pounds of pears)," which we write mathematically as

$$u(a, p) = 3a + 2p,$$

means that if you have to choose between two bundles of apples and pears, you will choose the bundle for which that function is greater. You will prefer 4 pounds of apples plus 3 pounds of pears (total utility = 18) to 3 pounds of apples plus 4 pounds of pears (total utility = 17).

If you are not familiar with the idea of functions, you may find the expression $u(a, p)$ confusing. All it means is "utility, which depends on a (the number of pounds of apples) and p (the number of pounds of pears)." The form of the dependence is then shown on the other side of the equality sign.

Several things are worth noting about such functions. The first is that we are very unlikely to know what someone's utility function actually is—we would have to know his preferences among all possible bundles of goods. The purpose of utility functions is to clarify our thinking by allowing us to build simplified pictures of how people act. Such **models** are not attempts to describe reality; they are attempts to set up a simplified situation with the same logical structure as the much more complicated reality in order to use the former to understand the latter. You should not confuse such models with large-scale econometric models—complicated sets of equations used (not very successfully) to try to predict the behavior of some real-world economy.

Section II   Price = Value = Cost

The second point to note is that the same pattern of behavior can be described by many different utility functions. In the example given above, suppose the utility function had been not u but

$$v(a,p) = 6a + 4p = 2 \times u(a,p).$$

The second function (v) is just twice the first (u); if the first is larger for one combination of apples and oranges than for another, so is the second. Since an individual always chooses the bundle that has higher utility, the two utility functions imply exactly the same behavior.

So far, we have assumed that your utility depends on only two goods. More generally we can write $u(x)$, where x is a bundle of goods. In the simple two-good case, x is the number of apples and of pears; we could write $x = (2,3)$ to describe a bundle of 2 apples and 3 pears. In the more general case of n goods, x is a longer list, describing how much of each good is in the particular bundle being considered. If we call the first good X_1 and the amount of the first good x_1, the second good X_2 and the amount of the second good x_2, and so on, and if the price of the first good is P_1 and similarly for the other goods, your income constraint—the requirement that the total bundle you purchase is worth no more than your total income—is the equation

$$I \geq P_1 x_1 + P_2 x_2 + \cdots + P_n x_n,$$

where the right-hand side of the equation is the amount you have to spend to buy that quantity of the first good (the quantity times its price— 3 pounds of apples at \$1/pound equals \$3), plus the amount for the quantity you are buying of the second good, plus . . ..

The point I made above about equivalent utility functions can be made more general by observing that if there are two functions, $u(x)$, $v(x)$, and if for any two bundles of goods, x_a, x_b, whenever $u(x_a) > u(x_b)$ then $v(x_a) > v(x_b)$ and vice versa, then the two utility functions describe exactly the same behavior and are equivalent. The purpose of a utility function is to tell which bundle of goods I prefer (the one for which the utility function gives a higher utility). Two different functions that always give the same answer to that question are equivalent—they imply exactly the same preferences.

My income and the prices of the goods I want define the alternatives from which I can choose; my utility function defines my preferences. Mathematically speaking, the problem of consumption is simply the problem of choosing the bundle of goods that maximizes your utility, subject to the income constraint—the requirement that the bundle you choose cost no more than your income. This, of course, is what we were doing earlier in the chapter. The utility function simply provides a more mathematically precise way of talking about it.

We have a utility function $u(x, y, z, \ldots)$ depending on the amount consumed of goods X, Y, Z, etc. We assume that the quantities x, y, z, ... can be continuously varied; that for x, y, z, $\ldots > 0$, u is a continuous function with continuous first derivatives, and that u is an increasing function of all its arguments (since they are goods, utility increases with increased consumption). u obeys the principle of declining marginal utility: $\partial u / \partial x$ decreases as x increases (and similarly for y, z, etc.), so $\partial^2 u / \partial x^2 < 0$. Our problem is to maximize u subject to the income constraint:

$$I \geq xP_x + yP_y + zP_z + \cdots$$

The general approach to solving such a problem (a constrained maximization) uses a mathematical device called a Lagrange multiplier, with which you may already be familiar. In this particular case, we can use a simpler and (to me) more intuitive approach. To begin with, note that $\geq$ in the income constraint can be replaced by $=$; since the only thing money is good for is buying goods and since more goods are always preferred to fewer goods, there is never any reason to spend less than your entire income.

We now consider varying x and y, while holding fixed the quantities of all other goods. If utility is at a maximum, an infinitesimal increase in x combined (because of the income constraint) with an infinitesimal decrease in y (such that total expenditure on x and y is unchanged) must leave utility unchanged, or in other words:

$$0 = du(x, y, z, \ldots) = \partial u / \partial x \, dx + \partial u / \partial y \, dy$$

From which it follows that

$$0 = du(x, y, z, \ldots)/dx = \partial u / \partial x + \partial u / \partial y \cdot dy/dx \qquad \text{(Equation 1)}$$

To find dy/dx we solve the income constraint for y in terms of x then take the derivative, thus:

$$y = (I - zP_z - \cdots - xP_x)/P_y$$

$$dy/dx = -(P_x/P_y)$$

Substituting this into Equation 1, we have

$$0 = \partial u / \partial x - (P_x/P_y) \, \partial u / \partial y$$

Rearranging this gives us

$$(\partial u/\partial x)/P_x = (\partial u/\partial y)/P_y \qquad \frac{\partial u/\partial x}{\partial u/\partial y} = \frac{P_x}{P_y}$$

which is the same relation that we derived earlier in the chapter, when we concluded that the price of an apple measured in oranges (P_a/P_o) is equal to the value of an apple measured in oranges. $\partial u/\partial x$ is the marginal utility of x and $\partial u/\partial y$ the marginal utility of y; their ratio is the value of x measured in y—the marginal rate of substitution. If a pound of X has a marginal utility of 3 and a pound of Y has a marginal utility of 1, then on the margin a pound of X is worth 3 pounds of Y. We could have made the same argument for X and Z instead of X and Y, or for any other pair of goods (holding consumption of everything else constant), so the equimarginal principle holds for all goods we consume.

It does not hold for goods we do not consume. As you may remember from a calculus course, the normal condition for a maximum, which is that the derivative is zero, does not apply if the maximum occurs at one end or the other of a variable's range. The situation is shown in Figure 3-14; $f(x)$, which is only defined for $x > 0$, has its maximum value at $x = 0$. Its derivative there is negative, but we cannot find higher values of f at lower values of x because there are no lower values of x. This is a corner solution; the maximum occurs at the corner (point A on Figure 3-14), where the function runs into the barrier $x = 0$.

A corner solution arises in consumption if there is a good X such that your maximum utility occurs when you are consuming none of it:

Figure 3-14

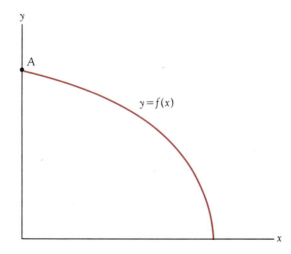

A corner solution. At A, $f(x)$ is maximum, but df/dx is not zero.

$x = 0$. Since it is a corner solution, the derivative of utility need not be zero even though utility is at a maximum; so Equation 1 need not hold. Put in words, that means that utility is still increasing as you decrease consumption of the good (and spend the money on other goods) up to the point where your consumption of X reaches 0. The marginal utility of X is less per dollar than the marginal utility of other goods, but you cannot increase your utility by consuming a dollar less of X and a dollar more of something else since you have already reduced your consumption of X to 0. So the equimarginal principle does not apply to goods you do not consume. This is the same point I made earlier and illustrated on Figures 3-3a and 3-3b. The picture of the corner is different, since it involves a utility function here and an indifference curve there, but the situation is the same.

Indifference Curves and Utility Functions

Next let us look at indifference curve analysis in terms of the utility function. Since we have only two dimensions, we will limit ourselves to a utility function with only two goods. Even in that case, showing two goods uses up the two dimensions we have available, leaving no place to show the utility function itself. With a third dimension, we could draw it as a surface, letting the height of the surface above any point (x, y) represent $u(x, y)$. Unfortunately this book is written on two-dimensional paper; Figure 3-15a is an attempt to overcome that limitation.

This is not a new problem; mapmakers face it whenever they try to represent a three-dimensional landscape on two-dimensional paper. The solution is a contour map. A contour map has one line through all points 100 feet above sea level, another through all points 200 feet above, and so on; by looking at the map you can, with practice, figure out the shape of the land in the third dimension. Where it is rising steeply, the contours are close together (the land rises 100 feet in only a short horizontal distance); where it is gently sloped, they are far apart.

The economist's equivalent of the contour on a topographical map is an indifference curve; it represents all of the points among which you are indifferent—or in other words, all of the bundles that give you the same utility. Figure 3-15a shows indifference curves U_1, U_2, and U_3, each labeled by its utility. Since u_1 is less than u_2, which in turn is less than u_3, points on U_3 are preferred to points on U_2, which are in turn preferred to points on U_1. The X-Y plane of Figure 3-15a corresponds to the indifference curve diagrams done earlier in the chapter.

Indifference curves do not completely describe the utility function from which they come. A curve is not labeled; it does not say "utility equals 9" on it. All the indifference curves tell us is which bundles we are indifferent among and which we prefer to which. They are in this sense less informative than the lines on a contour map, which tell us not only where the contour is but which contour (how many feet above sea

Figure 3-15

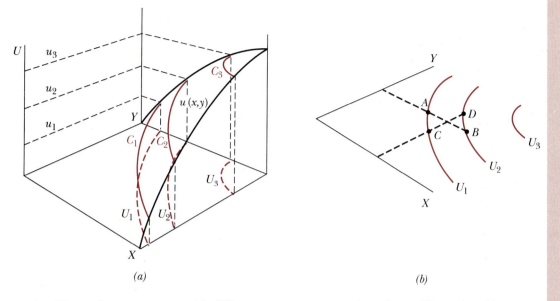

(a)   (b)

A utility surface, contours, and indifference curves. $u(x,y)$ shows how utility varies with consumption of X and Y. C_1, C_2, and C_3, are contours on U; U_1, U_2, and U_3 are the corresponding indifference curves. C_1 is the contour at a "height" of u_1; U_1 is the indifference curve joining all bundles with utility u_1. The same is true for C_2, U_2, and C_3, U_3.

level) it is. Hence one set of indifference curves may correspond to many different utility functions. The fact that, in spite of that, we can analyze consumption completely in terms of indifference curves corresponds to a point I made earlier—that different utility functions may describe exactly the same behavior.

As we move along an indifference curve, utility stays the same. Suppose (x, y) and $(x + dx, y + dy)$ are two points on the same indifference curve. We have:

$$u(x, y) = u(x + dx, y + dy) \approx u(x, y) + dx \cdot \partial u/\partial x + dy \cdot \partial u/\partial y.$$

As dy, $dx \rightarrow 0$, their ratio becomes the slope of the indifference curve, and the approximate equality becomes an equality. In that case,

$$dx \cdot \partial u/\partial x + dy \cdot \partial u/\partial y = 0$$

and

$$-(\partial u/\partial x)/(\partial u/\partial y) = dy/dx = \text{slope of the indifference curve.}$$

Chapter 3   The Consumer: Choice and Indifference Curves   73

This is equivalent, as you should be able to show, to the conclusion we reached earlier—that minus the slope of the indifference curve was equal to the value of apples (X) measured in oranges (Y).

U_1 in Figure 3–15b, like the indifference curves discussed earlier, slopes down to the right; its slope is negative. To keep utility constant, a reduction in the amount of one good must be balanced by an increase in the amount of another. Indifference curves sloping the other way would describe your preferences between two things, one of which is a good and one a bad—something for which $\partial u / \partial y > 0$. If this seems an odd thing to graph, consider representing your utility as a function of number of hours worked and number of dollars of income, the first a bad and the second a good, and deducing how many hours you will work at any given wage. Or consider the situation where production of a good results in undesirable waste products.

The slope of an indifference curve is usually negative because we are usually representing preferences between two goods. Its curvature, the fact that the slope of the indifference curves becomes shallower (i.e., less negative) as you move right or down on the diagram and steeper as you move left or up, is suggested by the principle of declining marginal utility but is not, strictly speaking, implied by it. Imagine that you move from A to B on Figure 3–15b. Quantity of Y stays the same and quantity of X increases, so $\partial u / \partial x$ must decrease. The slope of the indifference curve is $-(\partial u / \partial x)/(\partial u / \partial y)$, so the slope of the indifference curve through B is shallower than the slope of the indifference curve through A—unless $\partial u / \partial y$ decreases even faster than $\partial u / \partial x$ as x increases. There is no obvious reason why it should, but nothing in our assumptions makes it impossible. Similarly, as you move from C to D, y increases, x stays the same, $\partial u / \partial y$ decreases, and the slope of the indifference curves becomes steeper—unless, for some reason, an increase in the quantity of Y decreases the marginal utility of X even faster than it decreases the marginal utility of Y.

Here again, as several times before, our analysis is complicated by the possibility that consumption of one good may affect the utility of another. In most real-world situations, we would not expect such effects to be very large—we consume many different goods, most of which have little to do with each other. The exceptions are pairs of closely related goods—cars and bicycles, bread and butter, bananas and peanut butter. In some of these cases (**substitutes,** such as cars and bicycles) the more we have of one good the less we value the other; in other cases (**complements,** such as bread and butter or gasoline and automobiles) the more we have of one the more we value the other.

In such cases, we may expect indifference curves to be oddly shaped—some examples are given in the problems at the end of this chapter. In most other cases, we assume the **principle of declining marginal rate of substitution**—which means that the slope of the indifference curves becomes shallower as we move to the right on the diagram and steeper as we move up. As you can see from the previous discussion, this is close enough to the principle of declining marginal utility that for most practical purposes we may think of them as the same.

We have now derived the equimarginal principle directly from utility functions and shown the connection between utility functions and indifference curves. It is worth noting that although the argument was made in terms of money income and money prices, money has nothing essential to do with it. We could just as easily have started with a bundle of goods $(x, y, \ldots)$, and allowed you to exchange X for Y at a price (of Y in terms of X) of P_y/P_x, for Z at a price of P_z/P_x, and so on. Here, as elsewhere in price theory, the use of money and money prices simplifies exposition but does not affect the conclusions.

PROBLEMS

1. Near the beginning of the chapter, I gave some examples of bads. Do you agree with them? If not, is one of us necessarily wrong? Discuss.
2. Suppose my preferences with regard to hamburger and pens are as shown.

Options	Hamburger(pounds/year)	Pens/year	Utility(utiles/year)
A	100	30	50
B	108	29	50
C	118	28	50
D	200	30	75
E	?	29	75

    a. What is the value of a pound of hamburger to me (between points A and B)?

    b. In choosing between bundles A and B, which do I prefer? Between C and D?

    c. About how much hamburger should be in E to make me indifferent between it and D? Explain briefly.

3. Figure 3-16 shows your preferences between brandy and champagne. Which (if any) of the bundles shown do you prefer to point A? To which is A preferred? Which are equivalent to A? For which bundles can you not tell whether they are equivalent, better, or worse than A?
4. Answer the same questions for point B.
5. Figure 3-17 shows your indifference curves for cookies and bananas. You have an income of $100, the price of cookies is $1, and the price of bananas is $0.25. How many of each do you choose to consume?

Figure 3-16

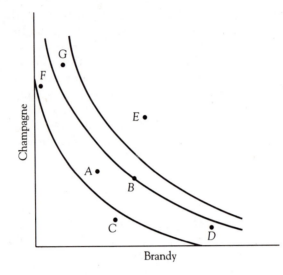

Indifference curves showing your preferences between brandy and champagne. For Problems 3 and 4.

Figure 3-17

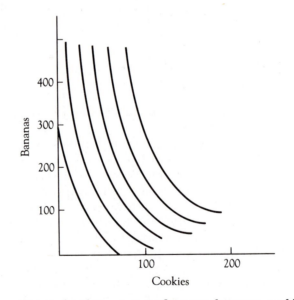

Indifference curves showing your preferences between cookies and bananas. For Problem 5.

Section II ′ Price = Value = Cost

Figure 3-18

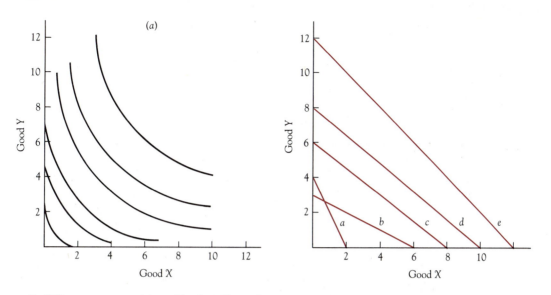

Indifference curves (*a*) and budget lines (*b*). For Problem 6.

6. Figure 3-18*a* shows a set of indifference curves; Figure 3-18*b* shows a set of budget lines. Your income is $12/week, the price of good *X* is $2, and the price of good *Y* is $4.
   a. Which line on Figure 3-18*b* is your budget line?
   b. Which point on Figure 3-18*a* do you prefer, among those available to you? In other words, how much of *X* and of *Y* do you choose to consume?

7. Figures 3-19*a*, *b*, *c*, and *d* show four different sets of indifference curves; in each case, points on U_3 are preferred to points on U_2, and points on U_2 are preferred to points on U_1. Describe verbally the pattern of preferences illustrated in each case. Yes, they are odd.

8. Figure 3-19*e* shows your preferences with regard to two goods—left shoes and right shoes. Explain why the indifference curves have the shape shown.

9. Draw a possible set of indifference curves for two things that are close, but not perfect, complements. An example might be bread and butter, if you much prefer your bread with butter but are willing to eat bread without butter (or with less than your preferred amount of butter).

10. Draw a possible set of indifference curves for two things that are perfect substitutes—butter and margarine for someone who cannot tell them apart. Draw another set for two things that are close, but not perfect, substitutes. An example might be chicken and turkey, if for some recipes you mildly prefer one or the other.

Figure 3-19

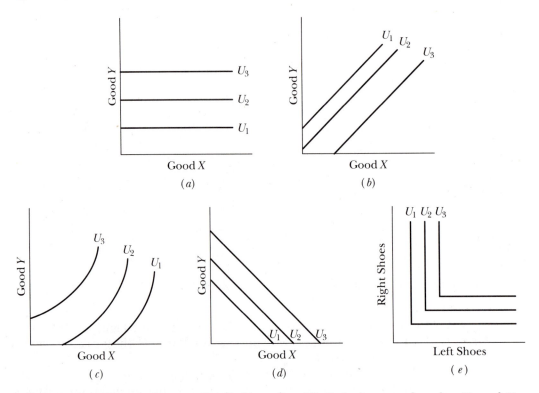

Some odd indifference curves. For Problems 7 and 8. U_3 is always preferred to U_2, and U_2 to U_1.

11. Figure 3-20 shows an indifference curve map and a budget line.
   a.   What is your marginal rate of substitution at points A, B, C?
   b.   What is the slope of the budget line at points A, B, C?
12. Use Figure 3-4 to derive an income-compensated demand curve for apples; B_1 on the figure should be one of your budget lines.
13. Use Figure 3-4 to derive an ordinary demand curve for apples; assume that your income is $100 and the price of oranges is $1.
14. William's income is $3/day; apples cost $0.50/apple.
   a.   Draw William's budget line, showing the choice between apples and expenditure on all other goods.
   b.   In order to reduce medical expenditures, the government decides to subsidize apples; for every dollar William spends on apples, he will be given $0.25 back. William pays no taxes. Draw William's budget line.
   c.   Instead of a subsidy, the government decides to use a voucher. The government provides William with $0.50/day, which can only

be spent on apples; any part of it that he does not spend on apples must be returned. William still pays no taxes. Draw his budget line. Be careful; it will not look like the other budget lines we have drawn.

15. The situation is the same as in the previous problem. Figure 3-21 shows William's indifference curves. How many apples a day does William consume:
   a. With neither subsidy nor voucher?
   b. With subsidy?
   c. With voucher?

16. Suppose that instead of subsidizing potatoes, as discussed in the text, we tax them; for every $2 you spend on potatoes, you must give an additional $1 to the government. The tax collected is then returned to the consumers as a *demogrant:* everyone gets a fixed number of dollars to add to his income. We assume that everyone has the same income and the same tastes.

   Would people be better or worse off than if there were no tax (and no subsidy)? Prove your answer.

Figure 3-20

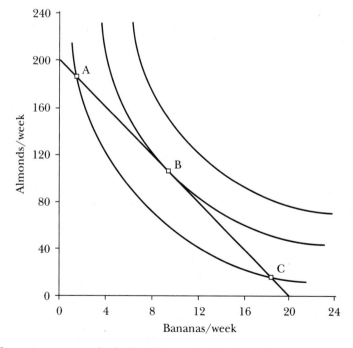

Indifference curves and a budget line.   For Problem 11.

Figure 3-21

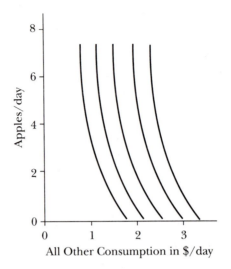

William's indifference curves showing his preferences between apples and all other goods.   For Problem 15.

The following problems refer to the optional section:

17. What testable proposition is suggested by the statement "*A* has more utility than *B* to me?"
18. Do each of a–d, *both* geometrically (you need not be precise) and using calculus. There are only two goods; x is the quantity of one good and y of the other. Your income is I. $u(x, y) = xy + x + y$.
    a. $P_x = \$1$; $P_y = \$1$; $I = \$10$. Suppose P_y rises to $\$2$. By how much must I increase in order that you be as well off as before?
    b. In the case described in part (a), if I does not change, what quantities of each good are consumed before and after the price change? How much of each change is a substitution effect? How much is an income effect?
    c. $P_x = \$1$; $I = \$10$. Graph the amount of Y you consume as a function of P_y, for values of P_y ranging from $\$0$ to $\$10$ (your ordinary demand curve for Y).
    d. With both prices equal to $\$1$, show how consumption of each good varies as I changes from $\$0$ to $\$100$.
19. Answer the following questions for the utility function:

$$u(x, y) = x - 1/y$$

Section II   Price = Value = Cost

a. $P_x = \$1$; $I = \$10$. Draw the demand curve for good Y, $\$1 < P_y < \$100$.
b. $P_x = \$1$; $I = \$10$. P_y increases from $\$1$ to $\$2$. Show the old and the new equilibria. The income effect could be eliminated either by changing I or by changing P_x and P_y while keeping their ratio fixed. What would the necessary change in I be? What would the necessary change in the prices be? Diagram both.
c. $P_x = \$1$. Draw the income-compensated demand curve for good Y. $\$1 < P_y < \$100$. Start with $P_y = \$1$ and $I = \$10$.
d. $P_x = \$1 = P_y$. Graph y against I for $\$0 < I < \$10$.

THE CONSUMER: MARGINAL VALUE, MARGINAL UTILITY AND CONSUMER SURPLUS

In Chapter 3 we used geometry, in the form of budget lines and indifference curves, to analyze the behavior of someone consuming only two goods. In this chapter we redo the analysis for a consumer buying many goods. We again use geometry, but in a different way. Each diagram shows on its horizontal axis quantity of one good, and on its vertical axis something related to that good (utility, value, marginal utility, marginal value) that varies with quantity.

We begin in the first part of the chapter by developing the concepts of marginal utility and marginal value and showing how they can be used to analyze the behavior of a consumer. The most important result of that analysis will be that the consumer's demand curve is identical to his marginal value curve. In the second part of the chapter, that result will be used to derive the concept of consumer surplus—the answer to the question "How much is it worth to me to be able to buy some good at a particular price—how much better off am I than if the good did not exist?" The remainder of the chapter is a collection of loosely related sections in which I rederive the equimarginal principle, examine more carefully exactly what we have been doing in the past two chapters, and use consumer surplus to analyze the popcorn puzzle discussed in Chapter 2.

MARGINAL UTILITY AND MARGINAL VALUE

So far, we have considered the consumption of only two goods—simple to graph but hardly realistic. We shall now consider the more general case of many goods. Since we only have two-dimensional graph paper, we imagine varying the quantity of one good while spending whatever income we have left on the optimal bundle of everything else.

Table 4-1 shows bundles, each of which contains the same quantity of all goods other than oranges, plus some number of oranges. In addition to showing the utility of each bundle, it also shows the **marginal utility** for each additional orange—the increase in utility as a result of adding that orange to the bundle. Figure 4-1 shows the same information in the form of a graph, with number of oranges on the horizontal axis and total

Table 4-1

Bundle	Oranges/Week	Total Utility	Marginal Utility
B	1	80	30
C	2	100	20
D	3	115	15
E	4	125	10
F	5	133	8
G	6	139	6
H	7	144	5
I	8	146	2
J	9	147	1
K	10	147	0
L	11	147	0
M	15	147	0
N	20	147	0

Figure 4-1

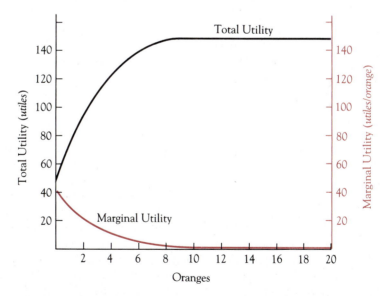

Total utility and marginal utility of oranges, assuming that it costs nothing to dispose of them. Total utility is shown in black, and marginal utility is shown in color. Because surplus oranges can be disposed of, marginal utility is never negative, and total utility never decreases with increasing number of oranges.

utility and marginal utility on the vertical axes. In comparing the table to the figure, you will note that on the table there is one value of marginal utility between 1 orange and 2, another between 2 and 3, and so forth, while on the figure marginal utility changes smoothly with quantity. The marginal utility shown on the table is really the average value of marginal utility over the corresponding range. For example, 20 is the average of marginal utility between 1 and 2 (oranges)—bundles B and C.

On a table such as Table 4-1, marginal utility is the difference between the utility of 1 orange and none, between 2 and 1, and so forth. On a graph such as Figure 4-1, it is the slope of the total utility curve. Both represent the same thing—the rate at which total utility increases as you increase the quantity of oranges. Since marginal utility is the slope of total utility, it is high when total utility is rising steeply, zero when total utility is constant, and negative if total utility is falling.

Total utility is stated in **utiles**—hypothetical units of utility. Since marginal utility is an increase in utility divided by an increase in oranges, it is measured in utiles per orange. That is why Figure 4-1 has two different vertical axes, marked off in different units. Both marginal utility and total utility depend on quantity of oranges, so both have the same horizontal axis. By putting them on the same graph, I make it easier to see the relationship between them.

The idea of total and marginal will be used many times throughout this book and applied to at least five different things—utility, value, cost, revenue, and expenditure. In each case, the relation between total and marginal is the same—marginal is the slope of total, the rate at which total increases as quantity increases. In this chapter, we use marginal utility and marginal value in order to understand consumer choice; in later chapters, production (both by individuals and by firms) will be analyzed in a similar way using marginal cost.

Declining Marginal Utility

You are deciding how many oranges to consume. If the question is whether to have one orange a week or none, you would much prefer one. If the alternatives are 51 oranges a week or 50, you may still prefer the additional orange, but the gain to you from one more orange is less. The marginal utility of an orange to you depends not only on the orange and you, but also on how many oranges you are consuming. We would expect the utility to you of a bundle of oranges to increase more and more slowly with each additional orange. Total utility increasing more and more slowly means marginal utility decreasing, as you can see from Table 4-1, so marginal utility decreases as the quantity of oranges increases. This is what I earlier called the principle of declining marginal utility. There may be some point (9 oranges a week on Table 4-1 and Figure 4-1) at which you have as many oranges as you want. At that point, total utility stops increasing; additional oranges are no longer a good. Their marginal utility is zero.

Figure 4-2

Total utility and marginal utility of oranges, assuming that it is costly to dispose of them. I want to eat only 10 oranges, so additional oranges have negative marginal utility. Total utility falls as the number of oranges increases beyond 10.

As long as one of the things we can do with oranges is throw them away, we cannot be worse off having more oranges; so oranges cannot be a bad. If it were costly to dispose of oranges (imagine yourself buried in a pile of them), then at some point the marginal utility of an additional orange would become negative—you would prefer fewer to more. Figure 4-2 shows your total and marginal utility for oranges as a function of the quantity of oranges you are consuming, on the assumption that it is costly to dispose of oranges.

From Marginal Utility to Marginal Value

Utility is a convenient device for thinking about choice, but it has one serious limitation—we can never observe it. We can observe whether bundle X has more utility to you than bundle Y by seeing which you choose, but that does not tell us *how much more* utility the bundle you prefer has. Since utiles are not physical objects that we can handle, taste, trade, and measure, we can never try the experiment of offering you a choice between an apple and 3 utiles in order to see whether the marginal utility of an apple to you is more or less than 3.

What we can observe are the relative marginal utilities of different goods. If we observe that you prefer 2 apples to 1 orange, we can conclude that the additional utility you get from the 2 apples is more than you get from the orange; hence the marginal utility per apple must be more than half the marginal utility per orange. If instead of measuring utility in utiles we measure it in units of the marginal utility of 1 apple, we can then say that the marginal utility of 1 orange is less than 2. If we observe that you are indifferent between 3 apples and 1 orange, we can say that the marginal utility of an orange is exactly 3.

What we are now dealing with is called **marginal value;** it is what one more unit of a good is worth to you in terms of other goods. Unlike marginal utility, it is in principle (and to some extent in practice) observable. We cannot watch you choose between apples and utiles, but we can watch you choose between apples and oranges. It is what I referred to in the previous chapter as the value of an orange (measured in apples). A more precise description would have been "the value of one more orange."

While we could discuss marginal value in terms of apples, it is easier to discuss it in terms of dollars. "The value to you of having one more orange is $1" means that you are indifferent between having one more orange and having one more dollar. Since the reason we want money is to buy goods with it, that means that you are indifferent between having one more orange and having whatever goods you would buy if your income were $1 higher. A graph showing total and marginal utility

Figure 4-3

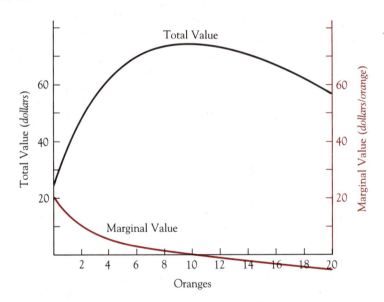

Total value and marginal value of oranges. The marginal utility of income is assumed to be 2 utiles per dollar, so total value is half as many dollars as total utility is utiles. The same is true for marginal value and marginal utility.

Section II Price = Value = Cost

(Figure 4-2) and the corresponding graph showing total and marginal value (Figure 4-3) appear the same, except for the scale; the vertical axis of one has utiles where the other has dollars, and $1 need not correspond to one utile. In drawing the figures, I have assumed that the marginal utility of income is 2 utiles/dollar (an additional $1 is worth 2 utiles), so a marginal utility of 20 utiles per orange corresponds to a marginal value of $10/orange, and a total utility of 60 utiles corresponds to a total value of $30.

This is an adequate way of looking at the relation between marginal value and marginal utility so long as we only consider situations in which the marginal utility of $1 does not change. If it does, then measuring utility in dollar units is like measuring a building with a rubber ruler. The resulting problems will be discussed in the optional section at the end of this chapter. For the moment, we will assume that the marginal utility of $1 can be treated as a constant. In that case, marginal value is simply marginal utility divided by the marginal utility of an additional dollar of income:

$$MV(\text{oranges}) = MU(\text{oranges})/MU(\text{income})$$

How Are Marginal Eggs Different from Other Eggs?   You eat some number of eggs each week. Suppose that the marginal value of the fifth egg (per week) is $0.50 (per week). This does not mean that there is a particular egg that is worth $0.50; it means that the difference between having 5 eggs per week and having 4 is worth $0.50/week. If we imagine that 5 eggs per week means 1 egg/day from Monday through Friday (cereal on the weekend), there is no reason why any one of those eggs should be valued more than another—but it seems likely that the extra value of 5 eggs a week instead of 4 is less than the extra value of 4 instead of 3. There is a marginal value of egg, not a marginal egg.

While this is the correct way of looking at marginal value in general, there are some particular cases in which one can talk about a **marginal unit**—a specific unit that produces the marginal value. Considering such cases may make it easier to understand the idea of marginal value. Once understood, it can then be applied to more general cases.

The Declining Marginal Value of Water.   Suppose, for example, that we use water for a number of different uses—drinking, washing, flushing, watering plants, swimming. The value of a gallon of water used in one way does not depend on how much water we are using in another; each is independent. To each use we can assign a value per gallon. If the price of water is $1/gallon, we use it only for those uses where it is worth at least that much; as the price falls, the number of uses expands. If water is worth $1/gallon to us for washing but only $0.10/gallon for swimming and $0.01/gallon for watering the lawn, then if its price is between $0.10 and $1 we wash but do not swim; if it is between $0.01

and $0.10 we wash and swim but do not water; and if it is below $0.01 we do all three. We can then talk of the marginal use for water—the use that is just barely worthwhile at a particular price.

If each additional unit of water goes for a different and independent use, there is an obvious justification for the principle of declining marginal utility. If you have only a little water, you use it for the most valuable purposes—drinking, for example. As you increase your consumption, additional water goes into less and less important uses, so the benefit to you of each additional gallon is less than that of the gallon before. In this particular case, declining marginal utility is not merely something we observe but also something implied by rationality. The difference between this and the egg case is that using water for a swimming pool does not change the value to us of using water to drink or to water the lawn, whereas eating an egg every Wednesday, in addition to the Monday, Tuesday, Thursday, and Friday eggs, may make us enjoy the other four eggs a little less.

The Declining Marginal Value of Money.   Consider, instead of water, money. There are many different things you can buy with it. Imagine that all of the things come in $1 packages. You could imagine arranging the packages in the order of how much you valued them—their utility to you. If you had $100, you would buy the 100 most valuable packages. The more money you had, the further down the list of packages you could go and the less valuable the marginal package would be. So additional money is worth less to you the more money you have.

While this way of looking at things is useful, it is not entirely correct, since goods are not independent; the possession of one may make another more or less valuable. One can imagine situations in which increasing your income from $3,000/year to $3,001 was more important than increasing it from $2,000 to $2,001. You may find it interesting to think up some examples. I will return to the subject in a later chapter.

Marginal Value and Demand

One of the objectives of this chapter is to derive a demand curve—a relation between the price of a good and how much of it a consumer chooses to buy. We are now in a position to do so. Imagine that you can buy all the eggs you want at a price of $0.80/egg. You first consider whether to buy 1 egg per week or none. If the marginal value to you of the first egg is more than $0.80 (in other words, if you prefer having one more egg to whatever else you could buy with $0.80), you are better off buying at least 1 egg. The next question is whether to buy 2 eggs or 1. Again, if the marginal value of one more egg is greater than $0.80, you are better off buying the egg and giving up the money. Following out the argument to its logical end, you conclude that you want to consume eggs at a rate such that the marginal value of an egg is $0.80. If you increased your consumption above that point, you would be paying $0.80 for an additional egg when consuming one more egg per week was worth less than $0.80 to you (remember declining marginal utility). You would be consuming an egg that was worth less than it cost. If you consumed less than that amount, you would fail to consume an egg that was worth more to you than it cost. This implies that (if you act rationally) the same points describe both your marginal value for eggs (value of having one more egg as a function of how many eggs per week you are consuming) and your demand for eggs (number of eggs per week you consume as a function of the price of eggs), since at any price you consume that quantity for which your marginal value of eggs equals that price. The relation is shown in Figures 4-4a and 4-4b. Note that your marginal value for eggs shows value

Figure 4-4

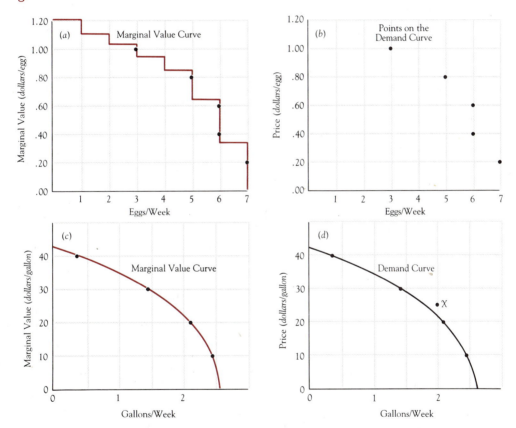

Marginal value and points on the demand curve. Panels (a) and (b) show a lumpy good. At any price, you buy a quantity for which marginal value equals the price, so the (price, quantity) points on the demand curve are the same as the (marginal value, quantity) points on the marginal value curve. Panels (c) and (d) show a continuous good. At any price, you buy a quantity for which marginal value equals the price; that is true for every price, so the demand curve is identical to the marginal value curve.

per egg as a function of quantity. Your demand curve shows quantity as a function of price.

Figures 4-4c and 4-4d show the same relation for a continuous good. As long as you are consuming a quantity of wine for which the marginal value of additional wine is greater than its price, you can make yourself better off by increasing your consumption. So you buy that quantity for which marginal value equals price. Since you do that for any price, your demand curve and your marginal value curve are the same.

By the principle of declining marginal utility, the marginal value curve should slope down; the more we have, the less we value additional quantities. I have just demonstrated that the demand curve is identical to the marginal value curve. It follows that demand curves slope down.

Some Problems. There is one flaw in this argument. So far, I have been assuming that the marginal utility of income—the increased utility from the goods bought with an extra dollar—is constant. But just as the marginal utility of apples depends on how many apples we have, the marginal utility of income depends on how much income we have. If our income increases, we will increase the quantities we consume (for normal goods), reducing the marginal utility of those goods. The marginal utility of a dollar is simply the utility of the additional goods we could buy with that dollar; so as income rises, the marginal utility of income falls.

A marginal value curve shows us what happens when we increase our consumption of one good *while holding everything else constant*. This does not quite correspond to what is shown by the demand curve of Figure 4-4d. That curve graphs quantity against price. As the price of the good falls and the quantity consumed increases, the total amount spent on that good changes—and so does the amount left to spend on other goods. Since the marginal value curve shows the value of a good measured in money, it should shift slightly as the change in that good's price changes the amount we have left to spend on other goods, and hence the marginal utility of money.

A similar difficulty in the analysis arises when the value to us of one good depends on how much we have of some other good. Bread is more valuable when we have plenty of butter, and butter less valuable when we have plenty of margarine. As price falls and quantity consumed rises in Figures 4-4b and 4-4d, the quantities of other goods consumed changes— which may affect the value of the good whose price has changed.

The problems here are the same as in the case of the Giffen good discussed earlier; a change in the price of one good affects not only the cost of that good in terms of others but also the consumer's total command over goods and services—a drop in price is equivalent to an increase in income. A full discussion of this would involve the income-compensated (Hicksian) demand curve discussed in the previous chapter.

A simpler solution, adequate for most practical purposes, is the one we used to justify the downward-sloping demand curve in the previous chapter. Since consumption is usually divided among many different

Section II Price = Value = Cost

goods, with only a small part of our income spent on any one, a change in the price of one good has only a very small effect on our real income and our consumption of other goods as compared to its effect on the cost of the good whose price has changed. If we ignore the small income effect, the complications of the last few paragraphs disappear. The demand curve is then exactly the same as the marginal value curve; since the latter slopes down (because of diminishing marginal utility), so does the former. The indifference curve argument gave us a downward-sloping demand curve for a consumer choosing between two goods; this argument gives one in the general case of a consumer buying many goods.

Warning. When I ask students taking an exam or quiz to explain why the demand curve is the same as the marginal value curve, most of them think they know the answer—and most of them are wrong. The problem seems to be a confusion based on an imprecise verbal argument. It sounds very simple: "Your demand is how much you demand something, which is the same as how much you value it" or, alternatively, "Your demand is how much you are willing to pay for it, which is how much you value it." But both of those explanations are wrong. Your demand curve shows not how much you demand it but how much of it you demand—a quantity, not an intensity of feeling.

Your demand curve does not show how much you are willing to give for the good. On Figure 4-4*d*, the point *X* (price = $25/gallon, quantity = 2 gallons/week) is above your demand curve. But if you had to choose between buying 2 gallons of wine a week at a price of $25/gallon or buying no wine at all, you would buy the wine; as we will see in a few pages, its total value is more than its cost. The demand curve shows the quantity you would *choose* to buy at any price, given that (at that price) you were free to buy as much or as little as you chose. It does not show the highest price you would pay for any quantity if you were choosing between that quantity and nothing.

What the height of your demand curve at any price is equal to is the amount you would be willing to pay for a little more of the good—your marginal value. That is true—but not because demand and value mean the same thing. The reason was given in the discussion of eggs and wine a few paragraphs earlier. It is also important; as you will see later in the chapter, the relation between demand and marginal value is essential in deriving consumer surplus, and as you will see later in the book, consumer surplus is an important tool in much of economics. I have emphasized the relationship between the two curves so strongly because it is easy to skip over it as obvious and continue building the structure of economics with one of its foundations missing.

Price, Value, Diamonds, and Water

In addition to the downward-sloping demand curve, another interesting result follows from the analysis of marginal value. As I pointed out earlier, there is no obvious relation between price (what you must give up to get something) and value (how much it is worth to you—what you are willing, if necessary, to give up to get it), a point nicely summarized in the saying that the best things in life are free. But if you are able to buy as much as you like of something at a per-unit price of P, you will choose, for the reasons discussed above, to consume that quantity such that an additional unit is worth exactly P to you. Hence in equilibrium (when you are dividing your income among different goods in the way that maximizes your welfare), the marginal value of goods is just equal to their price! If the best things in life really are free, in the sense of being things of which you can consume as much as you want without giving up anything else (true of air, not true of love), then their *marginal* value is zero!

This brings us back to the diamond-water paradox. Water is far more useful than diamonds, and far cheaper. The resolution of the paradox is that the total value to us of water is much greater than the total value of diamonds (we would be worse off with diamonds and no water than with water and no diamonds), but the marginal value of water is much less than that of diamonds. Since water is available at a low cost, we use it for all its valuable uses; if we used a little more, we would be adding a not very valuable use, such as watering the lawn once more just in case we had not watered it quite enough. Diamonds, being rare, get used only for their (few) valuable uses. Relative price equals relative marginal value; diamonds are much more expensive than water.

CONSUMER SURPLUS

This brings us to another (and related) paradox. Suppose you argued that "since the value of everything is equal to its price, I am no better off buying things than not buying, so I would be just as happy on Robinson Crusoe's island with nothing for sale as I am now." You would be confusing marginal value and average value; you are no better off buying the last drop of water at exactly its value but are far better off buying (at the same price) all the preceding (and to you more valuable) drops. Note that "preceding" describes order in value, not in time.

Can we make this argument more precise? Is there some sense in which we can define how much better off you are by being able to buy as much water as you want at $0.01/gallon or as many eggs as you want at $0.80/egg? The answer is shown in Figure 4-5a. By buying 1 egg instead of none, you receive a marginal value of $1.20 and give up $0.80; you are better off by $0.40. Buying a second egg provides a further increase in value of $1.10 at a cost of another $0.80. So buying 2 eggs instead of none makes you better off by $0.70.

This does not mean you have $0.70 more than if you bought no eggs—on the contrary, you have $1.60 less. It means that buying 2 eggs instead of none makes you as much better off as would the extra goods

Figure 4-5

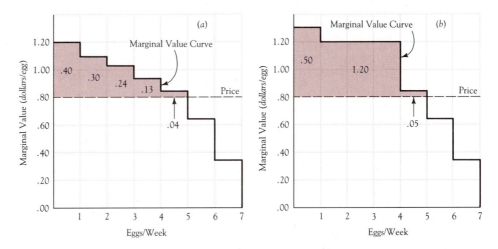

Marginal value curve and consumer surplus for a lumpy good. The shaded area under the marginal value curve and above the price equals the benefit to you of buying that quantity at that price. It is called *consumer surplus*.

you would buy if your income were $0.70 higher than it is. You are indifferent between having your present income and buying 2 eggs (as well as whatever else you would buy with the income) and having $0.70 more but being forbidden to buy any eggs.

Continuing the explanation of Figure 4-5a, we see that as long as you are consuming fewer than 5 eggs per week, each additional egg you buy makes you better off. When your consumption reaches 5 eggs per week, any futher increase involves buying goods that cost more than they are worth. The total gain to you from consuming 5 eggs at a price of $0.80 each instead of consuming no eggs at all is the sum of the little rectangles shown in the figure. The first rectangle is a gain of $0.40/egg times 1 egg, for a total gain of $0.40; the next is $0.30/egg times 1 egg, and so on.

Summing the area of the rectangles may seem odd to you. Why not simply sum their heights, which represent the gain per egg at each stage? But consider Figure 4-5b, which shows a marginal value curve for which the rectangles no longer all have a width of 1 egg per week. Gaining $0.40/egg on 3 eggs is worth 3 times as much as gaining $0.40/egg on 1 egg.

Finally, consider Figure 4-6a, where instead of a lumpy good such as eggs we show a continuous good such as wine (or apple juice). If we add up the gain on buying wine, drop by drop, the tiny rectangles exactly fill the shaded region *A*. That is your net gain from being able to buy wine at $8/gallon.

This area—representing the gain to a consumer from what he consumes—has a name. It is called **consumer surplus**. It equals the area under the demand curve and above the price—area *A* on Figure 4-6*a*. You will meet consumer surplus again—its derivation was one of the main purposes of this chapter. Its traditional use in economics is to evaluate the net effect on consumers of some change in the economic system, such as the introduction of a tax or a subsidy. As we will see in Chapters 10 and 16, it is also sometimes useful for helping a firm decide how to price its product.

Your consumer surplus from buying wine at some price is the value to you of being able to buy as much wine as you wish at that price— the difference between what you pay for the wine and what it is worth to you. The same analysis can be used to measure the value to you of other opportunities. Suppose, for example, that you are simply given 2 gallons per week for free, with no opportunity to either sell any of it or buy any more. The value to you of what you are getting is the value of the first drop of wine, plus the second, plus . . . adding up to the whole area under your demand curve—region *A* plus region *B* on Figure 4-6*a*. The situation is just the same as if you bought 2 gallons per week at a price of $8/gallon and were then given back the money. Area *A* is the consumer surplus on buying the wine; area *B* is the $16/week you spend to get it. The total value to you of the wine is the sum of the two, which is the area under the marginal value curve; total value is simply the area under marginal value.

If area *A* plus area *B* is the value to you of being given 2 gallons of wine per week, it is also the largest sum you would pay for 2 gallons per

Figure 4-6

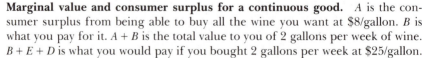

Marginal value and consumer surplus for a continuous good. *A* is the consumer surplus from being able to buy all the wine you want at $8/gallon. *B* is what you pay for it. *A* + *B* is the total value to you of 2 gallons per week of wine. *B* + *E* + *D* is what you would pay if you bought 2 gallons per week at $25/gallon.

Section II   Price = Value = Cost

week if the alternative were having no wine at all. Figure 4-6*b* shows that situation. Your surplus from buying 2 gallons per week for $25/gallon is the value to you of the wine—areas *A* plus *B* on the previous figure, equal to $C + E + B$ on Figure 4-6*b*—minus what you spend for it. You are spending $25/gallon and buying 2 gallons, so that comes to $50/week—the colored rectangle $D + E + B$ on Figure 4-6*b*. Subtracting that from the value of the wine ($C + E + B$) gives a surplus equal to region *C* minus region *D*. Your surplus is positive, so you buy the wine. This is the case mentioned earlier in the chapter where you would rather have a price/quantity combination that is above your demand curve than have nothing.

ODDS AND ENDS

Again the Equimarginal Principle

You are consuming a variety of goods; being rational, you have adjusted the amount you consume of each until you are consuming that bundle you prefer among all those bundles you can buy with your income. Consider two goods—apples and cookies. For each, consider the marginal utility to you of an additional dollar's worth of the good. Suppose it were larger for apples than for cookies. In that case, by spending $1 less on cookies and $1 more on apples, you could get a better bundle for the same amount of money! But you are supposed to have already chosen the best possible bundle. If so, no further change can improve your situation. It follows that when you have your optimal bundle, the utility to you of a dollar's worth of apples must be the same as the utility to you of a dollar's worth of cookies—or a dollar's worth of anything else. If it were not, there would be a better bundle with the same price, so the one you had would not be optimal.

Since that may seem confusing, I will go through it again with numbers. We start by assuming that you are consuming your optimal bundle of apples and cookies. Suppose apples cost $0.50 each and cookies (the giant size) cost $1 each. You are consuming 4 cookies and 9 apples each week; at that level of consumption, the marginal utility of a cookie is 3 utiles and the marginal utility of an apple is 2 utiles (remember that the marginal utility of something depends both on your preferences and on how much you are consuming). A dollar's worth of apples is 2 apples; a dollar's worth of cookies is 1 cookie. If you increased your consumption of apples by 2, your utility would increase by 4 utiles; if you then decreased your consumption of cookies by 1, your utility would go back down by 3 utiles. The net effect would be to make you better off by 1 utile ($4 - 3 = 1$). You would still be spending the same amount of money on apples and cookies, so you would have the same amount as before to spend on everything else. You would be better off than before with regard to apples and cookies and as well off with regard to everything else. But that is impossible; since you were already choosing the optimal bundle, no change in what you consume can make you better off.

I have proved that if the marginal utility per dollar's worth of the different goods you are consuming is not the same, you must not be choosing the optimal bundle. So if you are choosing the optimal bundle, the marginal utility of a dollar's worth of any of the goods you consume must be the same. In other words, the marginal utility of each good must be proportional to its price. If butter costs $4/pound and gasoline $2/gallon, and a dollar's worth of butter (1/4 pound) increases your utility by the same amount as a dollar's worth of gasoline (1/2 gallon), the marginal utility of butter (per pound) must be twice the marginal utility of gasoline (per gallon)—just as the price of butter (per pound) is twice the price of gasoline (per gallon).

This is now the fourth time I have derived this result. The third was when, in the process of showing that the marginal value curve and the demand curve are the same, I demonstrated that you consume any good up to the point where its marginal value is equal to its price. While I did not point out then that marginal value equal to price implies the equimarginal principle, it is easy enough to see that it does. Simply repeat the argument for every good you consume. If marginal value is equal to price for every good, then for any two goods, the ratio of their marginal values is the same as the ratio of their prices. Since marginal value is marginal utility divided by the marginal utility of income, the ratio of the marginal values of two goods is the same as the ratio of their marginal utilities.

This may be clearer if it is stated using algebra instead of English. Consider two goods X and Y, with marginal values MV_x and MV_y, marginal utilities MU_x and MU_y, and prices P_x and P_y. We have

$$MV_x = P_x;$$

$$MV_y = P_y;$$

$$MV_x \equiv MU_x/MU(\text{income})$$

$$MV_y \equiv MU_y/MU(\text{income})$$

Therefore,

$$P_x/P_y = MV_x/MV_y = MU_x/MU_y.$$

The left hand side of this equation corresponds to "the price of an apple measured in oranges" in Chapter 3 (minus the slope of the budget line; apples are X, oranges Y); the right hand side is the marginal rate of substitution (minus the slope of the indifference curve).

This is the final derivation of the principle in this chapter, but you will find it turning up again in economics (and elsewhere). The form in which we have derived it this time makes more obvious the reason for calling it the equimarginal principle. A convenient, if sloppy, misstatement of it is "Everything is equal on the margin."

It is important, in this and other applications of the equimarginal principle, to realize that it is a statement not about the initial situation (preferences, market prices, roads, checkout counters, or whatever) but about the result of rational decision. You may (as I do) vastly prefer Kroger chocolate chip cookies (the kind they used to bake in the store and sell in the deli section) to apples; if so, you may buy many more cookies than apples. What the equimarginal principle tells you is that you will buy just enough more cookies to reduce the marginal utility per dollar of cookies to that of apples.

Continuous Cookies

It may occur to some of you that there is a problem with the most recent argument by which I "proved" the equimarginal principle. I originally defined the marginal utility of something of which I have n units as the utility of $n + 1$ units minus the utility of n units; since marginal value is derived from marginal utility, it would be defined similarly. Applying this to my example of 9 apples and 4 cookies, the marginal value of an apple involves the difference between 9 and 10 and the marginal value of a cookie involves the difference between 4 and 5. But the change that I considered involved increasing the consumption of apples from 9 not to 10 but to 11, and decreasing the consumption of cookies from 4 to 3. Unless the marginal value of the eleventh apple is the same as that of the tenth (which it should not be, by our assumption of declining marginal utility) and the marginal value of the fourth cookie the same as that of the fifth (ditto), the argument as I gave it is wrong!

The answer to this objection is that although I have described the marginal utility of an apple or an orange as the difference between the utility of 10 and the utility of 9, that is only an approximation. Strictly speaking, we should think of all goods as consumed in continuously varying quantities (if this suggests applesauce and cookie crumbs, wait for the discussion of time in the next section). We should define the marginal utility as the increased utility from consuming a tiny bit more, divided by the amount of that tiny bit (and similarly for marginal value). Marginal value is then the slope of the graph of total value; in Figure 4-7 it is $\Delta V/\Delta Q$. If, when we are consuming 100 gallons of water per week, an additional drop (a millionth of a gallon) is worth one hundred-thousandth of a cent, then the marginal value of water is .00001 cents/.000001 gallons, which comes out to $0.10/gallon. The argument of the previous section can then be restated in terms of an increase in consumption of .002 apples and a decrease in consumption of .001 cookies. Since we do not expect

Figure 4-7

Total value and its slope. $\Delta V/\Delta Q$ is the average slope of total value between A and B. As ΔV and ΔQ become very small, A and B move together, and $\Delta V/\Delta Q$ approaches the slope of total value at a point—which is marginal value.

the marginal value of cookies to change very much between 4 cookies and 3.999 cookies, the argument goes through.

The precise definitions of marginal utility (see the optional section of Chapter 3) and marginal value require calculus—the marginal value of apples is the derivative of total value with respect to quantity. Since I am not assuming that all of my readers know calculus, I use the sort of imprecise language given above. Precisely the same calculus concept (a derivative) is implicit in such familiar ideas as speed and acceleration. You might carelessly say that, having driven 50 miles in an hour, your speed was 50 miles per hour—but you know that speed is actually an instantaneous concept and that 50 miles per hour is only an average (part of the time you were standing still at a stop light, part of it going at 50, part of it at 65). A precise definition of speed must be given in terms of small changes in distance divided by the small amounts of time during which they occur, just as a precise definition of marginal value is given in terms of small changes in value divided by the small changes in quantity that cause them.

Economics and Time

In talking or writing about economics, it is often convenient to describe consumption in terms of quantities—numbers of apples, gallons of water, and so forth. But 100 apples consumed in a day are not of the same value to me as 100 apples consumed in a year. The easiest way to deal with this problem is to think of consumption in terms of rates instead of quantities—6 apples per week, 7 eggs per week, and so on. Income is not a number of dollars but rather a number of dollars per week. Value is also a flow—6 apples per week are worth, not $3, but $3/week.

If we think of all quantities as flows and limit ourselves to analyzing situations in which income, prices, and preferences remain the same for long periods, we avoid most of the complications that time adds to economics. Many of these complications are important to understanding the nonstatic world we live in. But in solving a hard problem, it is often wise to solve the easier parts first; so in this section of the book, the problems associated with change are mostly ignored. Once we have a clearly worked-out picture of static economics, we can use it to understand more complicated situations—and will, starting in Chapter 12. Until then, we are doing economics in a perfectly static and predictable world, in which tomorrow is always like today and next year is always like this year. That is why, in drawing indifference curve diagrams, we never considered the possibility that the consumer would spend only part of his income in order to save the rest for a rainy day; either it is raining today or there are no rainy days.

Problems associated with time and change are not the only complications ignored at this point; you might find it interesting to make a list as we go along, and see how many get dealt with by the end of the book.

One advantage to thinking of consumption in eggs per year instead of just eggs is that it lets us vary consumption continuously. There are severe practical difficulties with changing the number of eggs you consume by $1/10$ of an egg at a time—what do you do with the rest of it? But it is easy enough to increase the rate at which you consume eggs by $1/10$ of an egg per week—eat, on average, 5 more eggs per year. Thus lumpy goods become continuous—and the consumption of continuous goods is, for mathematical reasons, easier to analyze than the consumption of lumpy goods. We can then define marginal utility and marginal value in terms of very small amounts of apples and cookies without first converting the apples into applesauce and the cookies into a pile of crumbs.

There is a second problem associated with time that we should also note. In describing the process of choice, I talk about "doing this, then doing that, then . . .." For example, I talk about increasing consumption from 4 apples to 5, then from 5 to 6, then from . . . and so on. It sounds as though the process happens over time, but that is deceptive. We are really describing not a process of consumption going on out in the real world but rather something happening inside your head—the process of solving the problem of how much of each good to consume. A more precise description would be "First you imagine that you choose to consume no apples and consider the resulting bundle of goods. Then you imagine that you consume 1 apple instead of none and compare that bundle with the previous one. Then 2 instead of 1. Then . . . Finally, after you have figured out what level of consumption maximizes your utility, we turn a switch, the game of life starts, and you put your solution into practice."

If you find it difficult to distinguish time in the sense of an imaginary series of calculations by which you decide what to do from the time in which you actually do it, you may instead imagine, as suggested before, that we are considering a situation (income, preferences, prices) that will be stable for a long time. We start by spending a few days experimenting with different consumption bundles to see which we prefer. The loss from consuming wrong bundles during the experiment can be ignored, since it is such a short period compared to the long time during which the solution is put into practice.

Money, Value, and Prices

Although prices and values are often given in terms of money, money has nothing essential to do with the analysis. In demonstrating the equimarginal principle, for example, I converted cookies into money (bought one less cookie, leaving me with an extra dollar to spend on something else) and then converted the money into apples (bought 2 apples for $1). The argument would have been exactly the same if there were no such thing as money and a cookie simply exchanged for 2 apples.

We are used to stating prices in money, but prices can be stated in anything of value. We could define all our prices as apple prices. The apple price of a cookie, in my example, is 2 apples—that is what you must give up to get a cookie. The apple price of an apple is 1 (apple). Once you have the price of everything in terms of apples, you also have the price of everything in terms of any other good. If a peach exchanges for 4 apples, and 4 apples exchange for 8 cookies, then the cookie price of a peach is 8.

There are two ways of seeing why this is true. The simpler is to observe that someone who has cookies and wants peaches will never pay more than 8 cookies for a peach, since he could always trade 8 cookies for 4 apples and then exchange the 4 apples for a peach. Someone who has a peach and wants cookies will never accept fewer than 8 cookies for his peach, since he could always trade it for 4 apples and then trade the 4 apples for 8 cookies. If nobody who is buying peaches will pay more than 8 cookies and nobody selling them will accept less, the price of a peach (in cookies) must be 8. The same analysis applies to any other good. So once we know the price of all goods in terms of one (in this example apples), we can calculate the price of each good in terms of any other.

This argument depends on an assumption that has so far been implicit in our analysis—that we can ignore all costs of buying and selling other than the price paid. This assumption, sometimes called **zero transaction costs**, is a reasonable approximation for much of our economic activity and one that will be retained through most of the book. Exceptions are discussed in parts of Chapters 6 and 18. It is not clear that the assumption is reasonable here. Imagine, for example, that you have 20 automobiles and want a house. The cookie price of an automobile is 40,000; the cookie price of a house is 800,000. It seems, from the discussion of the previous paragraph, that all you have to do to get your house is trade automobiles for cookies and then cookies for the house.

But where will you put 800,000 cookies while you wait for the seller of the house to come collect them? How long will it take you to count them out to him? What condition will the cookies be in by the time you finish? Clearly, in the real world, there are some problems with such indirect transactions.

This brings us to the second reason why relative prices—prices of goods in terms of other goods—must fit the pattern I have described. Trading huge quantities of apples, cookies, peaches, or whatever may be very costly for you and me. It is far less costly for those in the business of such trading—people who routinely buy and sell carload lots of apples, wheat, pork bellies, and many other outlandish things and who make their exchanges not by physically moving the goods around but merely by changing the pieces of paper saying who owns what, while the goods sit still. For such professional traders, the assumption of zero transaction costs is close to being correct. And such traders, in the process of making their living, force relative prices into the same pattern as would consumers with zero transaction costs—even if they never consume any of the goods themselves.

To see how this works, imagine that we start with a different structure of relative prices. A peach trades for 2 apples and an apple trades for 4 cookies, but the price of a peach in cookies is 10. A professional trader in the peach-cookie-apple market appears. He starts with 10,000 peaches. He trades them for 100,000 cookies (the price of a peach is 10 cookies), buys 25,000 apples with the 100,000 cookies (the price of an apple is 4 cookies), trades the apples for 12,500 peaches (the price of a peach in apples is 2). He has started with 10,000 peaches, shuffled some pieces of paper representing ownership of peaches, apples, and cookies, and ended up with 2,500 peaches more than he started with—which he can now exchange for whatever goods he wants! By repeating the cycle again and again, he can end up with as many peaches—and exchange them for as much of anything else—as he wants.

So far, I have assumed that such a transaction—the technical name for it is **arbitrage**—has no effect on the relative prices of the goods traded. But if you can get peaches, in effect, for nothing, simply by shuffling a few pieces of paper around, there is an almost unlimited number of people willing to do it. When the number of traders—or the quantities each trades—becomes large enough, the effect is to change relative prices. Everyone is trying to sell peaches for cookies at a price of 10 cookies for a peach. The result is to drive down the price of peaches measured in cookies—the number of cookies you can get for a peach. Everyone is trying to buy apples with cookies at 4 cookies for an apple. The result is to drive up the price of apples measured in cookies and, similarly, to drive up the price of peaches measured in apples. As prices change in this way, the profit from arbitrage becomes smaller and smaller. If the traders have no transaction costs at all, the process continues until there is no profit. When that point is reached, relative prices exactly fit the pattern described above—you get the same number of cookies for your peach whether you trade directly or indirectly via apples. If the traders have some transaction costs, the result is almost the same but not quite; discrepancies in relative prices can remain as long as they are small enough so that it does not pay traders to engage in the arbitrage trades that would eliminate them.

I have now shown that the price of peaches in terms of cookies is determined once we know the price of both goods in apples—precisely, if transaction costs are zero; approximately, if they are not. By similar arguments, we could get the exchange ratio between any two goods (how many of one must you give for one of the other) starting with the price of both of them in apples, or in potatoes, or in anything else. The equimarginal principle then appears as "the ratio of marginal utilities of two goods is the same as their exchange ratio." If 2 apples exchange for 1 cookie, then in equilibrium a cookie must have twice the marginal utility of an apple.

I used money in talking about values as well as in talking about prices. Here too, the money is merely a convenient expository device. The statement that the marginal value of something is $0.80 means that you are indifferent between one more unit of it and whatever else you would buy if you had an additional $0.80. Just as in the case of prices, the money serves as a conceptual intermediate—we are really comparing one consumption good with another. The arguments of this chapter could be made in "potato values" just as easily as in "dollar values." Indeed potato values are more fundamental than dollar values, as you can easily check by having a hamburger and a plate of french-fried dollars for lunch.

It is often asserted that economics is about money or that what is wrong with economics is that it only takes money into account. That is almost the opposite of the truth. While money does play an important role in a few areas of economics, such as the analysis of business cycles, price theory could be derived and explained in a pure barter economy without ever mentioning money.

A similar error is the idea that economists assume everyone wishes to maximize his wealth or his income. Such an assumption would be absurd. If you wished to maximize your wealth, you would never spend any money except for things (such as food) that you required in order to earn more money. If you wished to maximize your income, you would take no leisure (except that needed for your health) and always choose the highest paying job, independent of how pleasant it was. What we almost always do assume is that everyone prefers more wealth to less and more income to less, everything else held constant. To say that you would like a raise is not the same thing as to say that you would like it whatever its cost in additional work.

Conclusion: Consumption, Languages, and All That

In my analysis of consumption (Chapters 3 and 4), I have tried to do two things. The first is to show how rational behavior may be analyzed in a number of different ways, each presenting the same logical structure in a different language. The second is to use the analysis to derive three interrelated results.

The simplest of the three, derived once with indifference curves and once with marginal value, is that demand curves slope down—the lower the price of something, the more you buy. In both cases, there is a possible exception, based on the ambiguity between a fall in price and a rise in income; in both cases, the ambiguity vanishes if we insist on a pure price change—a change in one price balanced by either a change in the other direction of all other prices or a corresponding change in income. It also vanishes if we assume that any one good makes up a small enough part of our consumption that we may safely ignore the effect on our real income of a change in its price.

A second result is that the value to a consumer of being able to buy a good at a price, which we call consumer surplus, equals the area under the demand curve and above the price. At this point, that may seem like one of those odd facts that professors insist, for their own inscrutable reasons, on having students memorize. I suggest that instead of memorizing it, you go over the derivation of that result (eggs and wine) until it makes sense to you. At that point, you will no longer need to memorize it, since you will be able to reproduce the result for yourself. It is worth understanding, and not just for passing economics courses. As we will see in later chapters, consumer surplus is the essential key to understanding arguments about policy ("should we have tariffs?") as well as to figuring out how to maximize profits at Disneyland.

The third result from these chapters is the equimarginal principle, which tells us that, as a result of our own rational behavior, the ratio of the marginal utilities of goods is the same as the ratio of their prices. In addition to helping us understand consumption, the equimarginal principle in this guise is one example of a pattern that helps us understand how the high salaries of physicians are connected to the cost of medical school and the labors of interning, why we do not get ahead by switching lanes on the freeway, and how not to make money on the stock market.

POPCORN—AN APPLICATION

In Chapter 2, I asked why popcorn is sold at a higher price in movie theaters than elsewhere. While we will not be ready to discuss possible right answers until Chapter 10, we can at this point use the idea of consumer surplus to show that the obvious answer is wrong. The obvious answer is that once the customers are inside the theater, the owner has a monopoly; by charging them a high price, he maximizes his profit. What I will show is that far from maximizing profits, selling popcorn at a high price results in lower profits than selling popcorn at cost!

To do this, I require the usual economic assumption that people are rational, plus an important simplifying assumption—that all consumers are identical. While the latter assumption is unrealistic, it should not affect the monopoly argument; if the theater owner charges high prices because he has a monopoly, he should continue to do so even if the customers are all the same. Here and elsewhere, the assumption of identical consumers (and identical producers) very much simplifies our analysis. It is frequently a good way of getting a first approximation solution to an economic problem.

The theater owner is selling his customers a package consisting of the opportunity to watch a film, plus associated goods such as comfortable seats, clean rest rooms, and the opportunity to buy popcorn. He charges his customers the highest price at which he can sell the package. Since the customers are identical, there is one price that everyone will pay and a slightly higher price that no one will pay.

In order to decide what to put into the package, the owner must consider how changes will affect its value to the customers and hence the maximum he can charge the customers for a ticket. Suppose, to take a trivial case, he decides to improve the package by giving every customer a quarter as he comes in the door. Obviously this will increase the amount the customers are willing to pay for a ticket by exactly $0.25. The owner is worse off by the time and trouble spent handing out the coins.

Suppose the theater owner decides that since he has a monopoly on providing seats in the theater, he might as well charge $1 for each seat in addition to the admission price. Since everyone wants a seat, the consumer is paying (say) $4 for an admission ticket and another $1 for a seat. That is the same as paying $5 for admission. If the customer is not willing to pay $5 for the movie, he will be no more willing when the payment is divided into two pieces; if he is willing to pay $5, the theater owner should have been charging $5 in the first place.

Figure 4-8

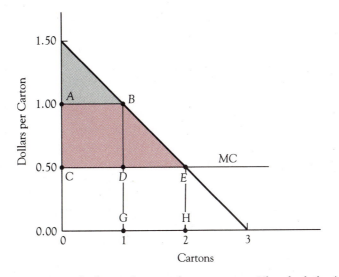

One theater customer's demand curve for popcorn. The shaded triangle is the consumer surplus from buying popcorn at $1/carton. The colored region (*ABEDC*) is the increase in his consumer surplus if price falls from $1/carton to $0.50/carton.

Now suppose the theater owner is trying to decide whether to sell popcorn in the theater at $1/carton or not sell it at all. One advantage to selling popcorn is that he gets money for the popcorn; another is that customers prefer a theater that sells popcorn to one that does not and are therefore willing to pay more for admission. How much more?

Figure 4-8 shows a customer's demand curve for popcorn. At $1/carton, he buys 1 carton. The shaded area is his consumer surplus—$0.25. That means (by the definition of consumer surplus) that the customer is indifferent between being able to buy popcorn at $1/carton and being unable to buy any popcorn but being given $0.25; the opportunity to buy popcorn at $1/carton is worth $0.25 to him. Making the popcorn available at that price is equivalent to handing each customer a quarter as he walks in the door; it makes the package offered by the theater (movie plus amenities—including popcorn) $0.25 more valuable to him, so the theater owner can raise the admission price by $0.25 without driving off the customers. The owner should start selling popcorn, provided that the cost of doing so is less than $1.25/customer. That is what he gets from selling the popcorn—a dollar paid for the popcorn plus $0.25 more paid for admission because the opportunity to buy popcorn is now part of the package.

Is $1/carton the best price? Assume that, as shown on Figure 4-8, the **marginal cost** to the owner of producing popcorn (the additional cost for each additional carton produced) is $0.50/carton. He can produce as many cartons as he likes, at a cost of $0.50 (for popcorn, butter, wages, and so forth) for each additional carton. Suppose he lowers the price of popcorn from $1 to $0.50. He is now selling each customer 2 cartons instead of 1, so his revenue is still $1/customer. His costs have risen by $0.50/customer, since he has to produce 2 cartons instead of 1. Consumer surplus, however, has risen by the colored area on Figure 4-8, which is $0.75; he can raise the admission price by that amount without losing customers. His revenue from selling popcorn is unchanged, his costs have risen by $0.50/ customer, and his revenue from admissions has risen by $0.75/customer, so his profits have gone up by $0.25/customer.

The argument is a general one; it does not depend on the particular numbers I have used. As long as the price of popcorn is above its marginal cost of production, profit can be raised by lowering the price of popcorn to marginal cost (*MC* on Figure 4-8) and raising the price of admission by the resulting increase in consumer surplus. The reduction in price reduces the owner's revenue on the popcorn that he was selling already by its quantity times the reduction—rectangle *ABDC*. The cost of producing the additional popcorn demanded because of the lower price is just covered by what the consumers pay for it, since the price of a carton of popcorn is equal to the cost of producing it; on Figure 4-8, both the additional cost and the additional revenue from selling popcorn are rectangle *DEHG*. Consumer surplus goes up by the colored area in the figure—rectangle *ABDC* plus triangle *BDE*. Since the owner can raise his admission price by the increase in consumer surplus, his revenue goes up by (*ABDC* + *BDE*) (increased admission) + (*DEHG* − *ABDC*) (change in revenue from selling popcorn). His cost goes up by *DEHG*, so his profit goes up by the area of triangle *BDE*.

The same argument can be put in words, without reference to the diagram: "So far as the popcorn already being sold is concerned, the price reduction is simply a transfer from the theater owner to the customer, so revenue from selling popcorn goes down by the same amount that consumer surplus goes up (*ABDC*). So far as the additional popcorn sold at the lower price is concerned, the customer pays the owner its production cost (*DEHG*) and is left with its consumer surplus (*BDE*). So if we lower the price of popcorn to its marginal cost, consumer surplus goes up by more than revenue from popcorn goes down. The theater owner can transfer the consumer surplus to his own pocket by raising the admission price to the theater; by doing so (and reducing popcorn to cost), he increases his profit by the consumer surplus on the additional popcorn (*BDE*)."

This shows that any price for popcorn above production cost lowers the profits of the theater owner, when the effect of the price of popcorn on what customers are willing to pay to come to the theater is taken into account.

We are now left with a puzzle. We have used economics to prove that a theater owner maximizes his profits by selling popcorn at cost. Economics also tells us that theater owners should want to maximize their profits and know how to do so. That implies that they will sell popcorn at cost. Yet they apparently do not. Something is wrong somewhere; there must be a mistake either in the logic of the argument, in its assumptions, or in our observation of what theaters actually do. We will return to that puzzle, and two possible solutions, in Chapter 10.

OPTIONAL SECTION

CONSUMER SURPLUS AND MEASURING WITH A (SLIGHTLY) RUBBER RULER

In using the equality between the marginal value curve and the demand curve to derive a downward-sloping demand curve earlier in this chapter, I discussed some of the problems of measuring value in goods instead of in utility. We are now in a position to see how the same problem affects the concept of consumer surplus.

Suppose a new good becomes available at price P. Consumer surplus, the area under the demand curve for the new good and above a horizontal line at P, is supposed to be the net benefit to me in dollars of being able to buy the new good—the increase in my utility divided by my marginal utility for a dollar. But as I increase my expenditure on the new good, I must be decreasing my total expenditure on all old goods. The less I spend on something, the less I consume of it; the less I consume, the greater its marginal utility. So after I have adjusted my consumption pattern to include the new good, the marginal utility of all other goods has risen. Since the marginal utility of a dollar is simply the utility of what I can buy with it, the marginal utility of a dollar has also increased. But the original discussion of marginal utility, marginal value, and consumer surplus treated the marginal utility of a dollar (usually called the marginal utility of income) as a constant.

The reason this is a good approximation for most purposes is shown in Figure 4-9. I assume that I am initially consuming 25 different goods, A–Y, and a twenty-sixth good, Z, becomes available at a price P_Z. The graphs show my marginal utility for goods A, B, and Z. In the initial situation (shown by the dashed lines), I am dividing all of my income among goods A–Y in such a way that the marginal utility of an additional dollar's worth of each good is the same. The price of good A is assumed to be $1/unit (the units could be pounds, gallons, or whatever, depending on what sort of good it is); of B, $2/unit.

After good Z becomes available, I rearrange my expenditure so that I again have the same marginal utility per dollar on each unit. Since some

Figure 4-9

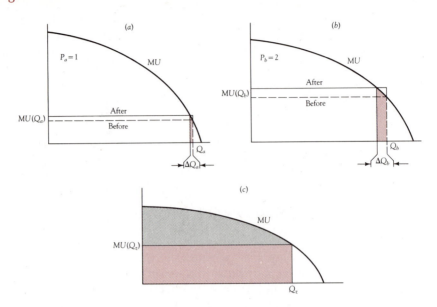

Marginal utility curves for three goods, showing the situation before and after the third good becomes available When good Z becomes available, the consumer buys less of goods A–Y and spends the money on Z instead. Colored regions show utility losses on goods A and B which (with similiar losses on C–Y, not shown) add up to the colored region representing expenditure on good Z.

of my income is now going to Z, I must be spending less on each other good, as shown by the solid lines in the figure. If I simply transferred all of the expenditure away from one good, its marginal utility per dollar would rise, the marginal utility per dollar of the other goods would stay the same, and I would no longer be satisfying the equimarginal principle and hence no longer maximizing my utility. So instead, I reduce my expenditure a little on each good, raising the marginal utility of each by the same amount. The result is that I am now consuming $Q_a - \Delta Q_a$, of good A, $Q_b - \Delta Q_b$ of good B, and so forth; by the equimarginal principle we have

$$MU(Q_a - \Delta Q_a)/P_a = MU(Q_b - \Delta Q_b)/P_b = \ldots = MU(Q_z)/P_z. \qquad \text{(Equation 1)}$$

Since total expenditure is unchanged, the reduction in expenditure on goods A–Y must equal the new expenditure on good Z, so

$$\Delta Q_a P_a + \Delta Q_b P_b + \ldots = Q_z P_z \qquad \text{(Equation 2)}$$

Since I am consuming 25 other goods, the decrease in consumption of each of them when I start consuming the new good as well is very small, as shown on the figures. So the marginal utility of a dollar's worth of the good is almost the same after the change as before.

To put the derivation of consumer surplus in terms of utility rather than in dollars (and so make it more precise), consider the narrow colored areas in Figures 4-9a and 4-9b. They represent the utility loss as a result of the decreased consumption of goods A and B. They are almost equal to the narrow rectangles whose height is $MU(Q - \Delta Q)$ and whose width is ΔQ, where "Q" is Q_a in Figure 4-9a and Q_b in Figure 4-9b. If you sum the areas of those rectangles (for all of goods A–Y), you get

$$\text{Total area} = MU(Q_a - \Delta Q_a)\Delta Q_a + MU(Q_b - \Delta Q_b)\Delta Q_b + \ldots$$

Substituting in from Equation 1 we have

$$= (MU(Q_z)/P_z) \times \{P_a \Delta Q_a + P_b \Delta Q_b + \ldots,$$

which by Equation 2

$$= (MU(Q_z)/P_z)(P_z Q_z) = MU(Q_z)Q_z = \text{colored area on Figure 4-9}c.$$

Since the total utility I get from consuming Q_z of Z is the area under the MU curve (the shaded area plus the colored area) my net gain is the shaded area—my consumer surplus measured in utiles.

The one approximation in all of this was ignoring the part of the narrow rectangles on Figures 4-9a and 4-9b that was shaded but not colored. That difference becomes smaller, relative to the colored part, the larger the number of different goods being consumed; as the number of goods goes to infinity, the ratio of shaded to colored goes to zero. So consumer surplus as we measure it (the area under an ordinary demand curve and above price) and consumer surplus as we define it (the value to the consumer of being able to buy the good) are equal for a consumer who divides his expenditure among an infinite number of goods, and are nearly equal for a real consumer, who divides his expenditure among a large but finite number of goods.

A mathematical argument is not really satisfactory unless it can be translated into English. This particular one translates into a short dialogue:

Query: "When a new good becomes available, you get consumer surplus by spending money on that good. But do you not lose the consumer surplus on the other goods you are now not buying with that money?"
Response: "If you are consuming many goods, you get the money to buy the new good by giving up a marginal unit of each of the others: the last

orange that was barely worth buying, the trip you weren't sure you wanted to take. The marginal unit is worth just what you pay for it—that is why it is marginal—so it generates no surplus."

PROBLEMS

1. Figure 4-10*a* shows a number of total utility curves and Figure 4-10*b* shows marginal utility curves.
   a. Which total utility curves correspond to goods? (There may be more than one.)
   b. Which marginal utility curve corresponds to total utility curve *b*? to total utility curve *e*?
   c. Which total utility curves and which marginal utility curves are consistent with declining marginal utility?
2. Figure 4-11*a* shows some total utility curves; draw the corresponding marginal utility curves.
3. Figure 4-11*b* shows some marginal utility curves; draw the corresponding total utility curves.
4. Figure 4-12 shows your marginal and total utility curves for persimmons. Are persimmons a good? A bad? Both? Explain.
5. Figure 4-13*a* shows your demand curve for Diet Coke.
   a. Approximately how much better off are you being able to buy all the Diet Coke you want at $5/gallon than not being able to buy any?

Figure 4-10

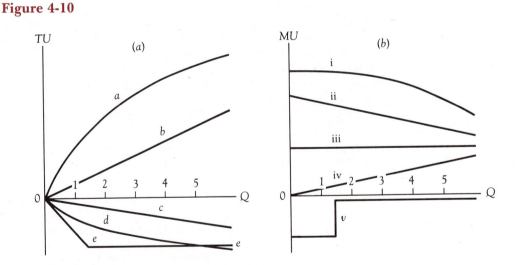

Total and marginal utility curves. For Problem 1.

Section II   Price = Value = Cost

Figure 4-11

Total and marginal utility curves.   For Problems 2 and 3.

Figure 4-12

Total and marginal utility curves for persimmons.   For Problem 4.

Chapter 4   Marginal Value, Marginal Utility, and Consumer Surplus   **111**

Figure 4-13

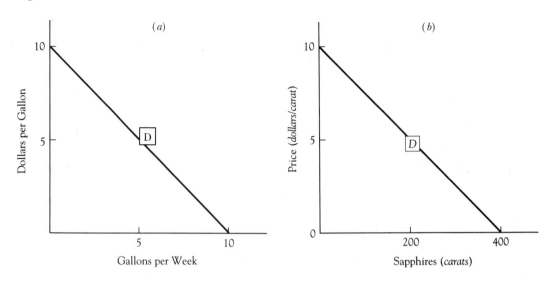

Your demand curves for Diet Coke and sapphires. For Problems 5 and 7.

    b.   How much better off are you being able to buy all the Diet Coke you want at $3/gallon than at $5/gallon?

6. Estimate, to within a factor of ten, what percentage of all water used in the United States is used to drink. Give your sources. Is the common conception of a water shortage as a situation where people are going thirsty an accurate one? What does this tell us about the difference between the marginal value of water at a quantity of a few gallons a week and the marginal value of water at the quantity we actually consume? (The numerical part of this cannot be answered from anything in the book; it is intended to give you practice in the useful art of back-of-the-envelope calculations—very rough estimates of real-world magnitudes—while at the same time connecting the abstract examples of the chapter to something real.)

7. Figure 4-13*b* shows your demand curve for sapphires. For religious reasons, sapphires can neither be bought nor sold. You accidentally discover 100 carats of sapphires. How much better off are you?

8. Figure 4-14*a* shows your demand curve for red tape. There is no market for red tape, but the government, which is trying to reduce its inventory, orders you to buy 50 pounds of it at $0.20/pound. How much better or worse off are you as a result?

9. You want colored marshmallows (purple, green, and gold) to put into the hot drinks at your Mardi Gras party; Figure 4-14*a* shows your demand curve. Colored marshmallows cost $1/bag.

Figure 4-14

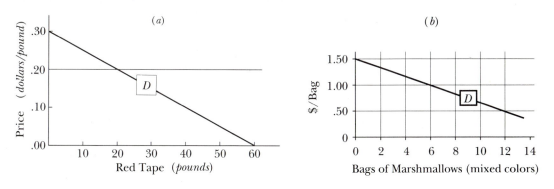

Your demand curves for red tape and marshmallows. For Problems 8 and 9.

   a. How many do you buy?
   After you have finished buying and paying for them, there is an announcement over the store's public address system; a special Mardi Gras sale has just started, and colored marsmallows are now only $0.50/bag.
   b. Do you buy more? If so, how many?
   c. What is your total consumer surplus from buying marshmallows— including those you bought initially and any others you bought during the sale?
10. In the example worked out in the text, how would profit be changed by a further reduction in the price of popcorn to $0.25/carton?

chapter 5

PRODUCTION

The preceding two chapters discussed consumption; this chapter discusses production. For simplicity we assume that there is only a single input to production, the producer's time, which may be used to produce any one of a variety of goods. You may think of these goods either as services, such as lawn mowing or dish washing, or as objects produced from raw materials that are freely available. Alternatively, you may want to think of the producer as an employee who produces some form of labor (assembling automobiles, painting houses) and sells it to a firm that combines labor with other inputs to produce goods.

Implicit in the assumption of a single input and a single output is the further assumption that the producer is indifferent between an hour spent mowing lawns and an hour spent washing dishes. Otherwise there would have to be either an additional input (unpleasantness of mowing lawns) or an additional (perhaps disvalued) output (getting grass all over my clothes), which would violate our assumption of only one input and one output.

In Chapter 9, we will analyze more complicated forms of production. Each production unit (a firm rather than a single worker) will have a **production function,** showing how it can combine inputs, such as labor and raw materials, to produce different quantities of output. The production decision will then involve several steps. The firm must first find, for any quantity of output, the lowest cost way (combination of inputs) to produce it; once it has done so, it will know the cost of producing any quantity (its total cost function). Given that information and the market price, the firm decides how much to produce in order to maximize its profit.

PART I—THE ARGUMENT

In Chapters 3 and 4, we derived the demand curve for a good from the preferences of the consumer; in this chapter, we will be deriving supply curves from the preferences and abilities of the producers. The first step is to see how a potential producer decides which good to produce. The next is to see how he decides how many hours to work. The final step is to consider the situation in which there are many different producers, so that the supply curve is the sum of their individual supply curves.

Choosing a Good to Produce

Table 5-1 shows the output per hour, the price, and the implicit wage for each of three goods—mowed lawns, washed dishes, and meals. The price for a mowed lawn is $10 and the producer can mow 1 lawn per hour, so the implicit wage is $10/hour. Similarly, washing 70 dishes per hour at $0.10/dish yields a wage of $7/hour, and cooking 2 meals per hour at $3/meal yields $6/hour. Since the only difference among the alternatives (from the standpoint of the producer) is the implicit wage, he chooses to mow lawns. Note that this decision depends on (among other things) the price. If the price for mowing a lawn were less than $7 (and the other prices were as shown in the table), he would wash dishes instead.

Table 5-1

	Lawn Mowing	Dish Washing	Cooking
Output	1 lawn/hour	70 dishes/hour	2 meals/hour
Price	$10/lawn	$0.10/dish	$3/meal
Wage	$10/hour	$7/hour	$6/hour

The Supply of Labor

Figure 5-1a shows a graph of the marginal *dis*value of labor as a function of the number of hours worked. If you were enjoying 24 hours per day of leisure (doing no work at all), it would take only a small payment ($0.50 in the figure) to make you willing to work for a single hour; you would be indifferent between zero hours a day of work and 1 hour of work plus $0.50. If, on the other hand, you were already working 10 hours a day, it would take a little over $10 to make you willing to work an additional hour.

Suppose the wage is $10/hour and you are working 5 hours per day. You would be willing to work an additional hour for an additional payment of about $3; since you can actually get $10 for it, you are obviously better off working the extra hour. The same argument applies as long as the marginal disvalue of labor to you is less than the wage, so you end up working that number of hours for which the two are equal. The number of hours of labor you supply at a wage of $10 is the number at which your marginal disvalue for labor is equal to $10. The same relation applies at any other wage, so your marginal disvalue for

Figure 5-1

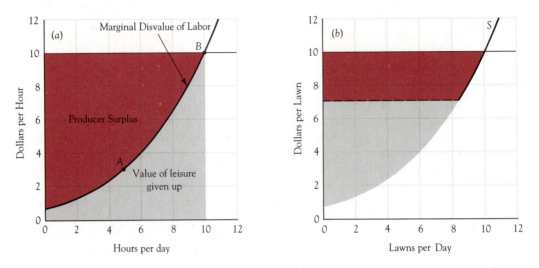

Producer surplus, the marginal disvalue for labor, and the supply curve for lawn mowing. The area above the marginal disvalue for labor curve and below $10/hour is the producer surplus from being able to work at $10/hour. The colored area above the supply curve for lawns and below the price is the producer surplus from mowing lawns at that price ($10/lawn). The supply curve is horizontal at the price at which you are indifferent between lawn mowing and your next most profitable production opportunity (dish washing).

labor curve is also your **supply curve for labor**, just as, in Chapter 4, your marginal value curve for a good was also your demand curve.

Presumably, leisure (like other goods) is worth less to you the more of it you have—it has declining marginal value. The cost to you of an hour of labor is giving up an hour of leisure—the less leisure you have, the greater that cost. So if leisure has decreasing marginal value, labor has increasing marginal disvalue. That fits my experience, and probably yours; the more hours a day I am working, the less willing I am to work an additional hour. Since the marginal disvalue of labor curve is increasing, the supply curve, showing how many hours you choose to work as a function of the wage you receive, is upward sloping as well. The more you are paid for each hour of labor, the more hours you choose to work.

Producer Surplus

We can now define producer surplus in a way analogous to consumer surplus. Suppose the wage is $10/hour. You are willing to work the first hour for $0.50; since you actually receive $10 for it, your net gain is $9.50. The next hour is worth about a dollar to you; you receive $10 for a gain of $9. Summing these gains over all the hours you work gives us the colored area of Figure 5-1a.

Section II   Price = Value = Cost

Note that the benefit to you of being able to work for $10/hour—your **producer surplus**—is not the same as the salary you get. Working 10 hours at a wage of $10/hour gives you a salary of $100/day. This is not, however, your gain from working. To find that, you must subtract out the cost to you of working—the value to you of the time that you spend working instead of doing something else. Your salary is the area of a rectangle 10 hours/day wide by 10 dollars/hour high—the sum of the shaded and the colored regions on Figure 5-1a. The value to you of your time—the total disvalue to you of working 10 hours a day—is the shaded area under the supply curve; you might think of it as how much worse off you would be if you were forced to work 10 hours per day and paid nothing. The rectangle minus the area under the supply curve is the area above the supply curve—your producer surplus, the amount by which you are better off working at $10/hour than not working at all.

The result, as you can see, is very much like the result for consumer surplus in the previous chapter. The consumer buys goods; their total value to him is measured by the area under his marginal value curve. He pays for them an amount equal to the rectangle price times quantity. His consumer surplus is the difference between the value of what he gets and what he pays—the area under the marginal value curve and above the price. The producer sells his leisure; its value to him is measured by the area under his marginal value for leisure curve, which is the same as his marginal disvalue for labor curve. He receives in exchange the rectangle wage times number of hours worked–the price for selling his leisure (working) times the amount of leisure sold (number of hours worked). His producer surplus is the difference between what he gets for his work and what it cost him—the value of the leisure he gives up—which is the area below the wage and above the marginal disvalue of labor curve. The marginal disvalue for labor curve is the supply curve for labor just as the marginal value for apples curve is the demand curve for apples.

The Supply of Goods—One Producer

We now have the supply curve for labor, but what we want is the supply curve for mowed lawns. Since I can mow 1 lawn per hour, a price of $10/lawn corresponds to a wage of $10/hour and a labor supply of 10 hours per day corresponds to mowing that many lawns. It appears that the supply curve for lawns and for labor are the same; all I have to do is relabel the vertical axis "price in $/lawn" and the horizontal axis "lawns/day."

Appearances are deceiving; the supply curve for lawns is not the same as for labor. My decision to mow lawns instead of spending my time producing something else depended on the price I could get for doing so. If that price drops below $7/lawn, my output of mowed lawns drops to zero; I am better off washing dishes instead. The resulting supply curve is shown on Figure 5-1b. The colored area is my producer surplus from producing mowed lawns at $10/lawn. To see why my producer surplus does not include the shaded area below the line at $7/lawn, consider what my producer surplus would be if I could get $7 for each lawn I mowed. How much better off am I being able to mow lawns at $7 than not mowing lawns? I am not better off at all; at that wage, I can do just as well washing dishes.

This is another example of the idea of opportunity cost, discussed in Chapter 3. The cost to me of mowing lawns is whatever I must give up in order to do so. If the best alternative use of my time is leisure, as it is for the solid part of curve S on Figure 5-1b, then the cost is the value of my leisure. If the best alternative use is washing dishes, as it is on the dashed part of S, then the cost is the money I would have gotten by washing dishes.

Going from the supply curve for labor to the supply curve for mowed lawns was particularly simple because the rate at which I mow is 1 lawn per hour. Suppose the grass stops growing, someone invents an automatic dishwasher, and I become a cook. Figure 5-2 shows my supply curve for meals, given that my supply curve for labor is as shown on Figure 5-1a.

To derive Figure 5-2, we note that each hour of work produces 2 meals (Table 5-1). Hence I earn $10/hour cooking if the price for meals is $5/meal. Working 10 hours/day, which is what I do if I get $10/hour, produces 20 meals/day. So point B on Figure 5-1a ($10/hour and 10 hours/day) corresponds to point b on Figure 5-2 ($5/meal and 20 meals/day); similarly point A corresponds to point a. The supply curve for meals is the same as the supply curve for labor except that it is "squished" vertically (by a factor of 2) and "stretched" horizontally (by a factor of 2). Unlike the supply curve for mowed lawns shown on Figure 5-1b, it has no horizontal segment—because, by assumption, meals are the only thing left to produce.

More Than One Producer

So far, I have considered the supply curve of a single producer. If we have more than one, there is no reason to assume they will all be equally good at producing the different goods, nor that they will all have the same supply curves for labor. If they do not, then their supply curves for mowed lawns—or other goods—will also be different, with the horizontal sections occurring at different prices according to their relative skills at different kinds of production. A producer who is very good at mowing lawns (many mowed per hour) or very bad at doing anything else will choose to mow lawns even if the price is low. A producer who is bad at mowing lawns (many hours per lawn) or good at something else will mow lawns only when the price is high. Figure 5-3 shows the supply curves for two such producers, A(nne) and B(ill), and their combined supply curve.

At prices below $2.50/lawn, neither Anne nor Bill produces. At prices above $2.50/lawn but below $5/lawn, only Anne produces; the combined

Figure 5-2

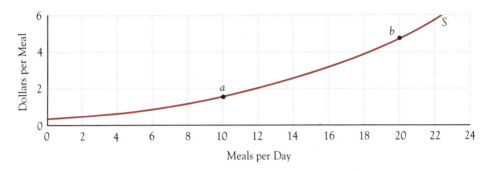

The supply curve for cooking meals. This supply curve is the same as the supply curve for labor, except that each hour worked corresponds to two meals cooked and each dollar per meal corresponds to $2/hour. Points *a* and *b* correspond to points *A* and *B* on Figure 5-1a.

supply curve is the same as her supply curve. At a price of $5, Bill abruptly enters the market, mowing 6 lawns per day; adding that to Anne's output of 9 gives a total output of 15. When the price goes from $5 to $6, Anne increases her output by another unit and so does Bill; so total output goes up by 2 to 17.

The combined supply curve is a *horizontal* sum. The summation is horizontal because we are summing *quantities* (shown on the horizontal axis) at each price. Both *A* and *B* can sell their products at the same price; whatever that price is, total quantity supplied is the (horizontal) sum of what they each produce. The same would be true if we were deriving a total demand curve from two or more individual demand curves. All consumers in a market face the same price, so total quantity demanded at a price is the quantity consumer *A* demands plus the quantity consumer *B* demands plus . . ..

The sum of the producer surplus that *B* receives at a price of $6 plus the producer surplus that *A* receives is equal to the producer surplus calculated from the combined supply curve—the area above their combined supply curve and below the horizontal line at $6. The reason is shown on Figures 5-3a through 5-3c. Consider the narrow horizontal rectangle *R* shown in Figure 5-3a. Its height is ΔP, its width is $Q_{A+B} = q_A + q_B$, so its area is $\Delta P \times (Q_{A+B}) = (\Delta P \times q_A) + (\Delta P \times q_B) = R_A + R_B$ on Figures 5-3b and 5-3c. The same applies to all of the other little horizontal rectangles that make up the producer surplus; in each case, the area of the rectangle on Figure 5-3a, showing the summed supply curve, is the sum of the areas of the rectangles on Figures 5-3b and 5-3c, which show the individual supply curves. So the shaded area on Figure 5-3a equals the sum of the shaded areas on 5-3b and 5-3c. The shaded areas are not precisely equal to the corresponding surpluses, since the rectangles slightly overlap the supply curve; but the thinner the rectangles are, the smaller the discrepancy. In the limit as the height of the rectangles (ΔP) goes to 0, the shaded areas become exactly equal to the corresponding producer surpluses; so the producer surplus calculated from the summed supply curve is the sum of the producer surpluses from the individual supply curves.

The result applies to any number of producers, as does a similar result for the consumer surplus of any number of consumers. So we can find the sum of the surpluses received by consumers or producers by calculating the surplus for their combined demand or supply curve just as if it were the demand or supply curve for a single individual. This fact will be important in Chapter 7, where we analyze the cost that taxes impose on producers and consumers, and elsewhere.

We now have two different reasons to expect that supply curves will slope up. The first is the increasing marginal disvalue of labor. The second is that as the price of a good rises, more and more people find that they are better off producing it than producing anything else. As each new producer comes in, the supply curve gets a new horizontal segment — the increased price results in increased quantity above and beyond any increased production by existing producers. This will prove important in the next section, where we see that the first reason for expecting supply curves to slope up is less powerful than it at first appears.

Figure 5-3

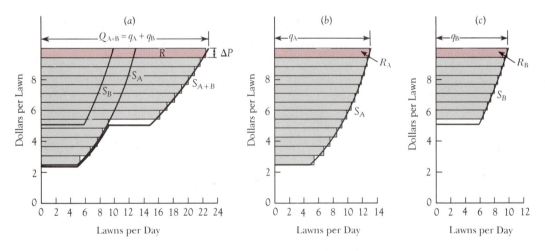

The producer surplus for a two-producer supply curve. The colored rectangle R is the sum of R_A and R_B, and similarly for the other rectangles. So the shaded area on Figure 5-3a is the sum of the shaded areas on Figures 5-3b and 5-3c. As ΔP approaches zero, the shaded area on each figure becomes exactly (instead of approximately) equal to the corresponding producer surplus. Hence the producer surplus calculated from the summed supply curve S_{A+B} is the sum of the producer surpluses calculated from S_A and S_B.

Look again at Figure 5-1a, and think about what it means. At a wage of $1/hour, the producer is working 2 hours per day and earning $2/day. It may be possible to live on an income of $730/year, but it is not easy. At a wage of $15/hour, the same individual chooses to work 12 hours per day and earn $65,700/year. There are probably people earning that kind of money who work those hours, but I suspect that for most of them the reason is more that they like working than that they want the money.

Income Effects in Production and the Backward-Bending Supply Curve for Labor

The mistake in the analysis that produced Figure 5-1a is the omission of what was described in Chapter 3 as the income effect. An increase in wages (say, from $10/hour to $11/hour) has two effects. It makes leisure more costly—each hour not worked means $11 less income instead of $10. That is an argument for working more hours at the higher salary. But at the same time, the increased wage means that the producer is wealthier—and is therefore inclined to consume more leisure. It is possible for the second effect to outweigh the first, in which case the increased wage causes a decrease in hours worked, as shown in Figure 5-4. This is called a **backward-bending supply curve for labor**; the backward-bending portion is from F to G (and presumably above G). The result, in the case of a single producer, would be a supply curve for goods that sloped in the wrong direction; for some range of goods, higher prices would generate less output instead of more.

This is not the first time we have seen a conflict between income and substitution effects; in Chapter 3, the same situation generated a Giffen good—a good whose demand curve sloped in the wrong direction. I argued that there were good reasons not to expect to observe Giffen goods in real life. Those reasons do not apply to the backward-bending supply curve for labor.

One of the reasons was that while we expect consumption of most goods to go up when income goes up, a Giffen good must be a good whose consumption goes down with increasing income—an inferior good. Indeed, it must be so strongly inferior that the income effect of an increase in its price (which, since we are buying it, is equivalent to a decrease in real income) outweighs the substitution effect. Our labor is something we are selling, not buying; an increase in its price (the wage rate) makes us richer not poorer, and so inclined to buy more leisure. So the backward-bending supply curve for labor only requires leisure to be a normal good.

The other reason a Giffen good is unlikely is that it must be a good on which we spend a large fraction of our income, in order that the decrease in its price can have a substantial effect on real income. This is implausible in the case of consumption, but not in the case of production. Most of us diversify in consumption but specialize in production; we divide our income among many consumption goods, but we get most of that income from selling one kind of labor. If the price we get for what we sell changes substantially, the result is a substantial change in our income. Hence the backward-bending supply curve for labor is far more likely to occur than is the Giffen good.

Economics is considerably simpler if demand curves always slope down and supply curves always slope up than if they insist on wriggling about as in Figure 5-4. Fortunately the argument for upward-sloping supply curves for goods does not entirely depend on upward-sloping supply curves for labor. If individuals supply less labor, and so mow fewer lawns, as the price of lawn mowing rises, their individual supply curves will slope backward. But if an increase in the price increases the number of people who find that lawn mowing yields a higher wage than any other alternative, the aggregate supply curve for lawns may still slope normally. It is particularly likely to do so in a large and complicated society. If many different goods are being produced, with the production of each employing only a small part of the population, even a small rise in the price of a good can induce some people to switch to producing it. It is still more likely if, as seems likely, only some of the producers are on the backward-bending portion of their supply curve for labor.

Marginal Value vs Marginal Utility

Another way of looking at the problem of the backward-bending supply curve for labor is as a result of the effect of a change in income on the

Figure 5-4

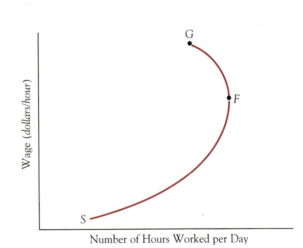

A backward-bending supply curve for labor. As the wage increases, the number of hours worked first increases (up to point *F*), then decreases.

Section II   Price = Value = Cost

relation between marginal value and marginal utility. When your wage increases from $10/hour to $11, you are being offered more dollars for your time than before, but since at the higher income each dollar is worth less to you (the marginal utility of income has fallen), you may actually be being offered less utility—$11 at your new, higher income may be worth less to you than $10 was before. If so, and if the marginal utility of leisure to you has not been changed by the increase in your income, you will choose to sell less of your time at the higher wage, and so work fewer hours. If the marginal utility of leisure has increased (you now have more money to spend on golf games and Caribbean vacations), the argument holds still more strongly.

The analysis of production given in the first part of this chapter (ignoring income effects) would correctly describe a producer whose income from other sources was large in comparison to his income from production. Changes in his wage would have only a small effect on his income, so we could legitimately ignore the income effect and consider only the substitution effect. The result would be the sort of curves shown in Figures 5-1a, 5-1b, and 5-2. It would also correctly describe a producer facing only a temporary change in his wage. He can transfer money from one year to another by saving or borrowing, so the value of money to him depends not on his current income but on some sort of lifetime average—his **permanent income**. His permanent income is changed only very slightly by changes in this week's wage, so the income effect of a temporary wage change is small.

The question of whether the supply curve for labor was or was not backward bending was a matter of considerable controversy 200 years ago, when Adam Smith wrote *The Wealth of Nations*, the book that founded modern economics. Some employers argued that if wages rose their employees would work fewer hours and the national income would fall; Smith argued that higher wages would mean better fed, healthier employees willing and able to work more in exchange for the higher reward. It is worth noting that Smith, who is usually described as a defender of capitalism, consistently argued that what was good for the workers was good for England and almost as consistently that what was good for the merchants and manufacturers (high tariffs and other special favors from government) was bad for England. He was a defender of capitalism—but not of capitalists.

PART 3—INDIFFERENCE CURVES AND THE SUPPLY OF LABOR

So far, we have analyzed the supply curve for labor, or for goods or services produced by labor, by using marginal value curves. Another way is by using indifference curves. The indifference curves on Figure 5-5 show an individual's preferences between leisure (defined, at this point, as any use of your time that does not bring in money) and income.

Using such a diagram, we can derive a supply curve for labor in a way that allows for the possibility that it may be backward bending. Figure 5-5a shows the production possibility sets (possible combinations of leisure and income) corresponding to wages of $5, $10, and $15/hour, along with the corresponding indifference curves and optimal bundles, for an individual with no other source of income. In each case, one possibility is 24 hours per day of leisure and no income. Another is no leisure and a daily income of 24 times the hourly wage. With a wage of $5/hour, for example, the line runs from 24 hours of leisure and no income to no leisure and an income of $120/day. The available combinations of leisure and income on Figure 5-5a correspond to points on the line between those two extremes. As the wage moves from $5 to $10 to $15/hour, the line moves from W_1 to W_2 to W_3 and the optimal bundle from A_1 to A_2 to A_3.

The indifference curves illustrated in Figure 5–5a imply a normal supply curve for labor, at least over the range of wages illustrated; as the wage rises, so does the number of hours worked (shown by a fall in the number of hours of leisure). Figure 5-5b illustrates a different set of indifference curves, leading to a backward-bending supply curve. Figure

Figure 5-5

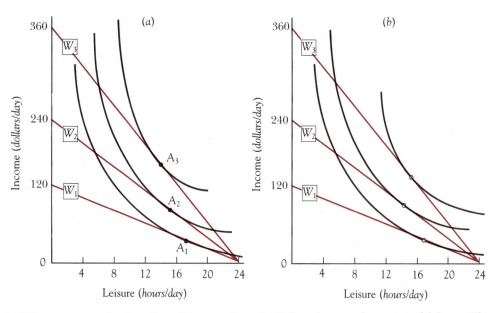

Indifference curve/budget line diagrams for calculating the supply curve of labor. The budget lines show the alternative bundles of leisure and income available to a producer at different wage levels; the indifference curves show his preferences among such bundles. The indifference curves of Figure 5-5a lead to a normally sloped supply curve for labor; those of Figure 5-5b lead to a backward-bending supply curve for labor.

Section II Price = Value = Cost

5-6 shows the two supply curves, S_1 (obtained from Figure 5-5a) and S_2 (from Figure 5-5b).

Students who try to redo the calculations shown on Figures 5-5a, 5-5b, and 5-6 in homework (or exam) problems frequently make the mistake of assuming that they can simply connect points such as A_1, A_2, and A_3 with a line, and then redraw the same line on another graph as the supply curve for labor. But the vertical axis of Figures 5-5a and 5-5b is income, while the vertical axis of Figure 5-6 is the wage rate; income is wage (dollars/hour) times number of hours worked. The wage on Figure 5-5a is not the height of a point but the slope of a line. W_1, for example, has a slope of (minus) $5/hour and shows the alternatives available to someone who can work at that wage. The point on Figure 5-6 that corresponds to A_1 on Figure 5-5a is C_1; its vertical coordinate is $5/hour (corresponding to the slope of W_1) and its horizontal coordinate is 7 hours per day (corresponding to the number of hours worked at A_1—24 hours per day total minus 17 hours per day of leisure). You may want to check for yourself the correspondence between A_2 and C_2 and between A_3 and C_3.

You may have realized by this point that what we are analyzing in this chapter is simply a special case of what we already analyzed in Chapters 3 and 4. Instead of talking about a supply of labor and a marginal disvalue for labor, we could have started with an individual who had an endowment of a good called leisure (24 hours per day), which he could

Figure 5-6

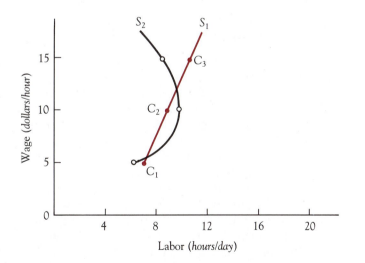

The supply curves for labor implied by Figures 5-5a and 5-5b. Points C_1, C_2, and C_3 correspond to points A_1, A_2, and A_3 on Figure 5-5a. Note that the vertical axis of this figure shows wage, not income; wage on Figures 5-5a and 5-5b is not the height of a point but the slope of a line.

sell at a price (his wage) and for which he had a marginal value curve. Just as in Chapter 4, the marginal value curve is identical to the demand curve. The marginal value for leisure curve is the same as the marginal disvalue for labor curve, and the demand curve for leisure is the same as the supply curve for labor, except that in each case the direction of the horizontal axis is reversed—increasing leisure corresponds to decreasing labor.

Our old friend the equimarginal principle applies here as well. The individual sells an amount of leisure (works a number of hours) such that the value of a little more leisure (the disvalue of a little more labor) is just equal to the price he is paid for it. In equilibrium, the wage equals the marginal value of leisure (marginal disvalue of labor).

PRODUCTION—MORE COMPLICATED CASES

So far, we have considered production under relatively simple circumstances. Producers sell their output on the market, so all they have to know in order to decide what to produce is how much it sells for. Amount of production, for any good, is simply proportional to amount of time spent producing it. In this section, we will consider some more complicated cases.

Production without a Market

So far in my discussion of production, I have assumed that the producer sells his output rather than consuming it himself. Figure 5-7 shows one way of analyzing the alternative—a situation where you consume your own output. *MV* is the marginal value to you of mowed lawns; *MdV* is the marginal disvalue of your labor. Your rate of output is 1 lawn per hour. The horizontal axis shows how many mowed lawns you produce and consume. You consume a mowed lawn by enjoying the view—I am not assuming that you eat grass.

If the quantity is less than Q_e, where the two curves cross, then the marginal value of the good is greater than the marginal disvalue of the labor used to produce it. That means that if you produced an additional unit, the value to you of the good would be more than the cost to you of the labor used to produce it, so you would be better off producing it. That remains true as long as quantity is less than Q_e, so you keep increasing your level of output (and consumption) until it reaches Q_e. Beyond that, additional units cost you more in labor than they are worth, so any further increase in output would make you worse off.

Section II   Price = Value = Cost

Figure 5-7

Marginal value/marginal cost diagram for a producer who consumes his output himself. On Figure 5-7, the marginal cost of production is the marginal disvalue of labor; since the output rate is one lawn per hour, the vertical axis can be read as either dollars per hour or dollars per lawn, and the horizontal axis can be read as either lawns per day or hours per day.

Figure 5-7 shows a case where only one kind of good can be produced. Figure 5-8 shows one way of analyzing a situation where that is no longer true. Two goods can be produced—meals and mowed lawns. The individual's preferences between them are shown by indifference curves, as in Chapter 3. If he chooses to work 10 hours per day, he can produce 10 lawns, or 20 meals, or any intermediate bundle; his **production possibility set** is the colored area on Figure 5-8. The optimal bundle is the point in the set that intersects the highest indifference curve—point *A* on the figure. The diagram is exactly the same as for an individual with an income of $10/day who is able to buy lawn mowing at $1/lawn and meals at $0.50/meal. In each case, the individual chooses the best bundle from a collection that includes 10 lawns (and no meals), 20 meals (and no lawns), and everything in between.

If you move back from the picture, however, and think about what it means, there is one important difference between the two cases. In discussing a consumer spending money, I argued that he would always spend his entire income, since the only thing money is good for is buying goods. The equivalent in the case of time is always working 14 hours per day—or perhaps 24!

Chapter 5   Production   **127**

Figure 5-8

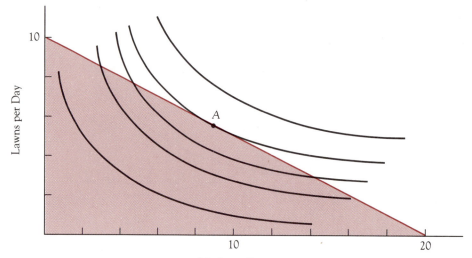

Indifference curves and production possibility set for an individual working 10 hours per day. The individual can produce 10 lawns per day and 20 meals per day; different points on the line between 10 lawns and 20 meals represent different divisions of time between producing lawns and producing meals. *A* is his optimal point.

The problem is that in drawing Figure 5-8, I implicitly assumed that the only things that matter to you are meals and mowed lawns—in particular, I assumed that you have no value at all for your own leisure. If that were true, you *would* work 24 hours per day. In drawing the figure, I have correctly translated the assumption into geometry without pointing out, until now, that the assumption itself is absurd. That is an example of why it is a good idea to move back and forth between mathematical and verbal descriptions, in order to make sure you know what your mathematics actually stands for. It is not unusual for articles to be submitted to economics journals that, when translated into English, turn out to make no sense. Some of them get published.

What the figure can be used for is to show what combination of the two goods the individual will choose to produce *if* he decides to work a certain number of hours. To find out how many hours he would choose to work, we would need to add a third dimension in order to show his preferences among meals, lawns, and leisure.

Nonlinear Production

Let us now drop another assumption. So far, the output of each good has been proportional to the time spent producing it. As a result, the frontier of the production possibility set for any pair of goods (total hours worked held constant, as in Figure 5-8) is a straight line, like a budget line. The similarity is not accidental. In Chapter 3, the consumer got goods by spending money; in this chapter, he gets them by spending time. In both cases, total expenditure is simply the sum of the price of one good (in money or in time) multiplied by the quantity of that good bought plus the price of the other good multiplied by the quantity of it bought.

Figure 5-9a shows a more complicated case—the production possibility set of someone who is more productive if he specializes. If he spends all his time mowing lawns, he can maintain his lawn-mowing skills at a high level and mow more lawns per hour than if he spends much of his time cooking. If he spends all his time cooking, he can maintain his culinary skills at a high level and produce far more meals per hour than if he spends most of his time mowing lawns. (Perhaps our measure of quantity of meals cooked should include some allowance for quality as well, so that a meal cooked by a professional mower of lawns is equivalent to $1/10$ of a meal cooked by a Cordon Bleu chef). Point J shows what happens if he tries to divide his time between lawn mowing and cooking, making himself a "jack of all trades and a master of none."

Figure 5-9b shows a production possibility set whose boundary curves in the opposite way. You may think of this as describing someone who could engage in two quite different kinds of production—digging ditches and writing sonnets. Digging ditches uses the producer's muscles; writing sonnets uses his mind. He can compose a few more sonnets per day if his mind is not distracted by ditch digging, and he can dig a few

Figure 5-9

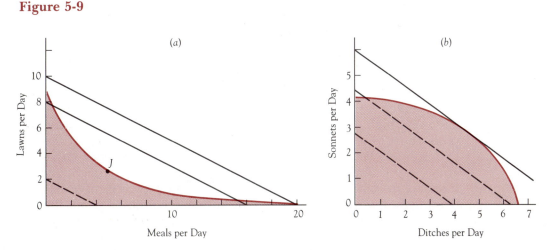

Two cases of nonlinear production. The individual is producing goods to sell. The shaded areas are the different bundles that he can produce. The straight lines are equi-income curves; each shows all the different bundles that sell for a given amount of money. The producer wants to produce the bundle that sells for the largest amount. That will be the point in the shaded region that touches the highest equi-income curve.

more ditches if he is not trying to find three more words that rhyme with "world" for the octave of a Petrarchan sonnet. But the two activities compete with each other only mildly, producing the curve shown in the figure.

Let us now go back to the problem with which we started this chapter—which good to produce. As in the earlier discussion, we assume the individual is producing goods to sell on the market rather than producing for his own consumption. We can reproduce the argument of Table 5-1, in this more complicated situation, by adding to our figure **equi-income lines**—lines that show the different bundles of goods that can be sold for the same total amount. These are indifference curves from the standpoint of the producer, since all that matters to him about his output is what he can sell it for. Unlike our usual indifference curves, these are straight lines. If lawn mowing sells for $10/lawn and meal cooking for $5/meal then if you start with a bundle of 10 lawns and want to construct other bundles that will bring you the same amount of money ($100), you find that each time you subtract 1 lawn, you must add 2 meals. The result is a straight line, as shown on Figures 5-9*a* and 5-9*b*. The slope of the line depends on the relative prices of the two goods. Picking the optimal set of goods to produce is easy. For any number of hours you consider working, find the highest line that touches the corresponding production possibility set; the point where they touch is the most valuable bundle you can produce with that amount of labor.

By looking at Figure 5-9*a*, you should be able to convince yourself that whatever the slope of the equi-income lines, the highest equi-income line that touches the production possibility set touches either at one end of the curve (all lawns) or at the other (all meals) or possibly at both, but never anywhere in the middle. This corresponds to what we usually observe—people specialize in production, spending all their time (aside from home production—cooking your own food and washing your own face) producing a single good or service. The situation of Figure 5-9*b*, on the other hand, while it can lead to specialization (if the slope of the line is either very steep or very shallow, implying that one of the goods has a very high price compared to the other), can also lead to diversified production, as in the case shown.

Figures 5-9*a* and 5-9*b* look very much like indifference curve diagrams, especially Figure 5-9*a*. In a way they are, but the straight line and the curve have switched roles. In an ordinary indifference curve diagram, the straight line is a budget line, showing what bundles of goods the consumer can choose among. The curve is an indifference curve, showing what bundles are equally attractive to him. On Figure 5-9, the curves are the equivalents of budget lines—they show the different bundles of goods the consumer can choose to produce. The straight line equi-income curves are indifference curves—since the goods are being produced for sale, the producer is indifferent between any two bundles that sell for the same amount.

From another standpoint, the straight line equi-income curve of Figure 5-9 and the straight budget line of Chapter 3 are the same line. Both show all bundles of goods that cost a given amount of money. From the standpoint of the consumer with a certain amount of money to spend, the line represents alternative bundles that he can buy with that amount of money. From the standpoint of the producer, it represents alternative bundles that he can sell to get that amount of money. It is the same transaction seen from opposite sides.

The logic of what we are doing here is essentially the same as in Chapter 3. An individual has objectives (utility from consumption for the consumer, utility from income and leisure for the producer) and opportunities. He chooses that one of the available opportunities that best achieves his objectives. The geometric apparatus of budget lines and indifference curves is simply one way of formalizing the definition of economics at the beginning of Chapter 1, one way of analyzing people who have objectives and tend to choose the correct way to achieve them.

PROBLEMS

1. Figure 5-10a shows your labor supply curve. Your wage is $10/hour. What is your producer surplus ? Give either a numerical or a graphical answer.
2. Figure 5-10a shows your marginal disvalue for labor curve. You can make $8/hour washing cars or $6/hour waiting on tables. What is your producer surplus from washing cars? In other words, how much worse off would you be if the carwash closed down?
3. Your rich uncle just died and left you, to your surprise, a $10,000/year trust fund. Figure 5-10a used to describe your supply curve for labor. What do you think your labor supply curve might look like now? Draw it.
4. You can produce 3 falchions/hour or 5 petards/hour. Figure 5-10b shows your supply curve for labor. Draw your supply curve for falchions, assuming that the price of a petard is $2. Draw your supply curve for petards, assuming that the price of a falchion is $4.
5. Some people, such as scoutmasters and PTA officials, are willing to work at jobs that pay nothing—even, in some cases, at jobs that pay less than nothing. Draw a labor supply curve for such a person.
6. In the text, I prove that the producer surplus calculated from the summed supply curve for two producers is the sum of the producer surpluses calculated separately. Prove the same result for consumer surplus.
7. Prove the same result for three producers.
8. Prove that the result applies to any number of producers.

Figure 5-10

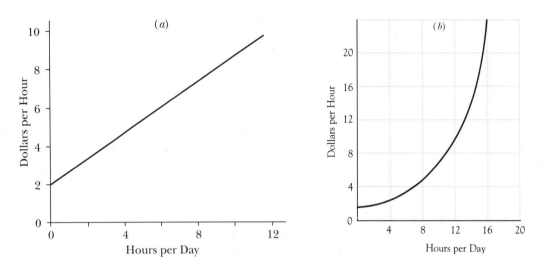

Supply curves or marginal disvalue curves for labor. For Problems 1, 2, 3, and 4.

9. In the examples discussed, producer surplus is always less than salary. Can you think of a situation where it would be greater? Discuss.

10. "At a cost of only $10,000,000 a year of public expenditure, this administration, by attracting new firms into the state, has increased the income of our citizens by $20,000,000. The citizens should be grateful; for every dollar of tax money they give us, we are providing them $2 of income." Assume the facts are correct; discuss the conclusion in terms of the ideas of this chapter.

11. The production possibility lines on Figure 5-5 were drawn on the assumption that if you spend no hours working you have no income. Draw a budget line for someone who receives $10/day from his parents and, in addition, can work as many hours as he wishes for $5/hour.

12. What are some other situations that the budget line you drew for the previous question might describe?

13. Draw a budget line for someone who can work as many hours as he wishes for $10/hour, but must pay $20/day interest on his accumulated debts.

14. What are some other other situations that the budget line you drew for the previous question might also describe?

15. In Chapter 4, I rejected the idea that economists assume individuals value only income. Draw a set of labor/leisure indifference curves for someone who always prefers more income to less, whatever the cost in other values. How many hours a day will he work?

Figure 5-11

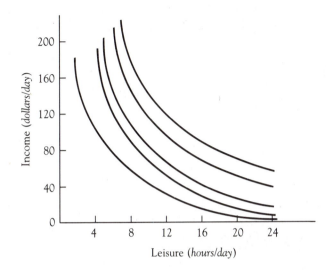

Indifference curves showing preferences with regard to income and leisure. For Problem 16.

16. Figure 5-11 is an indifference map showing your tastes for leisure and income. Draw the corresponding supply curve for labor over a range of wages from $1–$10/hour. How does it slope? Show how you calculated it.

The following problems refer to the optional section:

17. In the situation shown in Figure 5-7, how much worse off would you be if you were forbidden to produce anything? Discuss your answer in terms of producer surplus and consumer surplus.
18. Use indifference curves to explain why we usually do not specialize in consumption. Use indifference curves to show a situation where an individual does specialize in consumption. This particular kind of solution to the decision problem illustrated on an indifference curve diagram has a name; what is it?
19. Draw an indifference curve diagram showing the producer of Figure 5-9a producing goods for his own consumption. Where is his optimal point? Is he specializing or diversifying?
20. Draw an indifference curve diagram showing the producer of Figure 5-9b producing goods for his own consumption. Where is his optimal point? Is he specializing or diversifying?

chapter 6

SIMPLE TRADE

PART 1—POTENTIAL GAINS FROM TRADE

Individuals exchange goods. The benefits they receive depend on how much they exchange and on what terms—I am better off (and you worse off) if you buy this book for $100 than if you buy it for $1. We do not yet know how market prices are determined—that is the subject of the next chapter—so we cannot say much about how the gains from trade will be divided among the traders. We do, however, know enough to understand why **mutual gains from trade** are possible—why one person's gain is not necessarily another person's loss. In this part of the chapter, I will examine the origin of such gains—first in the case where each individual has a stock of goods that can be either consumed or traded for someone else's goods and then in the case where individuals produce goods in order to exchange them.

Trade without Production

I have 10 apples. You have 10 oranges. We have identical tastes, shown in Figure 6-1 and Table 6-1. Point F is my initial situation; point A is yours. Column 1 of the table shows the bundles that are equivalent to (have the same utility as) 10 oranges plus no apples, corresponding to indifference curve U_1 on Figure 6-1. Column 2 shows the bundles equivalent to 10 apples and no oranges, corresponding to U_2.

Suppose I trade 5 of my apples for 5 of your oranges. We are now both at point R, with 5 apples and 5 oranges each. Since point R must be on a higher indifference curve than either A or F, we are both better off. The same result can be seen from the table. I was indifferent between my initial 10 apples and a bundle of 5 apples plus 2 oranges. Since oranges are a good, I prefer more of them to fewer. It follows that I prefer 5 apples plus 5 oranges to 5 apples plus 2 oranges; I am indifferent

134

Table 6-1

Bundle	Column 1 Apples	Oranges	Utility	Bundle	Column 2 Apples	Oranges	Utility
A	0	10	5	F	10	0	10
B	1	6	5	G	7	1	10
C	2	3	5	H	5	2	10
D	3	1	5	K	4	3	10
E	4	0	5	L	3	5	10
				M	2	8	10
				N	1	12	10
				O	0	17	10

between having 5 apples plus 2 oranges and having 10 apples, hence I prefer 5 apples plus 5 oranges to my original 10 apples. Similarly, you were indifferent between having your original 10 oranges and having 4 apples plus no oranges; obviously you are better off with 5 apples plus 5 oranges. We have both gained from the trade. That is why we were both willing to make it.

There are many other trades we could have made instead that would also have benefited both of us. Since I am indifferent between my initial

Figure 6-1

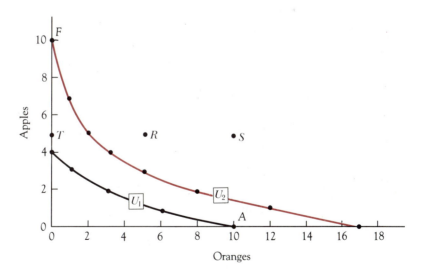

Indifference curves between apples and oranges, showing the same preferences as Table 6-1.

situation (10 apples) and having 5 apples plus 2 oranges, I gain by trading away 5 apples as long as I get more than 2 oranges in exchange. Similarly you gain by trading away all of your oranges as long as you get more than 4 apples in exchange. So if you give me 10 oranges for 5 apples, we are both better off than when we started (I am at point S on the figure; you are at point T). If you give me 3 oranges for 5 apples, we are also better off than when we started. Obviously I would prefer to get 10 oranges for my 5 apples, and you would prefer to give only 3. There is a **bargaining range**—a range of different exchanges, some more favorable to me and less favorable to you than others, but all representing improvements for both of us on the original situation. One consequence of the existence of a bargaining range is discussed in the section of this chapter on bilateral monopoly. Other consequences—and ways of dealing with the ambiguity as to which trade will actually occur—are discussed later in the optional section.

In the example I have been using, the gains from trade come about because we start with different **endowments**—different initial quantities of goods. The same gains could also occur if we had identical endowments—5 apples plus 5 oranges each, for example—but different preferences. Figure 6-2a shows my preferences (the colored indifference curves) and yours (the black indifference curves). We both have the same initial endowment—5 apples and 5 oranges apiece. The arrows show the results of my trading 4 of my apples for 4 of your oranges; both of us are better off. As in the previous case, there are a variety of alternative trades that would also benefit both of us.

It is even possible to draw indifference curves that allow two people with identical preferences and identical endowments to gain by trade. In order to do so, however, I must give the indifference curves a shape inconsistent with our usual assumptions, as shown in Figure 6-2b. The goods shown are beer and apples. G is just enough beer to get drunk (you are not interested in being half drunk), and H is just enough apples to make a pie for your dinner party. F, your original endowment, includes enough apples for too small a pie and enough beer to get you just drunk enough to burn it. You would prefer either G (all beer) or H (all apples) to F. If two people were in that situation, with identical tastes and identical endowments of beer and apples, they could both gain by trade. One would take all the apples, one would take all the beer, and both would be better off.

This is a situation in which your tastes violate the rule of declining marginal utility. One can think of other examples. If it takes a gallon of gasoline to get where you are going, increasing the amount you have from 1/2 gallon to 1 gallon benefits you more than increasing it from zero to 1/2 gallon did. While such situations are possible, we usually prefer to assume them away, since they add complications to the analysis that are usually unnecessary.

Figure 6-2

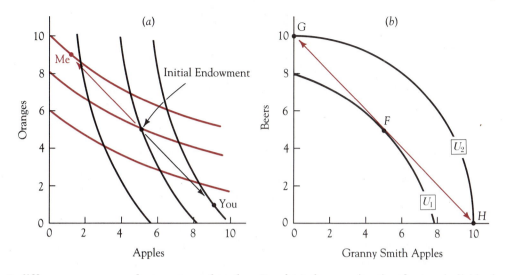

Indifference curves, endowments, and trade.   Panel (*a*) shows a situation for two individuals with different tastes but the same initial endowment. The colored indifference curves show my tastes; the black curves show yours. The figure shows a trade (you give me 4 oranges in exchange for 4 apples) which benefits both of us. In panel (*b*), we have the same tastes and identical endowments. The trade of 5 apples for 5 beers makes both parties better off, since both point *G* (10 beers) and point *H* (10 apples) are preferred to point *F* (5 of each).

Trade and Production — English Version

So far, we have been trading a fixed endowment of goods; now we will consider the combination of trade with production, first in a verbal form and later using geometry. We will find it convenient to consider only two traded goods while holding constant our consumption of all other goods (except leisure). In order to simplify the discussion, we assume that over the range of alternatives considered, we always consume the same amount of the traded goods. (Our demand for them is "perfectly inelastic," to use a term with which you will later become familar.) The benefit of trade then takes the form of increased leisure; if it takes less time to produce consumption goods, we have more time to spend enjoying them.

Assume it takes me 1 hour to mow my lawn and $1/2$ hour to cook a meal. You are a better cook; you can cook a meal in 15 minutes. You are also a worse mower; it takes you 2 hours to mow the same lawn. For both of us, production possibility sets are linear—it takes twice as long to produce 2 meals (or 2 mowed lawns).

Initially I am mowing my lawn once per day (the grass grows fast around here) and cooking 3 meals per day, for a total of $2\frac{1}{2}$ hours of work. You are doing the same, for a total of $2\frac{3}{4}$ hours.

I offer to mow your lawn in exchange for your cooking my meals. It will take me 2 hours to mow both lawns; it will take you 1½ hours to cook all 6 meals. We will both be better off. Just as in the earlier examples, there are a variety of other trades that would also be improvements for both of us on the initial situation. For example, I could offer to mow your lawn once in exchange for 4 meals (you would cook all my meals; I would mow your lawn three days out of four). Since it takes you 1 hour to cook 4 meals and 2 hours to mow the lawn, you are still better off making the trade.

I am better at mowing lawns than you are, so I mow the lawns; you are better at cooking, so you cook. Since "better" appears to mean "can do it in less time," it seems that I could be better than you at both cooking and mowing, and that if I were there would be no way in which I could benefit from trading with you.

This seems to make sense, but it is wrong—as a simple example will show. Suppose I can cook a meal in 15 minutes and mow a lawn in ½ hour. It takes you ½ hour to cook a meal and 2 hours to mow a lawn. I am better at everything; what can you offer me to trade?

Just as before, you offer to cook my meals in exchange for my mowing your lawn. Before the trade, you spent 1½ hours cooking 3 meals and 2 hours mowing your lawn, for a total of 3½ hours. After the trade, you spend 3 hours cooking meals for both of us. You are better off by ½ hour. What about me?

Before the trade, I spent 45 minutes per day cooking and ½ hour mowing, for a total of 1¼ hours. After the trade, I spend 1 hour per day mowing both lawns, for a total of 1 hour. I am better off too! How can this be? How can it pay me to hire you to do something I can do better?

The answer is that the relation between cost to me and cost to you in time has nothing to do with whether we can gain by trade; time is not what we are trading. The relevant relation is between my cost of mowing a lawn and yours in terms of meals cooked—our opportunity costs. We are, after all, trading mowed lawns for meals, not for time.

In the first example I gave, the opportunity cost to me of mowing a lawn was 2 meals, since mowing 1 lawn took the time in which I could have made 2 meals. The opportunity cost to you of mowing a lawn was 8 meals. Since lawn mowing cost much more to you (in terms of meals) than to me, it was natural for you to buy lawn mowing from me and pay with meals.

A different way of describing the same situation is to say that the cost to me of producing a meal was ½ lawn and the cost to you was ⅛ lawn. Since meals cost you much less than they cost me (in terms of lawns), it was natural for me to buy meals from you, using lawn mowing to pay you. These are two descriptions of the same transaction; when we trade lawn mowing for meal cooking, we can describe it as buying lawns with meals or meals with lawns, according to whose side we are looking at it from.

Since a lawn costs you 8 meals, you are willing to buy lawn moving for any price less than 8 meals per lawn—it is cheaper than producing it yourself. Since it costs me 2 meals, I am willing to sell for any price higher than 2. Obviously there is a wide range of prices at which we can both benefit—any price of more than 2 meals per lawn and less than 8 will do.

Now consider the second example, where I can cook a meal in 15 minutes and mow a lawn in 30, while you take 30 minutes to cook a meal and 2 hours to mow a lawn. The cost of mowing a lawn to me is 2 meals; the cost of mowing a lawn to you is 4 meals. I benefit by trading lawns for meals as long as I get more than 2 meals per lawn; you benefit by trading meals for lawns as long as you pay fewer than 4 meals per lawn. Again, there is room for both of us to benefit by trade.

Once we realize that the relevant cost of producing one good is measured in terms of other goods, it becomes clear that I cannot be better than you at everything. If I am better at producing lawns (in terms of meals), then I must be worse at producing meals (in terms of lawns). If this is not obvious when put into words, consider it algebraically.

Let L be the time it takes me to mow a lawn and L' the time it takes you. Let M be the time it takes me to cook a meal and M' the time it takes you. The cost to me of mowing a lawn (in terms of meals) is L/M; if a lawn takes 30 minutes and a meal 15, then a lawn takes the time in which I could produce 2 meals. The cost to you is L'/M'. But the cost to me of a meal in terms of lawns is, by the same argument, M/L; the cost to you is M'/L'. If $L/M > L'/M'$ then $M'/L' > M/L$. If you are better than I am at mowing a lawn, I must be better than you at cooking a meal.

To put the same argument in numbers, imagine that it costs me 3 meals to mow a lawn and costs you 2. $3 > 2$. I am a worse mower than you; it costs me more meals to mow a lawn. But $1/3 < 1/2$. I am a better cook than you. It costs me only $1/3$ lawn to cook a meal, and it costs you $1/2$ lawn.

Comparative Advantage. The general principle I have been explaining is called the **principle of comparative advantage**. It is usually discussed in the context of foreign trade. The principle is that two nations, or individuals, can both gain by trade if each produces the goods for which it has a comparative advantage. Nation A has a comparative advantage over Nation B in producing a good if the cost of producing that good in A relative to the cost of producing other goods in A is lower than the cost of producing that good in B relative to the cost of producing other goods in B.

The error of confusing **absolute advantage** ("I can do everything better than you can") with comparative advantage typically appears as the claim that because some other country has lower wages, higher productivity, lower taxes, or some other advantage, it can undersell our domestic manufacturers on everything, putting our producers and workers out of work. This is used as an argument for **protective tariffs**—taxes on imports designed to keep them from competing with domestically produced goods.

There are a number of things wrong with this argument. To begin with, if we were importing lots of things from Japan and exporting nothing to them (and if no other countries were involved), we would be getting a free ride on the work and capital of the Japanese. They would be providing us with cars, stereos, computers, toys, and textiles, and we would be giving them dollars in exchange—pieces of green paper which cost us very little to produce. A good deal for us, but not for them.

Here, as in many other cases, thinking in terms of money obscures what is really happening. Trade is ultimately goods for goods—although that may be less obvious when several countries are involved, since the Japanese can use the dollars they get from us to buy goods from the Germans who in turn send the dollars back to get goods from us. In terms of goods, the Japanese cannot be better at producing everything. If it costs them fewer computers to produce a car (translation: If the cost in Japan of all the inputs used to produce a car divided by the cost in Japan of all the inputs used to produce a computer is smaller than the corresponding ratio in the United States), then it costs them more cars to produce a computer. If they trade their cars for our computers, both sides benefit.

If you still find the claim that tariffs on Japanese automobiles are a way of protecting us from the Japanese in order to keep American workers from being replaced by Japanese workers plausible, consider the following fable.

Growing Hondas. *There are two ways we can produce automobiles. We can build them in Detroit or we can grow them in Iowa. Everyone knows how we build automobiles. To grow automobiles, we begin by growing the raw material from which they are made—wheat. We put the wheat on ships and send the ships out into the Pacific. They come back with Hondas on them.*

From our standpoint, "growing Hondas" is just as much a form of production—using American farm workers instead of American auto workers—as building them. What happens on the other side of the Pacific is irrelevant; the effect would be just the same for us if there really were a gigantic machine sitting somewhere between Hawaii and Japan turning wheat into automobiles. Tariffs are indeed a way of protecting American workers—from other American workers.

In Chapter 19, we will discuss tariffs again, demonstrating under what circumstances and in what sense American tariffs impose net costs on Americans and in what special cases they do not. At that point, we will also discuss why tariffs exist—and why the industries that actually get protected by tariffs are not the same as the industries that one might be able to argue, on economic grounds, ought to get protected.

There is a problem in using indifference curves to represent our preferences among two produced goods. With only two dimensions, there is no place to put leisure; if we are not careful, we may find that we are treating leisure as if it had no value at all. One way of solving the problem is to put leisure on one axis and all other goods—shown as the income available to buy them—on the other. This is what we did in Chapter 5 in order to use indifference curves to derive a supply curve for labor. While this was a useful diagram for analyzing the division of time between production and leisure, it is of no use for analyzing trade. In order to have trade, we must have two different goods to exchange. Since leisure itself cannot be traded, we need two goods *in addition to* leisure. With two-dimensional paper, we cannot graph three goods.

If we want to use the geometric approach to analyze trade, we will have to go back to graphing two different tradeable goods (or services) on the axes. We justify this by letting the indifference curves represent our preferences with regard to those two goods, given that we are also consuming some fixed amount of leisure (and possibly other goods). Such diagrams can be used to analyze the choice between two goods while ignoring decisions about how much of other goods (including leisure) we wish to consume.

Figure 6-3 shows the production possibility sets for me and you in the first example of the previous section. The only addition is the assumption that each of us is going to spend exactly 6 hours per day working. Both of us are assumed to have the same preferences, represented by indifference curves U_1, U_2, and U_3—point A is on the highest indifference curve that touches my opportunity set, point B on the highest curve that touches yours.

To see why our combined opportunity set is as I have drawn it and why it is so large, imagine that we start in the upper left-hand corner, at point D on Figure 6-3. All we are doing is mowing lawns—9 of them a day (6 by me and 3 by you).

How much must we give up (in terms of lawns mowed) in order to produce 1 meal? If I cook it, we must give up $1/2$ lawn mowed (it takes me 1 hour to mow a lawn, $1/2$ hour to cook a meal); if you do it, only $1/8$ of a lawn. Obviously we get the meal at lower cost by having you cook it. As we move down and to the right along the boundary of the opportunity set, we are giving up only $1/8$ lawn per meal—that is why the line slopes down so slowly.

Eventually we reach point E, where you are spending all of your 6 hours of working time cooking while I am still spending all my time mowing lawns. We are producing 24 meals and 6 mowed lawns per day (if this seems like more than we have any use for, remember that the nonsatiation assumption becomes more plausible when we expand our simple examples to fit a world with many more than two goods in it).

Figure 6-3

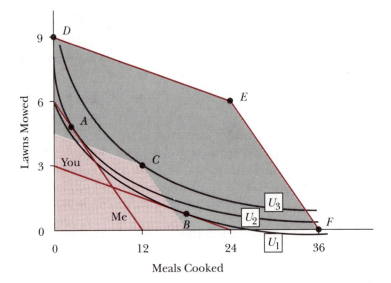

Production possibility sets for 2 individuals. The entire shaded and colored region shows the production possibility set for the combined output of two producers. The colored region shows the alternatives available to each producer if they divide their output evenly. *C*, the optimal point with joint production and even division, is preferred to *A*, my optimal point if I produce alone, and to *B*, your optimal point if you produce alone. This shows the possibility of mutual gains from trade.

If we wish to produce still more meals, I must cook them—at a cost of ½ lawn per meal. The boundary turns abruptly down, since my cost for cooking meals is higher than yours. Eventually we reach point *F*, where we are both cooking full time and producing 36 meals per day.

The entire shaded and colored area on Figure 6-3 shows the production possibility set available to the two of us together. The colored inner section shows how much each of us can have if we choose to split our output evenly, with each of us getting half of the lawns and half of the meals. *C* is the optimal point (for each of us) on that assumption. Note that it is on a higher indifference curve than either *A* or *B*, our optimal points without trade. Obviously many other divisions are possible. The point to note is how much bigger the consumption opportunity set becomes for each of us when we combine our efforts through trade. I am (relatively) good at mowing lawns, and you at cooking meals. Without trade, I cannot make full use of my comparative advantage—there are too many meals I want cooked and not enough lawns I want mowed. The situation is the same (in the opposite direction—too many lawns and not enough meals) for you. Through trade, we solve the problem.

PART 2—COMPLICATIONS OF TWO-PERSON TRADE

In the first part of this chapter, we saw why individuals can gain by trade. In this part, we will look a little more carefully at some of the problems associated with two-person trade—in particular, at problems associated with the conflict between the two traders over the division of the gains.

Bilateral Monopoly—The Serpent in the Garden

So far, I have presented an entirely optimistic view of trade, with individuals cooperating to their mutual benefit. There is one problem that may have occurred to you. In each of these cases, there are many different trades that benefit both parties; some are preferred by one, some by the other. What decides which trade actually occurs?

Consider the following very simple case. I have a horse that is worth $100 to me and $200 to you. If I sell it to you, there is a net gain of $100; the price for which I sell it determines how the gain is divided between us. If I sell it for $100, you get all the benefit; if I sell it for $200, I do. Anywhere in the bargaining range between these two extremes we divide the $100 surplus between us.

Bargaining Costs. If I can convince you that I will not take any price below $199, it is in your interest to pay that; gaining $1 is better than gaining nothing. If you can convince me that you will not pay more than $101, it is in my interest to sell it for that—for the same reason. Both of us are likely to spend substantial real resources—time and energy, among other things—trying to persuade each other that our bargaining positions (the amounts we say we will pay or take) are real.

One way I can do so is by trying to deceive you about how much the horse is really worth to me. When I set up the problem, I (the author of this book) told you (the reader of this book) what the real values were, but the you and I inside the problem do not have that information. Each of us has to guess how much the horse is worth to the other–and each has an incentive to try to make the other guess wrong. If I believe the horse is worth only $101 to you, there is no point in my trying to hold out for more.

One danger in such bargaining is that we may be too successful. If I persuade you that the horse is really worth more than $200 to me (and I may try to do so, in the false belief that you will, if necessary, pay that much for it), then you stop trying to buy it. If you persuade me that it is worth less than $100 to you (ditto, *mutatis mutandis*), then I stop trying to sell it. In either case, the deal falls through and the $100 gain disappears.

Strikes and Wars—Errors or Experiments? Consider a strike. When it is over, union and management will have agreed to some contract. Typically, both the stockholders whose interest management is supposed to represent and the workers whose interest the union is supposed to represent would be better off if they agreed, on the first day of bargaining, to whatever contract they will eventually sign, thus avoiding the cost of the strike. The reason they do not is that the union is trying to persuade management that it will only accept a contract very favorable to it and management is trying to persuade the union that no such contract will be offered. Each tries to make its bargaining position persuasive by demonstrating that it is willing to accept large costs—in the form of a strike—rather than give in.

Much the same is true of wars. When the smoke clears, there will be a peace treaty; one side or the other will have won, or some compromise will have been accepted by both. If the peace treaty were signed immediately after the declaration of war and just before the first shot was fired, there would be an enormous savings in human life and material damage. The failure of the nations involved to do it that way may in part be the result of differing factual beliefs; if each believes that its tanks and planes are better and its soldiers braver, then the two sides will honestly disagree about who is going to win and hence about what the terms of the peace treaty will be. In this situation, one may regard the war as an (expensive) experiment to settle a disagreement about the military power of the two sides.

But there are other reasons why wars occur. Even if both sides agree on the military situation, they may have different opinions about how high a price each is willing to pay for victory. It is said that when the Japanese government consulted its admiralty on the prospects of a war with the United States, the admiralty replied that they could provide a year of victories, hold on for another year, and would then start losing—a reasonably accurate prophecy. The Japanese attacked anyway, in the belief that the United States—about to become engaged in a more difficult and important war in Europe—would agree to a negotiated peace sometime in the first two years. An expensive miscalculation.

While bilateral monopoly bargaining is a common and important element in real-world economies, it is not the dominant form in which trade occurs. Fortunately (from the standpoint both of saving bargaining costs and of simplifying economic analysis), there are other and more important mechanisms for determining on what terms goods are exchanged, mechanisms that lead to a less ambiguous result as well as considerably lower transaction costs.

Getting "Ripped Off"

There seems to be a widespread belief that if someone sells something to you for more than he could have—if, for example, he could make a profit selling it to you for $5 but charges $6—he is somehow mistreating you, "ripping you off" in current jargon. This is an oddly one-sided way of looking at such a situation. If you pay $6 for the good, it is presumably worth at least $6 to you. (I am not now considering the case of fraud, where what you think you are getting and what you are really getting are different things.) If it costs him $5 and is worth $6 to you, then there is a $1 gain when you buy it; your claim that he ought to sell it to you for $5 amounts to claiming that you are entitled to get all of the benefit from the transaction. It would seem to make just as much (or as little) sense to argue that he should get all the benefit—that if you buy a good for $5 when you would, if necessary, have been willing to pay $6, then you are ripping him off. Yet I know very few people who, if they see a price of $4 on a new book by their favorite author for which they would gladly pay $10, feel obliged to volunteer the higher price—or even to offer to split the difference.

As it happens, substantial bargaining ranges are not typical of most transactions, for the same reasons that bilateral monopoly is not the dominant form of trade. Most of the goods you buy are sold at about cost (if cost is properly computed) for reasons you will learn in the next few chapters. Nonetheless, bilateral monopolies and bargaining ranges do exist. I am myself a monopolist: I give speeches and write articles on a variety of topics, and I believe that nobody else's speeches and articles are quite the same as mine. I enjoy writing and speaking. I would give some speeches and write some articles even if I did not get paid for them; indeed I do (sometimes) write articles and give speeches for which I am not paid. That is no reason why I should not charge for my services if I can. If someone is willing to pay me $500 for a speech I would be willing to give for free, then that is evidence that giving the speech produces a net gain of at least $500. I see no reason why I should feel obliged to turn all of that gain over to my audience.

OPTIONAL SECTION

THE EDGEWORTH BOX

In the case of two-person trade, there may be many different exchanges, each of which would be beneficial to both parties; some exchanges will be preferred by one person, some by the other. There are then two different questions to be settled. One is how to squeeze as much total gain as possible out of the opportunities for trade; the other is how that gain is to be divided. The two individuals who are trading have a common interest in getting as much total gain as possible but are likely to disagree about the division.

An ingenious way of looking at such a situation is the Edgeworth Box, named after Francis Y. Edgeworth, the author of a nineteenth century work on economics called *Mathematical Psychics* (which does not mean what it sounds like).

In the simplest two-person trading situation (such as the one discussed at the beginning of this chapter), there are only two goods and no production. There are then four variables—how much of good X I have (x_1), how much you have (x_2), how much of good Y I have (y_1), and how much you have (y_2). Since exchange does not change the total amounts of the two goods, we have two **constraints:** $x_1 + x_2 = x$ and $y_1 + y_2 = y$, where x and y are the total endowments of X and Y. Since we have four variables and two constraints, the constraints can be used to eliminate two of the variables, leaving us with two—which can be plotted on a two-dimensional surface such as this page. Here is how you do it.

How to Build a Box. First draw a box, such as Figure 6-4, with length x and height y (20 and 15). Any division of x and y between you and me can be represented by a point, such as point A. The horizontal distance from the *left-hand* edge of the box to A is x_1 ($=15$), the vertical distance from the *bottom* of the box is y_1($=3$); so A represents the amount of x and y I have, seen from the lower left-hand corner of the box (which is where the origin of a graph usually is). Since the length of the box is x ($=20$), the horizontal distance from A to the *right-hand* edge of the box is $x - x_1 = x_2$ ($=5$); the vertical distance from A to the *top* edge of the box is $y - y_1 = y_2$ ($=12$). So A also represents your holdings of X and

Figure 6-4

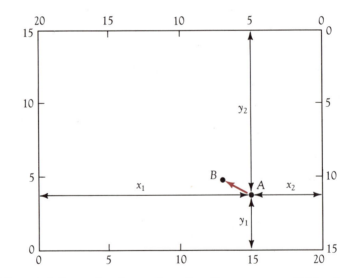

An Edgeworth Box. A point, such as A or B, represents a division between us of the total quantity of X and Y. x_1 is how much X I have, and x_2 is how much you have; similarly y_1 is how much Y I have, and y_2 is how much you have. My quantities are measured from the bottom left corner of the box; your quantities are measured from the top right corner.

Section II   Price = Value = Cost

Y—as seen, in an upside-down sort of way, from the upper right-hand corner of the box. Any point inside the box represents a possible division of the total quantity of *X* and *Y*, with my share measured from the lower left-hand corner, yours from the upper right-hand corner. Any possible trade is represented by a movement from one point in the box, such as *A*, to another, such as *B*. The particular trade that moves us from *A* to *B* consists of my giving you 2 units of X in exchange for 1 unit of Y.

The Edgeworth Box is the opportunity set of the two traders; it shows all the ways in which the existing stock of goods could be divided between them. Any trade simply moves them from one point in the box to another. In order to see what trades they will be willing to make, we also need their preferences. Figure 6-5 shows the same box, with my indifference curves (the thin lines—U_1, U_2, U_3) and yours (the thick lines—V_1, V_2, V_3) drawn in. Note that my indifference curves are shown in terms of my consumption (x_1, y_1), while yours are shown in terms of your consumption (x_2, y_2). Hence mine are convex to my origin at the bottom left-hand corner and yours to your origin at the top right-hand corner. My utility increases as I move up and to the right (increasing my consumption); yours increases as you move down and to the left (increasing your consumption).

Figure 6-5

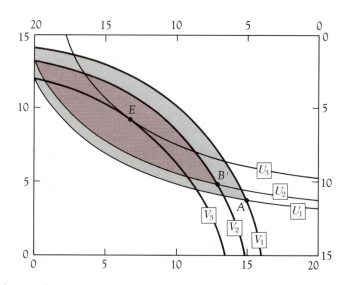

An Edgeworth Box showing indifference curves and possible gains from trade. Thin indifference curves show my preferences; thick ones show yours. The entire shaded and colored area is preferred to *A* by both of us; the colored area is preferred to *B* by both of us. Once we reach point *E*, no further trade can benefit both of us.

Trading. This makes it sound as though any trade must help one of us and hurt the other, but that is not the case. A trade that moves us down and to the right or up and to the left may put both of us on higher indifference curves. Consider the move from point *A* to point *B* on Figure 6-5. Since *B* is on a higher indifference curve for both of us than *A*, the trade benefits both of us. If we start at point *A*, any point in the shaded and colored areas bounded by U_1 and V_1 is preferred by both of us; we might both agree to a trade that moved us from *A* to such a point.

Suppose we make the trade that moves us from *A* to *B*. The points that are preferred to *B* make up a smaller area bounded by U_2 and V_2, shown colored in the figure. It is in our interest to make another trade. The process stops only when we reach a point such as *E*. At *E* our indifference curves are tangent to each other. Since they curve in opposite directions, this means that starting from point *E*, any point that is on a higher indifference curve for me must be on a lower curve for you; any trade that makes me better off makes you worse off. This is easier to see on the diagram than to explain in words.

The Contract Curve. The point *E* is not unique. Figure 6-6 shows the same box with the indifference curves drawn in such a way as to show

Figure 6-6

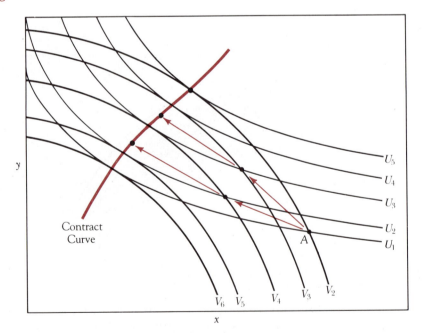

An Edgeworth Box showing the contract curve and ways of reaching it.
Starting at point *A*, the arrows show two possible sequences of trades that reach the contract curve.

Section II   Price = Value = Cost

the **contract curve**—the set of all points from which no further mutually beneficial trading is possible. As we saw in the previous paragraph, these are the points where one of my indifference curves is tangent to one of yours. If we continue trading as long as there is any gain to be made, we must eventually end up at some point on the contract curve. The arrows in the figure show two different series of trades, each starting at point *A*, leading to different points on the contract curve. Once we reach the curve, there is no further trade that can make both of us better off.

TRADE BALANCES, EXCHANGE RATES, AND FOSSIL ECONOMICS

In recent years, foreign trade has been a popular topic with newspaper writers and television commentators. The peculiar thing about the public discussion, which largely centers on the issue of trade deficits and American "competitiveness," is that most of it is based on ideas that have been obsolete for more than 150 years—at least since David Ricardo discovered the principle of comparative advantage. It is rather as though discussions of the space program started out by assuming that the earth was sitting still in the middle of the universe, with the sun, the other planets, and the stars rotating around it.

The discussion of trade earlier in this chapter provides the essential ideas necessary to understand why most of what you see on the subject in the media is nonsense. So far, we have examined those ideas in the context of two individuals or two nations, trading goods for goods; we have said nothing about issues such as exchange rates, money prices, or the balance of trade. In this section, I will try to show more clearly how the logic of comparative advantage works itself out in modern international trade.

It is useful to start with the frequently made claim that the United States is not competitive in international trade, and that the reason is that our production costs, and thus the prices at which we try to sell our goods, are too high relative to the cost of goods abroad. *A* fundamental problem with this claim is that American costs are in dollars and Japanese costs are in yen. In order to compare them, we must first know how many yen you can get for a dollar—the **exchange rate**. Until we understand how the exchange rate is determined, we cannot say to what extent the high cost of an American car in Japan, *measured in yen*, is a result of the number of dollars it takes to produce a car, and to what extent it is a result of the number of yen it takes to buy a dollar.

How is the exchange rate determined? Some people wish to trade dollars for yen, some wish to trade yen for dollars. The equilibrium price, as we will see in more detail in the next chapter, is the price at which buyers choose to buy as much as sellers choose to sell. If more yen are supplied than demanded, the price falls; if fewer, the price rises. When the two numbers are equal, the price is at its equilibrium level, just as on any other market.

Why do people want to trade dollars for yen, or vice versa? To simplify the analysis, we will start with a situation where there are no **capital flows**—Japanese do not want to buy U.S. government debt, or U.S. land, or shares in U.S. corporations, nor do Americans want to buy similar assets in Japan. The only reason for Japanese to want dollars is in order to buy American goods; the only reason Americans want yen is to buy Japanese goods.

Suppose that at some particular exchange rate, say 200 yen to the dollar, most goods are cheaper in Japan than in the United States—America is not competitive. In that case lots of Americans will want to trade dollars for yen in order to buy Japanese goods and import them, but very few Japanese will want to sell yen for dollars, since practically nothing in America is worth buying. The supply of yen is much lower than the demand, so the price of yen goes up. Yen now trade for more dollars than before, and dollars for fewer yen.

The fewer yen you get for a dollar, the more expensive Japanese goods are to Americans, since Americans have dollars and the Japanese are selling goods for yen. The more dollars you get for a yen, the less expensive American goods are to the Japanese. The exchange rate continues to move until prices are, on average, about the same in both countries—more precisely, until the quantity of dollars offered for sale by Americans equals the quantity that Japanese wish to buy. Since the only reason people in one country want the other country's money is to buy goods, that means that the dollar value of U.S. imports (the number of dollars we are selling for yen) is now the same as the dollar value of U.S. exports (the number of dollars they are buying with yen). Americans are now exporting those goods in which we have a comparative advantage (our production cost for those goods, relative to our production cost for other goods, is low compared to the corresponding ratio in Japan) and importing those goods in which the Japanese have a comparative advantage.

One implication of this analysis is that trade automatically balances. If the quality of one country's goods improves or their cost falls, the result is not an imbalance of trade but a change in the exchange rate. Improved production makes a country richer, but it does not make it more competitive.

This raises an obvious question: If trade automatically balances, how is it that the United States has a trade deficit? To answer that question, we must drop the assumption that there are no capital flows, that the only reason Japanese want dollars is to buy U.S. goods.

Suppose that, for some reason, the United States is an attractive place to invest. Foreigners—Japanese in our example—wish to acquire American assets: shares of stock, land, government bonds. To do so, they must have dollars. Demand for dollars on the dollar-yen market now consists in part of demand by Japanese who want dollars to buy American goods and in part of demand by Japanese who want them to buy land or stock. At the equilibrium exchange rate, American imports (supply of dollars) equal American exports plus Japanese investment (demand for dollars). America now has a trade deficit; our imports are more than our exports.

Seen from the standpoint of a firm trying to export American goods, the reason for the trade deficit is that our costs are too high—we cannot export as much as we import. But that "reason" confuses a cause with an effect. The fact that our dollar costs are high compared to Japan's yen costs is a statement not about our costs but about the exchange rate. The real reason for the trade deficit is the capital inflow; indeed, the capital inflow and the trade deficit are simply two sides of an accounting identity. If the exchange rate were not at a level at which the United States imported more than it exported, there would be no surplus of dollars in Japanese hands with which to buy capital assets from Americans.

One implication of this analysis is that terms such as trade deficit and unfavorable balance of payments are highly deceptive. There is nothing inherently bad about an inflow of capital. The United States had a capital inflow, and consequently an "unfavorable" balance of payments, through most of the nineteenth century; we were building our canals and railroads largely with European money.

Whether our present trade deficit should be viewed as a problem depends on what you think the reason for it is. If capital is flowing into the United States because foreigners think America is a safe and prosperous place to invest, then the trade deficit is no more a problem now than it was a hundred and fifty years ago. If capital is flowing into the United States because Americans prefer to live on borrowed money and let their children worry about the bill, then that is a problem; but the trade deficit is the symptom, not the disease.

PROBLEMS

1. Table 6-2*a* shows the utility to individual *A* of various bundles of apples and oranges. Table 6-2*b* shows the utility to *B* of various bundles of apples and oranges. Apples and oranges are goods for both *A* and B.

   a. Draw indifference curves for *A* and B.

   b. Suppose *A* starts with 10 apples and no oranges; she can trade apples for oranges at a price of 2 apples per orange. How many of each will she end up with?

   c. Suppose *B* starts with 10 oranges and no apples. He can trade apples for oranges at a price of ½ apple per orange. How many of each will he end up with?

Table 6-2

(a) Apples	Oranges	Utility	(b) Apples	Oranges	Utility
10	0	10	6.5	0	5
6	1	10	5	1	5
4	2	10	3.9	2	5
2	3	10	3	3	5
1	4	10	2.2	4	5
0	5	10	1.5	5	5
10	1	15	1	6	5
6	2	15	0	10	5
4.5	3	15	10	0	10
3	4	15	7	1	10
2.2	5	15	5.5	2	10
1.5	6	15	4	3	10
1	7	15	3	4	10
0	10	15	2.5	5	10
10	2	19	2.1	6	10
8	3	19	1.6	8	10
6.2	4	19	9	2	15
5	5	19	7.2	3	15
3.9	6	19	6	4	15
3	7	19	5	5	15
1.5	10	19	4.1	6	15
			3.4	7	15
			2.3	10	15

   d. *A* starts with 10 apples (and no oranges) and *B* with 10 oranges
       (and no apples). They engage in voluntary trade with each other.
       What can you say about the bundles they will end up with?
2. Person *A* of Problem 1 starts with 1 apple and 9 oranges. She can
   trade apples for oranges (or oranges for apples) at a rate of 1 apple
   for each orange. What bundle does she end up with?
3. Table 6-3 shows how many hours it takes each of three people to
   produce a table or a chair.
   a. If only *A* and *B* exist, will *A* buy chairs from *B*, sell chairs to *B*, or
       neither?
   b. If only *A* and *C* exist, will *A* buy chairs from *C*, buy tables from
       C, or neither?

Table 6-3

Time to Produce	A	B	C
1 Table	10 hours	15 hours	12 hours
1 Chair	2 hours	5 hours	6 hours

Section II   Price = Value = Cost

c. If only *B* and *C* exist, will *B* buy chairs from *C*, sell tables to *C*, or neither?

4. I am better than my wife at bargaining with contractors, repair people, and the like; with a given amount of time and effort, I am likely to get a lower price. Also, I rather enjoy such bargaining, while she dislikes it. Are these two separate reasons why I should do the bargaining and she should do other family work, or are they two parts of one reason? Discuss. Does the fact that my wife and I are not selfish with regard to each other (i.e., I have a high value for her happiness, and she for mine) mean that we should ignore the principle of comparative advantage in allocating household jobs? Does it simplify any of the problems normally associated with exchange (between us)?

5. I can write one economics textbook/year or discover one oil well every three years (including the time for me to learn enough geology to discover the oil well). My wife can discover one oil well per year or write an economics textbook every two years (ditto, *mutatis mutandis*).
   a. Draw my opportunity set for annual production of textbooks and oil wells.
   b. Draw hers.
   c. Draw our combined opportunity set.

6. The situation is as in the previous question.
   a. For each textbook we write we are paid $50,000. For each oil well we discover we are paid $75,000. All we care about is money (economists and geologists are mercenary types). Draw our combined opportunity set for producing textbooks and oil wells and the relevant indifference curves. Given that all we care about is money, what other term might you use for our indifference curves? How many textbooks do I write each year and how many oil wells do I discover? How about my wife?
   b. As before, we are paid $50,000/textbook. How high would the price we are offered to discover oil wells have to be to make us decide to produce no textbooks and spend all of our time discovering oil wells?
   c. We are paid $75,000/well to discover oil wells. How much would we have to be paid per textbook to make us decide to spend all our time writing textbooks?

7. After spending the mid-70s discovering oil wells, I decide I would prefer never to look at another well log. After spending the mid-80s writing textbooks, my wife decides she would prefer never to look at another indifference curve. After considering the matter at some length, we decide that we are not as mercenary as we thought. I decide to redraw our indifference curves, taking account of the fact that, for any given income, I would prefer to write textbooks and she would prefer to discover oil wells—although either one of us may be willing to do the other's job if paid enough. What do my indifference curves between oil wells produced and textbooks written look like (assume

the same prices as in part (a) of the previous question)? What do hers look like?

(Note: the question does not give enough information to tell you exactly what the indifference curves look like, but it does give enough that you should be able to draw some plausible ones.)

8. I have a very talented wife. She is as good as I am at writing textbooks (1/year) and phenomenally good at discovering oil wells (2/year). She is also very lazy; I cannot persuade her to work more than half time. My talents are the same as in Problem 5. Answer the same questions as in Problem 6. Discuss.

9. Suppose that instead of marrying my wife (Betty) I trade with her. I want to consume half an economics textbook and a quarter of an oil well each year (there's no accounting for tastes). I am such a good bargainer that I can get all of the benefit from trading with her, leaving her neither better nor worse off than if we had not traded.
   a. We have the same abilities as in Problem 5; how much of the year do I work?
   b. We have the same abilities as in Problem 8; how much of the year do I work?
   c. In answering parts (a) and (b), did you have to make any assumptions about Betty's tastes?
   d. What principle does this question illustrate? Explain.

10. Figure 6-3 corresponds to the first example in this chapter's verbal discussion of trade with production. Draw a similar figure corresponding

Figure 6-7

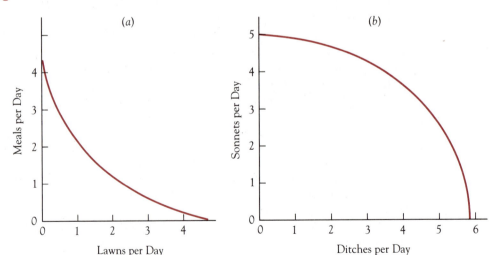

Nonlinear production possibility frontiers. Figure 6-7a represents the production possibility frontier for each of two identical individuals with identical preferences; so does Figure 6-7b.

Section II   Price = Value = Cost

to the second example (where I can cook a meal in 15 minutes and mow a lawn in ½ hour; it takes you ½ hour to cook a meal and 2 hours to mow a lawn.)

11. Figures 6-7a and 6-7b correspond to two possible situations discussed in the optional section of Chapter 5. Use them to show how two people with identical production possibility sets, identical preferences, and normally shaped indifference curves can still gain from trade. (Hint: It only works with one of the figures.)

12. When I do your work for you (in exchange for something else), I give up leisure and you get it. Why is this not quite the same thing as my trading leisure for whatever you are paying me for my work?

The following problem refers to the optional section:

13. Figure 6-8 shows an Edgeworth Box for individuals A and B; their initial situation is at point D.
    a. Show the region of possible trades—outcomes that both individuals prefer to D.
    b. Draw in the contract curve.
    c. Draw a possible series of trades leading to a point on the contract curve.

Figure 6-8

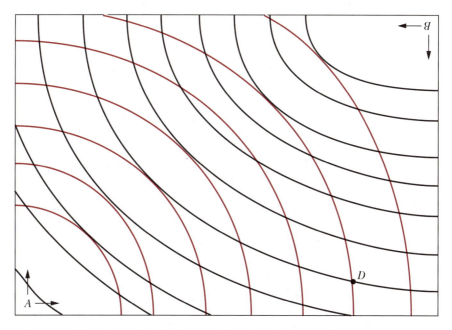

Edgeworth box for individuals A and B.   For Problem 13.

chapter 7

MARKETS—PUTTING IT ALL TOGETHER

In this chapter, we will combine what we learned about demand and supply curves in Chapters 3, 4, and 5 with the idea of trade discussed in Chapter 6, in order to understand how prices and quantities are determined.

In Chapter 3, we saw how the behavior of an individual consumer led to a demand curve, a relation between the price at which he could buy a good and the quantity he chose to buy. In most markets, all customers pay about the same price, so we can talk of a single market price and a single demand curve, representing the total demand of all consumers for the good as a function of its price. Since total quantity demanded at any price is the amount I want to buy at that price plus the amount you want to buy at that price plus the amount he wants to buy at that price plus . . ., the **market demand curve** is the horizontal sum of the individual demand curves, as shown in Figure 7-1.

In Chapter 4, I showed how we could analyze consumption in terms of continuously variable goods by thinking in terms of rate of consumption rather than number of units consumed—cookies per week rather than cookies. When we are considering the combined demand of a large number of people, we have a second reason for treating goods and curves as continuous. For lumpy goods such as automobiles, for which individual demand curves are step functions rather than curves (you buy one automobile or two, not 1.32 automobiles), even a very small drop in price will make a few consumers (out of millions) decide to buy a car instead of not buying one.

In Chapter 5, I showed how individual supply curves could be derived, starting with a producer's output rates for different goods plus either his marginal disvalue for labor curve or the indifference curves showing his preferences with regard to leisure and income. Just as the market demand curve is the horizontal sum of individual demand curves, so the market supply curve is the horizontal sum of the individual supply curves; having seen how to derive the individual supply curves for a good, we also know how to derive its total supply curve.

We are now ready to put supply curves and demand curves together. Figure 7-2a shows supply and demand curves for widgets, a hypothetical commodity consumed mostly by the authors of economics textbooks. The particular curves shown in the figure happen to be straight; as you may have guessed by now, the term curve, in the language of economists and mathematicians, includes straight lines. The vertical axis of the diagram is price, the horizontal axis is quantity; any point on the diagram, such as A, represents a quantity and a price (Q_A and P_A). What will the market price be and what quantity will be produced and consumed at that price?

As any experienced guesser could predict, the answer is point E, where the supply and demand curves cross. The interesting question is why.

Suppose the price were P_1 on Figure 7-2a. At that price, producers wish to produce and sell a quantity Q_1, while consumers only wish to purchase a (smaller) quantity Q_1'. Some of the producers find themselves with widgets that they cannot sell. In order to get rid of them, the producers are willing to cut the price. Price falls. It continues to do so as long as the quantity supplied is greater than the quantity demanded.

Figure 7-1

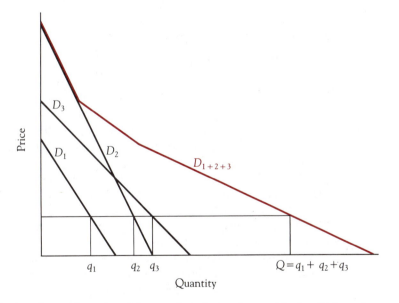

Market demand curve. The market demand curve is the *horizontal* sum of individual demand curves, since total quantity demanded at any price is the sum of my quantity demanded at that price plus your quantity demanded at that price plus . . ..

Figure 7-2

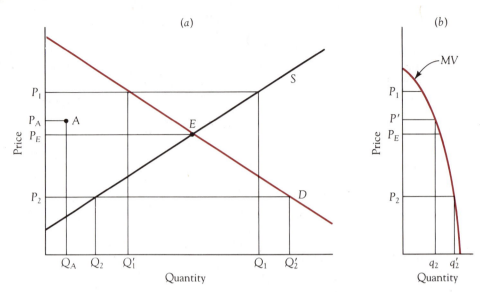

Market equilibrium.   At point E, price $= P_E$; quantity demanded equals quantity supplied. At lower prices, less is supplied; individuals are consuming quantities for which $MV > P$, as shown on Figure 7-2b, and so are willing to offer a higher price for additional quantities.

Suppose, instead, that the price were P_2 on Figure 7-2a. Now producers wish to produce a quantity Q_2, while consumers wish to purchase a (larger) quantity Q_2'. Consumers cannot consume goods that are not produced, so some of them are unable to buy what they want. They are willing to offer a higher price, so they bid the price up. Figure 7-2b shows what is happening in terms of the marginal value curve of one such consumer. At P_2 he would like to buy q_2' but finds he can only buy q_2. At that quantity, his marginal value for another widget is $P' > P_2$; he is willing to pay any price up to P' in order to get another widget, so the price is bid up.

If the price is below P_E, the price for which quantity supplied and quantity demanded are equal, it will be driven up; if it is above P_E, it will be driven down. So P_E is the **equilibrium price**. But P_E is the price for which quantity supplied (at price P_E) equals quantity demanded (at price P_E), so it is the price at the point where the two curves cross.

The idea of an **equilibrium**—a situation in which a system generates no forces that tend to change it—is common to many different sciences. It is often useful to distinguish three different sorts of equilibria. A **stable equilibrium** is one in which, if something does move the system slightly away from the equilibrium, forces are set in motion that move it back again. An **unstable equilibrium** is one in which, if something moves the system slightly away from the equilibrium, forces are set in motion that

Section II   Price = Value = Cost

move it even further away. A **metastable equilibrium** is one in which, if something moves the system slightly away from the equilibrium, no forces are set in motion at all—it remains in the new position, which is also an equilibrium.

The three sorts of equilibria can all be illustrated with a pencil. Hold the pencil by the point, with the eraser hanging down. It is now in a stable equilibrium—if someone nudges the eraser end to one side or another, it swings back. Balance the pencil on its point on your finger. It is now in an unstable equilibrium—if someone nudges it, it will fall over. Lay the pencil (a round one) down on the table. It is now in a metastable equilibrium—nudge it and it rolls over part way and remains in its new position. One sometimes encounters people, either human or feline, who appear to be in metastable equilibrium.

The equilibrium illustrated in Figure 7-2a and again in Figure 7-3 is stable—if you move the price and quantity away from E, forces are set in motion that move them back. In zone I (on Figure 7-3), quantity demanded is greater than quantity supplied, so price goes up; in zone III, quantity demanded is less than quantity supplied, so price goes down. In zone II, the quantity being produced is more than producers want to produce at that price, so they reduce their output; in zone IV, for similar reasons, they increase their output. The restoring forces are shown by the arrows in Figure 7-3.

We now have a simple rule for combining a supply curve and a demand curve to get a market price and quantity. The equilibrium occurs at the intersection of the two curves and is stable if the demand curve is falling and the supply curve rising—as we shall always assume that they are, for reasons discussed in Chapters 3, 4, and 5. We shall now use this rule to analyze the effects of shifts in demand and supply curves.

Figure 7-3

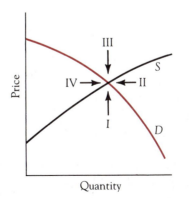

Stable equilibrium. The arrows show the directions of the forces moving the system back to equilibrium.

Elasticity—A Brief Digression

The effect on price and quantity of shifts in supply and demand curves depends, among other things, on how steep the curves are. Economists find it useful to discuss the steepness of curves in terms of their elasticity. The **price elasticity** of a demand or supply curve, at a point, is defined as the percentage change in quantity divided by the percentage change in price. If, for instance, a 1 percent increase in price results in a 1 percent increase in quantity supplied, we have:

$$\frac{\text{percent change in quantity}}{\text{percent change in price}} = \frac{1\%}{1\%} = 1$$

So, in this case, the supply elasticity is 1. Similarly, if we graphed quantity demanded against income with price held fixed (a rising curve for a normal good, a falling curve for an inferior good), we would define the **income elasticity** of the curve at a point as the percentage change in quantity divided by the percentage change in income that caused it.

For the purposes of this chapter, all you need to know is that very elastic means that a small change in price results in a large change in quantity while very inelastic means that a large change in price results in only a small change in quantity. The limiting cases are **perfectly elastic** (a horizontal supply or demand curve) and **perfectly inelastic** (a vertical curve). We will discuss the idea of elasticity in more detail in Chapter 10.

Shifting Curves

Figure 7-4a shows a supply-demand diagram with a shift in the demand curve from D_1 to D_2. One can imagine this resulting from a change in tastes (widgets become more popular), weather (it has been a hot summer and widgets work better in hot weather), the price of other goods (widgets use a lot of widget oil, the price of which has just fallen), consumer incomes, expected future prices, or whatever. The demand curve has shifted out. Demand has increased—at every price, the new quantity demanded is larger than the old. The result is to move the equilibrium point from E_1 to E_2. Both equilibrium price and equilibrium quantity increase.

In Figure 7-4b, the shift occurs in the supply curve. Supply has increased, perhaps because raw materials have become cheaper; at every price, the new quantity supplied is larger than the old. The result is an increase in quantity but a *decrease* in price. These results are completely general; as long as demand curves slope down and supply curves up, an increase in demand will increase both price and quantity, while an increase in supply will increase quantity but decrease price. Decreases in demand or supply have the opposite effects. You should be able to convince yourself of these relationships by examining Figures 7-4a and 7-4b.

Figure 7-4

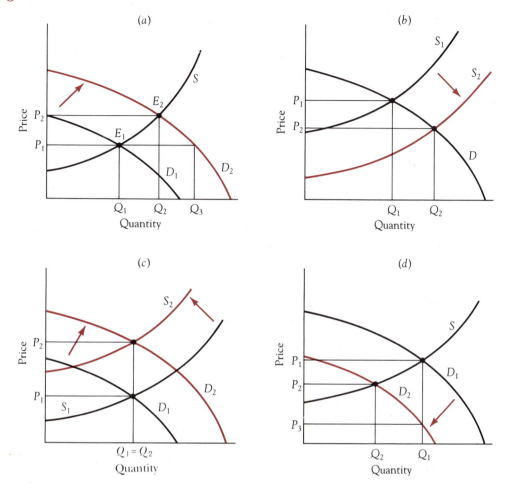

The effects of shifts in supply and demand curves. In Figures 7-4a and 7-4d, the demand curve shifts. In Figure 7-4b, the supply curve shifts. In each case, quantity demanded, quantity supplied, and price all change as a result. In Figure 7-4c, both the demand curve and the supply curve shift; price changes, but quantity stays the same.

It is important, in order to avoid confusion, to distinguish between **changes in supply** (the supply curve shifting, as in Figure 7-4b) and **changes in quantity supplied**. In Figure 7-4a, the supply curve stays fixed but the quantity supplied increases from Q_1 to Q_2. A supply curve (or a demand curve) is a relation between price and quantity; if the price changes because of a shift in the demand curve, the new price results in a new quantity supplied, even if the supply curve does not change. In Figure 7-4c, on the other hand, both the supply curve and the demand curve shift, while the quantity supplied stays exactly the same. The shift in the supply curve in this example is just enough to cancel the effect of the change in price, so the new price on the new supply curve yields the same quantity supplied as the old price on the old supply curve. One could easily enough construct other examples where a shift in both curves changed quantity but not price, or changed both.

One should distinguish similarly between **changes in demand** and **changes in quantity demanded**. By being careful about both distinctions, one can avoid some of the worst absurdities of newspaper discussions of economics. Consider, for example, the following paradoxes:

> *If demand increases, that bids up the price, so increased demand is associated with increased price. But if price rises, that decreases demand, so decreased demand is associated with increased price.*

Or:

> *If demand increases, that bids up the price, but the increased price drives demand back down again.*

Or:

> *If demand decreases, that drives down the price, which drives down the supply, which brings the price back up.*

Most such confusions can be avoided by drawing the relevant curves and distinguishing carefully between shifts of the curves (demand or supply moving out or in) and movements along the curves (quantity demanded or supplied changing because of a change in price). If the demand curve shifts, as in Figure 7-4a, while the supply curve stays fixed, that is a change in demand, which changes price, which changes quantity supplied—but supply (the supply curve) is still the same. A change in supply, as in Figure 7-4b, changes price and quantity demanded but not demand.

The first two paradoxes are illustrated on Figure 7-4a. An increase in demand (the demand curve shifts out) raises price; the increased price reduces quantity demanded below what it would have been if the demand curve had shifted but the price had remained the same (Q_3). The resulting quantity demanded (Q_2), although less than Q_3, is more than the old quantity demanded (Q_1). Q_2 must be greater than Q_1 because quantity demanded is equal to quantity supplied, the supply curve has not shifted, and a higher price applied to the same supply curve must result in a larger quantity supplied.

The third paradox is illustrated on Figure 7-4d. A decrease in demand (the demand curve shifts in) lowers the price; quantity supplied is now lower than it would have been at the old price ($Q_2 < Q_1$). But quantity supplied is equal to quantity demanded (at the new price on the new demand curve), so there is no reason for the price to go back up. What is true is that if the lower price had not reduced the quantity supplied,

Section II   Price = Value = Cost

price would have had to fall even further (to P_3 on Figure 7-4d) in order for quantity supplied and quantity demanded to be equal. It is only in this sense that the "reduced supply" (actually reduced quantity supplied) "brings the price back up" (reduces the amount by which the price falls).

Figures 7-5a through 7-5f show some interesting extreme cases. In Figures 7-5a and 7-5b, the supply curves are perfectly elastic. On Figure 7-5a, the industry will produce any quantity at a price P (or any higher price, but the price can never get higher since as soon as it does quantity supplied exceeds quantity demanded) and no quantity at any lower price. A shift in demand (Figure 7-5a) has no effect on price; it simply results in a different quantity at the old price. A shift in supply from S_1 to S_2, both perfectly elastic (Figure 7-5b), changes the price by the (vertical) amount of the shift and the quantity by the effect of that price change on quantity demanded along the old demand curve.

In Figures 7-5c and 7-5d, demand is perfectly elastic. Consumers are willing to buy an unlimited quantity at a price P on Figure 7-5c (or

Figure 7-5

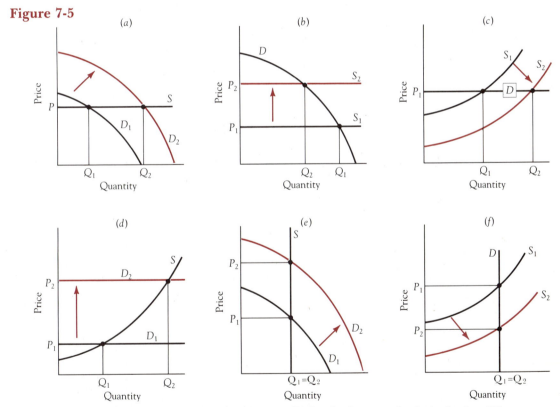

The effect of shifts when one curve is either perfectly elastic or perfectly inelastic. When one curve is perfectly elastic, a shift in the other changes quantity but not price (Figures 7-5a and 7-5c); when one curve is perfectly inelastic, a shift in the other changes price but not quantity (Figures 7-5e and 7-5f).

any lower price, but . . .) and nothing at any higher price. A shift in supply (Figure 7-5c) leaves price unaffected but changes quantity by the (horizontal) amount of the shift. A shift in demand (Figure 7-5d) changes price by the vertical amount of the shift and quantity by the effect of the price change on the quantity supplied.

In Figure 7-5e, the supply curve is perfectly inelastic—the quantity supplied does not depend on price. The supply of land is often thought of as perfectly inelastic—there are a certain number of square miles on the earth's surface, and that is that. The supply of labor is also perfectly inelastic—if we include the part of your labor that you supply to yourself (leisure). Defined in this way, the supply of labor is 24 hours per day times the population. It is fixed, at least over the short term. What we normally call the supply of labor is this minus the demand by the owners of the labor. I do not work 24 hours per day because I choose to consume some of my labor myself. Both of these examples will come up again in Chapter 14.

With a perfectly inelastic supply curve, a shift in the demand curve results in a corresponding change in price and no change in quantity, as shown in Figure 7-5e. With a perfectly inelastic demand curve (a "need" in the sense discussed and rejected in Chapter 2), a shift in the supply curve has a similar effect, as shown in Figure 7-5f.

One of the differences between economics as done by economists and economics as done by journalists, politicians making speeches, and others, is that the noneconomists often speak as though all supply and demand curves were perfectly inelastic. This is the same disagreement that I discussed earlier in the context of "needs" vs. "wants." The noneconomist tends to think of the demand for water as "the amount of water we need" and assumes that the alternative to having that amount of water is people dying of thirst. But, as you should know from answering one of the questions in Chapter 4, only a tiny fraction of the water we consume is drunk. While the demand for drinking water may be highly inelastic over a wide range of prices, demand for other uses is not. If the price of water doubles, it pays farmers to use water more sparingly for irrigation, chemical firms to use less of it in their manufacturing processes, and homeowners to fix leaky faucets more promptly than before. Nobody dies of thirst, but total consumption of water falls substantially.

Who Pays Taxes?

We are now ready to start answering one of the questions frequently asked of economists; the number of weeks and pages it has taken us to get this far may explain why answers that fit in a newspaper column or a 30-second news report are generally unsatisfactory. The question is "Who really pays taxes?" When the government imposes a tax on some good, does the money come out of the profits of those who produce the good or do the producers pass it along to the consumers in higher prices?

Section II   Price = Value = Cost

Suppose, for example, that the government imposes a lump sum sales tax of $1/widget; for every widget that is sold, the producer (assumed to be the seller—there are no middlemen at this stage of the analysis) must pay the government $1. The result is to shift the supply curve up by $1, from S_1 to S_2, as shown in Figure 7-6.

Why does a sales tax shift the supply curve in this way? What matters to the producer is how much he gets, not how much the consumer pays. A price of $6/widget with the tax gives the producer the same amount for each widget sold as a price of $5/widget without the tax. So he will produce the same quantity of widgets at $6/widget after the tax is imposed as he would have produced at $5 before, and similarly for all other prices. Each quantity on the new supply curve corresponds to a price $1 higher than on the old, so the supply curve is shifted up by $1.

This does not mean that the market price goes up $1. If it did, producers would produce the same amount as before the tax; consumers, at the higher price, would consume less than before, so quantity supplied would be greater than quantity demanded. If, on the other hand, price did not rise at all, quantity demanded would be the same as before the tax. Quantity supplied would be less (since producers would be getting a dollar less per widget), so quantity supplied would be less than quantity

Figure 7-6

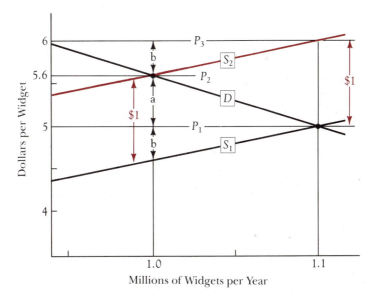

The effect of a $1 tax on widgets collected from the producers. The supply curve shifts up from S_1 to S_2 due to the tax; equilibrium price rises by a, from $5/widget to $5.60/widget. Quantity falls from 1.1 million widgets per year to 1 million widgets per year.

demanded. As you can see on Figure 7-6, the price rises, but by less than a dollar. All of the tax is collected from the producer in the literal sense that the producer hands the government the money, but in fact the price paid by the consumer has gone up by a and the price received by the producer has gone down by b.

To see why b on the figure equals the decrease in the price received by the producer, note that if the market price had gone all the way up to $P_3 = P_1 + \$1$, the producer's receipts, after paying the \$1 tax, would still be P_1 per widget, just as before the tax was imposed. Since the price only goes to $P_2 = P_1 + a$, the producer's receipts per widget (after tax) have fallen by the difference between P_3 and P_2, which is b. Put algebraically, we have:

$$P_3 - P_2 = (P_1 + \$1) - (P_1 + a) = \$1 - a = b.$$

As you can see by examining Figure 7-6, the way in which the burden of the tax is divided between consumers and producers depends on the slopes of the supply and demand curves. Figures 7-7a and 7-7b show two extreme cases. In Figure 7-7a, the supply curve S is perfectly inelastic; you cannot see the shift in S, since shifting a vertical line up moves it onto itself. Since quantity and the demand curve stay the same, the price must stay the same, so the entire burden of the tax is borne by the producers;

Figure 7-7

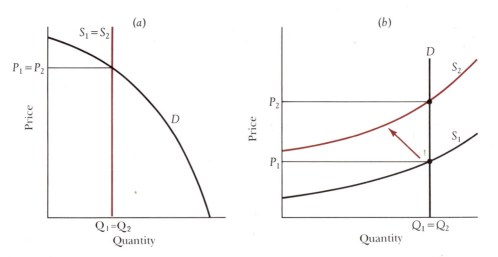

The effect of a tax when demand or supply is perfectly inelastic. In Figure 7-7a, the supply curve is perfectly inelastic and the entire burden of the tax is borne by the producers. In Figure 7-7b, the demand curve is perfectly inelastic and the entire burden is borne by the consumers.

　　　　　　　　　　　　　　　　Section II　Price = Value = Cost

Figure 7-8

Two ways of graphing the effect of a $1 tax on widgets. In Figure 7-8a, the tax is collected from consumers, shifting the demand curve down from D_1 to D_2. In Figure 7-8b, the demand curve is a function of price paid (market price plus any tax on consumers), and the supply curve is a function of price received (market price minus any tax on producers). The figure could show a $1 tax on either producer or consumer.

it is sometimes asserted that this is true of a tax on land. In Figure 7-7b, the demand curve is perfectly inelastic, and the price increases by the full dollar; the entire burden of the tax is borne by the consumers. Most real-world cases fall between these two extremes.

In Figure 7-8a, the initial demand and supply curves for widgets are the same as in Figure 7-6; what has changed is the form of the tax. Instead of taxing producers, the government has decided to tax consumers. For every widget you buy, you must pay the government $1. The result is to shift the demand curve instead of the supply curve—from D_1 down to D_2. The number of widgets you choose to buy depends on what it costs you to buy them—the price plus the tax. Suppose that before the tax was imposed you chose to buy 12 widgets at $5 apiece. With the tax, the price at which you would choose to buy 12 is $4, since at that price you are again paying $5/widget—$4 to the producer and $1 to the government.

This is an application of the principle that costs are opportunity costs, discussed in Chapter 3. The cost to you of buying a widget for $5 is the loss of the goods you would otherwise have bought with the money. So widgets at $5 with no tax cost you the same amount as widgets at $4 with a $1 tax, payable by the consumer; in each case you give up, for each widget purchased, the opportunity to buy $5 worth of something else. Since the cost to you of each widget is the same in both cases and since you decide how many widgets to purchase on the basis of cost and value, as described in the derivation of the individual demand curve in Chapter 4, you buy the same quantity in both cases. So does everyone else. So

Chapter 7   Markets—Putting It All Together   **167**

the total quantity demanded is the same at a price of $4 with the tax as it would be without the tax at a price of $5, and similarly for all other prices. The demand curve shifts down by $1—the amount of the tax.

Looking at Figure 7-8a, you can see that as a result of the shift in the demand curve, the price received by the producer has gone down by an amount b' and the amount paid per widget by the consumers has gone up by a'. To see why a' is the increase in what consumers are paying per widget, note that if price had fallen by a full dollar, to P_3', the consumers would have been no worse off—what they paid on the tax they would have made up on the lower price, making the cost to them of each widget the same as before. In fact, price has only fallen to $P_2' > P_3'$; hence the increase in what consumers are paying for each widget is $P_2' - P_3' = (P_1' - b') - (P_1' - \$1) = \$1 - b' = a'$.

If you compare Figure 7-8a with Figure 7-6, you can see that they are essentially the same figure; $b = b'$ and $a = a'$. Figure 7-8a is simply Figure 7-6 with everything shifted down by $1. The reason is that in Figure 7-6, the price shown on the vertical axis is price after tax, since the tax is paid by the producer; in Figure 7-8a, it is price before tax, since the tax is paid by the consumer. The difference between price before tax and price after tax is the amount of the tax: $1. In both cases, quantity supplied is determined by price received by the producer, quantity demanded by price paid by the consumer, and the effect of the tax is to make price paid by the consumer $1 higher than price received by the producer.

A third way of describing the same situation is shown in Figure 7-8b. Here supply is shown as a function of price received, demand as a function of price paid. Before the tax was instituted, market equilibrium occurred at a quantity (Q_1) for which price received was equal to price paid; after the tax was instituted, market equilibrium occurs at a quantity (Q_2) for which price received is a dollar less than price paid, with the difference going to the government.

If you look carefully at Figures 7-6, 7-8a, and 7-8b, you should be able to see that they are all the same; the only thing that changes from one to another is what is shown on the vertical axis. The figures are the same not just because I happen to have drawn them that way but because they have to be drawn that way; all three describe the same situation. The cost of widgets to the consumers (which is what matters to them), the amount received by the producers per widget sold (which is what matters to them), and the quantity of widgets sold are all the same whether the tax is collected from producers or consumers. How the burden of the tax is really distributed is entirely unaffected by who actually hands over the money to the government!

And for the Real Cost of Taxes . . .

The previous section started with the question of who really pays taxes. It seems we now have the answer. Using a supply-demand diagram, we can show how much of the tax is passed along to the consumer in the form of higher prices and how much appears as a reduction in the (after-tax) receipts of the producer. In any particular case, the answer depends on the relative elasticity of the supply and demand curves—on how rapidly quantity demanded and quantity supplied change with price, as indicated by the slope of the curves S and D on our diagrams.

We have answered *a* question, but it is not quite the right question. We know by how much the tax raises the cost of widgets to the consumer and by how much it lowers the revenue received by the producer for each widget he sells, but that is not quite the same thing as how much *worse off* it makes them. The cost to the consumer is not merely a matter of how much money he spends; it also depends on what he gets for it.

To see this in a particularly striking way, imagine that the government decides to impose a tax of $1,000/widget. Production and consumption of widgets drop to zero. The government receives nothing; producers and consumers pay nothing. Does that mean that a tax of $1,000/widget costs consumers (and producers) nothing?

Obviously not. The consumers could have chosen to consume zero widgets before the tax increase—the fact that they actually consumed 1,100,000 widgets at a price of $5/widget (Figure 7-9) indicates that they preferred that number of widgets at that price to zero widgets; hence the tax has made them worse off. Our mistake was in assuming that the cost of the tax to the consumers was simply the number of widgets they bought times the increase in the price of the widgets. We should also have included the loss due to the reduced consumption of widgets.

Let us now consider a more reasonable tax—$1/widget instead of $1,000/widget. This makes the cost of widgets to consumers $5.60 and the quantity demanded and supplied 1,000,000, as shown by P_2 and Q_2 on Figure 7-9. Before there was any tax at all, consumers bought 1,100,000 widgets per year; after the $1 tax was imposed, their consumption went down to 1,000,000. The extra 100,000 widgets were worth at least $5 apiece (which is why consumers bought them before the tax was imposed, when the price of widgets was $5 each) but less than $5.60 (which is why they no longer buy them when the price goes up to $5.60). The consumers are worse off by the benefit they no longer get from purchasing those 100,000 widgets per year at $5 apiece, as well as by the increased price they must pay for the 1,000,000 widgets per year they continue to purchase. Similarly, the producers are worse off by the profits they would have made on the additional 100,000 widgets, as well as by lost revenue on the 1,000,000 widgets they still produce.

What we left out of our initial analysis of the cost of taxation was consumer (and producer) surplus, which was introduced in Chapter 4 (and 5) to measure the benefit to a consumer (producer) of being able to purchase (sell) as much as he wanted of a good at a particular price. Before the tax, the consumer could purchase as many widgets as he wanted at $5 apiece; afterwards he could purchase as many as he wished at $5.60 apiece. The cost to him of the tax is the difference between the consumer surplus he received in the first case and the consumer surplus he received in the second. This is shown in Figure 7-9. The entire shaded and colored area of Figure 7-9 is the consumer surplus received before the tax. The darkly shaded area is the consumer surplus received after the tax. The colored area is the difference between the two—the cost of the tax. It is divided into two regions. R_1 is a rectangle whose height is the increase in the price and whose width is the quantity of widgets being consumed after the tax (1,000,000 per year). R_2 is an (approximate) triangle representing the lost consumer surplus on the 100,000 widgets per year that were consumed before the tax and are not consumed after the tax. R_1 is the amount of the tax paid by the consumers, in the sense discussed earlier in this chapter—the price increase times the quantity being consumed after the tax is imposed. R_2 is part of the **excess burden** of the tax. R_1 is a loss to the consumers and an equal gain (in tax revenue) for the government; R_2 is a loss for the consumers with no corresponding gain for anyone. It has often been argued that the ideal system of taxes is that which minimizes excess burden, thus collecting a given amount of revenue at the lowest possible cost.

Figures 7-10a and 7-10b show that the relation between R_1 and R_2 depends on the shape of the demand curve. If it is very flat (demand is *highly elastic*), then the increased price due to the effect of the tax (from P_1 to P_2) results in a large reduction in quantity demanded and a large

Figure 7-9

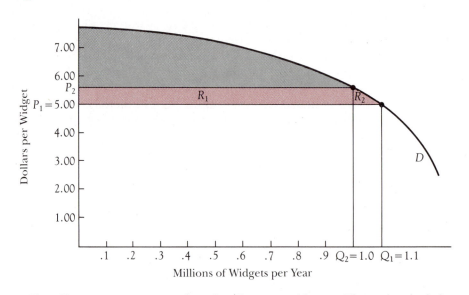

The effect on consumer surplus of a $1 tax on widgets. The entire shaded and colored area is consumer surplus before the tax; the darkly shaded area is consumer surplus after the tax. The colored area is the cost the tax imposes on consumers. R_1 is revenue collected by the tax; R_2 is excess burden.

Section II   Price = Value = Cost

loss of consumer surplus relative to the amount of tax revenue collected. P_3 on the diagram is the price at which quantity demanded is zero; for a tax that raises the price of the good that high, R_2 is substantial (the entire consumer surplus at P_1) and R_1 is zero. The effect of such a tax is all excess burden and no revenue at all.

If, on the other hand, the slope of the demand curve is very steep (demand is *highly inelastic*), as shown in Figure 7-10b, then the increased price results in only a small decrease in consumption, and R_2 is small compared to R_1. In the limiting case of perfectly inelastic demand, there is no reduction in consumption and hence no excess burden.

This has sometimes been used as an argument for taxing necessities instead of luxuries. The idea is that demand for necessities is very inelastic (you have to have them) while demand for luxuries is very elastic; hence taxes on necessities produce little excess burden compared to taxes on luxuries. Attempts to actually measure price elasticity of demand for different goods do not always bear out this presumption; the demand for cigarettes, for example, which are usually thought of as luxuries (and sinful ones at that—hence the object of "sin taxes"), seems to be relatively inelastic. In any case, even if taxes on necessities do minimize excess burden, there remains the objection that taxes on necessities "hurt the poor" while taxes on luxuries "soak the rich"—and the latter is generally more popular, at least as a political slogan, than the former.

So far in this discussion, I have concentrated on the cost of the tax to the consumer. A similar analysis could be applied to the producer, with producer surplus substituted for consumer surplus. The result would be similar; for consumers as well as for producers, the cost of the tax

Figure 7-10

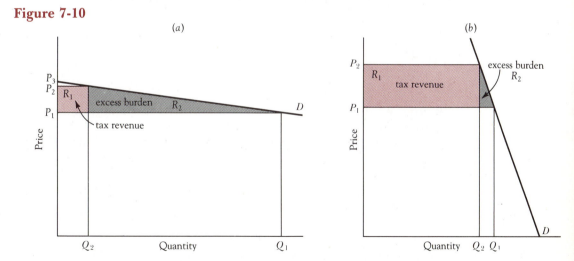

The effect of elasticity of the demand curve on the relation between revenue and excess burden. A very elastic demand curve (Figure 7-10a) produces a high ratio of excess burden to revenue; a very inelastic demand curve (Figure 7-10b) produces a low ratio.

includes an element of excess burden, and the relation between excess burden and the rest of the cost to the producers depends on the elasticity of the supply curves.

In discussing the excess burden imposed by taxes, or anything else that depends on elasticity of supply and demand, it is important to distinguish between short-run and long-run effects. Elasticities of both supply and demand are usually greater in the long run than in the short. If the price of gasoline rises, the immediate response of the consumer is to drive less. Given a longer time to adjust, he can also arrange a car pool, buy a smaller car, or move closer to his job. If the price of heating oil rises, he can adjust, in the short run, only by turning down his thermostat. In the long run, he can improve the insulation of his house or move to a warmer climate.

In the short run, the producer is stuck with his existing factory. If price falls, he may still prefer producing at the lower price to scrapping his machinery. In the longer term, supply is more elastic; at the lower price, it will no longer be worth maintaining the machines or buying new ones as the old ones wear out. If price rises, his short-run response is limited to trying to squeeze more output from the existing factory. In the longer run, he can build a bigger factory.

For all of these reasons, elasticities are generally greater in the longer run. High elasticity implies high excess burden, so the excess burden of a tax is likely to become larger, relative to the amount collected, as time goes on. A famous example is the window tax in London some centuries ago, which led to a style of houses with few windows. A similar and more recent example was a tax on houses in New Orleans that depended on the number of stories at the front of the house. That is supposed to be the origin of the "camelback" houses—one story in front, two in back. In the long run, dark houses in London and higher building costs in New Orleans were part of the excess burden of those taxes.

Landlords and Tenants—An Application of Price Theory

Suppose the government of Santa Monica decides that since landlords are bad and tenants good, every landlord must pay each of his tenants $10/month. In the short run, this benefits the tenants and hurts the landlords, since rents are set by contracts that usually run for a year or so; as long as the tenant is paying the same rent as before and receiving an additional $10, he is better off than before. In the longer run, however, the supply and demand curves for apartments are shifted by the new requirement, changing the equilibrium rent. The effect is shown in Figure 7-11a.

From the standpoint of the landlord, the new requirement is simply a tax of $10/month on each apartment rented. What matters to the landlord in deciding whether to rent out an apartment (as opposed to occupying it himself, turning it into a condominium, letting the building fall apart,

Figure 7-11

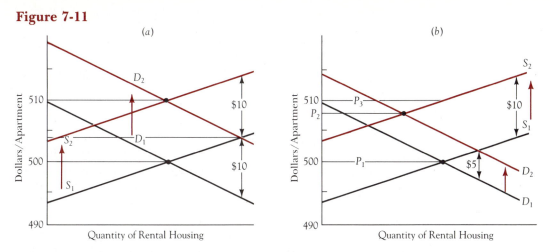

Effect of regulations on the rental market. Figure 7-11*a* shows the effect of a compulsory $10 transfer from landlords to tenants. Figure 7-11*b* shows the effect of requiring landlords to provide tenants with six months' notice. The requirement is equivalent to a $10 tax on landlords and a $5 subsidy to tenants.

not building it in the first place, or whatever other alternatives he has) is how much he ends up getting, not how much the tenant initially pays him. Since he has to give $10 back to the tenant, he actually gets rent minus $10. So the supply curve is shifted up by $10; at a rent of $510 per apartment per month, the quantity of apartments offered to rent is the same as it would have been before at a rent of $500/month.

From the standpoint of the tenant, the $10 is a subsidy—a negative tax. A positive tax would shift the demand curve down by the amount of the tax; the effect of the negative tax is to shift the demand curve *up* by $10. Whatever quantity of housing each tenant would have chosen to rent before at a price of $500/month (instead of buying a house, sharing an apartment with a friend, or moving to Chicago), that is now the quantity he will choose to rent if the rent is $510, since $510 in rent minus $10 from the landlord is a net cost to him of $500. If the rent is less than $510, he will choose to rent more housing than he rented before at $500; if the rent is more than $510, he will rent less.

Figure 7-11*a* shows the result; for simplicity we are treating housing as if it were a simple continuous commodity like water, and defining price and quantity in terms of some standard-sized apartment. Since both supply and demand curves shift up by $10, their intersection shifts up by $10 as well. The new equilibrium rent is precisely $10 higher than the old, so the law neither benefits the tenant nor hurts the landlord. If this result seems paradoxical to you, you are a victim of what I earlier called naive price theory. Once the assumption that prices are handed down from heaven in some mysterious manner is replaced by an understanding of how they are determined, the result is not only possible but obvious.

If every time you pay the rent, the landlord is required to go through a ceremony of extracting one $10 bill and giving it back to you, there is no reason why that requirement should affect the real rent you pay and he receives.

Let us now consider a different law—one that seems at first less arbitrary. The city government decides that it is unfair for landlords to "force" tenants to sign lease contracts that are "biased" in favor of the landlords, so it passes a law requiring landlords to give tenants six months' notice before evicting them, even if the tenants have agreed in the lease to some shorter period. Again we consider the effect after enough time has passed so that rents have had a chance to adjust themselves to the new equilibrium, as determined by the supply and demand curves after the change.

Suppose the landlords are all identical. The requirement of six months' notice increases their operating costs, since it makes it harder to evict undesirable tenants. From their standpoint, it is equivalent to a tax. Suppose it is equivalent to a tax of $10. Suppose, in other words, that landlords are indifferent between having to provide each tenant with six months' notice and having to pay a $10/month tax on each apartment. The supply curve for apartments shifts up by $10, as shown in Figure 7-11b.

From the standpoint of the tenants (who we will also assume are all identical to each other), the additional security of the six months' requirement is worth something; an apartment with that security is worth more than one without it. It is thus equivalent to them to receiving a subsidy—a negative tax. Suppose that it is equivalent to a subsidy of $5/month. Just as in the previous case, the result is to shift the demand curve up; the same tenant who was willing to pay $500/month for an apartment without six months' tenure is willing to pay $505 for one with the additional security. The curve shifts up by $5, as shown in Figure 7-11b. The result is similar to the $10 transfer shown on Figure 7-11a, but the demand curve shifts up only $5 instead of $10.

Looking at the figure, you can see that the new price is higher than the old by more than $5 and less than $10. This is not an accident. The exact price depends on the slope of the curves, but (as you should, with a little effort, be able to prove) the increase must be more than the smaller shift and less than the larger. Since the law increases the costs to landlords by more than it increases rents, landlords are worse off. Since it increases the value of the apartment to tenants by less than it increases rents, tenants are also worse off!

In setting up the problem, I assumed that the six months' notice requirement cost the landlords more than it was worth to the tenants; specifically, I assumed that it cost the landlords $10 and was worth $5 to the tenants. What happens if we make the opposite assumption? Suppose the law imposes a cost of $5 (shifting the supply curve up by $5) and a benefit of $10 (shifting the demand curve up by $10). In that case, as you should be able to demonstrate, the increase in rent is again between $5 and $10. Both parties are better off as a result of the law—the landlord gets an increase in rent greater than the increase in his costs, while the tenant pays an increase in rent less than the value to him of the improved contract.

In this case, however, the law is unnecessary. If there is no law setting the terms for rental contracts, a landlord who is renting out his apartment (without six months' security) for $500/month will find it in his interest to offer his tenant the alternative of the same apartment with six months' security at, say, $509/month. The tenant will accept the offer, since (by our assumption) he prefers $509 with security to $500 without; the landlord will be better off, since it only costs him, on average, $5/month to provide the security. Hence, even without the law, all rental contracts will provide for six months' notice before eviction. So in this case, the law has no effect; it forces the landlords to do something they would do anyway.

More generally, it will pay the landlord to include in the lease contract any terms that are worth more to the tenant than they cost him—and adjust the rent accordingly. Given that he has done so, any requirement that he provide additional security (or other terms in the contract) forces the landlord to add terms to the lease that cost him more than they are worth to the tenant. The ultimate result is a rent increase that leaves both landlord and tenant worse off than before.

In proving this result, I made a number of simplifying assumptions. One was that the cost per apartment imposed by such a requirement on the landlord did not depend on how many apartments he was renting out; the requirement, like a lump sum tax, shifted the supply curve up by the same amount all along its length. I also made the equivalent assumption for the tenants—that security was worth the same amount per apartment independent of how much apartment was consumed (the horizontal axis of the diagrams should really represent not number of apartments but amount of housing rented—rooms, square feet of apartment space, or some similar measure). Dropping these assumptions would make the diagrams and the analysis substantially more complicated. With some effort, one could construct situations where the requirement shifts the supply and demand curves in a way that benefits tenants at the expense of landlords, or landlords at the expense of tenants, but there is no particular reason to expect either to happen.

A second assumption was that all landlords were identical to each other, and similarly for all tenants. Dropping these assumptions changes the results somewhat. To see why, imagine that you are a landlord who is unusually good at recognizing good tenants. Offering six months' security costs you nothing—you never rent an apartment to anyone you will ever want to evict. Assume that the situation, with regard to the tenants and the other landlords, is as shown in Figure 7-11b. If there is no legal restriction on contracts, you find that by offering security you can get a rent of $505/month instead of $500; since the security costs you nothing, you do so. After the law changes to force all landlords to offer security, you find that the market rent, for apartments with the (required) six months' security, is more than $505 (as shown in Figure 7-11b). The restriction has actually helped you, by forcing your competitors (the other landlords) to add a feature (security) to their product that was expensive for them to produce but inexpensive for you. Their higher costs decreased the market supply curve and increased the market price, benefiting you.

One could construct similar cases involving tenants. The interesting point to note is that the effect of legal restrictions on contracts between landlords and tenants is not, as one might at first expect, a redistribution from one group (landlords) to another (tenants). Insofar as the groups are uniform, the restrictions either have no effect or injure everyone; insofar as the members of the groups differ from each other, the restriction may also result in redistribution within the groups—benefiting some members of one or both of the groups at the expense of other members of the same group.

One of the difficulties in teaching (and learning) economics is that so much of it seems to be simply plausible talk about familiar subjects. That is an illusion. In the course of this chapter, I have given proofs of two very implausible results—that it does not matter whether a tax is collected from producers or consumers and that restrictions on rental contracts "in favor" of tenants actually hurt both tenants and landlords.

The fact that economics seems to be merely plausible talk about familiar things poses a serious danger to the student. He may go through the first half of the course nodding his head from time to time at what seem like reasonable statements by the text or the professor, only to discover at the midterm that he has somehow failed to learn most of the structure of ideas that the lectures and text were supposed to be teaching—even though it all seemed to make sense when he heard it.

The best way to find out for yourself whether you really understand the ideas is to try to apply them to numerical examples. That is the significance of such examples. Whether you do or do not become an economist, it is unlikely that you will ever be faced with any real-world equivalent of a numerical problem on an economics exam; as we will see shortly, the real world rarely provides us with accurate graphs of supply and demand curves. What you will be faced with—whether as an economist or a participant in the economy—are problems similar to the problem of figuring out whether a restriction on lease contracts benefits or harms tenants. To do so, you must learn economics, not merely learn about economics; numerical problems are a way to check whether or not you have done so. In exactly the same sense, the right way to find out whether you have learned typing is not to see if you can tell someone about it, or remember what you have been taught, but to try to type something—even if it is only "The quick brown fox jumps over the lazy dog." Many of the problems in an economics text are about as closely related to the ways in which you will actually use economics as the quick brown fox is to the things you eventually expect to type—and serve much the same function.

PART 2—SUPPLY AND DEMAND—SOME GENERAL POINTS

In the first part of this chapter, we put together what we had done in Chapters 3–6 in order to show how equilibrium price and quantity are determined by demand and supply curves. We then applied the analysis to a variety of real-world issues. In the second part of the chapter, we will look back at what we have just done in order to clarify some points and avoid some common misunderstandings.

Mechanism versus Equilibrium

In economics (and elsewhere), there are often two different ways of approaching a problem—to work through a (possibly infinite) series of changes or to look at what the situation must be when all changes have ceased. The latter is often much easier than the former.

Consider a simple supply-demand problem. At a price of $1, purchasers of eggs wish to buy 1,000 eggs per week and producers wish to produce 900. The first way of analyzing the problem might go as follows:

Step 1: There are only 900 eggs to be purchased. The consumers bid against each other until they have driven the price up to $1.25; at that price, they only want to buy 900 eggs.
Step 2: At the new price, producers want to produce 980 eggs per week. They do so. They find that at $1.25, they cannot sell that many, so they compete against each other (by cutting the price) until the price falls to $1.05; at that price, consumers will buy 980 eggs.
Step 3: At $1.05, producers only want to produce 910 eggs per week. They do so. Consumers bid against each other . . .

As you can see, there are several things wrong with this approach. To begin with, the series may go on forever, with the prices gradually converging; indeed, with some demand and supply curves, the series would diverge—the swings in price would get wider and wider. Furthermore, the process as I have described it depends on producers and consumers always basing their decisions on what the price just was instead of trying to estimate what it is going to be. Once you drop that assumption, there are many possible sequences of events, depending on the detailed assumption you make about how producers predict the future. The alternative approach goes as follows:

If quantity supplied is greater than quantity demanded, the price will fall; if less, the price will rise. Price will therefore tend toward the point at which the two are equal. This is the equilibrium price—the intersection of supply and demand.

Shortages, Surpluses, and How to Make Them

To most noneconomists, a shortage is a fact of nature—there just isn't enough. To an economist, it has almost nothing to do with nature. Diamonds are in very short supply—yet there is no diamond shortage. Water is very plentiful; the average American consumes, directly or indirectly, more than 1000 gallons per day. Yet we see water shortages.

The mistake is in assuming that "enough" is a fact of nature—that we need a particular amount of land, water, diamonds, oil, or whatever. In fact, the amount we choose to consume (and that producers choose to produce) depends on the price; what we think of as our "need" is usually our quantity demanded at the price we are used to paying. A **shortage** occurs not when the amount available is small but when it is less than the amount we want; since the latter depends on price, a shortage simply means that a price is too low—below the level where quantity supplied would equal quantity demanded. Frequently this is the result of either government price control (gas and oil prices in the early seventies, for example) or the refusal by government to charge the market price for something it supplies (urban water). Sometimes it is the result of producers who misestimate demand (particular models of cars) and are unwilling or unable to adjust price or output quickly. An obvious example is where the seller is bound by an advertised price and finds that at that price he runs out.

One interesting case of a relatively stable supply-demand disequilibrium (a **surplus** rather than a shortage) occurred many years ago in Hong Kong. Rickshaws are small carts drawn by one person and used to transport another—a sort of human-powered taxi. They used to be common in Hong Kong. Casual observation suggested that the drivers spent most of their time sitting by the curb waiting for customers—quantity supplied was much larger than quantity demanded. Why?

The explanation appears to be that many of the customers were tourists from countries where the wage level was, at that time, much higher than in Hong Kong. The price it seemed natural to them to offer to pay was far above the price at which supply would have equaled demand. People were attracted into the rickshaw business until the daily income (one fourth of the day working for a high hourly payment, three fourths of the day sitting around) was comparable to that of other Hong Kong jobs. It is worth noticing that the tourists who paid $4HK for a ride that represented $1HK worth of labor were worse off by $3HK than if they had paid the lower price but that there was no corresponding gain to the recipients.

The Invisible Demand Curve

A careless reading of an economics textbook may give the impression that economists are people who go around measuring supply and demand curves and calculating prices and quantities from them. This is a complete

Section II   Price = Value = Cost

misunderstanding. What we observe are prices and quantities. To the extent that we know anything about particular demand curves, it is mostly deduced from such observations. For the most part, supply curves and demand curves are used not as summaries of information (like a table of atomic weights) but as analytical tools, ways of understanding the mechanism by which prices are determined.

Indeed, demand and supply curves are in a sense unobservable. We observe that this year there was a certain amount of wheat grown and it sold at a certain price. We make similar observations for other years. Can we plot the corresponding points on a graph and call them a demand curve ("When price was $1, demand was 4,000,000 bushels; when price was . . .")? No. If the demand curve and supply curve had stayed the same from year to year, price and quantity would have stayed the same as well. Since they did not, at least one of the curves must have shifted, and perhaps both. If the demand curve stayed the same and the supply curve shifted around (changes in the weather affecting the supply of wheat, for instance), then the observed points trace out the demand curve (Figure 7-12a), but if it was demand that shifted and supply that stayed fixed, then we have a graph of the supply curve instead (Figure 7-12b). If both curves shifted, we have a graph of neither (Figure 7-12c).

Demand or Supply?

One of the original puzzles of economics was whether price was determined by the value of a good to the purchaser (demand) or the cost of production (supply). You are now in a position to see that the answer is both. If the supply curve is horizontal at a price P, then P is the market price, whatever the demand curve may be—unless the quantity demanded at that price is zero, in which case nothing is sold and there is no market price. If demand is horizontal at a price P, then that will be the market price—whatever the supply curve (with the same exception). In the normal case, where neither line is horizontal, a shift in either will change the price.

The statement "Price is determined by both value to the consumer and cost of production" is also true in a more complicated sense; it is in a sense true that price is equal to both value to the consumer and cost of production—even in the extreme case of a horizontal supply curve, where price is determined entirely by supply.

How can this be true? It is true if value and cost mean marginal value and marginal cost. The consumer, faced with the opportunity to consume as much as he wants at a price P, chooses to consume that quantity of the good at which his marginal value for an additional unit is just equal to P. We saw that in Chapter 4, where we derived the demand curve from the consumer's marginal value curve. So price equals value—not because value determines price but because price (at which the good is available) determines quantity (that the consumer chooses to consume) and quantity

Figure 7-12

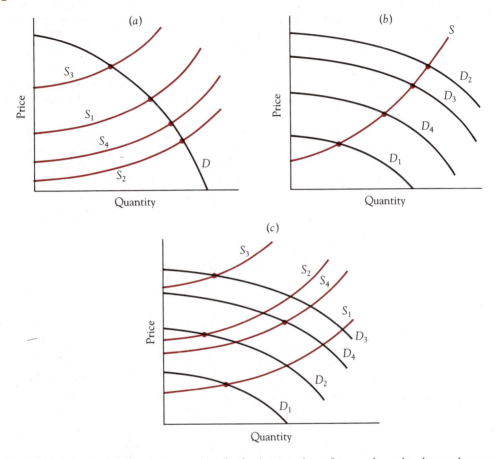

Invisible curves. What we observe is only the intersection of a supply and a demand curve. If the supply curve is shifting (Figure 7-12*a*), the intersections map out the demand curve; if the demand curve is shifting (Figure 7-12*b*), they map out the supply curve; and if both are shifting (Figure 7-12*c*), they show neither.

consumed determines (marginal) value. Seen from the other side, the producer, able to sell all he wants at a price *P*, expands output until his marginal cost of production (the marginal disvalue per hour of labor to him divided by the number of units he produces in an hour) is *P*. We saw that in Chapter 5 and will see it again, in the case of a firm rather than an individual producer, in Chapter 9. So price equals cost—not because cost determines price but because price (at which he can sell the good) determines quantity (that he produces) which determines (marginal) cost.

In considering a single consumer or a single producer, we may take price as given, since his consumption or production is unlikely to be large enough to influence it significantly. Considering the entire industry (made up of many producers) and the entire demand curve (made up of many individual demand curves), this is no longer true. The market price is that price at which quantity demanded equals quantity supplied. At the quantity demanded and supplied at that price, price equals marginal cost equals marginal value. Demand and supply curves jointly determine price and quantity; quantity (plus demand and supply curves) determines marginal value and marginal cost.

Warning

There are two somewhat subtle mistakes that I have found students often make in interpreting the material of this chapter. The first is a verbal mistake with regard to demand. It is easy to think of "my demand increasing" as meaning "I want it more." But demand (the demand curve) is a graph of quantity demanded as a function of price. If your demand increases, that means that at any price, you want more of it—not that you want it more. How much you want it is your marginal value, not your demand; it depends, among other things, on how much of it you have. That the two curves (demand and marginal value) are the same is not a matter of definition (they mean quite different things) but something that we proved in Chapter 4.

The other mistake has to do with why supply curves shift. We are used to thinking of prices as the result of bargaining between buyer and seller, with each claiming that the price he wants is fair. It is tempting to imagine that when a tax is imposed, the reason price rises is that the seller tells the buyer, "Look here. My costs have gone up, so it is only fair for you to let me raise my price." The buyer replies, "I agree that it is fair for you to raise your price, but I should not have to bear the whole cost of the tax, so let us compromise on a price increase that transfers part of the tax to me and leaves you paying the rest."

Such an imaginary dialogue has *nothing* to do with the process I have been describing in this chapter, and almost nothing to do with how prices are really determined. To begin with, I am assuming a market with many buyers and many sellers; each individual, in deciding how much to buy or sell, takes the price as given, knowing that nothing he does can much affect it. In such a context, bargaining has no place. If you do not like my price, I will sell to someone who does; if nobody will buy at the price I am asking, I must have made a mistake about what the market price was.

When a tax is imposed on the producers, each producer revises his calculation of how much it is in his interest to produce. Before the tax, when the price was, say, $10, he produced up to the point where producing an additional widget cost him as much, in time and effort, as $10 was worth to him. When a $1 tax is imposed, he finds that each additional widget is bringing him only $9—$10 for the widget minus $1 for the tax.

He is in the same situation as if there were a $9 price and no tax, so he reduces his production to what he would have produced if the price were $9 and there were no tax. He is not trying to bargain with anyone—he is simply maximizing his welfare under changed circumstances. All other producers act similarly—some by reducing production, some by leaving the industry and producing something else instead. Quantity supplied (at $10) is now less than quantity demanded, so price rises. As it rises, producers increase the amount they find it in their interest to produce; consumers decrease the amount they find it in their interest to consume. The price continues to rise until it reaches a level at which the quantity producers wish to produce is the same as the quantity consumers wish to consume.

PROBLEMS

1. Figures 7-13a and 7-13b each show demand curves for two individuals; in each case, draw the combined demand curve.
2. Figure 7-14 shows the supply curve for avocados. A tax of $0.50/avocado is imposed. Draw the new supply curve.
3. Figure 7-15 shows the demand curve for peanut butter. A consumption tax is imposed; every purchaser must pay the government $0.40 for every jar of peanut butter purchased. Draw the new demand curve for peanut butter.

Figure 7-13

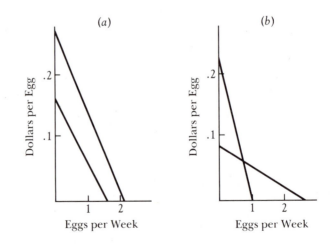

Demand curves for Problem 1.

Figure 7-14

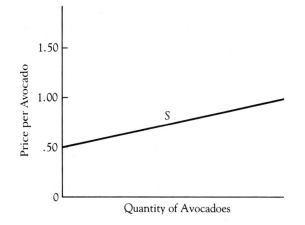

Supply curve for Problem 2.

Figure 7-15

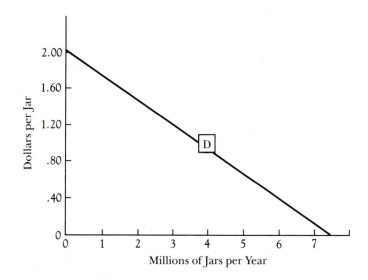

Demand curve for Problem 3.

4. Figure 7-16 shows demand and supply for potatoes in 1925. For each quote below, redraw the figure showing the change described. The parts are alternatives, not successive events. The authors of the quotes may be assumed to know as much economics as the average newspaper reporter. You may explain your answers if you wish.

a. *In 1926, the invention of the french fry caused a great increase in the demand for potatoes. The result was to increase the price of potatoes.*

Figure 7-16

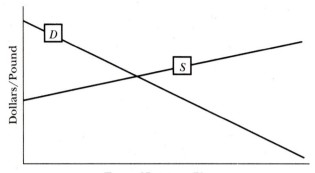

Tons of Potatoes/Year

Supply and demand curves for Problem 4.

> *The increased price increased the supply, which drove the price back down again.*

b. *In 1926, bad weather decreased the potato supply, driving up the price. The higher price decreased the demand, which drove the price down.*

5. Figure 7-17 shows the supply and demand curves for bananas.
   a. What are the equilibrium price, quantity, and total consumer expenditure?
      For parts (b–g), answer the following questions:
      i. What is the equilibrium price? Quantity? Consumer expenditure for bananas?

Figure 7-17

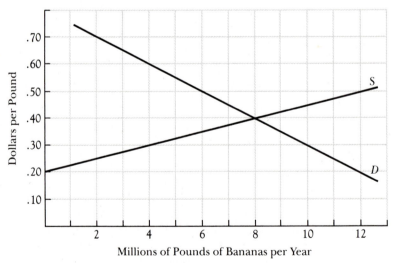

Supply and demand curves for Problem 5.

Section II   Price = Value = Cost

     ii. How much better or worse off are consumers than in part (a) (no tax)? Producers?

    iii. How much revenue does the government get?

  b. Consumers must pay a tax of $0.10/pound on bananas.

  c. Producers must pay a tax of $0.10/pound on bananas.

  d. Producers pay and consumers receive a tax of $0.10/pound.

  e. Producers and consumers each pay a tax of $0.05/pound.

  f. The government requires all bananas to be labeled with the date they were picked. This results in an increased cost to producers of $0.08/pound. Consumers are indifferent between unlabeled bananas at a price P and labeled bananas at a price P plus $0.03.

  g. As in (f), except that the cost to the producers is $0.03 and the value to the consumers $0.08. Comment on your results.

     (Note: Each of parts (b–g) is independent; in each case, we start with the same initial situation, make one change, and evaluate the result.)

6. Can a tax lower the total expenditure of consumers on bananas and at the same time hurt the consumers? If so, give an example. Explain.

7. Work out the effect of a tax in the case of a perfectly elastic supply curve. In the case of a perfectly elastic demand curve.

8. What are the relations between price elasticity of demand and supply and excess burden to the producers? Demonstrate your results with figures similar to Figures 7-5a through 7-5f, 7-10a, and 7-10b.

9. What is the exact mathematical relation between P_2 and P_3 in Figure 7-6 and P_2' and P_3' in Figure 7-8a?

10. I asserted that one could, with some effort, construct a situation where a restriction on rental contracts actually benefited landlords at the expense of tenants. Do so. You should assume that for every quantity, the demand curve shifts up less than the supply curve (the restriction costs the landlord more than it benefits the tenant), but you need not assume that the shift is uniform along the curve.

11. Social Security taxes are paid half by the employer and half by the worker. What do you think is the significance of that division? How would things be different if the tax were entirely on the worker or entirely on the employer or divided in some other way between them? Prove your answer.

12. Why do you think the present division of Social Security payments between employer and employee exists?

13. In discussing the surplus of rickshaws, I claimed that the high price paid by customers to rickshaw drivers was a cost to the customer but not a gain to the driver. Explain.

chapter 8

THE BIG PICTURE

SOLVING AN ECONOMY

Several chapters back, I described the economy as a complicated interdependent system and proposed to solve it by separately solving the parts. I have now done so, at least for a simple economy. The separate pieces are the consumer, the producer, and the market in which they interact. In discussing the consumer's behavior, in Chapters 3 and 4, we saw how the attempt to achieve his objectives leads to an individual demand curve, describing how much he will buy of a good at any price. The shape of this demand curve depends on the preferences of the individual, his income, and the prices of all other goods. Once we have the individual demand curves, we can sum them to get a market demand curve.

In Chapter 5, we saw how a similar argument leads to a supply curve. One new element was the addition of a production function—a relation between the time a particular producer spends producing things and how much he produces. In Chapter 5, the production function took the form of a table showing the rates at which a producer could produce each of various combinations of goods. The producer could use his time to produce goods, sell the goods for money, and, as a consumer, use the money to buy the goods he wished to consume.

Here, as in most of economics, money is not essential to the analysis, although it makes its presentation easier. We could analyze production and consumption in essentially the same way even if all trade occurred by barter, with individuals producing goods and exchanging them directly for other goods. The only difference would be that the system would appear more complicated, both to us and to the people inside it. Instead of talking about the price of apples, or meals, or lawn mowing, we would have to talk about the price of apples measured in meals or the price of lawn mowing measured in oranges; this would complicate both our description of the economy and the lives of the participants.

Another complication of barter, from the standpoint of individual traders, is the **double coincidence problem**. In an economy with money, an individual can sell the goods he produces to one person and use the money to buy what he wants from another. In a barter economy, the trader must find one person who both has what he wants and wants what he has. In almost all of the analysis so far, I have neglected the **transaction costs** associated with a market—the costs of finding someone to trade with and negotiating an exchange. That useful simplification would be less plausible in a barter market.

Having gotten demand curves (and consumer surplus) from the chapters on consumption, and supply curves (and producer surplus) from the chapter on production, we combined the two in Chapter 7 to describe how market prices are determined, how they are affected by changes in supply and demand, and the effects of the resulting changes in price and quantity on the welfare of consumers and producers. We now have all the pieces of an economy—supply, demand, and their combination. Let us see if we can assemble them.

Putting It Together: The First Try

Putting the pieces together appears very simple. We start with individual preferences, represented by indifference curves or utility functions, and the ability of individuals to produce goods—production functions. The preferences of consumers (and their incomes) give us demand curves, the preferences of producers (between leisure and income) plus production functions give us supply curves, the intersections of supply and demand curves give us prices (and quantities), and we are finished. We have derived prices and quantities from preferences and production functions.

It is not so simple. The intersection of supply and demand curves gives us prices. Prices (of the goods the individuals produce and sell) give us incomes. But we needed incomes to start with, since they were one of the things that determined demand curves!

The same problem appears if we stop talking about prices in general and talk instead about particular prices. We run through our supply and demand argument to get the price of widgets. We then do the same to get the price of cookies. But one of the things affecting the demand for widgets is the price of cookies (if cookies are inexpensive, you spend your money on them instead of on widgets). We could solve that problem by solving for cookies first—but one of the things affecting the demand for cookies might well be the price of widgets.

Why would we expect the demand curve for one good to depend on the price of another? There are two reasons. The first is that the goods may actually be related in consumption; this is the case of what are called **complements** and **substitutes**. Bread and butter, for example, are commonly used together, so the value of bread to you depends in part on the price of butter, and vice versa. Your demand curve for bread goes up when the price of butter goes down. Bread and butter are complements. Trains and airplanes both provide the same service—

transportation. Your demand curve for rail travel goes down when airline fares go down. Trains and airplanes are substitutes.

These possibilities may be assumed away when we are trying to describe a very simple economy. We can limit our analysis, as we did in most of Chapter 4, to people for whom the usefulness of one good never depends on how much they have of another, and then reintroduce such complications at a later stage of the analysis. We may assume, in other words, that the individual's utility function is simply the sum of a lot of little utility functions—utility of apples (which depends only on how many apples he has) plus utility of oranges plus utility of water plus . . ..
There is a second sort of interdependence that cannot be dealt with so easily. The demand curve of a good is identical to its marginal value curve, which tells us how many dollars are equivalent to a little more of the good. But dollars are valuable for the (other) goods that they can buy, so the value of a dollar depends on the price of those goods. If all prices go down, a unit of a good is still equivalent to the same amount of some other good but to fewer dollars; so the demand curve for one good depends on the prices of the other goods that money could be spent on. As I have pointed out before, a drop in the price of everything is just like an increase in income—and has similar effects on the demand curve for any particular thing.

In thinking about what determines the price of one good, it is convenient, and often correct, to treat all other prices as given and work through the effect of some change in demand or supply on the particular good we are interested in. We cannot follow the same procedure in understanding the whole interdependent system. Each price depends on all other prices, both directly, because the price of one good to a consumer may affect his demand curve for other goods, and indirectly, since the price of a good to its producer affects his real income, which in turn affects his supply and demand curves for other goods.

Nailing Jelly to a Wall

The interdependence of the different elements that make up the economic system is not wholly new; it is a more complicated example of a problem we have already met and dealt with. The error is in thinking that, having worked out the separate parts of the problem, we can then assemble them one part at a time—solve for one part of the system, then for another, then . . .. The discussion of the egg market in Chapter 7 started with a simpler form of the same mistake. I tried to solve the problem in a series of stages; at each stage, I solved part of the system while ignoring its effect on the rest. I started with a given quantity of eggs being produced, then found the price at which that was the quantity consumers wished to consume. At that point, I was solving for price, given the requirement that price must be such that quantity demanded (at that price) equals quantity produced. I next found the quantity that would be produced at that price; in other words, I solved for quantity, given the condition that quantity produced must be the quantity producers choose to produce, using the price derived in the previous stage of the argument. That gave me a different quantity produced, which had to be plugged back into the demand side of the analysis (the first step), yielding a different price, which must be plugged back into the supply side, yielding a different quantity . . . . The logical tangle that results is a (simple!) case of an attempt to solve an interacting system one piece at a time while ignoring the effect on all the other pieces.

The solution was to stop treating it as a mechanism and instead look for the equilibrium point. That occurs at the one price and quantity combination for which quantity supplied equals quantity demanded. In the more complicated case of the whole economy, we will follow essentially the same procedure.

Putting It Together: The Second Try

Our problem is to start with individual preferences and production functions and derive a complete set of equilibrium prices and quantities. The first step is to consider some list of prices—a price for every good. This initial list is simply a first guess, a set of prices chosen at random.

Since each supply curve is determined by the prices of the goods the producer would like to buy and of the other goods he could sell (and preferences and production functions, which know), we can calculate all supply curves. Since quantity supplied of any good is determined by the supply curve and the price of that good, we can calculate the quantity supplied of every good. Since income is determined by the prices of the goods we produce and the quantities we produce of them, we can calculate every producer's income. Since the demand curve for any particular good is determined by income (of the consumers, which they get as producers) and prices (of other goods), we can calculate all demand curves; since quantity demanded of any good is determined by the demand curve and the price of that good, we can calculate the quantity demanded of every good.

So, starting with preferences, production functions, and a list of prices, we can calculate all quantities supplied and demanded and compare the quantity demanded of every good with the quantity supplied. If the two are equal (for every good), we have the right list of prices—the list that describes the equilibrium of the system. If they are not equal, we pick another list of prices and go through the calculation again. We continue until we find the right list of prices. The logical sequence is diagrammed in Figure 8-1.

In practice, this would be a slow way of finding the right answer, rather like putting a thousand monkeys at a thousand typewriters and waiting for one of them to type out *Hamlet* by pure chance. After the first million years, they might have produced nothing better than "To be or not to be, that is the grglflx." There are faster ways, provided you have explicit descriptions of everybody's preferences and productive abilities;

Figure 8-1

How to solve an economy. Starting with prices of all goods, production functions, and preferences of all consumers, one can derive quantities supplied and demanded. If they are equal for all goods, the initial set of prices describes a possible market equilibrium—a solution for that economy.

the general mathematical problem is that of solving a set of n equations in n unknowns. Our simple egg example was a problem of two equations (quantity equals quantity producers choose to supply at the price; quantity equals quantity demanded at the price) in two unknowns (quantity and price). A problem with two unknowns can be solved in two dimensions, which happened to be the number we had available, so we were able to solve the problem graphically by finding the point where two lines (the supply and demand curves) intersected.

I have gone through right and wrong ways of solving an economy so fast that you may have lost the former in the latter. I will therefore repeat the very simple result.

> **To solve an economy, find that set of prices such that quantity demanded equals quantity supplied for all goods and services.**

That simple result—contrasted with the previous hundred and some pages—may remind you of the mountain that gave birth to a mouse. But without those pages, we would not have known how prices (and preferences) generate supply and demand curves, nor how supply and demand curves in turn determine prices.

Solving even a very simple real-world economy would involve thousands of equations; in practice, the problem is insoluble even with advanced mathematics and modern computers. But the point of the analysis is not actually to solve an economy and come up with a set of prices and quantities. Even if we could solve the equations we could not write them down in the first place, since we do not know everyone's preferences and abilities. What we observe are prices and quantities; we see the solution, not the problem. The point of the analysis is to learn how the system is interrelated, so that we can understand how any particular change (a tariff, a tax, a law, an invention) affects the whole system. Also for the fun of understanding the logical structure of the interrelated world around us.

Your response may be that we do not understand a system if our "solution" requires information and calculating abilities we do not have. But as I tried to make clear in Chapter 1, economists do not expect to know what people's objectives are, only what the consequences are of people rationally pursuing them. Nor, I might have added, are economists experts in the technology of production.

If you think economics is useless if it cannot actually solve an economy—predict what the entire set of prices and quantities is going to be—consider what we have already done. The book so far contains demonstrations of at least four strikingly counterintuitive results: (1) that a theater owner maximizes his profit by selling popcorn at cost; (2) that for a nation or individual to be better at producing one thing is logically equivalent to its being worse at producing something else (the principle of comparative advantage); (3) that the costs imposed by taxes on producers and consumers are unaffected by who pays the taxes; and (4) that legal restrictions on leases "in favor of tenants" either have no effect or hurt both tenants and landlords. Not one of those conclusions depended on our knowing any real-world demand or supply curve, nor any of the preferences and abilities from which those curves might have been derived.

Economics is not the only science that analyzes systems it cannot actually solve. The three-body problem—the problem of determining the behavior of three objects interacting by gravitational attraction according to the laws of Newtonian physics—has not yet been solved, but that does not prevent astronomers from studying the solar system, which contains at least nine planets, the sun, and a considerable number of moons, comets, and asteroids.

OPTIONAL SECTION

PARTIAL AND GENERAL EQUILIBRIUM

The kind of economics that we did in Chapter 7 is what economists call **partial equilibrium** analysis; we analyzed the effect of changes in the market for one good, whether widgets or apartments, while ignoring the effects on other goods. The kind of economics that we did in this chapter, when we saw how, in principle, an economy can be solved, is called **general equilibrium** analysis.

Most economic analysis, in this book and elsewhere, is partial equilibrium; one assumes that the effects one is interested in are limited to one or at most a few goods. In many situations, this is a legitimate assumption—not because it is precisely correct but because it leads to correct conclusions.

Consider a change that shifts the demand or supply curve for one good. The result is to change the price of the good and the quantity produced and purchased, as described in Chapter 7. It is very unlikely that, after the change, each consumer will be spending the same amount of money on the good at the new price as he did at the old.

If a consumer is spending more (or less) on the good whose price has changed, he must be spending less (or more) on all other goods. Hence the quantity demanded of those goods has changed. Hence the initial assumption, that only the one good was affected, is wrong.

It is wrong but, like the assumptions on which economics is built, useful. In most cases, such effects are spread among a large number of other goods, each of which is only slightly affected (this is not true in the special case of two goods that are close substitutes or close complements, which is why such goods must be treated together in such an analysis). Small changes in prices generally produce very small effects on total surplus—the sum of consumer and producer surplus. Roughly speaking, a $0.10 increase in price produces not one tenth the effect of a $1 increase but one hundredth. The reason is that when a price goes up, most of the resulting loss in consumer's surplus is a gain in producer surplus; only that part of the loss of (consumer and producer) surplus associated with the reduction in quantity produced and consumed is a net loss. Since the reduction in quantity associated with a price increase of $1 is about 10 times as great as that associated with a price increase of $0.10 (exactly 10 times if the relevant curve is a straight line) and since the average consumer surplus per unit on the lost consumption is also about 10 times as high, the product is 100 times as great.

It follows from this argument that while it may be important that a change in the price and quantity of one good results in a change of $1 in the price of another good, it is much less important if the change in one good results in a change of $0.10 in 10 other goods, and still less if it results in a $0.01 change in each of 100 other goods. Since such effects are typically spread over thousands of goods, it is usually legitimate to ignore them. This is one justification for using partial equilibrium analysis. The *reason* for doing so is that, as you have probably realized at this point, general equilibrium analysis is usually much harder.

IS THIS CHAPTER REALLY NECESSARY?

I have spent most of this chapter showing that the way in which we have been doing economics is not quite correct, explaining what the correct way would be, and then explaining why I am going to keep on using the "not quite correct but much easier" approach. It would seem that if I omitted the whole discussion, the book could continue in exactly the same way, saving the reader a chapter of work and a considerable amount of confusion. In that sense, this chapter is unnecessary; there is not a single problem anywhere else in the book that depends on understanding this chapter for its solution—and this chapter has no problems.

The justification for this chapter—and complications elsewhere that may seem equally unnecessary—is my belief that lying to students is bad pedagogy. If I am going to teach you a particular way of doing economic analysis, I ought to point out its problems and inconsistencies—as I have done in this chapter—instead of passing quietly over them in the hope that you will not notice. The argument by which I have tried to justify the way in which I am doing economics is really only a sketch of a much more complicated argument, one that those of you who decide to become economists will probably encounter again in a few years. In the rest of this book, I will limit myself to partial equilibrium theory; the purpose of this chapter was to explain why.

HALFTIME

WHAT WE HAVE DONE SO FAR

In Section I of this book, I defined economics as that approach to under-standing behavior that starts from the assumption that people have objec-tives and tend to choose the correct ways of achieving them. I went on to add several additional elements—the assumption that objectives were reasonably simple, the definition of value in terms of revealed prefer-ence, and the idea that the different things we value are all comparable. In Section II, I used economics to analyze individual behavior in order to show how prices and quantities are determined in a simple economy. The connections between the two sections may not always have been obvious; while Section II applied the ideas discussed in Section I, I usually did not bother interrupting the analysis to point out what assumption or defini-tion was being applied where. Since we are now at a sort of halfway point, finished with the analysis of a simple economy and about to launch our-selves into a sea of complications, this is a convenient place to look back at what we have done and trace out some of the connections.

The central assumption of rationality—the assumption that people tend to choose the correct means to achieve their objectives—has been applied throughout Section II. The approach used over and over again was first to figure out what a rational person would do—how he could best achieve his objectives—and then to conclude that that is what people *will* do.

In the analysis of production, for example, we first figured out which good it was in the individual's interest to produce, then concluded that that was the good he would produce. We went on to figure out how much it was in his interest to produce, given his preferences, and again concluded that that was what he would do. Similarly, in the analysis of consumption, the demand curve was equal to the marginal value curve because the individual took the actions that maximized his net benefit. In the analysis of trade, each individual only made those exchanges that

194

benefited him, and two individuals continued to trade as long as any exchanges that benefited both of them remained to be made.

One part of the assumption of rationality discussed in Chapter 1 was that people have reasonably simple objectives. This too has been used, although rarely mentioned, several times in Section II. Consider, for example, the discussion of budget lines and indifference curves in Chapter 3. Throughout that discussion, I assumed that the only reason someone wanted money was for the goods it would buy. In discussing the location of the optimal bundle, for example, I argued that the individual would spend his entire income—that, after all, is what money is for (the possibility of saving for future consumption did not come up, since we were assuming a static world in which each day was just like the next). But one could imagine an individual who liked the idea of living below his income—forever—and so chose to buy fewer goods than he might, while accumulating an ever-increasing pile of money. That may seem irrational to you, but remember that we have no way of knowing what people *should* want. Economics deals with the consequences of what they *do* want. I ignored the possibility of such behavior not because it was irrational in the normal sense of the word but because it violated the assumption that individual objectives were reasonably simple.

I again assumed that one desired money only for what it could buy when I discussed income effects and substitution effects; I asserted, as you may remember, that if your income doubled and the prices of everything you consumed also doubled, you would be in the same situation as before. But suppose that at some point in your life, you fell in love with the idea of being a millionaire. What you wanted was not a particular level of consumption but the knowledge that you had a million dollars. Doubling all incomes and prices would make it considerably easier for you to reach that goal. Here again, I assumed such situations away on the grounds that they would violate my assumption of reasonably simple objectives.

The definition of value in terms of revealed preference was also used in Section II. One could argue that it is revealed preference, not rationality, which implies that demand curves are equal to marginal value curves; your values are revealed by how much you choose to consume at any price—your demand curve. The principle of revealed preference and the assumption of rationality are closely connected; if we did not believe that people tended to choose the actions that best achieved their objectives, we would have a hard time deducing their objectives from the actions they chose. To say that you value an additional apple at a dollar means that given the choice between the apple and some amount of money less than a dollar, you will choose the apple; given the choice between an apple and some amount of money larger than a dollar, you will choose the money. From that, it follows that you will keep increasing your consumption of apples until you reach the point where the marginal value of an apple is equal to its price. Since you do that at any price, the graph of how much you buy at any price is the same as the graph of your marginal value at any quantity. The demand curve and the marginal value curve are identical.

Revealed preference appeared again in the derivation of consumer surplus. Later in Chapter 4, the combination of consumer surplus and rationality was used to prove that a profit-maximizing theater owner would sell popcorn at cost. The argument depended on the assumption that consumers would correctly allow for the price of popcorn in deciding how much they were willing to pay for a ticket. In classroom discussions of the popcorn problem, I find that students are frequently unwilling to accept that; they believe that consumers (irrationally!) ignore the price of popcorn and simply decide whether or not the movie is worth the price. Perhaps so. The applicability of economics to any form of behavior is an empirical question. What I demonstrated was that if the assumptions of economics apply to popcorn in movie theaters, then the obvious explanation of why it was expensive had to be wrong.

The assumption of rationality was used yet again in the popcorn problem, applied this time to the theater owner rather than to his customers. If the theater owner's rational policy is to sell popcorn at cost, then rationality implies that that is what he will do. The observation that theater owners apparently sell popcorn for considerably more than it costs them to produce it provides us with a puzzle. One may, of course, conclude that economics is wrong. In Chapter 10, I hope to persuade you that there are more plausible solutions to the puzzle.

One more economic idea was discussed in Section I—comparability, the idea that none of the goods we value is infinitely important in comparison to the others. While comparability was never mentioned in Section II, it was implicit in the way in which we drew up the tables and figures of Chapters 3, 4, and 5. Imagine drawing an indifference diagram for two goods, a "need" A on the horizontal axis and a "want" B on the vertical axis. Since no amount of B could make up for even a tiny reduction in A, the indifference curves would have to be vertical. But vertical indifference curves imply that you are indifferent between a bundle consisting of 5 units of A and 5 of B and a bundle consisting of 5 units of A and 10 of B—which is inconsistent with the assumption that you value B. It is possible to analyze such a situation—but not with indifference curves.

I have now shown you some examples of how the assumptions of Section I were used in the analysis of Section II. The same assumptions will continue to be applied throughout the rest of the book; just as in Section II, I will only occasionally point out which assumptions go into which arguments. One of the things I have learned in writing this book is that economics is considerably more complicated than I thought it was. In such an intricately interrelated system of ideas, pointing out every connection whenever it occurs would make it almost impossible to follow the analysis. Much of the job of tracing out how and where the different strands of the analysis are connected you will have to do for yourself.

That is not entirely a bad thing. It has been my experience that I only really understand something when I have figured it out for myself. Reading a book, or listening to a lecture, can tell you the answer. But until you have fitted the logical pattern together yourself, inside your own head, what you have read or heard is only words.

AND FOR OUR NEXT ACT

This brings us to the end of the first half of the book. The second half will be devoted to expanding and applying the ideas worked out so far. In Section III, I will introduce a series of complications to our simple model. The first, in Chapter 9, is the existence of the firm, an enterprise that serves as an intermediary between the ultimate producers and the ultimate consumers, buying productive services from the individuals who own them and selling consumption goods. Next, in Chapter 10, I drop the assumption that we are dealing with markets in which each individual producer and consumer is too small a part of the whole for his decisions to have a significant effect on market price; this will get us into discussions of monopoly and related complications—including, in Chapter 11, the complications of strategic behavior and the attempt to use game theory to deal with them. In Chapters 12 and 13, I add time and uncertainty to the analysis, bringing the world we are analyzing noticeably closer to the one we live in. Finally, having expanded the theory to include most of the essential complications of a real economy, I use it in Chapter 14 to answer one of the questions that economists are frequently asked—how the distribution of income is determined in a market economy.

Section IV begins by making explicit the criteria of "economic welfare," "efficiency," "desirability," and the like that have been introduced, or at least suggested, in the discussion of consumer and producer surplus. I then go on to show how such criteria can be used to judge alternative economic arrangements. Expanding on that subject, and on the results of dropping our normal assumption that prices are free to reach their supply/demand equilibrium, I will discuss the effects of various interferences in the workings of the market, some touched on already in earlier chapters.

At the end of Chapter 17 ("Market Interference"), you may be left with the impression that the market is a perfect mechanism for satisfying our desires and that there are no legitimate arguments for interfering with its natural workings. In Chapter 18, I attempt to dispel that impression by discussing **market failures**—ways in which failures of the market to conform to assumptions we have made (often implicitly) in our analysis may result in its failure to function as we would expect and wish. This chapter is an expansion of a point made in Chapter 1—that rational behavior by individuals does not necessarily produce rational behavior by groups.

Halftime   **197**

By the end of Section IV, all of the essential ideas of the course will have been covered. Section V consists of a series of chapters applying those ideas. A few of the applications will be conventional ones, such as the analysis of the effects of tariffs in Chapter 19. More of the applications will be of the sort that I find especially interesting—using economics to analyze the dating/sex/marriage market of which most of us are a part, for example, or to analyze the economics of theft.

The book ends with a final chapter in which I discuss how economics is done, what economics is good for—why, aside from passing a course, you should want to learn what I want to teach—and what economists do.

COMPLICATIONS, OR

section III

ONWARD TO REALITY

chapter 9

THE FIRM

So far, we have discussed production in the context of one person converting his time into some service such as lawn mowing. While that is a useful place to start, it ignores two important features of production—the use of more than one input in producing an output and the cooperation of more than one person in production. In this chapter, we will explore production in the more complicated case of the firm—a group of people combining inputs to produce an output.

Why do firms exist? Part of the reason is suggested in Chapter 6—because two people coordinating their production can do better for themselves than if they act independently. In Chapter 6, the coordination occurred through trade. Individuals produced independently but decided how much to produce of what by taking into consideration the possibility of trading it for something else. In a firm, the cooperation is closer. Typically many individuals work together to produce a single item. The obvious reason is that they produce more that way. This is, in large part, a result of the principle of division of labor—if each of us specializes in a particular part of the productive process, he can be much better at it, hence more productive, than if each of us has to do everything. It is difficult to imagine one worker, however skillful and well equipped, producing an automobile in a year entirely by himself, yet an automobile factory produces several automobiles per worker per year.

In the production of automobiles, some of the division of labor occurs within the firm and some between firms; General Motors does not, for example, produce the steel from which its cars are made. One could imagine a society in which there was a high degree of division of labor, all of which occurred between firms, with each firm participating in only one part of the productive process and perhaps consisting of only one person. That possibility, and the difficulties it would create, are discussed in the optional section at the end of this chapter.

In discussing consumption, we reduced the individual to a set of preferences and his environment to a set of prices and a budget constraint. In discussing the firm, we follow a somewhat similar process—how similar will be clearer by the end of the chapter. We start with a production function, which describes the ways in which the firm can convert inputs (labor, raw materials, the use of machinery) into its output (the product it produces); we assume, for simplicity, that each firm produces only one product. The production function, plus the assumption that the firm is trying to maximize its profits, describe the firm; the prices the firm faces, for both its inputs and its output, describe its environment. The combination of the two tells us what the firm will do—how much it will produce and how.

PART I—FROM PRODUCTION FUNCTION TO COST CURVES

We begin with a production function, which tells how a firm can transform its inputs into the goods it produces. You can think of a production function as an explicit function, $Q(x_1, x_2, x_3, \ldots)$, where Q is the amount produced and $x_1, x_2, \ldots$ are the amounts of all the different inputs that can be used to produce it. Alternatively, you can think of a production function as a very large table listing all possible combinations of inputs and, for each combination, the resulting quantity of output. Table 9-1 is

Table 9-1

Input Bundle	Labor (hours)	Cost of Labor ($10/hr)	Capital ($-years)	Cost of Capital (0.05/yr)	Clay (pounds)	Cost of Clay ($4/lb)	Total Cost	Output of Pots
A	1.00	$10.00	100	$ 5.00	1.00	$ 4.00	$ 19.00	1
B	0.25	2.50	400	20.00	4.00	16.00	38.50	1
C	4.00	40.00	25	1.25	0.25	1.00	42.25	1
D	2.00	20.00	200	10.00	2.00	8.00	38.00	2
E	4.00	40.00	100	5.00	1.00	4.00	49.00	2
F	1.00	10.00	100	5.00	16.00	64.00	79.00	2
G	1.00	10.00	1,600	80.00	1.00	4.00	94.00	2
H	3.00	30.00	300	15.00	3.00	12.00	57.00	3
I	9.00	90.00	100	5.00	1.00	4.00	99.00	3
J	4.00	40.00	100	5.00	5.06	20.24	65.24	3
K	4.00	40.00	225	11.25	2.25	9.00	60.25	3
L	1.00	10.00	8,100	405.00	1.00	4.00	419.00	3
M	4.00	40.00	400	20.00	4.00	16.00	76.00	4
N	9.00	90.00	178	8.89	1.78	7.12	106.01	4
O	0.946	9.46	94.6	4.73	1.18	4.72	18.92	1
P	1.89	18.90	189	9.45	2.36	9.44	37.84	2
Q	2.84	28.40	284	14.20	3.55	14.20	56.76	3
R	3.78	37.80	378	18.90	4.73	18.92	75.68	4

$$\text{Output} = \text{Labor}^{1/2} \times (\text{Capital}/100)^{1/4} \times \text{Clay}^{1/4}$$

part of such a table for a firm manufacturing clay pots; the explicit production function is given at the bottom. Each row of Table 9-1 shows the number of pots that can be produced in a year with a particular collection of inputs—so much labor, so much use of capital, so much clay.

The table also shows the cost of the inputs; we assume that the firm is a small enough part of the market that the prices at which it buys its inputs and sells its output are a given, not something affected by how much it buys or sells. The price of labor is $10/hour, the price of clay is $4/pound, and the price for the use of capital (strictly speaking, its rental) is .05/year. The meaning of the first two is obvious; the third, the price of capital, is an interest rate. If the interest rate is .05/year (or, more conventionally stated, 5 percent per annum), then using $100 worth of capital for a year costs you $5—the interest you would pay if you borrowed the money to buy the $100 worth of machinery that you must use for a year ($100 × 1 year = 100 dollar-years of capital) in order to produce a pot using input bundle A. At the end of the year, you could either resell the machinery and pay back the loan or keep the machinery for another year and use another 100 dollar-years worth of capital to produce another pot—at a cost, for capital, of another five dollars interest on your loan. If you find it odd that your inputs consist of pounds of clay but dollar-years of capital, and that you have used capital as an input even if you give back the machine when you have finished with it, consider that exactly the same thing is true of the third input—labor. Your input is not workers but worker-hours, and you return the worker (to himself) when you have finished employing him.

The firm must figure out how much to produce and how to produce it. A sensible first step, on the principle of dividing hard problems into manageable pieces, is to pick a level of output and figure out, given the production function and the prices of inputs, how to produce that quantity at the lowest possible cost. To do so, you start by considering all of the different combinations of inputs that would produce that quantity of output. On Table 9-1, for example, input bundles H, I, J, K, L, and Q can each be used to produce three pots. Next you calculate the cost of each bundle. This is just like calculating the cost of a consumption bundle; you multiply the quantity of each input by its price to find out how much you spend on that input, then add the figures for all the inputs to find the cost of the whole bundle, as shown on the table. Mathematically this gives us

$$C = P_1 x_1 + P_2 x_2 + P_3 x_3 + \ldots$$

C is the cost of that particular bundle. But there are usually many different combinations of inputs that will produce the same output. By using more labor, for example, you can minimize wastage and so reduce your consumption of raw material; whether that is worth doing depends on how expensive raw material is in comparison to labor. By using more machinery (ultimately capital—you will have to wait until Chapter 14 for a clearer explanation of what capital is), you may be able to economize on labor, raw material, or both. There are many kinds of raw material you can use (substituting among plastic, aluminum, and steel, for example, in making an automobile), and each of them comes in many different forms at different prices. Figuring out how to produce 73 television sets is an immensely complicated process with no single answer—there are many ways to do it. Typically, however, there is only one least expensive way, which is what the firm is looking for.

Comparing, on Table 9-1, the different bundles that can be used to produce one pot, you find that bundle O does it at the lowest cost; similarly bundle P is the least expensive way of producing 2 pots, Q of producing 3, and R of producing 4. Figure 9-1 shows the **total cost curve** (total cost as a function of quantity) implied by Table 9-1.

Since the table shows only a few of the possible ways of producing any particular number of pots, you cannot tell whether you have found the least costly input bundle or only the least costly of those shown. That is one of the problems with using a finite table to represent an infinite number of alternatives. In the optional section of this chapter, I show how one can use calculus to find the lowest cost bundles of inputs to produce various levels of output. The results of those calculations, for output levels of 1, 2, 3, and 4, are bundles O, P, Q, and R. They represent only a slight improvement over bundles A, D, H, and M, the lowest cost found without calculus. In this case, at least, one can come fairly close to achieving the perfectly rational decision by simple trial and error.

Figure 9-1

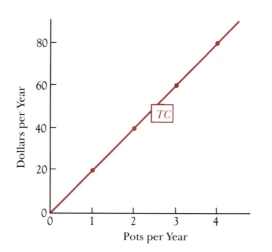

Total cost for producing clay pots. The figure shows the cost of the least-cost bundle of inputs for producing each quantity of pots.

It may have occurred to you that the way in which we use Table 9-1 to find the least-cost way of producing pots is very similar to the way in which a similar table was used in Chapter 3 to find the most attractive consumption bundle. The logic of the two problems is almost exactly the same. In Chapter 3, we compared all the consumption bundles with the same cost to find out which produces the greatest utility; in this chapter, we compare all the input bundles producing the same output to see which has the lowest cost.

Having analyzed the production function, there are now two directions to go. We will first analyze the firm's behavior as a buyer, in order to deduce its demand curve for steel, labor, and the other inputs it uses in production. We will then analyze its behavior as a producer and seller, in order to deduce its supply curve for its output. As you will see, the two sides are connected, since the price for which the firm can sell its output is one of the things determining its demand for inputs.

The Input Market

Geometry I: Isoquant Curves and Isocost Lines. In Chapter 3, after recognizing that the table showed only a tiny sample of the possible consumption bundles, we went on to analyze the same problem geometrically, using budget lines and indifference curves. The same approach applied to production is shown on Figure 9-2; just as in the case of consumption, the fact that we are drawing our curves on two-dimensional paper means that we can only show two variables at a time. Here the two variables are inputs—labor and clay, used to produce pots. We may imagine either that there are only two variables—that only two inputs are used to produce the output—or that we have already decided on the amount of the other inputs, such as capital, to be used.

In Chapter 3, the individual maximizes his utility subject to a budget constraint; here the firm minimizes its "budget"—its total expenditure— subject to a fixed level of production. These represent essentially the same process. The individual consumer tries to get as much of something (utility, happiness, "his objectives") as possible while spending a given amount of money; the firm tries to spend as little money as possible while getting a given amount of something (output). Figure 9-2 is the equivalent, for a firm, of the indifference curve diagrams of Chapter 3.

The contour Q_1 is called an **isoquant**. It shows the different combinations of the two inputs that can produce a given quantity of output (73 pots). The colored lines are **isocost** lines; each shows all the input bundles that can be bought at a given cost. The isocost line is straight for the same reason the budget line is; we are assuming that the firm buying inputs, like the consumer buying consumption goods, can purchase as much as it wants at a constant price per unit.

In Chapter 3, we had a given budget line and were looking for the highest indifference curve that touched it. Here we have a given isoquant and are looking for the lowest isocost line that touches it. That is why

Figure 9-2

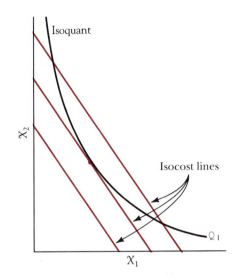

Isoquant

Isocost lines

Q_1

X_2

X_1

Isoquant/isocost diagram for two inputs. Each isocost line shows the different bundles of inputs that have the same cost. The isoquant, Q_1, shows the different bundles of inputs needed to produce a given quantity of output. The point of tangency is the optimal (i.e., lowest cost) input bundle for producing that quantity of output.

the figures in Chapter 3 showed one budget line and several indifference curves, while here Figure 9-2 shows one isoquant and several isocost lines. In Chapter 3, the solution was to find the (indifference) curve that was tangent to the (budget) line; the optimal consumption bundle was at the point of tangency. Here the solution is to find the (isocost) line that is tangent to the (isoquant) curve; the optimal input bundle, the lowest cost bundle of inputs to produce that quantity of output, is at the point of tangency.

Suppose the firm has figured out the lowest cost way of producing a particular output: 73 television sets, a million cars, three pots, or whatever. It repeats the calculation for every other level of output it might consider producing: 74 television sets, 50 television sets, 900 television sets. At the end of the process, it has converted its production function into a **total cost function**—a function that tells it how much it will cost to produce any level of output.

Figures 9-3*a* and *b* show how this would work for the case of two inputs, X and Y, with prices $P_x = 2, P_y = 3$. I have labelled the isoquants and some of the isocost lines on 9-3*a*. The points of tangency show the input bundles that would produce the various output quantities at the lowest cost. Line *SEP*, which links those points, is the **scale expansion path**; it shows how the consumption of the inputs X and Y would increase as output expanded. Figure 9-3*b* shows the resulting total cost curve.

Point *A* on Figure 9-3*b*, for instance, shows total cost of 30 for producing a quantity of 34. It corresponds to point *a* on Figure 9-3*a*, where the isoquant for producing 34 units is tangent to the isocost line for a cost of 30.

Figure 9-4 shows how the inputs used to produce a given quantity of output (34 widgets) would change if the price of the inputs changed.

Figure 9-3

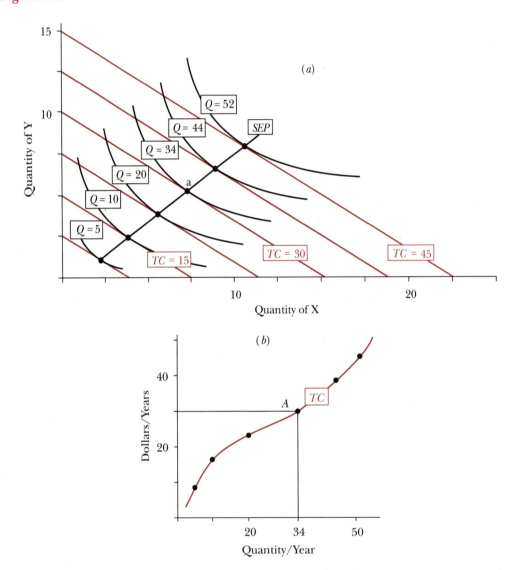

Scale expansion path and total cost curve for the case of two inputs. The scale expansion path (*SEP*) in Figure 9-3*a* indicates the input bundles that would produce the various output quantities at the lowest cost. Figure 9-3*b* shows the resulting total cost curve.

Section III   Complications, or Onward to Reality

Figure 9-4

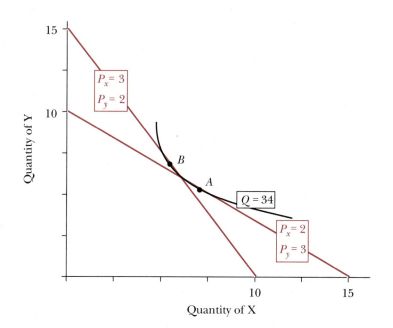

The effect of a change in input prices.   When the price of X rises and the price of Y falls, the optimal input bundle for producing 34 widgets changes from A to B. The firm substitutes the input that has become cheaper for the input that has become more expensive.

Point A shows the input bundle that produces 34 widgets at lowest cost if P_x is 2 and P_y is 3; point B shows the lowest cost bundle if we reverse the prices. As one would expect, when the prices change, the firm shifts to using more of the good that has become cheaper (Y) and less of the good that has become more expensive (X). This **factor substitution effect** is precisely analogous to the substitution effect in consumption described in Chapter 3. There we were rolling a budget line along an indifference curve; here we are rolling an isocost line along an isoquant.

In Chapter 3, we were able to use figures similar to this (3-8a and 3-9a) to derive the individual's demand curve for a good. Can we, in the same way, derive the firm's demand curve for its input?

The answer is no. Figure 9-4 shows the inputs that the firm would use to produce *a given quantity* of output at different input prices. But as input prices change, so does the cost to the firm of producing its output, and hence the quantity that it chooses to produce. We would have to take account of that effect if we wanted to derive demand curves for inputs.

How would we do so? We have just seen how, for a given set of input prices, the firm calculates a total cost curve. In the next section we will see how, from the total cost curve and the market price, the firm decides how much to produce. In order to calculate the firm's demand curve for

Chapter 9   The Firm   **207**

one input, say steel, we would simply repeat this analysis for a range of different steel prices, holding the prices of all other inputs fixed. For each price we would calculate the profit-maximizing quantity of output (say automobiles), and for that quantity we would calculate the quantity of steel in the least-cost bundle of inputs.

I Knew I Had an Equimarginal Principle Lying Around Here Somewhere.   The same argument that led us to the equimarginal principle in consumption applies in production as well, if we replace marginal value with **marginal product**—after first defining the latter.   The marginal product of an input is the rate at which output increases as the quantity of that input increases, all other inputs held constant. You may think of it as the increase in output resulting from one additional unit of that input. If adding one worker to a factory employing 1,000, while keeping all other inputs fixed, results in an additional 2 cars per year, then the marginal product of labor is 2 cars per worker-year.

How can you produce two more cars with no more steel? The answer is that for small variations in inputs, one factor can substitute for another—in this case, labor for raw materials. One of the things the additional labor may do is improve quality control, so that fewer cars have to be scrapped; another is to make possible a more labor-intensive production process that produces cars with slightly less steel in them. Table 9-1 shows the same thing happening with the manufacture of pots. As you go from bundle A to bundle E, for example, the amount of clay and of capital used stay the same; the amount of labor quadruples, and the output rises from 1 pot to 2. Perhaps what is happening is that in A, many of the pots crack when they are fired; in E, the workers are spending four times as much time on each pot, and as a result they have doubled the percentage that survive firing. Going from A to E, labor input increases by 3 worker-hours and output by 1 pot, so the marginal product of labor is 1/3 pot/worker-hour.

If we consider large changes in inputs, this becomes less plausible—it is hard to see how one could produce either pots or cars with no raw materials at all, however much labor one used. This is an example of the **law of diminishing returns**, which plays the same role in production as does the law of declining marginal utility in consumption. If you hold all factors but one constant and increase that one, eventually its marginal product begins to decline. Each additional worker-year increases the number of cars produced by less and less. However much fertilizer you use, you cannot grow the world's supply of wheat in a flowerpot. In just the same way, as you hold all other consumption goods fixed and increase one, eventually the additional utility from each additional unit becomes less and less. I will not trade my life for any number of ice cream cones.

The equimarginal principle in consumption tells us that if you have chosen the optimal consumption bundle, the value to you of an additional dollar's worth of any good in the bundle—anything you consume—is the same. The equimarginal principle in production tells us that if the firm is minimizing its costs for a given quantity of output, the additional output produced by a dollar's worth of any input it uses is the same. Algebraically, if MP_x is the marginal product of input x and similarly for input y, we have:

$$MP_x/P_x = MP_y/P_y$$

The argument, which should seem familiar, goes as follows: If the firm is already producing its output at the lowest possible cost, there can be no way of reducing its cost any further while producing the same quantity of output. Suppose there are two inputs whose marginal product per dollar's worth is different—an additional dollar's worth of input A increases output by 4 units; an additional dollar's worth of input B increases output by 3 units. To reduce cost while producing the same amount of output, use \$0.75 more of input A and \$1 less of input B. Output goes up by (4 units/\$'s worth) × (¾ \$'s worth) = 3 units, because of the increased input of A. It goes down by 3 units because of the decreased input of B. So the net effect is to produce the same output with \$0.25 less expenditure—which is impossible if the firm is already producing at minimum cost.

If you find it confusing to use a "dollar's worth" as a unit to measure the quantity of input, we can use physical units instead. Input A costs \$1/pound and its marginal product is 4 units per pound; input B costs \$2/pound and its marginal product is 6 units per pound. Use ¾ of a pound more of A, ½ pound less of B; output remains unchanged and expenditure has fallen by \$0.25.

In this case, just as in the similar proof in Chapter 4, the argument only works precisely if the amount of the change is infinitely small, so that the marginal product of an input is the same whether we consider an increase or a decrease. The larger the size of the changes in inputs we consider, the less precise the argument becomes. But in order to prove that the firm is not producing at minimum cost, all we need show is that there is some change that lowers cost while maintaining output—even a very small change will do.

We have shown that if the marginal product of a dollar's worth of input is not the same for all inputs, or in other words if the marginal products of inputs are not proportional to their prices, it is possible to alter the bundle of inputs in such a way as to reduce cost while maintaining the same output. It follows that for the *least-cost bundle*—the bundle that a profit-maximizing firm will choose—the marginal products of inputs are proportional to their prices. That is the equimarginal principle in production.

If you look back at Figure 9-2, you will see that we could have derived the same result there. The slope of the isocost line is the ratio of the prices of the two inputs. The slope of the isoquant at any point is the ratio of the marginal products of the two inputs: the **marginal rate of substitution in production**. It shows the rate at which inputs substitute for each other in the production function (how much you must increase one input to balance the output loss due to a unit decrease in another) just as the marginal rate of substitution in consumption showed the rate at which consumption goods substitute for each other in the utility function. At the point of tangency, the two slopes are equal: $P_x/P_y = MP_x/MP_y$. If, in equilibrium, it requires a two-unit increase in input B to make up for a one-unit decrease in input A, then input A must cost exactly twice as much per unit as input B.

Income comes from owning factors of production, such as your own labor, savings, land, or the like. The amount of income you get from the factors you own depends on how much you can sell or rent them for. The equimarginal principle in production, which tells us the relation between the prices of factors and their marginal product, will turn out to be of considerable interest when we discuss the distribution of income in Chapter 14.

Geometry II: Marginal Revenue Product and the Input Demand Curve. Just as in the case of consumption in Chapter 4, we can carry the argument one step further. The marginal product of an input, say steel, is measured in units of output: $1/2$ automobile/ton of steel, say. The **marginal revenue product** (*MRP*) of the input is its marginal product (sometimes called its **marginal physical product**) multiplied by the additional revenue the firm gets for each additional unit produced—the price at which it sells its output. If an automobile sells for $10,000 and an additional ton of steel increases output by half an automobile, then the marginal revenue product of steel is $5000/ton.

Suppose steel costs only $4000/ton. If the firm uses an additional two tons of steel while holding all other inputs constant, its production cost increases by $8000, its output increases by one automobile, its revenue increases by $10,000, and its profit increases by $2000. As long as the cost of steel is lower than its marginal revenue product, profit can be increased by using more steel. So the firm continues to increase its use of steel until the marginal revenue product of steel equals its price: $MRP = P$.

The argument should be familiar—it is the same one used in Chapter 4 to show that $P = MV$. There is one essential difference. Consumption goods are bought with money but used to produce utility. In order to go from marginal utility to marginal value, we needed to know the rate at which the consumer could convert dollars into utiles, which depended on the tastes and opportunities of that particular consumer. Input goods are bought with money and used to produce output goods—which are then sold for money. We could not predict how many dollars' worth of utility the consumer would get from a given quantity of apples, but we can predict how many dollars' worth of automobiles a firm will produce with a given quantity of steel. The rate at which the firm can convert automobiles into dollars is simply the price of automobiles.

This is one example of a more general difference between the analysis of individuals and of firms. While we assume that individuals have relatively simple objectives, we do not know just what those objectives are. The objective of the firm, on the other hand, is known—at least, it is known in economic theory, and the theory seems to do a reasonably good job of explaining the real world. The objective of the firm is to maximize its profit. From that assumption plus the firm's opportunities, as embodied in its production function, the prices of its inputs, and the price at which it can sell its output, we can calculate what the firm will do.

In Chapter 4, we used the relation $P = MV$ to derive the individual's demand curve from his marginal value curve. It would seem that we could, in exactly the same way, use the relation $P = MRP$ to derive the firm's demand curve for its inputs. We simply draw the MRP_s curve, showing marginal revenue product of steel as a function of its quantity. At any price, the firm buys that quantity of steel for which $P_s = MRP_s$. So the firm's demand curve for steel, D_s, equals the MRP_s curve, as shown on Figures 9-5a and b.

There is one problem with this. The marginal product of one input depends on the quantity of other inputs. In order to draw the curve MRP_s on Figure 9-5a, I must first discover, for any quantity of steel, how

Figure 9-5

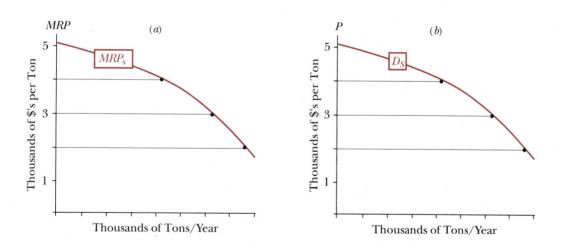

The marginal revenue product curve for steel and the demand curve for steel.

much of each other input—rubber, labor, capital—the firm would choose to use.

To answer that question we again use the equimarginal principle. We know that, in equilibrium, the marginal physical product per dollar's worth of every input the firm uses must be the same. So for any given amount of steel, we use the production function to find the quantities of the other inputs at which the ratio of marginal product to price is the same for all inputs. At those quantities, we calculate the marginal revenue product of steel and put it on the graph.

Why did we not do the same thing in Chapter 4, when we were calculating the demand curves for consumption goods? In principle, we should have. Where two goods are closely related in consumption—bread and butter, for example, or gasoline and automobiles—the demand curve for one must take account of that relation. To calculate the marginal value of bread one must allow for the fact that as you increase your consumption of bread you also increase your consumption of butter—otherwise (assuming that you only like buttered bread) your marginal value for bread would drop off rapidly as you ran out of butter.

But in the case of consumption, such interdependencies are the exception, not the rule, so we could and did ignore them in Chapter 4—especially since, at that point, we were trying to describe a very simple economy. In the case of production, the interdependency of inputs is far more important—the marginal product of steel drops off very rapidly if you cannot hire additional laborers to make it into cars.

Warning. You should not interpret what we have done so far in this chapter as implying that an actual firm, say General Motors, has a list somewhere describing every possible way of producing every conceivable quantity of output and a room full of computers busy twenty-four hours a day figuring the least-cost way of doing so. GM is profoundly uninterested in the cost of producing seven automobiles per year or 7 billion, and equally uninterested in the possibility of making them out of such inputs as bubble gum, lettuce, or the labor services of phrenologists.

Just as in the case of consumer behavior, our assumption is that people (and firms) tend to end up making the right decision, which in this case means producing goods at the lowest possible cost so as to maximize their profit. To figure out what that decision is, we imagine how it would be made by a firm with complete information and unlimited ability to process it. In practice, the decision is made by a much more limited process involving a large element of trial and error—but we expect that it will tend to produce the same result. If it does not, and some other practical method does, then some other firm will produce cars at lower cost than GM. Eventually GM will either imitate its competitor's method or go out of business.

The Output Market: Cost Curves

Figure 9-1 showed the total cost function for the pottery of Table 9-1. A total cost function is enormously simpler than a production function, since it has only one variable; you may, if you wish, think of it as the production function for producing automobiles (or anything else) using only one input—money. The single input is used to hire labor and machinery and to buy steel, glass, and other inputs, which are then used to produce automobiles. For most of the rest of this chapter, it is only the cost function and not the full production function that we will need in order to understand the firm's behavior.

Figure 9-6 shows total cost as a function of output for a hypothetical firm producing widgets. **Fixed cost** (*FC*) is the height of the total cost curve where it runs into the vertical axis—total cost as we approach zero output from the right. For the firm shown by TC_2, total cost goes to zero as output goes to zero. For the firm whose total cost curve is TC_1, the ability to produce anything at all involves a substantial cost (FC_1). An example of such a fixed cost would be the cost of designing a new computer, which the firm must pay whether it is going to produce a million computers or only one.

One of the things not shown on the figure is the influence of time on costs. Cost of production really depends on *rate of production* (automobiles

Figure 9-6

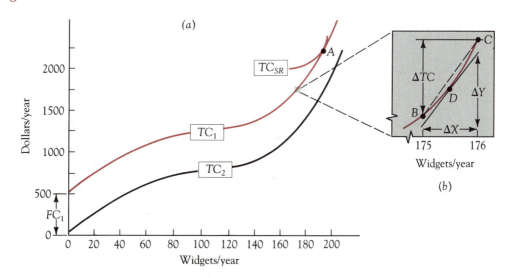

Total cost curves with (TC_1) and without (TC_2) fixed cost. 6*b* is an expanded view of the section of 6*a* inside the square, showing the relation between the precise definition of marginal cost (slope of total cost) and the approximate definition (increase in total cost with a one-unit increase in quantity).

per year) as well as on *amount of production* (automobiles); the cost of producing 1,000,000 automobiles in 10 years is very different from the cost of producing them in one year. The cost of producing different levels of output also depends on how much time the firm is given to adjust to changes. If GM has been producing 5,000,000 cars per year and suddenly decides to reduce output to 2,000,000, there will be many costs it cannot get out of—expensive factories standing empty, executives with long-term contracts who must be paid whether or not there is any work for them, and so on. If GM decides that over the next ten years its output will gradually fall to 2,000,000/year, it can gradually reduce its scale of operations to something more appropriate to the new rate of production.

Going in the other direction, if GM wishes to double its rate of output over a period of a few months, it will find it difficult and expensive; factories will be running all night, workers will have to be paid for overtime, and suppliers will have to be paid premium prices to get them to provide large quantities at short notice. If the same increase occurs gradually over a period of years, the cost is much less. In general, we would expect the total cost curve to rise more steeply with increasing quantity, and fall more gently with decreasing quantity, for short-term changes than for long-term changes. Curve TC_{SR} on Figure 9-6a shows such a pattern, with A the point at which the firm is presently producing.

While the distinction between long-run and short-run cost curves is worth noting at this point, it need not be dealt with here. At this point, we are still considering a perfectly static and predictable world in which tomorrow is always just like today. In such a world, production decisions are made once and for all and never changed. The cost curves in this chapter describe costs for a firm that expects to produce the same quantity of output in the same way forever. In Chapter 13, we will finally drop that assumption. At that point, it will be necessary to return to the distinction between long-run and short-run cost curves; until then, we can ignore it.

Figure 9-7 shows the **marginal cost** curve corresponding to TC_1 on Figure 9-6a. The relation between total cost and marginal cost is the same as the relation between total utility and marginal utility, total value and marginal value, or total product (quantity of output) and marginal product. Marginal cost is the rate at which total cost changes with output; it may be thought of, somewhat imprecisely, as the increase in total cost when output is increased by one unit. Just as marginal value is the slope of the total value curve, so marginal cost is the slope of the total cost curve.

Expressed in numbers, marginal cost at an output rate of 1,000 is the difference between the cost of producing 1,001 units and the cost of producing 1,000. Just as with marginal value, you should not try to associate marginal cost with a particular identifiable unit—a particular car, say. All the cars rolling off the assembly line are identical; the marginal

Figure 9-7

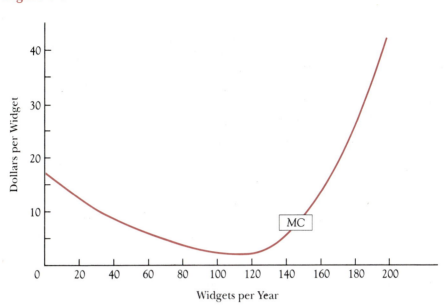

A marginal cost curve. *MC* is the marginal cost curve corresponding to TC_1 in Figure 9-6.

cost of another car is the cost of making the total number of cars coming off that line larger by one.

Figure 9-6*b* is an expanded view of the part of Figure 9-6*a* inside the square; it shows the relation between the precise definition of *MC* (the slope of *TC*) and the approximate definition (increase of cost with a one-unit increase in quantity). The slope of TC_1 at point *D* is $\Delta Y/\Delta X$. The increase in cost per unit increase in quantity, the slope of the dashed line *BC*, is $\Delta TC/\Delta X$. ΔX is one unit. The solid and the dashed line are almost exactly parallel, so their slopes are almost exactly equal.

So far, I have defined total cost (*TC*) and marginal cost(*MC*). There is a third kind of cost curve that we will find useful—**average cost** (*AC*). The average cost to produce any quantity of output is simply the total cost divided by the quantity; if it costs $10,000 to produce 500 widgets, then the average cost is $20/widget. Figure 9-8 combines curves from Figures 9-6*a* and 9-7 and adds *AC*, putting all three cost curves on one graph so as to make it easier to see the relations among them.

One thing you may notice about *AC* on Figure 9-8 is that it goes to infinity as quantity goes to zero. Why? As quantity goes to zero, total cost does not; the firm whose cost curves we are looking at has some fixed costs. Average cost is total cost divided by quantity; as quantity goes to zero, total cost approaches *FC*, so *TC/q* goes to *FC*/0—infinity. Figure 9-9 shows *TC*, *MC*, and *AC* for the firm represented by TC_2 on Figure 9-6;

Figure 9-8

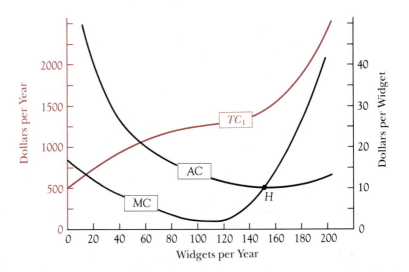

Total cost, marginal cost, and average cost for a firm. Because the firm has positive fixed cost, average cost goes to infinity as quantity goes to zero. Average and marginal cost intersect at point *H*, which is the minimum of average cost.

there are no fixed costs, and *AC* does not go to infinity as quantity goes to zero.

There is also a useful relation between *AC* and *MC* that you may have noticed on Figures 9-8 and 9-9. Where marginal cost is above average cost, average cost is rising; where marginal cost is below average cost, average cost is falling. Where marginal cost is equal to average cost, at

Figure 9-9

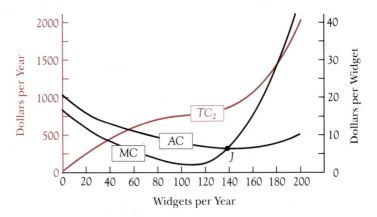

Total cost, marginal cost, and average cost for a firm with no fixed cost.

points *H* on Figure 9-8 and *J* on Figure 9-9, average cost is neither rising nor falling; it is horizontal.

Why? At an output of 150 widgets on Figure 9-8, total cost is $1,500 and marginal cost is $10/widget. Average cost is $1,500/150 widgets = $10/widget. If you increase output to 151, total cost increases by $10—that is what $MC = \$10$ means. But if the average is $10 and you increase quantity by 1 and cost by $10, the average stays the same; you are averaging in one more unit whose cost is exactly the average of the previous units. If average cost does not change when you add another unit, then average cost is independent of quantity—the line is horizontal, as at points *H* and *J*.

Consider a different point on the graph, one at which output is 100 widgets, total cost is $1,250, and marginal cost is $3/widget. Average cost is $1,250/100 widgets = $12.50/widget. If you increase output to 101, total cost increases by $3—that is what $MC = \$3$ means. But if the present average is $12.50 and you increase quantity by 1 and cost by $3, the average must fall. You are averaging in one more unit whose cost is less than the average of the previous units, so you are pulling the average down. The same thing would happen if you calculated the average height of a basketball team and then decided to average in the coach as well.

If *MC* is below *AC*, each additional unit of output pulls down the average. If an increase in quantity lowers average cost, then the *AC* curve is falling. So when marginal cost is below average cost, average cost is going down. Similarly, if marginal cost is higher than average cost, then increasing quantity means adding more expensive units to the average, which pulls the average up. So if marginal cost is above average cost, average cost is rising (getting higher as output gets higher).

Average cost is rising when it is below marginal cost, falling when it is above marginal cost, and level when it is equal to marginal cost. Now that you know the pattern, you should be able to see it easily enough on Figures 9-8 and 9-9. You should also be able to see that when average cost is at its minimum, it intersects marginal cost.

Why? Just before it reaches its minimum, average cost is falling; just after, it is rising. When it is falling, marginal cost must be below it; when it is rising, marginal cost must be above it. So marginal cost must cross average cost from below just at the minimum of average cost. A similar argument demonstrates that at a maximum of average cost, marginal cost crosses it from above. Running the same argument in the opposite direction, it is easy enough to show that these are the only two situations in which marginal cost can cross average cost; if the two curves cross, it must be at a minimum or maximum of average cost.

Students who try to memorize these relations frequently find them confusing; there are, after all, three different curves involved (*TC*, *MC*, *AC*) and two different kinds of characteristics (above/below, rising/falling). A better policy is to go over the argument until you can reproduce it for yourself, then do so when necessary. There are lots of relations that *could* exist among the curves, but only a few rather simple ones that *do*. While at this point they may seem to be the sort of thing that only a professor or textbook author could find of interest, they turn out to be surprisingly useful. In Chapter 16, the fact that marginal cost intersects average cost at the latter's minimum turns out to be a key element in the proof of what may be the most surprising, and important, result in all of economics. Stay tuned.

PART 2—FROM COST CURVES TO SUPPLY CURVES

We have now derived the cost curves of the firm from its production function and the prices of inputs. The next stage is to use the cost curves to derive the firm's *supply curve*—the relation between the price at which it can sell its output and the amount it chooses to produce. The final step in the analysis is to combine the supply curves of many firms into a supply curve for the entire industry; doing this will turn out to involve some additional complications.

The Firm's Supply Curve

In Chapter 4, we derived the demand curve of the consumer from his marginal value curve; now we will use almost exactly the same argument to derive the supply curve of the firm from its marginal cost curve. Figure 9-10*a* shows the same curves as Figure 9-8; the only addition is the price *P* at which the firm can sell its output. We assume (as I mentioned earlier) that the firm, like individual producers in Chapter 5, is producing only

Figure 9-10

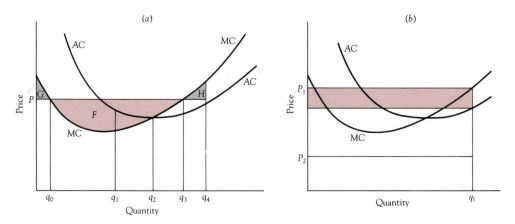

The effect of quantity on profit. If the firm produces q_3, where $MC = P$, profit is maximized. Expanding output to q_4 decreases profit by H; contracting output to q_0 decreases profit by F. Figure 9-10*b* shows another way of calculating profit—as quantity × (price − average cost).

a small fraction of the industry's total output, so that its decision of how much to produce has a negligible effect on P; from the firm's point of view, it can sell as much as it wishes at the market price and nothing at any higher price. For the same reason, we assume that the quantity of inputs the firm buys has no significant effect on the price it must pay for them. Each input has a market price; the firm can buy as much as it likes at that price and none at any lower price. These assumptions—that the firm cannot affect the price it can get for its output or the price it must pay for its input—are the central features of what economists call *perfect competition*. The effects of dropping those assumptions will be discussed in the next chapter.

The firm considers producing a quantity, q_1, at which MC is lower than price. If it increased its output from q_1 to $q_1 + 1$, it would sell one more unit, increasing its revenue by P and its cost by MC. Since P is larger than MC, revenue would go up by more than cost, so **profit**, which is revenue minus cost, would increase. Obviously q_1 is the wrong amount to produce. The same argument applies at q_2. It continues to apply as long as marginal cost is less than price—$MC < P$. So the firm should expand its output up to the point at which $MC = P$. That is q_3 on Figure 9-10a.

If a firm always produces that quantity for which $MC = P$, then its supply curve—the amount it produces as a function of price—is equal to its MC curve, just as a demand curve is equal to an MV curve for a consumer. This is almost correct, but not quite. Typically, MC first falls (as the increasing size of the firm produces advantages—more efficient production on a larger scale), then rises (the firm has taken full advantage of large-scale production; further increases in size mean more and more levels of administration between the president and the factory floor, leading to less efficient production). There may be prices at which, rather than producing a quantity for which $MC = P$, the firm prefers not to produce at all, thus saving the expense of producing units for which MC is higher than P. This occurs when, at the "optimal" quantity of output ($MC = P$), profit is still negative. One would get a similar effect with a demand curve if MV, instead of sloping steadily downward as shown on Figure 4-4, first rose and then fell. There would be prices at which, rather than consuming the quantity for which $MV = P$, the consumer would prefer to consume nothing in order not to have to pay for units whose marginal value was less than their price.

The firm's profit is the difference between what it takes in (**total revenue**—the quantity produced times the price for which it is sold) and what it spends (total cost). If there were no fixed cost, then total profit from producing quantity q_3 on Figure 9-10a would be the colored area F minus the shaded area G. Starting at an output level of zero and expanding output up to q_0, each additional unit costs more to produce than the price it sells for, contributing a (negative) profit of $P - MC$; adding all those little rectangles together gives us the area G. If the firm chose to produce a quantity q_0, its profit would be minus G. As it continues expanding output beyond q_0, the additional units sell for more than they cost to produce; again each unit increases profit by $P - MC$—but this time it is positive, since between q_0 and q_3 marginal cost is less than P. The profit from expanding output from q_0 to q_3 is the sum of all those little rectangles—the colored area F. So the total profit from producing a quantity q_3 is $F - G$.

Seen this way, it becomes obvious why producing the quantity for which $P = MC$ results in the maximum profit. If you produce less, you are giving up the opportunity to produce units that will sell for more than they cost to produce; if you produce more, expanding output to q_4, the additional units cost more than they sell for, lowering profit by the area H. The argument should be familiar; it is essentially the same as the derivation of consumer surplus in Chapter 4.

So far, we have calculated what profit would be if there were no fixed cost. Fixed cost is the amount you have to pay in order to produce anything at all; it does not depend on how much you produce. Total cost is fixed cost plus **variable cost**: $TC = FC + VC$. Since fixed cost does not depend on how much you produce, it has no effect on the marginal cost curve, which shows the additional cost of producing one more unit. It does affect the average cost curve, since average cost is total (including fixed) cost divided by quantity. And since profit is total revenue minus total cost, fixed cost also comes out of profit. So if we include the effect of fixed cost, profit on Figure 9-10a is $F - G - FC$.

Earlier I showed that the firm, if it produces at all, maximizes its profit by producing that quantity for which $MC = P$. It may have occurred to you, looking at Figure 9-10a, that there are two quantities (q_0 and q_3) for which $MC = P$. How does the firm decide which it should produce? The answer should be clear from the previous few paragraphs. If, in the region between the two points, the marginal cost curve is *below* the price line, then producing those units will increase profit—by area F on Figure 9-10a. So the firm is better off producing q_3 instead of q_0. If, in the region between the two points where marginal cost equals price, the marginal cost curve is *above* the price line, then the firm is losing money on those units and would be better off producing the lower quantity. As you should be able to see for yourself, this implies that the firm should produce a quantity at which the marginal cost curve crosses the price line *from below*—as it does at q_3 on Figure 9-10a.

Figure 9-10b shows another way of calculating profit—one that can be done from the figure without knowing the size of fixed cost. Average cost is, by definition, total cost divided by quantity. So total cost is average cost times quantity. Total revenue is price times quantity. So profit—total revenue minus total cost—is simply quantity times the difference between price (P_1) and average cost; it is shown as the shaded area on Figure 9-10b. That makes sense—price is what you get for each unit produced and average cost is what it costs you to produce it, so price minus average cost is your per-unit profit. Multiply that by quantity and you have total profit.

So profit is negative when price is below average cost; the firm would do better by shutting down entirely, eliminating its fixed cost by selling off all its facilities, and going out of business. If profit is negative for all quantities the firm could produce—if, in other words, the average cost curve is everywhere above the price line, as it would be if the price were P_2 on Figure 9-10b—the firm's optimal decision is to go out of business and produce nothing—or better yet, never to come into existence in the first place. Whether or not that situation exists depends both on the firm's cost curves and on the market price.

We now know, for any price, how much the firm will produce. We have deduced the firm's supply curve. The firm produces nothing if the price is below the minimum of average cost. If price is above minimum average cost then there is some range of output quantity for which the firm can make positive profits; the firm maximizes its profit by producing the quantity for which marginal cost equals price. So the firm's supply curve is the rising portion of its marginal cost curve above its intersection with average cost. Figure 9-11a shows a series of different prices, P_1, P_2, P_3, P_4, and for each, the quantity the firm chooses to produce. Figure 9-11b shows the resulting supply curve.

On Figure 9-11b, and on similar figures in Chapter 5 and later in this chapter, the horizontal section of the firm's supply curve is shown as a dashed line. This is to indicate that the supply curve does not really exist in that region; if price equals minimum average cost, the firm will produce either nothing at all or the quantity for which average cost is minimum—making a profit of zero in either case. It will not produce any intermediate quantity, since that would result in negative profit.

Figure 9-11

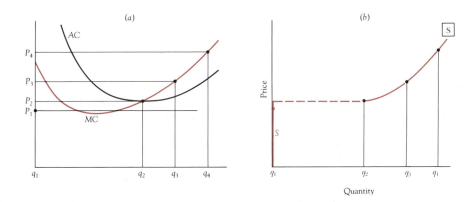

Deducing a supply curve from a marginal cost curve.   Figure 9-11a shows, for each price, the profit-maximizing quantity. Figure 9-11b shows the resulting supply curve, S.

The analysis we have just used to demonstrate the relation between the firm's marginal cost curve and its supply curve is the same used earlier to show that the individual's demand curve was equal to his marginal value curve. The only important difference is that we assumed marginal value always fell with quantity, while we expect marginal cost to first fall, then rise; the result is that the firm may have to produce over a range of output at which it is losing money on each additional unit (between zero and q_0 on Figure 9-10a, where marginal cost is greater than P) in order to reach a level of output where it is making money on additional units.

In this section, I have derived an important relationship linking the cost curves of the firm to its supply curve and to the amount of profit it makes. We will use these results repeatedly in this chapter and later in the book; you may want to go over the analysis again to be sure you understand it before continuing.

You may also find it useful to see how the analysis of the individual producer in Chapter 5 fits into this chapter as a special case—a one-person firm using a single input. The individual producer of Chapter 5 also had a supply curve that was equal to a marginal cost curve—the marginal cost to him of his own time. I explained the horizontal segment of a firm's supply curve by saying that below some price, the profit from producing is negative, so it is better not to produce. I explained the horizontal segment of the individual supply curve by the existence of a price for one good below which the producer is better off producing something else.

The two explanations seem different, but they are not. One cost of using your time to dig ditches is that you are not cooking meals at the same time. How great is that cost? It is equal to what you could make by cooking meals. If the hourly return from digging is less than the hourly return from cooking, then digging produces a negative profit—when the opportunity cost of not cooking is taken into account. In Chapter 5, it was convenient to think of the "cost of working" as the "disvalue of labor"— sore muscles, boredom, and the like. But that is only one example of a more general sort of cost. The cost of mowing lawns is whatever you give up in order to do so, whether that is the pleasure of lying in bed reading science fiction books or the income from washing dishes.

Industry Supply Curve: Closed Entry

We now know how to derive the supply curve of a firm from its cost curves. The next step is to go from the supply curve of a firm to the supply curve of an industry made up of many firms. In doing so, we will encounter a number of complications. I will start with the simplest case and build up from there.

We begin with an industry made up of ten identical firms. We assume that the number of firms is fixed by law; it is illegal for anyone to start a new one. Figure 9-12 shows the supply curve for a single firm, S_f, the supply curve for the industry, S_i, and the demand curve. S_i is simply

Figure 9-12

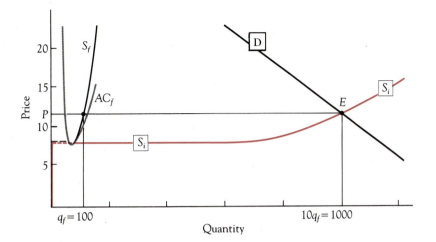

Deducing an industry supply curve from a firm supply curve in an industry with closed entry. The industry has ten identical firms. Its supply curve, S_i, is the horizontal sum of ten firms' supply curves, S_f. The figure assumes that the quantity of inputs used by the industry has no effect on their price.

S_f multiplied horizontally by 10—the number of firms. If, at a price P, a single firm produces a quantity q_f, then ten firms will produce $10 \times q_f$. We are adding together, horizontally, ten identical supply curves, just as we added supply curves in Chapter 5. To find the market price, we simply look for the intersection of the supply curve and the demand curve, as in Chapter 7. It occurs at point E on Figure 9-12.

A number of points are worth noting here. The first is that although price is independent of output from the standpoint of the firm, the same is not true from the standpoint of the industry. The output of any single firm is too small to affect the price significantly, so each firm takes the price as given and adjusts quantity accordingly. But the output of the industry as a whole does affect price. If all the firms increase output, price falls; if all the firms decrease output, price rises. In Chapter 11, we will see what happens if the firms act together to restrict output and drive up price. In this chapter, we assume that the number of firms is sufficiently large that each individual firm merely concerns itself with its own output and takes the behavior of the other firms as given.

If there are only ten firms, that assumption is a somewhat dubious one. I used ten firms in my example because for much larger numbers it becomes difficult to plot the firm supply curve and the industry supply curve on the same graph, as I did for Figure 9-12. You should really think of the analysis as applying to an industry with many more firms— hundreds or thousands of them. That is why, in drawing industry supply curves, I ignore the complications associated with small quantities of output—where there can be one firm producing, or two, but not one and a half.

In deriving the firm's supply curve, we assumed that both the price at which it sold its output and the prices at which it bought its inputs were unaffected by the firm's decisions. While this is a reasonable assumption from the standpoint of one firm in the industry, it is less reasonable for an entire industry. If one farmer decides to double the amount of wheat he plants, he need not worry about the effect of that decision on the price of fertilizer or the wages of farm laborers; but if every farmer decides to double his planting of wheat, both fertilizer prices and farm wages are likely to rise.

It may seem inconsistent to say that no firm affects the price of its inputs but that the industry, which is made up of all the firms, does. It is not. From the standpoint of a single firm in an industry containing many firms, the effect of its demand on the price of inputs may well be negligible, so it can ignore that effect in deciding how much to produce. The same is not true for the industry as a whole. Each increase in the purchases of one firm causes a small increase in prices, which must be paid by all the other firms as well; this is what is called a *pecuniary externality* (an **externality** is a cost or benefit imposed by one firm or individual on another) and will be discussed in Chapter 18. The effect on one firm of the increased price of inputs caused by the increase in that firm's consumption may be negligible, while the effect on all of the firms of the increased price of inputs caused by the increased consumption of all of the firms is not.

Figure 9-12 takes no account of any such effect. It was drawn on the (unstated) assumption that the cost of the industry's inputs was unaffected by the amount of them that the industry bought—or, in other words, that the supply curve for the inputs is horizontal. This assumption is reasonable for some inputs to some industries—increased production of watches is not likely to have much effect on the price of steel, although steel is used in making watches—but not for all.

Figures 9-13a and 9-13b show how we can, if necessary, deal with this complication. Figure 9-13a shows supply curves for a firm, one of whose inputs (iron) becomes more expensive as the industry uses more of it. S_1, S_2, and S_3 are three different supply curves for the same firm, corresponding to three different prices of iron—$1/pound, $2/pound, and $3/pound. Figure 9-13b shows the supply curve for iron. QI_1 on Figure 9-13b is the quantity of iron produced if the price of iron is $1/pound, and similarly for QI_2 ($2/pound) and QI_3 ($3/pound). Q_1 on Figure 9-13a is the quantity of output that results in the industry buying QI_1 of input; Q_2 and Q_3 are related to QI_2 and QI_3 similarly.

S, the supply curve of the industry on Figure 9-13a, goes through three points marked A_1, A_2, and A_3. A_1 shows the price (P_1) at which the industry will supply quantity Q_1. It is the price that corresponds to

Figure 9-13

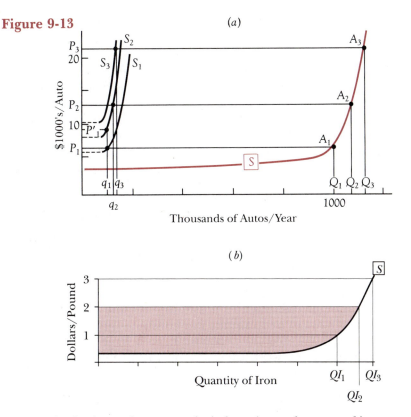

(a)

(b)

From the firm's supply curve to the industry's supply curve, taking account of effects on input prices. As in Figure 9-12, there are ten identical firms, and no new firms can enter. S_1, S_2, and S_3 are the firms' supply curves corresponding to prices of $1, $2, and $3/pound for iron. As total industry output expands from Q_1 to Q_2 to Q_3, the price of iron rises, as shown on Figure 9-13b, moving the firms from S_1 to S_2 to S_3.

quantity $q_1 = Q_1/10$ on firm supply curve S_1. Similarly, A_2 is at quantity Q_2 and price P_2, where P_2 is the price at which a firm with supply curve S_2 produces quantity $q_2 = Q_2/10$; A_3 has the same relation to Q_3, P_3, and S_3.

Each of the points A_1, A_2, and A_3 represents a possible price/quantity combination for the industry. In each case, at that quantity of output, the industry uses an amount of the input (QI_1, QI_2, QI_3) resulting in a price for the input ($1/pound, $2/pound, $3/pound) that results in a supply curve for the individual firm (S_1, S_2, S_3); the quantity produced by the industry (ten firms) is simply ten times the quantity that a firm with that supply curve would produce at that price.

In comparing Figures 9-12 and 9-13a, there are two things you should notice. The first is that S_2 on Figure 9-13a, the supply curve for the firm

Chapter 9 The Firm

225

when iron is at \$2/pound, is the same as S_f on Figure 9-12. The second is that S in Figure 9-13a rises more steeply than S_i in Figure 9-12. To make this clear, I have shown both S and S_i together on Figure 9-14.

To see why S rises more steeply than S_i on Figure 9-14, we must go back to Figure 9-13a. When quantity falls from $q_2 = Q_2/10$ to $q_1 = Q_1/10$, price must fall first to P_1', the price on S_2 corresponding to a quantity of q_1, then by an additional amount $P_1' - P_1$ to get from S_2 to S_1. At the lower quantity (q_1), the industry uses less iron, the price of iron is therefore only \$1/pound, and the firm's supply curve is lower—S_1 instead of S_2. Similarly, when quantity rises from q_2 to q_3, price must go up by enough to not only increase quantity on S_2 but also rise from S_2 to S_3. So price rises more rapidly as quantity is increased above Q_2 on S than it does on S_i, and it falls more steeply as quantity is decreased below Q_2. So S is steeper than S_i.

Why are S_1, S_2, and S_3 arranged in the way shown on Figure 9-13a? Because S_3 corresponds to a higher cost for the input than S_2, and S_2 higher than S_1. The higher the cost of the input, the higher the marginal cost of producing the output, hence the higher the supply curve.

By introducing the possibility that the industry may have to pay a higher price for its inputs if it consumes more of them, I have considerably complicated the problem; I could have saved both myself and you a good deal of work by assuming the problem away, just as I assumed,

Figure 9-14

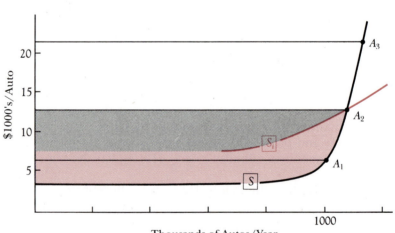

Thousands of Autos/Year

Industry supply curves with (S) and without (S_1) effects on input prices. The producer surplus calculated from S_i is equal to the summed producer surpluses of the ten firms of Figure 9-13a. It is less than the producer surplus calculated from S_i; the difference represents producer surplus going to the iron industry of Figure 9-13b.

for the purposes of this chapter, that variations in output by a single firm did not affect the prices at which it sold and bought. The reason I did not do so is that, in exchange for the additional complications of Figure 9-13a, we get two important results. One will be postponed to the next section; the other will be discussed here.

Back in Chapter 5, we saw that the producer surplus calculated from a supply curve representing the total supply of several producers was the same as the sum of the producer surpluses for all the individual supply curves of the individual producers. This is true for Figure 9-12; the industry supply curve is simply the firm supply curve multiplied horizontally by ten, so the producer surplus (profit) of the industry at any price is ten times the surplus of the firm. It does not, however, appear to be true for Figure 9-13a.

Suppose the price of autos is P_2. The auto industry produces a quantity Q_2 (point A_2 on Figure 9-13a). It consumes a quantity QI_2 of iron at a price of \$2/lb. At this price the firm's supply curve is S_2, which is identical to S_f on Figure 9-12 and so implies the same amount of producer surplus. But the industry supply curve S on Figure 9-13a is not the same as S_i on Figure 9-12, as you can see on Figure 9-14, which shows both. S and S_i intersect at point A_2 where price is P_2 and quantity is Q_2. Since S is steeper than S_i, the corresponding producer surplus at a price of P_2 (the colored and gray regions on Figure 9-14) is larger than the producer surplus at the same price calculated from S_i (the gray region). If the producer surplus for S_i is ten times that for S_f, the producer surplus for S must be more than ten times that for S_2. But S_2 is the supply curve faced by a firm in the situation described by point A_2 (price of iron = \$2/pound). There are ten such firms. It appears that the producer surplus of the industry is greater than the producer surplus of the firms that make it up! What have we missed?

The answer is on Figure 9-13b. The firms shown on Figure 9-13a are not the only producers who benefit from their output—there are also the producers of iron. The higher the quantity produced on Figure 9-13a, the higher the quantity of iron used—and the price (on Figure 9-13b) at which it sells. If we had drawn the figure precisely and to scale, using actual production functions, the colored area on Figure 9-13b, representing the producer surplus received by the producers of iron when the price of iron is \$2/pound, would just make up the discrepancy between the total producer surplus calculated from S on Figure 9-13a and the producer surplus per firm calculated from S_2.

I have asserted this result: I have not proved it, nor will I in this book. Figures 9-12 through 9-14 and the discussion of the last few paragraphs should make the result seem plausible, since they demonstrate that the discrepancy exists and that it is the result of the same fact—a rising supply curve for iron—which is responsible for the existence of producer surplus on Figure 9-13b. But a plausibility argument is not a proof.

Free Entry and the Industry Supply Curve

So far, I have considered an industry with a fixed number of firms; in that context, the supply curve of the industry can be seen as simply the horizontal sum of the supply curves of the individual firms—with appropriate allowance for the way in which the firm supply curves shift if changes in the industry's output affect the price of its inputs. It is now time to drop the assumption that the number of firms in the industry is fixed and consider an ordinary competitive industry with free entry; anyone who wishes may start a firm.

Now, when price increases, not all of the resulting increase in output need come from existing firms; some may come from new firms started to take advantage of the higher price. Hence the industry supply curve, which tells us how total output responds to changes in price, is not simply the firm supply curve multiplied by the number of firms. This is the same situation we encountered in Chapter 5, when we noted that as the price of a good increases, more and more people find that they are better off producing it than producing anything else, so a higher price results in output from new producers as well as increased output by those already producing that good. Seen from the standpoint of this chapter, the new producers of Chapter 5 are new one-person firms entering the industry.

The simplest way to derive an industry supply curve is to assume, as in the previous section, that existing firms all have the same production function and that there exist an unlimited number of potential firms each with the same production function as the existing firms. Just as at the beginning of the previous section, we will start by ignoring any effect that the actions of the industry may have on the price of its inputs.

In that situation, the industry supply curve is very simple. If existing firms are making positive profits—if their total revenue is larger than their total cost—it will pay new firms to come into existence. As new firms come into existence, supply expands, driving down the price. The process continues until profit is no longer positive. If, on the other hand, existing firms are making negative profits, then firms go out of business, reducing supply and driving price up—until profit is no longer negative. The equilibrium point is where profit is zero.

There is only one possible equilibrium price—the price at which revenue exactly covers cost. If revenue exactly covers cost, then average cost must be equal to price. We know, from our analysis of the supply curve of the firm, that each firm is producing an output for which marginal cost equals price. So the equilibrium of the whole industry occurs where price, marginal cost, and average cost are all equal.

If marginal cost equals average cost, then, as we saw earlier in the chapter, average cost is at a minimum (or a maximum, a possibility we shall for the moment ignore). Hence the equilibrium of the industry has each firm producing at minimum average cost and selling its product for a price that just covers all costs. That implies that the supply curve for

Figure 9-15

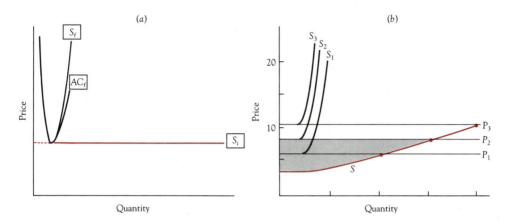

Deducing an industry's supply curve from a firm's supply curve in an industry with open entry. Figure 9-15a shows the case in which the industry's inputs are in perfectly elastic supply; Figure 9-15b shows the case where they are not.

the industry is a horizontal line at price equal to minimum average cost, as shown in Figure 9-15a. Increases in demand increase the number of firms and the quantity of output, with price unaffected. We have described a **constant-cost industry**—one for which the cost of an additional unit of production is independent of quantity.

You may be puzzled by the assertion that new firms come into existence as soon as existing firms start making a profit; surely entrepreneurs require not merely some profit but enough to reimburse them for the time and trouble of starting a new firm. But profit is defined, by economists if not by accountants, as revenue minus cost, where cost *includes* the cost to the entrepreneur of his own time and trouble. Hence if firms are making greater than zero profits, they are more than repaying their owners for the costs of starting them.

There is another way in which the ambiguity in the term profit can lead to confusion here; it is most easily illustrated in the case of a company owned by its stockholders. For accounting purposes, the profit of such a firm is what is left after paying for labor, raw materials, and the interest on money borrowed by the firm; it is what the stockholders get in exchange for their investment. For economic purposes, however, the capital provided by the stockholders must also be considered an input, and its **opportunity cost**—what the stockholders could have gotten by investing the same money elsewhere—is one of the costs of production. The firm makes an **economic profit** only if its profit in the accounting sense is enough to more than just pay the stockholders for the use of their capital—to give them a return greater than the normal market return on the amount they invested in the firm. Such a firm is more attractive than

Chapter 9   The Firm

alternative investments. So if firms in an industry are making positive economic profit, new firms enter that industry, driving the price down to the point where economic profit is again zero.

Two Roads to an Upward-Sloped Supply Curve

The supply curves that I described in Chapters 5 and 7 sloped up; the higher the price, the higher the output. The analysis of this chapter seems to imply a horizontal supply curve, with unlimited output available at one price, as shown in Figure 9-15a. What have we left out?

In discussing the supply curve of an industry with free entry, we have ignored the effect of increases in the size of the industry on the price of its inputs. It is now time to stop doing so. If the output of automobiles increases, so does the demand for steel, auto workers, and Detroit real estate. As the demand for these things increases, their prices rise. As the price of the inputs increases, so does average cost; the result is a rising supply curve. Figure 9-15b shows this; it corresponds to Figure 9-13a of the previous section—for an **increasing-cost industry** instead of a constant-cost industry.

What are the differences between the two situations—a competitive industry with open entry and a competitive industry with closed entry? One, which can be seen by comparing Figure 9-13a to Figure 9-15b, is in the relation between the firm supply curve and the industry supply curve. In Figure 9-15b, the individual firm is always at the bottom of its supply curve—receiving a price equal to average cost and making no economic profit. Increased price causes increased quantity not by sliding the firms up their supply curves but by pulling new firms into the market.

The other difference can be seen if we also look at Figure 9-15a. In the previous section, where we considered an industry with a fixed number of firms, the supply curve sloped up even before we took account of the effect of the industry on the prices of its inputs. In this section, it does not. In that section, the effect of a rising supply curve for the industry's inputs was to make a rising supply curve for its outputs rise more steeply than it otherwise would; in this section, it is to make a flat supply curve for the industry's outputs into a rising one.

In comparing the two sections, it is also worth noting the relevance of the earlier discussion of producer surplus to the situation discussed here. In a competitive industry with free entry, profit is competed down to zero, so the firms receive no producer surplus. But if the industry supply curve slopes up, the industry as a whole must have producer surplus—shown, for a price of P_2, as the shaded area on Figure 9-15b. The explanation is that all of the producer surplus passes through the firms to the suppliers of their inputs. If the suppliers are themselves competitive firms with free entry, it passes through them to their suppliers, until it eventually ends up in the hands of the ultimate suppliers—workers renting out their labor, landowners renting out their land, and so forth. This is a point that will become important in Chapter 14, where I discuss how incomes are determined by ownership of the factors of production—the ultimate inputs.

So far, I have explained upward-sloping supply curves, in the context of a competitive industry with free entry, as a result of upward-sloping supply curves for the industry's inputs. An alternative approach is to assume that some firms have access to "better" means of production than others, giving them better production functions. As the price rises, worse and worse firms are pulled into the market, with higher and higher minimum average costs. The price, at any level of production, must be high enough to cover the costs of the highest cost firm that is producing— the **marginal firm**—otherwise it will not produce. It must not be high enough to cover the costs of the next higher cost firm, the most efficient firm that is *not* producing—otherwise that firm would enter the market too. At a price at which marginal firms cover their costs, firms with lower costs than the marginal firms make net profits, unlike the zero-profit firms of the earlier analysis. Figure 9-16 shows how such a situation can be graphed. At a price P, firm 1, with the lowest cost curves, makes positive profits, shown by the colored area; firm 2 just covers its costs, and firm 3 has not yet come into existence.

These two ways of getting upward-sloping supply curves are really the same. The reason that input costs eventually rise with increasing demand for inputs is that there is not an unlimited supply of identical inputs.

Figure 9-16

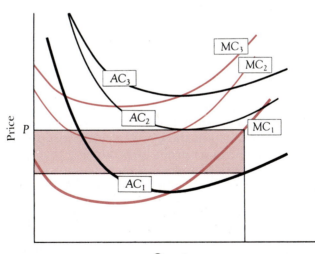

An industry in which different firms have different cost curves. Firm 1, with average cost AC_1 and marginal cost MC_1, is making positive profits. Firm 2 is the marginal firm and makes zero profit. Firm 3 does not exist; it is a potential firm that would come into existence only at a higher price.

There are only so many skilled widget makers willing to work for $8/hour. To get more, you must pay more, inducing those presently employed to work more hours and luring additional workers into the industry. The same applies to land, raw materials, and capital goods. The reason firms do not all have the same cost curves is that some possess inputs that others lack—a particularly skilled manager, an unusually good machine, a favorable location. It is the limited supply of those particular inputs which implies that increased production must use worse machines, less skillful managers, worse locations—or pay more in order to attract high-quality inputs away from wherever they are presently being used.

So long as the scarce inputs actually belong to the firm—consisting, for instance, of the talents of the firm's owner or real estate belonging to a corporation—the distinction between having a better production function and having scarce assets may not be very important. Seen one way, the firm receives positive profits from its operations and turns them over to its owners; seen the other, its profits are zero, but its owners receive income on scarce resources that they rent to the firm. It is a more important distinction when the scarce asset belongs to the firm's landlord or one of its employees; when the relevant contracts are next renegotiated, the firm is likely to find that its positive profit was purely a short-run phenomenon.

Summing It Up

We have spent most of this chapter deriving the supply curve for an industry made up of many firms; the process has been sufficiently lengthy and contained enough complications and detours that you may well have lost track of just how we did it. This is a convenient place to recapitulate.

We start with a production function—a description of what quantity of output could be produced with any bundle of inputs. For any given set of input prices, we then calculate a total cost curve by finding the cost of the least expensive bundle of inputs necessary to produce each level of output. From that total cost curve—total cost of production as a function of quantity produced—we calculate average cost and marginal cost curves. From those we calculate a supply curve for the firm; each firm maximizes its profit by producing that quantity for which marginal cost equals price—unless, at that quantity, price is still below average cost, in which case the firm produces nothing and exits the industry.

Once we have the supply curve for the firm, we are ready to find the supply curve for the industry. If the industry is closed—new firms are not permitted—the supply curve for the industry is simply the horizontal sum of the supply curves of the firms that make it up, with some possible complications due to the effect of the quantity that the industry produces on the price of its inputs. If the industry is open—new firms are free to enter—then in equilibrium profit must be zero, since positive profit attracts firms into the industry, driving down the market price, while negative profit drives firms out, raising the market price. In the simplest case—an unlimited supply of identical firms with horizontal (perfectly elastic) supply curves for their inputs—the result is a horizontal supply curve for the industry's output at a price equal to the minimum average cost of the firm. In the more complicated cases, the result is a rising supply curve. Price is still equal to minimum average cost—or if firms are not identical, it is between the minimum average cost of the highest cost firm that is producing and the minimum average cost of the lowest cost firm that is not.

Industry Equilibrium and Benevolent Dictation

The industry equilibrium we have just described—competitive equilibrium with free entry—has some interesting features. Suppose you were appointed dictator over the industry and told to produce the same output at the lowest possible cost. You would arrange things just as they are arranged in this solution—with each firm producing at minimum average cost.

From your standpoint, controlling the whole industry, there are two marginal costs for increasing output, corresponding to two different margins on which output can increase. One is the margin of the number of firms—output can be increased by having more firms. The cost of the extra units you get by adding an additional firm to the industry is that firm's average cost, so that is the marginal cost to the industry of increasing output on that margin. The other way of increasing output is by having each firm produce one more unit; the cost of those extra units is the firm's marginal cost. Marginal cost is the same on both margins—and must be if goods are being produced at minimum total cost. This is precisely analogous to the argument that showed that the marginal utility per dollar produced by different goods being consumed must be the same if utility is being maximized—it is one more application of the equimarginal principle. I leave the proof as an exercise for you; it is essentially the same as the last two or three times.

Another interesting feature of the competitive equilibrium is that price equals marginal cost; this implies that the price of a widget to a consumer deciding whether to consume one more is equal to the cost of producing it. He will choose to consume it only if it is worth at least that much to him—in which case it is, in some sense, "worth producing." This point will be discussed more precisely and in much more detail in Chapters 15 and 16.

Production and Exploitation

There is a sense in which nothing is produced. The laws of physics tell us that the sum total of mass and energy can be neither increased nor reduced. What we call production is the rearrangement of matter and energy from less useful to more useful (to us) forms.

It is sometimes said that only factories are really productive; middlemen (retailers and wholesalers) merely "move things about" while absorbing some of what others have produced. But all *anyone* does is to move things about—to rearrange from less to more useful. The producer rearranges iron ore and other inputs into automobiles; the retailer rearranges automobiles on a lot into automobiles paired up with particular customers. Both increase the value of what they work on and collect their income out of that increase.

It is often said that some participants in the economy "exploit" others—most commonly that employers exploit workers. This raises the question of what it means to exploit someone. Two different definitions are often used—simultaneously—in such discussions. The first is that I exploit you if I benefit by your existence. In this sense, I hope to exploit my wife and she hopes to exploit me; so far we have both succeeded. If that is what exploitation means, then it is the reason that humans are social animals and not, like cats, solitary ones.

The second definition is that I exploit you if I gain *and you lose* by our association. The connection between the two can be made either by claiming that the world is a "zero-sum game" in which the only way one person can gain is at another person's expense, or by arguing that if I gain by our association you deserve to have the gain given to you, so my refusal to give it to you injures you. The former argument is implausible. The second has a curious asymmetry to it. If I give you all the gain, you have now gained by our association and should obviously give it all back to me. It may be more sensible to keep the term exploitation out of economics and reserve it for political invective.

OPTIONAL SECTION

THE PUZZLE OF THE FIRM

Our analysis so far has shown how individuals coordinate their actions through the price system. This raises the question of why any other method is used. Why do firms exist? Why do we not observe an economy in which all producers are individuals, contracting with each other to buy and sell specific goods and services. Why do we observe instead firms, which buy people's time and then tell them what to do with it? Why is the capitalist beach made up of socialist grains of sand?

The simplest answer is that contracting can be costly. In Chapter 6, I described how bilateral monopoly (one buyer, one seller) can lead to costly bargaining as each party tries to get for himself as much as possible of the difference between the value of the good to the seller and to the buyer. While bilateral monopoly is in one sense rare, it is in another sense ubiquitous.

Consider a professor looking for a new job. There are, we will suppose, 20 universities as well suited to me as UCLA, and 200 economists as suitable for UCLA to employ as I am. Suppose I accept a job at UCLA, move to Southern California, buy a house, and spend a year or two learning to know and work with my colleagues and discovering how to teach UCLA undergraduates (by slipping lecture cassettes into their Sony Walkmen). When I came to UCLA, my salary was (say) $30,000/year. Two years later, I am just as productive as expected and enjoy UCLA exactly as much as I expected to. But a problem arises.

The chairman of the department realizes that if I was willing to come for $30,000, even though I had to pay the costs of moving and adjusting, then I would probably stay even if he reduced my salary to $25,000—after all, there is no way I can get my moving expenses back by leaving. He calls me into his office to discuss the tight state of the department's budget.

I am glad to have a chance to talk to the chairman, for I too have been considering the situation. For my first two years, my productivity was reduced by the need to learn the ropes at my new job. If they were willing to offer me $30,000/year, it was probably because, although I was really worth only $25,000/year for the first two years, they expected me to be worth enough more than $30,000/year thereafter to make up for the initial loss. Now that I have an opportunity to talk to the chairman, I will explain that, after considering the difficulty of the work I am doing, I believe I am entitled to a substantial raise. After all, there is no way he can get back the money he has lost on me during the first two years.

What we have here is a situation that was initially competitive but became a bilateral monopoly (with potential bargaining costs) once the trading parties had made costly adjustments to each other. The obvious solution is long-term contracting. When I come to UCLA, it is with an agreement specifying my salary for some years into the future.

This solution is itself costly—it constrains us even if circumstances change so that the contract *should* be renegotiated. There is no easy way to distinguish renegotiation motivated by a change in circumstances from renegotiation designed to take advantage of the bilateral monopoly created by our adjustments to each other. We could try to make the salary contingent on relevant circumstances (cost of living, university budget, alternative job offers), but there will never be enough small print to cover all of them.

The firm is a particular sort of long-term contract, in which the workers agree to do what they are told (within certain limits) for a stated number of hours a day in exchange for a fixed payment. The central problem of the firm is summed up in the Latin phrase *qui custodes ipsos custodiet*—"Who guards the guardians?" Since the workers receive a fixed wage, their objective is to earn it in the most enjoyable way possible; this is not necessarily the same behavior that maximizes the firm's profits. It is necessary to hire supervisors to watch the workers and make sure they do their job. Who then is to watch the supervisors? Who is to watch him?

One answer is to have the top supervisor be the **residual claimant**—the person who receives the firm's net revenue as his income. He watches the supervisors below him, they watch the ones below them, and so on. The residual claimant does not have to be watched in order to make him act in the interest of the firm—his interest and the firm's interest are the same.

What I have described is a firm run by its owner. This is a common arrangement in our economy. It makes sense in a situation where the worker whom it is most difficult for anyone else to supervise is the top supervisor; since he is the residual claimant, he supervises himself. While it is a common arrangement, it is not a universal one; not all firms are managed by their owners. In some, the worker whom it is most difficult and important to supervise is not the top manager but some skilled worker on whose output the firm depends—an inventor, for instance, with a firm built around him to support his genius (Browning, Ruger, Dolby). It may make sense for him to be the residual claimant—the owner of the firm—and for the top manager to be an employee; that is how such firms are sometimes organized. In other firms, there may be a group of skilled workers who can most easily be supervised by each other. You then get a workers' cooperative, although not necessarily one that includes all of the workers. An example is a law partnership.

There is another common solution to the problem of organizing a firm—a joint stock corporation, owned neither by its managers nor by its workers but by the stockholders who provide much of its capital, and controlled by the managers that those stockholders elect. Considering that solution brings us to some interesting problems—and a historical digression.

Even Homer Nods: Smith and the Corporation

Adam Smith, who in the eighteenth century produced the most influential economics book ever written, argued that corporations were almost hopelessly incompetent. With ownership widely dispersed, everybody's business is nobody's business; the managers can do what they like with the stockholders' money. Smith predicted that corporations would succeed only with government support, except in areas that required large amounts of money and very little skill—such as banking and insurance.

Smith was wrong; even where they have no special support from government (save for the privilege of limited liability)—even when government imposes special taxes on them—corporations have successfully competed with owner-run firms and partnerships in a wide range of fields. His mistake was in failing to predict the benign effects of the take-over bid.

Imagine you know that a corporation is being badly run. You buy as much stock as possible—enough to let you take over the corporation and install competent managers. Earnings shoot up. The market value of your stock shoots up. You sell out and look for another badly managed firm. Such behavior is discouraged by securities regulation and vituperated by existing managements, for obvious reasons. It (and its threat, which helps keep managers honest) may be the reason for the success of the corporation in the modern world.

This raises an interesting idea. The same arguments that show that the corporation cannot work apply with still greater force to democratic government. In a presidential election, the individual voter has one chance in several million of deciding the outcome—so why should he spend valuable time and energy studying the candidates and the issues before he votes? Here again, everybody's business is nobody's business. The result is that most voters do not even know the names of many of the politicians who "represent" them.

Is there a reason why the solution to the problems of the corporation—the take-over bid—does not solve the problems of democratic government? Yes. The difference between the two cases is that your "share" in the United States is not transferable property—which may be why, if casual observation is to be trusted, democratic governments are worse run than most corporations.

Your share in the United States is not transferable property—but perhaps it could be. Imagine that it were. Each citizen owns one citizenship, which includes one vote. You may leave the country and sell your citizenship to someone who wants to live here. If the country is badly run, someone can buy up a vast number of citizenships, elect a competent government, and make a fortune reselling the citizenships at a higher price. The country need not be emptied while the operation is going on; the operator can always rent his citizenships out between the time he buys them and the time he sells them.

PRODUCTION FUNCTION TO COST CURVE VIA CALCULUS

At the beginning of this chapter, I described the production function of a firm producing clay pots and showed how it could be used to find the total cost curve. One problem with the procedure described there was that Table 9-1 showed only a few of the possible bundles of inputs. Looking over the alternative bundles shown on the table to find the least costly way of producing any level of output only guarantees that you end up with the best alternative among those shown; there may be other bundles, not shown on the table, that are even less costly. Another problem is that the table shows bundles for producing only a few of the many possible levels of output.

Both problems can be eliminated if we use calculus instead of trial and error. The production function, which is given at the bottom of Table 9-1, tells us how much output we can produce from any combination of inputs:

$$Q = L^{1/2}(K/100)^{1/4}R^{1/4}. \qquad \text{(Equation 1)}$$

Here Q is the quantity of output (number of pots), L the amount of labor, K the amount of capital, and R the amount of raw material (clay). Since, according to Table 9-1, the price of labor is \$10/hour, the price of capital is .05/year (an interest rate of 5 percent), and the price of clay is \$4/pound, the cost (C) of any bundle of labor, capital, and raw material is:

$$C = 10L + .05K + 4R. \qquad \text{(Equation 2)}$$

Our problem is to find the values of L, K, and R that minimize C for a given Q.

The first step is to use Equation 1 to eliminate one of the variables. Rearranging the equation, we have:

$$R = 100Q^4/L^2K. \qquad \text{(Equation 3)}$$

Substituting that into Equation 2 gives us:

$$C = 10L + .05K + 400Q^4/L^2K. \qquad \text{(Equation 4)}$$

Minimizing Equation 4 by varying K and L while holding Q constant gives us two first-order equations:

$$0 = \partial C/\partial L = 10 - 800Q^4/L^3K$$

and

$$0 = \partial C/\partial K = .05 - 400Q^4/L^2K^2.$$

Solving those, we have:

$$L^3K = 400Q^4/5 = 80Q^4 \qquad \text{(Equation 5)}$$

and

$$L^2K^2 = 40,000Q^4/5 = 8,000Q^4. \qquad \text{(Equation 6)}$$

Taking the square root of Equation 6 gives us:

$$LK = 200Q^2/5^{1/2}. \qquad \text{(Equation 7)}$$

Dividing Equation 5 by Equation 7 gives us:

$$L^2 = 2Q^2/5^{1/2}.$$

Solving for L, we have:

$$L = 2^{1/2}Q/5^{1/4} = .946Q.$$

We can then plug that into Equation 7 and solve for K:

$$K = 20Q \times 2^{1/2}5^{3/4} = 94.6Q.$$

We then find R by plugging K and L into Equation 3; the result is:

$$R = Q(5^{3/4}/2^{3/2}) = 1.182Q.$$

We now have L, K, and R as functions of Q. For any value of Q, they tell us how much of each input is included in the least-cost bundle that can be used to produce that quantity of output; mathematical purists may wish to check the second-order conditions to make sure we have minimized cost instead of maximizing it. Inserting the expressions for L, K, and R into Equation 2 gives us the total cost curve—the cost of producing any quantity of output in the least expensive possible way.

$$TC(Q) = 10(.946Q) + .05(94.6Q) + 4(1.182Q)$$
$$= Q(9.46 + 4.73 + 4.73) = 18.92Q$$

Bundles O, P, Q, and R on Table 9-1 show the results of solving for $Q = 1, 2, 3,$ and 4; Figure 9-1 shows the total cost curve.

Production Functions and Returns to Scale

In analyzing the production of pots, our production function was:

$$Q(L, K, R) = L^{1/2}(K/100)^{1/4}R^{1/4}.$$

This is an example of a type of production function, called a **Cobb-Douglas production function** (after economist Paul Douglas and mathematician Charles Cobb), that is frequently used in economic theory—not because it describes actual firms better than alternative functions but because it has some convenient mathematical properties. The general Cobb-Douglas production function, for inputs X, Y, Z, ... is:

$$Q(X, Y, Z, \ldots) = AX^a Y^b Z^c \ldots \qquad \text{(Equation 8)}$$

Consider a function of this form for which the sum of the exponents equals one; for simplicity I assume only three inputs:

$$a + b + c = 1 \qquad \text{(Equation 9)}$$

We have:

$$Q(kX, kY, kZ) = A(kX)^a(kY)^b(kZ)^c = Ak^{(a+b+c)}X^a Y^b Z^c = kQ(X, Y, Z).$$

Put in words, this tells us that if the exponents sum to 1, then multiplying all inputs by a constant multiplies the output by the same constant. If we use twice as much labor, and steel, and rubber, we produce twice as many automobiles. A further result, which you could check by redoing our analysis of the pottery production function (Equation 1) for the more general case shown in Equations 8 and 9, is that as the amount you want to produce increases, the amount of each input in the optimal production bundle increases proportionally. If using particular quantities of labor, steel, and rubber is the lowest cost way of producing 100 automobiles, then using ten times those quantities is the lowest cost way of producing 1000.

Such a production function exhibits **constant returns to scale**. The corresponding total cost curve is a straight line through the origin; the average and marginal cost curves are horizontal and identical. Average cost is the same however many units you make.

If the exponents of a Cobb-Douglas production function sum to less than 1, doubling all inputs results in less than a doubling of output (**decreasing returns to scale**). If the exponents sum to more than 1, doubling inputs more than doubles outputs (**increasing returns to scale**). In all of these cases, just as in the constant returns to scale case, the ratio of the different inputs in the optimal input bundle stays the same as the scale of output increases. If 10 units of X, 20 units of Y, and 15 units of Z make up the least-cost bundle for producing 100 widgets, then 20 units of X, 40 units of Y, and 30 units of Z is also a least-cost bundle. Whether that bundle produces 200 widgets (constant return to scale), fewer than 200 (decreasing returns to scale) or more than 200 (increasing returns to scale) depends on the sum of the exponents in the production function.

This implies that, for a Cobb-Douglas production function, decreasing returns to scale (if all inputs are increased by the same factor, output increases by a smaller factor) imply **net diseconomies of scale** (the cost of producing a given quantity of ouput, using the least cost bundle, increases with quantity) and increasing returns to scale imply **net economies of scale**. For other production functions that relationship might not be true. One could imagine a case where doubling all inputs resulted in a less than doubling of output, but where doubling expenditure on inputs (and changing the mix of inputs) resulted in a more than doubling of output. Consider, for instance, a situation where one of the costs of production is designing the product; it is not necessary to double the input of designers in order to double the number of units of output.

PROBLEMS

1. My production function for grading finals is:

$$F = L^{1/2}O^{1/2}$$

where F is the number of finals graded, L is my labor, and O the number of hours I must spend at my optometrist's to make up for the damage done to my eyes. My labor grading exams is worth $15/hour, and the optometrist charges $45/hour.
   a. Draw isoquants for $F = 10$, and $F = 40$.
   b. Draw isocost lines for expenditures of $600 and $1200.
   c. Draw my total cost curve from $F = 10$ to $F = 100$. You may use trial and error (a spreadsheet helps), isoquants, or calculus, but you should find at least three points on the total cost curve.
2. Figure 9-17 shows isoquant curves for producing illuminated manuscripts; the inputs are parchment (price $P = 20$) and labor (price $W = 1$).
   a. What is the least cost way of producing 10 manuscripts?
   b. Show, as a table or a graph, how the number of parchments and hours used varies as the number of manuscripts produced goes from 5 to 30.
   c. Manuscripts can be sold for $40 apiece. About how many does the firm produce? How much labor does it hire? How many parchments does it buy?

Figure 9-17

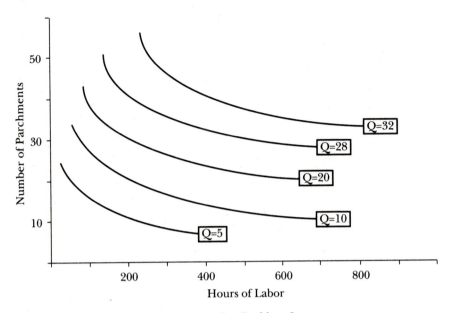

Isoquant curves for a scriptorium.   For Problem 2.

3. Figure 9-18 shows the average and marginal cost curves for a firm. At a price of \$6/widget, about how many widgets will the firm produce?

Figure 9-18

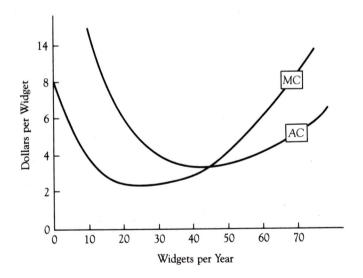

Cost curves for Problems 3 and 4.

Figure 9-19

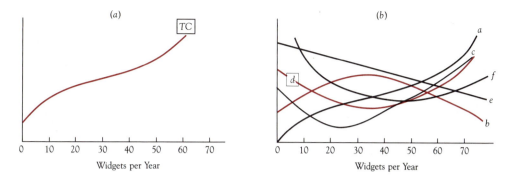

(a)

TC

0 10 20 30 40 50 60 70
Widgets per Year

(b)

a
c
d
f
e
b

0 10 20 30 40 50 60 70
Widgets per Year

Cost curves for Problem 5.

4. If additional firms like this are free to enter the market, what will the price of widgets eventually be?

5. Figure 9-19a shows a total cost curve (total cost of producing widgets as a function of quantity of widgets produced). Which of the curves shown in Figure 9-19b could be the corresponding marginal cost curve? Which could be the corresponding average cost curve? (The vertical axes of the figures are deliberately left unmarked; answering the question does not require that information.)

6. Figure 9-20 shows several pairs of MC and AC curves; which are possible?

7. How does the relation between MC and AC tell you whether AC is at a maximum or a minimum?

8. Demonstrate that the firm always prefers the point where MC intersects P from below to the point where it intersects it from above. What does this imply about the situation where marginal cost crosses average cost at the maximum instead of the minimum of average cost?

9. Figure 9-21 shows the supply curves for three types of potential firms—type 1, type 2, and type 3. Assume there are ten of each type; no additional firms are allowed to enter the market. Draw the industry supply curve. Assume that all of the industry's inputs have horizontal supply curves; the amount purchased does not affect the price.

10. What are the essential differences between the analysis of production in this chapter and of consumption in Chapters 3 and 4?

11. Figure 9-22 shows the supply curve for a pencil firm and the producer surplus that the firm receives if the price at which it can sell pencils is $0.10/pencil. As in several earlier figures, the supply curve is discontinuous; there is no price at which the firm chooses to produce more than zero and fewer than 10,000 pencils per week. The supply curve shows, for any price, the quantity the firm chooses to produce at that price, so in the range of quantity between 0 and 10,000, the supply curve does not exist.

Chapter 9   The Firm

243

Figure 9-20

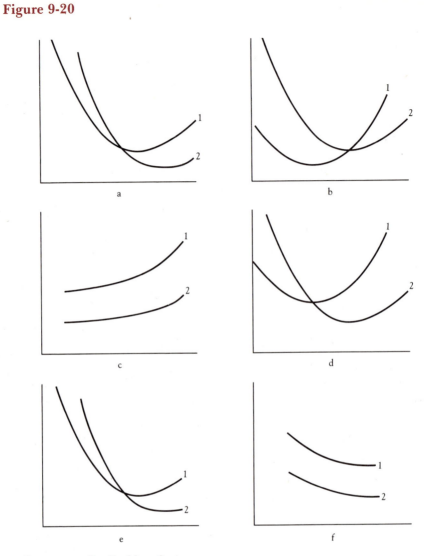

Cost curves for Problem 6.

Producer surplus is the area above the supply curve and below the price. In this case, between 0 and 10,000 pencils per week, there is no supply curve for it to be above. Nonetheless, here and earlier, the region representing producer surplus is drawn as if the supply curve had a horizontal section at the discontinuity—as if, in other words, the dashed line on the figure were really part of the supply curve.

Prove that this is the correct way of calculating producer surplus in this case. (This is a hard question.)

Section III   Complications, or Onward to Reality

Figure 9-21

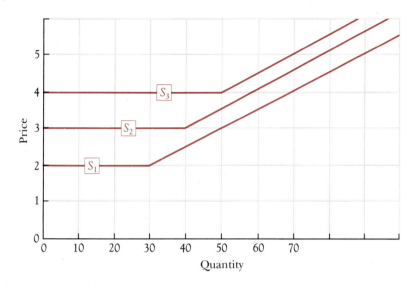

Supply curves for Problem 9.

(Hint: You will want to use both the marginal cost and the average cost curves of the firm in your proof. Second Hint: What is producer surplus at a price of $0.06/pencil? Why?)

Figure 9-22

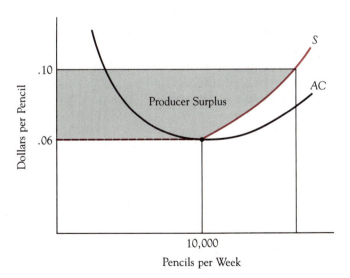

Supply curve and producer surplus for Problem 11.

12. The friends who rent our third floor are enthusiastic gardeners; we are not. The result is that we get free gardening and they get free use of a yard to garden in. Who is exploiting whom, in which sense? What might be a better term to describe the situation?
13. Who or what do cats exploit? In which sense or senses of the word?

The following problems refer to the optional section.

14. The production function is the same as for Table 9-1; the price of labor is $5/hour, the price of capital is .04/year, and the price of clay is $6/pound. Find and graph the total cost curve.
15. Prices are the same as in Problem 14; the production function is:

$$Q = L^{1/3} K^{1/3} R^{1/3}$$

Solve for L, K, R, and TC as functions of Q, for $1 \le Q \le 64$.
16. Your production function is as in Problem 15. You have decided to produce 100 pots; you have already bought 8 pounds of clay, so the only question is how much labor and capital to use. The wage rate is $10/hour, and the interest rate is 10 percent.
    a. Use calculus to find the optimal values of L and K.
    b. Solve the same problem using an isoquant-isocost diagram similar to Figure 9-2.

FOR FURTHER READING

Two interesting and original discussions of some of the questions raised in the optional section of the chapter are: Ronald Coase, "The Nature of the Firm," *Economica*, Vol. 4 (November, 1937), pp. 386–405, and Armen Alchian and Harold Demsetz, "Production, Information Costs, and Economic Organization," *American Economic Review*, Vol. 62 (December, 1972), pp. 777–795.

chapter 10

SMALL-NUMBERS PROBLEMS:
MONOPOLY AND ALL THAT

In everything I have done so far, except for parts of Chapter 6, I assumed that trade involved many individuals or firms on each side. In deciding how much to sell or buy, the effect of the decision on the market price could be ignored, since the amount bought or sold by a single firm or individual would have a negligible effect on the price. While the demand curve faced by an entire industry was downward sloping (the more they sold, the lower the price), the demand curve faced by a single firm was essentially horizontal; similarly the supply curve faced by a single consumer was essentially horizontal even though the market supply curve was rising.

An example may make this clearer. If there were 100 identical firms in an industry, a doubling in the output of any single firm would cause total quantity supplied (by the industry) to increase by only 1 percent. The resulting fall in price would be even less than we would expect from applying a 1 percent increase in quantity to the demand curve, since as price falls, not only does quantity demanded increase, but quantity supplied (by the other 99 firms) also decreases. From the standpoint of the firm, the demand curve is almost perfectly elastic; changes in the quantity of output it produces have almost no effect on the price at which it can sell that output.

A firm in such a situation is sometimes described as a **price taker**. The firm takes the market price as given and assumes it can sell as much as it wants at that price. The firms described in Chapter 9 were price takers. The horizontal line that I drew at price in some of the figures of that chapter may be thought of as a (perfectly elastic) demand curve—the demand curve faced, not by the industry, but by the firm.

Not all industries consist of hundreds of firms. In this chapter and the next we will discuss situations where there are only a few firms in the industry, starting with the simple case of a **monopoly**—a firm that is the only seller of some particular good or service. In Part 1 of this chapter, we consider a monopoly that sells all of its output at the same price—a **single-**

price monopoly. In Part 2, we consider a **discriminating monopoly**—a firm that is able to sell different units of its output at different prices. In Part 3, we discuss the different reasons why monopolies might exist. In Part 4, we expand the discussion to include other small-numbers cases. In Chapter 11 we will go on to discuss strategic behavior and game theory, and to apply what we learn to the difficult problem of analyzing **oligopoly**—a market with several sellers.

PART 1 — SINGLE-PRICE MONOPOLY

We start with a monopoly that finds it must sell all of its output at the same price; the reasons why it must do so will be discussed later, when we consider the problems faced by firms that try to sell at different prices to different customers. Consider the widget firm whose situation is shown in Figure 10-1*a*. *D* is the total demand curve for widgets; since there is only one firm producing widgets, it is also the demand curve faced by that firm. *MC* is its marginal cost curve. The firm is producing at a quantity where $MC = P$, just as Chapter 9 says it should. Quantity is 20 widgets per month; price is $10/widget.

Suppose the firm reduces its output from 20 widgets to 19 widgets per month. Its production cost falls by about $9.50/month (the shaded area). Price rises to $11/widget. Before, its revenue was $200/month; now it is $209/month. Costs are down and revenue up, so its profit must have increased!

How can this be? Did we not prove in the previous chapter that profit was maximized at a quantity where $P = MC$? No. We proved that it was

Figure 10-1

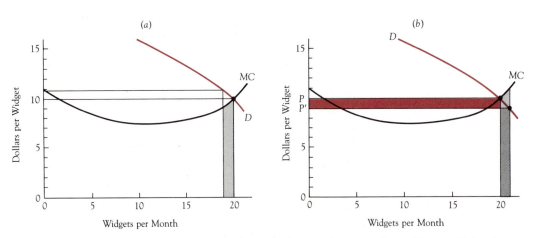

The effect of quantity on revenue and profit for a price searcher. Figure 10-1*a* shows the effect of reducing quantity from 20 to 19; Figure 10-1*b* shows the effect of increasing quantity from 20 to 21. On Figure 10-1*b*, the decrease in revenue is the colored area; the reduction in profit is that plus the lightly shaded area.

maximized at that quantity *for a price-taking firm*—a firm that could ignore the effect of its output on prices. If you go back to the relevant part of Chapter 9, you will see that we always took price as given.

The firm shown in Figure 10-1*a* is not a price taker but a **price searcher**. Rather than taking price as given and deciding how much to produce and sell at that price, it must decide how much to produce, knowing that by doing so it simultaneously determines both price and quantity—the more it produces, the lower the price.

When a price taker increases his output by one unit, he gains or loses according to whether the revenue from the additional unit is more or less than the cost of producing it. The revenue from one unit is the price it sells for, P, and the cost of producing one more unit is MC. So he gains if $P > MC$ and loses if $P < MC$. As long as $P > MC$, his profit increases with each additional unit, so he keeps expanding his output until it reaches a level at which MC is equal to P, as described in Chapter 9.

For a price searcher, the situation is more complicated. When he increases his output by one unit, one of the effects is a small reduction in the market price. Since (by assumption) all widgets are sold at the same price, this means that he gets a little less not only for the additional unit but also for each of the other units he is selling. His profit goes up by the price for which he sells the additional unit (P'), down by the cost of producing that unit (MC), and down by the initial quantity he was selling (Q) times the change in price ($P - P'$). The three terms are all shown on Figure 10-1*b*, for an increase in output from 20 widgets per month to 21. The increase in revenue—P' (times the additional number of units: 1)— is shown darkly shaded. The decrease in revenue, $20(P - P')$, is shown colored. The increased cost is the entire shaded area, light plus dark. The reduction in profit is the sum of the colored and the lightly shaded regions.

Students are often puzzled as to why the firm must reduce its price on the "previous" units just to sell an "additional" unit. The mistake they are making is to think of "previous" and "additional" as referring to an actual sequence of events taking place in the market. They are imagining that the firm first sells 20 units and then sells 1 more; why should the latter event affect the former? But we are describing a firm that is either going to sell 20 units per month for the next ten years or 21 units per month for the next ten years and is trying to decide which alternative will yield higher profits. If it chooses to sell 21 units, it must sell them at a price at which consumers are willing to buy that many—which means a lower price than if it sells only 20. "Previous" and "additional" describe the order in which we think about the alternatives, not the order in which things actually happen.

Marginal Revenue

To find out more exactly what the profit-maximizing quantity is for a single-price monopoly, we introduce a new concept—**marginal revenue**.

Marginal revenue is defined as the increase in revenue per unit of increased quantity for very small changes in quantity, just as marginal cost was defined as the increase in cost per unit of increased quantity for very small changes in quantity. Students familiar with calculus may prefer to think of marginal revenue as the derivative of total revenue with regard to quantity, and marginal cost as the derivative of total cost with regard to quantity—calculus for the same thing.

If quantity is increased by one unit, revenue changes for two reasons. There is an increase in revenue of P' from selling one more unit, and there is a reduction in revenue of $Q(P - P')$. Here P and Q are the price and quantity before the increase, P' the price after. The change in price caused by one additional unit is small compared to the total price—but in calculating the change in profit, the total price is only multiplied by one unit, while the change in price is multiplied by Q units. Figure 10-2a shows the two terms for an increase in output from 20 units to 21 units and shows marginal revenue as a function of quantity over a range of output. The shaded vertical rectangle is the gain from selling the additional unit; the colored horizontal rectangle is the loss from selling the other units at a lower price. Note that marginal revenue is always lower than price—by the lost revenue on the previous units resulting from the fall in price.

To express this with algebra instead of figures, note that the change in price caused by a one-unit increase in quantity is simply $\Delta P/\Delta Q$—the slope of the demand curve. So we have:

$$MR = P + Q(\Delta P/\Delta Q)$$

Figure 10-2

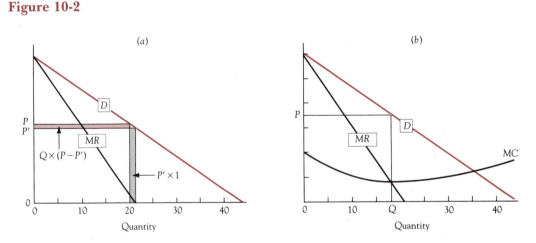

Using marginal revenue to find the profit-maximizing quantity. *MR* is the marginal revenue implied by the demand curve D. Figure 10-2a shows how *MR* could be calculated. Figure 10-2b shows the profit-maximizing quantity (*Q*)—where *MR* = *MC*. *P* is the price at which that quantity will sell.

Section III   Complications, or Onward to Reality

On Figure 10-2a, the demand curve is a straight line. I drew it that way to illustrate a particularly simple way of finding a marginal revenue curve. It so happens that for a straight-line demand curve, marginal revenue is also a straight line, running from the vertical intercept of demand (the price at which quantity demanded is zero) to one half the horizontal intercept (half the quantity that would be demanded at a price of zero) as shown on the figure. This fact is of no significance at all for economics, since there is no reason to expect real-world demand curves to be straight lines, but it is very convenient for solving economics problems. Those of you familiar with calculus should be able to prove the result; it is quite easy. For those unfamiliar with calculus, it is almost the only thing in this book that you will find useful to learn without knowing why it is true; feel free to forget it as soon as the course is over.

Now that we have a marginal revenue curve, maximizing the monopolist's profit is simple. If marginal revenue is higher than marginal cost, he should increase his output—the additional revenue (even allowing for the effect of the fall in price) is greater than the additional cost. If marginal revenue is lower than marginal cost, he should decrease output. If he has the correct (i.e., profit-maximizing) output, marginal revenue will be equal to marginal cost. This solution is shown on Figure 10-2b.

Note that we are solving for quantity and then using the demand curve to find the price at which that quantity will be sold. A mistake students often make in trying to solve this sort of problem is to confuse MR on the graph with P; they find quantity correctly at the intersection of MR and MC but then assume that the height of the point of intersection is the price. It is not; it is the marginal revenue. Price is the height of the demand curve at that quantity. Marginal revenue, marginal cost, and price are all in the same units (money divided by quantity—dollars per pound, for example, or pennies per gram), and they are all functions of quantity, so they can be and are shown as different curves on the same figure—but that does not mean that they are the same thing.

Price Searcher vs. Price Taker

The profit-maximizing rule for a price searcher—produce that quantity for which marginal revenue equals marginal cost—is also the correct rule for a price taker. Since the impact of a change in quantity on price is zero for a price taker (that is why he is a price taker), marginal revenue is equal to price; each additional unit he produces increases his revenue by the price he sells it for. Since for the price taker MR and P are the same, MR = MC and P = MC are for him the same thing. The price taker producing where price equals marginal cost is a special case of the price searcher producing where marginal revenue equals marginal cost.

In our analysis of price-taking firms in Chapter 9, one of our main objectives was to find supply curves—first the supply curve of a firm and then the supply curve of an industry made up of many firms. We cannot do the same thing here. We cannot find the supply curve of a price searcher because a price searcher does not have a supply curve.

A supply curve tells how much a firm or industry will produce as a function of the price it can get for its goods. But the amount a price searcher produces does not depend only on the price it is getting but also on the price it could get at other levels of output. Its output depends not just on a price—the height of the demand curve at one point—but on the shape of the whole demand curve.

To see this, compare Figures 10-3a and 10-3b, which show two different demand curves and the marginal revenue curves they imply. Both figures also show the same marginal cost curve. The market price that the firm chooses to charge is the same in both cases—P—but the quantity is different. This demonstrates that even if we know the cost curves of the firm and the price, we cannot predict the quantity. So the supply curve, which shows quantity supplied as a function of price, does not exist.

In deriving the supply curve of a firm from its cost curves in Chapter 9, the rule "produce a quantity for which $MC = P$" was only the first step. The second step was to observe that if profit was negative at that output, it could be increased by shutting down the firm and going out of business. This implies the additional rule "provided that at that quantity price is at least as high as average cost." That was why the supply curve was equal to the marginal cost curve only at and above its intersection with average cost.

The second rule applies to a monopoly as well; if the price for which the monopoly sells its products is less than its average cost, it would be better off going out of business. While the *marginal* revenue of a price

Figure 10-3

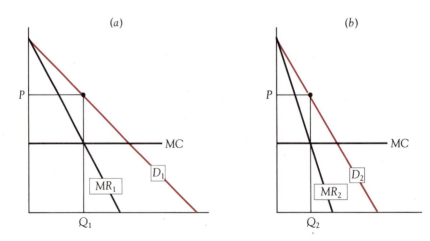

Two different demand curves that imply the same price but different quantities.

searcher is different from that of a price taker, the *average* revenue is the same—price. If you are selling 1,000 apples at $0.50 each, your total revenue is $500 and your average revenue (total divided by quantity) is $0.50/apple—whether or not the amount you produce affects the price. So a different way of stating the rule is "Go out of business if average revenue is less than average cost."

The third step in deriving the supply curve for a price taker took us from the firm to the industry; as long as profit was positive, it would pay other firms to enter the industry. By doing so, they would drive down price and profit. The result was that in equilibrium, profit (revenue minus all costs) was zero.

In the case of a monopoly, the firm and the industry are the same; for one or another of several reasons discussed later in the chapter, no additional firms can enter. The argument for zero profit appears to vanish, leaving us with the possibility of **monopoly profit**—which will be discussed later, after we have looked at the different reasons why a monopoly might exist.

Elasticity or How Flat Is Flat?

In several chapters, especially this one and Chapter 9, I have found it useful to describe curves—supply curves, demand curves, cost curves— as more or less flat. That is not an entirely adequate way of expressing the underlying idea; how flat a curve looks on a graph depends partly on how you choose to draw the vertical and horizontal scales. Figures 10-4*a* and 10-4*b* are graphs of exactly the same demand curve (for water); the difference is that the horizontal axis shows gallons per day in Figure 10-4*a* and gallons per week in Figure 10-4*b*. To check that the graphs are really the same, note that at a price of $0.10/gallon, quantity demanded is

Figure 10-4

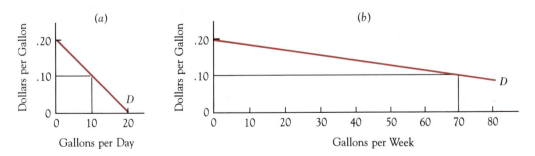

Two views of the same demand curve. Quantity is measured in gallons per day on Figure 10-4*a* and in gallons per week on Figure 10-4*b*. The same demand curve looks much flatter on Figure 10-4*b* than on Figure 10-4*a*.

10 gallons per day (on Figure 10-4*a*) and 70 gallons per week (on Figure 10-4*b*). Yet the demand curve appears much flatter on Figure 10-4*b* than on Figure 10-4*a*. By changing the scale of the horizontal axis we have stretched the curve horizontally, making it look flatter.

The solution to this problem is to replace "flatness" with "elasticity." Elasticity was explained briefly in Chapter 7, but the idea was used there only in a qualitative way; very flat demand and supply curves were described as very elastic, and very steep curves were described as very inelastic. In discussing the behavior of a monopoly, we will require a somewhat more precise understanding of elasticity—as a quantitative, and not merely a qualitative, concept.

The elasticity of a demand (or supply) curve at some quantity Q (remember that how flat a curve is may depend where on it you are) is defined as the percentage change of quantity divided by the percentage change of price, calculated for a very small change in price. For those familiar with calculus, it is $dQ/dP \times P/Q$. The rest of you may think of it as the percentage change in quantity resulting from a 1 percent change in price, or as P/Q divided by the slope of the curve. Some economists include a minus sign in the definition of demand elasticity so as to make both supply and demand elasticity positive numbers (quantity demanded *decreases* when price increases, so the percentage change in quantity is negative); I will follow that convention.

A highly elastic curve is one for which quantity changes a lot when price changes a little, whether the change is an increase or a decrease. A demand curve for which a price increase from $1.00 to $1.01 resulted in a decrease in quantity demanded from 100 widgets to 50 would be highly elastic; one for which a doubling of price caused only a 1 percent decrease in quantity demanded would be highly inelastic. One way of remembering this is to think about how much quantity demanded (or supplied) "stretches" when price changes—if the curve is very elastic, it stretches a lot. A **unit elastic curve** is one for which a 1 percent change in price results in a 1 percent change in quantity—elasticity equals 1. A curve is called **elastic** if its elasticity is more than that and **inelastic** if it is less. The elasticity of a curve typically varies along its length, so a supply curve may be elastic for one range of quantities, inelastic for another, and unit elastic at the point between the two ranges.

How flat a curve appears depends on how you draw it—changing the x axis from gallons per day to gallons per week flattens the curve considerably. This is not true of elasticity; if you change the units used to measure quantity by a factor of seven—as you do in going from gallons per day to gallons per week—both the quantity and the change in quantity are affected, but their ratio—the percentage change in quantity—remains the same. If a price drop of 1 percent causes you to increase your consumption of water by 10 percent, it does so whether consumption is measured in gallons per day or gallons per week. Elasticity is discussed further in the optional section of this chapter, where I show how to calculate it for various sorts of curves.

The concept of elasticity is useful in analyzing the behavior of a single-price monopoly. If elasticity is 1.0 at some point on a demand curve, that means that a 1 percent increase in price causes a 1 percent decrease in quantity. Since revenue is price times quantity, that means that where the demand curve is unit elastic a small change in price or quantity has no effect on revenue. The effect on revenue of an increase in price is just balanced by the effect of the resulting decrease in quantity, so marginal revenue is zero. A similar argument shows that where elasticity is greater than 1.0 (the elastic region of the demand curve), marginal revenue is positive; where elasticity is less than 1.0, it is negative. More generally, if we call the price elasticity of demand $e_p \equiv -(\Delta Q/Q)/(\Delta P/P)$, we have:

$$MR = P + Q(\Delta P/\Delta Q) = P + P(\Delta P/P)/(\Delta Q/Q) = P(1 + (\Delta P/P)/(\Delta Q/Q) = P(1 - 1/e_p)$$

The implications of this result for the relation between the elasticity of a demand curve and the behavior of a monopoly will be left as an exercise for the reader—in the form of problems at the end of this chapter.

PART 2 — DISCRIMINATORY PRICING

So far, we have assumed that the monopolist sells all of his output at the same price. To see why he might prefer not to do so, we start with the simple case of a monopolist with 1,000 customers, all identical. We can represent the total demand curve by the demand curve of a single individual, remembering that for the total, all quantities are 1,000 times larger. Figure 10-5 shows such a demand curve. The firm, following the prescription of Part 1, sells the customer 6 cookies per week at a price of $0.70/cookie. At that quantity marginal revenue equals marginal cost; for simplicity I have made marginal cost constant.

Looking at the figure, we—and the president of the cookie company— make the following observation. Additional cookies cost $0.40 each to make. Up to a quantity of 12 cookies per week, additional cookies are worth more than $0.40 each to the customer. (Remember that a demand curve for an individual is also his marginal value curve.) It seems a pity to lose those additional sales—and the money that could be made on them.

As long as the firm must sell all cookies at the same price, there is no solution to this dilemma; in order to sell the customer more cookies, the firm must lower its price, and that would decrease, not increase, its profit. The cookie president gets an idea.

As a special favor to our customers, and in order to celebrate the tricentennial of the invention of the cookie, we are cutting our prices. For the first six cookies per week purchased by each customer, the old price of $0.70 remains in effect, but additional cookies may be purchased for only $0.50 each.

Chapter 10   Small-Numbers Problems: Monopoly and All That   **255**

Figure 10-5

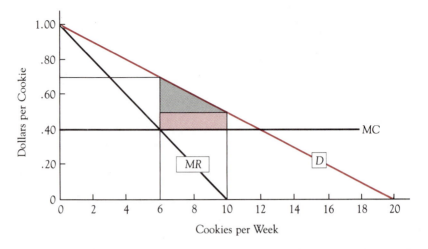

Discriminatory pricing in the cookie industry—first try. The profit-maximizing single price is $0.70/cookie. The firm charges each customer that price for the first 6 cookies but sells additional cookies for $0.50/cookie, increasing its profit by the colored area.

The result is shown on the figure. Each customer buys 10 cookies: 6 at $0.70 each and 4 more at the reduced price of $0.50. The customers are better off than before by the additional consumer surplus on the extra cookies (the gray area); the cookie company is better off by the profit on the additional cookies (the colored area). Since the additional 4 cookies cost $0.40 each to produce and are sold for $0.50, profit has increased by $0.40/customer/week (4 cookies × $0.10/cookie). With 1,000 customers, that comes to an additional $20,800/year. The cookie president has reason to be proud of himself.

That is no reason to rest on his laurels. Figure 10-6a shows the more elaborate price schedule released for the next year. The first 6 cookies per week are still sold for $0.70 each, but the rest are now on a sliding scale—$0.65 for the seventh cookie, $0.60 for the eighth, $0.55 for the ninth, $0.50 for the tenth, $0.45 for the eleventh, and $0.40 for the twelfth cookie. The increased profit (compared with the original single-price scheme) is again the colored area on the figure; as you can see, it has grown.

At this point, the cookie president's daughter, who took this course last year and has just joined the firm, enters the discussion. "Why," she asks, "should our customers get so much out of our business? We are the ones doing all the work, yet they end up with a large surplus—the gray area of Figure 10-6a. I don't mind losing the six little triangles—after all, they are entitled to a few crumbs—but surely we can do something about

Figure 10-6

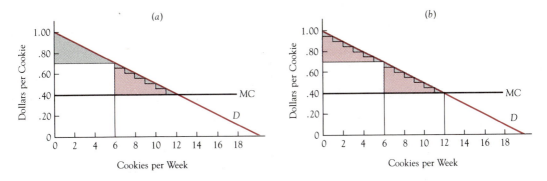

(a) / *(b)*

Discriminatory pricing in the cookie industry—improved versions. On Figure 10-6*a*, cookies are sold on a sliding scale starting at $0.70/cookie. On Figure 10-6*b*, the price starts at $0.95/cookie and is $0.05 less for each additional cookie.

the big one." Figure 10-6*b* shows the pricing scheme she comes up with for the next year.

Figure 10-6*b* is very close to **perfect discriminatory pricing**—a price schedule that transfers all of the consumer surplus to the producer. Its imperfection—the "crumbs" referred to in the previous paragraph—comes from the problem of describing a discontinuous variable (3 cookies or 4 cookies but never 3.141532 cookies) with concepts, such as marginal value, more suited to continuous variables (water—or wine). It is possible, by setting the price schedule perfectly, to use such a set of prices to end up with all the surplus, crumbs included.

Two-Part Pricing

There is an easier way to do the same thing. The next year, the company announces a new and much simpler pricing policy. Cookies will no longer be sold to the general public—only to members of the cookie club. Members can buy cookies at cost—$0.40/cookie—and may buy as many as they wish at that price. The membership fee is $3.60/week. That, by a curious coincidence, is the total consumer surplus received by a consumer who is free to buy as many cookies as he wants at a price of $0.40/cookie. This *two-part price* (membership plus per-cookie charge) first maximizes the sum of consumer and producer surplus (by inducing the consumer to buy every cookie that is worth at least as much to him as it costs to produce) then transfers the entire consumer surplus to the producer.

Before I go on to more complicated cases, let us look a little more carefully at the result so far. The firm maximizes its profit by charging a price equal to marginal cost and an additional membership fee equal to the entire consumer surplus. The effect of selling at *MC* is to maximize the sum of consumer and producer surplus; Figures 10-7*a* through 10-7*c* show that the sum for a price higher than *MC* (Figure 10-7*a*) or

Figure 10-7

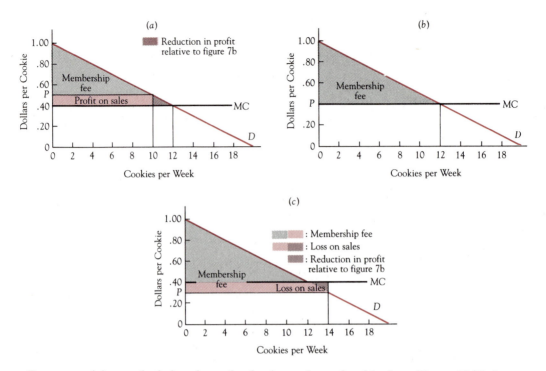

Two-part-pricing—calculating the optimal price and membership fee. Figure 10-7*b* shows the pattern that maximizes the firm's profits; the price per cookie is equal to marginal cost, and the membership fee is equal to the consumer surplus at that price. Figures 10-7*a* and 10-7*c* show that a higher or lower price results in less profit.

lower than *MC* (Figure 10-7*c*) is lower than for a price equal to *MC* (Figure 10-7*b*). Note that the colored area in Figure 10-7*c* is a loss resulting from selling below cost; it is larger than the increase in the lightly shaded area (membership fee) resulting from the lower price. The overall effect of reducing price below marginal cost is to reduce the firm's profits by the difference—the darkly shaded (and colored) triangle.

The conclusion can be simply stated. The effect of the entrance fee is to transfer the consumer surplus to the producer, giving him the sum of both surpluses—which he maximizes by setting price equal to marginal cost. If you think this sounds familiar, you are right. It is the same argument that was used at the end of Chapter 4 to show why movie theaters should sell popcorn at cost. For more on that subject, stay tuned. It is also the pattern of pricing often used by sellers of telephone services, electricity, and a variety of other goods and services.

So far, we have assumed that all customers are identical; under those circumstances, the seller may achieve something quite close to perfect discriminatory pricing, although there are some difficulties which we shall discuss later. I shall now complicate the problem by assuming that there are two different kinds of customer with different demand curves. Type A customers have demand curve D_A on Figure 10-8, which is the same as the demand curve shown on Figures 10-5 through 10-7c; type B customers have demand curve D_B. There are 500 customers of each type.

The cookie president and his daughter have a problem. If they continue their previous two-part pricing system ($0.40/cookie plus $3.60/week), customers of type A will continue to join the club and buy the cookies, but customers of type B, for whom the consumer surplus at $0.40/cookie is only $2.40/week, will find that the cookie club costs more than it is worth and refuse to join. If, on the other hand, the membership fee is reduced to $2.40/week (the consumer surplus for type B consumers), the cookie company will lose $1.20/week that it could have gotten from the type A customers at the higher price.

The revenue from selling cookies just covers the cost of producing them (since the per-cookie price is just equal to marginal cost), so whatever membership price the firm decides to charge, profit will be equal to the revenue from selling membership in the cookie club. At the higher price, that is $3.60 from each of 500 type A customers; at the lower price, it is $2.40 from each of 1,000 customers (both type A and type B). Profit is maximized by charging the lower price—while regretting the consumer surplus left, unavoidably, in the hands of the type A customers.

There are two ways in which the cookie president can try to improve on this result. One, which we will discuss later in this section, is to some-

Figure 10-8

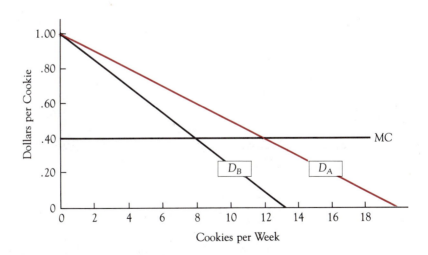

The case of nonidentical customers. D_A is the demand curve for type A customers; D_B is the demand curve for type B customers.

how figure out which customers are of which type and charge a higher membership fee to the type A customers—or rather, raise the membership fee to $3.60 and offer a "special discount membership" to the type B customers. The other is to raise the per-cookie price.

The reason he might raise the price can be explained verbally as follows: "At any price, type A customers eat more cookies. Hence raising the price is an indirect way of charging them more than the type B customers. The total surplus is reduced, for the reasons shown in Figures 10-7a through 10-7c, but since I am no longer receiving the total surplus, that is no longer a conclusive argument against raising price. The increase in my share of the surplus may outweigh the reduction in the total."

- The argument can be made more precisely with the use of graphs. I will limit myself to showing that there is a combination of higher price per cookie and lower membership fee that results in a higher profit in this particular case; this is shown on Figures 10-9a and 10-9b. Our previous solution (membership of $2.40) gave a profit of $2,400/week. The new solution is a price of $0.50/cookie and a membership fee of $1.667. Revenue on memberships totals $1,667; profits on cookie sales ($0.10/cookie times number sold) are $1/week on each type A customer and $0.667/week on each type B customer. Total profit is $2,500/week— $100 more than with the previous solution.

This example demonstrates that in at least one case—the one I have just described—a monopoly can increase its profits by selling its product for more than marginal cost, even though it is in a position to charge a two-part price. The example does not demonstrate that it always, or even usually, pays a monopoly to do so. Alfred Marshall, who put together

Figure 10-9

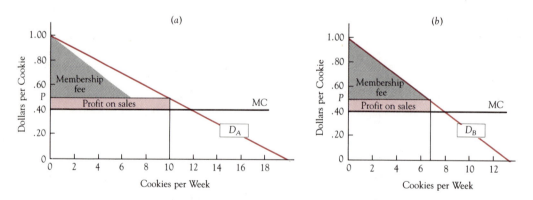

Price above marginal cost as a device for discriminatory pricing. The firm is charging a price higher than *MC* as an indirect way of charging more to type A customers (Figure 10-9a) than to type B customers (Figure 10-9b). The resulting profit is higher than with *P* = *MC*.

modern economics about 100 years ago, warned in an appendix to his *Principles of Economics* of the danger of deducing general principles from specific examples; it is always possible that in choosing the particular example you may, without realizing it, assume away one of the essential elements of the general problem. One should therefore, Marshall argued, base one's final conclusions not on examples but on proved theorems.

We have finally found a possible solution to the popcorn puzzle. (I only kept you in suspense for eight chapters.) In my previous discussions, I assumed that the theater customers were all identical; if that assumption holds, so does the conclusion—that the theater should sell popcorn at marginal cost and make its profit on admission tickets. But if customers are not identical and if those who are willing to pay a high price for a ticket tend to be the same ones who buy a lot of popcorn, then the combination of cheap tickets and expensive popcorn may be an indirect way of charging a high admission price to those who are willing to pay it without driving away those who are not.

Market Segmentation and Discriminatory Pricing

So far, most of the discriminatory pricing we have discussed was designed to charge different prices to the same person for different units consumed, thus taking advantage of the fact that the consumer has a higher marginal value for the first few units and will, if necessary, pay a higher price for them. This was done either by charging different prices for different units or by charging a two-part price—one price to buy anything and another for each unit bought. Only at the end of the previous section did we discuss attempts to discriminate between different customers, in the context either of a monopolist who knows exactly who has what demand curve and prices accordingly or one who uses a per-unit price higher than marginal cost as an indirect way of discriminating between high-demand and low-demand customers.

An alternative approach for the cookie company—or any monopolist selling to a diverse group of customers—is to try to find some indirect way of distinguishing between customers who are and are not willing to pay a high price. Discriminatory pricing of this sort is very common—so much so that some of us have gotten into the habit, whenever we see a pattern of behavior on the marketplace that does not seem to make sense, of trying to explain it in terms of price discrimination.

One familiar example is the policy of charging less for children than for adults at movie theaters. A child takes up just as much space as an adult—one seat—and may well impose higher costs, in noise and mess, on the theater and the other patrons. Why then do theaters often charge lower prices for children? The obvious answer is that children are (usually) poorer than adults; a price the theater can get adults to pay is likely to discourage children from coming—or parents with several children from bringing them.

A similar example is the youth fare that airlines used to offer. It was a low fare for a standby ticket, offered only to those under a certain age. The lower fare reflected in part the advantage to the airlines of using standby passengers to fill empty seats, but that does not explain the age limit. The obvious answer is that making the fare available to everyone might have resulted in a substantial number of customers "trading down"—buying a cheap standby ticket instead of an expensive regular one. Presumably the airlines thought that making it available to youths would result in their buying a cheap standby ticket on an airplane instead of taking the bus, driving, or hitching.

The same analysis that explains low fares for youths also explains special discounts for old people; they too are (often) poor. It also explains large price differences between "high-quality" and "low-quality" versions of the same product—hardcover books and paperbacks, first-class seats and tourist-class seats, and so on. The difference may merely reflect a difference in production cost—or it may be a device to extract as much consumer surplus as possible from those customers who are willing, if necessary, to pay a high price and are likely to prefer the luxury version of the product.

Another example of discriminatory pricing is the Book of the Month Club. A publisher who gives a special rate to a book club is getting customers most of whom would not otherwise have bought the book; since most of those who are willing to buy the book at the regular rate are not members of the club, he is only stealing a few sales from himself. Discount coupons and trading stamps in grocery stores may be another example. Customers with a high value for their own time do not bother with such things—and pay a higher price.

A firm engaged in this sort of discriminatory pricing faces two practical problems. The first is the problem of distinguishing customers who will buy the good at a high price from those who will not. In the examples I have given, that is done indirectly—by age, taste, membership in a discount book club, or the like. A more elegant solution is said to be used by optometrists. When the customer asks how much a new pair of glasses will cost, the optometrist replies, "Forty dollars." If the customer does not flinch, he adds "for the lenses." If the customer still does not flinch, he adds, "each." I use a similar technique in selling my services as a public speaker.

The second problem is preventing resale. It does no good to offer your product at a low price to poor customers if they then turn around and resell it to rich ones, thus depriving you of high-price sales. This is why discriminatory pricing is so often observed with regard to goods that are consumed on the premises—transportation, movies, speeches, and the like. If GM sells cars at a high price to rich customers and at a low price to poor ones, Rockefeller can send his chauffeur to buy a car for him. There is little point in having the chauffeur take a trip for Rockefeller or see a movie for him.

The problem of controlling resale also exists with the form of discriminatory pricing discussed earlier in the context of identical customers—discriminating between what the customer is willing to pay for his first cookie and what he is willing to pay for his tenth. The problem occurs when a cookie club member buys 48 cookies per week, eats 12, and sells 36 to friends who have not paid for membership in the cookie club. That is why two-part (or more generally multipart) pricing is more practical with electricity or health spa services than with cookies.

The ability of a firm to engage in successful discriminatory pricing also depends on its being a price searcher—having some degree of what is sometimes called monopoly power. In a market with many firms producing virtually identical products, price discrimination is impractical; if one firm tries to sell the product at an especially high price to rich customers (or customers who very much want the product), another firm will find it in its interest to lure those customers away with a lower price. Airlines do not wish to have their own customers trade down to a cheaper ticket—but Delta has no objection to getting a customer to give up a first-class ticket on Pan Am in order to buy a tourist ticket on Delta.

All of the cases I have described involve some element of monopoly. Youth fares existed at a time when airline fares were controlled by the Civil Aeronautics Board (CAB), a regulatory agency that provided government enforcement for a private cartel, keeping rates up and new firms out; they have since disappeared along with airline regulation. Copyright laws (and the economics of publishing) give each book publisher a monopoly—not of books, or even of a particular type of book, but at least of a particular book. The result is that publishers are price searchers; each knows that some customers are willing, if necessary, to pay a high price, while others will only buy the book if they can get it at a low price. Movie theaters have an element of monopoly, at least in areas where they are scarce enough that a customer cannot conveniently pick among several showing the same film.

This brings me to the question of why monopolies exist—which is the subject of the next part of the chapter.

PART 3 — WHY MONOPOLIES EXIST

Why do monopolies exist? Under what circumstances will there be only one firm in an industry? Why, if revenue is greater than cost, do not other firms choose to start producing the same product?

One answer may be that if they do, the monopolist will call the police. The original meaning of monopoly was a government grant of the exclusive right to sell something. Typically such monopolies were either sold by the government as a way of raising money or given to people the government liked, such as the king's mistresses (or their relatives). Monopolies of this sort are still common. One obvious example is the Post Office—a monopoly that is not only protected by the government (the Private

Express Statutes make competition illegal) but also run and subsidized by it.

A second possibility is a **natural monopoly**. This occurs when the shape of the firm's cost curve is such that a firm large enough to produce the total output of the industry can do so at a lower cost than could several smaller firms. Figure 10-10a shows an example of such a cost curve. A firm producing q_1 at price P has positive profits (price is greater than average cost), but a firm producing $q_2 = q_1/2$ at the same price does not. If one large firm is formed and sells at P, smaller firms will not find it worth their while to enter the market.

Another case very similar to the natural monopoly is the natural cartel. A **cartel** is a group of firms acting together as if they were a single monopoly. Cartels are most likely to occur in industries where **economies of scale** (advantages that allow large firms to produce more cheaply than small ones) are not quite sufficient to allow one giant firm to produce more cheaply than several large ones; such an industry is likely to consist of a few large firms. Figure 10-10b shows the sort of cost curves that might lead to a cartel; what is important is not simply the shape of the cost curves but their relation to the market demand curve—the fact that minimum average cost occurs at a quantity that is a large fraction of the quantity demanded at a price equal to minimum average cost. This guarantees that any firm producing less than (in this example) about one third of the industry's total production will have higher average costs than larger firms and so be at a competitive disadvantage.

As long as the firms in a cartel cooperate with each other, the cartel functions like a natural monopoly. Some of the difficulties in maintaining such cooperation will be discussed in Chapter 11. One common solution is a government-enforced cartel, such as the U.S. airline industry prior to deregulation or the U.S. rail industry from the end of the nineteenth century to the present.

Figure 10-10

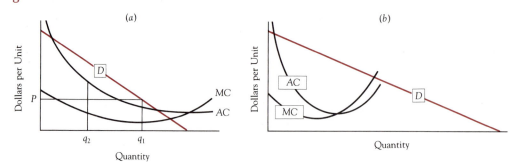

Cost curves for a natural monopoly (a) or natural cartel (b). Figure 10-10a shows cost curves for which a large firm producing the entire amount demanded has a cost advantage over smaller firms. Figure 10-10b shows the case where a firm large enough to produce a large fraction of total industry output has lower costs than smaller firms.

Section III   Complications, or Onward to Reality

Most people who think about natural monopolies imagine them as gigantic firms such as Bell Telephone or GM. It is widely believed that such firms, by taking advantage of mass production techniques, can produce more cheaply than any smaller firm; it has often been argued that, for this reason, free competition naturally leads to monopoly. As George Orwell put it, "The trouble with competitions is that somebody wins them."

This does not seem to be a correct description of the real world, at least at present. While there are advantages to mass production, in most industries a firm need not produce the entire world's output in order to take advantage of them. The steel industry, for example, produces in very large plants, but the largest firm (U.S. Steel) consists not of one gigantic steel mill but of over 100 large ones. A firm 1 percent of its size can operate one steel mill and take advantage of the same scale economies. The president of such a firm is closer to the worker pouring the steel by several layers of administration than is the president of U.S. Steel, which may be one reason that U.S. Steel has not, in recent decades, been one of the more successful firms in the industry.

Bell Telephone was until recently a government-enforced monopoly—it was illegal for another firm to try to compete by offering local phone service in an area served by Bell, or for Bell to compete in an area served by General Telephone or one of the smaller companies. GM is not a monopoly even within the United States, and such limited monopoly power as it does have in the U.S. market is largely a result of tariffs that restrict the ability of foreign auto producers to compete with it.

I am a more typical example of a natural monopoly than is GM. As a public speaker, I produce a product that is, I believe, significantly different from that produced by anyone else; if you want a certain sort of talk on certain sorts of subjects, you must buy it from me. The result is that I am a price searcher. Some groups are willing to pay a high price for my services, some a lower price; some would like me to speak but can offer nothing but expenses and dinner. If I sell my speeches at a fixed price, I must either price some of the customers out of the market (even though I might enjoy speaking to them, and so be willing to do so for free—at some levels of output, my marginal cost is negative) or else accept low fees from some groups that are willing to pay high ones. In fact, I engage in a considerable amount of discriminatory pricing, offering free or low-cost speeches to especially worthy (i.e., poor) groups. The same is true of my services as a writer; I have one outlet that pays a very high rate, but I recently wrote a column on something that interested me for a new magazine that paid nothing.

My monopoly over the production of certain kinds of speeches and articles is a far more common sort of natural monopoly than that of Bell or GM; it is due not to the huge scale of production but to the specialized nature of the product. Examples of similar monopolies would be the only grocery store in a small town or your favorite thriller writer. It is not only a more common sort of monopoly, it is also one much more important to those of you who expect to be in business. It is unlikely that you will ever be the head of GM or U.S. Steel, and if you are, you may find that the monopoly power of those firms is very limited. It is much more likely that you will find yourself selling a specialized product in a particular geographical area, and so functioning as a price searcher facing a downward-sloped demand curve. It is even more likely that some of the firms you deal with will be in such a position. If so, the analysis of this chapter should help you understand why they sell their product in the way they do.

Artificial Monopoly

There is one more sort of monopoly worth discussing—the **artificial monopoly**. An artificial monopoly is a very large firm that has no advantage in production efficiency over smaller firms but nonetheless manages to drive all of its competitors out of business, remaining the sole producer in the industry. A typical example is the Standard Oil Trust—not the real Standard Oil Trust as it actually existed in the late nineteenth and early twentieth centuries but the Standard Oil Trust as it appears in many high school history books. In the optional section, I discuss that case along with the general problem of maintaining a monopoly position without either a natural monopoly or a government grant of monopoly power. My conclusion there is that the artificial monopoly is largely or entirely a work of fiction; it exists in history books and antitrust law but is and always has been rare or nonexistent in the real world, possibly because most of the tactics it is supposed to use to maintain its monopoly position do not work.

Monopoly Profit

One important difference between an industry consisting of many firms and an industry consisting of one was mentioned earlier; in the former case, the equilibrium price is such as to make economic profit zero, since positive profits attract new firms and their output drives down the price. This is not the case for a monopoly industry. If it is a government-granted monopoly, new firms are forbidden by law; if it is a natural monopoly, there is only room for one firm.

The result is monopoly profit. If the government simply sells the right to be a monopoly to the highest bidder, the price should equal the full monopoly profit that the winner expects to make; if he had bid less, someone else would have outbid him. In this case, the monopoly firm makes no net profit, since its costs include what it paid to become a monopoly. What would have been monopoly profit all goes to the government. If instead of selling the monopoly privilege, the government gives it away, then the firm receives the monopoly profit—unless "giving away" really means selling for something other than money paid to the government. Examples might be the attentions of the king's mistress (old style) or discreet contributions to the reelection fund of the incumbent president (new style).

In the case of a natural monopoly, the situation is more complicated. Since the monopoly is not created by the government, there is no reason to expect the government to control who is the monopolist. Once a firm has the monopoly, it may be able to earn substantial monopoly profits without attracting competitors. A competitor would have to duplicate the initial firm's productive facilities, making the industry's capacity twice what it could sell at the price the existing monopoly was charging; the resulting price war might well hurt both firms, a possibility that may persuade the second firm not to try to enter the market.

This raises the question of how the first firm got its monopoly position in the first place. That question is discussed in Chapter 16, where it is shown that under at least some circumstances, the zero-profit condition does apply to natural monopolies, with the monopoly profit being competed away in the process of obtaining it.

PART 4 — OTHER FORMS OF PRICE SEARCHING

So far we have considered only one kind of price searcher—a monopoly, the only seller of a good or service. Our next step is to consider its mirror image. Having done so, we will go on to briefly discuss some harder cases.

Monopsony

I began this chapter by dropping the assumption that individuals can sell and buy as much as they like without affecting the price. So far, I have discussed monopolies—individuals and firms that are the only sellers of some good or service. An individual or firm that is the only buyer of a good or service is called a **monopsony**. An example might be the one large employer in a small town (a monopsony buyer of labor) or the DeBeers diamond cartel (a monopsony buyer of rough diamonds).

Just as a monopoly must consider how much its revenue from selling widgets increases when it sells one more widget, so a monopsony must consider how much its expenditure for widgets increases when it buys one more widget. A monopoly's marginal revenue is less than the price it sells its goods for because, in order to sell more, it must lower its price. A monopsony's **marginal expenditure** is more than the price it pays for each widget, because by buying more it bids up the price—not only for the additional widget but for all other widgets it buys.

A firm that buys its inputs in a competitive market buys that quantity for which price equals marginal revenue product, as we saw in Chapter 9. At any other quantity it could increase its profit by buying more (if $MRP > P$) or less (if $MRP < P$). A monopsony, by exactly the same argument, buys that quantity for which marginal expenditure equals marginal revenue product. Since marginal expenditure for a monopsony is higher than price, it will generally use less of the input of which it has a monopsony than if it were a price taker.

The monopsony's behavior is exactly analogous to that of a monopoly. The monopoly sells the quantity for which marginal revenue equals marginal cost, and thus sells less than if it were selling in a competitive market. The monopsony buys the quantity for which marginal expenditure equals marginal revenue product, and thus buys less than if it were buying in a competitive market. If you convert the monopoly into a competitor, its marginal revenue becomes equal to the price at which it sells its goods and we are back with $P = MC$ as in Chapter 9. If you convert the monopsony into a competitor, its marginal expenditure becomes the price for which it buys its input, and we are again back in Chapter 9 with $P = MRP$.

Figure 10-11 shows the result graphically. S is the supply curve for a good whose only purchaser is a monopsony. ME is the monopsony's marginal expenditure—the amount by which its expenditure on the input increases if it buys one more unit. The monopsony buys a quantity Q_m

Figure 10-11

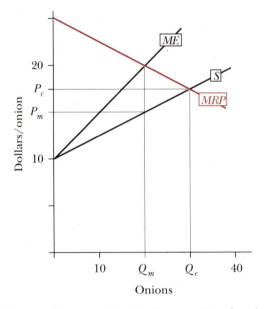

Using marginal expenditure to calculate the quantity of an input purchased by a monopsony. The monopsony, which uses onions as an input, purchases the quantity (Q_m) for which marginal expenditure on onions equals the marginal revenue product of onions. The price of onions is P_m, the price at which that quantity is supplied by onion producers, as shown by the supply curve S. An industry of competitive firms would have purchased Q_c at price P_c.

Section III Complications, or Onward to Reality

for which $ME = MRP$. If it behaved like a firm buying in a competitive market it would instead buy Q_c, the quantity where MRP crosses S and is thus equal to the price.

The Hard Problems

A market can have any number of buyers and any number of sellers. Most of my analysis so far has concentrated on the case of many buyers and many sellers; in this chapter, I have considered the cases of one seller and many buyers (monopoly) and one buyer and many sellers (monopsony). These are the easy cases, the ones for which economics gives relatively simple and straightforward solutions. The hard problems are the cases of oligopoly (several sellers and many buyers); oligopsony (several buyers and many sellers); bilateral monopoly (one buyer, one seller); bilateral oligopoly (several sellers, several buyers); one seller, several buyers (no name I know of); and one buyer, several sellers (ditto).

What all of these hard cases have in common is strategic behavior. In all of the analysis so far, except for the discussion of bilateral monopoly in Chapter 6, the individual or firm could decide what to do while taking what everyone else was doing as given. That is appropriate in a price taker's market; since my output is a negligible part of total output, it is not in the interest of any of my customers to say to me, "I want what you are selling at the price you are asking for it, but I will refuse to buy it, in order to force you to lower the price." If he tries that, I will sell it to someone else instead. It is also appropriate in the monopoly situation I have been discussing in this chapter, where there is one seller and many buyers—although selling my speeches, with one seller and a few buyers, approaches the case of bilateral monopoly.

But the assumption that we can ignore bargaining, strategic behavior, and the like is inappropriate in all of the hard cases. If there are several sellers and many buyers, everything a seller wants to know about the buyers' behavior is summed up in the demand curve, but a seller cannot use a supply curve to describe the behavior of the other sellers, since they do not have supply curves. Each has an incentive to try to persuade the others to keep their production down, in order that he can sell lots of output at a high price; each has an incentive to threaten that if the other producers expand their output, he will expand his. In the case of bilateral monopoly, the seller has an incentive to try to persuade the buyer to pay a high price by threatening not to sell at a low one, even if selling at the low price is better than not selling at all. For similar reasons, bargaining, threats, and the like are important elements in the other situations that do not consist of many people on one side and either one or many on the other.

As you will see in the next chapter, analyzing strategic bargaining is a hard problem. It is a subset of the more general problem of solving n-person games. *The Theory of Games and Economic Behavior* by Von Neumann and Morgenstern was an attempt to solve the general problem;

it is a great book but an unsuccessful attempt. Economists since have spent a good deal of effort trying to understand such situations, with rather limited success.

In addition to strategic behavior, this chapter has also ignored two other questions often associated with monopoly—is it a bad thing and if so what should we do about it? We take up those issues in Chapter 16, where we discuss why and under what circumstances monopolies produce undesirable outcomes, and the problems associated with trying to use government regulation to improve things.

PART 5 — APPLICATIONS

Disneyland

It is interesting to apply some of the ideas of this chapter to the problem faced by Disneyland in setting its pricing policies. Over the years, it has used various combinations of an entry fee plus per-ride charges. When I was last there, the per-ride charges were zero—the admission ticket provided unlimited rides. A few years earlier, when I was a visiting professor at the University of California at Irvine, the hospitality package that I received from the housing office included a card that permitted me to buy an unlimited ride ticket. I do not believe such cards were being sold to the general public, although they must have been very widely available.

How should Disney decide what combination of entry fee and per-ride ticket price to charge? To begin with, assume that all customers (and all rides) are identical. Figure 10-12 shows one customer's demand for rides. The horizontal axis shows the number of rides he buys as a function of the price he must pay for each ride.

Suppose Disneyland requires a ticket, costing $1, for each ride. The customer will choose to go on 5 rides, paying Disneyland $5. At a price of $0.40, he would choose 8 rides and pay $3.20. At a price of $1.60, he would choose 2 rides and pay $3.20. At a price of $2, he would choose zero rides and pay nothing. What price should Disney charge?

The problem of choosing a ticket price appears to be the same as the problem of the price searcher trying to pick a price and quantity, which was analyzed in Part 1 of this chapter. If so, we know the solution; choose price so as to sell that number of rides for which marginal revenue is equal to marginal cost. If Disneyland's marginal cost is zero (it costs the same amount to run a ride whether or not anyone is on it), Disney should choose the price at which marginal revenue is zero and total revenue is at its maximum—$1/ride in this example.

That is the wrong answer. Disneyland need not limit itself to charging a price for the rides; it can and does also charge a price to come into the park. The more expensive the rides are, the lower the price that people will be willing to pay to enter. What Disney wants to maximize is revenue

Figure 10-12

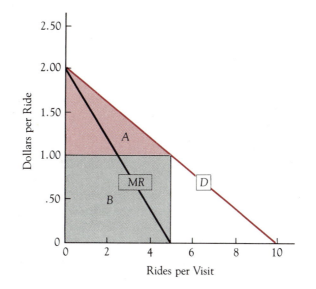

Demand for rides at Disneyland—the profit-maximizing price for a single-price monopoly. If the price for a ride is $1, which maximizes revenue from the rides, the consumer surplus, which is the amount that can be charged as an admission price, is area A.

from entry tickets plus revenue from ride tickets minus costs; it cannot do so by simply setting the price of the ride ticket so as to maximize revenue from ride tickets.

To figure out what combination of prices Disneyland should charge, we need to know exactly how the price people will pay for admission is affected by the price they are charged for the rides. Fortunately, we do. Area A on Figure 10-12 is the consumer surplus received by a consumer who is free to buy as many rides as he wishes at $1/ride. Since his consumer surplus is defined as the value to him of being able to buy rides at that price, it is also the maximum that he will pay for the right to do so—which he gets by entering Disneyland. Area A is the highest entry fee Disneyland can charge if it charges $1 for each ride; at any higher fee, customers will stop coming.

Area B on the figure is the number of rides the customer takes times the price of each ride ticket. So area B is the total revenue (from that customer) from ride tickets. Area A plus area B is Disney's total revenue from that customer—entry fee plus ride tickets. As you can easily see, the area is maximized if the ride price is zero, as shown in Figure 10-13a; the rides are free and all the money is made on the entry fee.

I have assumed that the cost to Disney of having one more person go on the ride is zero. Suppose that is not true; suppose it costs $0.20 more electricity to operate the ride with someone on it than with an empty seat. Figure 10-13*b* shows that situation, with price per ride set at $1. Area *A* is again consumer surplus (and maximum entry fee), but area *B* is now revenue from ride tickets minus the cost of those rides. Each ride the customer takes provides an extra $1 of income and an extra $0.20 of cost, for a net gain of $0.80. You should be able to satisfy yourself that the area *A* + *B* is now maximized by setting the price equal to $0.20 per ride—the marginal cost. The proof is the same one we have already seen twice—once in Chapter 4 for popcorn and once in this chapter for cookies.

There are at least two important complications we would have to add if we wanted to decide what the real Disneyland should do. One is that customers are not all identical; the admission price that one customer is more than willing to pay may be high enough to drive another customer away. If, on average, the customers who are willing to pay a high admission price are also the ones who go on a lot of rides, then a high price for rides is an indirect way of charging a high total price (rides plus admission) to those who are willing to pay it; this greatly complicates the problem of choosing an optimum ticket price.

The second important complication is that some rides may be used to capacity. In this case, my decision to go on one more ride imposes a cost—even if it takes no more electricity to run the ride full than empty. Since the ride is already full, the cost of my going on it is that someone

Figure 10-13

The profit-maximizing per-ride price with two-part pricing. At a price of zero, the sum of admission price (*A*) and revenue from rides (*B* = 0 on Figure 10-13*a*) is maximized. If *MC* = 0 for the ride, as shown on Figure 10-13*a*, this is the profit-maximizing arrangement; if *MC* = 0.20, as shown on Figure 10-13*b*, the profit-maximizing price is $0.20/ride.

Section III Complications, or Onward to Reality

else does not. My decision to take the ride lengthens the line of people waiting for it, imposing costs on everyone else in the line and persuading someone else to take one fewer ride.

This appears to be a cost imposed on the customers, not on the park; why should Disney care how long the customers stand in line? The answer is that how long they have to stand in line to go on a ride is one of the things affecting how much they value visiting Disneyland, hence how much they will pay for the admission ticket. By going on one more ride, you impose a cost directly on the other customers and indirectly on Disney; Disney should take that cost into account in deciding what price to charge for the ride. It turns out that (assuming all customers are identical) the optimal price is the one that just reduces the line to zero. You may find it easier to figure out why that is true after you finish Chapter 17.

The Popcorn Problem

In the discussion of popcorn at the end of Chapter 4, I showed that if customers are identical, theaters should sell popcorn at cost. One explanation of what we observe is that they do—that the high price of popcorn (and candy and soda) reflects high costs. Since the theater is selling food for only 20 minutes or so every two hours, perhaps its operating costs are much higher than those of other sellers.

In this chapter's discussion of discriminatory pricing, I suggested an alternative explanation, based on the fact that customers are not identical. If popcorn is expensive, the poor student who is just barely willing to pay $5 to see the movie will probably either do without or smuggle in his own, while the affluent student (or the one trying to impress a new date) will be willing both to pay a high price and to buy a lot of popcorn. The combination of cheap tickets and expensive popcorn is a way of keeping the business of the poor student while making as much as possible out of the rich one.

How could one find out which explanation is right? Discriminatory pricing is only possible if the seller has a considerable degree of monopoly; in a competitive industry, if you try to charge a higher price to richer customers, some other firm will undercut you. In a small town, there may be only one movie theater; even if there are several, it is unlikely that more than one is showing a particular movie at a particular time. Each theater is then a monopoly (with regard to its particular movie) and can engage in discriminatory pricing by, among other things, charging above-cost prices for food. In a large city, the customers can choose among many theaters, several of which may be showing the same film. If the discriminatory pricing explanation is correct, we would expect the difference between the price of popcorn or candy in a movie theater and its price elsewhere to be larger in small towns than in big cities. If, on the other hand, the difference reflects a difference in cost, we would probably expect the opposite result, since both labor and real estate—the two things that contribute to the high cost of a food concession in a theater that can only sell ten percent of the time—are generally more expensive in cities.

OPTIONAL SECTION

CALCULATING ELASTICITIES

Figure 10-14a shows how price elasticity varies with quantity along a straight-line demand curve. The figure has two vertical axes; the one on the left shows price, the one on the right elasticity. The slope of a straight line is the same everywhere ($-\frac{1}{2}$ for the demand curve shown on the figure) so $dQ/dP = 1/(dP/dQ) = 1/(-\frac{1}{2}) = -2$. Elasticity equals $-(P/Q)dQ/dP$; P/Q varies along the line. It is equal to infinity at the left end of D, where $P = 4$ and $Q = 0$; it is equal to zero at the right end, where $Q = 8$ and $P = 0$. Along the curve, elasticity varies as shown in Figure 10-14a. Points A, B, and C have been marked to allow you to check that the curve correctly shows the elasticity at those points.

Figure 10-14b shows the same information for a demand curve that is not a straight line. Both dP/dQ—the slope—and P/Q vary along the line. This time I have marked two points—a and b—so that you can check my calculations. In each case, the slope—dP/dQ—is calculated by taking the slope of a line tangent to the curve at that point. Table 10-1 shows the calculations for Figures 10-14a and 10-14b. ΔP and ΔQ are the vertical

Figure 10-14

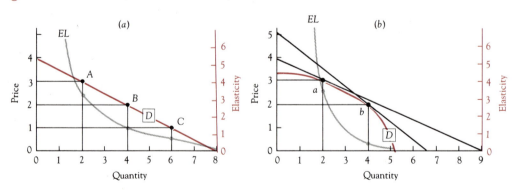

Calculating the elasticity of a demand curve. Each diagram shows demand and elasticity. Elasticity is calculated at three points on Figure 10-14a and two points on Figure 10-14b.

Section III   Complications, or Onward to Reality

Table 10-1

Point	Q	P	ΔQ	ΔP	$\Delta Q/\Delta P$	$-(P/Q)\Delta Q/\Delta P$
A	2	3	8	-4	-2	3
B	4	2	8	-4	-2	1
C	6	1	8	-4	-2	.33
a	2	3	9	-4	-2.25	3.38
b	4	2	6.5	-5	-1.3	.65

and horizontal intercepts of the tangent; their ratio is its slope, which is equal to dP/dQ.

Figure 10-15 shows a simpler way of calculating price elasticity. The triangles GEC, HFE, and OFC are all similar. From the similarity of HFE and OFC, we have:

$$EF/EH = CF/OC.$$

Hence

$$EF = EH(CF/OC). \qquad \text{(Equation 1)}$$

Figure 10-15

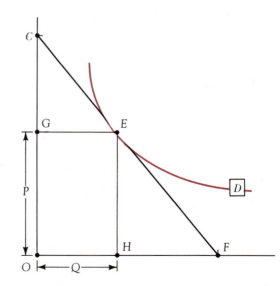

A simpler way of calculating elasticity. The elasticity of the curve at point E is EF/CE.

From the similarity of GEC and OFC, we have:

$$CE/GE = CF/OF.$$

Hence

$$CE = GE(CF/OF) \qquad \text{(Equation 2)}$$

Dividing Equation 1 by Equation 2, we have:

$$EF/CE = (EH/GE)(OF/OC). \qquad \text{(Equation 3)}$$

But, as you can see from the figure, $EH = P$, $GE = Q$, and OC/OF is minus the slope of the line CF. The slope of CF is equal to the slope of the demand curve at the point E—which is dP/dQ. So OF/OC is $-dQ/dP$, and Equation 3 becomes:

$$EF/CE = (P/Q)(-dQ/dP) = \text{elasticity of demand curve } D \text{ at point } E.$$

So one can calculate the elasticity of a demand curve by simply drawing the tangent and taking the ratio between EF (the distance from the point of tangency to the intersection with the quantity axis) and CE (the distance from the point of tangency to the intersection with the price axis). This gives us a simpler way of calculating the elasticity of a demand curve than the one shown on Table 10-1.

ARTIFICIAL MONOPOLY

Economies of scale are ways in which large firms can produce more cheaply than small ones; diseconomies of scale are the opposite. One important source of economies of scale is mass production; a firm that produces a million widgets per year can set up assembly lines, buy special widget-making machinery, and so forth. Another source may be economies of scale in administration; a large firm can afford to take advantage of specialization by having one executive deal with advertising and another with personnel. Economies of scale are usually important only up to some maximum size; that is why a large firm, such as GM or U.S. Steel, does not consist of one gigantic factory, as it would if such a factory could produce at a substantially lower cost than several large factories.

An important source of diseconomies of scale, as mentioned earlier, is the problem of coordinating a large firm. The fundamental organizational problem of a firm is the conflict between the interests of the employees and the interests of the owners. The owners want to maximize profits. The employees, while they have no objection to profits, would prefer to take more leisure, work less hard, or benefit themselves in other ways, even if the result is less profit for the owners. This problem is "solved" by supervisors who watch the employees, give raises to those who work hard, and fire those who do not. The supervisors are themselves employees and must themselves be monitored by a higher level of supervisors. Since such monitoring is neither costless nor perfectly effective, every additional layer increases costs and reduces performance. The more layers there are, the more the employees find themselves pursuing, not the interest of the firm, but what they think the person above them thinks the person above him thinks is the interest of the firm. Seen from this standpoint, the ideal arrangement is the one-person firm; if its sole employee chooses to slack off, he, being also the owner of the firm, pays the cost in reduced profits.

When I was choosing a publisher for this book, I had offers from two firms, one substantially larger and more prestigious than the other. I ended up choosing the smaller and less prestigious firm, in large part because in dealing with it I felt as though I was conversing with human beings—rather than being quoted to from a manual entitled *How to Deal With Aspiring Authors*. One reason for the difference may well have been that the people I dealt with at the smaller firm were a couple of layers closer to the top of their organization than were their opposite numbers at the larger firm.

If there were only diseconomies of scale, we would expect to see an economy of one-person firms, cooperating by trading goods and services with each other. Firms consisting of one person, one family, or a small number of individuals are common (writers, doctors, owners of small grocery stores), but so are much larger firms. It appears that diseconomies of scale are often balanced by economies of scale.

Consider an industry in which economies and diseconomies balance each other over a considerable range of production, giving the firm a cost function like that of Figure 10-16. Average cost is roughly constant over

Figure 10-16

A cost curve for an industry in which large and small firms have about the same average cost.

a large range of firm sizes, including a firm large enough to produce all of the output demanded at a price equal to average cost. It is widely believed that this is a common situation and one likely to lead to an artificial monopoly; the usual example is the Standard Oil Trust under John D. Rockefeller.

The argument goes as follows: I am Rockefeller and have somehow gotten control of 90 percent of the petroleum industry. My firm, Standard Oil, has immense revenues, from which it accumulates great wealth; its resources are far larger than the resources of any smaller oil company or even all of them put together. As long as other firms exist and compete with me, I can earn only the normal return on my capital and labor—economic profit equals zero. Any attempt to push up prices will cause my competitors to increase their production and may also draw additional firms into the industry.

I therefore decide to drive out my competitors by cutting prices to below average cost. Both I and my competitors lose money; since I have more money to lose, they go under first. I now raise prices to a monopoly level, calculated as if I were a natural monopoly (marginal cost equals marginal revenue). If any new firm considers entering the market to take advantage of the high prices, I point out what happened to my previous competitors and threaten to repeat the performance if necessary.

This argument is an example of the careless use of verbal analysis. "Both I and my competitors are losing money . . ." sounds very much as though we are losing the same amount of money. We are not. If I am selling 90 percent of all petroleum, a particular competitor is selling 1 percent, and we both sell at the same price and have the same average cost, I lose $90 for every $1 he loses.

My situation is worse than that. By cutting prices, I have caused the quantity demanded to increase; if I want to keep the price down, I must increase my production—and losses—accordingly. So I must actually lose (say) $95 for every $1 my competitor loses. Worse still, my competitor, who is not trying to hold down the price, may be able to reduce his losses and increase mine by reducing his production, forcing me to sell still more oil at less than production cost, and so lose still more money. He may even be able to close down temporarily and wait until I tire of throwing my money away and permit the price to go back up. Even if he has some costs that he cannot escape without going permanently out of business, he may be able to reduce his total losses by temporarily closing his older refineries, running some plants half time, and failing to replace employees who move or retire. If so, for every $95 or $100 I lose, he loses (say) $0.50.

But although I am bigger and richer than he is, I am not infinitely bigger and richer; I am 90 times as big and presumably about 90 times as rich. I am losing money more than 90 times as fast as he is; if I keep trying to drive him out by selling below cost, it is I, not he, who will go bankrupt first. Despite the widespread belief that Rockefeller maintained his position by selling oil below cost in order to drive competitors out of business (**predatory pricing**), a careful study of the record found no solid evidence that he had ever done so.

In one case, a Standard Oil official threatened to cut prices if a smaller firm, Cornplanter Oil, did not stop expanding and cutting into Standard's business. Here is the reply Cornplanter's manager gave, according to his own testimony:

> Well, I says, "Mr. Moffett, I am very glad you put it that way, because if it is up to you the only way you can get it (the business) is to cut the market (reduce prices), and if you cut the market I will cut you for 200 miles around, and I will make you sell the stuff," and I says, "I don't want a bigger picnic than that; sell it if you want to" and I bid him good day and left. That was the end of that.
>
> —quoted in John S. McGee, "Predatory Price Cutting: The Standard Oil (NJ) Case," *Journal of Law and Economics*, Vol. 2 (October, 1958), p.137.

In addition to predatory pricing, a variety of other tactics have been suggested for a firm trying to get and maintain an artificial monopoly. One is for the firm to buy out all of its competitors; it has been argued that this, rather than predatory pricing, is how Rockefeller maintained his position. The problem is that if every time someone builds a new refinery, Rockefeller has to buy him out, starting refineries becomes a very profitable business, and Rockefeller ends up with more refineries than he has any use for.

It is hard to prove that none of these tactics can ever work. If, for instance, Rockefeller can convince potential competitors that he is willing to lose an almost unlimited amount of money keeping them out, it is possible that no one will ever call his bluff—in which case it will cost him nothing. One can only say that the advantage in such a game seems to lie with the small firm, not the large, and that the bulk of the economic and historical evidence suggests that the artificial monopoly is mostly or entirely mythical.

One consequence of such myths may be to encourage monopoly. Selling at below cost is a poor way of driving your competitors out of business but may be a good way for a new firm to persuade customers to try its products. Under present antitrust law, a firm that does so risks being accused by its competitors of unfair competition and forced to raise its price. Laws that make life hard for new firms—or old firms entering new markets—reduce competition and encourage monopoly, even if they are called antitrust laws.

PROBLEMS

1. Economics is a competitive industry; my decision to become an economist or to teach one more course will not much affect the

salary of economists. Economists as a group face a downward-sloping demand curve; the more there are, the less they can expect to get for their services. But each individual economist faces an almost perfectly horizontal demand curve; his decision to teach more courses, write more books, do more consulting, or whatever will have a very small effect on the price he receives for doing so.

The argument does not apply to everything an economist does. This book, for example, may increase (or decrease!) your interest in becoming an economist; your decision to become an economist may affect the salary received by other economists—including me. How should that possibility affect my decision of how to write the book? If the book makes economics seem an attractive and interesting profession, what can you deduce about how many copies I expect to sell?

2. Figure 10-17 shows two demand curves; draw the corresponding marginal revenue curves.

3. One can draw two different demand curves D_1 and D_2 such that a single-price monopoly would charge the same price whether faced by D_1 or D_2, but produce different quantities. One can also draw two curves D_3 and D_4 that result in the same quantity but different prices. Assuming that the producer has the MC curve of Figure 10-3a, draw demand curves D_1–D_4.

4. Suppose a single-price monopoly has no production cost. What can you say about the elasticity of demand at the profit-maximizing quantity? Can you give an example of a monopoly with no production cost? With marginal cost equal to zero? If so, do.

Figure 10-17

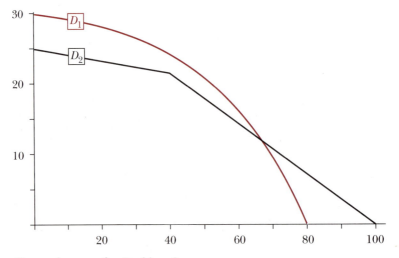

Demand curves for Problem 2.

5. Suppose a monopoly has $MC > 0$. What can you say about the elasticity of demand at the profit-maximizing quantity? Prove your result.

6. Suppose that some change in technology or input prices alters the fixed cost of a monopoly, while leaving the marginal cost curve unaffected. What is the effect on output and price? Does it depend on whether the monopoly can price discriminate? Explain your answer.

7. Quercus, Inc. has been accused of violating the antitrust laws by charging a monopoly price for acorns. The firm's lawyer argues as follows: "While it is true that we produce most of the world's acorns, it has been shown by independent studies that the demand curve for acorns is elastic. If we tried to take advantage of our position by raising the price, we would only hurt ourselves by losing sales."

    The lawyer for the antitrust division of the justice department replies: "I agree that, at the present price of acorns, the demand curve is elastic. That is evidence not that you are innocent but that you are guilty." Explain. Which lawyer is correct? Remember that evidence is not the same as proof; the question is only whether the observed elasticity of demand is evidence for or against the firm's guilt.

8. When I asked a realtor to find a house for me to buy, one of her first questions was, "How much do you want to spend?" This seems a rather odd question, since how much I want to spend, on houses or anything else, depends on what I can get for the money; even if I can buy a $200,000 house ($300,000 if enough of you buy this book), I might rather spend $100,000 if for that price I can get most of what I want. Why do you think the realtor puts the question this way? (Hint: Realtors are paid on commission; in most cities, they receive a fixed percentage of the value of the houses they sell.)

9. How should I answer the realtor in Problem 8? Should I tell her the maximum I am willing to spend for a house?

10. Figures 10-18a, 10-18b, and 10-18c show demand curves, marginal cost curves, and average cost curves for three single-price monopoly firms. In each case, how much should the firm produce and at what price should it sell in order to maximize its profit?

11. Suppose the firms in Problem 10 can engage in discriminatory pricing. Under what circumstances can they do so perfectly by using a two-part price? Assuming that they can do so, what should the two parts be for each firm—how large a per-unit charge and how large an admission charge? Assume that each firm has 100 customers.

12. Figures 10-19a and 10-19b show demand curves, marginal cost curves, and average cost curves for two monopolies. In the first case, there are 10 customers with demand curve D_A and 10 with D_B; in the second case, there are 10 type A and 5 type B customers. Note that average cost is shown as a function of total quantity produced, while each of the demand curves relates price to the quantity bought by a asingle customer.

Figure 10-18

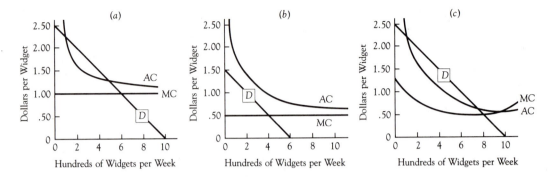

Demand and cost curves for Problems 10 and 11.

    a. In each case, draw the total demand curve and find the profit-maximizing price, assuming the firm is a single-price monopoly.

    b. In each case, find the optimal two-part price (per-unit charge plus membership fee for the right to buy any units at all) assuming the per-unit fee must equal marginal cost.

    c. In each case, find some two-part price that yields a higher profit than you got in part (b).

    d. Is any general principle suggested by your answers to (c)? If so, prove it if possible. (This is a hard problem.)

13. Figure 10-20 shows the cost curves for one firm in an industry. Can you tell whether the firm is or is not a natural monopoly? If not, what additional information do you need?

14. Figure 10-21a shows the supply curve for size 18 tractor tires. Super-Ox, a tractor company, is the only purchaser of such tires. *MRP* is the marginal revenue product of such tires for SuperOx.

Figure 10-19

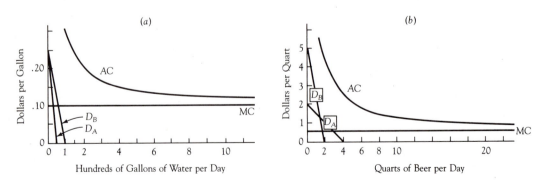

Demand and cost curves for Problem 12.

Figure 10-20

Cost curves for Problem 13.

a. Draw the marginal expenditure curve for buying tires.
b. How many tires should SuperOx buy?

15. The supply curve for size 18 tires is the same as in the previous problem. SuperOx sells tractors on a competitive market at $20,000 apiece. Inputs are used in fixed proportions; each tractor requires exactly four tires, plus a bundle of other inputs, which SuperOx purchases on a competitive market for $19,000.

a. Draw SuperOx's *MRP* curve. (Hint: It is not equal to *MRP* on Figure 10-21*a*.
b. How many tires should SuperOx buy?

16. The situation is the same as in the previous question, except that SuperOx is the only seller of tractors; the demand curve for tractors is shown on Figure 10-21*b*.

a. Draw SuperOx's *MRP* curve.
b. How many tires should SuperOx buy?

Figure 10-21

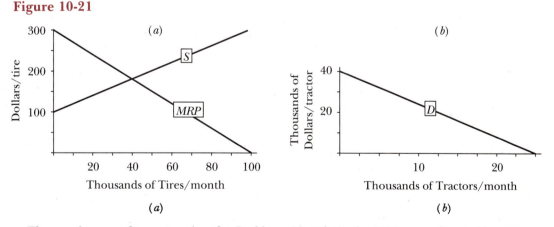

The supply curve for tractor tires for Problems 14 and 15, the *MRP* curve for Problem 14 only, and the demand curve for tractors in Problem 16.

Figure 10–22

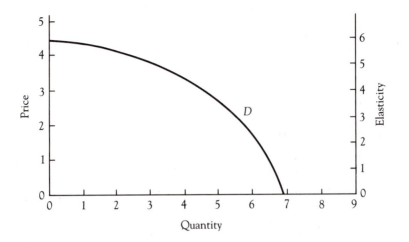

Demand curve for Problem 18.

17. Give a brief verbal explanation of how you would analyze the buying and selling decisions of a firm that was both a monopoly and a monopsony.

The following problem refers to the optional section:

18. Figure 10-22 shows a demand curve; graph the elasticity as was done on Figures 10-14*a* and 10-14*b*. You may use whichever method of calculating it you prefer.

FOR FURTHER READING

Students interested in a detailed and original analysis of monopoly and price discrimination may want to look at the classic discussion of the subject in A. C. Pigou, *The Economics of Welfare* (London: Macmillan, 1932), especially Chapters XIV–XVII. A more modern source would be George Stigler, *The Organization of Industry* (Chicago: University of Chicago Press, 1968).

I am not the first economist to think of applying economic theory to the Magic Kingdom. You may wish to read Walter Oi, "A Disneyland Dilemma: Two-Part Tariffs for a Mickey Mouse Monopoly," *Quarterly Journal of Economics*, Vol. 85 (February, 1971), pp. 77–96.

chapter 11

HARD PROBLEMS:
GAME THEORY, STRATEGIC BEHAVIOR,
AND OLIGOPOLY

"There are two kinds of people in the world: Johnny Von Neumann and the rest of us."

—Attributed to Eugene Wigner, a Nobel Prize winning physicist.

An economy is an interdependent system. In the process of solving it we have deliberately pushed that interdependency into the background. The individual, both as consumer and producer, is a small part of the market and can therefore take everyone else's behavior as given; he does not have to worry about how what he does will affect what they do. The rest of the world consists for him of a set of prices—prices at which he can sell what he produces and buy what he wants.

The monopolist of Chapter 10 is big enough to affect the entire market, but he is dealing with a multitude of individual consumers. Each consumer knows that what he does will not affect the monopolist's behavior. Each consumer therefore reacts passively to the monopolist, buying the quantity that maximizes the consumer's welfare at the price the monopolist decides to charge. From the standpoint of the monopolist, the customer is not a person at all; he is simply a demand curve.

Our analysis has thus eliminated an important feature of human interaction and of many markets—bargaining, threats, bluffs, the whole gamut of strategic behavior. That is one of the reasons why most of price theory seems, to many students, such a bloodless abstraction. We are used to seeing human society as a clash of wills, whether in the boardroom, on the battlefield, or in our favorite soap opera. Economics presents it instead in terms of solitary individuals, or at the most small teams of producers, each calmly maximizing against an essentially nonhuman environment, an opportunity set rather than a population of self-willed human beings.

There is a reason for doing economics this way. The analysis of strategic behavior is an extraordinarily difficult problem. John Von Neumann, arguably one of the smartest men of this century, created a whole new branch of mathematics in the process of failing to solve it. The work of his successors, while often ingenious and mathematically sophisticated, has not brought us much closer to being able to say what people will or should do in such situations. Seen from one side, what is striking about price theory is the unrealistic picture it presents of the world around us. Seen from the other, one of its most impressive accomplishments is to explain a considerable part of what is going on in real markets while avoiding, with considerable ingenuity, any situation involving strategic behavior. When it fails to do so, as in the analysis of oligopoly or bilateral monopoly, it rapidly degenerates from a coherent theory to a set of educated guesses.

What Von Neumann created, and what this chapter attempts to explain, is game theory. I start, in Part 1, with an informal description of a number of games, designed to give you a feel for the problems of strategic behavior. Part 2 contains a more formal analysis, discussing various senses in which one might "solve" a game and applying the solution concepts to a number of interesting games. Parts 3 and 4 show how one can attempt, with limited success, to apply the ideas of game theory to specific economic problems.

PART 1—STRATEGIC BEHAVIOR

"Scissors, Paper, Stone" is a simple game played by children. At the count of three, the two players simultaneously put out their hands in one of three positions: a clenched fist for stone, an open hand for paper, two fingers out for scissors. The winner is determined by a simple rule: Scissors cut paper, paper covers stone, stone breaks scissors.

The game may be represented by a 3×3 **payoff matrix**, as shown in Figure 11-1. Rows represent strategies for Player 1; columns represent strategies for Player 2. Each cell in the matrix is the intersection of a row and a column, showing what happens if the players choose those two strategies; the first number in the cell is the payoff to Player 1, the

Figure 11-1

		Player 2		
		Scissors	Paper	Stone
Player 1	Scissors	0, 0	+1, −1	−1, +1
	Paper	−1, +1	0, 0	+1, −1
	Stone	+1, −1	−1, +1	0, 0

The payoff matrix for Scissors, Paper, Stone.

second the payoff to Player 2. It is convenient to think of all payoffs as representing sums of money, and to assume that the players are simply trying to maximize their expected return—the average amount they win—although, as you will see, game theory can be and is used to analyze games with other sorts of payoffs.

The top left cell shows what happens if both players choose scissors; neither wins, so the payoff is zero to each. The next cell down shows what happens if Player 1 chooses paper and Player 2 chooses scissors. Scissors cuts paper, so Player 2 wins and Player 1 loses, represented by a gain of one for Player 2 and a loss of one for Player 1.

I have started with this game for two reasons. The first is that, because each player makes one move and the moves are revealed simultaneously, it is easily represented by a matrix such as Figure 11-1, where one player chooses a row, the other chooses a column, and the outcome is determined by their intersection. We will see later that this turns out to be a way in which any two-person game can be represented, even a complicated one such as chess.

The second reason is that although this is a simple game, it is far from clear what its solution is—or even what it means to solve it. After your paper has been cut by your friend's scissors, it is easy enough to say that you should have chosen stone, but that provides no guide for the next move. Some quite complicated games have a winning strategy for one of the players. But there is no such strategy for Scissors, Paper, Stone. Whatever you choose is right or wrong only in relation to what the other player chooses.

While it may be hard to say what the correct strategy is, one can say with some confidence that a player who always chooses stone is making a mistake; he will soon find that his stone is always covered. One feature of a successful strategy is unpredictability. That insight suggests the possibility of a deliberately randomized strategy.

Suppose I choose my strategy by rolling a die, making sure the other player is not watching. If it comes up 1 or 2, I play Scissors; 3 or 4, paper; 5 or 6, stone. Whatever strategy the other player follows (other than peeking at the die or reading my mind), I will on average win one third of the games, lose one third of the games, and draw one third of the games.

Can there be a strategy that consistently does better? Not against an intelligent opponent. The game is a symmetrical one; the randomized strategy is available to him as well as to me. If he follows it, then, whatever I do, he will on average break even, and so will I.

One important feature of Scissors, Paper, Stone is that it is a **zero-sum game**; whatever one player wins the other player loses. While there may be strategy of a sort in figuring out what the other player is going to do, much of what we associate with strategic behavior is irrelevant. There is no point in threatening to play stone if the opponent does not agree to play scissors; the opponent will refuse, play paper, and cover your stone.

Bilateral Monopoly, Nuclear Doom, and Barroom Brawls

Consider next a game discussed in an earlier chapter—bilateral monopoly. The rules are simple. You and I have a dollar to divide between us, provided that we can agree on a division. If we cannot agree, the dollar vanishes.

This game is called bilateral monopoly because it corresponds to a market with one buyer and one seller. I have the world's only apple and you are the only person in the world not allergic to apples. The apple is worth nothing to me and $1 to you. If I sell it to you for $1, I am better off by $1 and you, having paid exactly what the apple is worth, are just as well off as if you had not bought it. If I give it to you, I gain nothing and you gain $1. Any price between one and zero represents some division of the dollar gain between us. If we cannot agree on a price, I keep the apple and the potential gain from the trade is lost.

Bilateral monopoly nicely encapsulates the combination of common interest and conflict of interest, cooperation and competition, typical of many human interactions. The players have a common interest in reaching agreement but a conflict over what the terms of the agreement will be. The United States and the Soviet Union have a common interest in preserving peace but a conflict over how favorable the terms of that peace will be to each side. Husband and wife have a common interest in preserving a happy and harmonious marriage but innumerable conflicts over how their limited resources are to be spent on things that each values. Members of a cartel have a common interest in keeping output down and prices up but a conflict over which firm gets how much of the resulting monopoly profit.

Bilateral monopoly is not a zero-sum game. If we reach agreement, our gains sum to $1; if we fail to reach agreement, they sum to zero. That makes it fundamentally different from Scissors, Paper, Stone; it permits threats, bargains, negotiation, bluff.

I decide to get 90 cents of the dollar gain. I inform you that I will refuse to accept any less favorable terms; you may choose between 10 cents and nothing. If you believe me, you give in. If you call my bluff and insist that you will only give me 40 cents, I in turn, if I believe you, have the choice of 40 cents or nothing. Each player is trying to get a better outcome for himself by threatening to force an outcome that is worse for both.

One way to win such a game is to find some way to commit oneself, to make it impossible to back down. A child with good strategic instincts might announce "I promise not to let you have more than 20 cents of the dollar, cross my heart and hope to die." If the second player believes that the oath is binding—that the first player will not back down because no share of the dollar is worth the shame of breaking the oath—the strategy works. The second player goes home with 20 cents and a resolution that next time he will get his promise out first.

The strategy of commitment is not limited to children. Its most dramatic embodiment is the doomsday machine, an idea dreamed up by Hermann Kahn and later dramatized in the movie *Doctor Strangelove*.

Suppose the United States decides to end all worries about Soviet aggression once and for all. It does so by building a hundred cobalt bombs, burying them in the Rocky Mountains, and attaching a fancy geiger counter. If they go off, the cobalt bombs produce enough fallout to eliminate all human life anywhere on earth. The geiger counter is the trigger, set to explode the bombs if it senses the radiation from a Soviet attack.

We can now dismantle all other defenses against nuclear attack; we have the ultimate deterrent. In an improved version, dubbed by Kahn the Doomsday-in-a-hurry Machine, the triggering device is somehow equipped to detect a wide range of activities and respond accordingly; it could be programmed, for instance, to blow up the world if the Soviets invade West Berlin, or West Germany, or anywhere at all—thus saving us the cost of a conventional as well as a nuclear defense.

While a doomsday machine is an elegant idea, it has certain problems. In *Doctor Strangelove*, it is the Russians who build one. They decide to save the announcement for the premier's birthday. Unfortunately, while they are waiting, a lunatic American air force officer launches a nuclear strike against the Soviet Union.

The doomsday machine is not entirely imaginary. Consider the situation immediately after the United States detects the beginning of an all-out nuclear strike by the Soviet Union. Assume that, as is currently the case, we have no defenses, merely the ability to retaliate. The threat of retaliation may prevent an attack, but if the attack comes anyway retaliation will not protect anyone. It may even, by increasing fallout, climactic effects, and the like, kill some Americans—as well as millions of Russians and a considerable number of neutrals who have the misfortune to be downwind of targets.

Retaliation in such a situation is irrational. Nonetheless, it would probably occur. The people controlling the relevant buttons—bomber pilots, air force officers in missile silos, nuclear submarine captains—have been trained to obey orders. They are particularly unlikely to disobey the order to retaliate against an enemy who has just killed, or is about to kill, most of their friends and family.

Our present system of defense by retaliation is a doomsday machine, with human beings rather than geiger counters as the trigger. So is theirs. So far both have worked, with the result that neither has been used. Kahn invented the idea of a doomsday machine not because he wanted the United States to build one but because both we and the Soviet Union already had.

Between "cross my heart and hope to die" and nuclear annihilation, there is a wide range of situations where threat and commitment play a key role. Even before the invention of nuclear weapons, warfare was often a losing game for both sides. A leader who could persuade the other side that he was nonetheless willing to play, whether because he was a madman, a fanatic, or merely an optimist, was in a strong bargaining position. They might call his bluff—but it might not be a bluff.

Another example was mentioned in the discussion of artificial monopoly in the previous chapter. If Rockefeller can somehow convince potential entrants to the refining business that if they build a refinery he will drive them out whatever the cost, he may be able to maintain a monopoly. If someone calls his bluff and he really has committed himself, he may have to spend his entire fortune trying, perhaps unsuccessfully, to carry out his threat.

There are many examples of the same logic on a smaller scale. Consider a barroom quarrel that starts with two customers arguing about baseball teams and ends with one dead and the other standing there with a knife in his hand and a dazed expression on his face. Seen from one standpoint, this is a clear example of irrational and therefore uneconomic behavior; the killer regrets what he has done as soon as he does it, so he obviously cannot have acted to maximize his own welfare. Seen from another standpoint, it is the working out of a rational commitment to irrational action—the equivalent, on a small scale, of a doomsday machine going off.

Suppose I am strong, fierce, and known to have a short temper with people who do not do what I want. I benefit from that reputation; people are careful not to do things that offend me. Actually beating someone up is expensive; he may fight back, and I may get arrested for assault. But if my reputation is bad enough, I may not have to beat anyone up.

To maintain that reputation, I train myself to be short-tempered. I tell myself, and others, that I am a real he-man, and he-men don't let other people push them around. I gradually expand my definition of "push me around" until it is equivalent to "don't do what I want."

We usually describe this as an aggressive personality, but it may make just as much sense to think of it as a deliberate strategy rationally adopted. Once the strategy is in place, I am no longer free to choose the optimal response in each situation; I have invested too much in my own self-image to be able to back down. In just the same way, the United States, having constructed a system of massive retaliation to deter attack, is not free to change its mind in the ten minutes between the detection of enemy missiles and the deadline for firing our own. Not backing down once deterrence has failed may be irrational, but putting yourself in a situation where you cannot back down is not.

Most of the time I get my own way; once in a while I have to pay for it. I have no monopoly on my strategy; there are other short-tempered people in the world. I get into a conversation in a bar. The other guy fails to show adequate deference to my opinions. I start pushing. He pushes back. When it is over, one of us is dead.

Two men are arrested for a robbery. If convicted, each will receive a jail sentence of two to five years; the actual length depends on what the prosecution recommends. Unfortunately for the district attorney, he does not yet have enough evidence to get a conviction.

The DA puts the criminals in separate cells. He goes first to Joe. He tells him that if he confesses and Mike does not, the DA will drop the burglary charge and let Joe off with a slap on the wrist—three months for trespass. If Mike also confesses, the DA cannot drop the charge but he will ask the judge for leniency; Mike and Joe will get two years each.

If Joe refuses to confess, the DA will not feel so friendly. If Mike confesses, Joe will be convicted and the DA will ask for the maximum possible sentence. If neither confesses, the DA cannot convict them of the robbery, but he will press for a six-month sentence for trespass, resisting arrest, and vagrancy.

After explaining all of this to Joe, the DA goes to Mike's cell and gives the same speech, with names reversed. Figure 11-2 shows the matrix of outcomes facing Joe and Mike.

Joe reasons as follows:

If Mike confesses and I don't, I get five years; if I confess too, I get two years. If Mike is going to confess, I had better confess too.

If neither of us confesses, I go to jail for six months. That is a considerable improvement on what will happen if Mike squeals, but I can do better; if Mike stays silent and I confess, I only get three months. So if Mike is going to stay silent, I am better off confessing. In fact, whatever Mike does I am better off confessing.

Joe calls for the guard and asks him to send for the DA. It takes a while; Mike has made the same calculation, reached the same conclusion, and is in the middle of dictating his confession.

This game has at least two interesting properties. The first is that it introduces a new solution concept. Both criminals confess because each calculates, correctly, that confession is better than silence whatever the

Figure 11-2

		Joe	
		Confess	Say Nothing
Mike	Confess	2 years, 2 years	3 months, 5 years
	Say Nothing	5 years, 3 months	6 months, 6 months

The payoff matrix for prisoner's dilemma.

other criminal does. We can see this on Figure 11-2 by noting that the column "Confess" has a higher payoff for Joe than the column "Say Nothing," whichever row Mike chooses. Similarly, the row "Confess" has a higher payoff for Mike than the row "Say Nothing," whichever column Joe chooses.

If one strategy leads to a better outcome than another whatever the other player does, the first strategy is said to **dominate** the second. If one strategy dominates all others, then the player is always better off using it; if both players have such dominant strategies, we have a solution to the game.

The second interesting thing is that both players have acted rationally and both are, as a result, worse off. By confessing, they each get two years; if they had kept their mouths shut, they each would have gotten six months. It seems odd that rationality, defined as making the choice that best achieves the individual's ends, results in both individuals being worse off.

The explanation is that Joe is only choosing his strategy, not Mike's. If Joe could choose between the lower right-hand cell of the matrix and the upper left-hand cell, he would choose the former; so would Mike. But those are not the choices they are offered. Joe is choosing a column, and the left-hand column dominates the right-hand column; it is better whichever row Mike chooses. Mike is choosing a row, and the top row dominates the bottom.

We have been here before. In Chapter 1, I pointed out that rationality is an assumption about individuals, not about groups, and described a number of situations where rational behavior by the individuals in a group made all of them worse off. This is the same situation in its simplest form—a group of two. Prisoners confess for the same reason that armies run away and students take shortcuts across newly planted lawns.

To many of us, the result of prisoner's dilemma and similar games seems deeply counterintuitive. Armies do not always run away, at least in part because generals have developed ways of changing the structure of rewards and punishments facing their soldiers. Burning your bridges behind you is one solution; shooting soldiers who run away in battle is another. Similarly, criminals go to considerable effort to raise the cost to their co-workers of squealing and lower the cost of going to jail for refusing to squeal.

But none of that refutes the logic of prisoner's dilemma; it merely means that real prisoners and real soldiers are sometimes playing other games. When the net payoffs to squealing, or running, do have the structure shown in Figure 11-2, the logic of the game is compelling. Prisoners confess and soldiers run.

Repeated Prisoner's Dilemma

One obvious response to the analysis of the prisoner's dilemma is that its result is correct, but only because the game is being played only once.

Many real-world situations involve repeated plays. Mike and Joe will eventually get out of jail, resume their profession, and be caught again. Each knows that if he betrays his partner this time around, he can expect his partner to treat him similarly next time, so they both refuse to confess.

The argument is persuasive, but it is not clear if it is right. Suppose we abandon Joe and Mike, and consider instead two people who are going to play a game like the one represented by Figure 11-2 a hundred times. To make their doing so more plausible, we replace the jail sentences of Figure 11-2 with positive payoffs. If both players cooperate, they get $10 each. If each betrays the other, they get nothing. If one betrays and the other cooperates, the traitor gets $15 and the patsy loses $5.

A player who betrays his partner gains $5 in the short run, but the gain is not likely to be worth the price. The victim will respond by betraying him on the next turn, and perhaps several more. On net, it seems that both players are better off cooperating every turn.

There is a problem with this attractive solution. Consider the last turn of the game. Each player knows that whatever he does, the other will have no further opportunity to punish him. The last turn is therefore an ordinary prisoner's dilemma. Betraying dominates cooperating for both players, so each betrays the other and each gets zero.

Each player can work through this logic for himself, so each knows that the other will betray him on the hundredth move. Knowing that, I know that I need not fear punishment for anything I do on the ninety-ninth move; whatever I do, you are in any case going to betray me on the next (and last) move. So I betray you on the ninety-ninth move—and you, having gone through the same calculation, betray me.

Since we know that we are both going to betray one another on the ninety-ninth move, there is now no punishment for betraying on the ninety-eighth move. Since we know we are going to betray each other on the ninety-eighth, there is no punishment for betraying on the ninety-seventh. The entire chain of moves unravels; if we are rational we betray each other on the first move and every move thereafter, ending up with nothing. If we had been irrational and cooperated, we would each have ended up with $1000.

If you find the result paradoxical, you have lots of company. Nonetheless, the argument is correct. It is only a minor relief to note that the analysis depends on the players knowing how many moves the game will last; if they are playing a finite but indefinite number of times, cooperation may be stable. We will return to this particularly irritating game at the end of Part 2 of this chapter.

Three-Person Majority Vote

So far, all of our games have had only two players. Consider the following very simple three-person game. There are three people—Anne, Bill, and Charles—and $100. The money is to be divided by majority vote; any allocation that receives two votes wins.

Think of the play of the game as a long period of bargaining followed by a vote. In the bargaining, players suggest divisions and try to persuade at least one other player to go along. Each player is trying to maximize his own return—his share of the money.

Bill starts by proposing to Anne that they divide the money between them, $50 for each. That sounds to her like a good idea—until Charles proposes a division of $60 for Anne and $40 for himself. Charles makes the offer because $40 is better than nothing; $60 is better than $50, so Anne is happy to switch sides.

The bargaining is not ended. Bill, who is now out in the cold, suggests to Charles that he will be happy to renew his old proposal with a different partner; Charles will get $50, which is better than $40, and Bill will get $50, which is better than nothing.

The potential bargaining is endless. Any division anyone can suggest is dominated by some other division, and so on indefinitely. A division that gives something to everyone is dominated by an alternative with one player left out and his share divided between the other two. A division that does not give something to everyone is dominated by another in which the player who is left out allies with one of the previous winners and they split the share of the third player between them.

In Part 2, we will see how game theorists have tried to deal with such problems. For the moment, it is worth noting two concepts that we have introduced here and will use later. One concept is a division—what we will later call an **imputation**—an outcome of the game, defined by who ends up with what. The other is a new meaning for dominance: One division dominates another if enough people prefer it to make it happen.

PART 2—GAME THEORY

The idea of game theory, as conceived by Von Neumann and presented in the book that he coauthored with economist Oskar Morgenstern, was to find a general solution to all games. That did not mean learning to play chess, or bridge, or poker, or oligopoly, perfectly. It meant figuring out how you would figure out how to play those games, or any others, perfectly. If one knew how to set up any game as an explicit mathematical problem, the details of the solution of each particular game could be left to someone else.

Seen from this standpoint, chess turns out to be a trivial game. The rules specify that if no pawn is moved and no piece taken for 40 moves, the game is a draw. That means that the total number of moves, and thus the total number of possible chess games, is limited—very large but finite. To play chess perfectly, all you need do is list all possible games, note on each who wins, and then work backward from the last move, assuming at each step that if a player has a move that leads to an eventual win he will take it.

This is not a very practical solution to the problem of beating your best friend at chess. The number of possible games is much larger than the number of atoms in this galaxy, so finding enough paper to list them all would be difficult. But game theorists, with a few exceptions, are not interested in that sort of difficulty. Their objective is to figure out how the game would be solved; they are perfectly willing to give you an unlimited length of time to solve it in.

In analyzing games, we will start with two-person games. The first step in solving them will be to show how any two-person game can be represented in a reduced form analogous to Figure 11-1. The next step will be to show in what sense the reduced form of a two-person fixed-sum game can be solved. We will then go on to discuss a variety of different solution concepts for games with more than two players.

Two-Person Games

We normally think of a chess game as a series of separate decisions; I make a first move, you respond, I respond to that, and so forth. We can, however, describe the same game in terms of a single move by each side. The move consists of the choice of a strategy describing what the player will do in any situation. Thus, one possible strategy might be to start by moving my king's pawn forward two squares, then if the opponent moves his king's pawn forward respond by . . . , if the opponent moves his queen's pawn instead respond by . . . , ... The strategy would be a complete description of how I would respond to any sequence of moves I might observe my opponent making (and, in some games, to any sequence of random events, such as the fall of a die or what cards happen to be dealt).

Since a strategy determines everything you will do in every situation, playing the game—any game—simply consists of each side picking one strategy. The decisions are effectively simultaneous; although you may be able to observe your opponent's moves as they are made, you cannot see inside his head to observe how he has decided to play the game. Once the two strategies are chosen, everything is determined. One can imagine the two players writing down their strategies and then sitting back and watching as a machine executed them. White makes his first move, black makes his prechosen response, white makes his prechosen response to that, and so on until one side is mated or the game is declared a draw.

Seen in these terms, any two-person game can be represented by a payoff matrix like Figure 11-1, although it may require enormously more rows and columns. Each row represents a strategy that Player 1 could choose; each column represents a strategy that Player 2 could choose. The cell at the intersection shows the outcome of that particular pair of strategies. If the game contains random elements, the cell contains the expected outcome—the average payoff over many plays of the game. In game theory, this way of describing a game is called its **reduced form**.

This is not a very useful way of thinking about chess if you want to win chess games; there is little point wasting your time figuring out in advance how to respond to all the things your opponent might conceivably do. It

Chapter 11   Game Theory, Strategic Behavior, and Oligopoly   **295**

is a useful way of thinking about chess, and poker, and craps, if you want to find some common way of describing all of them in order to figure out in what sense games have solutions and how, in principle, one could find them.

What is a solution for a two-person game? Von Neumann's answer is that a solution (for a zero-sum game) is a pair of strategies and a value for the game. Strategy S_1 guarantees Player 1 that he will get at least the value V; strategy S_2 guarantees Player 2 that she will lose at most V. V may be positive, negative, or zero; the definition makes no assumption about which player is in a stronger position.

Player 1 chooses S_1 because it guarantees him V, and Player 2, if she plays correctly (chooses S_2) can make sure he does no better than that. Player 2 chooses S_2 because it guarantees her $-V$, and Player 1, if he plays correctly (chooses S_1) can make sure she does no better than that.

Two obvious questions arise. First, is this really a solution; is it what a sufficiently smart player would choose to do? Second, if we accept this definition, do all two-person games have solutions?

The Von Neumann solution certainly does not cover everything a good player tries to do. It explicitly ignores what bridge players refer to as stealing candy from babies—following strategies that work badly against good opponents but exploit the mistakes of bad ones. But it is hard to see how one could eliminate that omission while constructing a better definition of a solution. There are, after all, many different opponents one might play and many different mistakes they might make; how do you define a "best" strategy against all of them? It seems reasonable to define a solution as the correct way to play against an opponent who is himself playing correctly.

Whether a solution exists for a game depends on what its reduced form looks like. Figure 11-3 shows the reduced form of a game that has a solution in this sense.

The central cell is the solution; it is the result of Bill choosing strategy B and Anne choosing strategy II. You can see that it is a solution by

Figure 11-3

		Bill		
		A	*B*	*C*
Anne	I	−4, +4	0, 0	−1, +1
	II	+2, −2	+1, −1	+2, −2
	III	+1, −1	0, 0	+4, −4

The payoff matrix for a game with a Von Neumann solution.

checking the alternatives. Given that Bill is choosing *B*, Anne is correct to choose *II*; anything else wins her zero instead of one. Given that Anne is choosing *II*, Bill is correct to choose *B*; anything else loses him two instead of one. The value of the game is -1. By choosing strategy *B*, Bill guarantees that he will not lose more than 1; by choosing strategy *II* Anne guarantees that she will win at least 1.

A strategy of this sort is sometimes called a **minimax strategy**. It is called a minimax because, seen from Bill's standpoint, he is minimizing the maximum amount he can lose; he acts as if he were assuming that, whatever he does, Anne will pick the right strategy against him. If he chose *A*, Anne could choose *II*, in which case he would lose 2; if he chose *C*, Anne could choose *III*, in which case he would lose 4. Precisely the same thing is true from Anne's standpoint; strategy *II* is her minimax as well. The Von Neumann solution has the interesting characteristic that each player acts as if the other one knew what he was going to do. One player does not in fact know what strategy the other is choosing, but he would do no better if he did.

Unfortunately, there is no reason to expect that all games will have such a solution. A simple counterexample is Scissors, Paper, Stone. If you look back at Figure 11-1, you will see that there is no cell with the characteristics of the solution shown on Figure 11-3. If, for example, Player 1 chooses scissors, then Player 2's best response is stone; but if Player 2 chooses stone, scissors is 1's worst response; he should choose paper instead. The same is true for any cell. A minimax strategy does not provide a solution.

Nonetheless, there is a Von Neumann solution, and we have already seen it. The trick is to allow players to choose not only **pure strategies**, such as *A*, *B*, *C*, or Scissors, Paper, Stone, but also **mixed strategies**. A mixed strategy is a probability mix of pure strategies—a 10 percent chance of *A*, a 40 percent chance of *B*, and a 50 percent chance of *C*, for instance. The solution to Scissors, Paper, Stone, as described in Part 1, is such a mixed strategy—an equal chance of following each of the three pure strategies. A player who follows that mixed strategy will lose, on average, zero, whatever his opponent does. A player whose opponent follows that strategy will win, on average, zero, whatever he does. So the Von Neumann solution is for each player to adopt that strategy. It is not only a solution but the only solution; if the player follows any one pure strategy (say stone) more frequently than the other two, his opponent can win more often than he loses by always picking the pure strategy (paper) that wins against that one.

We have now seen what a Von Neumann solution is and how a game that has no solution in terms of pure strategies may still have a mixed-strategy solution. Von Neumann's result is a good deal stronger than that. He proved that every two-person fixed-sum game has a solution, although it may require mixed strategies. He thus accomplished his objective for that class of games. He defined what a solution was, proved that one always existed, and in the process showed how, in principle, you would find it—provided, of course, that you had enough computing power and unlimited time. He also did his part to deal with at least the former proviso; one of the other things Von Neumann helped invent was cybernetics, the mathematical basis for modern computers.

If you look at Figures 11-1 and 11-3, you will note that both of the games are zero-sum. The numbers in each cell sum to zero; whatever one player wins the other loses. A zero-sum game is a special case of a **fixed-sum game**, one for which the total return to the two players, while not necessarily zero, is independent of what they do. As long as we limit ourselves to fixed-sum games, the interest of the two players is directly in conflict, since each can increase his winnings only by reducing the other player's.

This conflict is an important element in the Von Neumann solution. Bill chooses the strategy that minimizes his maximum loss because he knows that Anne, in choosing her strategy, is trying to maximize her gain—and her gain is his loss. The Von Neumann solution is not applicable to two-person variable-sum games such as bilateral monopoly or prisoner's dilemma, nor to many-person games.

Many-Person Games

For games with more than two players, the results of game theory are far less clear. Von Neumann himself proposed a definition of a solution, but not a very satisfactory one; it, and another solution concept growing out of Von Neumann's work, will be discussed in the optional section of this chapter. In this section, we will discuss another solution—a generalization of an idea developed by a French economist/mathematician early in the nineteenth century.

Consider an *n*-person game played not once but over and over, or continuously, for a long time. You, as one player, observe what the other players are doing and alter your play accordingly. You act on the assumption that what you do will not affect what they do, perhaps because you do not know how to take such effects into account, perhaps because you believe the effect of your play on the whole game is too small to matter.

You keep changing your play until no further change will make you better off. All the other players do the same. Equilibrium is finally reached when each player has chosen a strategy that is optimal for him, given the strategies that the other players are following. This solution to a many-player game is called a **Nash equilibrium** and is a generalization by John Nash of an idea invented by Antoine Cournot more than 100 years ago.

Consider, as a simple example, the game of driving, where choosing a strategy consists of deciding which side of the road to drive on. The U.S. population is in a Nash equilibrium; everyone drives on the right. The situation is stable, and would be stable even with no traffic police to enforce it. Since everyone else drives on the right, my driving on the left would impose very large costs on me (as well as others); so it is in my interest to drive on the right too. The same logic applies to everyone, so the situation is stable.

In England, everyone drives on the left. That too is a Nash equilibrium, for the same reason. It may well be an undesirable Nash equilibrium. Since in most other countries people drive on the right, cars have to be specially manufactured with steering wheels on the right side for the English market. Foreign tourists driving in England may automatically drift into the right-hand lane and discover their error only when they encounter an English driver face to face—and bumper to bumper. This is particularly likely, in my experience, when making a turn; there is an almost irresistible temptation to come out of it on what your instincts tell you is the correct side of the road.

If all the English drivers switched to driving on the right, they might all be better off. But any English driver who tried to make the switch on his own initiative would be very much worse off. A Nash equilibrium is stable against individual action even when it leads to an undesirable outcome.

A Nash equilibrium may not be stable against joint action by several people; that is one of the problems with using it to define the solution to a many-person game. The Swedish switch to driving on the right is an extreme example; everyone changed his strategy at once. In some other games, a particular outcome is stable as long as everyone acts separately but becomes unstable as soon as any two people decide to act together. Consider the case of a prison guard with one bullet in his gun, facing a mob of convicts escaping from death row. Any one convict is better off surrendering; the small chance of a last-minute pardon or successful appeal is better than the certainty of being shot dead. Any two convicts are better off charging the guard.

A Nash equilibrium is not, in general, unique, as the case of driving shows; both everyone driving on the left and everyone driving on the right are equilibria. There is also another and more subtle sense in which a Nash equilibrium may not be unique. Part of its definition is that my strategy is optimal for me, given the strategies of the other players; I act as if what I do has no effect on what they do. But what this means depends on how we define a strategy. My action will in fact affect the other players; what response by them counts as continuing to follow the same strategy? As you will see in Part 4 of this chapter, different answers to that question correspond to different Nash equilibria for otherwise identical games.

While this is the first time we have discussed Nash equilibrium, it is not the first time we have used the idea. The grocery store and the freeway in Chapter 1 and the markets in Chapter 7, with price where supply crossed demand, were all in Nash equilibrium; each person was acting correctly, given what everyone else was doing.

In each of these cases, it is interesting to ask how stable the equilibrium is. Would our conclusions be any different if we allowed two or three or ten people to act together, instead of assuming that each person acts separately? Does our result depend on just how we define a strategy? You may want to return to these questions after seeing how Nash equilibrium is used to analyze monopolistic competition in Part 3 of this chapter and the behavior of oligopolies in Part 4.

Bounded Rationality

In everything we have done so far, the players have been assumed to have an unlimited ability to calculate how to play the game—even to the extent of considering every possible chess game before making their first move. The reason for that assumption is not that it is realistic; obviously for most games it is not. The reason is that it is relatively straightforward to describe the perfect play of a game—whatever the game, the perfect strategy is the one that produces the best result.

It is much more difficult to create a theory of just how imperfect the decisions of a more realistic player with limited abilities will be. This is the same point made in Chapter 1, where I defended the assumption of rationality on the grounds that there is usually one right answer to a problem but a large number of wrong ones. As long as the individual has some tendency to choose the right one, we may be better off analyzing his behavior as if he always chose it than trying to guess which of the multitude of wrong decisions he will make.

There have been numerous attempts by economists and game theorists to get around this problem, to somehow incorporate within the theory the idea that players have only a limited amount of memory, intelligence, and time with which to solve a game. One of the most interesting attempts involves combining game theory with another set of ideas also descending, in large part, from John Von Neumann's fertile brain—the theory of computers. We cannot clearly define what kind of mistake an imperfect human will make, but we can clearly define what sort of strategies a particular computer can follow. If we replace the human with a computer, we can give precise meaning to the idea of limited rationality. In doing so, we may be able to resolve those puzzles of game theory that are created by the "simplifying assumption" of unlimited rationality.

Suppose we have a simple game—repeated prisoner's dilemma, for instance. The game is played by humans, but they must play through computers with specified abilities. Each computer has a limited number of possible states, corresponding to its limited amount of memory; you may think of a state as representing its memory of what has so far happened in the game. The computer bases its move on what has so far happened, so each state implies a particular move—cooperate or betray in the case of prisoner's dilemma.

The history of the game after any turn consists of the history before the turn plus what the opponent did on the turn, so the computer's state after a turn is determined by its state before and the opponent's move. Each player programs his computer by choosing the state it starts in, what move each state implies, and what new state results from each state plus each possible move the opponent could make. The players then sit back and watch the computers play.

One attractive feature of this approach is that it gives a precise meaning to the idea of bounded rationality; the intelligence of the computer is defined as the number of possible states it can be in. One can then prove theorems about how the solution to a particular game depends on the intelligence of the players.

Consider the game of repeated prisoner's dilemma with 100 plays. Suppose it is played by computers each of which has only 50 possible states. The state of the computer is all it knows about the past; with only 50 states the computer cannot distinguish the 100 different situations corresponding to "it is now the first move," "it is now the second move,". . . "it is now the last move." Put in human terms, it is too stupid to count up to 100.

The cooperative solution to repeated prisoner's dilemma is unstable (with a fixed number of plays) because it always pays to betray the other person on the last play. Knowing that, it pays to betray the other person on the next-to-last play, and so on back to the beginning. But you cannot adopt a strategy of betraying on the hundredth round if you cannot count up to 100. With sufficiently bounded rationality the cooperative solution is no longer unstable.

Experimental Game Theory

So far, I have discussed only theory. Games can also be analyzed by the experiment of watching people play them and seeing what happens; such work is done by both psychologists and economists.

Recently, a new and different experimental technique has appeared. A few years ago, a political scientist named Robert Axelrod conducted a prisoner's dilemma tournament. He invited all interested parties to submit strategies for repeated prisoner's dilemma; each strategy was to take the form of a computer program. He loaded all of the strategies into a computer and ran his tournament, with each program playing 200 rounds against each other program. When the tournament was over he summed the winnings of each program and reported the resulting score.

Sixteen programs were submitted, some of them quite complex. The winner, however, was very simple. It cooperated on the first round, betrayed the opponent in any round if the opponent had betrayed it in the round before, and cooperated otherwise. Axelrod named it "tit-for-tat," since it punished betrayal by betraying back—once.

Axelrod later reran the tournament in a number of different versions, with different collections of programs. Tit-for-tat always came in near the top, and the winner was always either tit-for-tat or something very similar. Playing against itself, tit-for-tat always produces the cooperative solution—the players cooperate on every round, maximizing their combined winnings. Playing against a strategy similar to itself, tit-for-tat usually produces the cooperative solution. Axelrod reported his results in a book called *The Evolution of Cooperation.*

It is hard to know how seriously to take such results. They do not give the same sort of certainty as a mathematical proof, since how well a strategy does depends in part on what strategies it is playing against; perhaps some killer strategy that nobody thought of would do even better than tit-for-tat. In the first version of Axelrod's tournament, for instance, a strategy that played tit-for-tat for the first 199 moves and then betrayed its opponent on the last move would have done a little better than tit-for-tat did. In later versions the number of rounds was indefinite, with a small probability that each round would be the last, in order to eliminate such end-game strategies.

On the other hand, strategies in the real world must be adopted and followed by real people; the people submitting strategies for Axelrod's tournament were at least as clever as the average criminal defendant bargaining with the DA. And the success of tit-for-tat was sufficiently striking, and sufficiently unexpected, to suggest some new and interesting ideas about strategies in repeated games.

This sort of experiment may become more common now that computers are inexpensive and widely available. One of its advantages is that it may, as in this case, produce a striking result that would never have occurred to a game theorist, even the one setting up the experiment. Observing behavior in the real world serves the same function for economists, providing an *is* to check their *ought to be.*

Before ending this part of the chapter, I should add one important qualification. Game theory is an extensive and elaborate branch of mathematics, and not one in which I am an expert. Even if I knew enough to produce a complete description of the present state of game theory, I could not fit it into one chapter. I have therefore in several places deliberately simplified the theory by implicitly assuming away possible complications. One example is the assumption that one member of a coalition in a many-person game can freely transfer part of his winnings to another member. That is true if the game is three-person majority vote; it is very much less true if the game is the marriage market discussed in Chapter 21.

Von Neumann's analysis of many-person games considered games both with and without such side payments; my description of it did not. Readers interested in a more extensive treatment may wish to go to the book by Luce and Raiffa cited at the end of the chapter. Readers who would like to witness the creation of game theory as described by its creator should read *The Theory of Games and Economic Behavior* by Von Neumann and Morgenstern. It is an impressive and interesting book, but not an easy one.

Economic Applications

You have probably realized by now that the term "game theory" is somewhat deceptive; while the analysis is put in terms of games, the applications are broader than that suggests. The first book on game theory was called *The Theory of Games and Economic Behavior*. Even that understates the range of what Von Neumann was trying to do. His objective was to understand all behavior that had the structure of a game. That includes most of the usual subject matter of economics, political science, international relations, interpersonal relations, sociology, and quite a lot more. In economics alone, there are many applications, but this is already a long chapter, so I shall limit myself to two: monopolistic competition and oligopoly, two quite different ways of analyzing situations somewhere between monopoly and perfect competition.

PART 3 — MONOPOLISTIC COMPETITION

We saw in Chapter 9 that a firm in a competitive industry — a price taker — would produce where marginal cost was equal to price, and that, if the industry was open, firms would enter it until profit was driven down to zero. In Chapter 10, we saw that a single-price monopoly — a price searcher — would produce where marginal cost was equal to marginal revenue, and might receive monopoly profit.

We will now consider the interesting and important case of an industry made up of price-searching firms with open entry. The condition $P = MC$ does not hold, but the zero-profit condition does. The situation is called **monopolistic competition**. It typically occurs when different firms produce products that are close but not perfect substitutes. A simple example is the case of identical services produced in different places. We will start by working through one such case in some detail, then go on to see how the results can be generalized.

The Street of Barbers

Figure 11-4 shows part of a long street with barbershops distributed along it. The customers of the barbershops live along the same street; they are evenly distributed with a density of 100 customers per block. Since all of the barbers are equally skilled (at both cutting hair and gossiping), the only considerations determining which barbershop a customer goes to are how much it costs and how far it is from his home. The customers are all identical, all of them get their hair cut once a month, and all regard walking an extra block to a barbershop and back again as equivalent to $1; they are indifferent between going to a barber N blocks away and paying him a price P or going to a barber $N + 1$ blocks away and paying $P - \$1$.

Consider the situation from the standpoint of barbershop B. Its nearest competitors, A and C, both charge the same price for a haircut: $8. A

Figure 11-4

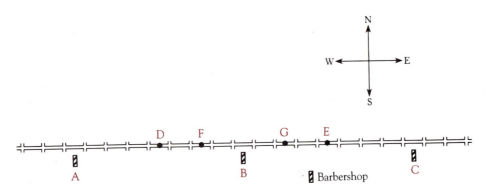

The street of barbers. There is one barbershop every eight blocks.

is located eight blocks west of *B*; *C* is located eight blocks east. How does *B* decide what price to charge?

Suppose he also charges $8. In that case, the only difference among the barbershops, so far as the customers are concerned, is how close they are; each customer goes to whichever one is closer. Anyone living west of point *D* will go to barbershop *A*; anyone between *D* and *E* will go to *B*; and anyone east of *E* will go to *C*. From *D* to *E* is eight blocks, and there are 100 customers living on each block, so barbershop *B* has 800 customers—and sells 800 haircuts a month.

Suppose barber *B* raised his price to $12. A customer at point *F* is two blocks from *B* and six from *A*. Since a walk of a block and back is equivalent to him to a $1 price difference, the two barbershops are equally attractive to him; he can either walk six blocks and pay $8 or walk two blocks and pay $12. For any customer between *F* and *B*, *B* is the more attractive option; the shorter walk more than balances the higher price. The same is true for any customer between *B* and *G*. There are four blocks between *F* and *G*, so at the higher price, *B* has 400 customers.

Similar calculations can be done for any price between $16 (no customers) and zero; every time *B* raises his price by a dollar he loses 50 customers to *A* and 50 to *C*. Figure 11-5 shows the relation between the price *B* charges and the number of customers he has—the demand curve for *B*'s services. The figure also shows the corresponding marginal revenue curve and the barbershop's marginal cost, assumed constant at $4/haircut.

Looking at Figure 11-5 and applying what we learned in Chapter 10, we conclude that the barber should produce that quantity for which marginal revenue equals marginal cost; he should provide 600 haircuts a month at a price of $10 each.

So far as barber *B* is concerned, we seem to have finished our analysis. We know that he maximizes his profit by charging $10/haircut. The only remaining question is whether, at that price, he more than covers his total

Figure 11-5

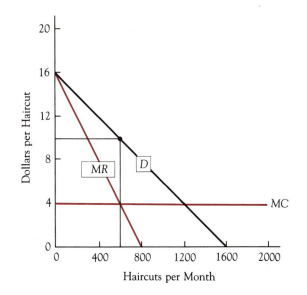

How to calculate the profit-maximizing price for a haircut. We calculate the profit-maximizing price for one barber, assuming that adjacent barbers charge $8 for a haircut.

cost; to answer that we would have to know his average cost curve. If he covers total cost, he should stay in business and charge $10; if not, he should go out of business.

We are not done. So far, we have simply assumed that A and C charge $8 haircut. But they too wish to maximize their profits. They too can calculate their marginal revenue curves, intersect them with marginal cost, and pick price and quantity accordingly. If we assume that barbershops are spaced evenly along the street and that they all started out charging the same price, then A and C started in the same situation as B—and their calculations imply the same conclusion. They too raise their price to $10—and so does every other barbershop.

We are still not done. Figure 11-5 was drawn on the assumption that shops A and C were charging $8. When they raise their prices, the demand curve faced by B shifts, so $10 is no longer his profit-maximizing price.

We have been here before; the street of barbers is beginning to look very much like the egg market of Chapter 7. Once again we are trying, unsuccessfully, to find the equilibrium of an interdependent system by changing one thing at a time. Every time we get the jelly nailed solidly to one part of the wall we find that it has oozed away somewhere else.

Here, as there, we solve the problem by figuring out what the situation must look like when the equilibrium is finally reached. The analysis is more complicated than simply finding the intersection of a supply curve and a demand curve, so I shall start by sketching out the sequence of steps by which we find the equilibrium.

The Solution—A Verbal Sketch

Each barber and potential barber must make a threefold decision: whether to be a barber, what price to charge, and where to locate his shop. His answer to those three questions defines the strategy he is following. We are looking for a set of consistent strategies: a Nash equilibrium. That means that each barber is acting in the way that maximizes his profit, given what all of the other barbers are doing.

To simplify things a little, we will start by looking for a symmetrical solution—one in which the barbershops are evenly spaced along the street and all charge the same price. The advantage of doing it this way is that if we can find an equilibrium strategy for one barber consistent with the adjacent barbers following the same strategy, we have a solution for the whole street. If we fail to find any such solution, we might have to look for one in which different barbers follow different strategies. Even if we do find a symmetrical solution, there might still exist one or more asymmetrical solutions as well; as we saw in considering which side of the road to drive on, a game may have more than one Nash equilibrium.

If the barbershops are evenly spaced and all charge the same price, we can describe the solution with two numbers—d, the distance between barbershops, and P, the price they all charge. Our problem is to find values of d and P that satisfy three conditions, corresponding to the three decisions that make up the barber's strategy. The first is that it does not pay anyone to start a new barbershop, or any old barbershop to go out of business. The second is that if all the barbers charge a price P, no individual barber would be better off charging some other price. The third is that it does not pay any barber to move his shop to a different location. If we find values of d and P for which all three conditions hold, we have a Nash equilibrium.

The first condition implies that economic profit is zero, just as for a competitive industry with open entry. The second implies the profit-maximizing condition for a price searcher: Produce a quantity such that marginal cost equals marginal revenue. We will return to the third condition later.

The Solution

Figure 11-6 shows the solution. It corresponds to Figure 11-5, with three changes. I have added an average cost curve, so that we can see whether profit is positive or negative. I have set d to a value (six blocks) that results in a profit of zero. I have found a price P ($=10$) such that if the adjacent barbershops (A and C) are distance d away and charge P, the profit-maximizing price for barbershop B is also P.

Figure 11-6

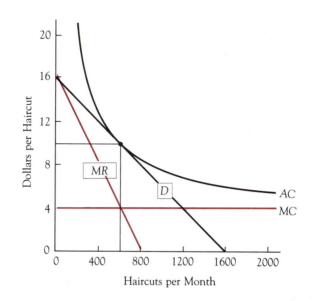

The solution—the equilibrium price of haircuts and density of barbershops.

I have given the solution rather than deriving it, since the derivation is somewhat lengthy. Students who would like to try solving the problem for themselves should start by picking an arbitrary value of d and finding $P(d)$, the price such that if the barbershops on either side of barbershop B are d blocks away and charge P, P is also the profit-maximizing price for B to charge. Then find $Q(d)$, the quantity that barbershop B produces if it charges $P(d)$. Plot $P(d)$ against $Q(d)$ on a graph that also shows AC as a function of quantity. The two curves intersect at a quantity and price where $P = AC$ and profit is therefore zero, giving you the solution.

Metastable Equilibrium?

There is one minor flaw in our solution to the barbershop problem. We have assumed that barbershops space themselves evenly along the block. In the problem as given, there is no reason for them to do so; as you can check for yourself, barbershop B can move left or right along the street without changing the demand curve it faces. As long as it does not move past either A or C, it gains as many customers from the competitor it moves towards as it loses to the competitor it moves away from.

From B's standpoint, the situation is what I described in Chapter 7 as a *metastable equilibrium*. B has no reason to move and no reason not to; his situation is the same either way. If he does move, that will affect A and C; their responses will have further effects for the barbershops farther along the street in both directions. If B decides to sit where we have put him—and everyone else does the same—we have a solution; if he does not, it is unclear just what will happen. So our solution is stable with regard to the first element of the strategy (whether to be a barber—the zero-profit condition) and the second (how much to charge), but only metastable with regard to the third condition (where to locate).

This problem could be eliminated by adding one more element to the situation—the customers' demand curve for haircuts. We have so far let the price charged affect which barber the customer goes to but not how often he has his hair cut; we have implicitly assumed that the demand curve for haircuts is perfectly inelastic. If we assume instead that at a higher cost (in money plus distance) customers get their hair cut less often, each barber will find that he maximizes his profit by locating halfway between the two adjacent barbers. If he moves away from that point, the number of customers stays the same but the average distance they must walk increases, so quantity demanded at any price, and the barber's profit, fall.

If the demand curve faced by a single barbershop depends not only on the location and prices of its competitors but also on the distance its customers must walk, we must redraw Figures 11-5 and 11-6. That would make the problem considerably more complicated without altering its essential logic—which is why I did not do it that way in the first place. You may, if you wish, think of Figure 11-6 as showing an almost exact solution for customers whose demand curves are almost, but not quite, perfectly inelastic. Any elasticity in the demand curve, however slight, gives the barbershops an incentive to spread themselves evenly. If the elasticity is very small, it will produce only a tiny effect on the demand curve faced by the barbershop (D), so the solution shown in the figure will be almost, although not precisely, correct.

Are We Really Just Talking about Barbershops?

So far, we have discussed only one example of monopolistic competition—barbershops along a street. The same analysis applies to many other goods and services for which the geographic location of seller and buyer is important—goods and services that must be transported from the producer to the consumer and those, such as haircuts or movies, for which the consumer must be transported to the producer.

Any such industry is a case of monopolistic competition, provided that firms are free to enter and leave the industry and are sufficiently far apart so that each has, to a significant degree, a captive market—customers with regard to whom the firm has a competitive advantage over other firms. This may mean that the firm can deliver its wares to those customers at a lower cost than can its more distant competitors, or it may, as in the barbershop case, mean that it costs the customers less, in time or money, to go to one firm than to another. In such a situation, the firm finds that it is a price searcher—it can vary its price over a significant range, with higher prices reducing, but not entirely eliminating, the quantity it can sell.

Firms whose product is consumed on the premises have been mentioned before—in Chapter 10. Because such firms are in a good position to prevent resale, they may also be in a good position to engage in discriminatory pricing. We could (but will not) examine the case of monopolistic competition with price discrimination; in doing so, we might produce a reasonably accurate description of movie theaters, lawyers and physicians in rural areas, private schools, and a number of other familiar enterprises.

There is another form of monopolistic competition that has nothing to do with geography or transport costs. Consider a market in which a number of firms produce similar products. An example might be the market for microcomputers. Any firm that wishes is free to enter, and many firms have done so. Their products, however, are not identical; some computers appeal more to people who have certain specific needs, certain tastes for computing style, experience with particular computers or computer languages, or existing software that will only run on particular computers. Hence different microcomputers are not perfect substitutes for each other. As the price of one computer goes up, those customers who are least "locked into" that particular brand shift to something else, so quantity demanded falls. But over a considerable range of prices, the company can sell at least some computers to some customers—just as a barbershop can raise its price and still retain the customers who live next door to it.

If the manufacturers of all computers appear to be making positive profits, new firms will enter the industry; if existing firms appear to be making negative profits, some will exit the industry—just as with barbershops. If one type of computer appears to be making large positive profits, other manufacturers will introduce similar designs—just as high profits on one part of the street of barbers, due to an unusually high ratio of customers to barbershops on that part of the street, would give barbershops elsewhere on the street an incentive to move closer.

Consider the recent history of the microcomputer industry. When Apple first introduced the Macintosh it was the only mass market machine designed around an intuitive, graphic, object-oriented interface. In early 1985, Jack Tramiel, president of Atari, announced what was to become the Atari 520ST; the press dubbed it the "Jackintosh." At about the same time, Commodore introduced the Amiga. Over the next few years it became clear that there were a lot of customers living on that particular part of the street of computers—a lot of users who, once introduced to such a computer, preferred it to the more conventional designs. In 1988, IBM finally moved its barbershop, introducing a new line of computers (PS/2) and a new operating system (OS/2) based on essentially the same ideas.

One reason why IBM chose to move may have been that its own portion of the street was getting crowded. During the years after IBM introduced its PC, XT, and AT, a large number of other companies introduced "IBM compatibles"—computers capable of running the same software, in many cases faster, and usually less expensive. By the time IBM finally abandoned the PC line, a sizable majority of IBM-compatible computers were being made by companies other than IBM.

The situation of the computer manufacturers is very similar to the situation of the barbershops—and both can be analyzed as cases of monopolistic competition. The same is true for other industries where the products of one firm are close but not perfect substitutes for the products of another (**product differentiation**), where some customers prefer one style of product and some another, where manufacturers are free to alter the style of their product in response to profitable opportunities, and where firms are free to enter or leave the industry.

PART 4—OLIGOPOLY

Oligopoly exists when there are a small number of firms selling in a single market. The usual reason for this situation is that the optimal size of firm, the size at which average cost is minimized, is so large that there is only room for a few such firms; this corresponds to the sort of cost curves shown on Figure 10-10b. The situation differs from perfect competition because each firm is large enough to have a significant effect on the market price. It differs from monopoly because there is more than one firm. It differs from monopolistic competition because the firms are few enough and their products similar enough that each must take account of the behavior of all the others. The number of firms may be fixed, or it may be free to vary.

So far as their customers are concerned, oligopolies have no more need to worry about strategic behavior than do monopolies. The problem is with their competitors. All of the firms will be better off if they keep their output down and their prices up. But each individual firm is then better off increasing its output in order to take advantage of the high price.

One can imagine at least three different outcomes. The firms might get together and form a cartel, coordinating their behavior as if they were a single monopoly. They might behave independently, each trying to maximize its own profit while somehow taking account of the effect of what it does on what the other firms do. Finally, and perhaps least plausibly, the firms might decide to ignore their ability to affect price, perhaps on the theory that in the long run any price above average cost would pull in competitors, and behave as if they were in a competitive market.

Cooperative Behavior: The Cartel

Suppose all the firms decide to cooperate in their mutual benefit. They calculate their costs as if they were a single large firm, produce the quantity that would maximize that firm's profits, and divide the gains among themselves by some prearranged rule.

Such a cartel faces three fundamental problems. First, it must somehow keep the high price it charges from attracting additional firms into the market. Second, it must decide how the monopoly profit is to be divided among the firms. Third, it must monitor and enforce that division.

Preventing Entry.   The cartel may try to deter entry with the threat that, if a new firm enters, the agreement will break down, prices will plunge, and the new firm will be unable to recoup its investment. The problem with this, as with most threats of retaliation, is that once the threat has failed to deter entry it no longer pays to carry it out.

The situation faced by the cartel and the new entrant can be illustrated with a payoff matrix, as shown on Figure 11-7a. All payoffs are measured relative to the situation before the new firm enters, so the bottom right cell of the matrix, showing the situation if the new firm stays

Figure 11-7

Payoff matrices for a cartel and a new firm threatening entry.   Figure 11-7b shows the case where the cartel has somehow raised entry costs; Figure 11-7c shows the case where the cartel has raised the cost to itself of giving in.

out and the cartel maintains its monopoly price, contains zeros for both players.

The cartel contains ten firms and is currently making a monopoly profit of 1,100. If the new firm enters the industry and is permitted its proportional share of the profit (100), the existing firms will be worse off by 100. It will cost the new firm 50 to enter the industry, so it makes a net gain of +50 (100 monopoly profit − 50 entry cost) if it enters and the cartel does not start a price war (bottom left cell).

If the new firm enters and the cartel starts a price war, it loses the monopoly profit and the new firm loses its entry costs (upper left cell). If the firm does not enter and the cartel for some reason starts a price war anyway, driving prices down to their competitive level, the monopoly profit is eliminated, making the cartel worse off by 1,100 (upper right cell).

A crucial feature of this game is that the new firm moves first; only after it enters the industry does the cartel have a chance to respond. So the new firm enters, knowing that if the cartel must choose between losing 100 by sharing its profit and losing 1,100 by eliminating it, the former option will be chosen.

How might the cartel alter the situation? One way would be to somehow increase the entrance cost above 100. The result would look something like Figure 11-7b. Staying out dominates entering for the new firm.

The simplest and most effective way of raising entrance costs is probably through government. Consider the trucking industry under Interstate Commerce Commission (ICC) regulation. In order for a new carrier to be allowed to operate on an existing route, it had to get a certificate from the ICC saying that its services were needed. Existing carriers would of course argue that they already provided adequate service. The result would be an expensive and time-consuming dispute before the commission.

Another approach to preventing entry is for the cartel somehow to commit itself—to build the economic equivalent of a doomsday machine. Suppose the ten firms in the cartel could sign legally binding contracts guaranteeing their customers a low price if an eleventh firm enters the industry. Having done so, they then point out to potential new firms that there is no point in entering, since if they do there will be no monopoly profit for anyone.

This particular solution might run into problems with the antitrust laws, although, as we will see shortly, similar devices are sometimes used by cartels to control their own members. A more plausible solution might be for the cartel members to somehow commit their reputations to fighting new entrants, thus raising the cost of giving in. By doing so they alter the payoff matrix, making it more expensive to themselves to choose the bottom left cell; doing so will destroy their reputation for doing what they say, which may be a valuable business asset. Figure 11-7c shows the case where the firms in the cartel will lose reputation worth 2000 if they give in.

Looking at the payoff matrix, it seems that the firms have only hurt themselves; they have made their payoff worse in one cell and left it the same in the others. But the result is to make them better off. The new firm observes that, if it enters, the cartel will fight. It therefore chooses not to enter. The situation is precisely analogous to the earlier cases of commitment. Just as in those cases, the player who commits himself is taking a risk that the other player may somehow misread the situation, call the bluff, and discover that it is no bluff, thus making both players worse off.

Dividing the Gains.   The second problem a cartel faces is deciding how the monopoly profit is to be divided among the member firms. In doing so, it is engaged in a game similar to bilateral monopoly but with more players. If the firms all agree on a division, there will be a monopoly profit to be divided; if they cannot agree, the cartel breaks up, output rises, prices fall, and most of the monopoly profit vanishes.

Here again, the cartel may attempt to defend itself by the equivalent of a doomsday machine—a commitment to break up entirely and compete prices down to marginal cost if any firm insists on producing more than its quota. How believable that threat is will depend in part on how much damage the excess production does. If Algeria decides to increase its oil production from 1 percent to 2 percent of total OPEC output, the threat by Saudi Arabia to double its production in response and eliminate everyone's profit, its own included, may not be taken very seriously. Figure 11-8 shows the corresponding payoff matrix. As before, all payoffs are measured relative to the initial situation.

One great weakness of a cartel is that it is better to be out than in. A firm that is not a member is free to produce all it likes and sell it at or just below the cartel's price. The only reason for a firm to stay in

Figure 11-8

Payoff matrix showing the consequence of output increases by Saudi Arabia and Algeria.

Chapter 11   Game Theory, Strategic Behavior, and Oligopoly   **313**

the cartel and restrict its output is the fear that if it does not, the cartel will be weakened or destroyed and prices will fall. A large firm may well believe that if it leaves the cartel, the remaining firms will give up; the cartel will collapse and the price will fall back to its competitive level. But a (relatively) small firm may decide that its production increase will not be enough to lower prices significantly; even if the cartel threatens to disband if the small firm refuses to keep its output down, it is unlikely to carry out the threat.

So in order for a cartel to keep its smaller members, it must permit them to produce virtually all they want, which is not much better than letting them leave. The reduction in output necessary to keep up the price, and the resulting reduction in profits, must be absorbed by the large firms. In the recent case of the OPEC oil cartel, it appears that the reduction of output has been mostly by Saudi Arabia and the United Arab Emirates. One consequence is that it is the Saudis who are the most reluctant to have OPEC raise its price, since it is they who pay in reduced sales for any resulting reduction in the quantity demanded.

Enforcing the Division.　The cartel must not only agree on the division, it must somehow monitor and enforce the agreement. Each member has an incentive to offer lower prices to favored customers—mostly meaning customers who can be lured away from other firms and trusted to keep their mouths shut about the deal they are getting. By doing so, the firm covertly increases its output above the quota assigned to it, and thus increases its profit. Such behavior destroyed many of the attempts by railroad companies to organize cartels during the nineteenth century—sometimes within months of the cartel's formation.

A number of devices may be adopted to prevent this. One is for all members of the cartel to sell through a common marketing agency. Another is for the firms to sign legally binding contracts agreeing to pay damages to each other if they are caught cheating on the cartel agreement. Such contracts are neither legal nor enforceable in the United States, but they are in some other countries.

Another and more ingenious solution is for all of the member firms to include a **Most-Favored-Customer clause** in their sales contracts. Such a clause is a legally binding promise by the seller that the purchaser will get as low a price as any other purchaser. If a firm engages in chiseling—selling at below the official price to some customers—and is eventually detected, customers that did not get the low price can sue for the difference. That makes chiseling a very expensive proposition unless you are sure you will not get caught, and thus helps maintain the stability of the cartel.

Figure 11-9 shows the payoff matrix for a two-firm cartel before and after the firms add Most-Favored-Customer clauses to their sales contracts. Before (Figure 11-9a), the firms are caught in a prisoner's dilemma; the equilibrium outcome is that both of them chisel. After (Figure 11-9b), the cost of chiseling has been increased, making it in

Figure 11-9

(a)

		Firm 2	
		Abide	Chisel
Firm 1	Abide	0, 0	−400, +200
	Chisel	+200, −400	−300, −300

(b)

		Firm 2	
		Abide	Chisel
Firm 1	Abide	0, 0	−400, −100
	Chisel	−100, −400	−500, −500

Payoff matrices for a two-firm cartel, before and after adding a Most-Favored-Customer clause. The clause raises the cost of chiseling to either firm, changing the dominant strategy from the lower right cell (both firms chisel) to the upper left (both firms abide by the cartel agreement).

both firms' interest to abide by the cartel price. Just as in the case shown by Figure 11-7c, the firms have made their alternatives less attractive, lowering the payoffs in some of the cells, and have benefited themselves by doing so.

There are many other contractual devices that can be used by a cartel to control cheating by its members. A **Meet-or-Release clause** is an agreement by which a seller guarantees that if the customer, after agreeing to buy, finds a lower price elsewhere, the seller will either meet the price or release the customer from his agreement. Such a clause gives the customer an incentive to report chiseling by other firms, in order to get a low price for itself; it thus makes such chiseling more risky and less profitable.

A particularly elegant device for controlling cheating is **cross-licensing of patents**. Suppose there are two firms in the widget industry, each with a variety of patents covering particular parts of the production process. Each firm can, if it wishes, produce widgets without infringing the other firm's patents. Instead, the firms cross-license; each agrees that, in exchange for permission to use the other firm's patents, it will pay the other firm $10 for every widget it produces.

The effect of the agreement is to raise marginal cost for each firm by $10/widget. At the higher marginal cost, each firm finds it in its interest to produce less. If their combined output is still too high, they raise the licensing fee and continue doing so until output reaches the profit-maximizing level—the level that would be produced by a single monopoly firm.

The beauty of this solution is that as long as the licensing fee is paid, there is no need for each firm to check on what the other firm is doing. It is in the private interest of each firm, given that it must pay the license fee, to keep its output down. Average cost is unaffected by the fee, assuming the firms produce the same amount, since each receives as much as it pays. But marginal cost is raised by the amount of the fee, and it is marginal cost that determines output.

Mergers

There is at least one more way that a cartel may try to control its members—by turning itself into a monopoly. If the firms in the cartel merge, many of the cartel's problems disappear. The disadvantage of merging is that it may raise costs; presumably the reason there were several firms initially instead of a single natural monopoly was that the efficient scale for a firm was less than the full size of the market. That is a price the individual firms may be willing to pay, if in exchange they get to sell at a monopoly price without worrying about chiseling by other members of the cartel or threats by some members to pull out unless they receive a larger share of the market.

Of course, in forming the merger, there is still a bargaining problem; the owners of each firm want to end up with as large a fraction as possible of the new monopoly's stock. It may be hard for each firm to judge just how much it can ask for its participation in the merged firm. When J. P. Morgan put together U. S. Steel, one crucial step was buying out Andrew Carnegie for $400 million. Morgan is said to have commented later that if Carnegie had held out for $500 million, he would have paid it.

One problem that merger does not eliminate is the problem of entry by new firms. Indeed, it may increase that problem. Threats by one large firm to increase output and drive down prices if a new firm enters are even less believable than threats by a group of firms, for the same reason that the Saudis are in a weak position in bargaining with Algeria or Venezuela. And if the larger firm has higher costs than the new entrant, its position is weaker still. When U.S. Steel was put together in 1901, its market share was about 61 percent. By 1985 it was down to 16 percent.

There Ought'a Be a Law

I have discussed a variety of different devices that cartels use to control cheating by their members. Such cheating is a bad thing from the standpoint of the cartel's members, but a good thing from the standpoint of the rest of us—their customers. This raises the question of why devices such as Most-Favored-Customer clauses and cross-licensing of patents are not illegal.

The general issue of regulating monopolies will be discussed at some length in Chapter 16. For the moment, it is sufficient to point out that all of these devices may also be used for other purposes. A Most-Favored-Customer clause may be a way of guaranteeing the customer that he will not be the victim of price discrimination by a supplier in favor of his competitors. A cross-licensing agreement may permit firms to lower their costs by each taking advantage of the other's technology. It is easy enough for me, writing a textbook, to assume that the widget firms can each produce widgets just as well using only its own patents, but there may be no easy way for a court to determine whether that is true for real firms in a real industry. A merger may be intended to give the new firm a monopoly at the expense of a higher production cost, but it may also be a way of lowering production costs by combining the different strengths of several different firms.

This does not, of course, mean that the government makes no attempt to regulate such behavior. Mergers between large firms have often been the target of antitrust suits. One problem is, as I suggested in the previous chapter, that such intervention may do more harm than good; while it may make it more difficult for oligopolies to charge monopoly prices, it may also make it more difficult for new firms to form that would compete with existing monopolies. A second problem is that, for reasons that will be discussed in Chapter 19, it may often be in the interest of the government doing the regulation to support the producers against their customers rather than the other way around.

There Is a Law—Government to the Rescue

> . . . the high price for the crude oil resulted, as it had always done before and will always do so long as oil comes out of the ground, in increasing the production, and they got too much oil. We could not find a market for it . . . of course, any who were not in the association were undertaking to produce all they possibly could; and as to those who were in the association, many of them men of honor and high standing, the temptation was very great to get a little more oil than they had promised their associates or us would come. It seemed very difficult to prevent the oil coming at that price.
>
> —John D. Rockefeller, discussing an unsuccessful attempt to cartelize the production of crude oil. Quoted in McGee, op. cit.

Rockefeller was too pessimistic; there is a way of keeping a high price from drawing more oil out of the ground. The solution is a monopoly in the original sense of the term—a grant by government of the exclusive right to produce.

Consider the airline industry. Until the recent deregulation, no airline could fly a route unless it had permission from the Civil Aeronautics Board. The CAB could permit the airlines to charge high prices while preventing new competitors from entering and driving those prices down. From the formation of the CAB (originally as the Civil Aeronautics Administration) in 1938 until deregulation in the late 1970s, no major scheduled interstate airline came into existence.

Even if the airlines, with the help of the government, were able to keep out new firms, what prevented one airline from cutting its fares to attract business from another? Again the answer was the CAB; under airline regulation it was illegal for an airline to increase or reduce its fares without permission. The airline industry was a cartel created and enforced by the federal government, at considerable cost to the airlines' customers.

In order for a private cartel to work, the number of firms must be reasonably small; otherwise the smaller firms will correctly believe that an expansion in their output will increase their sales with only a negligible effect on price. That is not true for a governmentally enforced cartel. The government can provide protection against both the entry of outsiders and expanded output by those already in the industry, thus providing an industry of many small price-taking firms with monopoly profits—at the expense of its customers. If the government prevents entry but does not control output, we have one of the situations discussed in Chapter 9—a competitive industry with closed entry.

One form such arrangements often take is professional licensing. The government announces that in order to protect the public from incompetent physicians (morticians, beauticians, poodle groomers, egg graders, barbers, . . .), only those with a government-granted license may enter the profession. Typically the existing members of the profession are assumed to be competent and receive licenses more or less automatically. The political support for the introduction of such arrangements comes, almost invariably, not from the customers, who are supposedly being hurt by incompetent practitioners, but from the members of the profession. That is not as odd as it may seem; the licensing requirement makes entry to the profession more difficult, reducing supply and increasing the price at which those already in the profession can sell their services.

Time

In discussing the problems a cartel faces, I have so far ignored the element of time. Supply curves are usually much less elastic in the short run than in the long. If the price of oil rises sharply, it may be years before the additional investment in exploration and drilling generated by the opportunity to make high profits has much effect on the amount of oil being produced. The same is true for demand. In the short run, we can adjust to higher oil prices by taking fewer trips, driving more slowly, or lowering our thermostats. In the medium run, we can form carpools. In the long run, we can buy smaller and more fuel-efficient cars, live closer to our jobs, and build better insulated homes.

So even if a cartel can succeed in raising the price—and its profits— for a few years, in the long run both the price and the cartel's sales are likely to fall as customers and potential competitors adjust. In the case of OPEC, the process of adjustment was somewhat delayed by the Iran-Iraq war—during which the combatants reduced each other's petroleum output by blowing up refineries, pipelines, and ports.

Noncooperative Behavior: The Nash Equilibrium

So far we have been considering outcomes in which the firms in an oligopolistic industry agree to cooperate, although we have assumed that each will violate the agreement if doing so is in its interest. An alternative approach is to assume that the oligopoly firms make no attempt to work together. Perhaps they believe that agreements are not worth making because they are too hard to enforce, or that there are too many firms for any agreement to be reached. In such a situation, each firm tries to maximize its profit independently. If each firm acts independently, entirely ignoring the effect of what it does on what other firms do, the result is a Nash equilibrium.

Part of the definition of Nash equilibrium is that each player takes what the other players are doing as given when deciding what he should do; he holds their behavior constant and adjusts his to maximize his gains. But if one firm increases its output, the other firms must adjust whether they choose to or not. If they continue to charge the same price, they will find that they are selling less; if they continue to produce the same amount, the price they can sell it for will fall. The firms, taken together, face a downward-sloping demand curve, and there is no consistent way of assuming it out of existence.

This means that, in describing the game, we must be careful what we define a strategy to be; as you will see, different definitions lead to different conclusions. The two obvious alternatives are to define a strategy by quantity or by price. In the former case, each firm decides how much to sell and lets the market determine what price it can sell it at; in the latter, the firm chooses its price and lets the market determine quantity. We will try to find the Nash equilibrium for an oligopoly first on the assumption that a firm's strategy is defined by the quantity it produces and then on the assumption that it is defined by the price the firm charges.

Strategy as Quantity—Version One

On this interpretation of Nash equilibrium, each firm observes the quantities being produced by the other firms and calculates how much it should produce to maximize its profit, assuming that their output stays the same. Figure 11-10 shows the situation from the standpoint of one firm. D is the demand curve for the whole industry. Q_{other} is the combined output of all the other firms in the industry. Whatever price the firm decides to charge, the amount it will sell will equal total demand at that price minus Q_{other}; so D_f, D shifted left by Q_{other}, is the **residual demand curve**, the demand curve faced by the firm. The firm calculates its marginal rev-

Figure 11-10

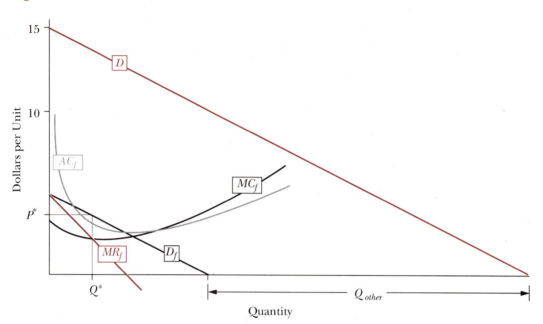

One firm in an oligopoly calculates its profit-maximizing quantity of output where marginal revenue equals marginal cost. Marginal revenue is calculated from the residual demand curve D_f. Other firms are assumed to hold the quantity they produce constant.

enue from that, intersects it with marginal cost, and produces the profit-maximizing quantity Q^*.

We are not quite finished. If the situation is a Nash equilibrium, then not only this firm but every firm must be producing the quantity that maximizes its profit, given the quantities produced by the other firms. If all firms are identical, then all firms will find the same profit-maximizing output. On Figure 11-10, Q_{other} is eight times Q^*, so the situation is a Nash equilibrium provided there are exactly nine firms in the market. Each firm produces Q^*, so from the standpoint of any one firm there are eight others, with a total output of $Q_{other} = 8Q^*$.

We have not yet considered the possibility of new firms entering the industry in response to the opportunity to make above-market profits. If entry is forbidden by law, we can forget that problem. If entry is legal and anyone who wishes can start a new firm with the same cost curves as the old one, then there is one more step to solving the problem. With nine firms, price is above average cost, so profit is positive. Redo the problem with ten firms; if price is still above average cost, try eleven. When you reach a number of firms for which price is below average cost, you have gone too far; if the number is twelve, then in equilibrium there will be eleven firms. The twelfth will not enter because it knows that if it does, it, along with the existing firms, will make negative profits.

Section III   Complications, or Onward to Reality

We are now back at something very much like monopolistic competition—marginal cost equal to marginal revenue and profit (approximately) equal to zero. The one difference is that we are assuming all firms produce identical products, so Firm 1 is just as much in competition with Firm 12 as with Firm 2.

Version Two—Reaction Curves

Another way of solving the same problem is in terms of **reaction curves**—, functions showing how one firm behaves as a function of the behavior of the other firms. The more firms in the industry, the more dimensions we need to graph such functions. Since we have only two dimensions available, we will consider the simple case of **duopoly**—an industry with two firms. This is, as it happens, the case analyzed by Cournot, who invented the fundamental idea more than a century before Nash.

Figure 11-11 shows the situation from the standpoint of one of the firms. D is the demand curve for the industry. D_1 is the residual demand curve faced by Firm 1, given that Firm 2 is producing a quantity $Q_2 = 40$; D_1 is simply D shifted left by Q_2. Q_1 is the quantity Firm 1 produces,

Figure 11-11

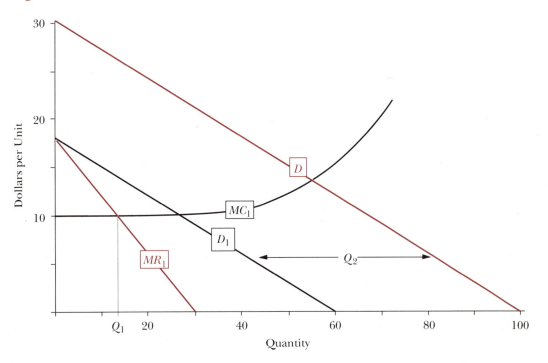

Calculating one point on Firm 1's reaction curve. If Firm 2 produces $Q_2 = 40$, Firm 1 maximizes its profit by producing $Q_1 = 13$.

calculated by intersecting the marginal revenue curve calculated from D_1 with the firm's marginal cost curve MC_1.

By repeating this calculation for different values of Q_2, we generate RC_1 on Figure 11-12—the reaction curve for Firm 1. It shows, for any quantity that Firm 2 chooses to produce, how much Firm 1 will produce. Point A is the point calculated using Figure 11-11. The same analysis can be used to generate RC_2, the reaction function showing how much Firm 2 will produce for any quantity Firm 1 produces. Since the two firms are assumed to have the same cost curves, their reaction curves are symmetrical. The Nash equilibrium is point E on Figure 11-12. At that point and only at that point, each firm is producing its optimal quantity given the quantity the other firm is producing.

Suppose the firms start instead at point A. Firm 1 is producing its optimal quantity (13) given that Q_2 is 40, but 40 is not the optimal quantity for Firm 2, given that Q_1 is 13. So Firm 2 shifts its output to put it on its

Figure 11-12

Using reaction curves to find a Nash equilibrium. E, where the two curves cross, is the equilibrium point. Starting at A, Firm 2 would reduce its output in order to get to its reaction curve at B. Firm 1 would then increase its output, moving to C. The sequence moves the system towards E, showing that the equilibrium is stable.

reaction curve at point *B*. Now its output is optimal, given what Firm 1 is doing. But Firm 1 is no longer on its reaction curve; 13 units is not its optimal output, given what Firm 2 is now doing, so Firm 1 increases Q_1, moving to point *C*.

As you can see, the two firms are moving closer and closer to point *E*. In Chapter 7, we saw that the point where a downward-sloped demand curve crosses an upward-sloped supply curve is a stable equilibrium: If prices and quantities are moved away from that point, they tend to come back. We have just shown that the same thing is true for the reaction curves of Figure 11-12.

The disadvantage of this approach to finding the equilibrium as compared to the first approach we used is that while reaction curves make mathematical sense for any number of firms, it is hard to graph them for more than two. The advantage is that this approach can be applied to a much wider range of problems. We have applied it to a situation where strategy is quantity produced. It could just as easily be applied to two firms each picking a location at which to build its store, or two political parties each choosing a platform and a candidate, or two nations each deciding how many missiles to build. In each case, the reaction curve shows what strategy one player chooses, given the strategy of the other. Nash equilibrium occurs where the two curves intersect, since only there are the strategies consistent—each optimal against the other.

Strategy as Price

We will now redo the analysis of oligopoly with one small change— defining a strategy as a price instead of a quantity. Each firm observes the prices that other firms are charging and picks the price that maximizes its profit on the assumption that their prices will not change.

Since all of the firms are producing identical goods, only the firm charging the lowest price matters; nobody will buy from any other. Figure 11-13 shows the situation from the standpoint of one firm. P_1 is the lowest of the prices charged by the other firms.

The firm in this situation has three alternatives, as shown by D_f. It can charge more than P_1 and sell nothing. It can charge P_1 and sell an indeterminate amount—perhaps $Q(P_1)/N$, if there are N firms each charging P_1. It can charge less than P_1, say one penny less, and sell as much as it wants up to $Q(P_1)$. It is easy to see that the last choice maximizes its profit. It is facing the horizontal portion of the demand curve D_f, so the quantity it sells (up to $Q(P_1)$), which on this figure is more than it wants to sell) does not affect the price. It maximizes its profit by producing Q^* and selling it for just under P_1.

We are not yet done; in a Nash equilibrium, not only this firm but every firm is maximizing its profit. That is not what is happening here. Each other firm also has the option of cutting its price, say by two cents, and selling all it wants. Whatever price the other firms are charging, it is

Figure 11-13

One firm in an oligopoly chooses its profit-maximizing price. All other firms are assumed to hold their prices constant; the lowest such price is P_1. The firm maximizes its profit producing Q^* and selling it for just under P_1.

in the interest of any one firm to charge a penny less. The process stops when the price reaches a level consistent with each firm selling where price equals marginal cost. If there are enough firms, or if additional identical firms are free to enter the industry, the process stops when price gets down to minimum average cost, at which point each firm is indifferent between selling as much as it likes at that price and selling nothing at all.

Bertrand Competition

Oligopolistic firms that produce where price equals marginal cost, just as if they were in a competitive industry, are engaged in **Bertrand competition**. This seems a peculiar thing to do if we define an oligopoly as a market where the individual firm is large enough so that its output has a significant effect on price. Firms are assumed to maximize their profit; they do so, as we saw in the previous chapter, by producing the quantity for which marginal revenue equals marginal cost. If the firm's output affects price, then marginal revenue is below price, so it intersects

Section III Complications, or Onward to Reality

marginal cost at a lower quantity, so the firm produces less than the competitive output.

Bertrand competition is less unrealistic if we define oligopoly as a market with only a few firms. In some such markets, the firm may be able to affect price only in the very short run. If there are lots of other firms that can easily enter the industry—and will if price is high enough to make doing so profitable—the situation may be equivalent to a competitive market.

We have just seen another possible explanation of Bertrand competition. If firms believe that other firms react to them by holding price constant and varying output, they end up producing the quantity for which price equals marginal cost, just as in a competitive market.

The Hand Is Quicker Than the Eye

We are now just about finished with the enterprise of using Nash equilibrium to analyze oligopoly. In order to describe a Nash equilibrium, we must define a strategy. We have considered two alternative definitions, one in which a firm picks a quantity to sell and one in which it picks a price to sell at. We have shown that those two definitions produce two quite different predictions for what the firms will end up doing—how much they will produce and what the price will be.

We could, if we wished, continue the process using more complicated strategies. Perhaps we could find a third solution to oligopoly, and a fourth, and a fifth. But there is not much point in doing so. We already have two answers to one question, and that is enough. More than enough.

FINAL WORDS

I hope I have convinced you that game theory is a fascinating maze. It is also, in my judgment, one that sensible people avoid whenever possible. There are too many ways to go, too many problems that have either no solution or an infinite number of them. Game theory is very useful as a way of thinking through the logic of strategic behavior, but as a way of actually doing economics it is a desperation measure, to be used only when all easier alternatives fail.

Many mathematical economists would disagree with that conclusion. If one of them were writing this chapter, he would assure you that only game theory holds out any real hope of introducing adequate mathematical rigor to economics, that everything else is a tangle of approximations and hand waving. He might concede that game theory has not produced very much useful economics yet, but he will assure you that if you only give him enough time wonderful things will happen.

He may be right. As you have probably gathered by now, I have a high opinion of John Von Neumann. When picking problems to work on, ones that defeated him go at the bottom of my list.

OPTIONAL SECTION

THE VON NEUMANN SOLUTION TO A MANY-PERSON GAME

Although the only solution concept for a many-person game used in the chapter was the Nash equilibrium, a variety of other solutions have been derived by game theorists and used by economists. Two of the most important are the Von Neumann stable set and the core.

Consider a fixed-sum game played by n players. Suppose that, after some negotiation, a group of m of them decide to ally, playing to maximize their combined return and then dividing the gains among themselves by some prearranged rule. Further suppose that the remaining players, observing the coalition, decide to cooperate in their own defense, and also agree to some division of what they can get among their members.

We have now reduced our n-person game to a two-person game—or rather, to a large number of different two-person games, each defined by the particular pair of coalitions playing it. Since fixed-sum two-person games are, in principle, a solved problem, we may replace each of them by its outcome—what would happen if each coalition played perfectly, as defined by the Von Neumann solution to the two-person game.

We now have a new n-person game—coalition formation. Each coalition has a value—the total winnings its members will receive if they play together against everyone else. How much each player ends up getting depends on what coalitions are formed and on how the coalition of which he is a member agrees to divide up its combined take. Three-person majority vote, which we discussed earlier, is an example of a simple coalition game; the value of any coalition with two (or three) members is $100, since a majority could allocate the money. The value of a coalition with one member is zero.

Von Neumann defined an **imputation** as a possible outcome of the game, defined by how much each player ended up with. An imputation X was said to dominate another imputation Y if there was a group of people all of whom were better off with X than with Y and who, if they formed a coalition, could guarantee that they got X. In other words, X dominates Y if

i. There is some coalition C such that X is a better outcome than Y for everyone in C (each person gets more), and
ii. The value of C, the combined winnings that the members of C will get if they cooperate, is at least as great as the amount that X allocates to the members of C.

We have now stated, in a more formal way, the ideas earlier applied to three-person majority vote. We may express the imputations in that game in the form (a,b,c), where a is the amount going to Anne, b to Bill, c to Charles. The imputation (50,50,0) means that $50 goes to Anne, $50 to Bill, and nothing to Charles.

Suppose we start by considering the imputation (50,50,0). It is dominated by the imputation (60,0,40), since Anne and Charles are both better off under the new division and their two votes are enough to determine what happens. The imputation (60,0,40) is in turn dominated by (0,50,50), and so on in an endless cycle. This is the sequence of bargains discussed for this game in Part 1.

Von Neumann tried to solve this problem by defining the solution to a many-person game not as a single imputation but as a group of imputations (called a **stable set**) such that within the group no imputation dominated another and every imputation outside of the group was dominated by one inside. One Von Neumann solution to three-person majority vote is the set of imputations:

(50,50,0),(50,0,50),(0,50,50)

It is fairly simple to show that no one of them dominates another and that any other imputation is dominated by at least one of them.

There are, however, some problems with this definition. To begin with, the solution is not an outcome but a set of outcomes, so it tells us, at most, that some one of those outcomes will occur. It may not even tell us that; there is no reason to assume that one game has only one solution. Three-person majority vote in fact has an infinite number of solutions, many of which contain an infinite number of imputations!

Consider the set of imputations $(x, 100-x, 0)$, $0 \le x \le 100$. It contains an infinite number of separate imputations, each defined by a different value of x. Examples are (10,90,0), (40,60,0), and (4.32,95.68,0), corresponding to $x = 10, 40$, and 4.32. It is simple to show that this set is also a solution; none of the infinite number of imputations within it is dominated by another, and every imputation outside the set is dominated by one inside the set.

Put in words, this solution corresponds to a situation where Anne and Bill have agreed to cut Charles out of the money and divide it between themselves in some one of the infinite possible ways. This is called a discriminatory solution; Charles is the victim of the decision by Anne and Bill to discriminate in favor of themselves and against him. There are lots of such discriminatory solutions, each containing an infinite number of imputations. They include two more in which one player is cut out entirely, plus an infinite number in which one player is given some fixed amount between zero and 50 and the other two divide the rest between themselves in all possible ways.

You may by now have concluded that Von Neumann's definition of a solution to the many-person game is more confusing than useful, since it may, and in this case does, generate an infinite number of solutions, many (in fact an infinite number) of which each contain an infinite number of outcomes. If so, I agree with you; Von Neumann's solution is a gallant try, but unlike his solution to two-person games it does not tell us much about the outcomes of games, even games played by perfect players with infinite calculating ability.

Before going on to discuss other solution concepts, it is worth pausing for a moment to see what Von Neumann did and did not accomplish. In analyzing two-person fixed-sum games, he first showed that all such games could be reduced to one—a matrix of outcomes, with each player choosing a strategy and the outcome determined by the intersection of the two strategies. He then solved that game. Within the limits of his definition of a solution, we now know how to solve any two-person fixed-sum game, although we do not happen to have enough computing power actually to solve any save very simple ones.

In analyzing many-person games, Von Neumann followed a similar strategy. He first showed that all such games could be reduced to one— a game in which players negotiate to form coalitions and divide the resulting gains, against a background defined simply by how much each coalition, if formed, can win. That is as far as he got. He failed to find a solution to that negotiation game that is of any real use in understanding how people do or should play it.

THE CORE

If you think that conclusion is evidence against my earlier description of John Von Neumann as one of the smartest people in this century, I suggest you try to produce a better definition for a solution to a many-person game. Many people have. The solution concept currently most popular with economists who do game theory is a somewhat different one, also based on Von Neumann's work. It is called **the core** and is defined as the set containing all imputations not dominated by any other imputation.

The core has two advantages over the Von Neumann solution. First, since it is defined as containing all undominated imputations, it is unique; we do not have the problem of choosing among several different cores for the same game. Second, since imputations in the core are undominated, once you get to one of them you may plausibly be expected to stay there; there is no proposal by the losers that can both benefit them and lure enough of the winners away to produce a new winning coalition. But while the core is unique, it may contain more than one imputation, so it still does not tell you what the outcome will be.

Furthermore, there is no guarantee that the core will contain any imputations at all. Three-person majority vote has *no* undominated imputations; whatever outcome is agreed upon, there is always some new proposal that benefits two of the players at the expense of the third. One of the things that economists who use game theory do is to prove whether the game describing a particular hypothetical economy does or does not have an empty core—whether there are any undominated imputations. This turns out to be closely related to the question of whether there is a competitive equilibrium for that economy.

PROBLEMS

1. Some games, including Scissors, Paper, Stone, are often played by children for negative stakes; the winner's reward is to be permitted to slap the loser's wrist. It is hard to see how such behavior can be understood in economic terms. Discuss what you think is going on, and how you would analyze it economically.

2. Birds (and other animals) compete for scarce food. When two birds find the same piece of food, each has the choice to fight or to flee. If only one is willing to fight, he gets the food at no cost. If neither is willing to fight, each has a 50 percent chance that the other will start running first, leaving him with the food. If both fight, each has a 50 percent chance of getting the food but also some chance of being injured.

   Suppose there are two varieties of a species of bird, differentiated only by their willingness to fight; in all other ways they are identical. The "hawk" variety always fights; the "dove" always flees. The two live in the same environment. Whichever variety on average does better at food gathering will tend to increase in numbers relative to the other.

   Getting a piece of food is worth a gain of 10 calories. If a hawk fights another hawk over a piece of food, the damage is on average the equivalent of -50 calories. Draw the corresponding payoff matrix.
   a. In equilibrium, what are the relative numbers of hawks and doves?
   b. Explain why.
   c. What part of the chapter does this problem relate to? Explain.

3. Suppose that having an "aggressive personality" pays; almost all of the time other people back down and give you what you want. What do you think will happen to the number of people who adopt that strategy? What will be the effect of that on the payoff to the strategy? Discuss.

4. Figure 11-14 shows marginal cost and average cost for an avocado firm; it also shows demand, D, for avocados. Answer each question first on the assumption that a strategy is defined as a quantity and again on the assumption that it is defined as a price.
   a. Firms can freely enter the avocado industry. In Nash equilibrium, how many firms are there; what is the price; what is the quantity? What is the profit for each firm?

Figure 11-14

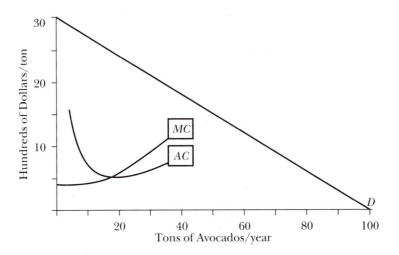

Cost curves for an avocado farm, Problem 4.

    b.   There are two avocado firms; no more are permitted. In Nash equilibrium what is the price; what is the quantity? What is the profit for each firm?

5.   The game of matching pennies is played as follows. Each player puts a penny on the table under his hand, with either the head or the tail up. The players simultaneously lift their hands. If the pennies match (both heads or both tails), Player *A* wins; if they do not match, Player *B* wins.

    a.   Figure 11-15*a* shows the payoffs. Is there a Von Neumann solution? What is it? What is the value of the game?

    b.   Figure 11-15*b* shows a different set of payoffs. Answer the same questions.

    c.   If the players both picked heads or tails at random, they would break even under either set of payoffs. Does this imply that both sets of payoffs are equally fair to both players? Discuss.

6.   There are two firms in an industry; the industry demand curve (*D*) and cost curves of each firm (*MC$_f$*, *AC$_f$*) are as shown on Figure 11-10. A strategy is defined as a price, not a quantity. Find the equilibrium, using reaction curves.

7.   There are two firms in an industry; industry demand (*D*) and firm cost (*MC$_f$*, *AC$_f$*) curves are as shown in Figure 11-10. The firms decide to control output by cross-licensing. What fee should they charge to maximize their profit:

    a.   Assuming that they will end up in a Nash equilibrium with strategies defined as quantities?

    b.   Assuming that they will engage in Bertrand competition?

Figure 11-15

(a)

		Player B	
		Heads	Tails
Player A	Heads	−1, +1	+1, −1
	Tails	+1, −1	−1, +1

(b)

		Player B	
		Heads	Tails
Player A	Heads	−1, +1	+2, −2
	Tails	+2, −2	−3, +3

Payoff matrices for the game of matching pennies, Problem 5.

8. The level of noise at a party often gets so loud that you have to shout to make yourself heard. Surely everyone would be better off if everyone kept his voice down. Discuss the logic of the situation from the standpoint of the ideas of this chapter.
9. Apply the idea of monopolistic competition to a discussion of the market for economics textbooks, with particular reference to this one.

FOR FURTHER READING

The plot of *Doctor Strangelove* was apparently borrowed from the novel *Red Alert* by Peter George (writing under the pseudonym Peter Bryant). In many ways, the novel gives the more interesting version. The air force officer who launches the attack is a sympathetic character, an intelligent and thoughtful man who has decided that a preemptive strike by the United States is the only way out of a trap leading eventually to surrender or mutual destruction. He arranges the attack in such a way that only he can cancel it, notifies his superiors, pointing out that since they cannot stop the attack they had better join it, and then commits suicide. The one flaw in his plan is that the Russians have built a doomsday machine.

At several points in this chapter, I have described the player of a game as choosing a strategy, giving it to a computer, and watching the computer play. There is in fact at least one computer game that works just that way. It is an old game for the Apple II called *Robot War*. The players each program an imaginary robot, then watch their robots fight it out on the computer screen, each following his programming. Not only is it a concrete example of one of the abstractions of game theory, it is also a brilliant device for using a computer to teach programming; when your robot loses, you figure out why and modify your program accordingly.

My description of how a computer can be used as a metaphor for bounded rationality is based on a talk I heard by Ehud Kalai on his recent work, some of which is described in the paper by Kalai and Stanford listed below.

For a discussion of strategic behavior, the original source is John Von Neumann and Oskar Morgenstern, *Theory of Games and Economic Behavior* (Princeton: Princeton University Press, 1944). An easier introduction is R. Duncan Luce and Howard Raiffa, *Games and Decisions: Introduction and Critical Survey* (New York: John Wiley & Sons, 1957).

An original set of essays on strategic problems is Thomas Schelling, *The Strategy of Conflict* (Cambridge: Harvard University Press, 1960).

Other works of interest are:

Robert Axelrod, *The Evolution of Cooperation*, NY: Basic Books, 1984.

E. H. Chamberlin, *The Theory of Monopolistic Competition*, Cambridge, MA: Harvard University Press, 1933.

A. Cournot, *Researches into the Mathematical Principles of the Theory of Wealth*, NY: Macmillan & Co., 1897. This is a translation of a book originally published in French in 1838.

H. Hotelling, "Stability in Competition," *Economic Journal* 39 (Mar. 1929),41–57.

Ehud Kalai and William Stanford, "Finite Rationality and Interpersonal Complexity in Repeated Games," *Econometrica* 56 (1988), 397–410.

John F. Nash Jr. , "Non-cooperative Games," *Annals of Mathematics* 54 (1951), 289–95.

J. Robinson, *The Economics of Imperfect Competition*, London: Macmillan, 1933.

P. Sraffa, "The Laws of Returns under Competitive Conditions," *Economic Journal* 36 (1926), 535–50.

chapter 12

TIME . . .

In earlier chapters I have ignored, so far as possible, two of the major complications of economics (and life)—time and uncertainty. While I have described production as occurring over time ("widgets per hour"), I have also assumed an unchanging world in which each hour is like the last. In relaxing those assumptions, I will first—in this chapter—describe how the picture must be altered to allow for a changing but still certain world, a world in which people never make mistakes, since they know exactly what is going to happen. In Chapter 13, I will describe some of the effects of further changing the picture to fit the uncertain world in which we live.

TIME AND INTEREST RATES

The simplest way to introduce time into the picture is by recognizing that a good is *when* as well as *what*. An apple today and an apple tomorrow are two different goods, as any hungry child will tell you. Not only is there a price for apples today in terms of oranges today, there is also a price for apples today in terms of apples next year. If I trade 100 apples today for 110 next year, I am receiving an "apple interest rate" of 10 percent, since giving you goods now in exchange for goods in the future is the same thing as loaning you goods in exchange for the goods plus interest in the future. The interest rate (in apples for a one-year loan) is the price of apples today measured in apples a year from now ($110/100 = 1.10$) minus one: $1.10 - 1.00 = .10 = 10\%$.

The price of apples today in terms of apples a year from now—the rate at which apples today exchange for apples a year from now—is determined in the same way as other prices. If you want to consume fewer apples now and more in the future, you sell apples now in exchange for apples in the future, contributing to the supply of the former and the demand for the latter. If you want to consume now and pay later, you sell future apples in exchange for present ones, contributing to the supply of future apples and the demand for present apples. There is some price—some apple interest rate—at which quantity supplied (of current apples to be exchanged for future apples) equals quantity demanded (of current apples to be exchanged for future apples). That is the market interest rate.

Investing Apples

So far, I have assumed that all loans are consumption loans; people buy present apples with future apples (borrow) in order to eat the apples. Another reason is to plant them. Suppose you can take 10,000 apples, remove the seeds from some of them, and trade what is left for the labor of workers who will plant the seeds, water the baby apple trees when they come up, pull weeds, and eventually pick 11,000 apples from your new orchard. If you can do all this in a year (very fast-growing apple trees), you will produce 11,000 future apples using 10,000 present apples as input.

If the apple interest rate is below 10 percent, this is a profitable investment. You borrow 10,000 apples, plant them, pay back 10,000 plus interest a year from now, and have some left over. By doing so, you provide an additional demand for present apples and supply of future apples, which must be included in the total demand and supply determining the apple interest rate. By buying present apples (borrowing apples now), "investing" them, and paying with future apples, you drive up the price of present apples in terms of future apples—the apple interest rate.

As long as the apple interest rate is below 10 percent, planting orchards is profitable. More and more orchards are planted. Each one increases the demand for present apples and the supply of future apples, driving the interest rate (the price of present apples measured in future apples) up. So if you, and everyone else, can convert 10 present apples into 11 future apples by planting an orchard, the apple interest rate cannot stay below 10 percent.

One way of producing future goods from present goods is by planting apple trees; another way is to put the present goods somewhere safe and wait. For goods without significant storage costs (gold bars—provided nobody knows you have them), you can produce one unit of the future good from one unit of the present good, so the interest rate for such goods cannot be less than zero. You would never give 10 ounces of gold in exchange for 9 a year from now, since you could always hide your 10 ounces and have 10 ounces a year from now. That is not true for perishable goods (tomatoes) or for goods that are expensive to store (gold bars—if everyone knows you have them). For such goods, negative interest rates are possible.

Apple Interest Rate = Orange Interest Rate

So far, I have talked only about apple interest rates, leaving open the possibility that there may be a different interest rate for every good. Whether this happens depends on what happens to relative prices (the price of apples now in terms of oranges now, for instance) over time. If the relative prices of all goods stay the same over time (so it always costs the same number of oranges to buy an apple, or a cookie, or a car, or anything else), then all goods must have the same interest rate. If the relative price of one good measured in another is changing, on the other hand, then the two goods will have different interest rates.

To see why this is true, imagine that the apple interest rate is 10 percent and that an apple always trades for two oranges. What is the orange interest rate?

Suppose you have 200 oranges now and want oranges a year from now. You trade your 200 oranges for 100 apples. You then trade your 100 apples today for 110 apples a year from now—lend them out for a year at an apple interest rate of 10 percent. Finally, you trade 110 apples a year from now for 220 oranges. You have, indirectly, exchanged 200 present oranges for 220 future oranges.

The sequence of transactions is shown in Figure 12-1a. The solid arrows show the actual transactions; the dashed arrow shows the overall effect. The rates at which the exchanges occur are shown in parentheses.

If you (and everyone else) can trade present oranges for future oranges indirectly at an interest rate of 10 percent (1 present orange for 1.1 future oranges), nobody will be willing to trade a present orange for

Figure 12-1

Arbitrage over time—converting present oranges into future oranges, using apples as intermediates. Solid arrows show actual transactions; dashed arrows show the net effect.

less than 1.1 future oranges, so the orange interest rate cannot be *less* than 10 percent. If you reverse the arrows on Figure 12-1*a* and run the cycle backward (borrow 100 apples and trade them for 200 oranges, then pay the debt a year from now with 110 apples that you get by trading 220 oranges for them), you convert future oranges into present oranges at an interest rate of 10 percent (1.1 future oranges for 1 present orange). If you (and anyone else) can get present oranges in this way at a cost of 1.1 future oranges each, nobody will pay more than 1.1 future oranges for a present orange, so the orange interest rate cannot be *more* than 10 percent.

Since the orange interest rate cannot be more or less than 10 percent, it must be 10 percent. So the orange interest rate and the apple interest rate are the same. Precisely the same argument applies for any other goods. If the relative prices of two goods stay the same over time, they must have the same interest rate; if the relative prices of all goods stay the same over time, all goods must have the same interest rate. This is what economists call the **real interest rate**, in contrast to the **nominal interest rate**—the rate at which you can exchange dollars today for dollars a year from now—the interest rate reported in the daily paper.

Apple Interest Rate ≠ Orange Interest Rate

We now know what happens if relative prices stay the same over time. What happens if they do not? Suppose that the price of apples measured in oranges is falling; an apple buys 2 oranges today, but a year from now, 1 apple will exchange for only 1.5 oranges. Running through the same example (present oranges to present apples to future apples to future oranges), you find that you have traded 200 present oranges for 165 future oranges, for an orange interest rate of about −17.5 percent. The cycle is shown on Figure 12-1*b*. Just as on Figure 12-1*a*, you can run through the cycle in either direction, lending or borrowing oranges at an interest rate of about −17.5 percent.

It may have occurred to you that this is not the first time you have seen this kind of argument. We used exactly the same procedure in Chapter 4 to show that if you knew the price of all goods in terms of one good, you could deduce the price of any good in terms of any other good. The process that we have illustrated here in Figures 12-1*a* and 12-1*b* was described there in a somewhat less complicated form; it is called **arbitrage**. All we have done is to expand the argument to apply to goods that are labeled by *when* they are as well as by *what* they are.

Real and Nominal Interest Rates

The real interest rate is the rate at which you can convert goods now into goods next year—whether by trading goods for goods directly or by converting goods into money, converting money this year into money next year (lending it out), and converting money next year into goods next year. The nominal interest rate is the rate at which you can convert dollars this year into dollars next year. If the real interest rate is 10 percent, that means that if instead of consuming 10 apples, or oranges, or automobiles you save them and lend them out, you will be paid back eleven next year. If the nominal interest rate is 10 percent and you lend out $10, you will get $11 back.

Real and nominal interest rates are equal if, as we shall assume throughout most of this chapter, the price of goods measured in money is not changing—the inflation rate is zero. If there is a positive inflation rate, the nominal rate is higher than the real rate; you get more future dollars for present dollars than future goods for present goods, but future dollars buy fewer goods than present dollars. We consume apples and oranges and automobiles, not dollars, so it is the real, not the nominal, interest rate that is relevant to the decision of whether to spend now or save for the future.

In most economies, relative prices change over time, so the apple interest rate and the automobile interest rate are likely to be different. The real interest rate is then a weighted average of the interest rates for different goods, with the weighting based on how much of each good the individual consumes. This leads to further complications, since the amount of each good consumed is also changing over time.

PRESENT VALUES

You have 6 oranges, 3 apples, and an ice cream cone. If markets exist for oranges, apples, and cones, and if, as we generally assume, the costs of arranging to buy and sell goods are negligible, you can transform that bundle of goods into any other bundle with the same total price—by selling what you have and buying what you want. You are therefore indifferent between any two such bundles—not in the sense of being equally willing to consume each, but in the sense of being able to transform one into the other by market transactions. So one useful way of summing up what you have is by calculating what it is worth; this makes it possible to compare (for purposes of buying and selling but not of consuming) very disparate bundles. I do not like diamonds and do like ice cream cones, but I would rather have a one-carat diamond than an ice cream cone—even Baskin-Robbins's Pralines and Cream. In this sense, $110 worth of anything is preferred to $100 worth of anything else.

The same method can be used to evaluate bundles across time. Suppose I am offered two employment contracts: one consists of $40,000/year for ten years, the other of $31,000 the first year and a $2,000 raise for each of the next nine. Each contract is a bundle of ten different goods. The different goods are "money this year," "money next year," and so on. How can I compare them?

I can compare them by using the price of "money this year" in "money next year" (or "money two years from now" or . . .) to find a single market value for the bundle, just as I do for a bundle of different goods at the same time. Suppose the interest rate, at which I can either borrow or lend, is 10 percent. In that case, I can convert $1,000 this year into $1,100 next year (by lending) or $1,100 next year into $1,000 this year (by borrowing). In the first case, I lend out the $1,000 (losing the use of it now) and get $1,100 ($1,000 plus $100 in interest) a year from now; in the second case, I borrow $1,000 this year, and pay back the principal plus $100 in interest with the $1,100 I will have next year.

The difference between money this year and money next year is not the same as the difference between how much money will buy this year and how much it will buy next year. Even if we expect prices to stay the same, most of us would rather have a dollar now than a dollar in the future, just as most of us would rather have an apple now than an identical apple in the future. So even when there is no inflation, the nominal interest rate is usually positive—if you give up a dollar this year, you can get more than a dollar next year in exchange.

The **present value** of a series of payments is their total value measured in terms of money in a single year. Suppose, in the example I gave, I want the present value in Year 1 of the series of payments associated with the first employment contract. Forty thousand dollars at the beginning of Year 1 is worth $40,000 in Year 1, so the present value of the first term is easy. Forty thousand dollars in Year 2 can be converted into $(1/1.1) \times \$40,000$ in Year 1; if I borrowed that sum in Year 1, I could exactly pay it off with my Year 2 income. Forty thousand dollars in Year 3 is equivalent to $(1/1.1) \times (1/1.1) \times \$40,000$ in year 1, and so on. The third column of Table 12-1 shows the present values of the payments in the first series. Adding them up we find that the present value of the first series of payments is $270,362. That is the sum I could borrow in Year 1 and exactly pay off with the entire ten-year stream of payments.

Table 12-1

1	2	3	4	5	6	7
	Pay-		Pay-			
Year	ment(1)	Present Value(1)	ment(2)	Present Value(2)	Save	Accumulate
1	$40,000	$40,000	$31,000	$31,000	$9,000	$ 9,000
2	$40,000	$36,364	$33,000	$30,000	$7,000	$16,900
3	$40,000	$33,058	$35,000	$28,926	$5,000	$23,590
4	$40,000	$30,053	$37,000	$27,799	$3,000	$28,949
5	$40,000	$27,321	$39,000	$26,638	$1,000	$32,844
6	$40,000	$24,837	$41,000	$25,458	-$1,000	$35,128
7	$40,000	$22,579	$43,000	$24,272	-$3,000	$35,641
8	$40,000	$20,526	$45,000	$23,092	-$5,000	$34,205
9	$40,000	$18,660	$47,000	$21,926	-$7,000	$30,626
10	$40,000	$16,964	$49,000	$20,781	-$9,000	$24,688
		$270,362		$259,892		$24,688

I can, in the same way, calculate the present value of the second series of payments (Table 12-1, column 5). It turns out that it is smaller. This implies that the first stream of income could, by appropriate borrowing and lending, be converted into the second with something left over. So the first stream of income is unambiguously preferable to the second, just as a bundle of goods worth $100 is unambiguously superior to a bundle worth $90, since one can sell the former, buy the latter, and have $10 left.

How would I convert the first stream of payments into the second? The answer is shown on columns 6 and 7 of the table. I would save (and lend out) $9,000 of my first year's salary (leaving me with $31,000 to spend, just as in the second stream), $7,000 of the second year's, $5,000 of the third, $3,000 of the fourth, $1,000 of the fifth. At that point I would have accumulated $25,000 plus interest. In the sixth year, I would pay myself $1,000 from my savings, in the seventh $3,000, and so on, for a total of $25,000. Column 7 of Table 12-1 shows, for each year, the accumulated savings, including interest. At the end, I would have had the same amount to spend each year as with the second employment contract and would have $24,688 left over.

So far I have been describing present value in words with numerical examples. Translated into algebra, we have the following formula:

$$PV(t) = \sum_{i=0}^{i=n} \frac{y_i}{(1 + r)^{i-t}}$$

Here $PV(t)$ is the present value at time t of an n-year stream of payments; y_i is the payment in year i and r is the market interest rate. $\sum$ is the mathematical symbol for "sum"; in general:

$$\sum x_i \equiv x_1 + x_2 + x_3 + \cdots$$

with the sum being over as many different x_is as there are values of i. If we wish to evaluate the present value as of the beginning of the stream of payments, we have $t = 0$,

$$PV(0) = \sum_{i=0}^{i=n} \frac{y_i}{(1 + r)^i}$$

Present value calculations provide a way of evaluating any project, employment contract, or the like that can be described as a stream of payments, positive (revenue) or negative (cost), through time. If the present value of a stream is positive, then it is worth having if you do not have to give up something else, such as an alternative job with a higher positive present value, in order to get it. If it is negative, it is not worth having. If you must choose between two, the one with the higher present value is preferable.

Using the idea of opportunity cost introduced in an earlier chapter, we can reduce the previous paragraph to one simple sentence: "Choose any alternative that has a positive present value." If taking one job means not taking another, then not getting what you would have earned in the second job is the (opportunity) cost of taking the first and should be included in the present value calculation. If the result is still positive, then the present value of the income stream is higher for the first job than for the second, so you should take it.

One interesting present value is the present value of $1/year forever, which turns out to be $1 divided by the interest rate. To see why this is so, note that if you lend out $10 at 10 percent interest (10 equals 1/0.10), you can collect $1/year forever. Just collect the interest and keep reinvesting the $10. We shall use this fact shortly.

ECONOMICS IN A CHANGING WORLD

In the previous 11 chapters we have analyzed the economics of an unchanging world, where every year is exactly the same as the year before. In that context, a question such as "If we sell widgets, will we make a profit?" reduces to the question "Will we make a profit this year?" Since every year is the same, if you make a profit this year you will make a profit every other year as well. In the real world, things are not so simple; a firm may choose to take a loss for several years in order to get profits in the future.

By using present values, we reduce the more complicated problem of choice in a changing world to the simpler problem that we have already solved. A firm trying to decide whether to produce widgets converts all of its future gains and losses into present values and adds them up. If the sum is positive (a net profit), it ought to produce; if the sum is negative (a net loss), it ought not to. Similar calculations can be made by a firm deciding how much to produce, what mix of inputs to use, and so forth. It compares the alternatives in terms of the present value of all gains and losses and chooses the one for which it is highest.

Suppose, to take a particularly simple example, that a firm is considering an investment (a factory, a piece of land, a research project) that lasts forever and produces the same return each year. If the present value of the annual profit made possible by the investment is greater than the cost of the investment, it is worth making; otherwise it is not. As we just saw, the present value of a permanent income stream of $X is X/r, where r is the market interest rate. So if an investment of $1,000,000 yields an annual return of more than $(r) \times $1,000,000$, it is worth making. If, in other words, the investment pays more than the going interest rate, it is an attractive one.

The calculation is more complicated if you are investing in something that will eventually wear out; in that case, the investment must pay at least the interest rate plus its own replacement cost to be worth making. The corresponding present value calculation is to compare the present value of the stream of income generated by the investment ($X per year for as many years as the machine lasts) with the initial expense plus the present value of any future expenses (maintenance, for example); if the present value of the payments is larger than the expense (the **net present value** is positive), the investment is worth making.

Redoing the previous 11 chapters in these terms would make this a very long chapter indeed, so I will restrict myself to working out the logic of one particularly interesting case.

DEPLETABLE RESOURCES

Consider a depletable resource, say petroleum. There is a certain amount of it in the ground; when it has all been pumped up, there will never be any more. Firms that own oil wells must decide how to allocate their production over time in order to maximize profits. What will be the result?

Assume, for simplicity, that it costs nothing to produce oil; if you own an oil well containing 1,000,000 barrels of oil, your problem is simply to decide when to sell how much. Further assume that the oil wells are owned by many firms, each with only a few wells, so that each firm is a price taker.

What the firm takes is not a single price but a pattern of prices over time—P_1 at the beginning of the first year, P_2 at the beginning of the second year, P_3 at the beginning of the third year, and so on. Since we are considering a world with change but no uncertainty, at the beginning of the first year everyone already knows what the entire pattern of prices over time is going to be. Suppose that the market interest rate is 10 percent, the first year's price (P_1) is $10.00/barrel, and the second year's price (P_2) is $12.00/barrel. A firm that sells some of its oil at the beginning of the first year gets a present value (measured in Year 1) of $10.00/barrel. A firm that sells oil a year later gets a present value (again measured in Year 1 so that we can compare the two) of $12.00/1.1 = $10.91/barrel. Under those circumstances, all firms would prefer to sell their oil in the second year. If they hold money for a year, they get 10 percent; if they hold oil for a year, they get 20 percent.

But if no oil were offered for sale in the first year, the price would be much more than $10.00/barrel. The price structure I have just described—$10.00/barrel in Year 1, $12.00/barrel in Year 2, and an interest rate of 10 percent—is inconsistent with rational behavior. If it existed, it would make people behave in a way such that it could not exist.

The only way to avoid such inconsistencies is for the pattern of prices over time to be such that P_2 is exactly 1.1 times P_1, so that the present value a firm gets by selling a barrel of oil is the same whether it sells it in the first year or the second. If it sells it in the first year, it gets $10.00; if it sells it in the second, it gets $11.00. The same argument applies to all future years. The price of oil must go up, year by year, at the interest rate.

You may find this way of describing what "must" happen confusingly abstract. The alternative is to try to describe the process by which an equilibrium set of prices is reached. In doing so, we will ignore the fact that in the perfectly predictable world we are assuming, everyone knows everything in the first minute of the first year, so equilibrium establishes itself immediately.

Imagine, then, that firms are considering a pattern of oil sales that does not lead to the pattern of prices I have described (price rising at the interest rate). A firm notices that it does better by selling its oil in Year 2 than it would by selling it in Year 1 and investing the money. So the firm changes its plans, transferring any production it had planned to make in Year 1 to Year 2. The result is to drive down the price in Year 2 and drive up the price in Year 1, moving both prices towards the pattern I have described. If the present value of the Year 2 price is still greater than the present value of the Year 1 price, another firm changes its plans. The process continues until the Year 2 price is equal to the Year 1 price times $1 + r$. The same argument applies for the relation between the Year 2 price and the Year 3 price, the Year 3 price and the Year 4 price, and so on.

Deducing the Current Price

Suppose you knew the demand curve for petroleum, the total amount that now exists, and the interest rate. How would you calculate the price? The easiest way is to work backward. The intersection of the demand curve with the vertical axis tells you the highest price petroleum can sell for—the price it will sell for the day the last well goes dry. Call that price P_{max} and that year T_{dry}. A year earlier, in year $T_{dry} - 1$, the price must be lower by a factor of $1/(1+r)$, two years earlier it must be lower by a factor of $1/(1+r)^2$ and so forth.

How do we find the date of T_{dry}? Since we know the price of petroleum in year $T_{dry} - 1$ and the demand curve, we know how much was consumed that year. The same applies for year $T_{dry} - 2$ and for each earlier year. Add up consumption year by year, starting at T_{dry} (quantity demanded $= 0$) and working back. When the total quantity consumed adds up to the total that now exists, you have reached the present. Since you now know how many years separate the year that we run out of oil from the present year, you know when we will run out. The calculations are shown in Figure 12-2a, where price is calculated from the demand curve, and Figure 12-2b, where quantity is added up year by year. The figures assume an initial quantity of oil of a billion barrels.

Section III Complications, or Onward to Reality

Figure 12-2

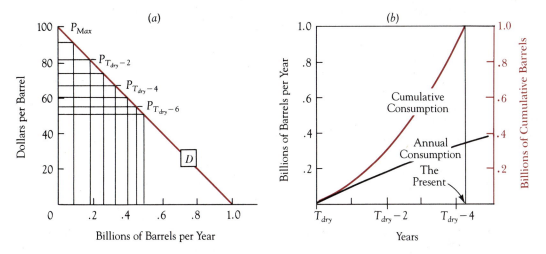

Calculating the price of a depletable resource by working backward from the date at which it is exhausted. T_{dry} is the year the last oil well runs dry. Working backward from T_{dry}, price falls at the interest rate, as shown on Figure 12-2a. Figure 12-2b shows the annual and cumulative consumption; when cumulative consumption reaches the total amount now existing, we have reached the present.

As you may have realized, I have simplified the problem somewhat by assuming implicitly that everything happens at the beginning of each year, so that quantity consumed depends only on price at that instant. One could solve the problem a little more precisely by letting price rise and quantity demanded fall continuously through the year. Doing that would involve either using calculus or making the geometric calculations even more complicated than they are, which is why I did not do so. I have also assumed that D, the demand curve for oil, is stable over time—quantity demanded changes as a result of the changing price, but not as a result of changing automobile technology, population, weather, and so forth. That assumption could also be dropped, but again at the cost of making the calculations more complicated.

In solving the problem, I assumed that the demand curve intersects the vertical axis—that there is some maximum price people will pay for petroleum. An alternative assumption is that as quantity goes to zero, price goes to infinity—people keep buying less and less petroleum at a higher and higher price per gallon. The calculation in that case is more complicated, since it involves an infinite sum (of smaller and smaller quantities of petroleum), but the logic of the problem is essentially the same.

Chapter 12   Time . . .   343

It is interesting to ask how our solution would change if we changed one of the variables. Suppose, for instance, that oil producers have adjusted to an interest rate (present and anticipated) of 5 percent. Some unexpected event raises the interest rate (now and forever after) to 10 percent. What happens to current and future prices and consumption of oil?

You should be able to work out the answer for yourself. At the old rate of production (before the change), oil prices were rising at 5 percent a year; an oil producer got the same return holding oil as holding money. With that pattern of production after the change, producers find that it is more profitable to produce a gallon of oil this year and invest the money, ending up next year with this year's price plus 10 percent, than to hold the oil and produce it next year, ending up with this year's price plus 5 percent. Oil producers alter their plans, shifting production to earlier years. As they do so, the price falls in the early years, since more oil is being produced then, and rises in the later years. When equilibrium has been reestablished, current production is higher and the current price lower than before the change, but the price is rising faster than it was before—10 percent a year instead of 5 percent. After adjusting to the higher interest rate, we are using oil faster than before and will run out sooner—as you can easily prove by starting at T_{dry} and working back to the present at the higher interest rate.

Efficient Allocation across Time

In discussing a competitive industry in Chapter 9, I pointed out that the structure of the industry was exactly that which would be chosen by a dictatorial administrator ordered to produce the same quantity at the lowest possible cost. A similar statement can be made about a competitive industry producing a depletable resource. The interest rate represents the rate at which goods this year can be converted into goods next year— as shown in the example of the apple orchard earlier in this chapter. The price of petroleum in any year is equal to its marginal value, for reasons explained back in Chapter 4. If the price of petroleum next year is less than $1+r$ times the price this year (if, say, $P_1 = \$10.00$ and $P_2 = \$10.50$), that means that the marginal barrel this year goes to someone with a marginal value for it of $10 and the marginal barrel next year goes to someone with a marginal value of $10.50/barrel. By choosing to produce a barrel next year that we could have produced this year, we are choosing a value of $10.50 next year instead of a value of $10 this year. But if the interest rate is 10 percent, someone who gives up $10 this year can convert it into $11 next year, so it is wasteful to give up $10 this year in exchange for only $10.50 next year. Following out this argument, a wise and benevolent administrator will allocate a depletable resource so as to make its price rise at the interest rate. As long as he does not do so, there is some way of reallocating production over time that produces a net gain.

This is only a sketch of an argument that cannot be made precisely until after the discussion of economic efficiency in Chapters 15 and 16. If you find the discussion of what a wise and benevolent administrator would do confusing, you may want to come back to it after reading those chapters.

Oil Prices and Insecure Property Rights

Before I leave the subject of depletable resources, several more points are worth making. The first is that the analysis I have given depends on the assumption that the owners of the resource have secure property rights—that they can confidently expect that petroleum they do not sell this year will still be theirs to sell next year.

Suppose that is not true; suppose, for example, that anyone who owns an oil well this year has a 10 percent chance of being expropriated next year. In that case, the same analysis implies that the price of petroleum will increase each year by a factor of $1.1 \times (1+r)$. Owners of oil wells will sell petroleum next year instead of this year only if the price is enough higher to compensate them both for the interest they lose by not selling the oil until next year and for the chance that when next year arrives, the oil will no longer belong to them.

Most oil, at present, belongs to governments; most of those governments are at least somewhat unstable. The present rulers of Saudi Arabia, for example, would be foolish to base their plans on the assumption that they will still rule Saudi Arabia ten years from now—especially with the fate of the Shah of Iran still recent history. They should be, and doubtless are, aware that money in Switzerland is a more secure form of property than oil in Saudi Arabia.

The effects of insecure property rights are not limited to distant sheiks. The American government may be stable, but its economic policies are not; the imposition of special taxes (such as the windfall profits tax) on oil companies is, in effect, a partial expropriation. If oil companies expect such taxes to increase, it is in their interest to produce oil now instead of saving it for the future—or, to put the conclusion more precisely, it is in their interest to produce more now and less in the future than they would if they did not expect such taxes to increase.

One implication of this argument is that the price of oil at present may be too low! If most of it belongs to people with insecure property rights, they have an incentive to produce more now (driving the present price down) and less in the future (driving the future price up) than if property rights were secure. If, as I claim, the solution under secure property rights is in some sense optimal ("efficient" in the sense to be defined in Chapter 15), then insecure property rights create a less desirable outcome. Initially oil prices are too low and consumption too high; later prices are too high and consumption too low. The allocation of the resource over time is inefficient; too much is consumed now and too little saved for later.

Is Oil a Depletable Resource?

It may occur to some readers to ask whether the price of oil *has* been increasing at the interest rate over, say, the last 50 or 100 years. The answer is no. From about 1930 to about 1970, the **real price** of oil—the price allowing for inflation—fell substantially. The OPEC boycott brought the real price most of the way back up to where it had been in 1930, but events since have brought it back down to about what it was before the boycott—far below where it would be if it had been rising at the interest rate from 1930 to 1970.

There are at least three possible explanations for the apparent divergence between theory and fact. The first is that the economic theory of depletable resources is wrong. The second is that the theory is logically correct but that one of its assumptions—a predictable world—does not apply. If, for example, each year people overestimated future demands and/or underestimated future supplies, future prices would consistently turn out lower than expected and price would fail to rise over time at the interest rate. Economists are generally skeptical of such an explanation because it requires not merely mistakes but consistent mistakes; one would expect that after a decade or two of overestimating future oil prices, people would learn to do better—especially people who own oil wells.

The third, and most interesting, explanation of the observed pattern of prices is that oil is not a depletable resource! If this seems like an odd idea, consider that the world has been "about to run out of oil" for most of the past century; for most of that time, proven reserves have been equal to between 10 and 20 years of production.

I started my analysis of a depletable resource by assuming that there were no production costs, so that the price of the resource was entirely due to the limited quantity. Suppose I had not made that assumption. How would the existence of production costs affect the conclusion?

Assume that production costs can be predicted with certainty. In that case, we can repeat our previous analysis, simply substituting "price minus production cost" for price. Price minus production cost is what the owner of an oil well ultimately gets by selling his oil. If it rises faster than the interest rate, all producers are better off holding their oil for future production; if it rises more slowly than the interest rate, all producers are better off selling everything immediately—or at least as fast as they can get the oil out of the ground without raising production cost substantially in the process. In equilibrium, price minus production cost must rise at the interest rate—provided the owners of oil wells have secure property rights.

So one explanation of what has actually happened to oil prices is that most of the price is production cost—where that includes not only the cost of pumping the oil but also the cost of finding it. If production cost in that sense has been falling over time, then price could be falling as well—even if price net of production cost was rising.

In the previous discussion, we were considering a **pure depletable resource**—a resource whose price was entirely determined by its limited supply. Consider, at the other extreme, a resource of which only a limited amount exists but for which production costs are substantial and for which that limited amount is very large compared to the quantity demanded at a price sufficient to cover the cost of production. The amount is so large that technology, law, and political institutions will have changed beyond recognition long before the supply is exhausted.

Under those circumstances, saving the good now in order to sell it when supplies run short is not a very attractive idea—before that happens we may have stopped using it, the owner may have been expropriated, or the world may have ended. Changes in its price over time will be almost entirely determined by changes in production cost. The good is, strictly speaking, depletable, but that fact has no significant effect on its price. The pattern of oil prices over the past 90 years or so suggests that that may well be how the market views petroleum.

If so, then the insecure property rights discussed earlier imply almost exactly the opposite of what they implied before. If the price of oil is determined by the cost of finding and producing it, then insecure property rights make the price of oil higher, not lower, than it would otherwise be. If someone who invests in finding and drilling an oil well has a 50 percent chance of having his well expropriated as soon as it starts producing, his return if he does keep the well must be at least twice his costs in order for him to be willing to make the investment. His return depends on the price he sells the oil for, so the price of oil will be higher in a world of insecure property rights. The same condition that makes the present price of a depletable resource (more precisely, a resource whose price is mostly due to its limited total quantity rather than to its cost of production) lower makes the present price of a resource whose price is mostly due to cost of production higher!

PRICE = VALUE THROUGH TIME AND SPACE

If an individual can buy apples for $0.50 apiece, he will adjust his consumption of apples until the marginal utility of an apple to him, the utility he gets from consuming one more apple, is the same as the marginal utility to him of $0.50—or, in other words, until the marginal value of an apple is $0.50. That is the argument by which we demonstrated, back in Chapter 4, that price equals marginal value: $P = MV$.

An interest rate is also a price. If the apple interest rate is 10 percent, the price of an apple this year is 1.1 apples next year. So I will adjust my consumption of apples in both years until the increased utility I get from consuming one more apple this year is the same as the increased utility I get from consuming 1.1 additional apples next year.

Impatience . . .

On a list of the differences between Lily and me it would be near the top that I park so I won't have to back out when I leave and she doesn't.

—Archie Goodwin

Why would an apple next year give me less utility than an apple this year? There are two major reasons. The first is impatience. Most of us, given the choice between the same pleasure now or in the future, would prefer to have it now. If so, then in comparing alternative patterns of pleasure over time—alternative utility streams—we will discount utility just as we discount income. If, in making a choice today, I am indifferent between a 100-utile pleasure now or a 105-utile pleasure next year, I may be said to have an **internal discount rate** (for utility) of 5 percent.

My internal discount rate—my impatience—is a characteristic of my tastes; it describes my preferences between pleasures now and pleasures in the future, just as my utility function describes my preferences between apples and oranges. The market interest rate depends not merely on my tastes but on the tastes and productive abilities of everyone else as well. There is no particular reason why the two rates should be equal. Impatience may explain why the value to me of an apple now is greater than the value to me (now) of an apple a year from now, but it does not explain why the ratio of the two is exactly equal to the market interest rate.

. . . And Equilibrium

The equality between price and marginal value is not a characteristic of the consumer's tastes; it is a result of his rational behavior in deciding how much of what good to consume. This is true when the choice is between the same good at different times just as much as when it is between different goods at the same time. I will use Figure 12-3 to show how this works for a consumer whose internal discount rate is zero in a world where the market interest rate is 10 percent.

Suppose the consumer whose marginal utility curve is shown on Figure 12-3 consumed the same number of apples each year—say 1,000 (he likes apples). The marginal utility of apples would be 10 utiles per apple, as shown on the figure. Since he consumes the same number of apples each year, he receives the same pleasure from consuming one more apple whichever year he consumes it. Since his internal discount rate is zero, he is indifferent between equal pleasures now and in the future. So he is indifferent between consuming an apple this year, next year, or in any future year.

The apple interest rate is assumed to be 10 percent, so he can trade 10 apples this year for 11 apples next year. Giving up 10 apples this year costs him about 100 utiles; consuming 11 more apples next year gives

Figure 12-3

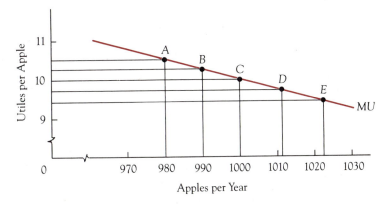

A consumer's marginal utility for apples. The consumer follows a pattern of consumption over time for which the present value (discounted at the discount rate for utility) of the marginal utility of an apple consumed next year equals $1/(1 + r)$ times the marginal utility of an apple consumed this year, where r is the apple interest rate. If the consumer's discount rate for utility equals the apple interest rate, he consumes the same number of apples each year (point C).

him about 110—the numbers are approximate because marginal utility will change a little over the range of quantities from 990 apples per year to 1,011 apples per year. He is indifferent between utiles this year and utiles next year, so losing 100 of the former and gaining 110 of the latter is a net gain. The consumer revises his consumption plans; instead of consuming 1,000 apples each year, he decides to consume 990 this year (point B on Figure 12-3) and 1,011 next year (point D).

Since he is now going to consume fewer apples in the first year than he had initially planned, their marginal utility will be higher. Since he is going to consume more apples in the second year, their marginal utility will be lower. As you can see from the figure, the marginal utility of apples in Year 1 (990 apples per year) is about 10.25 utiles per apple; the marginal utility in Year 2 (1,011 apples per year) is about 9.75 utiles per apple. Even with the revised plan, 11 apples next year are still worth more, in utiles, than 10 apples this year. So long as this is true—so long as the marginal utility of apples in Year 1 is not at least 10 percent greater than in Year 2—the consumer can improve his situation by revising his consumption plan and transferring consumption from Year 1 to Year 2. If the marginal utility of apples in Year 2 were more than 10 percent greater than in Year 1, he could improve his situation by revising in the opposite direction—transferring consumption from Year 2 to Year 1. He will achieve his optimal plan only when the amount he consumes in each year is such that the ratio of the marginal utility of apples in Year 1 to the marginal utility of apples in Year 2 is 1.1—equal to the price of apples in Year 1 measured in apples in Year 2. This, of course, is our old friend the equimarginal principle:

$$\frac{MU(\text{apples in Year 1})}{MU(\text{apples in Year 2})} = \frac{Price(\text{apples in Year 1})}{Price(\text{apples in Year 2})}$$

The ratio of prices, measured in some common unit (say dollars in Year 1), is equal to the price of Year 1 apples measured in Year 2 apples. The solution is shown on Figure 12-3 as points A (first year) and E (second year). The marginal utilities are about 10.5 and 9.5, so their ratio is about 1.1.

The analysis can easily be generalized to more than two years. We have shown that the ratio of marginal utilities between Year 1 and Year 2 must be 1.1. The same argument applies between Year 2 and Year 3, Year 3 and Year 4, and so forth. Consumption of apples rises, year by year, in such a way as to make the marginal utility of apples fall by 10 percent per year.

So far, we have done our calculations on the assumption that the consumer has an internal discount rate of zero—he is indifferent between identical pleasures now and in the future. Now let us consider a consumer who has an internal discount rate of 5 percent. He too will adjust his consumption plans until he is indifferent between an additional 10 apples this year and an additional 11 apples next year. Since he regards 10 utiles this year as equivalent to 10.5 next year, his optimal consumption plan will be one for which 11 apples next year produce 5 percent more utility next year than 10 apples this year produce this year. His consumption for this year will be point B on Figure 12-3; his consumption for next year will be point D.

Finally, consider a consumer whose internal discount rate is 10 percent. His consumption will be point C this year and point C next year. Each year he consumes 1,000 apples and receives a marginal utility of 10 utiles per apple. Since he regards 10 utiles this year as equivalent to 11 next year, he can benefit neither by increasing his present consumption (10 apples more this year, 11 fewer next year) nor by decreasing it.

We have now answered the question that started this discussion. The marginal value of a future apple, measured in present apples, will be the same as the price of a future apple, measured in present apples; $MV = P$. Hence the internal discount rate for apples will be equal to the apple interest rate—and similarly, the internal discount rate for dollars will be equal to the dollar interest rate. The internal discount rate for apples is the sum of the internal discount rate for utility and the rate at which the marginal utility of apples declines with time. The rational consumer will adjust his consumption plans until that sum equals the apple interest rate.

Beyond Apples: Savings, Investment, and the Interest Rate

We have also provided a way of looking at another question of considerable interest—what determines how much people save or borrow. The individual consumer has a flow of income, an internal discount rate, a utility function, and an interest rate at which he can borrow or lend. His objective is, by appropriate borrowing and lending, to arrange his consumption over his lifetime in such a way as to maximize the present value of his utility. That is simply a more formal statement of what we have just been doing with apples—rearranging consumption wherever doing so gets us more utility, discounted at the individual's internal discount rate back to time zero, than it costs us.

Consider an individual—a professional baseball player, say—who will have a very high income in the early part of his life and a much lower one later on. If he spends his money as it comes in, he will consume $100,000 a year at age 25 and only $20,000 a year at age 50. The utility from the last $1,000 of $100,000 is probably much less than the utility from adding $1,000 plus 25 years of accumulated interest to $20,000. So he reduces his expenditure in the early years, invests the money at the market interest rate, and spends it when his income falls.

The same argument applies in reverse to someone with the opposite income pattern—a medical student, say, who has very little income through about age 25 but expects to be doing very well at age 50. He adjusts in the opposite direction, transferring consumption from the later years to the earlier years by borrowing.

We can describe the behavior of such individuals a good deal more precisely by applying the results of the previous section to dollars instead of apples. Assuming, as usual, rational individuals and a predictable world, each consumer will borrow and lend in such a way as to make his internal discount rate for dollars equal to the market interest rate—the rate at which he can borrow or lend dollars.

This implies that the individual's marginal utility for income, discounted back to the present at his internal discount rate for utility, should fall year by year at the interest rate. A dollar spent now will give him the same discounted utility as a dollar plus interest spent next year; the increase in the money exactly balances the fall in its discounted marginal utility. If that were not the case, he could make himself better off by increasing or decreasing his savings. We are again back with the equimarginal principle, applied over time instead of space.

Figure 12-4 shows how the allocation of consumption over time can be analyzed using budget lines and indifference curves. Consider someone who has $40,000 and is deciding how to divide his consumption between this year and next year. If he spends it all now, he will have $40,000 of consumption this year and none next. If he consumes nothing this year, he can lend it all out at an interest rate of 25 percent and con-

Figure 12-4

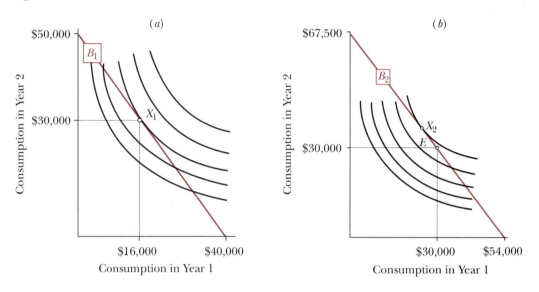

Budget line diagrams for intertemporal choice. B_1 on Figure 12-4a shows a consumer with $40,000 in Year 1 or $50,000 in Year 2. B_2 on Figure 12-4b shows a consumer with $30,000 each year. On both figures, the interest rate is 25 percent.

sume $50,000 next year. The budget line B_1 on Figure 12-4a shows the alternatives available to him. He maximizes his utility (at X_1) by spending $16,000 this year and lending out the other $24,000. Next year he gets back $24,000 in principal plus $6,000 in interest, for a total of $30,000, all of which he consumes. His demand for loans, at an interest rate of 25 percent, is −$24,000. The minus sign means that he is making loans— he is a supplier, hence he is "demanding" a negative quantity.

The same figure could just as easily show someone who has nothing this year but will get $50,000 next year. By borrowing against his future income (at 25 percent), he can consume $40,000 in Year 1 and nothing (his debt just cancels his income) in Year 2. Alternatively, he can consume nothing this year and the whole $50,000 next year. B_1 shows the alternative patterns of consumption available to him. His alternatives, and therefore his optimum pattern of consumption, are exactly the same as in the previous case. He borrows and consumes $16,000 in Year 1. After paying back $20,000 in principal and interest, he has $30,000 left to consume in Year 2. His demand for loans at 25 percent is +$16,000.

Why does the same figure represent both situations? In both, the consumer has the same wealth—a present value of $40,000 in Year 1. As we showed earlier, if the consumer can freely borrow or lend at the same interest rate, all income streams with the same present value are equivalent.

352   **Section III   Complications, or Onward to Reality**

Figure 12-4b shows a consumer with an income of $30,000 each year. If he consumes his income as it comes in, he will be at point E—his **initial endowment**. He maximizes his utility by instead saving $6,000 from his first $30,000. His consumption (point X_2) is $24,000 in Year 1 and $37,500 in Year 2. His demand for loans at 25 percent is $-$6,000$.

We could, if we wished, use diagrams like these to derive the demand curve for loans of a single individual, just as we derived a demand curve from indifference curves back in Chapter 3. We would start with an indifference curve map representing the individuals taste for two "goods"— consumption in Year 1 and consumption in Year 2. For a given endowment—a stream of income—we would draw a series of budget lines corresponding to different interest rates. For each budget line we would find the optimal point and calculate how much the individual would borrow or lend in order to get there from his initial endowment. We would end up with a curve showing amount borrowed as a function of the interest rate. Since the paper we draw the curves on only has two dimensions, we would be limited to analyzing behavior in a two-period world. The mathematics could be generalized easily enough to a many-period world, but we could no longer draw the diagrams.

In all of these cases, just as in the indifference curve diagrams of Chapter 3, the optimum point occurs where the budget line is tangent to an indifference curve. The slope of the budget line shows the rate $(1 + r)$ at which consumption in Year 1 can be exchanged for consumption in Year 2. The slope of the indifference curve shows the rate $(1 + d,$ where d is your internal discount rate for dollars) at which you are *just willing* to exchange consumption in Year 1 for consumption in Year 2. At the point of tangency the two slopes are equal, so the internal discount rate for dollars is equal to the market interest rate. We have derived the equimarginal principle over time in exactly the same way we derived it between goods in Chapter 3.

Figure 12-5a shows a somewhat different case—a consumer with an endowment F who can lend (again at 25 percent) but cannot borrow— perhaps because nobody trusts him to pay the money back. If he could borrow he would, putting him at point X; since he cannot, the best he can do is to stay at F, spending each year's income that year. Figure 12-5b shows a similar situation, but one in which the consumer's inability to borrow has no effect; even if he could borrow, he wouldn't. Finally, Figure 12-5c shows the more realistic case of an individual (again with endowment F) who can both borrow and lend, but at different rates. He can lend at 10 percent, but must pay 25 percent if he wishes to borrow.

So far we have been analyzing the decision to borrow or lend by a single consumer. If we add up the behavior of all consumers, we get the total supply and demand for loans by consumers. The higher the interest rate is, the more consumers shift consumption towards their later years, since a higher interest rate increases the amount you can get later if you

Figure 12-5

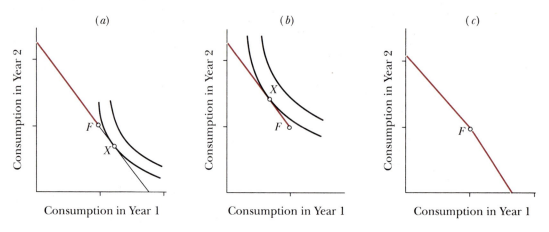

(a)   (b)   (c)

Consumption in Year 2 | Consumption in Year 1 (for each panel)

Budget line diagrams for a consumer whose ability to borrow is limited. Figures 12-5*a* and 12-5*b* show a consumer who cannot borrow; in Figure 12-5*b*, this has no effect on his consumption choices. Figure 12-5*c* shows a consumer who can borrow, but only at a higher interest rate than he lends.

give up a dollar now. So a higher interest rate decreases the **net demand** (demand minus supply) for loans by consumers.

What are the factors that determine the shape of the net demand curve for loans—the relation between the interest rate, which is what the lender is paid for the use of his money, and the amount consumers choose to lend or borrow? One factor is the pattern of lifetime earnings and of expenditure opportunities. If the number of careers that, like medicine, require lengthy training increases, then so will the demand for loans. We saw this effect on Figure 12-4*a*, where the same individual changed from net lender to net borrower when his income was shifted from Year 1 to Year 2. If medical technology improves in a way that gives old people new and very valuable ways of spending their money, the utility function for income to the elderly rises. Individuals choose to spend less of their income when young in order to save it to pay medical bills when they are old. Since they must lend out the money they save in order to get interest on it, the supply of loans increases.

A second factor is the internal discount rate. If some cultural change makes people more concerned about their own (or their children's) future, their savings will go up and their borrowing down. If everyone decides to enjoy life today whatever the consequences, savings go down and borrowing up.

If all lending and borrowing were of this sort, then total borrowing and total saving would have to be equal; you cannot borrow a dollar unless someone else saves it and lends it to you, so net demand for loans (at the equilibrium interest rate) must be zero. In that situation, changes in the net demand schedule end up as changes in the market interest rate. If demand for loans rises and supply falls, the interest rate goes up until quantity demanded and quantity supplied are again equal.

All lending and borrowing is not of this sort. In addition to individuals borrowing or lending in order to adjust their consumption patterns over time, there are also firms borrowing in order to invest—the equivalent, in my earlier example, of using apples to grow apple trees. As we saw earlier, the decision of whether or not to make a particular investment is based on a present value calculation. The higher the market interest rate, the lower the present value of a future return. So if interest rates are high, firms will only invest in projects that have a very high return relative to the initial investment. The lower the interest rate, the larger the number of projects that yield a positive net present value. So the demand curve for loans by firms is downward sloped—quantity of loans demanded increases as the interest rate falls.

Just as we can use indifference curves to analyze intertemporal choice of consumption by individuals, so we could use isoquant curves and isocost lines to analyze the corresponding decision by firms. Just as the firms in Chapter 9 chose the lowest cost bundle of inputs to produce a given quantity of output, so here firms choose the lowest cost combination of Year 1 inputs (purchased by borrowing against Year 2 income) and Year 2 inputs with which to produce Year 2 output. Different interest rates imply different slopes for the isocost lines, different lowest cost combinations of inputs, and thus different amounts of borrowing by firms.

Individuals and firms are not the only participants on the capital market. Governments borrow, both from their citizens and from foreigners, in order to finance present expenditures with future taxes. And capital may flow into (or out of) the country—foreigners may find they get a better return in America than at home and therefore choose to lend money to American consumers, firms, or governments. Individuals, firms, and governments both here and abroad all contribute to the supply and demand curves that determine the market interest rate.

OPTIONAL SECTION

IMPATIENCE AND THE BALANCE OF PAYMENTS

In the optional section of Chapter 6, I showed that a trade deficit is equivalent to a net inflow of capital and argued that whether our current deficit is a good or a bad thing depends on why that inflow is occurring. We are now in a position to state the argument a little more clearly.

A capital inflow occurs because foreign investors can get more for their money here than at home—it reflects relatively high real interest rates. If the reason is, as sometimes asserted, that Americans have become increasingly impatient, unwilling to give up present utility for future utility, then it is a symptom of a change that will ultimately make us poorer—we are consuming our future income and some day the bill will come due. If the reason is that American firms have lots of good investment opportunities and are therefore happy to offer higher rates than Japanese firms, the bill will still come due, but we will have the returns from those investment opportunities to pay it with.

The fact that real interest rates have become relatively high here may reflect a change, not here, but abroad. Perhaps Japanese savers have become less impatient, or wealthier, or Japanese firms have fewer good investment opportunities than before, or the Japanese government has stopped borrowing money from its people. Any of those changes would lower Japanese real interest rates, making America a more attractive place to invest. The result would be a capital inflow and hence a trade deficit.

PROBLEMS

1. One of my examples of goods that are inexpensive to store was "gold bars—provided nobody knows you have them." Why are gold bars expensive to store if people know you have them?

2. What does your answer to Problem 1 suggest might be one of the factors affecting interest rates?

3. The apple interest rate is zero, the peach interest rate is 10 percent. Currently the price of a peach is 1 apple. What will the price of a peach be next year? The year after?

4. According to the numbers at the bottom of Table 12-1, the first stream of income is worth $270,362, the second is worth $259,892, and their difference, the amount you would have if you received the first while simultaneously paying out the second, is $24,688. The numbers do not appear to add up. What is wrong? Show that the numbers are actually consistent.

5. You have a choice between two jobs. One of them pays you $20,000/year for four years, with the payment coming at the end of each year. The other pays you $19,000/year for four years, plus a "recruitment bonus" of $3,000 at the beginning of the first year. The market interest rate is 10 percent. Which job should you take?

6. Some years ago, a prominent consumer magazine ran an article on how to choose a mortgage. Different ways of borrowing a given amount of money (with or without down payment, short term or

long term, etc.) were compared according to the total number of dollars you had to pay out during the term of the mortgage—the fewer dollars the better.

    a. What sort of conclusion do you think they reached? According to their criterion, what is the best kind of mortgage?

    b. Do you agree with their criterion? Can you describe two mortgages for the same amount of money, one of which results in your paying out more total dollars but is clearly better? If so, do. Assume that your income is sufficient to pay either mortgage.

7. You can build a factory for $1,000,000 that will permit you to manufacture 100,000 widgets per year at a cost of $1/widget (not counting the cost of the factory). The market interest rate is 10 percent.

    a. The factory will last forever; you do not expect the price of widgets to change. What is the lowest price for widgets at which the factory is worth building?

    b. The factory will last only three years. What is the lowest price for widgets at which the factory is worth building?

8. The government borrows money by selling at auction $1,000 bonds, payable in two years, with no interest payments. The market interest rate is 10 percent.

    a. How much will the bonds sell for?

    b. Even though the bonds do not "pay interest" (the buyer receives $1,000 when the bonds mature and nothing before that), buyers still end up receiving interest on their investment. Explain.

    c. What interest rate are buyers of the bonds actually receiving on their investment? Explain.

9. A bank offers you the following deal. Deposit $1,000 with them and they will give you a pair of binoculars. Five years later, you get your $1,000 back—but no interest. Assuming that the market interest rate is 5 percent, how much are you really paying for the binoculars?

10. A bank offers you the following deal. Deposit $10,000 with them and they will give you a savings bond worth $2,000. Four years later, they will give you your money back—but no interest. What interest rate are you really getting?

11. The following is a list of prices for wheat futures printed in February; the price for a wheat future is the price you pay now in exchange for delivery of a bushel of wheat at some future date.

March	May	July	September	November	January
$2.40	$2.70	$1.20	$1.50	$1.80	$2.10

    a. When is the new crop harvested? Explain.

    b. About how much does it cost to store a bushel of wheat for a month? Explain. For both parts you may, if you wish, assume that the interest rate is zero. (Note: This problem requires some original thinking by you; it has not been done anywhere in the chapter. The correct analysis is, however, similar to the analysis of other problems that are in the chapter.)

12. I can borrow as much as I want at 10 percent; I can lend as much as I want at 8 percent. What can you say about my internal discount rate for money in a year when I borrow money? A year when I lend money?

13. Is my internal discount rate for utility determined by my tastes, my opportunities, or both? Is my internal discount rate for money determined by my tastes, my opportunities, or both? Explain.

14. I am trying to decide whether to have my wisdom teeth out. I estimate the cost, in time, pain, and money, at 10,000 utiles. The benefit is a reduction in minor dental problems of about 1 utile a day. I expect that I, my teeth, and my dental problems will last forever.
    a. I decide not to have my wisdom teeth out. What can you say about my internal discount rate?
    b. I decide to have my wisdom teeth out. What can you say about my internal discount rate?

15. What effect would each of the following have on interest rates?
    a. A new religion spreads that preaches the virtues of thrift; converts save their money for their old age.
    b. A new religion spreads that preaches that the end of the world is imminent.

16. Figure 12-4a shows the same budget line corresponding to two possible situations—one in which income is $40,000 in Year 1 and nothing in Year 2, and one in which it is nothing in Year 1 and $50,000 in Year 2.
    a. Redraw (or photocopy) the figure, showing the endowments E_1 and E_2 corresponding to the two situations.
    b. For each situation, calculate the demand curve over a range of interest rates.
    c. Give another initial endowment that would also correspond, at an interest rate of 25 percent, to the same budget line.

FOR FURTHER READING

The analysis of depletable resources given in this chapter is not a product of recent concerns with the problem, summarized in phrases (and book titles) such as "limits to growth" and "spaceship earth." It was produced more than 50 years ago by Harold Hotelling. His original article is:

"The Economics of Exhaustible Resources," *Journal of Political Economy* 39 (1931), 137–75.

chapter 13

...AND CHANCE

I returned and saw under the sun, that the race is not to the swift, nor the battle to the strong, neither bread to the wise, nor yet riches to men of understanding, nor yet favour to men of skill; but time and chance happeneth to them all.

—Ecclesiastes 9.11

PART 1—SUNK COSTS

So far, I have introduced time into the economy, but not uncertainty; everything always comes out as expected. The real world is not so simple. One of the consequences of uncertainty is the possibility of mistakes; another is the problem of what to do about them.

You see an advertisement for a shirt sale at a store 20 miles from your home. You were planning to buy some new shirts, and the prices are substantially lower than in your local clothing store; you decide the savings are enough to make it worth the trip. When you arrive, you discover that none of the shirts on sale are your size; the shirts that are your size cost only slightly less than in your local store. What should you do?

You should buy the shirts. The cost of driving to the store is a **sunk cost**—once incurred, it cannot be recovered. If you had known the prices before you left home, you would have concluded that it was not worth making the trip—but now that you have made it, you must pay for it whether or not you buy the shirts. Sunk costs are sunk costs.

There are two opposite mistakes one may make with regard to sunk costs. The first is to treat them as if they were not sunk—to refuse to buy the shirts because their price is not low enough to justify the trip even though the trip has already been made. The second is to buy the shirts even when they are more expensive than in your local store, on the theory that you might as well get something for your trip. The something you are getting in this case is less than nothing. This is known as throwing good money after bad.

When, as a very small child, I quarrelled with my sister and then locked myself in my room, my father would come to the door and say, "Making a mistake and not admitting it is only hurting yourself twice." When I got a little older, he changed it to "Sunk costs are sunk costs."

In discussing firms' cost curves, one should distinguish between fixed costs and sunk costs—while the same costs are often both fixed and sunk, they need not always be. **Fixed costs** are costs you must pay in order to produce anything—the limit of total cost as a function of quantity when quantity approaches zero. One could imagine a case where such costs were fixed but not sunk, either because the necessary equipment could be resold at its purchase price or because the equipment was rented and the rental could be terminated any time the firm decided to stop producing.

The significance of sunk costs is that a firm will continue to produce even when revenue does not cover total cost, provided that it does cover nonsunk costs (called **recoverable costs**), since nonsunk costs are all the firm can save by closing down. All costs, ultimately, are opportunity costs—the cost of doing one thing is not being able to do something else. Once a factory is built, the cost of continuing to run it does not include what was spent building it, since whatever you do you will not get that back. It does include the cost of not selling it to someone else—which may be more or less than the cost of building it, depending on whether the value of such factories has gone up or down since it was built.

In deriving the supply curve of a competitive industry with open entry in Chapter 9, I assumed that the same cost curves possessed by one firm were available to an unlimited number of others. The conclusion was that firms would always produce at the minimum of average cost, where it crossed marginal cost. The reason was that if, at the quantity for which marginal cost equaled price (where profit is maximized for a price taker), price were above average cost, economic profit would be positive; it would pay other firms to enter the industry. They would do so until price was driven down to the point where it equaled both MC and AC, which occurs where they cross at the minimum of AC.

Does the relevant average cost include sunk costs? That depends on whether we are approaching the equilibrium from above or below and on how long a time we consider. If prices start out above the equilibrium price, firms will only enter the industry as long as the price is above average cost including sunk cost—costs are not sunk until they are incurred, and the new firm starts out with the option of not incurring them. The equilibrium will be reached when price equals average total cost.

If we approach the equilibrium from below—if there are too many firms (perhaps because demand has recently fallen) and price is insufficient to cover even the average of nonsunk costs—firms will leave the market. They will continue to do so until price gets up to average nonsunk cost.

If the assets bought with the sunk costs (factories, say) wear out over time, then the number of factories will gradually decline and the price will gradually rise. Until it reaches average total cost, nobody will build any new factories. Eventually price will be equal to average total cost, just as it was when we reached the equilibrium from above, but it may take much longer to get there; it usually takes longer to wear out a factory than to build one.

In the next two sections, I will work through the logic of such situations in some detail while trying to show how it is related to the logic of a different sort of situation that was briefly discussed several chapters ago.

Upside, Downside, Cost Equals Price

In analyzing the industry supply curve in Chapter 9, I assumed an unlimited number of potential firms, all with the same cost curve; if existing firms make a profit, new firms come into existence until the profit is competed down to zero.

One objection to this that I discussed is that firms are not all identical. Some power companies own special pieces of real estate—Niagara Falls, for example—not available to their competitors. Some corporations are run by superb managers or possess the services of an inventive genius such as Browning or Kloss. Surely such fortunate firms can, as a result, produce their output at a lower cost than others—and can therefore make profits at a price at which it does not pay less fortunate firms to enter the industry.

But although firms that have, in this sense, low cost curves appear to make positive profits when less fortunate firms just barely cover their costs, that is an illusion. One should include in cost the cost of using the special assets (location, administrator, inventor, or whatever) that give that firm its advantage. The value of those assets is what the firm could sell them for or, in the case of human assets, what a competitor would pay to hire them away. One of the firm's (opportunity) costs of operating is not selling out, and one of the costs to an inventor of running his own firm is not working for someone else's firm. If the possession of those special assets gives the firm an additional net revenue of, say, $100,000/year (forever—or almost), then the market value of those assets is the present value of that income stream. The interest on that present value is then the same $100,000/year. Since giving up that interest is one of the costs to the firm of staying in business, the firm should subtract it from revenue in calculating its economic profit.

Suppose, for example, that the firm is making an extra $100,000/year as a result of owning its special asset and that the interest rate is 10 percent. The present value of a permanent income stream of $100,000/year is $1 million, and the interest on $1 million is $100,000. By using the asset this year, the firm gives up the opportunity to sell it and collect interest on the money it would get for it. We should include $100,000/year as an additional cost—forgone interest. Doing so reduces the profit of the firm to zero—the same as the profit of an ordinary firm. In one sense, this argument is circular; in another sense, it is not.

The same argument applies in the opposite direction to firms whose revenues fail to cover their sunk costs (firms whose revenues fail to cover their recoverable costs go out of business). Suppose a widget factory costs $1 million to build and lasts forever; further suppose the interest rate is 10 percent, so that the factory must generate net revenue of $100,000/year to be worth building. At the time the factory is built, the price of widgets is $1.10/widget. The factory can produce 100,000 widgets per year at a cost (not including the cost of building the factory) of $0.10/widget, so it is making $100,000/year—just enough to justify the cost of building it. Further suppose that the factory can be used for nothing but building widgets; its scrap value is zero.

Widget

FIMBRIATED
GIDGET

The invention of the fimbriated gidget drastically reduces the demand for widgets. Widget prices fall from $1.10 to $0.20. At a price of $0.20, the firm is netting only $10,000/year on its $1 million investment. So are all the other (identical) firms. Are they covering costs?

The factory is a sunk cost from the standpoint of the industry, but any individual firm can receive its value by selling it to another firm. How much will it sell for? Since it generates an income of $10,000/year and since at an interest rate of 10 percent an investment of $100,000 can generate the same income, the factory will sell for $100,000. So the cost of not selling it is $100,000—and the annual cost of not selling it is $10,000, the interest forgone. Ten thousand dollars is the firm's revenue net of costs before subtracting the cost of the factory, so net revenue after subtracting the cost of the factory—economic profit—is zero.

Again the argument is circular but not empty, since it tells us, among other things, what determines the price of a factory in a declining industry. In the case I have just described, the firm loses $900,000 the day the price of widgets drops, since that is the decrease in the value of its factory. Thereafter it just covers costs, as usual.

The assumptions used in this example, although useful for illustrating the particular argument, are not quite consistent with rational behavior. In the market equilibrium before the price drop, economic profit was zero. That is an appropriate assumption for the certain world of Chapters 1–12, but not for the uncertain world we are now discussing. If there is some possibility of prices falling, then firms will bear sunk costs only if the *average* return justifies the investment. Prices must be high enough that the profit if they do not fall balances the loss if they do. The zero-profit condition continues to apply, but only in an average sense—if the firms are lucky, they make money; if they are unlucky, they lose it. On average they break even. This point will be discussed at greater length later in the chapter.

Sunk Costs in the Shipping Industry

You may find it helpful to work through another example. Consider ships. Suppose that the total cost of building a ship is $10 million. For simplicity we assume that operating costs and the interest rate are both zero. Each ship lasts 20 years and can transport 10,000 tons of cargo each year from port A to port B. We assume, again for simplicity, that the ships all come back from B to A empty. It takes a year to build a ship. The demand curve for shipping cargo is shown in Figure 13-1a.

We start with our usual competitive equilibrium—price equals average cost. There are 100 ships and the cost for shipping cargo is $50/ton. Each ship makes $500,000 a year; at the end of 20 years, when the ship collapses into a pile of rust, it has just paid for itself. Every year five ships are built to replace the five that have worn out. If the price for shipping were any higher, it would pay to build more ships, since an investment of $10 million would produce a return of more than $10 million; if it were lower, no ships would be built. The situation is shown in Figure 13-1a.

Figure 13-1b shows the effect of a sudden increase in the demand for shipping—from D to D'. In the short run, the supply of shipping is perfectly inelastic, since it takes a year to build a ship. The price shoots

Figure 13-1

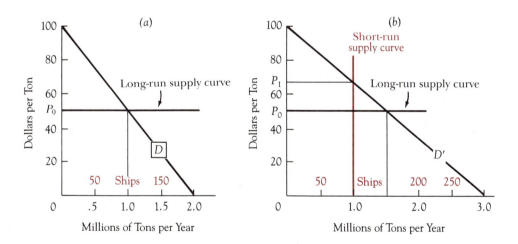

Supply and demand curves for shipping, showing the effect of an unanticipated increase in demand. Figure 13-1a shows the situation before the increase and Figure 13-1b after. The horizontal axis shows both quantity of cargo carried each year and the equivalent number of ships. The short-run supply curve is vertical at the current number of ships (and amount of cargo they carry). The long-run supply curve is horizontal at the cost of producing shipping (the annualized cost of building a ship divided by the number of tons it carries).

up to P_1, where the new demand curve intersects the short-run supply curve.

Shipyards immediately start building new ships. At the end of a year, the new ships are finished and the price drops back down to the old level. Figure 13-2 shows the sequence of events in the form of a graph of price against time.

Looking again at Figure 13-1b, note that it has two supply curves—a vertical short-run supply curve and a horizontal long-run supply curve. No ships can be built in less than a year, so there is no way a high price can increase the supply of shipping in the short run. Since operating costs are, by assumption, zero, it pays shipowners to operate the ships however low the price; there is no way a low price can reduce the supply of shipping in the short run. So in the short run, quantity supplied is independent of price for any price between zero and infinity.

The situation in the long run is quite different. At any price where ships more than cover their construction cost, it pays to build ships; so in the long run, the industry will produce an unlimited quantity of shipping at any price above $P_0 = \$50$/ton. As ships are built, the short-run supply curve shifts out. At any price below P_0, building a ship costs more than the ship is worth, so quantity supplied falls as the existing ships wear out. So the long-run supply curve is horizontal. It is worth noting that on the "up" side—building ships—the long run is a good deal shorter than on the "down" side.

Suppose that instead of the increase in demand shown in Figure 13-1b, there is instead a decrease in demand, from D to D'', as shown

Figure 13-2

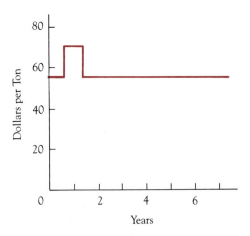

A possible pattern of freight rates over time. At $T = 0$ there is an unexpected increase in demand, as shown on Figure 13-1b; price rises above its long-run equilibrium, then falls back when additional new ships are completed.

Section III   Complications, or Onward to Reality

Figure 13-3

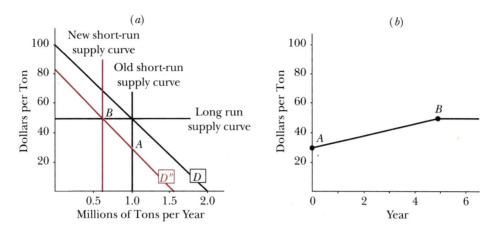

The effect of an unexpected decrease in demand for shipping. Figure 13-3*a* shows the situation after the demand curve shifts. Figure 13-3*b* shows the resulting pattern of prices over time.

in Figure 13-3*a*. Price drops. Since there are no operating costs, existing ships continue to carry cargo as long as they get any price above zero. The price is at the point where the old (short-run) vertical supply curve intersects the new demand curve *(A)*.

Building a ship is now unprofitable, since it will not, at the new price, repay its construction costs. No ships are built. Over the next five years, 25 ships wear out, bringing the long-run quantity supplied (and the short-run supply curve) down to a point where the price is again $50/ton *(B)*. Figure 13-3*b* shows how the price and the number of ships change with time.

There is one thing wrong with this story. The initial equilibrium assumed that the price of shipping was going to stay the same over the lifetime of a ship—that was why ships were produced if and only if the return at current prices, multiplied by the lifetime of the ship, totaled at least the cost of production. The later developments assumed that the demand curve, and hence the price, could vary unpredictably.

If shipowners expect random changes in future demand and believe that future decreases will be at least as frequent and as large as future increases, the price at which they are just willing to build will be more than $50/ton. Why? Because ships can be built quickly, so that the gain from an increase in demand is short-lived, but wear out slowly, so that the loss from a decrease in demand continues for a long time. Compare the short period of high prices in Figure 13-2 with the long period of low prices in Figure 13-3*b*. If the current price is high enough (P_e on Figure 13-4) that any increase causes ships to be built, then an increase

Figure 13-4

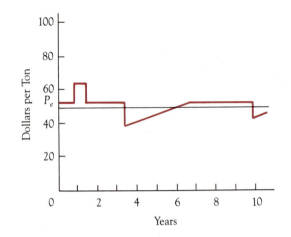

A possible pattern of freight rates over time. Unlike Figure 13-2, this figure assumes that the producers expect unpredictable shifts in demand. The average return from carrying freight must be enough to just cover the costs.

in demand will hold prices above P_e for only a year. A decrease can keep prices below P_e for up to 20 years. If P_e were equal to $50/ton, the price at which ships exactly repay the cost of building them, the average price would be lower than that and ships, on average, would fail to recover their costs. So P_e must be above $50/ton.

This is the same point that I made earlier in describing the effect of sunk costs in the widget industry. In order to make the behavior of the shipowners rational, we must assume that they do not start building ships until the price is high enough that the profits if demand does not fall make up for the losses if it does. The pattern of price over time in the industry then looks something like Figure 13-4.

How to Lie While Telling the Truth— A True Story

Many years ago, while spending a summer in Washington, I came across an interesting piece of economic analysis involving these principles. The congressman I was working for had introduced a bill that would have abolished a large part of the farm program, including price supports for feed grains (crops used to feed animals). Shortly thereafter the agriculture department released a "study" of the effects of abolishing those particular parts of the farm program. Their conclusion, as I remember, was that farm income would fall by $5 billion while the government would save only $3 billion in reduced expenditure, for a net loss of $2 billion.

The agriculture department's calculations completely ignored the effect of the proposed changes on consumers—although the whole point of the price support program was (and is) to raise the price of farm products and thus of food. Using the agriculture department's figures, the proposed abolition would have saved consumers (as I remember) about $7 billion, producing a net gain of $5 billion. The agriculture department, which of course opposed the proposed changes, failed to mention that implication of its analysis.

Another part of the report asserted that the abolition of price supports on feed grains would drive down the prices of the animals that consumed them. It went on to say that the price drop would first hit poultry producers, then producers of pork and lamb, and finally beef producers. All of this, to the best of my knowledge, is correct. The conclusion that appears to follow is that poultry producers will be injured a great deal by the abolition, lamb and pork producers somewhat less, and beef producers injured least of all. This is almost the precise opposite of the truth.

If you think about the situation for a moment, you should be able to see what is happening. Removing price supports on feed grains lowers the cost of production for poultry, pork, lamb, and beef—feed grains are probably the largest input for producing those foods. In the case of poultry, the flocks can be rapidly increased, so the poultry producers will receive an above-normal profit (cost of production has fallen, price of poultry has not) for only a short time. Once the flocks have increased, the price of chickens falls and the return to their producers goes back to normal. The herds of pigs and sheep take longer to increase, so their producers get above-normal returns for a longer period, and the beef producers get them for longer still. The situation is just like the situation of the shipowners when demand increases, except that there is a drop in production cost rather than an increase in the demand schedule. The agriculture department appeared to be saying that the beef producers would receive the least injury and the poultry producers the greatest injury from the proposed change; what their analysis actually implied was that the beef producers would receive the largest benefit and the poultry producers the smallest benefit.

PART 2—LONG-RUN AND SHORT-RUN COSTS

So far, we have been analyzing the influence of uncertainty on prices by taking account of the effect of sunk costs on the behavior of profit-maximizing firms. A more technical description of what we are doing is that we are analyzing the effect of uncertainty in terms of Marshallian **quasi-rents**—"Marshallian" because this approach, along with much of the rest of modern economics, was invented by Alfred Marshall about 100 years ago and "quasi-rents" because the return on sunk costs is in many ways similar to the rent on land. Both can be viewed as the result of a demand curve intersecting a perfectly inelastic supply curve—although in the case of sunk costs, the supply curve is inelastic only in the short run.

The more conventional way of analyzing these questions is in terms of short-run and long-run cost curves and the resulting short-run and long-run supply curves. I did not use that approach in Chapter 9, where supply curves were deduced from cost curves, and so far I have not used it here. Why?

The reason I ignored the distinction between long-run and short-run costs in Chapter 9 was explained there; in the unchanging world we were analyzing, long run and short run are the same. The reason I did not introduce the ideas of this chapter in that form is that the way in which I did introduce it provides a more general and more powerful way of analyzing the same questions. It is more general because it allows us to consider productive assets—such as ships and factories—with a variety of lifetimes and construction times, not merely the extreme (and arbitrary) classes of "short-" and "long-"lived. It is more powerful because it not only gives us the long-run and short-run supply curves but also shows what happens in between, both to the price of the productive assets and to the price of the goods they produce.

The simplest way to demonstrate all of this—and to prepare you for later courses that will assume you are familiar with the conventional approach—is to work out the short-run/long-run analysis as a special case of the approach we have been following. While doing so, we will also be able to examine some complications that have so far remained hidden behind the simplifying assumptions of our examples.

Factory Size and the Short-Run Supply Curve

We start with an industry. Since we used up our quota of widgets earlier in the chapter, we will make it the batten industry. Battens are produced in batten factories. There are many batten firms, so each is a price taker. A firm entering the industry—or a firm already in the industry that is replacing a worn-out factory—must choose what size factory to build. A small factory is inexpensive to build but expensive to operate—especially if you want to produce a large amount of output. Larger factories cost more to build but are more efficient for producing large quantities. A firm can only operate one factory at a time.

Figures 13-5 through 13-7 show the cost curves for three different factories. The first costs $1 million to build, the second costs $3 million, and the third costs $5 million. A factory has no scrap value, so the investment is a sunk cost. Each factory lasts ten years. The interest rate is zero, so the annual cost associated with each factory is one tenth the cost of building it. One could easily enough do the problem for a more realistic interest rate, but that would complicate the calculations without adding anything important.

Total cost is the sum of fixed cost and **variable cost**. The figures are drawn on the assumption that the only fixed cost in producing battens is the cost of building the factory; all other costs are variable. Since this

Figure 13-5

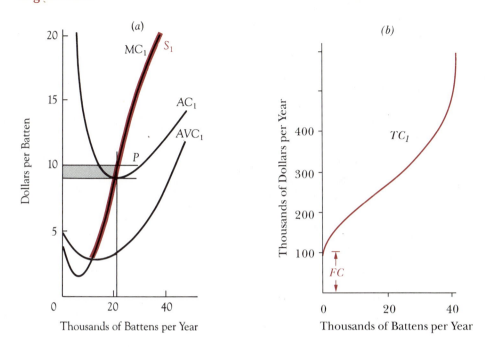

Cost curves and the resulting supply curve for a small batten factory. The factory costs $1 million to build. Since it lasts for ten years, the annualized fixed cost (*FC*) is $100,000/year. The shaded area shows the profit at a price of $10/batten.

implies that the fixed cost and the sunk cost are identical, so are variable cost (total cost minus fixed cost) and recoverable cost (total cost minus sunk cost). The figures show average variable cost *(AVC)*; it might just as well have been labeled *ARC* for "average recoverable cost."

Each pair of figures shows four cost curves—total cost *(TC)*, marginal cost *(MC)*, average cost *(AC)*, and average variable cost *(AVC)*. Total cost includes the (annualized) cost of the factory; since that is assumed to be the only fixed cost, total cost at a quantity of zero is the annualized cost of the factory—$100,000/year on Figure 13-5*b*. Since average cost is defined as total cost over quantity, it too includes the cost of the factory. Average variable cost, on the other hand, does not include the cost of the factory, since that is fixed.

So far as marginal cost is concerned, it does not matter whether or not we include the cost of the factory. Marginal cost is the slope of total cost; adding a constant term to a function simply shifts it up without affecting its slope.

Suppose the batten firm has built the factory of Figure 13-5. The market price of a batten is *P*; the firm must decide how many to produce each year. Just as in Chapter 9, the firm maximizes its profit by producing

Figure 13-6

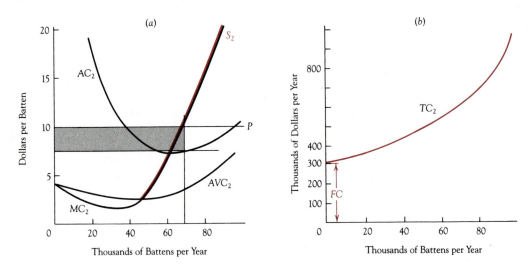

Cost curves and the resulting supply curve for a medium-sized batten factory. The factory costs $3 million to build. Since it lasts for ten years, the annualized fixed cost (*FC*) is $300,000/year. The shaded area shows the profit at a price of $10/batten.

Figure 13-7

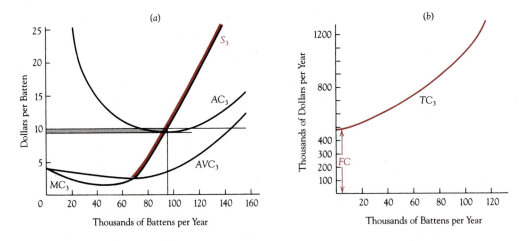

Cost curves and the resulting supply curve for a large batten factory. The factory costs $5 million to build. Since it lasts for ten years, the annualized fixed cost (*FC*) is $500,000/year. The shaded area shows the profit at a price of $10/batten.

the quantity for which $MC = P$—provided that at that quantity it is not losing money.

In Chapter 9, we could see whether the firm was making or losing money by comparing price to average cost; if average cost is greater than price, then profit is negative and the firm should go out of business. This time we have two average costs—AC and AVC. Which should we use?

We should use AVC. The firm already has the factory; it is deciding whether or not to shut it down. If the firm shuts down the factory, it will not get back the money that was spent to build it—that is a sunk cost. What it will save is its variable cost. If the savings from shutting down the factory are greater than the loss from no longer having any battens to sell, then the factory should be shut down. Otherwise it should continue to operate. So as long as price is greater than average variable cost, the firm continues to operate the factory, producing the quantity for which marginal cost equals price. If price is lower than average cost, the factory is not paying back its cost of construction and should never have been built—but it is too late to do anything about that. Sunk costs are sunk costs.

The curves labeled S_1–S_3 on Figures 13-5 through 13-7 are the supply curves implied by the previous two paragraphs. Each S runs along the marginal cost curve, starting at its intersection with average variable cost. For any price lower than that, quantity supplied is zero.

The Long-Run Supply Curve

These are the **short-run supply curves**. They correctly describe the behavior of a firm that already owns a functioning factory. But in the long run, factories wear out and must be replaced. A firm that is about to build a factory is in a different situation, in two respects, from a firm that already has a factory. First, the cost of building the factory is not yet sunk—the firm has the alternative of not building and not producing. The firm will build only if it expects price to be above average cost—including in the average the cost of building the factory.

The second difference is that a firm about to build can choose which size of factory it prefers. Its choice will depend on what the price is. So the long-run supply curve must take account of the relation between the price of battens and the size of the factories in which they will be produced.

How do we find the long-run supply curve of a firm? We consider a firm that is about to build a factory and expects the market price of battens to remain at its present level for at least the next ten years— the lifetime of the factory. The firm's long-run supply curve is then the relation between the quantity the firm chooses to produce and the price.

We solve the problem in two steps. First we figure out, for each size of factory, how many battens the firm will produce if it decides to build a factory of that size. Then we compare the resulting profits, in order to find out which factory the firm will choose to build. Once we know which factory the firm chooses to build and how much a firm with a factory of that size chooses to produce, we know quantity supplied at that price. Repeat the calculation for all other prices and we have the firm's long-run supply curve.

Figures 13-5 through 13-7 show the calculations for a price of $10/batten. As we already know, if a price-taking firm produces at all, it maximizes its profit by producing a quantity for which $MC = P$. So for each size of factory, a firm that chose to build that factory would produce the quantity for which marginal cost was equal to price.

Having done so, what would the firm's profit be? Profit per unit is simply price minus average cost. The firm should include the cost of building the factory in deciding which factory to build, so the relevant average is average cost, not average variable cost. Total profit is profit per unit times number of units—the shaded rectangle in each figure. It is largest for Figure 13-6, so the firm builds a $3 million factory and produces that quantity for which, in such a factory, price equals marginal cost.

Figure 13-8 shows the result of repeating the calculations for many different prices. As I have drawn the curves, the less expensive factories have a lower average cost for low levels of output and a higher average cost for high levels. The result is that as price (and quantity) increase, so does the optimal size of the factory. The long-run supply curve for the firm (Figure 13-8b) is then pieced together from portions of the short-run supply curves of Figures 13-5 through 13-7. In doing so, we limit ourselves to the part of each short-run supply curve above the corresponding average cost (AC not AVC), since that is the long-run

Figure 13-8

The short-run average cost curves and the short-run and long-run supply curves for a firm producing battens. *AC* and *S* are drawn on the assumption that there are only three possible factory sizes, corresponding to Figures 13-5, 13-6, and 13-7. For any price, the firm builds the factory that produces the largest profit at that price.

Section III   Complications, or Onward to Reality

supply curve for that size of factory. We end up with the long-run supply curve for a firm that is free to vary factory size as well as other inputs.

Looking at Figure 13-8b, we see that the smallest size of factory is irrelevant to the firm's supply curve, since there is no price of battens at which it would be worth building such a factory. If the market price is below P_0, none of the three sizes of factory can make enough money to justify the cost of building it, so the firm produces nothing. For prices between P_0 and P_1 on Figure 13-8b, the firm maximizes its profit by building a $3 million factory and producing the quantity for which the marginal cost (MC_2 on Figure 13-6a) equals the price. For prices above P_1, it does better building a $5 million factory and producing along the MC_3 curve of Figure 13-7a. So S is the firm's long-run supply curve.

An alternate way of deriving the long-run supply curve of the firm is to consider the factory itself as one more input in the production function. Just as in Chapter 9, one then calculates the lowest cost bundle of inputs for each level of output; the result tells you, for any quantity of output, how much it costs to produce and what inputs—including what size of factory—you should use. You then go on to calculate average cost (the same curve shown on Figure 13-8a), marginal cost, and the supply curve. Since we are considering the long-run supply curve, we are (temporarily) back in the unchanging world of Chapters 1–11.

Figure 13-9a shows what the firm's long-run average cost curve would be like if, instead of limiting the firm to only three sizes of factory, we allowed it to choose from a continuous range of factory sizes. The solid line LAC on the figure is the resulting long-run average cost curve; the gray lines are average cost curves for several different factory sizes,

Figure 13-9

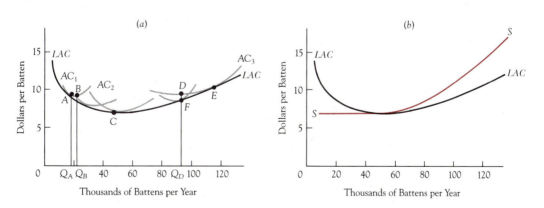

The long-run average cost curve and supply curve for a firm producing battens. *LAC* and *S* are drawn on the assumption that there is a continuous range of possible factory sizes. For any level of output desired, the firm builds the factory that produces that output at the lowest cost. For any price, it builds the factory that produces the largest profit at that price.

including those shown on Figures 13-5 through 13-7. Since for any quantity, the firm chooses that factory size which produces that quantity at the lowest possible cost, the average cost curve for a factory can never lie below the average cost curve for the firm. Every point on the firm's long-run average cost curve is also on the average cost curve for some size of factory—the size the firm chooses to build if it expects to produce that quantity of output. The result is what you see on Figure 13-9a; the average cost curves for the different factory sizes lie above the firm's long-run average cost curve and are tangent to it.

One feature of figures such as 13-9a that some people find puzzling is that the point where a factory average cost curve touches the firm's long-run average cost curve is generally not at the minimum average cost for that size of factory. AC_1, for example, touches LAC not at point B, which is its minimum, but at point A, and similarly for all the others except AC_2. Mathematically, the reason for this is quite simple. AC_1 is tangent to LAC at point A. At the point of tangency, the two curves have the same slope. Unless LAC is at its minimum—as it is at point C, where it touches AC_2—its slope is not zero. Since the slope of LAC is not zero at the point of tangency, neither is the slope of AC_1; so AC_1 cannot be at its minimum. The same applies to all of the points of tangency except C.

As I have commented before, one can read through a proof without ever understanding why the conclusion is correct; for some of you, the previous paragraph may be an example of that. Another way of putting the argument is to point out that while the firm that chooses to produce quantity Q_A could lower its average cost by expanding output to Q_B, it would then be producing a larger quantity; if it wished to produce that quantity, it could do so at an even lower average cost by using a bigger factory. B shows the minimum average cost for producing *in a $1 million factory*. It does not show the minimum average cost for producing a quantity Q_B; so it does not show what the average cost would be for a firm that wished to produce that quantity and was free to build whatever size factory it preferred. Similarly, D is the minimum point on AC_3, but there is another (unlabeled) average cost curve lying below it, providing a lower cost way of producing Q_D—at point F.

Figure 13-9a shows the short-run and long-run average cost curves for a firm that can choose from a continuous range of factory sizes. Figure 13-9b shows the long-run average cost curve and the long-run supply curve for such a firm. Every time the price goes up a little, the optimal size of factory shifts up as well. The result is the smooth supply curve of Figure 13-9b.

In Chapter 9, after finding the supply curve for a firm, we went on to find the supply curve for an industry made up of many such firms. We can do the same thing here. In the short run, the number of factories is fixed; there is not enough time to build more or for existing factories to wear out. So the short-run supply curve for the industry is simply the horizontal sum of the short-run supply curves for all the existing

Figure 13-10

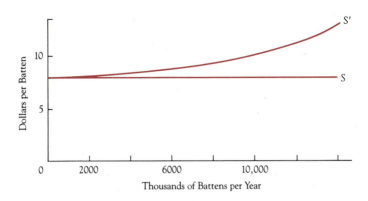

Two possible long-run supply curves for the batten industry. *S*, which is horizontal at a price equal to minimum average cost, is drawn on the assumption that inputs are available in perfectly elastic supply. *S'* is drawn on the assumption that as quantity increases, input prices are bid up.

factories—just as in the case of the competitive industry with closed entry discussed in Chapter 9.

In the long run, the number of factories can vary; firms may build new factories or fail to replace existing factories as they wear out. Unless there are barriers to entry, such as laws against building new factories, we are in the second case of Chapter 9—a competitive industry with free entry. If the inputs to the industry are in perfectly elastic supply so that their price does not depend on industry output, the (constant-cost) industry's long-run supply curve is *S* on Figure 13-10—a horizontal line at price = marginal cost = minimum average cost. If the price of some of the inputs rises as the industry purchases more of them (an increasing-cost industry), the result is an upward-sloped supply curve, such as *S'*.

Part 1 vs. Part 2—Two Approaches Compared

The short-run supply curve tells us how the firm will respond to changes in price over periods too short to make it worth changing the size of its factory; the long-run supply curve tells how the firm will respond to what it regards as permanent changes in price. We have now solved for both. In doing so, what have we learned that we did not already know?

The most important lesson is how to calculate the behavior of the firm over the short run. In all of the earlier examples of this chapter, the firms had simple all-or-none patterns of production. A widget factory either produced at capacity or shut down; a ship continued to carry a full load of freight as long as it got anything at all for doing so. We were, in effect, assuming the cost curves shown in Figures 13-11*a* and 13-11*b*—

Figure 13-11

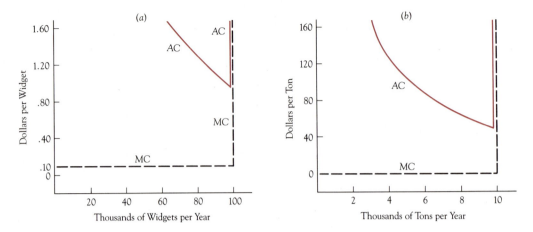

Cost curves for widgets and shipping. The figures show the cost curves for the widget (11*a*) and shipping (11*b*) industries discussed in Part 1 of the chapter.

marginal cost constant up to some maximum level of production and infinite beyond that. We were also assuming that there was only one kind of factory and one kind of ship.

In analyzing the batten factory, we allowed for more realistic cost curves. By doing so, we saw how, even in the short run, quantity supplied can vary continuously with price. We could have done the same thing in the earlier analysis; I chose not to. All-or-none production was a simplifying assumption used to avoid complications that were, at that point, inessential. The discussion of long-run and short-run supply curves was a convenient point at which to drop that simplification.

What are the disadvantages of the short-run/long-run approach? One of them is that it encourages students to confuse sunk costs and fixed costs. In the examples that are used, the two are generally the same, but there is no reason why they have to be.

In the batten industry, as I pointed out earlier, the curve labeled average variable cost could also have been labeled average recoverable cost, since the two are equal. I labeled it *AVC* in deference to convention; that is how you will generally see it in other textbooks. It would have been more correct to have labeled it *ARC*. It is the fact that the cost is recoverable, not the fact that it is variable, that is essential to the way in which the curve is related to the short-run supply curve. If we were considering a situation in which variable cost and recoverable cost were not the same, we could have simply drawn the *ARC* curve and forgotten about *AVC*.

One of the faults of the short-run/long-run approach is that it encourages confusion between fixed and sunk costs. One of its limitations is that it distinguishes between only two kinds of costs—short-run and long-run.

The more general approach to sunk cost, which we developed earlier in the chapter, can be used to analyze a much broader range of situations, including ones in which there are several long-lived productive assets with different lifetimes.

A second limitation is that the short-run/long-run approach says nothing about what happens to price between the two periods—how it adjusts over time to unexpected changes in demand. If we know how many factories of what size exist, the short-run supply curve allows us to calculate price and quantity; whether or not we know how many factories exist, the long-run supply curve tells us what price and quantity must eventually be if the situation remains stable for long enough. But the approach does not explain how to calculate the path by which price and quantity move from the one value to the other—which is one of the things we did in analyzing the widget and shipping industries.

None of this means that the short-run/long-run approach is wrong. Both in using economics and in teaching it, one must balance the costs and benefits of different degrees of simplicity. The short-run/long-run approach described in this section has the advantages and the disadvantages of greater simplicity; it is easier to teach but tells us less of what we want to know than the approach used earlier in the chapter.

In one sense, the difference is entirely pedagogical. Once you understand either approach, you can develop the other out of it. Starting with short- and long-run cost curves, you could, with a little ingenuity, figure out how to analyze more complicated cases or how to trace the path of price and quantity over time. Starting with sunk costs, you can work out short-run and long-run cost curves as special cases—not only in the shipping industry of Figures 13-1 through 13-4 but in more complicated situations as well. By teaching the material in both ways, I hope I have allowed you to learn it in whichever way you found more natural. That is a benefit. Its cost is measured in additional pages of book and additional hours of time—mine in writing and yours in reading. The production of textbooks involves the same sort of trade-off between costs and benefits as does the production of anything else—or any other action requiring choice.

PART 3—SPECULATION

It is difficult to read either newspapers or history books without occasionally coming across the villainous speculators. Speculators, it sometimes seems, are responsible for all the problems of the world—famines, currency crises, high prices.

How Speculation Works

A speculator buys things when he thinks they are cheap and sells them when he thinks they are expensive. Imagine, for example, that you decide there is going to be a bad harvest this year. If you are right, the price of grain will go up. So you buy grain now, while it is still cheap. If you are right, the harvest is bad, the price of grain goes up, and you sell at a large profit.

There are several reasons why this particular way of making a profit gets so much bad press. For one thing, the speculator is, in this case at least, profiting by other people's bad fortune, making money from, in Kipling's phrase, "Man's belly pinch and need." Of course, the same might be said of farmers, who are usually considered good guys. For another, the speculator's purchase of grain tends to drive up the price, making it seem as if he is responsible for the scarcity.

But in order to make money, the speculator must sell as well as buy. If he buys when grain is plentiful, he does indeed tend to increase the price then; but if he sells when it is scarce (which is what he wants to do in order to make money), he increases the supply and decreases the price just when the additional grain is most useful.

A different way of putting it is to say that the speculator, acting for his own selfish motives, does almost exactly what a benevolent despot would do. When he foresees a future scarcity of wheat, he induces consumers to use less wheat now. The speculator gets consumers to use less wheat now by buying it (before the consumers themselves realize the harvest is going to be bad), driving up the price; the higher price encourages consumers to consume less food (by slaughtering meat animals early, for example, to save their feed for human consumption), to import food from abroad, to produce other kinds of food (go fishing, dry fruit, . . .) and in other ways to prepare for the anticipated shortage. He then stores the wheat and distributes it (for a price) at the peak of the famine. Not only does he not cause famines, he prevents them.

More generally, speculators (in many things, not just food) tend, if successful, to smooth out price movements, buying goods when they are below their long-run price and selling them when they are above it, raising the price towards equilibrium in the one case and lowering it towards equilibrium in the other. They do what governmental "price-stabilization" schemes claim to do—reduce short-run fluctuations in prices. In the process, they frequently interfere with such price-stabilization schemes, most of which are run by producing countries and designed to "stabilize" prices as high as possible.

Cui Bono

Why indeed should we welcome you, Master Stormcrow? Lathspell I name you, ill-news; and ill news is an ill guest they say.

—Grima to Gandalf in *The Two Towers* by J.R.R. Tolkien

At least part of the unpopularity of speculators and speculation may reflect the traditional hostility to bearers of bad news; speculators who drive prices up now in anticipation of a future bad harvest are conveying the fact of future scarcity and are forcing consumers to take account of it. Part also may be due to the difficulty of understanding just how speculation works. Whatever the reason, ideas kill, and the idea that speculators cause shortages must be one of the most lethal errors in history. If speculation is unpopular it is also difficult, since the speculator depends for his profit on not having his stocks of grain seized by mob or government. In poor countries, which means almost everywhere through almost all of history, the alternative to speculation in food crops is periodic famine.

One reason people suspect speculators of causing price fluctuations is summarized in the Latin phrase *cui bono*; a loose translation would be "Who benefits?" If the newspapers discover that a gubernatorial candidate has been receiving large campaign donations from a firm that made $10 million off state contracts last year, it is a fair guess that the information was fed to them by his opponent. If a coup occurs somewhere in the Third World and the winners immediately ally themselves with the Soviet Union (or the United States), we do not have to look at the new ruler's bank records to suspect that the takeover was subsidized by Moscow (or Washington).

While *cui bono* is a useful rule for understanding many things, it is not merely useless but positively deceptive for understanding price movements. The reason is simple. The people who benefit from an increase in the price of something are those who produce it, but by producing, they drive the price not up but down. The people who benefit by a price drop are those who buy and consume the good, but buying a good tends to increase its price, not lower it. The manufacturer of widgets may spend his evenings on his knees praying for the price of widgets to go up, but he spends his days behind a desk making it go down. Hence the belief that price changes are the work of those who benefit by them is usually an error and sometimes a dangerous one.

Speculators make money by correctly predicting price changes, especially those changes that are difficult to predict. It is natural enough to conclude, according to the principle of *cui bono*, that speculators cause price fluctuations.

The trouble with this argument is that in order to make money, a speculator must buy when prices are low and sell when they are high. Buying when prices are low raises low prices; selling when prices are high lowers high prices. Successful speculators decrease price fluctuations, just as successful widget makers decrease the price of widgets. Destabilizing speculators are, of course, a logical possibility; they can be recognized by the red ink in their ledgers. The Hunt brothers of Texas are a notable recent example. A few years ago, they lost several billion dollars in the process of driving the price of silver up to what turned out to be several times its long-run equilibrium level.

It is true, of course, that a speculator would like to cause instability, supposing that he could do so without losing money; more precisely, he would like to make the prices of things he is going to sell go up before he sells them and of things he is going to buy go down before he buys them. He cannot do this by his market activities, but he can try to spread misleading rumors among other speculators; and, no doubt, some speculators do so. His behavior in this respect is like that of a producer who advertises his product; he is trying to persuade people to buy what he wants to sell. The speculator faces an even more skeptical audience than the advertiser, since it is fairly obvious that if he really expected the good to go up he would keep quiet and buy it himself. So the private generating of disinformation, while it undoubtedly occurs, is unlikely to be very effective.

I once heard a talk by an economist who had applied the relationship between stabilization and profitable speculation in reverse. The usual argument is that speculators, by trying to make a profit, provide the useful public service of stabilizing prices. The reverse argument involved not private speculators but central banks. Central banks buy and sell currencies, supposedly in order to stabilize exchange rates (an exchange rate is the price of one kind of money measured in another). They are widely suspected (by economists and speculators) of trying to keep exchange rates not stable but above or below their market clearing levels.

If profitable speculation is stabilizing, one might expect successful stabilization of currencies to be profitable. If the banks are buying dollars when they are temporarily cheap and selling them when they are temporarily expensive, they should be both stabilizing the value of the dollar and making a profit. One implication of this argument is that the central banks are superfluous—if there are profits to be made by stabilizing currencies, speculators will be glad to volunteer for the job. A second implication is that we can judge the success of central banks by seeing whether they in fact make or lose money on their speculations. The conclusion of the speaker, who had studied precisely that question, was that they generally lost money.

OPTIONAL SECTION
CHOICE IN AN UNCERTAIN WORLD

In Chapters 1–11, we saw how markets work to determine prices and quantities in a certain and unchanging world. In Chapter 12, we learned how to deal with a world that was changing but certain. In such a world, any decision involves a predictable stream of costs and benefits—so much this year, so much next year, so much the year after. One simply converts each stream into its present value and compares the present values of costs and benefits, just as we earlier compared annual flows of costs and benefits.

Section III   Complications, or Onward to Reality

The next step is to analyze individual choice in an uncertain world. Again our objective is to convert the problem we are dealing with into the easier problem we have already solved. To describe an uncertain world, we assume that each individual has a **probability distribution** over possible outcomes. He does not know what *will* happen but he knows, or believes he knows, what *might* happen and *how likely* it is to happen. His problem, given what he knows, is how to achieve his objectives as successfully as possible.

The Rational Gambler

Consider, for example, an individual betting on whether a coin will come up heads or tails. Assuming the coin is a fair one, half the time it will come up heads and half the time tails. The gambler's problem is to decide what bets he should be willing to take.

The answer seems obvious—take any bets that offer a payoff of more than $1 for each $1 bet; refuse any that offer less. If someone offers to pay you $2 if the coin comes up heads, on condition that you pay him $1 if it comes up tails, then on average you gain by accepting the bet and should do so. If he offers you $0.50 for the risk of $1, then on average you lose by accepting; you should refuse the bet.

In these examples, you are choosing between a certain outcome (decline the bet—and end up with as much money as you started with) and an uncertain outcome (accept the bet—end up with either more or less). A more general way of putting the rule is that in choosing among alternatives, you should choose the one that gives you the highest **expected return**, where the expected return is the sum of the returns associated with the different possible outcomes, each weighted by its probability. In the particular case where you are choosing between two alternatives, one of which consists of doing nothing, that implies that you should accept a bet if the expected return from doing so is positive and decline it if the expected return is negative.

Maximizing Expected Return. This is the correct answer in some situations but not in all. If you make a 50-50 bet many times, you are almost certain to win about half the time; a bet that on average benefits you is almost certain to give you a net gain in the long term. If, for instance, you flip a fair coin 1,000 times, there is only a very small chance that it will come up heads more than 600 times or fewer than 400. If you make $2 every time it comes up heads and lose $1 every time it comes up tails, you are almost certain, after 1,000 flips, to be at least $200 ahead.

The case of the gambler who expects to bet many times on the fall of a coin can easily be generalized to describe any game of chance. The rule for such a gambler is "Maximize expected return." Since we defined expected return as the sum, over all of the possible outcomes, of the return from each outcome times the probability of that outcome, we have:

$$<R> \equiv \sum p_i R_i. \qquad \text{(Equation 1)}$$

Here p_i is the probability of outcome number i occurring, R_i is the return from outcome number i, and $<R>$ is the expected return.

When you flip a coin, it must come up either heads or tails; more generally, any gamble ends up with some one of the alternative outcomes happening, so we have:

$$\sum p_i = 1. \qquad \text{(Equation 2)}$$

In the gamble described earlier, where the gambler loses $1 on tails and gains $2 on heads, we have:

$$p_1 = 0.5; R_1 = +\$2 \text{ (heads)}$$

$$p_2 = 0.5; R_2 = -\$1 \text{ (tails)}$$

$$<R> = (p_1 \times R_1) + (p_2 \times R_2) = [0.5 \times (+\$2)] + [0.5 \times (-\$1)] = +\$0.50.$$

Here p_1 and p_2, the probabilities of heads and tails respectively, are each equal to one half; your expected return is $0.50. If you play the game many times, you will on average make $0.50 each time you play. The expected return from taking the gamble is positive, so you should take it—provided you can repeat it many times. The same applies to any other gamble with a positive expected return. A gamble with an expected return of zero—you are on average equally well off whether or not you choose to take it—is called a **fair gamble**.

We now know how a gambler who will take the same gamble many times should behave. In choosing among several gambles, he should take the one with the highest expected return. In the particular case where he is accepting or declining bets, so that one of his alternatives is a certainty of no change, he should take any bet that is better than a fair gamble.

Maximizing Expected Utility. Suppose, however, that you are only playing the game once—and that the bet is not $1 but $50,000. If you lose, you are destitute—$50,000 is all you have. If you win, you gain $100,000. You may feel that a decline in your wealth from $50,000 to zero hurts you more than an increase from $50,000 to $150,000 helps you. One could easily enough imagine situations in which losing $50,000 resulted in your starving to death while gaining $100,000 produced only a modest increase in your welfare.

Such a situation is an example of what we earlier called declining marginal utility. The dollars that raise you from zero to $50,000 are worth more per dollar than the additional dollars beyond $50,000. That is precisely what we would expect from the discussion of Chapter 4. Dollars are used to buy goods; we expect goods to be worth less to you the more of them you have.

When you choose a profession, start a business, buy a house, or stake your life savings playing the commodity market, you are betting a large sum, and the bet is not one you will repeat enough times to be confident of getting an average return. How can we analyze rational behavior in such situations?

The answer to this question was provided by John Von Neumann, the same mathematician mentioned in Chapter 11 as the inventor of game theory. He demonstrated that by combining the idea of expected return used in the mathematical theory of gambling (probability theory) with the idea of utility used in economics, it was possible to describe the behavior of individuals dealing with uncertain situations—whether or not the situations were repeated many times.

The fundamental idea is that instead of maximizing expected return in dollars, as in the case described above, individuals maximize expected return in utiles—expected utility. Each outcome i has a utility U_i. We define expected utility as:

$$<U> \equiv \sum p_i U_i. \qquad \text{(Equation 3)}$$

Your utility depends on many things, of which the amount of money you have is only one. If we are considering alternatives that only differ with regard to the amount of money you end up with, we can write:

$$U_i = U(R_i).$$

Or, in other words, the utility you get from outcome i depends only on how much more (or less) money that outcome gives you. If utility increases linearly with income, as shown on Figure 13-12, we have:

$$U(R) = A + (B \times R);$$

$$<U> = \sum p_i U_i = \sum p_i (A + BR_i) = A \sum p_i + B \sum p_i R_i.$$

$$= A + B <R>. \qquad \text{(Equation 4)}$$

Comparing the left- and right-hand sides of Equation 4, we see that whatever decision maximizes $<R>$ also maximizes $<U>$. In this case— with a linear utility function—the individual maximizing his expected utility behaves like the gambler maximizing his expected return.

A Methodological Digression.   In going from gambling games to utility graphs, we have changed somewhat the way in which we look at expected return. In the case of gambling, return was defined relative to your initial situation—positive if you gained and negative if you lost. That was a convenient way of looking at gambling because the gambler always has the alternative of refusing to bet and so ending up with a return of zero. But in an uncertain world, the individual does not usually have that alternative; sometimes—indeed almost always—he is choosing among alternatives all of which are uncertain. In that context, it is easier to define zero return as ending up with no money at all and to measure all other outcomes relative to that. We can then show the utility of any outcome on a graph such as Figure 13-12 as the utility of the income associated with that outcome. If you start with $10,000 and bet all of it at even odds on the flip of a coin—heads you win, tails you lose—then the utility to you of the outcome "heads" is the utility of $20,000. The utility to you of the outcome "tails" is the utility of zero dollars.

A second difficulty with Figure 13-12 is the ambiguity as to just what is being graphed on the horizontal axis—what is utility a function of? Is it income (dollars per year) or money (dollars)? Strictly speaking, utility is a flow (utiles per year) that depends on a flow of consumption (apples per year). The utility we get by consuming 100 apples, or whatever else we buy with our income, depends in part on the period of time over which we consume them.

If I were being precise, I would do all the analysis in terms of flows and compare alternatives by comparing the present values of those flows, in dollars or utiles. This would make the discussion a good deal more complicated without adding much to its content. It is easier to think of Figure 13-12, and similar figures, as describing either someone who starts with a fixed amount of money and is only going to live for a year, or,

Figure 13-12

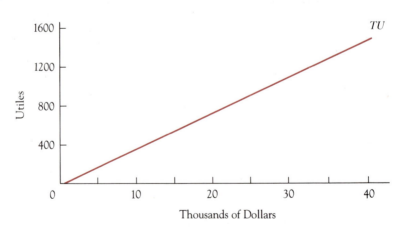

Total utility of income for a risk-neutral individual.

alternatively, someone with a portfolio of bonds yielding a fixed income who is considering gambles that will affect the size of his portfolio. The logic of the two situations is the same. In the one case, the figure graphs the utility flow from a year's expenditure; in the other case, it graphs the present value of the utility flow from spending the same amount every year forever. Both approaches allow us to analyze the implications of uncertainty while temporarily ignoring other complications of a changing world. To make the discussion simpler, I will talk as if we are considering the first case; that way I can talk in "dollars" and "utiles" instead of "dollars per year" and "utiles per year." The amount of money you have may still sometimes be described as your income—an income of x dollars/year for one year equals x dollars.

Risk Preference and the Utility Function, or, As I Was Saying When I So Rudely Interrupted Myself

Figure 13-12 showed utility as a linear function of income; Figure 13-13a shows a more plausible relation. This time, income has declining marginal utility. Total utility increases with income, but it increases more and more slowly as income gets higher and higher.

Figure 13-13

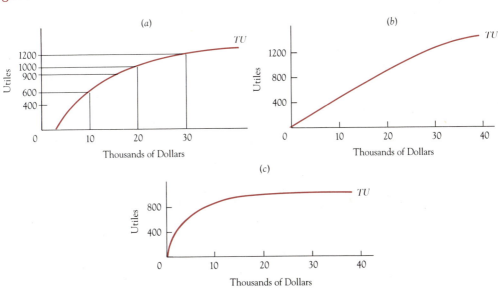

Total utility of income for a risk-averse individual. Figure 13-13b corresponds to an individual who is only slihtly risk averse; he will refuse a fair gamble but accept one that is slightly better than a fair. Figure 13-13c corresponds to an individual who is very risk averse; he will accept a gamble only if it is much better than a fair gamble.

Chapter 13 ... and Chance 385

Suppose you presently have $20,000 and have an opportunity to bet $10,000 on the flip of a coin at even odds. If you win, you end up with $30,000; if you lose, you end up with $10,000.

In deciding whether to take the bet, you are choosing between two different gambles. The first, the one you get if you do not take the bet, is a very simple gamble indeed—a certainty of ending up with $20,000. The second, the one you get if you do take the bet, is a little more complicated—a 0.5 chance of ending up with $10,000 and a 0.5 chance of ending up with $30,000. So for the first gamble, we have:

$$p_1 = 1; R_1 = \$20,000; U_1 = U(R_1) = U(\$20,000) = 1,000 \text{ utiles}$$
(from Figure 13-13a)

$$<U> = p_1 \times U_1 = 1,000 \text{ utiles}.$$

For the second gamble, we have:

$$p_1 = 0.5; R_1 = \$10,000; U_1 = U(R_1) = U(\$10,000) = 600 \text{ utiles}$$
(from Figure 13-13a)

$$p_2 = 0.5; R_2 = \$30,000; U_2 = U(R_2) = U(\$30,000) = 1,200 \text{ utiles}$$
(from Figure 13-13a)

$$<U> = (p_1 \times U_1) + (p_2 \times U_2) = (0.5 \times 600 \text{ utiles}) + (0.5 \times 1,200 \text{ utiles})$$

$$= 900 \text{ utiles}.$$

The individual takes the alternative with the higher expected utility; he declines the bet. In money terms, the two alternatives are equally attractive; they have the same expected return. In that sense, it is a fair bet. In utility terms, the first alternative is superior to the second. You should be able to convince yourself that as long as the utility function has the shape shown in Figure 13-13a, an individual will always prefer a certainty of $1 to a gamble whose expected return is $1.

An individual who behaves in that way is **risk averse.** A utility function that is almost straight, such as Figure 13-13b, represents an individual who is only slightly risk averse. Such an individual would decline a fair gamble but might accept one that was a little better than fair—bet $1,000 against $1,100 on the flip of a coin, for example. An individual who was extremely risk averse (Figure 13-13c) might still accept a gamble—but only one with a very high expected return, such as risking $1,000 on the flip of a coin to get $10,000.

Figure 13-14a shows the utility function of a **risk preferrer.** It exhibits increasing marginal utility. A risk preferrer would be willing to take a gamble that was slightly worse than fair—although he would still decline one with a sufficiently low expected return. An individual who is neither a

Figure 13-14

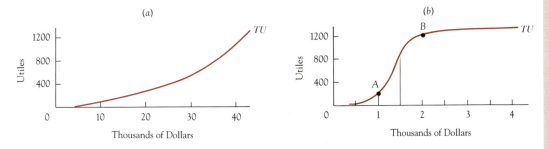

(a) *(b)*

Total utility of income for a risk preferrer and for someone who is risk preferring for some incomes and risk averse for others. Figure 13-14*b* shows total utility of income for someone who requires about $1,500 to stay alive. Below that point, the marginal utility of income (the slope of total utility) increases with increasing income; above that point, it decreases.

risk preferrer nor a risk averter is called **risk neutral**. The corresponding utility function has already been shown—as Figure 13-12.

Consider an individual who requires a certain amount of money in order to buy enough food to stay alive. Increases in income below that point extend his life a little and so are of some value to him, but he still ends up starving to death. An increase in income that gives him enough to survive is worth a great deal to him. Once he is well past that point, additional income buys less important things, so marginal utility of income falls. The corresponding utility function is shown as Figure 13-14*b*; marginal utility first rises with increasing income, then falls.

Such an individual would be a risk preferrer if his initial income were at point *A*, below subsistence. He would be a risk averter if he were starting at point *B*. In the former case, he would, if necessary, risk $1,000 to get $500 at even odds. If he loses, he only starves a little faster; if he wins, he lives.

In discussing questions of this sort, it is important to realize that the degree to which someone exhibits risk preference or risk aversion depends on three different things—the shape of his utility function, his initial income, and the size of the bet he is considering. For small bets, we would expect everyone to be roughly risk neutral; the marginal utility of a dollar does not change very much between an income of $19,999 and an income of $20,001, which is the relevant consideration for someone with $20,000 who is considering a $1 bet.

The Simple Cases. The expected return from a gamble depends only on the odds and the payoffs; the expected utility depends also on the tastes of the gambler, as described by his utility function. So it is easier to predict the behavior of someone maximizing his expected return than of someone maximizing expected utility. This raises an interesting question—under what circumstances are the two maximizations equivalent?

When does someone maximize his utility by maximizing his expected return?

We saw one answer at the beginning of this section of the chapter. An individual who makes the same gamble many times can expect the results to average out. In the long run, the outcome is almost certain—he will get something very close to the expected value of the gamble times the number of times he takes it. Since his income at the end of the process is (almost) certain, all he has to do in order to maximize his expected utility is to make that income as large as possible—which he does by choosing the gamble with the highest expected return.

There are three other important situations in which maximizing expected utility turns out to be equivalent to maximizing expected return. One is when the individual is risk neutral, as shown on Figure 13-12. A second is when the size of the prospective gains and losses is small compared to one's income. If we consider only small changes in income, we can treat the marginal utility of income as constant; if the marginal utility of income is constant, then changes in utility are simply proportional to changes in income, so whatever choice maximizes expected return also maximizes expected utility.

One can see the same thing geometrically. Figure 13-15 is a magnified version of part of Figure 13-13a. If we consider only a very small range of income—between $19,900 and $20,000, for instance—the utility function is almost straight. For a straight-line utility function, as I showed earlier, maximizing expected utility is equivalent to maximizing expected return. So if we are considering only small changes in income, we should act as if we were risk neutral.

Figure 13-15

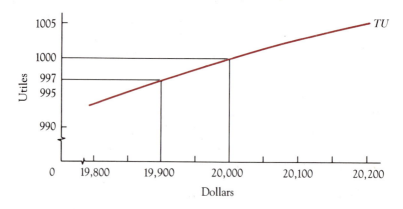

Magnified version of part of Figure 13-13a. Although the total utility curve shown on Figure 13-13a is curved, corresponding to risk aversion, any small section of it appears almost straight. This corresponds to the fact that the marginal utility of income is almost constant over small ranges of income; individuals are almost risk neutral for small gambles.

Next consider the case of a corporation that is trying to maximize the market value of its stock—as the discussion of takeover bids in the optional section of Chapter 9 suggests that corporations tend to do. In an uncertain world, what management is really choosing each time it makes a decision is a probability distribution for future profits. When the future arrives and it becomes clear which of the possible outcomes has actually happened, the price of the stock will reflect what the profits actually are. So in choosing a probability distribution for future profits, management is also choosing a probability distribution for the future price of the stock.

How is the current market value of a stock related to the probability distribution of its future value? That is a complicated question—one that occupies a good deal of the theory of financial markets; if you are an economics major, you will probably encounter it again. The short, but not entirely correct, answer is that the current price of the stock is the expected value of the future price—the average over all possible futures weighted by the probability of each. The reason is that the buyer of stock is in the same position as the gambler discussed earlier; he can average out his risks by buying a little stock in each of a large number of companies. If he does, his actual return will be very close to his expected return. If the price of any particular stock were significantly lower than the expected value of its future price, investors would all want to buy some of it; if the price were higher than the expected value of its future price, they would all want to sell some. The resulting market pressures force the current price toward the expected value of future prices.

If, as suggested above, management wishes to maximize the present price of its stock, it must try to maximize the expected value of its future price. It does that by maximizing the expected value of future profits. So it acts like the gambler we started with; it maximizes expected returns.

This is true only if the firm is trying to maximize the value of its stock. The threat of takeover bids has some tendency to make it do so. It is not clear how strong that tendency is—how closely that threat constrains management. To the extent that management succeeds in pursuing its own goals rather than those of the stockholders, the conclusion no longer holds. If the firm takes a risk and goes bankrupt, the (present and future) income of the chief executive may fall dramatically. If so, he may well be unwilling to make a decision that has a 50 percent chance of leading to bankruptcy even if it also has a 50 percent chance of tripling the firm's value.

Insurance. The existence of individuals who are risk averse provides one explanation for the existence of insurance. Suppose you have the utility function shown in Figure 13-13a. Your income is $20,000, but there is a small probability—0.01—of some accident that would reduce it to $10,000. The insurance company offers to insure you against that accident for a price of $100. Whether or not the accident happens, you give them $100. If the accident happens, they give you back $10,000. You now have a choice between two gambles—buying or not buying insurance.

If you buy the insurance, then, whether or not the accident occurs, the outcome is the same—you have $20,000 minus the $100 you paid for the insurance (I assume the accident only affects your income). So for the first gamble, you have:

$$p_1 = 1; R_1 = \$19,900; <U> = p_1 \times U(R_1) = 997 \text{ utiles.}$$

If you do not buy the insurance, you have:

$$p_1 = 0.99; R_1 = \$20,000; U(R_1) = 1,000 \text{ utiles;}$$

$$p_2 = 0.01; R_2 = \$10,000; U(R_2) = 600 \text{ utiles;}$$

$$<U> = [p_1 \times U(R_1)] + [p_2 \times U(R_2)] = 990 \text{ utiles} + 6 \text{ utiles} = 996 \text{ utiles.}$$

You are better off with the insurance than without it, so you buy the insurance.

In the example as given, the expected return—measured in dollars—from buying the insurance was the same as the expected return from not buying it. Buying insurance was a fair gamble—you paid $100 in exchange for one chance in a hundred of receiving $10,000. The insurance company makes hundreds of thousands of such bets, so it will end up receiving, on average, almost exactly the expected return. If insurance is a fair gamble, the money coming in to buy insurance exactly balances the money going out to pay claims. The insurance company neither makes nor loses money; the client breaks even in money but gains in utility.

Insurance companies in the real world have expenses other than paying out claims—rent on their offices, commissions to their salespeople, and salaries for their administrators, claim investigators, adjusters, and lawyers. In order for an insurance company to cover all its expenses, the gamble it offers must be somewhat better than a fair one from its standpoint. If so, it is somewhat worse than fair from the standpoint of the company's clients.

The clients may still find that it is in their interest to accept the gamble and buy the insurance. If they are sufficiently risk averse, an insurance contract that lowers their expected return may still increase their expected utility. In the case discussed above, for example, it would still be worth buying the insurance even if the company charged $130 for it. It would not be worth buying at $140. You should be able to check those results for yourself by redoing the calculations that showed that the insurance was worth buying at $100.

Earlier I pointed out that with regard to risks that involve only small changes in income, everyone is (almost) risk neutral. One implication of this is that it is only worth insuring against large losses. Insurance is worse than a fair gamble from the standpoint of the customer, since the insurance company has to make enough to cover its expenses. For small losses, the difference between the marginal utility of income before and after the loss is not large enough to convert a loss in expected return into a gain in expected utility.

The Lottery-Insurance Puzzle. Buying a ticket in a lottery is the opposite of buying insurance. When you buy insurance, you accept an unfair gamble—a gamble that results, on average, in your having less money than if you had not accepted it—in order to reduce uncertainty. When you buy a lottery ticket, you also accept an unfair gamble—on average, the lottery pays out in prizes less than it takes in—but this time you do it in order to increase your uncertainty. If you are risk averse, it may make sense for you to buy insurance—but you should never buy lottery tickets. If you are a risk preferrer it may make sense for you to buy a lottery ticket—but you should never buy insurance.

This brings us to a puzzle that has bothered economists for at least 200 years—the lottery-insurance paradox. In the real world, the same people sometimes buy both insurance and lottery tickets. Some people both gamble when they know the odds are against them and buy insurance when they know the odds are against them. Can this be consistent with rational behavior?

There are at least two possible ways in which it can. One is illustrated on Figure 13-16. The individual with the utility function shown there is risk averse for one range of incomes and risk preferring for another, higher, range. If he starts at point *A*, in between the two regions, he may be interested in buying both insurance and lottery tickets. Insurance

Figure 13-16

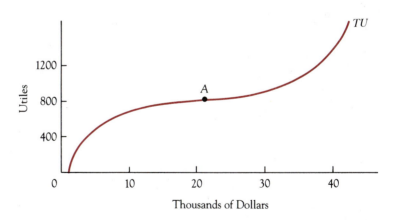

One solution to the lottery-insurance puzzle. The total utility function shows declining marginal utility of income (risk aversion) to the left of point *A* and increasing marginal utility of income (risk preference) to the right. An individual at *A* may increase his expected utility by buying both insurance and lottery tickets.

protects him against risks that move his income below A—where he is risk averse. Lottery tickets offer him the possibility (if he wins) of an income above A—where he is risk preferring.

This solution is logically possible, but it does not seem very plausible. Why should people have such peculiarly shaped utility functions, with the value to them of an additional dollar first falling with increasing income then rising again? And if they do, why should their incomes just happen to be near the border between the two regions?

Another explanation of the paradox is that in the real-world situation we observe, one of the conditions for our analysis does not hold. So far, we have been considering situations where the only important difference among the outcomes is money; the utility of each outcome depends only on the amount of money it leaves you with. It is not clear that this is true for the individuals who actually buy lottery tickets.

Consider the lotteries you have yourself been offered—by *Reader's Digest*, Publisher's Clearinghouse, and similar enterprises. The price is the price of a stamp, the payoff—lavishly illustrated with glossy photographs—a (very small) chance of a new Cadillac, a Caribbean vacation, an income of $20,000 a year for life. My rough calculations—based on a guess of how many people respond to the lottery—suggest that the value of the prize multiplied by the chance of getting it comes to less than the cost of the stamp. The expected return is negative.

Why then do so many people enter? The explanation I find most plausible is that what they are getting for their stamp is not merely one chance in a million of a $40,000 car. They are also getting a certainty of being able to daydream about getting the car—or the vacation or the income—from the time they send in the envelope until the winners are announced. The daydream is made more satisfying by the knowledge that there is a chance, even if a slim one, that they will actually win the prize. The lottery is not only selling a gamble. It is also selling a dream—and at a very low price.

This explanation has the disadvantage of pushing such lotteries out of the area where economics can say much about them; we know a good deal about rational gambling but very little about the market for dreams. It has the advantage of explaining not only the existence of lotteries but some of their characteristics. If lotteries exist to provide people a chance of money, why do the prizes often take other forms; why not give the winner $40,000 and let him decide whether to buy a Cadillac with it? That would not only improve the prize from the standpoint of the winner but would also save the sponsors the cost of all those glossy photographs of the prizes.

But many people may find it easier to daydream about their winnings if the winnings take a concrete form. So the sponsors (sometimes) make the prizes goods instead of money—and provide a wide variety of prizes to suit different tastes in daydreams. This seems to be especially true of "free" lotteries—ones where the price is a stamp and the sponsor pays for the prizes out of someone's advertising budget instead of out of ticket receipts. Lotteries that sell tickets seem more inclined to pay off in money—why I do not know.

In Chapter 1, I included in my definition of economics the assumption that individuals have reasonably simple objectives. You will have to decide for yourself whether a taste for daydreams is consistent with that assumption. If not, then we may have finally found something that is not an economic question—as demonstrated by our inability to use economics to answer it.

Von Neumann Utility

Near the beginning of this section, I said that John Von Neumann was responsible for combining the ideas of utility and choice under uncertainty. So far, I have shown how the two ideas are combined but have said very little about exactly what Von Neumann (in conjunction with economist Oskar Morgenstern) contributed. You may reasonably have concluded that the great idea was simply to assert "People maximize expected utility" and keep talking—in the hope that nobody would ask "Why?"

What Von Neumann and Morgenstern actually did was both more difficult and more subtle than that. They proved that if you assume that individual choice under uncertainty meets a few simple consistency conditions, it is always possible to assign utilities to outcomes in such a way that the decisions people actually make are the ones they would make if they were maximizing expected utility.

Von Neumann and Morgenstern start by considering an individual choosing among "lotteries." A lottery is a collection of outcomes, each with a probability. Some outcome must occur, so all the probabilities together add up to one. Just as, in considering ordinary utility functions, we assume that the individual can choose between any two bundles, so they assumed that given any two lotteries L and M, the individual either prefers L to M, prefers M to L, or is indifferent between them. They further assumed that preferences are transitive; if you prefer L to M and M to N, you must prefer L to N.

Another assumption was that in considering lotteries whose payoffs are themselves lotteries—probabilistic situations whose outcomes are themselves probabilistic situations—people combine probabilities in a mathematically correct fashion. If someone is offered a ticket giving him a 50 percent chance of winning a lottery ticket, which in turn gives him a 50 percent chance of winning a prize, he regards that **compound lottery** as equivalent to a ticket giving a 25 percent chance of winning the same prize—and similarly for any other combination of probabilities.

The remaining two assumptions involve the continuity of preferences. One is that if I prefer outcome A to outcome B, I also prefer to B any lottery that gives me some probability of getting A and guarantees that if I do not get A, I will get B. The final assumption is that if I prefer outcome A to outcome B and outcome B to outcome C, then there is some probability mix of *A* and *C*—some lottery containing only those outcomes—that I consider equivalent to *B*. To put it in different words, this says that as I move from a certainty of *A* to a certainty of *C* via various mixtures of the two, my utility changes continuously from $U(A)$ to $U(C)$. Since by assumption $U(A) > U(B) > U(C)$—that is what the "if" clause at the beginning of this paragraph says—as my utility moves continuously from $U(A)$ to $U(C)$ it must at some intermediate point be equal to $U(B)$.

All of these assumptions seem reasonable as part of a description of "rational" or "consistent" behavior under uncertainty. If an individual's behavior satisfies them, it is possible to define a **Von Neumann utility function**—a utility for every outcome—such that the choices he actually makes are the choices he would make if he were trying to maximize his expected utility. That is what Von Neumann and Morgenstern proved.

In the optional section of Chapter 3, I pointed out that utility as then defined contained a considerable element of arbitrariness; utility functions were supposed to describe behavior, but exactly the same behavior could be described by many different utility functions. We could deduce from observing individuals' choices that they preferred *A* to *B*, but not by how much. Even the principle of declining marginal utility, to which I several times referred, is, strictly speaking, meaningless in that context; if you cannot measure the amount by which I prefer one alternative to another, then you cannot say whether the additional utility that I get when my income increases from $9,000/year to $10,000 is more or less than when it increases from $10,000 to $11,000. Declining marginal utility then has content only in the form of the declining marginal rate of substitution—a concept that, as I pointed out at the time, is closely related but not equivalent.

Once we accept the Von Neumann-Morgenstern definition of utility under uncertainty, that problem vanishes. The statement "I prefer outcome *C* to outcome *B* by twice as much as I prefer *B* to *A*" is equivalent to "I am indifferent between a certainty of *B* and a lottery that gives me a two-thirds chance of *A* and a one-third chance of *C*."

To see that the two statements are equivalent, we will work out the expected utilities for the two alternatives described in the second statement and show that the first statement implies that they are equal, as follows:

Let Lottery 1 consist of a certainty of *B*, Lottery 2 of a two-thirds chance of *A* and a one-third chance of *C*. We have for Lottery 1:

$$p_1 = 1; U_1 = U(B); <U> = U(B).$$

We have for Lottery 2:

$$p_1 = {}^2\!/_3; U_1 = U(A);$$

Section III   Complications, or Onward to Reality

$$p_2 = \frac{1}{3}; U_2 = U(C);$$

$$<U> = p_1 U_1 + p_2 U_2 = \frac{2}{3} U(A) + \frac{1}{3} U(C).$$

Statement 1 tells us that:

$$U(C) - U(B) = 2 \times \{ U(B) - U(A) \}.$$

Rearranging this gives us:

$$U(C) + \{ 2 \times U(A) \} = 3 \times U(B);$$

$$\frac{2}{3} U(A) + \frac{1}{3} U(C) = U(B). \qquad \text{(Equation 5)}$$

The left-hand side of Equation 5 is the expected utility of Lottery 2, and the right-hand side is the expected utility of Lottery 1, so the expected utilities of the two alternatives are the same; the individual is indifferent between them.

We have now shown that Statement 1 implies Statement 2. We could equally well have started with Statement 2 and worked backward to Statement 1. If each statement implies the other, then they are equivalent.

So using utility functions to describe choice among probabilistic alternatives makes the functions themselves considerably less arbitrary. In our earlier discussion of utility, the only meaningful statements were of the form "A has more utility to me than B" or, equivalently, "I prefer A to B." Now the statement "Going from A to B increases my utility by twice as much as going from C to D" (or, equivalently, "I prefer A to B twice as much as I prefer C to D") has meaning as well. If we can make quantitative comparisons of utility differences, we can also make quantitative comparisons of marginal utilities, so the principle of declining marginal utility means something. We saw exactly what it meant a few pages ago; the statement "My marginal utility for income is declining" is equivalent to "I am risk averse." Similarly, the statement "My marginal utility for ice cream cones is declining" is equivalent to "I am risk averse if expected return is in ice cream cones rather than in dollars. I would not accept a gamble that consisted of a 50 percent chance of getting an ice cream cone and a 50 percent chance of losing one."

We have eliminated much of the arbitrariness from utility functions but not all of it. Nothing we have done tells us how big a utile is, so a change in scale is still possible. If I say that I prefer A to B by 10 utiles, B to C by 5, and C to D by 2, while you insist that the correct numbers are 20, 10, and 4, no possible observation of my behavior could prove one of us right and one wrong. We agree about the order of preferences; we agree about their relative intensity—all we disagree about is the size of the unit in which we are measuring them.

It is also true that nothing we have done tells us where the zero of the utility function is. If I claim that my utilities for outcomes A, B, and C are 0, 10, 30, while you claim they are −10, 0, and 20, there is again no way of settling the disagreement. We agree about the order, we agree about the differences—all we disagree about is which alternative has zero utility. So changes in the utility function that consist of adding the same amount to all utilities (changing the zero), or multiplying all utilities by the same number (changing the scale), or both, do not really change the utility function. The numbers are different, but the behavior described is exactly the same. This means, for those of you who happen to be mathematicians, that utility functions are arbitrary with respect to linear transformations.

My own preference, in discussing utility, is to define zero as nonexistence or death; that, after all, is the one outcome in which one gets, so far as I know, neither pleasure nor pain. A friend and colleague once commented to me that she was not certain whether the present value of utility at birth was positive or negative—meaning that she was not sure whether, on net, life was worth living. I concluded that her life had been much harder than mine.

Buying Information

You have decided to buy a car and are choosing between two alternatives: a Honda Accord and a Nissan Stanza. From previous experience, you expect that you will like one of the cars better than the other, but unfortunately you do not know which. If forced to state your opinions more precisely, you would say that you think your consumer surplus would be $500 higher if you bought the better car, and the probability that the Accord is better than the Stanza is exactly 0.5.

You consider two strategies. You can randomly choose one of the cars and buy it. Alternatively, you can rent an Accord for your next long trip, a Stanza for the trip after that, and then decide which to buy. You believe that after having driven each car a substantial distance, you will know with certainty which you like better. Since it is more expensive to rent a car than to use a car you own, the second strategy will cost you an extra $200. Should you do it?

The answer depends on your utility function. You are choosing between two lotteries. The first has payoffs of $0 and $500, each with probability 0.5. The second has a certain payoff of $300, since you get the extra consumer surplus but pay $200 for it. If you are risk neutral or risk averse, you prefer a certainty of $300 to a 0.5 chance of $500, so you rent the cars before you buy. If you are a strong risk preferrer, you prefer the gamble, so you buy without renting.

This simple problem illustrates the general idea of buying information. By paying some **search cost** you can reduce uncertainty, improving, on average, the outcomes of your decisions. To decide whether the search cost is worth paying, you compare expected utility without search to expected utility with search, remembering to include the cost of the search in your calculation.

In this particular case you had only two alternatives, to search or not to search, and searching gave you complete information—you knew with certainty which car you preferred. In more general cases you may have to decide just how much searching to do; the more you search, the better your information. The correct rule is to search up to the point where the value of the marginal increase in your expected utility from searching a little more is just equal to the cost.

One example of such behavior that has received a great deal of attention is the problem of job search. Many people who consider themselves unemployed could find a job almost instantly—if they were willing to wait on tables, or wash dishes, or drive a cab. What they are looking for is not a job but a good job. The longer they look, the better, on average, will be the best job opportunity they find. Their rational strategy is to keep looking as long as they expect to gain more from additional search than it costs them. Such **search unemployment** makes up a significant fraction of the measured unemployment rate.

One implication of this is that increases in unemployment compensation tend to increase the unemployment rate. The reason is not that the unemployed are lazy bums who prefer collecting unemployment to working, but that they are rational searchers. The higher the level of unemployment compensation is, the lower the cost of being unemployed while searching for a job. The less it costs to search, the more searching it pays to do.

Issues associated with acquiring and using information provide some of the most interesting and difficult questions in economics. They first appeared back in Chapter 1, where I briefly mentioned the problem of incorporating information costs into the definition of rationality, and will reappear in Chapter 18.

Where We Are Now

In the first 11 chapters of this book, we used economics to understand how markets work in a certain and unchanging world. It may have occurred to you that doing so was a waste of time, since we live in a world that is uncertain and changing.

Looking back at what we have done in Chapters 12 and 13, you may now see why the book is organized in this way. In Chapter 12, we learned how to analyze choice in a changing (but certain) world using the same tools developed for an unchanging world—simply evaluate costs and benefits in terms of present values instead of annual flows. Now we have learned how to analyze choice in an uncertain world by again using the same tools; we merely evaluate costs and benefits by comparing the expected utilities of probabilistic outcomes instead of the utilities of certain outcomes. Combining the lessons of the two chapters in order to analyze choice in a world that is both changing and uncertain would be straightforward—evaluate choices in terms of the present value of expected utility.

What we have done is to first solve economics in a simple world and then show that the more complicated and realistic world can, for purposes of economic analysis, be reduced to the simple one. Introducing time and change does create some new problems, such as those associated with sunk costs. Yet it is still true that in learning to deal with the simple world of Chapters 1–11 we learned most of the basic ideas of economics, and that in Chapters 12 and 13 we have taken a large step towards making those ideas applicable to the world we live in.

A Philosophical Digression

The concept of utility originated during the nineteenth century among thinkers interested in both philosophy and economics. It was proposed as an answer to the question "What should a society maximize?" The utilitarians asserted that a society should be designed to maximize the total utility of its members.

Their position has been heavily criticized over the years and is now in poor repute among philosophers. One of the major criticisms was that although we can, in principle, determine whether you prefer A to B by more than you prefer C to D, there seems to be no way of determining whether I prefer A to B by more than *you* prefer C to D. There is no way of making **interpersonal comparisons of utility**, no way of deciding whether a change that benefits me (gives me A instead of B) and injures you (gives you D instead of C) increases or decreases total utility.

One possible reply to this criticism of utilitarianism goes as follows. Suppose we define utility in the sense of Von Neumann and Morgenstern and use it to evaluate some question such as "Should the United States abolish all tariffs?" It turns out that the utilitarian rule—"Maximize total utility"—is equivalent to another rule that some find intuitively more persuasive: "Choose that alternative you would prefer if you knew you were going to be one of the people affected but had no idea which."

Why are the two equivalent? If I have no idea who I am going to be, I presumably have an equal probability p of being each person; if there are N people involved, then $p = 1/N$. If we write the utility of person i as U_i, then the lottery that consists of a probability p of being each person has an expected utility:

$$<U> = \sum p_i U_i = \sum p U_i = p \sum U_i.$$

But $\sum U_i$ is simply the total utility of the society, so whichever alternative maximizes total utility also maximizes $<U>$.

PROBLEMS

1. How should the developers of a new airliner take account of the plane's design costs in deciding whether to design and build the plane? In determining the price to charge airline companies? Should they suspend production if they find that they cannot obtain a price that will cover design costs?

2. After reading this chapter, you are considering dropping this course. What costs should you take into account in deciding whether to do so? What costs that you should ignore in that decision should you have taken into account in deciding to take the course in the first place?

3. Figure 13-17a shows the cost curves for producing typewriters in a typewriter factory. The inputs are available in perfectly elastic supply; all firms are identical and there are no restrictions on starting new firms. Each firm can run one factory.

   a. Draw the supply curve for one firm; label it S_f. Draw the supply curve for the industry, label it S_i. D_a is the demand curve for typewriters; everyone expects it to stay the same forever. How many are sold at what price? How many firms are there?

   b. The demand curve shifts up to D_b. It takes a year to build a new typewriter factory. Draw the *short-run* supply curve S_{SR}, showing price as a function of quantity over times too short to build more factories. A month after the change, how many typewriters are sold at what price?

Figure 13-17

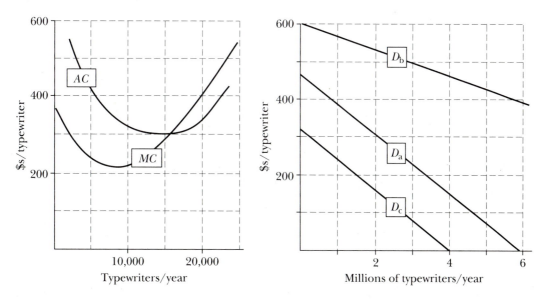

Cost curves for a typewriter factory and demand curves for typewriters. For Problem 3.

Chapter 13 ... and Chance

c. *AC* on Figure 13-17*a* includes the cost of building a typewriter factory, which is three million dollars. Factories last for 10 years; the interest rate is zero and factories have no scrap value. After the industry has adjusted to D_b, the word processor is invented and the demand curve for typewriters suddenly shifts down to D_c. Everyone expects it to remain there forever. Immediately after the change, what is the price of a typewriter?

d. The demand curve remains at D_c. Fifty years later, what is the price of a typewriter? How many are produced each year?

4. Long-run total cost includes both short-run and long-run expenses, so for any quantity long-run total cost must be larger than short-run total cost. True or false? Discuss.

The following problems refer to the optional section:

5. You have $30,000; your utility function is shown by Figure 13-12. There is one chance in a hundred that your house will be struck by lightning, in which case it will cost $10,000 to repair it. What is the highest price you would be willing to pay, if necessary, for a lightning rod to protect your house?

6. Answer Problem 5 for the utility function of Figure 13-13*a*.

7. Figure 13-18 is identical to Figure 13-13*a*, with the addition of a line connecting two points—*A* and *E*—on the utility function. I claim that point *C*, halfway between points *A* and *E*, represents the utility (vertical axis) and expected return (horizontal axis) of a 50-50 gamble between *A* ($10,000) and *E* ($30,000); the fact that *C* is below the graph of the utility function indicates that you prefer a certainty with the same expected return ($20,000) to such a gamble. Similarly, I claim that point *B* represents a gamble with a 75 percent chance of giving you *A* and a 25 percent chance of giving you *E*, and that point *D* represents a gamble with a 25 percent chance of *A* and

Figure 13-18

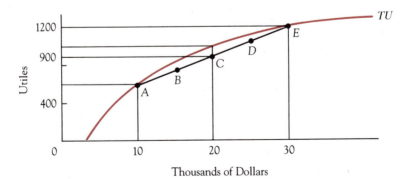

For Problem 7—total utility of income for a risk-averse individual.

Section III Complications, or Onward to Reality

a 75 percent chance of E. Prove that these claims are true—that the vertical position of each point equals the expected utility of the corresponding gamble and that the horizontal position equals the expected return.

8. In the text, I asserted that declining marginal utility of income was equivalent to risk aversion and that increasing marginal utility of income was equivalent to risk preference. While I gave examples, I did not prove that the assertion was true in general. Use the result of Problem 8 to do so.

9. In discussing risk aversion, I have only considered alternatives that are measured in money. Suppose you are gambling in apples instead. Is it possible for someone to be a risk preferrer in terms of dollars and a risk averter in terms of apples? Vice versa? Does it depend on whether there is a market on which you can buy and sell apples?

10. In one episode of *Star Trek*, Spock is in an orbiting landing craft that is running out of fuel and will shortly crash. Captain Kirk and the *Enterprise* are about to leave the planet, having somehow misplaced one landing craft and one science officer. Spock fires his rockets, burning up all the remaining fuel, in the hope that the *Enterprise* will notice the flare and come rescue him. Later Kirk twits the supremely logical Spock with irrationality, for having traded his last few hours of fuel for a one in a hundred chance of rescue. Is Kirk correct? Was Spock's behavior irrational?

FOR FURTHER READING

The original discussion of Von Neumann utility is in John Von Neumann and Oskar Morgenstern, *Theory of Games and Economic Behavior* (Princeton: Princeton University Press, 1944), Chapter 1.

A classic discussion of the lottery-insurance paradox is Milton Friedman and Leonard J. Savage, "The Utility Analysis of Choices Involving Risk," *Journal of Political Economy*, Vol. 56, No. 4 (August, 1948), pp. 279–304.

For discussions of some of the philosophical issues associated with what, if anything, the good society would maximize, you may wish to look at two important books: Robert Nozick, *Anarchy, State and Utopia* (New York: Basic Books, Inc., 1974) and John Rawls, *A Theory of Justice* (Cambridge: Harvard University Press, 1971). You may also be interested in an essay of mine on the question of what you should maximize if one of the variables is the number of people; in that situation maximizing total utility and maximizing average utility lead to different results. It is:

"What Does Optimum Population Mean," *Research in Population Economics*, *Vol. III* (1981), Eds. Simon and Lindert.

chapter 14

THE DISTRIBUTION OF INCOME AND THE FACTORS OF PRODUCTION

PART 1—THE DISTRIBUTION OF INCOME

Three questions that are often asked of economists are: What is the distribution of income? What determines the distribution of income? Is it fair? In this part of the chapter, I will have a little to say about the first question and a good deal to say about the second. Whether what I say has anything to do with the third, you will have to decide for yourself.

Measuring the Distribution of Income

Curve G on Figure 14-1a is a graph of the cumulative income distribution for some imaginary society. The horizontal axis shows a fraction of the population, ranked by income; the vertical axis shows what fraction of national income goes to that part of the population. Point A on the figure shows that the bottom 25 percent of the population receives about 15 percent of national income; point B shows that the bottom 85 percent of the population receives about 80 percent of national income.

Curve H on Figure 14-1b is a similar graph for a society in which everyone has the same income. It is a straight line. Since everyone has the same income, the "bottom" 10 percent of the population has 10 percent of the income, the bottom 50 percent has 50 percent, and so on. Line G on Figure 14-1a, which shows an unequal distribution, must lie below line H, since for an unequal distribution the bottom n percent of the population must have less than n percent of the income. Hence the colored area **M** in Figure 14-1a must be less than the colored area **N** in Figure 14-1b; their difference is the shaded area **L**. To make this clearer, I have also shown H on Figure 14-1a.

Twice the area of **L** on Figure 14-1a, called the **Gini coefficient**, is a simple measure of how unequal the income distribution of Figure 14-1a is. Since the graph is a 1×1 square, its entire area, equal to twice the triangle **N** on Figure 14-1b, is simply 1. So the Gini coefficient can also be defined as the ratio of area **L** to area **N**, or as the ratio of **L** to **L**+**M**. The

Figure 14-1

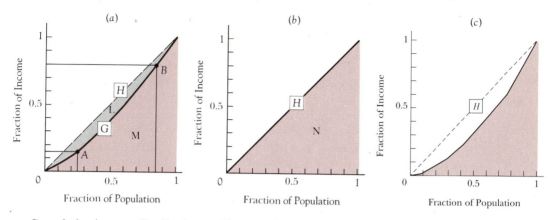

Cumulative income distributions.   Figure 14-1*b* shows the distribution for a population where everyone has the same income. Twice the shaded area **L** on Figure 14-1*a* is the Gini coefficient for the distribution shown. Figure 14-1*c* describes a population where lifetime incomes are all equal but current incomes are not.

closer that ratio is to zero, the more nearly equal the income distribution. Various estimates of what the Gini coefficient is for the United States at present and how it has varied over time have been made.

One problem with most such estimates is that they measure current income rather than lifetime income. To see why this is a problem, imagine that we have a society in which everyone follows an identical career pattern. From ages 18 to 22 everyone is a student, earning $5,000/year at various part-time jobs. From 23 to 30 everyone has a job with a salary of $20,000/year. From 31 to 50 everyone makes $30,000/year; from 51 to 65 everyone makes $40,000/year and then retires on a pension of $15,000/year and lives to 77. Figure 14-1*c* shows the resulting income distribution, seen at a single instant. If you calculate a Gini coefficient from the figure, it is about 0.23.

This is a perfectly egalitarian society, since everyone's income follows the same pattern; but the income distribution appears far from equal on the graph, and the Gini coefficient is not equal to zero, as it should be if all incomes are equal. The reason is that, at any one instant, some people are students, some are employees with varying degrees of experience, and some are retired. So if you look at a cross section of the society at a single instant, incomes appear quite unequal. Both the cumulative income distribution shown on Figure 14-1*c* and the corresponding Gini coefficient are the same as for a society where one twelfth of the people have an income of $5,000/year, two tenths have $15,000/year, and so on—with everyone having the same income for his whole lifetime. The Gini coefficient as usually calculated tells us how unequal incomes are at one instant in time but does not distinguish between inequality due to different people being in different stages of their earning cycle and inequality due to some people being richer or more talented than others.

Most estimates of the income distribution are done in this way, which suggests that most estimates considerably overstate actual inequality. One study I saw that tried to allow for such effects concluded that they roughly doubled the measured Gini coefficient. If that result is correct, then if you consider lifetime income rather than income at one instant in time, the U.S. income distribution is about half as unequal as conventional estimates suggest.

A similar problem arises when one tries to figure out whether some particular program, such as social security, redistributes from the rich to the poor or from the poor to the rich. To see how the problem arises, we will start by considering a social security program that has no redistributional effect at all; everyone gets back just what he paid in, plus accumulated interest. (This is not the way the real social security system works.) Since payments are made when you are employed and benefits received when you are retired, payments are made by someone with a higher income than the person who receives the benefits—not because the money is going from rich to poor but because it is going from you when you have a higher income to you in a later year when you have a lower income. If you look at a cross section of the population, it appears that social security redistributes from rich to poor—the people who are paying are richer than those receiving—even though, in this case, there is no redistribution at all.

It is not clear what the distributional effect of the real social security system is; it may actually redistribute from lower to higher income workers. The higher income worker typically starts working—and paying in—at an older age, which reduces his total payments, and lives longer, which increases his total benefits. Whether these effects are outweighed by other features of the system that provide relative advantages to the poor is not clear. What is clear is that a comparison of the incomes of those who in any particular year are receiving social security to the incomes of those who are paying for it always shows the system transferring income from richer to poorer—and that result tells us almost nothing about the real effect of the system on the distribution of income.

A third problem arises when we try to measure changes in the distribution of income over time. To do so, we require statistics on what incomes are and were. The obvious source for such statistics is the Internal Revenue Service (IRS). But IRS statistics tell us not what people earned but what they reported. Over the past 70 years, the rate at which income is taxed has increased enormously. The higher the tax rate, the higher the incentive for people with high incomes to make them appear lower than they are, at least when the IRS is looking. So IRS figures almost certainly underestimate how well the rich are doing in recent decades as compared to the earlier part of the century. The recent tax reform act substantially lowered the tax rate on the highest brackets; it will be interesting to see if one result is an increase in the number of people who confess to having high incomes, and thus in (measured) income inequality.

The conclusion from all of this is that statements about the income distribution, about how it has changed over time, and about how it is changed by particular government programs, should be viewed with considerable skepticism.

What Determines the Income Distribution?

You are a worker. What determines your salary? One answer is "the most you are worth to any employer." Another is "the least you are willing to work for." Both are true—for exactly the same reason that the price of a good is equal both to its value to the consumer and to its cost of production.

To Each According to His Product. Consider the president of a pants company, trying to decide how many workers to hire. Holding all other inputs constant, he calculates how many extra pairs of pants the firm produces for each extra worker hired; the answer is five pairs per day. Five pairs of pants per day is the marginal physical product of a worker, as explained in Chapter 9.

Suppose a pair of pants sells for $10. The marginal revenue product of a worker is then $50/day. If an employer hires one more worker, output rises by five pairs of pants per day, the firm sells them for $10/pair, so revenue increases by $50/day. Since marginal product is defined with all other inputs held constant, cost rises by what the firm has to pay the extra worker. As long as the cost of hiring another worker is less than $50/day, the firm increases its profit by hiring him. As it hires more workers, their marginal product drops, because of the law of diminishing returns. The firm stops hiring when marginal revenue product equals the wage it must pay to get more workers. So a worker's wage equals what he produces—the value of the extra production from adding one more worker while keeping all other inputs fixed. If we consider a range of different wages, this implies, as we saw back in Chapter 9, that the firm's demand curve for an input is simply that input's marginal revenue product curve.

The logic of the situation is the same that gave us demand curves from marginal value curves and supply curves from marginal cost curves. It applies not only to workers but to all inputs—as was pointed out in Chapter 9. As long as the producer can buy as much of an input as he likes at some price—as long, in other words, as he is a price taker on the market for his inputs—he will buy it up to the point where its marginal revenue product equals its price. Hence the prices received by the owners of all inputs to production—the wages of labor, the rent of land, the interest on capital—are equal to the marginal revenue products of those inputs. Since income ultimately comes from selling inputs, this appears to be an explanation of the income distribution.

To Each According to His Cost.   That each factor receives its marginal revenue product is a true statement about the income distribution (provided we are only considering price takers—there are additional complications for price searchers), but it is not an explanation of the income distribution. One way of seeing that is to note that it is also true that each factor gets its marginal cost of production. A worker who can choose how many hours he wants to work will work up to the point where his wage equals the marginal value of his leisure—the cost, to him, of working an additional hour. Hence his wage is equal to what it costs him to work. Just as we saw back in Chapter 5, the worker's supply curve for his own labor equals his marginal disvalue of labor (value of leisure) curve. Similarly, individuals will save (producing capital) up to the point at which the cost of giving up a little more present consumption in exchange for future consumption just balances what they gain by doing so—the interest rate. So the interest on capital is equal to the marginal cost of producing it.

One Explanation Too Many?   We appear to have two explanations of the distribution of income—which some might consider one explanation too many. But neither is complete by itself. Labor receives its marginal product—but the marginal product of labor is determined in part by how much labor (and capital and land and . . .) is being used; the law of diminishing returns tells us that as we increase the amount of one input while holding the others constant, the marginal product of that input eventually starts to go down. Labor is paid its marginal cost of production—but that cost depends in part on how much labor is being sold; the law of declining marginal utility, applied to leisure, implies that the cost of working one more hour depends in part on how many hours you are working.

What we actually have is a description of equilibrium on the market for inputs—the same description we got some chapters earlier when we were considering the market for final goods. The full explanation of the income distribution is that the price of an input is equal to both its marginal cost of production and its marginal revenue product, and the quantity of the input sold and used is that quantity for which the marginal cost of production and the marginal revenue product are equal. (Marginal) cost equals price equals (marginal) value.

This conclusion is useful for seeing how various changes affect the distribution of income. Suppose the number of carpenters suddenly increases, due to the immigration of thousands of new carpenters from Mexico. Both before and after the change, carpenters receive their marginal revenue product. Both before and after, they receive a wage equal to the marginal value of the last hour of leisure they give up.

But the wage after the migration is lower than the wage before. Since the supply of carpenters is higher than before, the equilibrium wage is lower. At that lower wage more carpenters are hired and their marginal product is therefore lower. With lower wages, the existing carpenters work fewer hours (assuming a normally shaped supply curve for their labor) and, when they are working fewer hours, have more leisure and value the marginal hour of leisure less. Some carpenters—those with particularly good alternative occupations—find that, at the lower wage, they are better off doing something else. The marginal cost to the worker of working an additional hour falls, either because the marginal hour is worked by one of the old carpenters who is now working fewer hours or because the marginal carpenter is now one of the new immigrants.

The change is shown on Figure 14-2. D is the demand curve for the services of carpenters ("carpentry") in the United States. S_{US} is the supply curve for the services of U.S. carpenters before the new immigrants arrive; its intersection with D gives us the equilibrium price (P_{old}) and quantity (Q_{US}^{old}) for carpentry before the immigration. $S_{Immigrant}$ is the supply curve of the new immigrants. S_{Total} is the total supply curve— the horizontal sum of S_{US} and $S_{Immigrant}$. Its intersection with D gives us

Figure 14-2

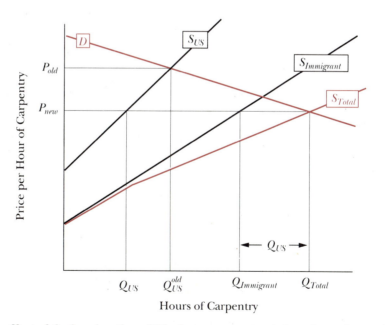

The effect of the immigration of Mexican carpenters on the price and quantity of carpentry in the United States. S_{Total} is the supply curve for the services of U.S. carpenters plus immigrants. Immigration reduces the equilibrium price to P_{new} and increases the equilibrium quantity to Q_{Total}. The quantity supplied of carpentry services by the U.S. carpenters falls to Q_{US}.

the equilibrium price (P_{new}) and quantity (Q_{Total}) for carpentry after the immigration.

Looking at the figure, we observe that the wages of carpenters (the price of carpentry) have fallen. Some of the old carpenters have left the profession, some (Q_{US}) remain. Back in Chapter 5 we saw that the supply curve for labor is equal to the horizontal sum of the marginal cost curves of the laborers. So the marginal carpenter before the change valued his time at P_{old} and the marginal carpenter after the change valued it at $P_{new} < P_{old}$. In the case shown, $Q_{US} > 0$; some U.S. carpenters remain in business, so marginal carpenters include both immigrants and U.S. carpenters willing to do some carpentry even at the lower wage.

In the short run, the additional carpenters are combined with the same quantity of other inputs—wood, hammers, saws—with the result that each additional carpenter produces considerably less than before. Over time, other inputs adjust. But in the new equilibrium, carpenters are cheaper than before, so it pays to use more of them relative to other inputs—and when more of them are used, their marginal revenue product is lower. Wages drop less in the long run than in the short run, but they are still lower than before the immigration.

Immigration is not the only thing that can affect the wage rate. Increases in the other factors of production will tend to increase the marginal product of labor, and hence its wage; decreases will have the opposite effect. Changes in technology can also alter the marginal product of labor or other inputs. If someone invents a computer program that does a better job than a human of teaching children basic skills, perhaps by converting reading, writing, and arithmetic lessons into exciting video games, a substantial amount of human labor will have been replaced by capital. The demand for labor has decreased, the demand for capital has increased, so when equilibrium is reestablished wages will be a little lower than before the change and the return on capital, the interest rate, a little higher.

Is It Just?

Once we know who owns inputs and how much each of the inputs gets, we also know the distribution of income. If I own 100 acres of land and land rents for $50/acre, I receive an income of $5,000/year from my land. If I also sell 2,000 hours per year of my own labor at $20/hour, I receive an income of $40,000/year from my labor. If these are the only inputs to production that I own, my total income is $45,000/year. We can in the same way calculate everyone else's income, giving us the distribution of income for the whole society.

One question often asked is, "Is this distribution just?" Supporters of the market system sometimes defend it by arguing that everyone gets what he produces, which seems fair. The wages of the laborer are equal to the market value of the additional output resulting from his labor, the interest received by the capitalist is equal to the value of the additional output resulting from the capital he has saved and invested, and so on. If the initial distribution of the ownership of inputs is just and if the principle "you are entitled to what you produce" is a legitimate one, it seems that the final distribution of income has been justified.

Even if you argue, as many would, that some inputs belong to the wrong people—for instance, that much of the land in the United States was unjustly stolen from the American Indians and should be given back—the argument still seems to justify a large part of the existing division of income. In a modern economy such as that of the United States at present, most income goes to human inputs—labor and the human capital embodied in learned skills—and most people would agree that a worker legitimately owns himself.

Another way in which one might try to justify the present distribution of income is by appealing to the second half of the market equality—price equals cost of production. If the principle "to each according to what he has sacrificed in order to produce" is appealing to you, you can argue that the capitalist deserves the interest he receives because it represents the cost to him of postponing his consumption—giving up consumption now in exchange for more consumption later—and that the worker deserves his salary because it just makes up to him for the leisure he had to give up in order to work.

If you are completely satisfied by either of these arguments, you have probably not entirely understood them. The product and the cost that equal price are marginal product and marginal cost. The worker's salary just compensates him for the last hour he works—but he gets the same salary for all the hours he works. The interest collected by the capitalist equals the value of the additional production made possible by the addition of his capital—but the marginal revenue product of capital depends, in part, on how much labor, land, and other inputs are being used. Pure capital, all by itself, cannot produce much.

We are left with the problem of how to define a fair division of goods when the goods are produced not by any single person but by the combined efforts of many. While "payment according to marginal product" is a possible rule for division, and one that describes a large part of what actually happens in a market economy, it is far from clear whether it is a fair rule, or even what fairness means in such a context. Fortunately, determining what is fair is one of the (few?) problems that is not part of economics.

What Hurts Whom?

So far, we have used our analysis of the distribution of income to try to determine whether it is just. The same analysis can also be used to help us answer a question of considerable interest to many of us: How do I find out whether some particular economic change helps or hurts me? The answer, put simply, is that an increase in the supply of an input I own drives down its price (and marginal revenue product) and so decreases my income. The same is true for an increase in the supply of an input that is a close substitute for an input I own. If I happen to own an oil well, I will regard someone else's discovery of a new field of natural gas—or a process for producing power by thermonuclear fusion—as bad news.

An increase in the supply of an input used with the input I own (a **complement in production**) has the opposite effect. As the relative amount of my input used in production declines, its marginal product increases (the principle of diminishing returns, applied in reverse). If I own an oil well, I will be in favor of the construction of new highways.

Economic changes can affect what I buy as well as what I sell. Increases in the supply of goods I buy, or of inputs used to produce goods I buy, lower the price of those goods and so tend to benefit me. Decreases in their supply tend to make me worse off, for the same reason.

This may help answer the practical question of what things I ought to be for or against in some cases, but not in very many. It is clear enough that if I am a (selfish) physician, I should be in favor of restrictive licensing laws that keep down the number of physicians, and that if I am a (selfish) patient, I should be against them. It is much less clear how I should view the effect on my welfare of government deficits, restrictions on immigration, laws controlling the use of land, or any of a myriad of other things that do not directly affect the supply of the particular inputs I happen to own.

And for Our Next Act

You may by now have realized that economics involves a continual balancing act between unrealistic simplification and unworkable complication. Chapter 8 was a prime example of the latter; the attempt to fully describe even a simple economy involves a system of equations whose solution is well beyond the capacity of any existing computer.

In Part 2, I will swing us back in the other direction by showing how even a relatively complicated economy, such as the one we live in, can be viewed for some purposes as having only three inputs to production. This approach makes it possible to say something about how a particular person is affected by changes in the supply, demand, and price of goods that he neither buys nor sells.

PART 2—THE FACTORS OF PRODUCTION

Consider apples. For most purposes, we talk about the "supply of apples," the "price of apples," and so on. But, strictly speaking, a Golden Delicious apple, a Jonathan apple, and a Granny Smith apple are three different things. Even more strictly speaking, two Jonathan apples are different things; one is a little prettier, a little sweeter, or whatever. Even if we considered two identical apples, they would still be in different places, and the location of a good is one of its important characteristics; oil companies spend large sums converting crude petroleum two miles down into (identical) crude petroleum in a tank above ground.

For some purposes, it is convenient to make very fine distinctions, for others it is not; one cost of fine distinctions is that they make analysis more complicated. It is more precise to treat Golden Delicious apples and Red Delicious apples as two different goods that happen to be close substitutes; it is simpler to treat them as the same good.

Treating goods as close substitutes has almost the same effect as treating them as the same good. If they are the same good, an increase in the price of one implies an exactly equal increase in the price of the other, since they must sell for the same price. If they are substitutes, an increase in the price of one leads to an increase in the demand for the other, and hence an increase in its price. If they are sufficiently close substitutes—and if one unit of one good substitutes for one unit of the other—then an increase in the price of one produces an almost equal increase in the price of the other. To say that two things are both units of the same good is equivalent to saying that they are perfect substitutes for each other, as one piece of paper is a perfect substitute for another even though the two pieces are not literally identical—they would look slightly different under a microscope.

One could make a simple picture complicated by viewing each apple as a different good. I am instead going to make a complicated picture simple by viewing many different things as one good. This is how it works.

How to Simplify the Problem

Consider three kinds of land—type *A*, type *B*, and type *C*. Suppose type *A* land is especially good for growing wheat, type *C* for growing soybeans, and type *B* good for both; for simplicity let an acre of *A* or *B* be equally good at producing wheat, and an acre of *B* or *C* equally good at producing soybeans. Further suppose supply and demand conditions are such that all the type *A* land is used for wheat, all the type *C* for soybeans, and some type *B* for each.

Under these circumstances, the prices of all three grades of land must be the same. The price of an acre of type *A* land is the present value of the net revenue (revenue minus production costs) of producing wheat on it; so is the price of an acre of type *B* land being used to produce wheat. Since types *A* and *B* land are equally good at producing wheat, the two prices must be the same. The price of an acre of type *C* land is the present value of the net revenue from producing soybeans on it—so is the price of an acre of type *B* land that is used for producing soybeans.

But all type *B* land must have the same price, whatever it is used for. If it did not, if, for instance, land used to produce soybeans was worth more than identical land used to produce wheat, then land would shift out of wheat production and into soybean production, driving the price of soybeans down and the price of wheat up. This process would continue until either the land was equally valuable in both uses or all of the type B land was used for soybeans.

Suppose a flood wipes out 100 acres of type A land. The initial effect is to raise the market price of wheat and of land growing wheat. Some type B land is now shifted from soybeans to the (more profitable) wheat. The quantity of wheat supplied increases, driving the price of wheat part of the way back down toward what it was before the flood. The quantity of soybeans supplied decreases, since some land that had been producing soybeans is now producing wheat; the price of soybeans rises. When equilibrium is reestablished, the prices of all three kinds of land are again the same. If they were not, more B land would shift from one crop to the other until they were. The final effect on the prices of wheat, soybeans, and land is the same as if the flood had wiped out 100 acres of type C land or of type B land.

Figures 14-3a, 14-3b, and 14-3c show the argument in graphical form; they illustrate the market for land used to grow wheat and soybeans. D_{Wheat} and D_{Soy} are the demand curves not for wheat and soybeans but for land used to grow them. The quantity of land used for wheat (Q_W) is measured from the left axis, the quantity used for soybeans (Q_S) from the right axis. Wheat land consists of all of the type A land (Q_A) plus part of the type B land; soybean land consists of the rest of the type B land plus all of the type C land (Q_C). The type B land is divided between wheat and soybeans in such a way as to make its price the same in either use.

Figure 14-3a shows the initial situation; the price of land in either use is P_0. Figure 14-3b shows the situation after a flood has eliminated 100 acres of type A land, reducing its total quantity to $Q_A' = Q_A - 100$. Figure 14-3c shows what happens if the flood hits the type B land instead; quantity of type A land is back to Q_A, but quantity of type B land is now $Q_B' = Q_B - 100$. You should be able to satisfy yourself that the price of land, P_1, is and must be the same on Figures 14-3b and c (and greater than the original price P_0), and the same for both uses of the land.

Figure 14-3d shows a situation where the prices of land used for wheat and land used for soybeans are no longer the same. The demand curves have shifted. There is no longer any way of dividing the type B land between the two uses that will make the price equal in both; even with all of it used to grow wheat, the price of wheat land (P_W) is still higher than the price of soybean land (P_S). No more land shifts from soybeans to wheat because the only land still being used to grow soybeans is type C land, which is badly suited for growing wheat.

As long as we only consider changes in supply and demand (of land, wheat, and soybeans) that leave some type B land growing soybeans and some growing wheat, as on 14-3a, b, c but not d, the situation is the same as if all the land were identical! We cannot directly replace type A land with type C land (or vice versa), but we can do so indirectly by replacing type A land with some type B land (converting it from soybeans to wheat)

Figure 14-3

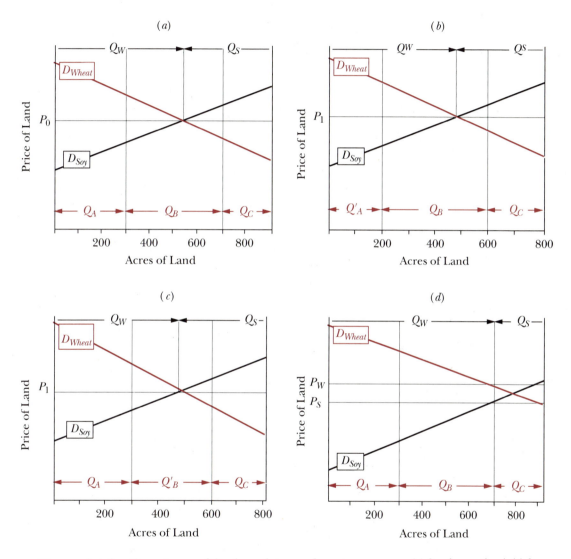

The market for three types of land used to produce two crops. 14-3*a* shows the initial situation. Type *A* land is well suited for growing wheat; type *C* for growing soybeans; type *B* for both. As long as we only consider situations in which some type *B* land is used for each crop, the price of land is the same in both uses and is determined only by the total quantity of land (14-3*a,b,c*).

and replacing the type *B* land with type *C* land. The price of all three kinds of land is the same, and all we need to know is the total supply of land. In analyzing this particular economy, we can reduce three different inputs—types *A*, *B*, and *C* land—into one.

This somewhat oversimplifies the situation that really exists with regard to land. There is a wide range of types of land (and crops); some land is very well suited for one crop and very badly for many others, while some land can grow any of several crops. The qualitative result, however, still holds. For many purposes, we can think of land as a single good with a single price and quantity—not because all land is the same, or even because any piece of land is a good substitute for any other piece (it is not), but because there are always some pieces of land that are "on the margin" between being used for one purpose or another.

When the supply of land suited for one crop—say, corn—decreases, the price of that crop goes up. Land that, at the old price of corn, was used to grow some other crop that brought in a slightly higher income now generates more income by producing corn, so such land shifts out of other crops and into corn. By doing so, it transmits the decreased supply (and increased price) to the land used for what such *marginal* land was previously producing. A decrease in the supply of any one kind of land ultimately raises the price of all land, as does an increase in the demand for any one kind of land.

Land is not the only "good" that can be treated in this way. There are three traditional **factors of production**—land, labor, and capital. Each is really a group of goods that substitute for each other sufficiently well to be treated, for many purposes, as a single good. In each case, what is essential is not that every unit can directly substitute for every other unit, but that there are always some marginal units that can shift from one use to another so as to transmit changes affecting one good in the group to all the others.

Most of the inputs to production can be classified as either land, labor, or capital, although not always in the way a noneconomist might expect—a surgeon, for example, is largely capital! So this approach allows us to view even a very complicated economy as if it had only three inputs to production. For analyzing short-run changes, the approach is not very useful—an increased demand for economists is unlikely to have much immediate effect on either the wages of ditchdiggers or the interest on bonds, although economists are a mixture of labor and capital, the wages of ditchdiggers are a measure of the price of labor, and the interest on bonds is a measure of the price of capital.

In the longer run, it is easier to transform one form of labor or capital into another. If the demand for economists increases, then more people will become economists—instead of ditchdiggers or political scientists or secretaries. Training additional economists will require that people—the economics students themselves, their parents, investors lending them money for their education, or the government—spend money now for a return in the future. So less money will be available to be spent now for a future return in other ways—to build factories, do research, or train people in other professions. Labor and capital are being shifted into producing economics and out of producing ditches, cars, and many other things.

In the short run, the economy is less flexible than in the long run, as has been pointed out before. In the short run, the only people who can do economics are economists; the only ways to produce more economics are by getting some economists presently producing economics to produce more of it, or by getting economists who are presently doing other things—writing textbooks, for example, or loafing on the French Riviera—to go back to doing economics. In the long run, the factors of production can be used to produce more economists, hence more economics—and similarly with anything else. So the factors of production are more useful for understanding what happens in the long term than for understanding what happens in the short term.

In the next few sections of the book, I will discuss the three traditional factors of production—labor, land, and capital—so that you can see what they are and how they differ from each other.

Labor

Workers combine in themselves two different factors of production—**raw labor** and **human capital**. To produce a steelworker, one requires both a person and training; the latter, like any other investment, involves consuming inputs now in exchange for future returns, so it is properly classified as a form of capital. The wages of a worker can then be divided into the return on raw labor and the return on the laborer's human capital.

People are not all identical; even before training, a 6-foot man can probably dig more ditches per day than a 5-foot woman. To some extent, one can deal with this by thinking of different people as containing different amounts of raw labor. The situation would be simple if the person who could dig twice as many ditches could also type twice as many pages and treat twice as many patients; you could then say that one person contained two units of labor and the other contained one. In the real world, it is more complicated.

One way of transforming one type of labor (secretaries) into another (ditchdiggers) is by having those few secretaries who are either 6-foot males or very strong females switch jobs—or, if we consider long-term changes, having more of the people physically capable of being ditchdiggers become ditchdiggers and fewer of them become secretaries. That will not produce many ditchdiggers. A more indirect way is to convert secretaries into truck drivers and (other) truck drivers into ditchdiggers. Truck driving, despite its macho image, is a job that does not require a great deal of physical strength; it can be and often is done by women.

Suppose you are a potential secretary (currently doing something else) who is just as productive as the marginal secretary—the one who would become a truck driver if the wages of truck drivers went up a little (or the wages of secretaries went down a little). Suppose the marginal truck driver—the one who would become a ditchdigger if the wages of ditchdiggers went up a little—can dig twice as many ditches per day as the average ditchdigger. Two ditchdiggers retire. The wages of ditchdiggers rise slightly. The marginal truck driver becomes a ditchdigger, the marginal secretary becomes a truck driver, and you become a secretary. You have substituted for two ditchdiggers. You contain twice as much labor as the average ditchdigger—even if you cannot lift a shovel.

In the short run, the total supply of labor is fixed; neglecting differences among workers, it is equal to the population times 24 hours per day. But in the long run, the population can change. The originators of modern economics—Adam Smith at the end of the eighteenth century, Thomas Malthus and David Ricardo at the beginning of the nineteenth—made this fact a central part of their analysis. They believed that the higher the wages of labor were, the more willing the mass of the population would be to have children—and the higher the growth rate of the population.

If everyone were poor, the cost of having a child would be giving up things that potential parents valued highly—such as food or clothing for themselves. So most people would marry late and, once married, try to avoid having children. The result would be a low birthrate, a decline in the quantity of labor relative to the other two factors of production, and an increase in wages.

If, on the other hand, wages were high, people would be more willing to have children. The result would be an increase in population and a decline of wages. Hence, the classical economists argued, there was an **equilibrium wage**—the wage at which the population just maintained itself. Wages above that increased the population, pushing the wage rate back down; wages below that decreased the population, pushing the wage rate back up.

Reaching the equilibrium might take a while. An economy in which the stock of capital was growing could maintain wages for an extended period of time above their equilibrium level, with population and capital growing together. But the limited supply of land, combined with the principle of diminishing returns, would eventually bring growth to a standstill and wages back to their long-run equilibrium level. This was called the **iron law of wages**. One conclusion Ricardo drew from this was that it would be a good thing if the poor acquired expensive tastes. They would then require a higher standard of living before they would be willing to bear the cost of having children, so the equilibrium wage would be higher.

Modern economics has tended to abandon such discussions and limit itself to considering an economy with a given population. One reason may be that wages have risen enormously, and fairly continuously, from Ricardo's day to ours, suggesting that there is no long-term equilibrium wage. Very recently, with rising concern about overpopulation and limited resources, there has been some revival of interest in economic theories that include changes in population as one of the variables included in the analysis.

Land

I started my discussion of the factors of production by showing how different types of land could be treated as if they were all the same good. For simplicity I set my assumptions up so that an acre of each kind of land was equivalent to an acre of each other kind. I could as easily have assumed that one acre of type A land produced the same return as two acres of type B land used for growing wheat, and that one acre of type B land used for growing soybeans produced as much as two acres of type C land. In that case, the price of an acre of A land would have been twice the price of an acre of B land and four times the price of an acre of C land. We would then think of A land as containing four units of land per acre, B as containing two, and C as containing one. We could then analyze land as if it were all the same—with the total quantity of land equal to the amount of type C land plus twice the amount of type B land plus four times the amount of type A land. This is much like the situation discussed earlier with regard to labor; types A, B, and C land correspond to secretaries, truck drivers, and ditchdiggers, respectively, in the earlier example.

There are a certain number of square miles on the surface of the earth; the number has not changed significantly in the past 100,000 years, and, short of some massive redesign of the planet, it will not change significantly in the next 100,000. So if we consider only **raw land** and classify investments that increase its productivity (fertilizing, draining, clearing) as capital, the supply of land, unlike the supply of most other things we have discussed, is almost perfectly inelastic.

If the supply of land is perfectly inelastic, the supply curve for land is vertical, which implies that a tax on land, whether "paid" by owner or renter, is entirely borne by the owner, with none of it passed on to the renter. It also implies that a tax on land generates no excess burden—as you showed (I hope) in your answer to Problems 8 and 9 of Chapter 7. Both results are shown on Figure 14-4, where the tax is paid by the consumers. I drew it that way because a tax paid by the producer shifts the vertical supply curve vertically, which is difficult to show; the shifted curve would be identical to the unshifted one.

These facts have sometimes been used to argue that land is the ideal thing to tax—there is no excess burden, and all of the tax is borne by the landowners. One difficulty with this proposal is that in order to tax something, you must measure it. Raw land may be in perfectly inelastic

Figure 14-4

The effect of a tax on land. Since the supply curve is perfectly inelastic, quantity and consumer surplus are unaffected by the tax. The loss of producer surplus is equal to the tax revenue collected.

supply, but the land we actually use—to live on, grow our food on, build our roads on—is not. It is a combination of raw land and other resources—labor used to clear the land, capital invested in improving it, and so on. One measure of the difference between land in use and raw land is the fact that only about one tenth of the land area of the earth is under cultivation—and the amount used for houses, roads, and the like is even less.

If you tax the market value of land, you discourage people from increasing the value of raw land by using capital and labor to improve it; the supply curve for improved land is by no means perfectly inelastic. So in order to impose the so-called single tax (a tax on the value of unimproved land, proposed as a substitute for all other taxes), you first have to find some way of estimating what the land would have been worth without any improvements—which is difficult.

Rent and Quasi-Rent

Because land is the standard example of a good in perfectly inelastic supply and because payment for the use of land is called rent, the term **rent** has come to be used in economics in two different ways. One is to mean payment for the use of something, as distinguished from payment for ownership (price). In this sense, one buys cars from GM but rents them from Avis. The other is to mean payment for the use of something in fixed (i.e., perfectly inelastic) supply—or, more generally, to mean payments above what is needed to call something into existence.

In this second sense, rent can be applied to many things other than land. Scarce human talents—the abilities of an inventive genius or the combination of good coordination and very long legs—can be thought of as valuable resources in fixed supply and without close substitutes; the wages of Thomas Edison or Wilt Chamberlain may be analyzed as a sort of rent. Rent in this sense is a price that allocates the use of something among consumers but does not tell producers how much to produce, since the good is not being produced. The opposite case is payment for something with a horizontal supply curve—in that case, payment is simply equal to cost of production.

Just as one can argue for taxing away the rent on the site value of land, on the grounds that since land is in perfectly inelastic supply the tax will result in no excess burden, so one can argue for taxing away the rent on scarce human talents. Here again, problems arise when you try to identify what you want to tax. It is not clear how the IRS can tell which athletes and which inventors will continue to exercise their abilities even if they are paid no more than the normal market wage, and which will decide to do something else.

The shape of a supply curve depends on how much time producers have to adjust their output. In the very short run, practically everything is in fixed supply. In the longer run, many things are; and in the very long run, practically nothing is. One may even argue that if certain talents produce high incomes, the possessors of those talents will be rich and have lots of children, thus increasing the supply of those talents, or that a sufficiently high rent on land will encourage the exploration and development of other planets, thus increasing the quantity of land. So the economic analysis developed to explain the rent on land may be inapplicable to anything—even land—in the (very) long run. But it can be used to explain the behavior of many prices in the (sufficiently) short run—which may be a day for fresh fish and 30 years for houses.

In the previous chapter, I discussed goods whose cost of construction was a sunk cost, such as ships or factories. As long as the price shipowners get for carrying freight is high enough that their ships are worth something and not high enough to make it worth building more ships, the supply of ships is perfectly inelastic. The number of ships does not change with price, although it does gradually shrink as ships wear out. The same is true for prices at which it is worth building more ships—if we limit ourselves to times too short to build them. So the returns on ships can be thought of as a sort of rent—called a quasi-rent—provided we limit ourselves to a sufficiently short-term analysis. That is just what we did in Chapter 13.

Capital

The third factor of production is capital. The meanings of labor and of land (more generally, unproduced natural resources) seem fairly obvious; the meaning of capital is not. Does producing capital mean saving? Building factories? Investing your savings? What is capital—what does it look like?

One (good) answer is that using capital means using inputs now to produce outputs later. The more dollar-years required (number of dollars of inputs times number of years until the outputs appear—a slight oversimplification, since it ignores the effect of compound interest, but good enough for our purposes), the more the amount of capital used. Capital is productive because it is (often) possible to produce more output if you are willing to wait than if you are not—to spend a week chipping out a flint axe and then use the axe to cut down lots of trees instead of spending two days scraping through a tree with a chunk of unshaped flint, or to make machines to make machines to make machines to make cars instead of simply making cars. Capital is expensive because people usually prefer consumption now to consumption in the future and must be paid to give up the former in exchange for the latter. **Capital goods** are the physical objects (factories, machines, apple trees) produced by inputs now and used to produce outputs in the future.

The essential logic of the market for capital was described in Chapter 12, where we discussed the individual's decision of how much to borrow or save and the firm's decision of what investment projects were worth making. The higher the market interest rate, the more willing consumers are to give up consumption now in exchange for consumption in the future, since a higher interest rate means more future goods in exchange for a given quantity of present goods; so we expect the net supply of capital by consumers to increase with the interest rate—the supply curve slopes up. The higher the market interest rate, the lower the present value of a future stream of income, and thus the harder it is for an investment project to justify, in present value terms, its initial cost. So a higher interest rate means fewer investment projects that are worth making, and thus less money borrowed by firms—the demand curve slopes down. At some interest rate the two curves cross—the quantity consumers want to lend equals the quantity firms want to borrow. That is the market interest rate.

Describing capital as a single good is both less and more legitimate than is a similar simplification for land or labor. It is less legitimate because once capital goods are built, they are not very flexible; there is no way an automobile factory can produce steel or a milling machine grow grain. In the case of labor and land, we argued that one variety could substitute for another through a chain of intermediates—from secretary to ditchdigger in the one case, from wheat to soybeans in the other. Finding a chain to connect a steel mill to a drainage canal, or an invention (capital in the form of valuable knowledge produced by research) to a tractor, would be more difficult.

But treating all capital as one good is more legitimate than treating all labor or all land as one, if we consider capital before it is invested. A steel mill cannot be converted into a drainage canal—but an investor can decide whether he will use his savings to pay workers to build the one or the other. So the anticipated return on all investments—the interest rate—must be the same. If investors expected to make more by investing a dollar in building a steel mill than by investing a dollar in digging a drainage canal, capital would shift into steel; the increased supply of steel would drive down the price of steel and the return on investments in steel mills. The reduced supply of capital in canal building would, similarly, increase the return on investments in canals. Investors would continue to shift their capital out of the one use and into the other until the returns on the two were the same.

A reduction in the supply of steel mills—the destruction of 100 mills by a war or an earthquake, say—will drive up the price of steel, increase the return on investments in steel mills, attract capital that would otherwise have gone elsewhere into the steel industry, and so drive up the general interest rate. Thus in the long run, there is a single quantity of capital and a single price for the use of capital—the interest rate. All capital is the same—before it is invested.

After it is invested, capital takes many forms. One of the most important is one that noneconomists rarely think of as capital—human capital. A medical student who invests $90,000 and six years in becoming a surgeon is bearing costs now in return for benefits in the future, just as he would be if he had invested his time and money in building a factory instead. If the salary of surgeons were not high enough to make investing in himself at least as attractive as investing in something else, he would have invested in physical capital instead. So the salary of a surgeon should be considered in part the wages of labor, in part the rent on certain scarce human talents, and in part interest on his human capital.

There is one important respect in which human capital differs from other forms of capital. If you have an idea for building a profitable factory but not enough money of your own to pay for it, you can raise more money either by letting other investors be part-owners of the factory or by borrowing, putting up the factory itself as your security. Your ability to invest in your own human capital is much more limited. You cannot sell shares of yourself because that would violate the laws against slavery—you cannot put yourself up as collateral for the same reason. You can borrow money to pay for your training—but after the money is spent, you may, if you wish, declare bankruptcy. Your creditors have no way of repossessing the training that you bought with their money.

In a market economy, investments in physical capital that can be expected to yield more than the normal market return will always be made. The same is not true for investments in human capital. They will be made only if the human in question (or his parents or someone else who values his future welfare or trusts him to pay back loans) can provide the necessary capital. In that respect, the market for human capital is an imperfect one.

The source of the imperfection was discussed in Chapter 12—insecure property rights. In Chapter 12, the property rights of owners of oil were insecure because of the possibility of expropriation—one consequence was to discourage investment in finding oil and drilling oil wells. Here the property rights of lenders are insecure because of the possibility of bankruptcy; the result is to discourage investment in (someone else's) human capital. The existence of this imperfection provides, on the one hand, an argument for government provision (or guarantees) of loans for education, and on the other hand, an argument for relaxing the prohibition against (self-chosen) slavery—to the extent of limiting the ability of people who borrow for their education to declare bankruptcy.

The Factors—Similarities and Differences

We have now looked at all three of the factors of production—labor, land, and capital. How are they similar? How are they different?

One respect in which factors differ is in the degree to which each is property. Land and physical capital are entirely property; they may be bought, sold, transferred, lent. Labor and human capital are property of a very limited sort, at least in our society. They may be rented out, but the contract can almost always be canceled at the will of the owner— the worker can always quit. Neither labor nor human capital can be sold, and neither can be used as collateral, since there is no way the lender can collect.

A second difference is in supply. Land is in absolutely fixed supply. Labor is also in fixed supply, if we include an individual's demand for his own labor (i.e., leisure) as part of demand rather than as something affecting supply. The quantity of labor changes over time because of changes in population; but since the producers of new labor (parents) do not own it and cannot sell it, it is not clear whether or not an increase in the price of labor will increase the supply, even in the long run. The quantity of capital changes as a result of saving; individuals who consume less than their income have the remainder available to invest. The higher the interest rate, the more you get next year in exchange for what you save this year, so we would expect the supply of new capital to increase with the interest rate—though for capital, as for labor, a backward-bending supply curve is not logically impossible.

We have now finished our sketch of the three factors of production. In ending, it is worth noting that there are some inputs to the productive process that do not fit comfortably into our categories. Two examples would be unproduced raw materials—iron ore, for instance—and special human abilities. Both *behave like* land, in the sense of being in fixed supply. But neither *is* land, since neither is a close substitute for the other things that are contained in the collection of related goods called land.

PART 3—APPLICATIONS

In Part 1 of this chapter, I showed how the distribution of income was determined and discussed how I might decide whether or not some particular change was in my interest by how it affected my share in the distribution. The conclusion was that I can expect to benefit by any change that raises the price of the productive inputs I sell or lowers the price of the goods I buy; I can expect to lose from any change that lowers the price of the inputs I sell or raises the price of the goods I buy.

The problem, as I pointed out at the time, is that many potential changes whose effects I might want to know cannot be evaluated in this way. They have no direct effect on the particular inputs I own and sell or the particular goods I consume, and the net consequence of their numerous indirect effects is hard to judge. The factors of production were introduced as a solution to this problem; when all inputs have been simplified down to three, it may be possible to judge both how some change affects each of the three factors and how a change in the prices of the factors affects my welfare.

That is what we will be doing in Part 3. We will consider three different public policy issues—immigration restrictions, limitations on foreign investment in poor countries, and governmental controls on land use. In each case, the question we are primarily interested in is not whether the policy is good or bad but who gains and who loses. In each case, we will try to answer that question by looking at the effect of the policy on the factors of production.

Immigration

We can combine Parts 1 and 2 of this chapter in order to analyze a number of interesting questions; we will start with the effect of increased immigration on the welfare of the present inhabitants of the United States. Prior to the 1920s, the United States followed a general policy of open immigration, except for some restrictions on immigration of Orientals. The result was a flood of immigrants that at its peak exceeded a million a year. Suppose we went back to open immigration. Who would benefit and who would lose?

Immigrants have, on average, less human and physical capital than the present inhabitants of the United States; they are less skilled and poorer. So one result of increased immigration would be an increase in the ratio of labor to capital in the United States. Immigrants bring labor and some capital but no land, so another result would be to decrease the ratio of land to both labor and capital. Hence, increased immigration would decrease the price of labor and increase the price of land; the effect on the price of capital is ambiguous, since it becomes scarcer relative to labor and less scarce relative to land. My guess is that since the additional immigrants who would come in under a policy of unrestricted immigration would bring very little capital with them—rich immigrants can come in under present laws—the return on capital would increase.

The net result would probably be to injure the most unskilled American workers. It might well benefit many or even most other workers, since what they are selling is not pure labor but a mixture containing a large amount of human capital. People who were net buyers of land would be injured by the increased price of land; people who were net sellers of land would be benefited. Net lenders would be benefited if the return on capital (the interest rate) increased; net borrowers would be injured.

Can we say anything about the overall effect on those presently living in the United States? Yes—but to do so, we must bring in arguments from a previous chapter. One way of looking at immigration restrictions is as barriers to trade; they prevent an American consumer from buying the labor of a Mexican worker by preventing the worker from coming to where the labor is wanted. The same comparative advantage arguments that were discussed in Chapter 6 and will be discussed again in Chapter 19 apply here as well. Since there is a net gain to trade, the abolition of immigration restrictions will produce a net benefit for present Americans, although some will be worse off—just as the abolition of tariffs produces a net benefit, although American auto workers (and GM stockholders) may be injured. These net benefits are in addition to the (very large) benefits to the new immigrants that are the reason they come.

Figure 14-5 shows the net effect of the immigration of Mexican carpenters discussed earlier; it corresponds to Figure 14-2 with the consumer and producer surpluses shown. Note that the darkly shaded area, representing the loss of producer surplus to existing carpenters, is included in, and therefore smaller than, the total shaded area (light and dark) representing the gain of consumer surplus to their customers. This implies that on net there is an increase in surplus even if we ignore the colored area, which represents the gain to the new immigrants.

A more precise discussion of what we mean by net benefits would carry us into the next chapter—which is about just such questions. A more rigorous explanation of why open immigration produces net benefits would carry us beyond the limits of this course. There are, however, two more points worth making before we finish with the question of immigration.

So far in my discussion of immigration, I have assumed a private property society in which the only way to get income is to sell labor or other inputs. In fact there are at least two other ways—from government (in the form of welfare, unemployment payments, and the like) and by private violation of property rights (theft and robbery). To the extent that new immigrants support themselves in those ways, they impose costs on the present inhabitants without providing corresponding benefits; in such a situation, the demonstration that new immigrants provide net benefits no longer holds.

It is unclear what, if any, connection there is between that argument and the abandonment of open immigration by the United States. It is tempting to argue that immigration restrictions were one of the consequences of the welfare state. As long as it was clear that poor immigrants would have to support themselves, they were welcome; once they acquired the right to live off the taxes of those already here, they were not. The argument neatly links two of the major changes of the first half of this century—and does so in a way that fits nicely with my own ideological prejudices.

Figure 14-5

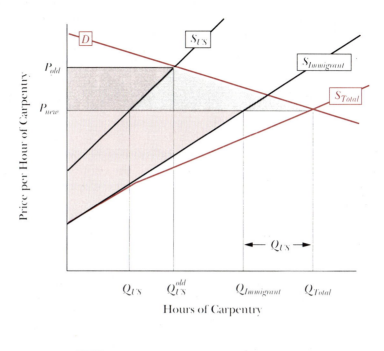

Producer Surplus Loss of U.S. Carpenters
Consumer Surplus Gain of U.S. Consumers
Producer Surplus Gain of Immigrant Carpenters

The effect of the immigration of carpenters on consumer and producer surplus. The gain in consumer surplus exceeds the loss of producer surplus to existing U.S. carpenters. A further benefit is the gain in producer surplus to immigrants.

Unfortunately for the argument, immigration restrictions were imposed in the early 1920s, and the major increase in the size and responsibility of government occurred during the New Deal—about a decade later. At most one might conjecture that both resulted from the same changing view of the role of the state.

Whether or not there was any historical connection between the rise of the welfare state in the United States and the end of unrestricted immigration, it seems clear that present objections to immigrants often involve the fear that, as soon as they arrive, they will go on welfare. It is much less clear that that fear is justified; a good deal of evidence seems to suggest that new immigrants are more likely to start working their way up the income ladder—in response to the opportunity to earn what are, from the standpoint of many of them, phenomenally high wages.

My final comment on free immigration concerns its distributional effects. Opponents of immigration argue that it "hurts the poor and helps the rich," since the obvious losers are unskilled American workers. If we limit our discussion to those presently living here, they are probably right. But the big gainers from immigration would be the immigrants—most of whom are very much poorer than the American poor. From a national standpoint, free immigration may hurt the poor; from an international standpoint, it helps them. By world standards, the American poor are, if not rich, at least comfortably well off.

Economic Imperialism

The term **economic imperialism** has at least two meanings. It is applied by some economists to the use of the economic approach to explain what are traditionally considered noneconomic questions. We are imperialists trying to conquer the intellectual territory presently held by political scientists, sociologists, psychologists, and the like. Much more commonly, it is used by Marxists to describe—and attack—foreign investment in "developing" (i.e., poor) nations. The implication of the term is that such investment is only a subtler equivalent of military imperialism—a way by which capitalists in rich and powerful countries control and exploit the inhabitants of poor and weak countries.

There is one interesting feature of such "economic imperialism" that seems to have escaped the notice of most of those who use the term. Developing countries are generally labor rich and capital poor; developed countries are, relatively, capital rich and labor poor. One result is that in developing countries, the return on labor is low and the return on capital is high—wages are low and profits high. That is why they are attractive to foreign investors.

To the extent that foreign investment occurs, it raises the amount of capital in the country, driving wages up and profits down. The effect is exactly analogous to the effect of free migration. If people move from labor-rich countries to labor-poor ones, they drive wages down and rents and profits up in the countries they go to, while having the opposite effect in the countries they come from. If capital moves from capital-rich countries to capital-poor ones, it drives profits down and wages up in the countries it goes to and has the opposite effect in the countries it comes from.

The people who attack "economic imperialism" generally regard themselves as champions of the poor and oppressed. To the extent that they succeed in preventing foreign investment in poor countries, they are benefiting the capitalists of those countries by holding up profits and injuring the workers by holding down wages. It would be interesting to know how much of the clamor against foreign investment in such countries is due to Marxist ideologues who do not understand this and how much is financed by local capitalists who do.

I should warn you that in the last few paragraphs I have used the term profit in the conventional sense of the return to capital, that being the way it is usually used in such discussions. A better term would be interest. That way, one avoids confusing profit in the sense of the return on capital with profit in the sense of economic profit—revenue minus all costs, including the cost of capital.

Land-Use Restrictions

In the United States and in similar societies elsewhere, there are often extensive limitations on how property owners can use their land. Many of these limitations can be defended in terms of externalities—a subject that will be discussed in Chapter 18. Whether or not the restrictions are justified, it is interesting to analyze their distributional effects.

Suppose the English government requires (as it does) that "greenbelts" be established around major cities—areas surrounding the urban center within which dense populations are prohibited. The result is to reduce the total amount of residential land available in such cities. The result of that is to increase rents. A law that is defended as a way of protecting urban beauty against greedy developers has as one of its effects raising the income of urban landlords at the expense of their tenants. It would be interesting to analyze the sources of support for imposing and maintaining greenbelt legislation, in order to see how much comes from the residents whose environment the legislation claims to protect and how much from the landlords whose income it increases.

PART 4—WAGE DIFFERENTIALS

So far, we have been using the ideas of Parts 1 and 2 of this chapter to determine who is injured or benefited by various policies. The same ideas can also be used to answer another question: What determines the different wages in different professions?

We begin with the observation from Part 2 that in equilibrium all sorts of labor are in some sense the same, as are all sorts of capital and land. If so, then one would expect that all jobs would receive the same pay. Obviously this is not so. Why?

Disequilibrium

The first answer is that we may not be in long-run equilibrium. Equilibrium is created and maintained by the fact that when one profession is more attractive than another, people tend to leave the less attractive profession and enter the more attractive one and new workers coming onto the market tend to enter the more attractive profession. As workers enter the attractive professions, they drive down their wages; as workers leave the unattractive ones, the wages in those professions rise. The process stops only when all professions are equally attractive.

All of this takes time. An individual who has spent considerable time and money training himself for one profession will switch to another only if the return is not only larger but large enough to justify the cost of the move. This is less of a problem for new workers coming onto the market, since they have not yet made the investment—but it may take a long time before the reduced inflow of new workers has much effect on the total number in the profession. So if an unexpected reduction in the demand for some particular type of labor pushes wages in that field below their long-run equilibrium level, it may be years before they come all the way back up. Similarly, an unexpected increase in demand for some particular sort of labor may keep wages above the normal level for some time, especially if the profession is one that requires lengthy training. The logic of the situation is essentially the same as in Chapter 13, applied to people instead of ships.

Differing Abilities

A second answer is that differing wages may reflect differing abilities. If, for example, intelligence is useful in practically any field and if nuclear physicists are, on average, more intelligent than grocery store clerks, then they will also have higher wages. The individual nuclear physicist may, in this case, earn no more than he would if he were a clerk—but the same man who is an average physicist, earning an average physicist's salary, would be an above-average clerk, earning an above-average clerk's salary. This is the case I described earlier as one person "containing more labor" than another. One hour of the intelligent worker's time may be equivalent to two hours of the average worker's time.

If this were the whole story, there is no obvious reason why nuclear physicists would be more intelligent than clerks—the intelligent individual would get the same return in either profession. In fact, of course, intelligence—and other abilities—are more useful in some fields than in others. Being seven feet tall is very useful if you are a basketball player; if you are a college professor, it merely means that you bump your head a lot.

Differences in such specialized abilities may not matter very much if the abilities are in sufficiently large supply. If 10 percent of the population consisted of men who were seven feet tall and well coordinated, basketball players would not get unusually high salaries—there would be too many tall clerks, tall professors, and tall ditchdiggers willing to enter the profession if they did. Similarly, whether the talents that make a good salesman bring high salaries to their possessors depends on both the supply of and demand for those talents. If equilibrium is reached only when all of the people who have those talents, plus some of those who do not have them, are salesmen, then the return to selling must be high enough to make it a reasonably attractive profession even to those who are not unusually talented at it—and a very attractive profession to those who are. If, on the other hand, in equilibrium all of the salesmen are talented and only some of those with the appropriate talents are salesmen, then talented salesmen will receive only a normal return for their efforts.

The logic of the situation is the same as in our earlier discussion of growing wheat and soybeans. Figure 14-6 shows the argument in graphical form. On Figure 14-6a the number of tall people (Q_{tall}) is more than enough to bring the wages of basketball players down to the wages

Figure 14-6

(*a*)

Quantity of People

(*b*)

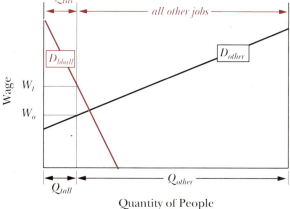

Quantity of People

The demand for basketball players and all other jobs and the number of tall people and all other people. On Figure 14-6*a* there are enough tall people to bring the wages of basketball players down to the wages for other jobs; on Figure 14-6*b* there are not. Quantities at the bottom of each figure show the fixed quantities of tall people (Q_{tall}) and ordinary people (Q_{other}) available. Quantities at the top of the figure show how many are actually being hired to play basketball (Q_{BB}) and for all other jobs.

Chapter 14   The Distribution of Income and the Factors of Production

of other jobs, so all jobs receive the same wage (W). On Figure 14-6b basketball has become more popular; the demand for basketball players (D_{bball}) has increased to the point where even with all the tall people playing basketball, their wage (W_t) is above the wage for other jobs (W_o).

We are now discussing what I earlier described as rents on scarce human abilities. If, to take an extreme case, only people who are over seven feet tall can play basketball, and if the demand for basketball players at a price equal to the wage in other professions is higher than the total number of people over seven feet tall, then the wages of basketball players can never be driven down to the ordinary wage rate. Nobody can move from other professions to basketball because everybody over seven feet tall is already playing basketball. Just as in the earlier discussion of land, the price is determined by the point where the demand curve intersects a perfectly inelastic supply curve.

Equal Net Advantage

We have now discussed two reasons why different professions might not, on net, be equally attractive—disequilibrium and differential abilities. There remains the possibility that even if neither of those factors is important—even if all professions are equally attractive—they may still be attractive in different ways.

Consider a group of professions. We assume that none of them requires any special human abilities; indeed, to make the situation even simpler, we assume that all individuals start with the same abilities. We also assume that the economy is in equilibrium; there have been no unexpected changes in the demand for different sorts of labor, so everyone is getting about the wage he expected to get when he chose his field.

Even in this situation, we may observe wide variations in the wages received by people in different professions. What is equal in equilibrium is the net advantage in each field, not the wage. If, for example, a particular profession, such as economics, is much more fun than other professions, it will also pay less. If it did not—if its wages were the same as those in less enjoyable fields—then on net it would be more attractive. People who were leading dull lives as ditchdiggers, sociologists, or lawyers would pour into the field, driving down the wage.

The argument applies not only to professions that are more fun but also to professions that have other nonpecuniary advantages. If, for example, many people want to be film or rock stars, not because the job is fun but because they like the idea of being watched by adoring multitudes, that will tend to drive down the wages of those professions. The same argument also works in reverse, for professions that have nonpecuniary disadvantages. That is why it costs more to hire people to drive trucks loaded with dynamite than trucks loaded with dirt.

A second factor that makes wages unequal even when net advantage is equal is the difference in the cost of entering different professions.

Becoming a checkout clerk requires almost no training; becoming an actuary requires years of study. If both professions earned the same wages, few people would become actuaries. In equilibrium the wage of the actuary must be enough higher to repay the time and expense invested in learning the job. Since the cost of training occurs at the beginning of his career and the return occurs later, the actuary must receive enough extra income to pay not only the cost of his training but also the interest on his investment in himself. If he did not, he would be better off investing his money in something other than himself and becoming a clerk instead. The wages of actuaries must pay for their human capital as well as their raw labor.

There is one more element that should be taken into account in explaining wage differentials—uncertainty. In some professions, the wage is fairly predictable; in others it is not. Movie stars make very large incomes, but the only actress I ever knew personally supported herself largely by temporary secretarial work. In a profession where most people are failures, at least from a financial standpoint, it is not surprising that the few successes do very well.

PROBLEMS

1. Suppose you wanted to calculate the Gini coefficient properly; further suppose you had complete information about everyone's income from birth to death. Exactly how would you solve the problem (confusion of changing income over time with changing income across people) discussed at the beginning of this chapter? (Hint: Use a concept from Chapter 12.)

2. The chapter discusses ways in which one might try to justify the distribution of income produced by a market. What do you believe is a just distribution? What should determine who gets how much?

3. Why is a backward-bending supply curve more plausible for labor considered as a factor of production than for any particular kind of labor (table making) or the product of such labor?

4. My wife is a geologist employed by an oil company. We spend less than 1 percent of our joint income for gasoline and several percent more for heating (gas) and power. Do you think we are better or worse off if the price of oil goes up? Would your answer be very much different if we had oil heat? If she was a geologist employed by a university? Discuss.

5. The government decides there are too many buildings in America and proposes a 50 percent tax on constructing new buildings. Which of the following groups will support the tax? Which will oppose it? Why?

a. Investors who own buildings.   d. Landlords

b. Building contractors.   e. Owners of undeveloped land

c. Tenants.

6. The concern with population questions in recent decades has been fueled in part by the belief that poor countries are poor mainly because they are overpopulated. Look up population densities (people per square mile) and income figures for China, Japan, India, West Germany, Belgium, Taiwan, and Mexico. Does it look as though poverty is mainly a function of population density? Looking at other countries, does the conclusion suggested by these cases seem to be typical? Discuss.

7. There are some people who very much want to be actors and will enter the profession even if they receive barely enough to live on. Discuss, as precisely as possible, under what circumstances actors will make barely enough to live on, under what circumstances they will make about the same wages as people in other fields, and under what circumstances they will make more. You may wish to simplify the problem by ignoring the probabilistic element—assume all actors make the same amount. You may find it useful to consider the effect on wages of different possible supply and demand curves for actors.

8. We described the additional salary received by someone who possesses scarce human talents as a sort of rent. What similar term might be used to describe the additional salary received by someone in a profession where wages are temporarily above their long-run equilibrium? Discuss.

FOR FURTHER READING

The classic discussion of the economics of wage differentials was published in 1776. It can be found in Chapter X, Book I, of Adam Smith, *An Inquiry into the Nature and Causes of the Wealth of Nations* (New York: Oxford University Press, 1976). The book is still well worth reading.

Students interested in a much more advanced treatment of one of the subjects raised in this chapter may want to look at Gary Becker, *Human Capital: A Theoretical and Empirical Analysis* (2nd ed; New York: Columbia University Press, 1975).

The most famous supporter of the idea of taxing the site value of land, Henry George, stated his argument in *Progress and Poverty* (New York: Robert Schalkenbach Foundation, 1984).

JUDGING
section IV
OUTCOMES

chapter 15

ECONOMIC EFFICIENCY

POSITIVE VS NORMATIVE

Positive statements are statements about what is; **normative** statements are statements about what ought to be. Economics is a positive science. An economist who says (correctly or incorrectly) that a $1 increase in the minimum wage will increase the unemployment rate by half a percentage point is expressing his professional opinion. If he goes on to say, "Therefore we should not increase the minimum wage," his statement is no longer only about economics. In order to reach a "should" conclusion, he must combine opinions about what is, which are part of economics, with **values**, opinions about what ought to be, which are not.

Of course, one of the main reasons people learn what *is* is in order to decide what *ought to be*. Economists have values just as everyone else does. Those values affect both their decision to become economists instead of ditchdiggers or political scientists and the questions they choose to study. But the values themselves, and the conclusions that require them, are not part of economics.

Economists frequently use terms, such as "efficient," that sound very much like "ought" words. Once one has proved that something leads to greater efficiency, it hardly seems worth asking whether it is desirable. Such terms, however, have a precise positive meaning, and it is quite easy to think of reasons why efficiency in the economist's sense might not always be desirable.

My own interpretation of why we use such terms is as follows. People keep coming to economists and asking them what to do. "Should we have a tariff?" "Should we expand the money supply?" The economist answers, "Should? I don't know anything about 'should.' If you have a tariff, such and such will happen; if you expand the money supply, . . . " The people who ask the questions say, "We don't want to know all that. On net, are the results good or bad?" The economist finally answers as follows:

As an economist, I have no expertise in good and bad. I can, however, set up a "criterion of goodness" called efficiency, that has the following characteristics. First, it has a fairly close resemblance to what I suspect you mean by "good." Second, it is so designed that in many cases I can figure out, by economics, whether some particular proposal (such as a tariff) is an improvement in terms of my criterion. Third, I cannot think of any alternative criterion closer to what I suspect you mean that also has the second characteristic.

One could object that the economist, defining efficiency according to what questions he can answer rather than what questions he is being asked, is like the drunk looking for his wallet under the street light because the light is better there than where he lost it. The reply is that an imperfect criterion of desirability is better than none.

The point of this story is to show how it is that economists claim to be positive scientists yet frequently use normative-sounding words. Three of these words are "improvement," "superior," and "efficient." They are used in a number of different ways in economics, and it is easy to confuse them.

IMPROVEMENT AND EFFICIENT

While the terms "improvement," "superior," and "efficient" are used in a number of different ways in different contexts—we shall discuss five in this chapter—the three words always have the same relation to each other. An **improvement** is a change—in what is being produced, in how it is produced, in who gets it, or whatever—that is in some way desirable. Situation B is **superior** to situation A if going from A to B is an improvement. A situation is **efficient** (in some particular respect) if it cannot be improved—if, in other words, there is no possible situation that is superior to it.

We will start by explaining what it means to produce one good efficiently. The next step is to apply the concept to two goods produced for one individual, seeing in what sense producing more of one and less of the other might be a net improvement. The final and most difficult step is to apply the idea of efficiency to something that affects two or more people.

Production Efficiency

We start with production efficiency. An improvement in production means using the same inputs to produce more of one output without producing less of another (**output improvement**), or producing the same outputs using less of one input and no more of any other (**input improvement**). As long as both inputs and outputs are goods, an improvement in this sense is obviously desirable; it means you have more of one desirable thing without giving up anything else. An output process is **production efficient** (sometimes called **X-efficient**) if there is no way of changing it that produces an output or input improvement. Production improvements and production efficiency provide a way of evaluating different outcomes that does not depend on our knowing the relative value of the different goods to the consumer. As long as both are goods, a change that gives more of one without less of the other is an improvement.

Figure 15-1*a* shows a production possibility set for producing two goods, X and Y, using a fixed quantity of inputs; every point in the colored region represents a possible output bundle. The curve F is the frontier of the set; for any point in the set that is not on F (such as A), there is some point on the frontier (B) that represents an improvement; in the case illustrated, B contains more of both X and Y than A. The points on the frontier are all output efficient; starting at B, the only way to produce more X is by producing less Y, as at C, and the only way to produce more Y is by producing less X, as at D.

This is the first time I have talked about the idea of production efficiency, but not the first time I have used it. From Chapter 3 on, I have been drawing figures with possibility sets and frontiers. A budget line, for example, is the frontier of a possibility set—the set of bundles it is possible to purchase with a given income. In indifference curve analysis, we only consider points on the budget line, not points below it, even though points below it are also possible—we could always throw away part of our income. Figure 15-1*b* shows this. The shaded area is the

Figure 15-1

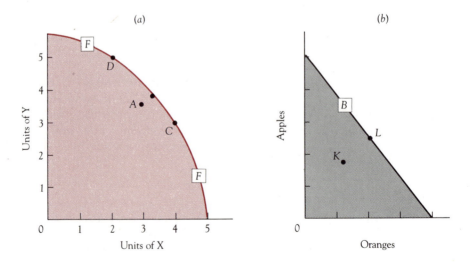

Possibility sets and frontiers. Figure 15-1*a* shows a production possibility set; F is its frontier. Figure 15-1*b* shows the set of alternative bundles available to a consumer; the budget line B is its frontier.

consumption possibility set. The line B is the **consumption possibility frontier**, alias the budget line.

But since insatiability implies that there is always something we want more of, we would never choose to throw away part of our income. Any point in the interior of the possibility set is dominated by a point on the frontier representing a bundle with more of both goods. Point K on Figure 15-1b is dominated by point L, just as A is dominated by B on Figure 15-1a. So if we are looking for the best bundle, we need only consider points on the frontier.

Similar considerations explain why, in diagrams such as Figures 5-9a and 5-9b of Chapter 5, we only considered output bundles on the frontier of the production possibility set (the number of lawns that could be mowed and meals cooked or ditches dug and sonnets composed with a given amount of labor). If you are going to work that number of hours, you might as well get as much output as possible, not spend some of the time walking around in circles instead of either mowing lawns or cooking meals.

Utility Efficiency

So long as we only consider output efficiency, there is no way of choosing between points B, C, and D on Figure 15-1a, all of which are output efficient. To do that, we must introduce preferences. Figure 15-2a is

Figure 15-2

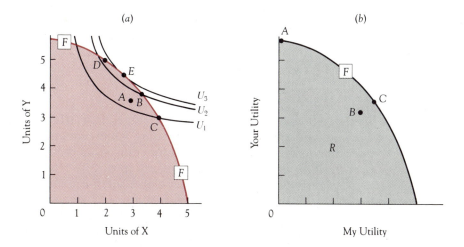

Efficient and inefficient outcomes. On Figure 15-2a, the alternatives are different output bundles to be consumed by an individual whose tastes are shown by the indifference curves; on Figure 15-2b, they are different allocations of goods (and hence utility) to two individuals. In each case, points on the frontier are efficient and points not on the frontier are not, but the former are not necessarily superior to the latter.

Figure 15-1a with the addition of a set of indifference curves. If I am producing X and Y for my own consumption, I can use my indifference curves to compare different efficient points. Point D, for example, is on a higher indifference curve than point C; I would rather consume 5 units of Y and 2 of X (point D) than 3 units of Y and 4 of X (point C).

A **utility improvement** is a change that increases my utility—moves me to a higher indifference curve. A situation is **utility efficient** if no further such improvements are possible. On the diagram, point E is the only point in the production possibility set that is utility efficient.

The fact that one point is output efficient and another is not does not mean that the first point is either output or utility superior to the second. On the diagram, point C is output efficient and point A is not—but A is on a higher indifference curve than C! A is inefficient because B is superior to it (more of both X and Y). B is also on a higher utility curve than A; it must be, since X and Y are both goods. C is efficient not because it is output superior to A (it is not—C has more X but less Y, so neither is output superior to the other) but because nothing is output superior to it. Since C is not output superior to A, there is no reason why it cannot be utility inferior to it—and in fact it is. If someone argued that "You should produce at C instead of at A, since C is efficient and A is not," his argument would sound plausible but be wrong.

On first reading, the previous paragraph may seem both confusing and irrelevant. It is there because the same point will be crucial to understanding the use (and misuse) of another and very important form of improvement and efficiency—Pareto efficiency—which I shall describe later in the chapter. The relevant concept—that the fact that A is not efficient and C is does not imply that C is an improvement on A—is easier to understand in the context of output efficiency than in the context of Pareto efficiency, so I advise you to try to understand it at this point.

SUMMING UTILITIES: THE PROBLEM

So far, we have been considering changes that affect only one person. The fundamental problem in defining what economic changes are, on net, improvements is the problem of comparing the welfare of different people. If some change results in my having two more chocolate chip cookies and one less glass of Diet Coke, there is a straightforward sense in which that is or is not an improvement; I do or do not prefer the new set of goods to the old (utility improvement). But what if the change results in my having two more cookies and your having one less glass of Diet Coke? It is an improvement from my standpoint, but not from yours.

The usual solution to this problem is to base the definition of efficiency on the idea of a **Pareto improvement** (named after the Italian economist Vilfredo Pareto)—defined as a change that benefits one person and injures nobody. A system is then defined as **Pareto efficient** if there is no way it can be changed that is a Pareto improvement. The problem with this approach is that it leaves you with no way of evaluating changes that are not Pareto improvements; the attempt to get around that problem while retaining the Paretian approach leads to serious problems, which I will discuss later.

One reason so many examples in earlier chapters involved identical producers and identical consumers was that I wanted to avoid the problem of balancing a loss to one person against a gain to another. If everyone is identical, any change that is in any sense an improvement must be a Pareto improvement: if it benefits anyone, it must benefit everyone. Early in the book, with the discussion of efficiency still many chapters in the future, that was very convenient.

Output efficiency is analogous to Pareto efficiency, with different people's utilities in the latter case corresponding to outputs of different goods in the former. A situation is Pareto efficient if there is no way of changing it that benefits one person and harms nobody—increases someone's utility without decreasing anyone else's. A situation is output efficient if there is no way of changing it that increases one output without decreasing some other output. Figure 15-2b shows the similarity; the axes are my utility and your utility, the region R consists of all possible combinations (the **utility possibility set**), and the frontier of that region, the curve F, consists of all the Pareto-efficient combinations.

In the case of output, we have a common measure by which to compare various points on the boundary: the utility of the individual consuming the output. This lets us compare two alternative output bundles, one of which contains more of one output and less of another. The important difference between Figure 15-2b and Figure 15-2a is the absence of indifference curves on 15-2b. The problem in comparing outcomes that affect several people is that there is no obvious way of comparing two different outcomes, one of which produces more utility for me and less for you than the other.

Some economists have tried to deal with such problems by imagining a social equivalent of the individual utility function (called a **social welfare function**). A social welfare function would give the welfare of the whole society as a function of the utilities of individuals, just as the utility function gives the welfare of the individual as a function of the quantities of goods he consumes. If we knew the social welfare function for the two-person society shown on Figure 15-2b, we could draw a set of social indifference curves on Figure 15-2b, just as we drew individual indifference curves on Figure 15-2a.

If we assume there is a social welfare function, we can try to analyze the outcome of different economic arrangements in terms of social preferences without actually knowing what the social preferences are—just as we have analyzed situations involving individual preferences without knowing what any particular real-world individual's preferences actually are. Some of the difficulties with this approach are discussed in the optional section of this chapter.

PARETIAN AND MARSHALLIAN EFFICIENCY

Another way of approaching the problem is to claim that although we have no way of deciding which of two Pareto-efficient outcomes is preferable, at least we should prefer efficient outcomes to inefficient ones. This argument is often made and sounds reasonable enough, but it runs into the difficulty that I discussed earlier in the context of output efficiency. While we may all agree that a Pareto improvement is an unambiguously good thing, it does not follow that a situation that is Pareto efficient is superior to one that is not.

Consider a world of two people, you and me, and two goods, cookies and Diet Cokes (20 of each). The situation is shown on Figure 15-2b; the axes are not Diet Cokes and cookies but my utility (which depends on how many of the Diet Cokes and cookies I have) and your utility (which depends on how many you have). One possible situation (A on Figure 15-2b) is for you to have all the cookies and all the Diet Cokes. That is Pareto efficient; the only way to change it is to give me some of what you have, which makes you worse off and so is not a Pareto improvement. Another possible situation (B) is for each of us to have 10 cookies and 10 Diet Cokes. That may be inefficient; if I like cookies more, relative to Diet Cokes, than you do, trading one of my Diet Cokes for one of your cookies might make us both better off (move us to C). The first situation is (Pareto) efficient and the second is not, yet it seems odd for you to say that the first situation is better than the second and expect me to agree with you.

The problem is that situation B is inefficient not because changing from B to A is a Pareto improvement (it is not) but because changing from B to C (I have 9 Diet Cokes and 11 cookies, you have 11 Diet Cokes and 9 cookies) is; it is hard to see what that has to do with A being better than B.

As this suggests, there are serious difficulties with the Paretian solution to the problem of evaluating different outcomes. They are sufficiently serious to make me prefer a different solution, proposed by the British economist Alfred Marshall; while he did not use the term "efficiency," his way of defining an improvement is an alternative to Pareto's, and I shall use the same terms for both. In most practical applications, the two definitions turn out to be equivalent, for reasons that I shall explain in the next section; but Marshall's definition makes it clearer what "improvement" means and in what ways it is only an approximate representation of what most of us mean by describing some economic change as "a good thing," "desirable," or the like. I have introduced the Paretian definition here because it is what most economics textbooks use; you will certainly encounter it if you study more economics.

To understand Marshall's definition of an improvement, we consider a change (the abolition of tariffs, a new tax, rent control, . . .) that affects many people, making some worse off and others better off. In principle we could price all of the gains and losses. We could ask each person who was against the change how much money he would have to be given so that on net the money plus the (undesirable) effect of the change would leave him exactly as well off as before. Similarly we could ask each gainer what would be the largest amount he would pay to get that gain, if he had to. We could, assuming everyone was telling us the truth, sum all of the gains and losses, reduced in this way to a common measure. If the sum was a net gain, we would say that the change was a **Marshall improvement**. If we had a situation where no further (Marshall) improvement was possible, we would describe it as efficient.

This definition does not correspond perfectly to our intuition about when a change is good (or makes people "on average, happier") for at least two reasons. First, we are accepting each person's evaluation of how much something is worth to him; the value of heroin to the addict has the same status as the value of insulin to the diabetic. Second, by comparing values according to their money equivalent, we ignore differences in the utility of money to different people. If you were told that a certain change benefited a millionaire by an amount equivalent for him to $10 and injured a poor man by an amount equivalent for him to $9, you would suspect that in some meaningful sense $10 was worth less to the millionaire than $9 to the poor man and therefore that "net human happiness" had gone down rather than up. The concept of efficiency is intended as a workable approximation of our intuitions about what is good; even if we could make the intuitions clear enough to construct a better approximation, it would still be less useful unless we had some way of figuring out what changes increased or decreased it.

How do we find out what changes produce net benefits in Marshall's sense? The answer is that we have been doing it, without saying so, through most of the book. Consumer (or producer) surplus is the benefit to a consumer (or producer) of a particular economic arrangement (one in which he can buy or sell at a particular price) measured in dollars according to his own values.

Several chapters back, I showed that the area under a summed demand curve was equal to the sum of the areas under the individual demand curves. So when we measure consumer surplus as the area under a demand curve representing the summed demands of many consumers, we are summing benefits—measured in dollars—to many different people. If we argue that some change in economic arrangements results in an increase in the sum of consumer and producer surplus, as we shall be doing repeatedly in the next few chapters, we are arguing that it is an improvement in the Marshallian sense.

The essential problem we face is how to add different people's utilities together in order to decide whether an increase in utility to one person does or does not compensate for a decrease to another. Marshall's solution is to add utilities as if everyone got the same utility from a dollar. The advantage of that way of doing it is that since we commonly observe people's values by seeing how much they are willing to pay for something, a definition that measures values in money terms is more easily applied in practice than would be some other definition.

Alfred Marshall was aware of the obvious argument against treating people as if they all had the same utility for a dollar: the fact that they do not. His reply was that while that was a legitimate objection if we were considering a change that benefited one rich man and injured one poor man, it was less relevant to the usual case of a change that benefited and injured large and diverse groups of people: all consumers of shoes and all producers of shoes, all the inhabitants of London and all the inhabitants of Birmingham, or the like. In such cases, individual differences could be expected to cancel out, so that the change that improved matters in Marshall's terms probably also "made things better" in some more general sense.

There is another respect in which Marshall's definition of improvement is useful, although it is one that might not have appealed to Marshall. If a situation is inefficient, that means that there is some possible change in it that produces net (dollar) benefits. If so, that suggests that a sufficiently ingenious entrepreneur might be able to organize that change, paying those who lose by it for their cooperation, being paid by those who gain, and pocketing the difference. If, to take a trivial example, you conclude that there would be a net improvement, in Marshall's sense of the term, from converting the empty lot on the corner into a McDonald's restaurant, one conclusion you may reach is that the present situation is inefficient. Another is that you could make money by buying the lot, buying a McDonald's franchise, and building a restaurant.

MARSHALL, MONEY, AND REVEALED PREFERENCE

There are several ways in which it is easy to misinterpret the idea of a Marshall improvement. One is by concluding that since net benefits are in dollars, "Economics really is just about money." Dollars are not what the improvement is but only what it is measured in. If the price of apples falls from \$10 apiece to \$0.10 apiece and your consumption rises from zero to 10/week, you have \$1/week less money to spend on other things, but you are better off by the consumer surplus on 10 apples per week—the difference between what they cost and what they are worth to you. Money is a convenient common unit for measuring value; that does not mean that money itself is the only, or even the most important, thing valued. The definition of a Marshall improvement does not even require that money exist; all values could have been stated in apples, water, or any other tradable commodity. As long as the price of apples is the same for all consumers, anything that is a net improvement measured in apples must also be a net improvement measured in money. If, for instance, apples cost \$0.50, a gain measured in apples is simply twice as large a number as the same gain measured in dollars, just as a distance measured in feet is three times the same distance measured in yards.

A second mistake is to take too literally the idea of "asking" everyone affected how much he has gained or lost. Basing our judgments on people's statements would violate the principle of revealed preference, which tells us that values are measured by actions, not words. That is how we measure them when analyzing what is or is not a Marshall improvement. Consumer surplus, for example, is calculated from a demand curve, which is a graph of how much people do buy at any price, not how much they say they think they should buy.

If we decided on economic policy by asking people how much they valued things, and if their answers affected what happened, they would have an incentive to lie. If I really value a change (say, the imposition of a tariff) at $100, I might as well claim to value it at $1,000. That will increase the chance that the change will occur, and in any case I do not actually have to pay anything for it. That is why, in defining a Marshall improvement, I added the phrase "assuming everyone was telling us the truth." What they were supposed to be telling the truth about was what they would do—how much they would give, if necessary, in order to get the result they preferred.

MARSHALL DISGUISED AS PARETO

The conventional approach to economic efficiency defines a situation as (Pareto) efficient if no Pareto improvements are possible in it. At first glance, that definition appears very different from the one I have borrowed from Marshall, which compares losses and benefits measured in dollars and defines a situation as efficient if no net improvement can be made in it. The Paretian approach appears to avoid any such comparison by restricting itself to the unobjectionable statement that a change that confers only benefits and no injuries is an improvement. The problem comes when one tries to apply this definition of efficiency to judging real-world alternatives.

Consider the example of tariffs. The abolition of tariffs on automobiles would make American auto workers and stockholders in American car companies worse off. Buyers of cars and producers of export goods would be better off. It can be shown that under plausible simplifying assumptions, there exists a set of payments from the second group to the first that, combined with the abolition of tariffs, would leave everyone better off. The payments by members of the second group would be less than their gain from the abolition; the receipts by members of the first group would be more than their losses from abolition.

This is equivalent to showing, as I shall do in Chapter 19, that the dollar gains to the members of the second group total more than the dollar losses to the members of the first group—that the abolition of tariffs is an improvement in Marshall's sense of the term. If I gain by $20 and you lose by $10, it follows both that there is a net (Marshall) improvement and that if I paid you $15 the payment plus the change would leave us both better off (by $5 each), making it a Pareto improvement. So a Marshall improvement plus an appropriate set of transfers is a Pareto improvement; and any change that, with appropriate transfers, can be converted into a Pareto improvement must be a Marshall improvement.

The abolition of auto tariffs by itself, however, is not a Pareto improvement: auto workers and stockholders are worse off. How then can Pareto efficiency be used to judge whether the abolition of tariffs would be a good thing? By the following magic trick.

The abolition of tariffs plus appropriate payments from the gainers to the losers would be a Pareto improvement. Actually arranging the payments is probably impossible, since there is no practical way of discovering exactly who gains or loses by how much. Since the situation with tariffs could be Pareto improved (by abolition plus compensation), it is not efficient. The situation without tariffs cannot be Pareto improved (I have not proved this; assume it is true). Hence abolition of tariffs moves us from an inefficient to an efficient situation. Hence it is an improvement.

If you believe that, I have done a bad job of explaining, earlier in this chapter, why a movement from an inefficient to an efficient situation need not be an improvement—a point made once in the context of output efficiency and again in the context of Pareto efficiency. A world without tariffs (and without compensation) is efficient, and a world with tariffs is not; but it does not follow that going from the latter to the former is an improvement. The situation with the tariff is being condemned not because it is Pareto inferior to the situation without the tariff but because it is Pareto inferior to yet a third situation: abolition of the tariff plus compensating payments.

Half of the trick is in confusing "going from a Pareto-inefficient to a Pareto-efficient outcome" with "making a Pareto improvement." The other half is in the word "possible." Imagine that someone asserted that tariffs are inefficient because there is a possible change—abolition plus compensating payments—that would be a Pareto improvement. If arranging the payments is impossible (or costly enough to wipe out the net gain), then the Pareto improvement is really not possible, so the initial situation is not really Pareto inefficient. The concept of Pareto improvement, and the associated definition of efficiency, can be applied to judge many real-world situations inefficient if you assume that compensating payments can be made costlessly (i.e., with no cost other than the payments themselves). Without this assumption, which is usually not made explicit, the Paretian approach is of much more limited usefulness.

One way to get out of this trap while retaining the trappings of the Paretian approach is to describe the abolition of the automobile tariff (without compensation) as a **potential Pareto improvement** or **Kaldor improvement**, meaning that it has the potential to be a Pareto improvement if combined with appropriate transfers (the **compensation**

principle—it is an improvement if the gainers could compensate the losers, even though they don't). This, as I pointed out above, is equivalent to saying that it is an improvement in Marshall's sense.

I prefer to use the Marshallian approach, which makes the interpersonal comparison explicit, instead of hiding it in the "could be made but isn't" compensating payment. To go back to the example given earlier, a change that benefits a millionaire by $10 and costs a pauper $9 is a potential Pareto improvement, since if combined with a payment of $9.50 from the millionaire to the pauper it would benefit both. If the payment is not made, however, the change is not an actual Pareto improvement. The "potential Paretian" approach reaches the same conclusion as the Marshallian approach and has the same faults; it simply hides them better. That is why I prefer Marshall. From here on, whenever I describe something as an improvement or an economic improvement, I am using the term in Marshall's sense unless I specifically say that I am not.

It is worth noting that although a Marshall improvement is usually not a Pareto improvement, the adoption of a general policy of "Wherever possible, make Marshall improvements" may come very close to being a Pareto improvement. In one case, the Marshall improvement benefits me by $3 and hurts you by $2; in another it helps you by $6 and hurts me by $4; in another . . . . Add up all the effects and, unless one individual or group is consistently on the losing side, everyone, or almost everyone, is likely to benefit. That is one of the arguments for such a policy and one of the reasons to believe that economic arrangements that are Marshall efficient are desirable.

EFFICIENCY AND THE BUREAUCRAT-GOD

In describing some economic arrangement as efficient or inefficient, we are comparing it to possible alternatives. This raises a difficult question: What does "possible" mean? One could argue that only that which exists is possible. In order to get anything else, some part of reality must be different from what it is.

But one purpose of the concept of efficiency is to help us decide how to act—how to change reality to something different than it now is. So any practical application of the idea of efficiency must focus on some particular sorts of changes. What sorts of changes are and should be implicit in the way we use the term?

One could argue that however well organized the economy may be, it is still inefficient. A change such as the invention of cheap thermonuclear power or a medical treatment to prevent aging would be an unambiguous improvement—and surely some such change is possible. That might be a relevant observation—if this were a book on medicine or nuclear physics. Since it is a book on economics, the sorts of changes we are concerned with involve using the present state of knowledge (embodied for our purposes in production functions, ways of converting inputs to outputs) but changing what is produced and consumed by whom.

One way of putting this that I have found useful is in terms of a **bureaucrat-god**. A bureaucrat-god has all of the knowledge and power that anyone in the society has. He knows everyone's preferences and production functions and has unlimited power to tell people what to do. He does not have the power to make gold out of lead or produce new inventions. He is benevolent; his sole aim is to maximize welfare in Marshall's sense.

An economic arrangement is efficient if it cannot be improved by a bureaucrat-god. The reason we care whether an arrangement is efficient is that if it is, there is no point in trying to improve it. If it is not efficient, there still may be no practical way of improving it—since we do not actually have any bureaucrat-gods available—but it is at least worth looking.

At this point, it may occur to you that while efficiency as I have defined it is an upper bound on how well an economy can be organized, it is not a very useful benchmark for evaluating real societies. Real societies are run not by omniscient and benevolent gods but by humans; however rational they may be, both their knowledge and their objectives are mostly limited to things and people that directly concern them. How can we hope, out of such components, to assemble a system that works as well as it would if it were run by a bureaucrat-god? Is it not as inappropriate to use "efficiency" in judging the performance of human institutions as it would be to judge the performance of race cars by comparing their speed to its theoretical upper bound—the speed of light?

The surprising answer is no. As we will see in Chapter 16, it is possible for institutions that we have already described, institutions not too different from those around us in the real world, to produce an efficient outcome. That is one of the most surprising—and useful—implications of economic theory.

WARNING

While the way in which this textbook teaches economics is somewhat unconventional, the contents—what is taught—are not very different from what many other economists believe and teach. This chapter is the major exception. While Alfred Marshall was, in other respects, a much more important figure in the history of economics than Vilfredo Pareto, Marshall's solution to the problem of deciding what is or is not an improvement has largely disappeared from modern economics; virtually all elementary texts teach the Paretian approach. Both the Marshallian approach and the Paretian, as it is commonly applied, have, under almost all circumstances, the same implications for what is or is not efficient. What differs is the justification given for the conclusions that both imply.

I am by no means the only contemporary economist who feels uncomfortable with the Paretian approach, but I may be the first to put that discomfort, and the Marshallian solution, into a textbook. In that respect, this chapter is either "on the frontier" or "out of the mainstream," according to whether one does or does not agree with it.

OPTIONAL SECTION

SOCIAL WELFARE AND THE ARROW IMPOSSIBILITY THEOREM

Earlier in this chapter, I mentioned that one "solution" to the problem of evaluating outcomes that affect different people is to assume that there exists a social welfare function—a procedure for ranking such outcomes—without actually specifying what it is. This is somewhat like the way we handle individual preferences; we assume a utility function that allows the individual to rank alternatives that affect him, although we have no way of knowing exactly what that function is.

But in the case of the utility function, although we cannot predict it, we can observe it by observing what choices the individual actually makes. There seems to be no equivalent way to observe the social welfare function, since there is no obvious sense in which societies make choices. We could try to describe a particular set of political institutions in this way, substituting "the outcome of the political process" for "what the individual chooses." But while this might be a useful way of analyzing what those institutions *will* do, it tells us nothing about what they *should* do—unless we are willing to assume that the two are identical. This leaves the social welfare function as an abstract way of thinking about the question, with no way of either deducing what it should be or observing what it is.

Even as an abstract way of thinking about the problem, the social welfare function has problems; not only is it an unobservable abstraction, it may well be a logically inconsistent one. To explain what I mean by that, I will start by showing how we can eliminate a particular candidate for a social welfare function—majority rule. I shall then tell you about a similar and much stronger result that eliminates a broad range of possible social welfare functions.

A social welfare function is supposed to be a way of ranking outcomes that affect more than one person; it is intended to be the equivalent, for a group, of an individual's utility function. There are two different ways in which one could imagine constructing a social welfare function. One is to base social preferences on individual preferences, so that what the society prefers depends, perhaps in some complicated way, on what all of the individuals prefer. The other is to have some external standard: what is good according to correct philosophy, in the mind of God, or the like. Economists, knowing very little about either the mind of God or correct philosophy, are reluctant to try the second alternative, so they have usually assumed that social preferences are built on individual preferences.

One advantage to defining social preferences in terms of individual preferences is that individual preferences express themselves in individual actions. Perhaps if we could set up the right set of social institutions, the choices made by all the individual members of society would somehow combine to produce the "socially preferred" outcome for the society. That, in a way, is the idea of democracy: Let each individual vote for what he prefers and hope that the outcome will be good for the society. Seen in this way, majority rule is a possible social welfare function. For each pair of alternatives, find out which one more people like and label that the socially preferred choice.

One problem with this was pointed out several centuries ago by Condorcet, a French mathematician. Majority vote does not produce a consistent set of preferences. Consider Table 15-1, which shows the preferences of three individuals among three outcomes. Individual 1 prefers outcome A to outcome B and outcome B to outcome C; Individual 2 prefers B to C and C to A; Individual 3 prefers C to A and A to B. Suppose we consider a society made up of only these three people and try to decide which outcome is preferred under majority rule. In a vote between A and B, A wins two to one, since Individuals 1 and 3 prefer it. In a vote between B and C, B wins two to one, since 1 and 2 prefer it. It appears that we have a social ranking; A is preferred to B and B to C.

If A is preferred to B and B to C, then A must also be preferred to C. But it is not. If we take a vote between A and C, Individual 1 votes for A but both 2 and 3 vote for C—so C wins. We have a system of social preferences in which A is preferred to B, B to C, and C to A! This is what mathematicians call an **intransitive ordering**; obviously it does not produce a consistent definition of what is socially preferred.

This **Condorcet Voting Paradox** eliminates majority rule as a possible definition of social welfare. A similar and much more general result proved by Kenneth Arrow, called the **Arrow Impossibility Theorem**, eliminates practically everything else. Arrow made a few plausible

Table 15-1

Ranking	Individual 1	2	3
First	A	B	C
Second	B	C	A
Third	C	A	B

assumptions about what a social welfare function must be like and then proved that no possible procedure for going from individual preferences to social preferences could satisfy all of them.

What are the assumptions? One is nondictatorship; the social welfare function cannot simply consist of picking one individual and saying that whatever he prefers is socially preferred. Another has the long name **independence of irrelevant alternatives**. It says that if the social welfare function, applied to individuals with a particular set of individual preferences, leads to the conclusion that alternative A is preferred to alternative B, then a change in preferences that does not affect anyone's preferences between A and B cannot change the social preference between A and B. Another assumption is that social preferences are positively related to individual preferences; if some set of individual preferences lead A to be preferred to B, a change in the preference of one of the individuals from preferring B to preferring A cannot make the social preference change in the other direction. The society cannot switch to preferring B as the result of an individual switching to preferring A. Finally the social welfare function must lead to a consistent set of preferences; if A is preferred to B and B to C, then A must be preferred to C.

What Arrow proved was that no rule for going from individual preferences to group preferences could be consistent with all of those assumptions.

> Economics Joke #2: *A physicist, a chemist, and an economist were shipwrecked on a desert island. After a while, a case of canned beans drifted to shore; the three began discussing how to open the cans. The chemist (a physical chemist) suggested that if they started a fire and put a can of beans on it, he could calculate at what point the resulting pressure would burst the can. The physicist said that he could then calculate the trajectory the beans would take as they spouted out of the burst can and put a clean palm leaf down for them to land on. "That's too much trouble," the economist said. "Assume we have a can opener."* (This is a joke about the social welfare function.)

The Arrow Impossibility Theorem does not quite prove that a social welfare function is logically impossible. For one thing, the theorem only applies to social preferences based on individual preferences; a social welfare function that says, "Socially preferred means what God wants" or "Socially preferred means what a philosopher can prove that we all ought to want," is not eliminated by the theorem. Furthermore it applies to social welfare functions based on preferences but not to those based on utility functions. The only form in which utility functions are observable is as preferences; we can observe that you prefer a cookie to a Diet Coke (because given the choice, you take the cookie), but we cannot observe by how much you prefer it. Even the Von Neumann version of utility discussed in the optional section of Chapter 13, while allowing quantitative statements about my preferences, does not allow quantitative comparisons between my preferences and yours.

If, in deciding what was socially preferred, we could use not only the fact that I preferred A to B but also that I preferred A to B by 7 utiles and B to C by 2, while you preferred B to A by 1 utile and C to B by 3, the Impossibility Theorem would no longer hold. In this case, the obvious social welfare function would be total utility: Add up everyone's utility for each outcome and use the sum as your social welfare function. This rule for defining what is desirable, called utilitarianism by philosophers, played an important role in the development of economics (and philosophy). Alfred Marshall, for instance, was a utilitarian who proposed what I have called Marshall efficiency as an approximate rule for maximizing the (unobservable) total utility.

AMBIGUITIES IN THE CONCEPT OF IMPROVEMENT

For most purposes, improvement in Marshall's sense provides an adequate working rule for applying our rather vague ideas of what is or is not a net improvement, but there are situations in which it can lead to apparently inconsistent results. Imagine a society of two people, you and me. There is one good in this society that is immensely valuable: a life-extension pill that doubles the life expectancy of whichever one of us takes it. There are also other goods. Suppose we want to use Marshall's approach to decide which of us should have the pill.

If I have the pill, there is no sum you could offer me that would make me willing to give it up; the pill plus the goods I already have are worth more to me than all of the other goods (mine plus yours) without the pill. The maximum you would be willing to offer me for the pill is less than all of your goods, since there is no advantage to you in taking the pill and then starving to death. So the dollar value of the pill to me (the amount I would have to be paid to give it up) is greater than its dollar value to you (the amount you would pay to get it). Leaving me with the pill is then, by Marshall's criterion, the preferred outcome; more precisely, taking the pill away from me is not an improvement.

But suppose we start with you having the pill. Following exactly the same argument, we find that leaving you with the pill is the preferred outcome! The problem is that since the pill is immensely valuable to both of us, whoever has it is, in effect, much wealthier than if he did not. He is wealthier not because he has more money but because he already has the most important thing that he would want money to buy: the pill. Since he is wealthier, the utility of money to him is less. So the money value of anything to him—what he would be willing to pay to get other goods or what he would have to be paid to give up the pill—is higher than it would be if he did not start out owning the pill. Since we are measuring utility by how much money (or goods) someone is willing to give to get something or willing to accept in exchange for giving something up, we get different results according to who we assume starts off with the pill.

Most applications of Marshall's definition of improvement do not involve this problem. If, for example, we consider the desirability of tariffs, it probably does not matter whether we start by assuming that tariffs exist and ask how people would be affected by abolishing them (measuring the amount of gains and injuries by their dollar equivalents) or start by assuming they do not exist and ask how people would be affected by imposing them. One reason it would not matter is that most of the gains and losses are themselves monetary; the dollar value to you of a $1 increase in your income is the same however rich you are. Another reason is that even if some of the gains and losses were nonmonetary, the abolition (or institution) of tariffs would have a relatively small effect on most people's income, hence a small effect on the monetary equivalent to them of some nonmonetary value.

This sort of problem is not limited to the Marshallian approach. Under the strict Pareto definition (an improvement means a Pareto improvement: someone is benefited and no one is hurt), most alternatives are incomparable; not only is there no way of deciding who should get the life-extension pill, there is no way of deciding whether tariffs should be abolished. As long as the abolition makes one person worse off, it is not a Pareto improvement. Under the "potential Pareto" criterion (a change is an improvement if there is some set of transfers from gainers to losers that, combined with the change, results in a Pareto improvement), one gets exactly the same problems as with Marshall's criterion.

PROBLEMS

1. In Figure 15-3a, the production possibility set for a worker working eight hours per day is shown as the shaded area. Which labeled points are output efficient? Which labeled points are output superior to point A?
2. In Figure 15-3b, the shaded area shows possible outcomes in terms of the resulting divisions of income between two people, John and Lisa; nobody else exists. Which labeled points are Pareto efficient? Which are Marshall efficient? Which are Pareto superior to point A? Which are Marshall superior to point A? Which are *potentially* Pareto superior to point A?
3. Figure 15-3c is similar to Figure 15-3b. What do you think is the significance of the difference between the shapes of the shaded areas in Figures 15-3b and 15-3c? (Warning: This question requires original thought.)

Figure 15–3

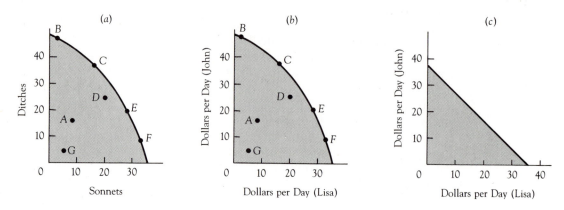

Opportunity sets for Problems 1–3.

4. The shaded area on Figure 15-4a is the possibility set for a worker working eight hours a day cutting down trees and making sawdust. Which labeled points are output efficient? Which are output superior to A? to B? to D? Which labeled points is A output superior to? What about D?

5. The shaded area on Figure 15-4b shows possible outcomes in terms of their effect on the incomes of two people, Ann and Bill; nobody else exists. Which labeled points are Pareto efficient? Which are Marshall efficient? Which are Pareto superior to point A? Which are Marshall superior to point A? Which are *potentially* Pareto superior to point A?

6. Draw the Pareto-efficient part of the shaded area in Figure 15-4b.

Figure 15-4

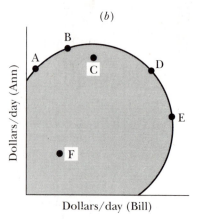

Figures for Problems 4–6.

Section IV Judging Outcomes

7. In this chapter, I gave one example of a Marshall improvement that many people would consider undesirable: a change that benefited a rich man by $10 and injured a poor man by $9. Give at least two other examples of Marshall improvements that many people (including well-informed people not themselves affected) would consider undesirable, where the reason for the conflict between the Marshall criterion and desirability does not depend on differences in income or wealth among the people affected.

8. One obvious objection to Marshall's definition of improvement is that we should take into account distributional effects; if a policy is a slight Marshall worsening but helps the poor it might still be desirable from a utilitarian standpoint. In order to take account of such effects, we must know what they are; this is not always easy. For each of the following policies, first describe what you think its distributional effect is (makes incomes more equal or makes incomes less equal) then give at least one reason why it might have the *opposite* effect.
   a. Agricultural price supports.
   b. Minimum wage laws.
   c. Tax-supported state universities.

9. The government imposes a tax of $0.10/pound on artichokes; the money is used to give everyone $5 for Christmas. Assume that people are not all identical. Is the law a Pareto improvement? A Marshall improvement? Would its abolition be a Pareto improvement? A Marshall improvement? Explain.

10. Do Problem 9 on the assumption that people are all identical.

11. The government imposes a $0.10/pound tax on artichokes; the supply and demand curves are shown in Figure 15-5. The money is used to finance research on thermonuclear power. Each dollar spent on such research produces $2 worth of benefits. Answer as in Problem 9.

Figure 15-5

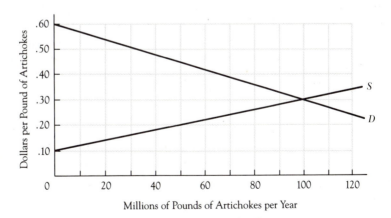

Supply and demand for artichokes—Problem 11.

12. The situation is as in Problem 11, except that you can vary the level of tax. How would you find the (Marshall) efficient level? Approximately what is it? (Warning: This is a hard problem. A verbal explanation requires original thought. A numerical answer may require either more mathematics than some of you have or a good deal of trial and error.)

FOR FURTHER READING

The ideas I have described as "Marshall improvement" and "Marshall efficiency" are more commonly derived from the idea of a potential Pareto improvement and referred to as the *Hicks/Kaldor criterion*. For the original, interesting, and readable discussion of those ideas, you may want to look at Alfred Marshall, *Principles of Economics*, (8th. ed.; London: Macmillan, 1920), Chapter VI.

Some other important papers on the Hicks/Kaldor criterion include: Nicholas Kaldor, "A Note on Tariffs and the Terms of Trade," *Economica* (November, 1940); John R. Hicks, "The Foundations of Welfare Economics," *Economic Journal* (December, 1939); and Tibor Scitovsky, "A Note on Welfare Propositions in Economics," *Review of Economic Studies* (November, 1941).

The Arrow Impossibility Theorem is proved in Kenneth Arrow, *Social Choice and Individual Values*, 2nd ed., (New Haven, CT: Yale University Press, 1970).

At several points in this chapter, I have asserted that the Marshallian and potential Paretian (Kaldor/Hicks) definitions of efficiency lead to the same conclusion; any situation that is efficient by one definition is efficient by the other. That is not quite true, as I discovered after the first edition of this book was published. For a description of circumstances under which an outcome can be Kaldor efficient but not Marshall efficient, see: David Friedman, "Does Altruism Produce Efficient Outcomes? Marshall vs Kaldor," *Journal of Legal Studies*, Vol. XVII (January, 1988).

chapter 16

WHAT IS EFFICIENT?

In Chapter 15, I explained the idea of Marshall efficiency and suggested that it could be used as a benchmark for evaluating different economic arrangements. In this chapter we do so, starting with the competitive industry of Chapter 9 and going on to the single-price and discriminating monopolies of Chapter 10. The objective in each case is to prove either that the outcome is efficient or that it is not. To prove that it is efficient, I must show that it cannot be improved by a bureaucrat-god. If it is not efficient, I will prove its inefficiency by showing how a bureaucrat-god could improve it. That may also give us some idea of why it is inefficient and how, even without a bureaucrat-god, the inefficient institutions might be improved.

A COMPETITIVE INDUSTRY

We assume an industry made up of many identical price-taking firms. The industry sells its output to consumers at a price P; it buys its inputs from the owners of the factors of production: workers, landlords, capitalists. All those involved—firms, consumers, owners—are price takers.

An efficient outcome is, by definition, one that cannot be improved by a bureaucrat-god. We will therefore consider the ways in which a bureaucrat-god might change the outcome produced by the market; if we can show that no possible change is a Marshall improvement, then the original equilibrium must have been efficient.

There are three ways in which the market outcome could be changed. The bureaucrat-god could have the same quantity of the good produced in the same way, while changing its *allocation*—who gets it. He could produce the same quantity and allocate it to the same people, while changing how it is produced. Finally, he could change the quantity.

Allocation

We begin by considering a change in allocation, quantity held constant. Initially, since the good is sold at a price P, everyone who values it at P or higher gets it and everyone to whom it is not worth at least P does not. Figures 16-1a and 16-1b show the marginal value curves of two consumers, Uno and Duo; each is buying the quantity (Q_1, Q_2) at which his marginal value is equal to P. The total value each of them gets from his consumption is the area under his marginal value curve; his consumer surplus is that total value minus what he pays. To change the allocation we must reduce the quantity consumed by one consumer and increase the quantity consumed by another. Figures 16-1a and 16-1b show the effect of transferring one unit from Uno to Duo.

If we change the allocation without changing any of the associated payments, Uno is worse off by area A_1 and Duo is better off by area A_2; as you can see from the figure, A_1 must be larger than A_2. To prove this mathematically, note that since the marginal value curve MV_1 is above

Figure 16-1

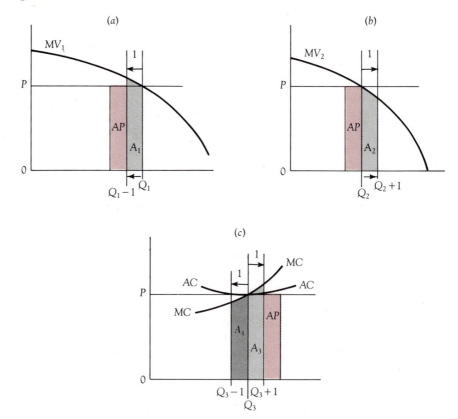

Effects of changing the quantity or allocation of output by one unit. Figures 16-1a and 16-1b show the effects of transferring one unit of output from Uno (1a) to Duo (1b). Figure 16-1c shows the increased (decreased) cost to a firm of producing one more (less) unit of output.

P to the left of Q_1, and the marginal value curve MV_2 is below P to the right of Q_2, A_1 must be greater than a rectangle P high and one unit wide (AP), and A_2 must be less than that same rectangle; so $A_1 > A_2$. P is a height on the graph (dollars/unit), while A_1 and A_2 are areas (dollars), so we had to convert P into the area $P \times 1$ unit in order to compare it to the areas A_1 and A_2. You should be able to satisfy yourself that the same relation holds however large the transfer and whatever the shape of the MV curves; the gain to Duo is less than the loss to Uno. Hence the transfer is a Marshall worsening.

The same argument can be made verbally. Before the transfer, everyone is consuming up to the point where $MV = P$. A transfer from Uno to Duo takes away from Uno units that were worth at least P to him, since at a price P he chose to buy them. It gives to Duo units that are worth less than P to him, since at a price of P he chose not to buy them. Each unit transferred is worth more to the person who loses it (Uno) than to the person who gets it (Duo), so the change is a worsening.

I am measuring value, as usual, by the amount an individual is willing to give up to get something. Some of you may respond that taking steak from a rich man who is willing to pay $4 for it and giving it to a poor man who is willing to pay only $3 is really an improvement, since something worth $3 to the poor man is more important than something worth $4 to the rich man. That is one of the objections to the Marshall criterion discussed in Chapter 15. What it is really saying is that we should maximize total utility rather than total value. But utility cannot be observed and value can. Hence we can describe (and perhaps construct) institutions that maximize total value but not ones that maximize total utility; the former may be regarded as a workable means for approximating the latter.

We have now seen that no reallocation of the existing quantity of output can be a Marshall improvement. The allocation produced by selling the good to all comers at the price at which quantity demanded equals quantity supplied allocates units of the good to those who most value them; any reallocation must transfer from someone who values the units of the good he is losing at more than their price to someone who values the units he is gaining at less. The conclusion holds not only for the quantity of output produced by a competitive industry but for *any* quantity of output; however much is produced, selling it at the price at which that quantity is demanded is the efficient way to allocate it.

Production

The next question is whether a bureaucrat-god could produce an improvement by changing the way in which the (fixed) quantity of output is produced; after that, we will consider whether he can produce an improvement by changing that quantity.

There are two ways in which the cost to an industry of producing a given quantity of output might be lowered. One is for some firm to produce the same output as before at a lower cost; the other is to change the division of output among firms. But in the initial situation, each firm is already producing its output in the least costly way: Any reduction in cost would increase the firm's profits and so would already have been made. As you may remember from Chapter 9, a firm gets its total cost curve from its production function by finding, for each level of output, the least expensive way of producing it. So there is no way the bureaucrat-god can reduce the cost to the firm of producing a given quantity of output.

What about reallocating production among firms: closing down one firm and having each of the others produce a little more or creating a new firm and having each firm produce a little less? Neither of these changes can decrease cost. In equilibrium, as you may remember from Chapter 9, the firms in a price-taking industry are producing at the minimum of their average cost curves—at Q_3 on Figure 16-1c. Since the firms are producing at minimum average cost, any change in output per firm must raise average cost, not lower it. Here again, just as in the case of allocation, the result is not limited to the particular price and quantity actually produced. If the demand curve shifted out, increasing price and quantity, the new quantity would again be produced in the least costly way.

We now know that no change in how output is produced or in how it is allocated can be an improvement. In at least these two dimensions, the competitive industry is efficient in the strong sense discussed in Chapter 15; no change that a bureaucrat-god could impose can be an improvement. The one remaining possibility for improvement is a change in the quantity produced.

Quantity

To see why this also cannot be an improvement, consider Figures 16-1b and 16-1c, which show the marginal value curve of a consumer and the marginal cost curve of a producer. The producer is producing a quantity Q_3 for which $P = MC = $ Minimum AC. If he increases output to $Q_3 + 1$, the additional cost will be the area A_3. If the additional unit goes to Duo, it will increase his consumption to $Q_2 + 1$; the value to him of the additional consumption is area A_2. As you can see from the figure, A_3 is greater than AP and A_2 is less than AP, so $A_3 > A_2$. It follows that the change is a worsening; the gain to the consumer from the additional output is less than the cost of producing it.

The same argument applies if we decrease output instead of increasing it; this time, look at Figures 16-1a and 16-1c. The reduction in output by the firm saves it area $A_4 < AP$, and the loss in consumption to Uno costs him area $A_1 > AP$; again there is a net loss.

What if, instead of increasing output by having one firm produce an additional unit, we increase it by adding one more firm (producing Q_3

units) to the industry? The cost per unit of additional output is now only P. But since the value per unit to the consumer of the additional units is less than P, the net result is still a worsening. The same is true if instead of adding a firm and increasing output by Q_3, we close down a firm and decrease output by Q_3.

The argument can be put verbally as well as graphically. In competitive equilibrium, the price of the good is just equal to the cost of producing a little more or less: $P = MC$. But since, in competitive equilibrium, consumers buy the good up to the point where its marginal value to them is P, any reduction costs the consumers more than P per unit and any increase benefits them by less. Hence any reduction in output saves the firms less than it costs the consumers, while any increase costs the firms more than it saves the consumers. In competitive equilibrium, consumers are consuming up to the point where each unit is worth exactly its cost of production. Any further increase involves producing units that cost more to produce than they are worth to the consumers; any reduction means failing to produce units that are worth more to the consumers than they cost to produce.

So far, we have only considered changing one variable at a time: allocation, production, or quantity. Could the bureaucrat-god perhaps create a Marshall improvement by changing two or three variables at once? No. We proved that the market allocation rule (sell at the price at which consumers want to buy exactly the amount produced) is the efficient way to allocate any quantity of output and that the way in which a competitive industry produces is the efficient way to produce any quantity of output. So whatever the quantity produced, allocation and production should be done in the way they would be done by a competitive industry. That leaves only one variable—quantity—and we just proved that if output is produced and allocated in that way, the efficient quantity is the quantity a competitive industry chooses to produce.

We are done. We have shown that no change in the outcome produced by an industry of competitive, price-taking firms can be a Marshall improvement. The outcome of a competitive market is efficient.

Filling In Details

In presenting the proof that the outcome of a competitive market is efficient, I have deliberately ignored a number of details in order to make it easier for you to see the whole pattern without being distracted by a series of lengthy digressions. I will now go back and fill in the missing points. Two of them are missing pieces of the proof; one is an explanation of something about the proof that you may have found confusing.

Dollar Cost, Value Cost. In demonstrating that the outcome of a competitive market could not be improved, I showed that no change in how the industry produces the output can lower the cost of production. This is not quite the same thing as showing that no change can be a Marshall improvement. A change in cost of production, after all, is merely a change in the number of dollars paid by the firms to the owners of the inputs. What is the connection between showing that a change raises the number of dollars paid ("raises cost") and showing that it is a Marshall worsening ("net loss of value")?

That connection comes from Chapter 5, where we saw that the price of an input (labor in that case) was equal to the cost to the individual of producing it. The marginal disvalue of labor (a.k.a. "the marginal value of leisure") was equal to the wage rate. If a producer changes his production process by using an extra hour of labor, the price he must pay for that labor, its cost in dollars, is also the cost to the worker of working the extra hour, its cost in value. By paying the worker his wage, the firm transfers the cost to itself. The worker is neither better nor worse off as a result of working the extra hour (and being paid for it), and the firm is worse off by the amount it has paid. The same analysis applies if the firm uses an hour less of labor—the money saved by the firm is just equal to the value to the worker of the extra leisure he gets. The analysis also applies to the other factors of production, as described in Chapter 14.

What about inputs for which the alternative to consumption by the firm is consumption by individual consumers—apples that can either be turned into applesauce or eaten as apples? Each consumer consumes a quantity of apples for which the marginal value of the last apple is just equal to its price, so if he eats one less apple (because the firm has bought it to make applesauce), the loss of value to him is the same as the dollar cost to the firm. The situation with regard to apples is the same as with regard to labor. If the firm buys an hour of my leisure, I reduce my consumption of leisure by an hour; the cost of doing so is my marginal value of leisure, which in equilibrium equals the price of leisure: my wage. The same is true with apples if we substitute "apples" for "leisure" and "price of apples" for "wage."

This implies that the total cost to the firm of any method of production—any set of inputs—is equal to the sum of the disvalues involved in producing (or not consuming) those inputs. So a change that lowers (dollar) cost also lowers the total value cost of producing the goods—the disvalues of producing the inputs—and a change that increases dollar cost also increases the total disvalues. It follows that a change that raises total cost as measured by firms and changes nothing else must also be a Marshall worsening.

One possibility I have not yet considered is that if the industry uses an additional unit of input, it might get it by bidding it away from some other industry. If the steel industry chooses to use more labor, that may mean not that workers have less leisure but that some workers move from producing autos to producing steel.

What is the cost to the auto industry of losing a worker? It is the worker's marginal revenue product: the increase in output, measured in dollars, from employing him. That, as we saw in Chapter 9, is equal to his wage. His wage is what the steel industry must pay to get him. So the cost in dollars to the firm hiring the input is again the same as the cost in value elsewhere; this time, the loss of value takes the form of lost output in another industry rather than of lost leisure to the worker.

The same argument applies to the other factors of production as well. A firm that increases its use of land by building one-story factories instead of three-story ones does not impose any cost on the land—land does not, like labor, consume its own leisure. It does impose a cost on whoever else is, as a result, not able to use the land. That cost is equal to the rent the firm must pay for the land. A similar analysis holds for a firm that increases its consumption of capital at the expense of other firms.

I have now shown that cost of production as measured by the firms in dollars they spend is the same as the total loss of value from their use of their inputs. Since the competitive industry produces its output at the minimum cost in dollars, it also produces it at the minimum cost in value. So any change in how it produces that quantity of output (everything else held fixed) must be a Marshall worsening.

Shuffling Money. One element in my proof of the efficiency of a competitive equilibrium that may have confused you is the way in which many of the arguments seemed to ignore money payments. I described the cost of an extra hour of labor as its marginal disvalue to the worker, but I then went on to say that the worker was no worse off, since he was paid for his time. I calculated costs and benefits to consumers Uno and Duo by looking at the area under their *MV* curves rather than by looking at their consumer surplus—the area under the curve and above price. I described the cost to a firm of producing an extra unit as *MC*, while ignoring the income it got from selling that unit.

All of these features of the proof have the same explanation. A transfer of money from one person to another is neutral in terms of the Marshall criterion, neither a gain nor a worsening. One person gains by a dollar, another loses by a dollar. The only way we can produce improvements or worsenings is by changing what happens with goods: how they are produced, how much of them is produced, who gets them. So when calculating net gains or losses in order to discover whether something is a Marshall improvement or a worsening, we can ignore flows of money.

In discussing the effect of reallocating goods to consumers, for example, I assumed that Uno and Duo continued to pay the same amount of money to the producer as before: The bureaucrat-god simply took one unit of the good from Uno and gave it to Duo. Since there was no transfer of money involved, Uno lost the value of the good to him and Duo gained its value to him.

I could just as easily have assumed that the bureaucrat-god took a unit of the good from Uno and gave it to Duo while at the same time taking P dollars from Duo and giving them to Uno; that would correspond to ordering Uno to buy one fewer good and ordering Duo to buy one more, both at the price P. In that case, Uno would have lost his consumer surplus on one unit (area B_1 on Figure 16-2a) while Duo gained his (negative) consumer surplus on one unit (he loses area B_2 on Figure 16-2b). He loses because he is buying units for more than they are worth to him, making him worse off than if he did not have to buy them. As you should be able to see from the figures, the net loss if we do it this way, $B_1 + B_2$, is the same as $A_1 - A_2$ on Figures 16-1a and 16-1b, which was the loss when there was no transfer of money. A_1 is $AP + B_1$ and A_2 is $AP - B_2$; so AP, the amount of money transferred, cancels, giving us $A_1 - A_2 = B_1 + B_2$.

The same explanation applies to the other cases that may seem puzzling. If a worker is ordered to work another hour and is not paid for it, his cost is equal to his MV of labor. If he is paid for the hour, the cost is transferred to whoever pays him. Net cost is unaffected—we are simply shuffling money.

The same rule of ignoring money payments because they have no effect on what is or is not a Marshall improvement takes care of another problem that may have occurred to you. If a firm decides to increase its consumption of labor, one effect is that a worker works an additional hour. Another effect is that wages rise a little—that is why the worker increases the number of hours he chooses to work. That small increase in wages can be ignored by the firm, since as a price taker it finds the effects of its actions on the prices of the things it buys to be negligible. But for the industry as a whole, or the economy as a whole, that small

Figure 16-2

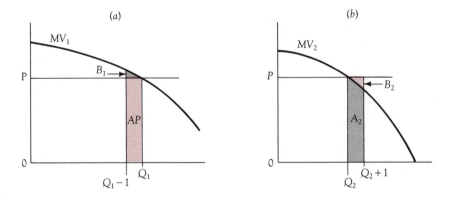

Effect of ordering Uno to buy one unit less and Duo one unit more. AP is the amount spent for one unit; B_1 is the consumer surplus loss to Uno and B_2 the consumer surplus loss to Duo as a result of the change.

increase in the wage rate must be multiplied by all of the hours worked by all workers—and the result may not be negligible. Should I not take that into account in calculating the costs and benefits that result from increasing the firm's input of labor by one unit?

The answer is no. The increase in wages is a transfer between the sellers and the buyers of labor. Each dollar that one person loses, someone else gets. There is no net gain or loss, hence no effect on whether the change is or is not a Marshall improvement. Such "pecuniary externalities" will be discussed in Chapter 18.

One problem with a proof of this sort is that I must present calculus arguments in verbal and graphical form. Strictly speaking, much of the analysis should be put in terms of infinitely small changes: working an extra second rather than an extra hour or consuming one millionth of an apple more or less. Since any large change can be broken up into an infinite number of infinitely small changes, a proof showing that each small change makes things worse also implies that large changes do so. Putting things that way is a good deal harder in a verbal argument than in a mathematical one, but the failure to limit ourselves to infinitesimal changes occasionally introduces errors or confusions into the argument.

It would be possible to give a precise verbal statement of the proof that a competitive equilibrium is efficient, but it would make the proof considerably more difficult than it already is. The proof as given is, I think, sufficiently precise to give you a clear understanding of why the result is true. Readers who feel comfortable with calculus may find it of interest to try to translate the proof into that more precise language.

Competitive Layer Cake. So far, I have described an economy in which there is only a single layer of firms between the ultimate producers and the ultimate consumers. Most real economies are more complicated than that. Many of the outputs of firms—steel ingots, typewriters, railroad transport—are inputs of other firms. While this makes the situation harder to describe, it does not change its essential logic, nor does it invalidate our conclusion that a competitive equilibrium is efficient.

To see why, we will start one layer up from the bottom. Consider an industry that buys its inputs from their original owners (workers, landowners, owners of capital) and produces as output a good used as an input by another firm. The price at which it sells that good equals its marginal cost of production; as we have shown, this is the same as the ultimate cost to those who give up the inputs used in producing it. So when a firm one layer further up uses that good in its production process, the price it must pay for the good is equal to the disvalues involved in producing the good, just as it would be if the good were one of the factors of production instead of something produced by another firm. So our proof of the efficiency of competitive equilibrium applies to the second layer of industry too. We can repeat the argument for as many layers as necessary, thus showing that the whole competitive layer cake is efficient.

A number of other simplifications also went into our argument. One, which has hardly been mentioned so far, is the assumption that each firm produces only one kind of good. Dropping that would make things considerably more complicated and would introduce an interesting set of puzzles involving **joint products** (things produced together, such as wool and mutton, or two metals refined from the same ore), quality variations among goods, and the like, many of which you may encounter in more advanced texts. It would not change the result.

What about introducing the complications of time and uncertainty that were discussed in Chapters 12 and 13? As I explained there, the effect of time in a certain world can be taken into account by doing all calculations using present values of future flows of revenue, cost, and value. Having done so, we could reproduce the proof we have just gone through and so demonstrate that a competitive equilibrium was efficient in a changing (but perfectly predictable) world.

Efficiency in an uncertain world is a more complicated issue, for two reasons. The first is that, in evaluating outcomes in an uncertain world, we must be careful to specify just what the bureaucrat-god is assumed to know–what sort of "perfect" economy we are using as our benchmark. If the bureaucrat-god knows the future and the real participants in the market do not, he can easily improve on their performance. But in defining the bureaucrat-god, we assumed that he had all of the information any person had, and only that information. That implies that he, like bureaucrats in the real world, has no better a crystal ball than the rest of us. The efficiency proof then holds in an uncertain world as well as in a certain one.

There is another sort of problem introduced by uncertainty that takes us beyond the bounds of this chapter. So far, we have ignored **transaction costs**, the costs of negotiating contracts, arranging to buy and sell goods, and the like; the only exception was the discussion of bilateral monopoly in Chapter 6. In order to get an efficient outcome in an uncertain world, one must assume that firms can buy and sell a very complicated set of goods—there must be a complete set of markets for **conditional contracts**. An example of a conditional contract would be my agreement to give you 1,000 gallons of water next year if the price of grain was above $2/bushel and rainfall in Iowa was less than 14 inches.

Such conditional contracts are useful in an uncertain world—you may be an Iowa farmer who only wants the water if both of those conditions hold. But the assumption that there are markets for all of the conditional contracts one can imagine and that on all of those markets transaction costs are negligible is implausible. It is far more implausible than the assumption that in a certain world, where we know what is going to happen next year, there are markets for all goods and that transaction costs on those markets are negligible. Here, as elsewhere, the introduction of transaction costs may invalidate proofs of the efficiency of a competitive equilibrium—or other arrangements. Inefficiencies connected with transaction costs will be discussed at somewhat greater length in Chapter 18.

Competitive Efficiency—Summing Up

At the end of Chapter 15, I raised the question of whether efficiency might be an unreasonable standard for judging real-world economies. You are now in a position to see to what degree that is or is not true. I have shown you how a set of institutions—competitive markets—can generate an efficient outcome, in the full sense in which the term is used in Chapter 15—an outcome that cannot be improved by a bureaucrat-god. I have also, I hope, given you some feeling for why that is only an approximation, although not a wildly unreasonable one, of a real economy.

Throughout the argument, I have assumed that everyone concerned—firms, owners of the factors of production, and consumers—is a price taker. If even a single participant in the market is not, then somewhere in the chain of argument a link fails and we can no longer prove efficiency.

As you may suspect from the amount of space I have spent on this discussion and the number of different things from different chapters that have fed into it, the efficiency of a competitive market is an important result. Insofar as one is interested in using economics to improve the well-being of mankind, it is probably the most important single result of economic theory. While we cannot expect any real-world economy to fit the requirements of the proof precisely, many economies, or at least many parts of many economies, come close enough to make us suspect that they are very close to being efficient—closer than under any alternative institutions. Where the assumptions necessary to prove efficiency break down, as in the case of the price-searching firms discussed in Chapter 10, understanding why the failure of the assumption leads to a failure of the proof is the obvious starting point for anyone who wishes to figure out how the situation could be improved.

MONOPOLY

So far, we have been analyzing the efficiency of the outcome of a competitive industry, an industry in which all participants are price takers. We will now consider the case of a monopolistic industry. Just as in Chapter 10, we will start with a single-price monopoly and then go on to more complicated cases.

One of the difficulties in teaching (and learning) economics is that many students start out believing they already know it. The subject is the world we all live in, and many of the words are ones whose meaning everyone already knows. It is easy to forget that a term such as "efficient" or "competitive," when used in economics, is a technical term with a meaning quite different from the same term used in ordinary conversation.

One of my favorite examples of this problem is the sentence "Monopoly is inefficient." The natural response of a student hearing or reading that sentence is, "Of course; I already knew that. Monopolists are rich and lazy; they have no competitors to put pressure on them, so they run their firms badly."

As you will see shortly, rich and lazy monopolists running their firms badly have nothing at all to do with what an economist means when he says that monopoly is inefficient. Indeed, in the sense in which "efficient" is used in ordinary conversation, economic theory suggests that monopolies should be just as efficient as competitive firms. It is only in the very different sense of "efficient" discussed in the previous chapter that we have reasons to expect at least some kinds of monopolies to be inefficient—not because the monopolist runs his firm badly, but because he runs it well.

Single-Price Monopoly

Consider the firm whose marginal cost, marginal revenue, and average cost are shown on Figure 16-3, along with the demand curve for its product. It costs the firm $1,000 to produce any widgets at all and $10/widget for each additional widget it produces, so its fixed cost is $1,000/year and its marginal cost is $10/widget. Since the firm has positive

Figure 16-3

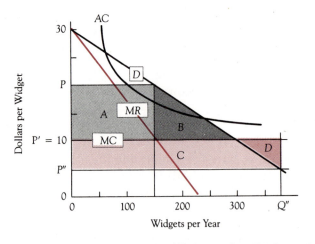

The profit-maximizing price (P) and the efficient price (P') for a single-price monopoly. Lowering the price from P to P' lowers the monopoly's profit by A but increases consumer surplus by A + B for a net gain of B. A further reduction to P'' would cost the monopoly C + D and benefit consumers by C, for a net loss of D.

fixed cost and constant marginal cost, average cost is lower the more the firm produces; the more widgets it is divided among, the lower the fixed cost per widget. The result is a natural monopoly; the larger the firm, the lower its average cost. As we saw in Chapter 10, the firm maximizes its profit by producing a quantity for which marginal revenue equals marginal cost.

Is this efficient? Our proof of the efficiency of a competitive industry involved three parts: efficient allocation of output, efficient production of output, and efficient quantity of output. So far as allocation is concerned, the proof applies to the single-price monopoly as well; it, like a competitive industry, sells its goods at the price for which quantity demanded equals quantity produced. Any reallocation of the existing quantity of output must transfer a good from someone to whom it is worth at least its price to someone to whom it is not, so it must be a Marshall worsening.

The proof also holds with regard to production efficiency. If the firm could produce the same quantity of output at a lower cost it would, since a reduction in cost would increase profits. Nor can the cost of production be lowered by a change in the number of firms. Since we are starting out with only one firm, any reduction means no firms and no output. Since the firm is a natural monopoly, any increase in the number of firms must raise average cost. So the monopoly industry is efficient both in how it allocates its output and in how it produces it.

What about the quantity it chooses to produce? The firm charges a price P at which $MC = MR$, since that maximizes its profit. If it lowered its price to $P' = MC = \$10$/widget, its profit on the 150 widgets per year that it had been selling for a price P would decline by the area A, since it would be selling those widgets for a price of only P'. At a price of P', it would also be producing and selling an additional 150 widgets per year, for a total of 300. It would neither make nor lose money on those additional widgets, since they would each cost \$10 to produce (MC) and would each be sold for \$10.

The drop in price would benefit consumers by area A plus area B— the increase in their surplus. Area A is the savings on the widgets they would have bought at the old price; area B is the consumer surplus on the additional widgets. Since the change benefits the consumers by more than it costs the producer, the decrease in price from P to P' is, on net, an improvement.

Would lowering the price even further improve things even more? No. A further price change to $P'' = \$5$/widget, as shown in Figure 16-3, would cost the producer an amount equal to the area of the entire colored rectangle $C + D = Q'' \times (P' - P'')$ and benefit consumers by the lightly colored area C; there would be a net loss equal to the area D. You should be able to convince yourself that at any price above or below $P' = MC$, net benefit is less than at P'. The efficient arrangement is for the monopoly to charge a price equal to marginal cost.

The same argument can be made verbally without using the figure. As long as price is above marginal cost, there are people who value an additional widget at more than it would cost to produce it; producing that additional widget and giving (or selling) it to such a person produces a net benefit. If the price were below marginal cost, some people would be consuming widgets that were worth less to them than the cost of production; reducing the production and the consumption of such a person by one widget would produce a net benefit. So we get an efficient outcome only with price equal to marginal cost. This is the same rule that defines the efficient price for a competitive industry.

But while price equal to marginal cost maximizes net benefit, it does not maximize the monopoly's profit; if the monopoly shown on Figure 16-3 sold at $10/widget ($MC$), it would just cover its variable cost and lose $1,000/year of fixed cost. It prefers to charge price P, corresponding to a quantity for which marginal cost equals marginal revenue, instead of $P' = MC$. So a single-price monopoly will charge an inefficiently high price—not because the monopolist does not know how to maximize his profit, but because he does.

A competitive firm, on the other hand, charges a price equal to marginal cost; the same argument shows that that is the efficient arrangement. It would seem to follow that there is an efficiency gain to breaking up a single monopoly firm into many small firms.

A glance at AC on Figure 16-3 should convince you that that is wrong; if the firm is broken up into ten smaller firms, average cost will be much higher and the price will go up instead of down. Not only that, but the situation will be unstable. Since average cost falls as output increases, one of the firms will expand, driving (or buying) out the others. We will then be back where we started, with a single monopoly firm.

What the demonstration does imply is that if the cost curves are consistent with competition, as in Figures 16-4a and 16-4b, a competitive industry results in a greater net benefit than a monopoly. This is an argument not against natural monopolies but against government-enforced monopolies (or cartels) in naturally competitive industries, such as trucking or agriculture. In Figure 16-4a, the average cost for a large firm (producing Q_2) and a group of small firms (producing Q_1 each) are the same, so the loss resulting from a government-enforced monopoly is the loss of the area B, the consumer surplus on the goods that would be produced if the industry were competitive and sold at marginal cost but are not produced when it is a monopoly. In Figure 16-4b, the large firm has larger costs than the small, as we would expect in a naturally competitive industry, so there is the additional loss of the area B', equal to the difference in average cost between five small firms and one large one times the monopoly output.

The same analysis also demonstrates the undesirability of artificial monopoly and so provides an argument in favor of government antitrust measures designed to discourage it. I argued in the optional section of Chapter 10 that attempts to establish artificial monopolies, monopolies formed and maintained in industries where a monopoly firm has no

Figure 16-4

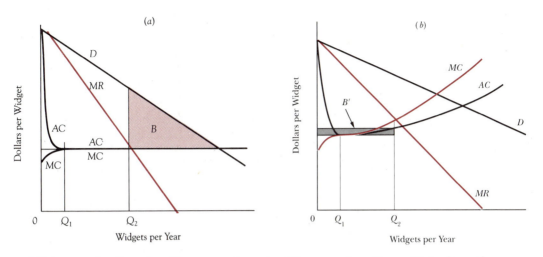

Efficiency gains from breaking up an "unnatural" monopoly. Figure 16-4a shows the case where a large firm has the same average cost as a small firm; B is the gain from increased output when the industry becomes competitive. Figure 16-4b shows the case where cost is larger for a larger firm; breaking up the monopoly then also reduces total production cost for the first Q_2 units by B'.

advantage in production costs over a smaller firm, are unlikely to succeed. If that conclusion is correct, there is no need for antitrust laws to prevent them; if it is wrong, the argument for the inefficiency of monopoly is an argument for antitrust.

What about the hard case: the natural monopoly illustrated in Figure 16-3? The government could pass a law requiring the firm to sell at a price equal to marginal cost—but the firm would respond by going out of business, since at that price it is losing money.

One solution is for the government either to regulate the monopoly or to run it, charging a price equal to marginal cost and making up any loss out of tax revenues. This leads to a number of additional problems.

Regulation and the Second Efficiency Condition. In the previous section, I demonstrated one efficiency condition for a monopoly: Price equals marginal cost. That condition determines how much a monopoly should produce, since price (and the demand curve) determines quantity. There is a second efficiency condition, which determines whether the monopoly should produce anything at all. Figure 16-5a shows cost curves and a demand curve for a firm whose fixed cost is so great that average cost is always above the demand curve. Whatever quantity of output it chooses, its average cost of production will be higher than the price at which it can sell that quantity. Such a firm will never come into

Figure 16-5

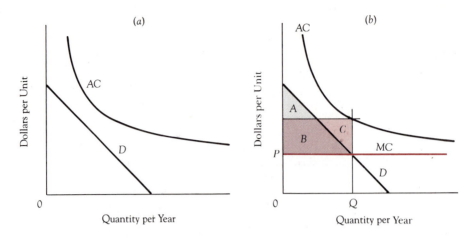

A natural monopoly that cannot cover its costs. Since for any quantity of output, AC is above the price that quantity sells for, a single-price monopoly cannot cover its costs. If such a monopoly operates and sells at $P = MC$, $A + B$ is the gain to its customers and $B + C$ the loss to the monopoly firm.

existence, or if it does (due to an error), it will go out of business as soon as its owners recognize the situation.

Should such a firm come into existence? Will net benefit be higher if it exists? That depends. If it produces a quantity Q at price $P = MC$, as shown on Figure 16-5*b*, the firm will lose its fixed cost and its customers will gain their consumer surplus. If the consumer surplus is larger than the fixed cost, there is a net benefit (although the firm still loses money); if the consumer surplus is less than the fixed cost, there is a net loss. Our first efficiency condition was "Price equals marginal cost"; our second is "Produce only if, at the quantity for which price equals marginal cost, consumer surplus plus profit is positive" or, in other words, consumer surplus is larger than the loss to the firm, if any.

Looking at a graph such as Figure 16-5*b*, how can one tell whether the loss to the firm is more or less than the gain to its customers? We know that if the firm exists, it should produce quantity Q. If it does, consumer surplus will be the shaded triangle $A + B$. On average, the firm makes $P - AC$ on each of Q units; since P is less than AC, it is losing the colored rectangle $B + C$. If $A + B$ is larger than $B + C$, or in other words if A is larger than C, the firm is producing a net benefit. If C is larger than A, it produces a net loss.

A private, profit-maximizing monopoly will only produce when profit is positive (or zero), in which case profit *plus* consumer surplus must be positive. So it will never produce when, according to the second efficiency condition, it should not. It may, however, fail to produce when it should—if profit is negative but the loss to the firm is less than the gain to its customers. In addition, as pointed out above, such a firm will not meet the first efficiency condition, since it will set marginal revenue equal to marginal cost instead of price equal to marginal cost.

Can a government-owned or government-regulated monopoly do better? It is not obvious that it can. There are two sorts of problems that it faces. First, there are problems associated with getting the regulatory agency to do what it "should" do. There is no obvious reason to expect the commissioners of a regulatory agency, or the official in charge of a government monopoly, to have any more interest in maximizing net benefit than the owner of a private monopoly. Regulators may well find it in their interest to regulate a monopoly in some way other than that recommended by economists. They might choose to allow the monopoly to make large profits in exchange for political contributions to the incumbent administration or future high-paying jobs for the regulators, or they might force the monopoly to provide service at a price below marginal cost in order to buy popularity with consumer-voters at the expense of the monopoly firm's stockholders. A regulator, or an official running a government monopoly such as the U.S. Post Office, is presumably trying to maximize some combination of private benefit to himself and political benefit to the administration of which he is a part; it is not obvious that he does either by maximizing net benefit to producers and consumers.

Government regulation or ownership of monopolies is what economics textbooks have traditionally offered as the cure for the efficiency problems of private monopoly. What is wrong with this traditional analysis is that it treats the owners and managers of a private monopoly as part of the economic system, acting to achieve their own objectives, but treats government officials as if they were benevolent bureaucrat-gods, standing outside the system. There seems no good reason for such an asymmetrical treatment of the two alternatives. In Chapter 19, we will see the results of including government within our analysis, applying the same assumptions to the participants in the political market as to the participants in the ordinary market.

Suppose, however, that the regulators do have the best of intentions; their only objective is to maximize net benefits by forcing the firm to follow the prescription of the two efficiency conditions: Charge marginal cost, provided that at that price net benefit is positive. They will find it difficult to do so.

In order to keep the regulated firm of Figure 16-5 in business, someone, presumably the government, has to make up the firm's losses: the difference between what it costs the firm to produce its output and what it is allowed to sell it for. If the government simply provides a subsidy equal to the difference between the regulated firm's revenue and its costs, the management of the firm has no incentive to keep down costs—especially the cost of things that can be used to make the life of management easier. If, instead, the regulatory agency estimates what marginal cost and average cost ought to be and offers the firm a fixed subsidy to cover the difference (while ordering it to sell at marginal cost), the firm has an incentive to misrepresent its cost function so as to make average cost appear as high as possible. This will either permit the firm to charge a price higher than the true marginal cost (if it makes marginal cost appear larger than it is) or get the firm a larger subsidy (by making the difference between average cost and marginal cost appear larger than it is). The regulators must come very close to running the firm themselves if they are to guarantee both that price equals marginal cost and that the total cost for producing whatever level of output can be sold at that price is as low as possible.

Suppose we assume these problems away too; we assume not only that the regulatory commission is trying to maximize net benefit but also that it knows the firm's cost curves. Even under these rather implausible assumptions, there is still a problem with the conventional regulatory solution to natural monopoly.

The problem is the second efficiency condition. The combination of marginal cost pricing plus a subsidy to cover the resulting loss will permit a monopoly to stay in business even if it does not meet the second efficiency condition—even if its costs are larger than the value to its customers of what it produces. In order for the regulatory agency to subsidize only those monopolies that should stay in business, it must know not only the cost curves of the firm but also the demand curve for its output, so that it can calculate what consumer surplus will be if the firm sells at marginal cost. If the consumer surplus is less than the required subsidy, the firm should be allowed to go out of business. But all the agency can observe directly is one point on the demand curve: quantity demanded at a price equal to marginal cost. That point gives very little information about consumer surplus; through the same point, one can draw two demand curves (D_1 and D_2 on Figure 16-6), one of which yields

Figure 16-6

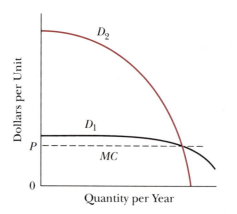

Two different demand curves that result in the same quantity demanded at $P = MC$.

almost no consumer surplus at a price equal to marginal cost and one of which, at the same price, yields a very large consumer surplus.

Can the regulatory agency determine the demand curve by asking the monopoly's potential customers how much they would buy at each price? Not if the customers are rational. However much the customers say they would pay, if the monopoly produces, they will only be charged marginal cost. It is in their interest to have the monopoly produce, since the customers receive all the benefit and pay only a small part of the taxes for the subsidy; so it is also in their interest to lie about how much it is worth to them, exaggerating the figure in order to induce the agency to subsidize the monopoly.

It seems that even a benevolent and well-informed regulatory agency faces a nearly insuperable problem in deciding which monopolies should be subsidized in order to keep them in business. An unregulated single-price monopoly may sometimes face a very similar problem. Consider the case of an unregulated railroad deciding whether to build a new rail line, and contrast it to the case of a regulatory agency deciding whether to subsidize the construction of a new rail line. The regulatory agency wants to maximize total value; the unregulated monopoly wants to maximize its profit. Each, in order to achieve its goal, must first estimate demand and then decide whether the rail line should be built.

There is one important difference between the two cases. The unregulated monopoly discovers, after the line is built, whether its decision was correct; there either is or is not some price at which the monopoly can make a profit on the new line, and it soon learns which. Since it can recognize success and failure, it can continually improve whatever techniques it uses to estimate demand; crudely speaking, if it builds a line and loses money, it can fire the market researchers who told it to build the line. The regulatory commission has no comparable test; even after the line is built, the commission never learns whether the line was worth building, since all the commission observes is quantity demanded at price equal to marginal cost.

Nationalized Monopoly.   It is sometimes suggested that the government, instead of regulating natural monopolies, should nationalize them and run them itself "for the public good." This solves one of the problems of regulated monopoly. The regulatory agency no longer has to duplicate the work of management in order to get the information necessary to regulate; now the agency *is* the management of the firm. It does not solve the incentive problem; it is by no means obvious that the interests of the managers of a nationalized firm, or of the politicians who appoint them, are the same as the interests of the population as a whole. Nor does it solve the problem of satisfying the second efficiency condition.

There is at least one important respect in which both regulation and nationalization may be worse than unregulated single-price monopoly. So far in this chapter, I have described natural monopoly as if it were an all-or-nothing matter. In fact, there are many intermediate points between perfect competition and natural monopoly, and the location of a particular industry along that continuum may change. In the case of an unregulated natural monopoly, if conditions change so that it becomes possible for smaller firms to enter the industry successfully, they will do so; the monopoly will gradually break down. If the industry is regulated or nationalized, the regulatory agency or the nationalized industry may use the force of law to control or prevent new competitors, thus converting the industry into a government-enforced monopoly. An example is the regulation of transportation by the Interstate Commerce Commission. In the absence of regulation, the transportation industry would have become competitive when trucking developed as a major competitor to rail transport, since large trucking firms have no important advantage in production cost over small ones. The ICC regulated—and to a considerable degree cartelized—the trucking industry in order to protect its original regulatees, the railroads.

Discriminatory Monopoly: The Solution?

So far, we have only considered single-price monopolies; we will now shift to the opposite extreme and consider a perfectly discriminating monopoly. Since it can sell at different prices to different customers, or sell to a single customer at a range of prices, it always pays the monopoly to produce and sell to any customer who is willing to pay, for one more unit, more than its marginal cost. So it sells the same amount, to the same people, as it would if it were selling at marginal cost.

The difference is that what would be consumer surplus for the single-price monopoly selling at marginal cost becomes revenue for the perfectly discriminating monopoly. Since the monopoly is collecting the sum of producer and consumer surplus, it is in the monopoly's interest to maximize that sum; so a perfectly discriminating monopoly satisfies both the first and second efficiency conditions! The information needed to satisfy the second efficiency condition—the shape of the demand curve—is part of the information that a firm needs in order to be a perfectly discriminating monopoly. And unlike the regulatory commission, the firm, having made an estimate of the shape of the demand curve, tests it by its pricing scheme. If, for example, the firm uses two-part pricing (per widget plus entry fee), an overestimate of consumer surplus will result in too high an entry fee and no customers.

This result holds only for a perfectly discriminating monopoly. Monopoly with imperfect price discrimination not only fails to produce an efficient outcome, it may produce a worse outcome than single-price monopoly. Since it charges different prices to different customers, it, unlike a single-price monopoly, allocates its output inefficiently. If two customers paying different prices each buy up to the point where price equals marginal value, the high-price customer will value his marginal unit more than the low-price customer, so a transfer from low-price to high-price customer would produce a net benefit. This inefficiency in allocation may or may not be balanced by an increase in output, relative to what would be produced without price discrimination, depending on the details of the situation.

Rent Seeking

The arguments I have given so far suggest that a perfectly discriminating monopoly, insofar as it is feasible, is the ideal solution to the problem of natural monopoly. It is ideal in that it maximizes total value, although it does so in a way that gives all the net value resulting from the monopoly's activities to the monopoly instead of leaving some of it with the customers. If we look at this situation from a point of view sufficiently broad to give the same weight to the interests of the stockholders of the monopoly firm as to those of its customers, the only defects to this solution seem to be the considerable difficulties in actually running a perfectly discriminating monopoly.

There is another and more profound difficulty with this solution. A perfectly discriminating monopoly, or even an ordinary single-price monopoly, receives profits above and beyond the normal return on capital. Firms therefore compete to become monopolies. If we consider such competition as itself an ordinary profit-maximizing economic activity, we expect that a firm will be willing to spend, in the attempt to become the monopoly, anything up to the full value of the expected profits. Insofar as this expenditure does not produce anything for anyone (aside from getting that firm, instead of another firm, the monopoly), it is sheer waste. If the firm consumes the full value of the monopoly in the process of getting it, and if, as in the case of perfectly discriminating monopoly, that value is the entire value to all concerned from the existence of the industry (consumer plus producer surplus), then the private perfectly discriminating monopoly, rather than being the best possible solution to the problem of natural monopoly, is the worst. The industry generates no net value to anyone.

This point can be clarified by an example. Suppose there is a certain valley into which a rail line could be built. Further suppose that whoever builds the rail line first will have a monopoly; it will never pay to build a second rail line into the valley. To simplify the discussion, we assume that the interest rate is zero, so we can ignore complications associated with discounting receipts and expenditures to a common date. Assume that if the rail line is built in 1900, the total profit that the railroad will eventually collect will be $20 million. If the railroad is built before 1900, it will lose a million dollars a year until 1900, because until then, not enough people will live in the valley for their business to support the cost of maintaining the rail line. Lastly, suppose that all of these facts are widely known in 1870.

I, knowing these facts, propose to build the railroad in 1900. I am forestalled by someone who plans to build in 1899; $19 million is better than nothing, which is what he will get if he waits for me to build first. He is forestalled by someone willing to build still earlier. The railroad is built in 1880—and the builder receives nothing above the normal return on his capital for building it.

This phenomenon—the dissipation of above-market returns in the process of competing to get them—has recently become known as **rent seeking**. It is a new and somewhat complicated subject; the results are not always as perverse as in this example. One can, for instance, add the additional assumption that there exists a strip of land that controls the only potential rail access to the valley. In this case the $20 million profit, instead of being dissipated by building the railroad early, goes to the person who owns that strip of land and auctions it off to the highest bidder—who then waits until 1900 to build his railroad, making perfect discriminatory pricing again the perfect solution to the problem of natural monopoly.

The analysis of rent seeking suggests that, at least under some circumstances, monopoly profit is not a transfer to the firm from its customers but a net loss. The higher the monopoly profit, the more resources the firm will burn up (by, in our example, premature construction of the railroad) in the process of getting it. If so, perhaps the best solution to the problem posed by monopoly is not regulation but taxation—taxation not of output but of profit.

Suppose the government imposes a 50 percent tax on the economic profit of a monopoly. Since the firm still gets 50 cents out of every dollar of profit, it is still in its interest to make profit as large as possible; so it behaves exactly as it would without the tax—produces the same quantity at the same price. Since the tax has no effect on the behavior of the firm, there is no excess burden. If the firm would otherwise have spent the present value of its anticipated monopoly profit in gaining the monopoly, then the knowledge that it will get only half as much will cut in half the amount it spends in rent-seeking behavior—the railroad, in our example, will not be built until 1890. In this case, the tax not only has no excess burden, it has no burden at all! What the government collects would otherwise have been wasted in premature construction.

The most obvious difficulty with this proposal is that in order to tax something you must first be able to identify it, and monopoly profit is easier to identify on a figure in a textbook than in the real world. A firm that appears to be making large profits may be a successful monopoly, but it may also be a firm in a competitive industry that gambled on a new product or a more efficient method of production and won. If profits above the market rate are automatically identified as a sign of monopoly and taxed accordingly, one result will be to reduce the incentive for such innovations.

There is an elegant solution to this problem. Suppose we know in 1900 that, starting in 1920, the American aluminum industry will be a natural monopoly. Let the government auction off the monopoly—the right to produce aluminum after 1920—to the highest bidder. Aspiring monopolists should be willing to bid up to the full present value of the future monopoly profits, so the government will have collected a 100 percent tax on monopoly profits, as estimated by the (prospective) monopolist.

This solution again has a problem—it depends on our being able to identify natural monopolies, and to do it even before they exist. If we guess wrong, we have just auctioned off a monopoly of a potentially competitive industry, and thus produced a governmental monopoly with its associated costs.

Even if we could identify natural monopolies correctly, it is not clear we would. The arguments of the last few paragraphs could, after all, provide elegant camouflage for a government that wanted to create monopolies, either as a source of revenue or in exchange for political support by favored firms and industries. It is worth remembering that the term "monopoly" originated in just this context—to describe otherwise competitive industries, such as the sale of salt, where one producer had bought from the government the right to exclude all others.

The Problem

The great mistake in most discussions of the problem of natural monopoly is the assumption that the problem is monopoly. The problem is a particular kind of production function: one for which minimum average cost occurs at a quantity not much less than the total amount of the good produced and sold. A single-price private unregulated monopoly is one (imperfect) solution to the problem posed by such a cost curve. It is imperfect because although it is efficient in the sense of producing a given quantity of output at the lowest possible cost, it is inefficient in both the quantity it produces (too low) and its decision of whether to produce at all (sometimes it will not when it should). Regulated private monopoly is another imperfect solution, one that may do better than unregulated private monopoly with regard to quantity but worse with regard to least-cost production, and that is less likely to disappear when and if the problem disappears. Government-run monopoly is yet another imperfect solution, with many of the same problems. Perfectly discriminating monopoly, to the extent it is possible, is an elegant solution that avoids the defects of the other solutions only to introduce a potentially worse defect in the form of rent seeking.

Patents and Efficiency

In several places in the text, you have been told that a single-price monopoly is inefficient; since it sells at a price above marginal cost, there will be some customers willing to pay more than the cost of production who do not get the good. If the monopoly lowered its price to MC and increased production accordingly, there would be a transfer from it to its present customers plus a net gain on the increased production.

This is true for the monopoly resulting from a patent or copyright, just as for other monopolies. The owner of a patent or copyright charges a licensing fee to the producer for each unit produced; this raises the price above the true marginal cost, since part of the cost the producer pays on each unit is simply a transfer to the inventor. The marginal cost of the inventor's contribution is zero; it costs no more to invent something of which a million will be manufactured than something of which one will be manufactured. So patents result in the same sort of inefficiency as other monopolies.

Just as with other monopolies, one way of eliminating this inefficiency is discriminatory pricing. Assume that is not practical. Before condemning patents and arguing that all license fees should be set to zero, you should remember that there are two efficiency conditions. One determines the optimal quantity of a good to produce if it is produced at all, the other whether it should be produced. If license fees are zero, which is the appropriate marginal cost, inventors have no incentive to invent (except to the extent that they can keep the invention secret or take advantage of having it first). This is one of the problems with government regulation of monopoly: If the monopoly must charge MC, it does not pay it to operate at all. If the government solves the problem by offering to pay the fixed cost (or the inventor's salary), government has the problem of deciding which goods are worth producing or which inventions are worth trying to invent.

PROBLEMS

1. In analyzing competition, single-price monopoly, and efficiency we have noted a number of equalities involving price, marginal value, marginal revenue, marginal cost, and average cost. Which equality or equalities:
   a. Are implied by a firm, in a competitive market, choosing to produce the quantity that maximizes its profit?
   b. Are implied by a single-price monopoly choosing the quantity that maximizes its profit?
   c. Are implied, in a competitive industry, by the ability of firms to enter the industry if economic profits are positive or leave if they are negative?
   d. Are implied by a rational consumer on a competitive market choosing the quantity to purchase?
   e. Are necessary for efficiency?

2. Figures 16-7a through 16-7c show average cost, marginal cost, and demand curves for three industries. Answer the following questions for each figure:
   a. If the industry is a single-price monopoly, will it choose to exist?
   b. If it is a perfectly discriminating monopoly, will it choose to exist?
   c. Should it exist (in the sense of Marshall)?
   d. Suppose the government auctions off the right to be the single firm in the industry. How much will it get if the firm is to be a single-price monopoly? A perfectly discriminating monopoly?

Figure 16-7

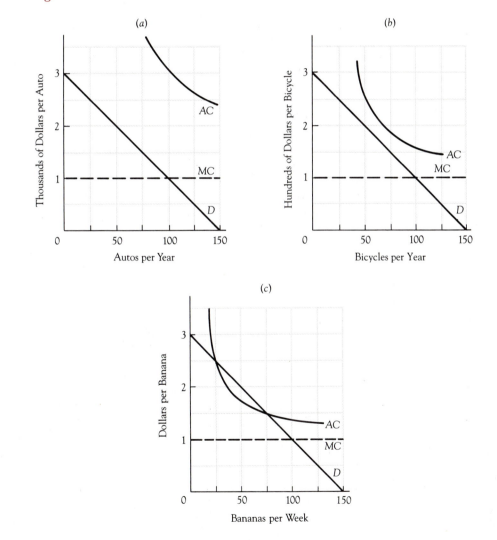

Three monopoly firms—Problems 2 and 3.

You may assume that the interest rate is 10 percent and that the curves shown are expected to remain the same forever.

3. In each of the cases shown on Figures 16-7a through 16-7c, how large is the net loss (to consumers, producers, and government) if the firm operates as a private, profit-maximizing, single-price monopoly (or, if it cannot cover its costs, does not exist) instead of following the rule for efficient production suggested in this chapter?

   By "net loss" here, I mean the number of dollars per year that, divided in some way between producers and consumers, could leave them exactly as well off with the private monopoly as they would be without the extra money but with an efficient monopoly. Note that one way of dividing $100 between me and you is to give me $200 and take $100 from you: $200 + (−$100) = $100.

4. Figures 16-8a and 16-8b show two alternative sets of cost curves that the Minnokarp fish farm might face. Answer the following questions for each:

   a. If the firm is a monopoly and cannot price discriminate, how much does it produce? What is the price?
   b. If the government put the firm out of business, how much worse off would the consumers be?
   c. At what price and quantity would a bureaucrat-god want the fish farm to produce?

5. Much of the United States became private property through homesteading. Whoever first claimed the land and worked it for a fixed number of years owned it. As the frontier moved west, any particular piece of land was first not worth farming (costs higher than benefits),

Figure 16-8

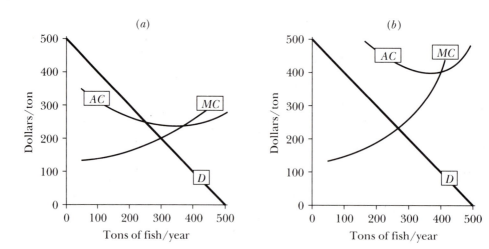

Demand and cost curves for Minnokarp fish farm—Problem 4.

then just worth farming, and then more than worth farming (benefits higher than costs). Under the homesteading law, at what point in this process would settlers start to farm the land? What can you say about the efficiency of this way of turning over the land to private ownership? Compare it to the alternative of auctioning off the land and using the income to reduce taxes.

6. Do you think that this book was sold to you at a price equal to the marginal cost of producing it? If not, would you be better or worse off if there were a law requiring publishers to sell books at marginal cost? Discuss.

7. We have not discussed the efficiency of monopolistic competition or oligopoly. Do you think they are efficient? Justify your answer.

FOR FURTHER READING

Two interesting discussions of rent seeking are:

Terry Anderson and P. J. Hill, "Privatizing the Commons: An Improvement?" *Southern Economic Journal*, Vol. 50, No. 2 (October, 1983), pp. 438–450.

Gordon Tullock, "The Welfare Costs of Tariffs, Monopolies and Theft," *Western Economic Journal*, Vol. 5 (June, 1967), pp. 224–232. This is, so far as I know, the first and best analysis of rent seeking.

chapter 17

MARKET INTERFERENCE

PRICE CONTROL

So far, we have analyzed markets in which price is free to move to the point at which quantity supplied equals quantity demanded. That may not be true if the government imposes a legal maximum or minimum price, or both. If the price control is binding—meaning that the supply/demand equilibrium price is above the maximum or below the minimum permitted—we have a new situation.

You cannot consume something unless someone produces it, so even under price control, quantity consumed and quantity produced must be the same (except in the short run, when you can consume stocks of the good accumulated in the past). If the quantity consumers wish to consume is greater than the quantity producers wish to produce, some mechanism other than price must allocate the limited supply.

In Chapter 2, I briefly discussed one such situation: price control on gasoline. I shall now redo that argument more precisely, using some of what you have learned since.

The Gasoline Paradox

Figure 17-1 shows demand (*D*) and supply curves for gasoline; they intersect at a price of $1/gallon and a quantity of 20 billion gallons per year. The government imposes price control on gasoline; the maximum price is $0.80/gallon. At that price, producers only want to pump, refine, and sell 17 billion gallons per year, but consumers want to buy 26 billion. Consumers cannot, for very long, use 9 billion gallons per year more than is being produced; gas stations rapidly run out of gasoline. When they do so the cost of gasoline goes up, even though its price does not.

How? One way of making sure you get as much as you want of the limited supply is by getting up early in the morning and arriving at the station shortly after the tank truck leaves. If everyone tries to do that, the result is a long line. Having to wait in line raises the cost of gasoline

Figure 17-1

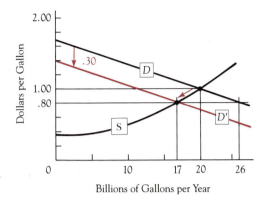

The effect of price control on gasoline. Price control at $0.80/gallon produces a shortage; quantity demanded is larger than quantity supplied. Lines grow until their cost shifts demand down to D'. Consumers are paying $0.20/gallon less in money and $0.30/gallon more in time.

to the consumer, adding a **nonpecuniary cost** (a cost in some form other than money, in this case, time) to the cost he is already paying in money.

Increased costs due to price control will come in other forms as well. One example is uncertainty—you can never be sure of getting gas when you want it. Every time you take a long trip, you risk being stranded in Podunk. Another additional cost (in time) is making more frequent visits to the gas station in order to be sure your tank is always full. Another may be bribes to the station owner. In at least one case during the gasoline shortage created by the price control of the early seventies, a prominent figure bought his own gas station in order to be sure he and his friends would get gas.

It does not matter, for the present argument, exactly what form the additional cost takes, although it is convenient to think of it, as in the discussion of Chapter 2, in terms of waiting in lines. All we need in order to analyze the effect of price control is the assumption that the additional cost is proportional to the amount of gasoline used (the more you use, the more times you have to wait in line to fill your tank) and is the same for all users. Given those assumptions, we can analyze the effect of price control, using techniques that we developed in Chapter 7 to analyze the effect of taxes.

If I must pay $0.80 in money plus $0.30 in waiting time and other inconveniences for each gallon of gasoline I buy, I will buy the same amount as I would if the price were $1.10/gallon ($0.80 + $0.30). The additional cost is equivalent to a $0.30/gallon tax on consumers; like such a tax, it shifts the demand curve down by $0.30, as shown on Figure 17-1. The time I spend in line is a cost to me but not a benefit to the producers of gasoline; they are still receiving only $0.80/gallon. The effect, on quantity produced and on the welfare of consumers and producers, is the same as if we had simply imposed a $0.30/gallon tax. The only difference is that none of the loss comes back as government revenue.

Thirty cents is not a number picked at random. As you can see on the figure, a $0.30 shift in the demand curve is just enough to make quantity demanded equal quantity supplied at the controlled price. If the cost (of lines and other inconveniences) to the consumers was less than $0.30, quantity demanded would still be more than quantity supplied. The attempts of individuals to compete against each other for the limited supply would drive the cost up further; in the simple example, lines would grow longer.

The startling thing about this analysis is that price control at a below-market price has not only, as one might expect, injured the producers, it has also raised the cost of gasoline to the consumers—by $0.10 / gallon. This result does not depend on the details of the diagram. As long as the supply curve slopes up, price plus nonpecuniary cost with price control must be more than price without, although the amount of the increase depends on the relative slopes of the supply and demand curves. In Figure 17–1, the supply curve is twice as steep as the demand curve. Since price determines how much is produced, it is the height of the supply curve at the equilibrium quantity; since cost, pecuniary plus non-pecuniary, determines how much consumers want, it is the height of the demand curve at the equilibrium quantity. As you move left on the figure, the demand curve rises $0.50 for every $1.00 the supply curve falls, so the increase in total cost to the consumers due to price control is half the reduction in price.

The analysis does depend on my assumption that the additional cost is, like a price or a tax, a per-gallon cost—that the increase in the marginal cost of gasoline to the consumer is the same as the increase in the average cost. Usually when we discuss costs to consumers we are talking about prices; the price of a gallon of gasoline is both the marginal cost to you of buying one more gallon of gasoline and the average cost of all the gasoline you buy. That may not always be the case for nonpecuniary costs.

Rationing

To see why this is important, consider a system of gasoline rationing. The price of gasoline is set at $0.80/gallon, and each year everyone receives ration tickets allowing him to buy 85 percent of what his annual consumption of gasoline was before price control. Anyone who tries to buy more than his ration is shot. Average cost for buying rationed gas is now only $0.80/gallon, but marginal cost beyond the rationed amount is very high—your life for the first pint. People buy until marginal cost equals marginal value—which happens at a quantity equal to what they have ration tickets for, since at that point marginal cost abruptly increases.

Figure 17-2

The cost of gasoline under rationing. The consumer can purchase at the controlled price 85 percent of what he consumed before price control; additional purchases are illegal.

The situation, for one consumer, is shown in Figure 17-2. The analysis (consumer buys up to that point at which marginal cost equals marginal value) was first done in Chapter 4; the only change is that marginal cost of gasoline to the consumer is no longer independent of quantity and no longer necessarily equal to price.

Once we allow the marginal cost of gasoline to the consumer (which determines how much he buys) to differ from the average cost (which determines how much he pays for it), our proof that price control must injure the consumer is no longer valid. That does not mean that price control plus rationing will necessarily benefit the consumer. He gets gasoline at a lower price, but he also gets less gasoline. He is better off if the shaded area $A + C$ in Figure 17-3 (consumer surplus after price control plus rationing) is greater than the area $A + B$ (consumer surplus without price control) and worse off if it is less.

In more complicated real-world cases, one should also take account of the cost of running and enforcing a rationing scheme and adjusting it to a changing world. During the period of price control and gasoline shortage in the seventies, gasoline was not rationed to individuals but was rationed to regions, on the basis of past consumption; the Department of Energy, in effect, decided how much went where. It has been argued that part of the shortage was caused by the resulting misallocation; the formula used did not take proper account of population movements that were altering the relative demands of different areas of the country.

Gasoline price control—and gasoline shortages—are for the moment only memories, but other forms of price control are still with us. One of the most common, rent control, provides an interesting case for discussing the distinction between allocational and distributional effects.

Figure 17-3

Gains and losses to the consumer caused by price control with rationing.
Consumer surplus is *A* + *B* before price control and *A* + *C* after; the consumer
is better off under price control if *C* > *B*, worse off if *C* < *B*.

DISTRIBUTION VS ALLOCATION

Economists find it useful to distinguish two sorts of issues, to which they
have given the confusingly similar names of "allocation" and "distribution." **Allocation** is the allocation of goods to people (I get a car with
manual transmission; you get a car with automatic transmission; he gets
a bicycle: who gets what) or of particular inputs to producing particular outputs (make it this way instead of that way). **Distribution** is the
distribution of real income, including both pecuniary and nonpecuniary
benefits (who gets how much). Noneconomists tend to think of issues as
distributional: If cars are sold on the market, rich people get them and
poor people do not; if we have private schools, rich kids get educated
and poor kids don't. Economists tend to think of issues as allocational:
Consider two people with the same income but different tastes. Let cars
and education both be sold. One person buys a car and no education;
one buys education and no car.

Economists tend to focus on allocational issues not because distribution is unimportant but because they have less to say about it. Allocational
changes typically do—or at least can—benefit (or harm) everyone, so we
can evaluate them without worrying about how to balance gains to one
person against losses to someone else. Distributional changes are just the
opposite. Pure redistribution (I lose a dollar; you gain a dollar; there are
no other effects) is neither a gain nor a loss in Marshall's sense. Efficiency
is unaffected, and efficiency is the least unsatisfactory criterion we have
for judging what is or is not an improvement.

Consider, as a humble example, the common household rule: You made the mess, you clean it up. In any single case, its effects are distributional, since it determines who has to do a particular unpleasant task. Over the long run, however, the distributional effect averages out (unless some members of the household are inherently much messier than others); its main effect is to give people who might make messes an incentive not to do so, and thus produce a more efficient allocation of effort to preventing messes.

Rent Control

One example of the distinction between allocation and distribution and of the difficulty in changing one without affecting the other is rent control. Suppose the city government of Santa Monica decides to impose rent control and sets the maximum rent for each apartment below what its market level would be. The obvious effect is distributional: landlords are worse off and tenants are better off. The less obvious effect is allocational. At the controlled rent, quantity of apartments demanded is higher than quantity supplied (since at the market rent they were equal). If you are already occupying a rented apartment, you have a good deal; if you are looking for an apartment to rent, you have a problem.

Normally, as families change, they move. A young couple has children and moves from a four-room to a six-room apartment; an older couple moves from a six-room to a four-room apartment after the children leave home. But suppose that, under rent control, the older couple has a six-room apartment for (say) $600/month; controlled four-room apartments rent for $400, and at that price the couple would be happy to move, since the additional rooms are no longer worth $200 to them. But since quantity demanded at the controlled price is larger than quantity supplied, there are no four-room apartments for rent in Santa Monica. Uncontrolled four-room apartments outside of Santa Monica rent for $600. The couple stays in the six-room apartment even though it has two rooms more than they want.

The same problem exists for people who would normally move from a four-room apartment in one part of town to an apartment the same size but in a different location—perhaps because they have changed where they work. If rent control remains in effect for a long time, where people live becomes determined more and more by where they used to live and less and less by where (size and location of apartment) it is now appropriate for them to live. This is an allocational problem: It makes some people worse off without making other people better off.

There is a simple solution. Allow tenants to sublet their apartments—for whatever rent they can get. There will now be two rents for any apartment: the controlled rent ($600 for a six-room apartment in the example we have been discussing) and the rent that a sublessee would pay the original tenant ($800, say), which is what the market rent would have been in the absence of rent control. The cost to an elderly couple of remaining in their six-room apartment is not $600 but $800. If they moved out, they would not only save $600 in rent for themselves, they would also make an additional $200 by continuing to pay rent at $600 and subletting to someone else at $800. Hence they are willing to pay (say) $600 to someone who will sublet a four-room apartment to them, just as (if there were no rent control) they would have been willing to move from an $800 apartment (six rooms) to a $600 apartment (four rooms).

What the combination of rent control plus uncontrolled subletting has done is to permit a free market in apartments while giving the original tenant part ownership of the apartment that he occupied when rent control was imposed. In effect, the tenants of the six-room apartment are quarter owners; if they choose to sublet, they receive $800; three fourths of that goes to the landlord as rent and one fourth they keep. This appears to be a way of producing a *distributional* effect (which may be "desirable" for political or other reasons) without any undesirable *allocational* effects.

There are several problems with this. The first is that landlords have almost no incentive to maintain their apartments. In an uncontrolled market, it pays the landlord to make any repairs or improvements that are worth more to the tenant than they cost; he can expect to get the money back in increased rent. Under rent control, all that matters to the landlord is that the apartment be in sufficiently good shape to command the controlled rent. If (as in the example) that is three fourths of the market rent, he can let the apartment deteriorate to three fourths of its previous market value at no cost to himself. The fall in its market rent will all be paid for by his original tenants. If they live in the apartment themselves, they will pay by living in a deteriorated apartment (or maintaining it themselves); if they sublet it to someone else, the deterioration will lower the difference between the rent they pay the owner and the rent they receive from the sublessee.

When rent control has been in effect for a while, apartments start to deteriorate; this results in laws (if they do not already exist) specifying how landlords must maintain apartments. A system of uncontrolled rents in which the landlord was led by his own interest to make those repairs and improvements that were worth making has been replaced by a system of rent control in which uniform standards are set and enforced in order to force landlords to do things that it is no longer in their interest to do voluntarily.

An allocational problem also arises with regard to new construction. Rent control means, in effect, that part of the value of a new apartment building is automatically given to the first set of tenants; they get to rent the apartment from the landlord at the controlled price and to the sublessees at an uncontrolled price. That discourages construction. The obvious solution is to make rent control apply only to buildings that already exist and exempt new construction.

But the same forces that made it politically profitable to impose rent control on existing housing this year (while promising not to control new housing) can be expected to make it profitable, five years hence, to impose rent control on the buildings built during that interval—while promising to leave future construction uncontrolled. Unless the politician not only promises that new housing will not be controlled but also finds some convincing way of committing himself, forcing himself to keep the promise in the future whether or not he still wants to, builders may not believe his promise—and not build. Even if the politician can bind himself, that may merely mean that, five years hence, he will be defeated by another politician running on a platform of controlling the "unfairly" uncontrolled new buildings.

Price Control: A Summary Schema

Figure 17-4 shows demand and supply curves for a good whose price is controlled; P_c is the controlled price. To avoid having to shift lines around on the figure, we use a trick introduced in Chapter 7, when we were analyzing the effect of taxes. The supply curve shows quantity produced as a function of price received by the producer; the demand curve shows quantity consumed as a function of cost—price plus nonpecuniary costs—to the consumer.

We begin with price control and no rationing. Lines (or other nonpecuniary costs) grow until they are large enough to reduce quantity demanded to quantity supplied. The nonpecuniary costs are shown on the graph as the difference between price received by the producer and

Figure 17-4

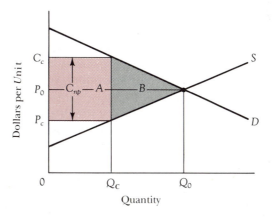

Costs associated with price control. *B* is a net loss of surplus due to reduced quantity produced and consumed. *A* is the nonpecuniary cost if there is no rationing. It is the total market value of ration tickets if there is rationing with transferable tickets.

cost paid by the consumer: C_{np} on Figure 17-4. The cost of the good to the consumer is the sum of the controlled price and the nonpecuniary cost: $C_c = P_c + C_{np}$. Quantity falls from Q_o, the quantity at the market price, to Q_c, the quantity supplied by the producers (at a price of P_c) and demanded by consumers (at a price of C_c). The net loss as a result of price control is area B (loss of consumer and producer surplus on goods no longer produced) plus area A (nonpecuniary costs per unit—time waiting in lines and the like—multiplied by the number of units consumed) plus any costs of administering and enforcing the controls.

We now add a rationing system such as that shown in Figure 17-2. Each consumer receives a fixed number of ration tickets, proportional to his previous year's consumption. In order to buy one unit of the good, say one gallon of gasoline, he must pay one ration ticket plus the controlled price of the good.

Under this system, the lines disappear, so the nonpecuniary cost A is eliminated, but new costs are introduced because of the misallocation produced by the rationing system. If, for example, I have just moved from the suburbs to the city, my ration of gas—my previous year's consumption times the ratio of current production to last year's production—is as much as I want at P_c. If the price were any higher, I would not use my full ration. You, on the other hand, have just moved from the city to the suburbs and are desperate for gas. Since your allocation—that same fixed fraction of your previous year's consumption—is far less than you want, you would gladly pay several times the controlled price to get additional gallons. Since I am consuming gas that is worth more to you, we have an inefficient allocation. This time the inefficiency is not only in how much is produced but also in who gets it.

In an ordinary market, producers have an incentive to maintain the quality of their products in order to sell them. Under price control, quantity demanded is greater than quantity supplied; producers find that they can save money by producing a lower quality product and still sell as much as they want at the controlled price. The price control system may be able to prevent some of the more obvious ploys, such as selling three-quart gallons at $0.80/gallon, but it is hard to measure and control less obvious dimensions of the product, such as the courtesy and quality of the service provided with the gasoline or the cleanliness of the station's rest rooms. So another cost of price control will be a level of quality below what customers would be willing to pay for on an uncontrolled market—just as one cost of rent control is that landlords no longer have an incentive to maintain their buildings.

Figure 17-4 shows total demand as a function of price; in order to show the effects of inefficient allocation among consumers, we would need to know their individual demand curves and allocations. There is no way to tell from Figure 17-4 how large the resulting loss is; it depends on how accurately the rationing scheme fits the actual demands of the consumers. Net loss resulting from rationing is now area B plus an unknown additional loss due to misallocation among consumers and inefficiently low quality, plus the costs of running and enforcing the rationing system.

There is an easy way to eliminate the misallocation: Make the ration tickets marketable. If you want gasoline more than I do, I sell you some of my ration. Under such a system, ration tickets have a market price; at that price, anyone can buy or sell as many as he wishes. Just as for any other good, the price of the ticket will be that price at which quantity supplied equals quantity demanded. The cost of buying gasoline is then the price of gasoline plus the price of a ration ticket. This is obviously true for consumers who use more than their ration and must buy additional tickets: If they want another gallon of gasoline, they must buy both the gasoline and the ticket. It is equally true for consumers who use some of their ration tickets and sell the rest. By consuming a gallon of gasoline from their own ration, they give up the opportunity to sell a ration ticket. The cost to them of consuming the gallon is then its price, P_c, plus the price they could have gotten for the ration ticket they used in buying it.

We know that the quantity of gasoline supplied is Q_c. The cost to the consumer at which that quantity is demanded is C_c on Figure 17-4. Since the cost to the consumer is the price of the gasoline plus the price of the ration ticket, it follows that the price of the ration ticket is C_{np}—what the non-pecuniary cost would have been without rationing. The price of the ration ticket is serving exactly the same function that the cost of waiting in line served before: reducing the quantity of gasoline that consumers demand to the quantity producers supply. The area A is now equal to the market value of the ration tickets: the number of tickets times the value of one ticket. The net cost is the area B plus costs associated with inefficiently low levels of quality (for gasoline sold at the controlled price) plus any costs of administering and enforcing the rationing.

Aside from adminstrative costs, the system is precisely equivalent to a tax of C_{np} imposed on producers, with the revenue from the tax distributed to consumers in proportion to their previous year's consumption—the same way that the ration tickets are distributed. In both cases, the price received by the producers, the controlled price in the one case or the market price net of tax in the other, is P_c. In both cases, the cost to the consumers of a gallon of gas is C_c. In the one case, consumers get ration tickets with a market value of C_{np} dollars each; in the other case, they get an equivalent amount of money.

Why is it that rationing systems usually do not permit individuals to buy and sell ration tickets? Perhaps because that would make the effect of price control plus rationing more obvious—and harder to defend. It is fairly easy to argue that, as a matter of justice, national hardships should be borne by everyone—that if there is "not enough" gasoline, everyone should be allowed to have as much gas as he "needs" and no more—and that the gasoline companies should not be allowed to profit from the shortage. That is a (favorable) description of price control plus a simple rationing system. It is much harder to argue for the peculiar system of taxes and subsidies described in the previous paragraph—which is equivalent to a rationing system after it is improved by making the ration tickets transferable. Yet it is hard to see how one can argue against making ration tickets transferable, since that change benefits everyone: buyers (who get additional tickets for less than they are worth to them) and sellers (who give up tickets for more than they are worth to them).

Can one improve rationing even further in order to eliminate the lost surplus B? Perhaps. The solution is to ration production as well as consumption. Producers must sell a quantity Q_c at the controlled price to consumers with ration tickets; any additional production sells at the market price to anyone who wants it (no tickets required). The quantity producers produce depends on their marginal revenue, which is now equal to the market price (since that is the price at which additional units can be sold), so output expands up to Q_0, the old uncontrolled output. Having a ration ticket allows you to buy gasoline at the controlled price instead of the market price, so the price of a ticket is the difference between the two prices: $P_0 - P_c$. The system has become a pure transfer of producer surplus to the consumers—very much like the transfer of consumer surplus to the producer under perfect discriminatory pricing. The details of who actually pays are complicated; they depend on how the production ration is divided up among producers and how new producers are treated.

During the oil price control of the 1970s, the U.S. government used such a system of production rationing to control the sale of crude oil to refineries. "Old oil," meaning oil produced by conventional methods from wells that were already producing, was controlled at a low price. "New oil"—oil from new wells, or additional oil produced from old wells in expensive ways, or imported oil—was uncontrolled (the system was actually somewhat more complicated; this is only a rough sketch). Of course, all refiners wanted to buy cheap old oil instead of expensive new oil, so the government rationed the old oil. The rationing rule used was that refiners got allocations of old oil proportional to the total amount of oil they refined. So for each barrel of uncontrolled foreign oil the refiner used, he was entitled to buy a certain amount of cheap, price-controlled domestic oil. These allocations were transferable ration tickets like those discussed above, and were valuable. The government was, in

Section IV   Judging Outcomes

effect, paying refiners to import foreign oil, with the payments coming out of the revenue of the domestic (old) oil producers—a peculiar way of reducing America's dependence on foreign oil.

Back in Chapter 9, we saw that firms in a competitive industry earn no economic profit; if they did, more firms would enter the industry, driving down price and thus profit. The producer surplus of the industry goes not to the firms but to the owners of inputs, such as land or labor. If price control transfers income from the industry to consumers, it must ultimately come not from the firms but from the owners of inputs. In the case of the oil industry, the distinction is in part an artificial one, since oil wells, which are an important input, generally belong to oil companies. What price control of oil expropriated was not the economic profit of the oil companies but part of the quasi-rent that the stockholders of the oil companies were receiving from their past investments in finding and drilling oil wells.

So far, I have considered the distinction between distributional and allocational effects of government decisions in the context of price control; the same distinction is relevant to other issues. Just as in the case of price control, the noneconomist is likely to perceive the issue as purely distributional, the economist as mostly allocational.

Liability Rules

One example of this is the issue of who should be liable for injuries caused by defective products. Consider two liability rules: *caveat emptor* and *caveat venditor*. *Caveat emptor* (Latin for "let the buyer beware") means that the seller or producer is not responsible for defects in his product; *caveat venditor* ("let the seller beware") means that he is.

One's first instinct is to suppose that if the law changes from *caveat emptor* to *caveat venditor*, consumers gain (and producers lose) the amount the producers have to pay the consumers to compensate them for defective products. But this conclusion depends on a hidden assumption: that the change in the law will not affect the price at which the goods are sold. That is most unlikely; the new legal rule raises the cost to the producer (when he sells the good, he becomes liable to pay if it is defective) and the value of the good to the consumer. Both the supply curve and the demand curve shift up, so the price must rise.

One's next guess might be that there is no effect at all—the consumers, on average, pay in higher prices just as much as they receive for defective products. This is closer but still not quite right. If the producer is liable for defective products, that gives him an incentive to make the product better. If the consumer is liable, that gives him an incentive to treat the products more gently and to take more precautions to minimize the cost of accidents: wearing safety glasses while using power tools, for instance.

To the extent that the consumer knows how good products are before he buys them, the first incentive is unnecessary—even if the producer is not liable, he will still try to avoid defects in order to make consumers willing to buy his product. Just as in similar cases discussed earlier, the producer will find it in his interest to make any improvements in quality that are worth more to the consumers than they cost him to make, since he can more than cover the additional costs with the increased price the consumers will be willing to pay for the improved product. But to the extent that the cost to consumers of evaluating the products they buy is high enough that they choose to buy in partial ignorance, the incentive provided to the producer by *caveat venditor* may serve a useful purpose.

This seems to imply that the rule should be *caveat emptor* where the main danger is from careless use by the consumer or where the consumer can readily inform himself of the quality of the good. It seems to imply that the rule should be *caveat venditor* where the consumer cannot readily judge quality and the best way to avoid problems is for the producer to produce better goods.

A still better solution is the combination of either *caveat emptor* or *caveat venditor* with freedom of contract. Suppose the rule is *caveat emptor*, and further suppose that consumers would much prefer to buy under a rule of *caveat venditor*, even at a price that compensated the producers for the cost of that rule. In that case, producers will find that selling their product with a guarantee (at a higher price) is more profitable than selling it without a guarantee. In effect, the producer who offers a guarantee is converting the rule for his product into *caveat venditor*—he is voluntarily making himself liable for product defects.

Suppose instead that the rule is initially *caveat venditor*. The consumer can, if he wishes, convert it to *caveat emptor* in exchange for a lower price—by signing a waiver in which he agrees not to sue. One area where such waivers could make a very large difference is in medical malpractice. Given the high cost of malpractice suits and malpractice insurance, a doctor might offer a much lower price to a patient who signed an agreement not to sue—or even an agreement only to sue in case of gross negligence. Under present law, unfortunately, such a waiver is unenforceable; the patient can sign it before the operation then "change his mind" and sue anyway. That is one example of the general movement of our legal system in recent decades away from freedom of contract, a change that some critics regard as a major cause of the "liability crisis"— the recent sharp increase in the size and frequency of liability suits and the cost of liability insurance.

ALLOCATION, DISTRIBUTION, AND THE EFFECTS OF INTERVENTION IN THE MARKET

In discussing gasoline price control, I assumed that all consumers were affected alike by the nonpecuniary costs resulting from a below-market price. A more realistic description would allow for the difference between the cost of waiting in line to a busy professional and the cost to a student who can study while waiting. The nonpecuniary cost must still be high enough to drive quantity demanded down to quantity supplied, but it does so by imposing low costs on some customers (and reducing the quantity they demand only slightly) and high costs on others. The average effect is to injure consumers of gasoline (the increase in nonpecuniary costs is greater than the decrease in price), but there may be many individual exceptions.

Similarly, under rent control, tenants who start with rent-controlled apartments are benefited at the expense of landlords, at least until and unless the apartments are allowed to deteriorate substantially; those who move into the area later, or wish to move from one apartment to another, are injured. There is an obvious distributional transfer from landlords to tenants and a less obvious allocational loss—resulting from misallocation of people to apartments, inefficient levels of construction and maintenance of apartments, and the like.

The same is also true of the change from one liability rule to another. The particular consumer who is injured by an exploding Coke bottle may be better off under a rule of *caveat venditor*—but the consumers who are not injured must pay a higher price because the legal rule raises the producer's cost, the value of the product to the consumer, and hence the supply curve, the demand curve, and the equilibrium price. So they are worse off as a result of *caveat venditor*. As in the case of gasoline price control, consumers and producers are, on average, worse off as a result of the rule—or of a rule imposing *caveat emptor*. Both groups would be benefited by freedom of contract.

What these examples suggest is that the effect of market interference is almost the opposite of what one might at first think. One would expect the effect to be mostly distributional, with price control, rent control, or *caveat venditor* benefiting buyers at the expense of sellers. In fact, it is mostly allocational; the restrictions have as their main effect a less efficient allocation of resources, a smaller pie to be divided up. Such distributional effects as do occur are (except in the rent control case) mostly among consumers and among producers rather than between producers and consumers.

Why is it that rent control, unlike price control of gasoline, has substantial distributional effects? There are two reasons. One is that the supply of housing is, in the short run, very inelastic; landlords do not start tearing down apartment buildings when rents fall by 10 percent. The short-run effect of rent control on the supply of housing is small compared to the effect of gasoline price control on the supply of gasoline.

The other reason is that the tenant who has an apartment when rent control is imposed is like the purchaser of gasoline under a rationing system. He can consume a certain amount of housing and no more (use the apartment he is presently renting) at the controlled price. The additional costs that reduce quantity demanded to quantity supplied affect him only when he wants to move to another apartment. In the short run, rent control is accompanied by a built-in system of rationing: Allocate each apartment to the tenant presently living in it. In the very long run, the case of rent control is the same as the case of price control on gasoline—but the short run is long enough so that many individuals benefit for a period of years and sometimes decades, which may explain why it is more popular than most other forms of price control.

DISTRIBUTION VS ALLOCATION: THE PROGRESSIVE INCOME TAX

In discussing rationing, we found it useful to distinguish between costs that were, like prices, proportional to the amount purchased and costs that were not. In discussing taxes in Chapter 7, I assumed that the tax you paid on something was proportional to the amount of it you bought or sold. That is true of most sales taxes, but it is not true of income taxes in the United States at present.

Under a **graduated income tax**, your income is divided into brackets, each with a different tax rate. In a **progressive** system, the higher the bracket, the higher the rate. In a **regressive** system, the higher the bracket, the lower the rate. While "progressive" sounds as though it means something good and "regressive" something bad, the terms are simply descriptions of two sorts of graduated taxes: one in which rates rise (progress) with income and one in which they fall (regress).

The graduated income tax system of the United States at present is progressive. To simplify the discussion, I will consider a progressive system with a simpler set of brackets and tax rates than we actually have. The first bracket will be from 0 to $10,000/year, the second from $10,000/year to $20,000/year, and the third from $20,000/year up. You pay nothing on income in the first bracket, 40 percent on income in the second, and 80 percent on income in the third.

So if your income is below $10,000/year, you pay no tax; if it is between $10,000/year and $20,000/year, you pay 40 percent of any income above $10,000/year. If you make $25,000/year, you pay 40 percent of your income in the second bracket (0.40 × $10,000/year = $4,000/year) plus 80 percent of your income in the third bracket (0.80 × $5,000/year = $4,000/year), for a total tax of $8,000/year.

An alternative that has been widely discussed is a **flat-rate tax**. In its purest form, this means that everyone pays a fixed percentage of his income. In considering the effect of shifting from one system to the other, we will discuss first allocational and then distributional effects.

Allocation

One way of eliminating distributional effects in order to focus on allocational ones is to analyze a situation in which everyone is identical. Suppose, to start with, that everyone has an income of $25,000/year.

Under the graduated tax, everyone is paying $8,000/year, which is 32 percent of his income. What would happen if the graduated system were replaced by a flat rate of 32 percent? Would people be better or worse off?

If your answer is "They are paying the same amount in taxes as before, so the change has no effect," you have not yet finished learning to think like an economist. Once people have adjusted to the new tax system, they will be paying more taxes than before—and they will be better off!

Just as the sales taxes analyzed in Chapter 7 affected the amount producers sold and consumers bought, so an income tax affects the amount of their leisure that workers choose to sell. Suppose the wage rate is $10/hour. Under the graduated system, with everyone in the 80 percent bracket, an individual who chooses to sell more leisure—to work more hours—receives only $2 for each extra hour worked; the other $8 goes to the IRS. An individual who sells less leisure—works fewer hours—loses only $2 for each hour less he works. We showed in Chapter 5 that a rational individual chooses to work a number of hours such that the marginal value of his leisure (alias the marginal disvalue of labor) is equal to the wage he receives for working. So each individual works up to the point where the marginal disvalue of one more hour is $2/hour.

Under the new flat-rate tax system, the marginal (and average) tax rate is only 32 percent instead of 80. An individual who works an extra hour at $10/hour receives $6.80 of extra income. After the tax law changes, every worker increases the amount he works (increases the amount of his leisure that he sells, decreases the amount he consumes himself) until the marginal value of his leisure rises from $2/hour to $6.80/hour. The workers are working more hours, receiving more income, paying more in taxes, and are better off.

They are making more because they are working more hours. They are paying more in taxes because 32 percent was the flat rate that would have yielded the same amount as the previous system of rates if incomes had stayed the same. Incomes have risen, so 32 percent of the new income is more than the amount produced by the old system. They are better off not simply because they have more money—that must be balanced against the additional hours they are working—but because each person has chosen an outcome, a bundle of a certain amount of income plus a certain amount of leisure, that he prefers to what he had before.

How do I know that? Under the new system, each individual could choose to work the same number of hours as before and pay the same tax—that, after all, is how the tax rate was calculated. That he does not choose to do so demonstrates that he now has an alternative he prefers. To put the argument more formally, the old optimal bundle is still in his new opportunity set; the fact that it is no longer optimal means that the new opportunity set contains a bundle he prefers to it.

If we now readjust the tax rate (down) so that everyone ends up paying the same tax as under the graduated system ($8,000/year), people are even better off. The flat-rate system now yields government the same revenue while giving every taxpayer an outcome (28 percent, say) that he prefers to the outcome under a flat rate of 32 percent—which he preferred to the old system. The change is not only a Marshall improvement, it is even (under our assumption that everyone is identical) a Pareto improvement.

So far, I have presented the argument in words. Figure 17-5 is a translation of part of it into geometry—specifically, the geometry of budget lines and indifference curves. It shows the alternatives available to an individual who works 250 days a year at \$10/hour; each hour/day he works increases his income by \$2,500/year. B_p is his budget line under the initial system of progressive taxes. If he works for 4 hours a day (consumes 20 hours/day of leisure) he pays no tax, so he can consume all of the \$10,000/year that he earns. On the next \$10,000, he pays 40 percent. By working 8 hours/day instead of 4 he increases his income to \$20,000 but his consumption to only \$16,000; the extra \$4000 goes in taxes. His optimum is at point A, where B_p is tangent to indifference curve U_1. He chooses to work 10 hours/day, pay \$8000 in taxes, and consume \$17,000.

Figure 17-5

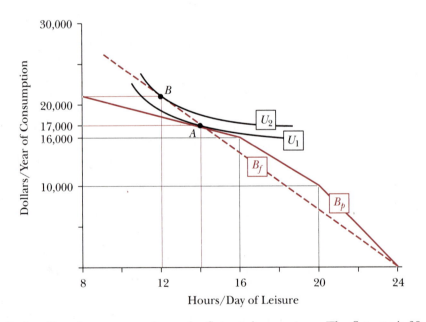

Budget lines for a progressive and a flat-rate income tax. The flat rate is 32 percent, which would bring in the same amount of money as the progressive tax if the taxpayer worked the same number of hours under both. In fact, under the flat-rate tax, the taxpayer works more hours, pays more tax, and is better off.

B_f shows his situation under a flat-rate tax of 32 percent. If he does not work at all he will have no consumption, so B_f, like B_p, intersects the horizontal axis at 24 hours/day of leisure. If he earns exactly $25,000/year he will pay $8000 in taxes and consume $17,000, just as under the graduated system; so B_f goes through point A.

Since B_f at A has a steeper slope than B_p it must intersect U_1 as shown, being above U_1 to the left of A and below it to the right. It must therefore be tangent to another and higher indifference curve: U_2 at point B. Since U_2 is above U_1, the taxpayer is better off under the flat-rate system. Since the two systems yield the same taxes at point A and B is to the left of A (less leisure, more labor, more income) the taxpayer at B under the flat-rate system is paying more taxes than at A under the progressive system. He is working more hours, paying more taxes, and on a higher indifference curve.

Some Complications

In proving this result—that a flat-rate tax is unambiguously superior to a progressive tax if all taxpayers are identical—I have skipped over a number of complications. The most important is the effect of the change in the tax law on the wage rate. Unless the demand for labor is perfectly elastic, one effect of an increased supply of labor (everyone is working more hours because of the change in the tax law) will be a fall in the wage rate. A full analysis of the effects of the change would have to take this into account, just as the analysis of the effect of taxes in Chapter 7 included the resulting change in price.

Including that effect would not change the essential result, however; it would simply transform some of the gain from producer surplus (going to the sellers of labor) to consumer surplus (going to the buyers). If everyone is identical, everyone ends up with an equal share of consumer and producer surplus. The analysis would be a little more complicated, but the net effect would still be a gain.

A further complication is the fact that selling leisure is not the only way of getting income; there are other factors of production. The same argument would apply to them as well. An income tax reduces the landowner's incentive to rent out his land, since if he consumes it himself (lives on it) he will get his return in an untaxed form, just as the worker avoids taxes by consuming his leisure instead of selling it. The effect is larger the higher the tax rate. In the same way, an income tax reduces the individual's incentive to save, since part of the interest on his savings will go to the government instead of to him.

One could imagine a variety of other complications as well. So far as I know, none would alter the result. The essential logic of the situation is quite simple. In deciding whether to earn an additional dollar of income, the relevant consideration is how much of that dollar the income earner will be able to keep, so it is the **marginal tax rate**—the rate paid on each additional dollar of income—that determines how much the taxpayer chooses to earn. Under a progressive system, the marginal rate must be higher than the average rate, hence higher than the flat rate that would yield the same revenue from the same income. From the standpoint of efficiency, the optimal rate is zero, since at a tax rate of zero the individual sells his leisure (or anything else) if and only if its value to the buyer is greater than its value to him—which is the efficient outcome. The flat-rate system has a lower marginal rate, hence is closer to the efficient arrangement, than a progressive system with the same average rate. Since at a lower marginal rate individuals choose to earn more income, the flat rate can actually be below the average of the graduated system and still yield the same tax revenue, making it still more attractive.

The principle here is exactly the same as in the solution to the hero problem of Chapter 1. The hero, as you may remember, is being pursued by 40 bad guys and has only 10 arrows. The solution is to shoot the bad guy in front. Then shoot the bad guy in front. Then shoot the bad guy in front. Then the bad guys start competing to see who can run slowest.

What we have here, just as with the graduated tax (and the ideal rationing system discussed earlier in the chapter) is a discrepancy between an *average* cost and a *marginal* cost. On average, the hero can only kill a fourth of his pursuers. But on the margin, the margin of who runs fastest, he can kill all of them—until he runs out of arrows. No one is willing to face a certainty of death just to give the survivors the pleasure of killing the hero. So once he has made it clear what he is doing, they all decline the honor of running in front.

That is also, as you may remember from Chapter 1, how Jarl Sigurd lost the battle of Clontarf: He ran out of men who were willing to carry the banner and accept a certainty of being killed. It is also how you impose a very large penalty for consuming gasoline without actually punishing anyone; if everyone believes he will be shot for exceeding his ration, nobody exceeds it and nobody is ever shot.

Distribution

As long as we limit ourselves to a world of identical individuals, the case against a progressive tax system is overwhelming. The argument *for* such a tax system is a distributional one—it is a way of imposing higher tax rates on individuals with higher incomes. In discussing efficiency, I pointed out that most people believe a dollar is worth more to a poor man than to a rich man. If so, a tax system that shifts more of the tax burden onto the rich may produce net benefits—in utility although not in dollars—even if, because of the allocational problems I have just discussed, the rich man is (say) $2 worse off for each $1 benefit to the poor man.

The declining marginal utility of income provides one reason why some people might wish to benefit the poor at the expense of the rich, even if there are efficiency costs to doing so. There are others. In Chapter 14, we discussed, but did not resolve, the question of whether the distribution of income produced by the market is in some sense just. For those who decide that it is not, one possible conclusion is that the tax system should be designed to equalize incomes for reasons not of utility but of justice.

Whatever the reason, if one wishes to make the after-tax income distribution more equal than the before-tax distribution, a progressive tax is an obvious—if costly—way to do so. It is not, however, entirely clear whether the tax system that presently exists in the United States has that effect. In analyzing the allocational effects of the two systems, I asserted, and to some degree demonstrated, that complicating the system did not change the essential result. It is less clear whether the same is true of the distributional effects.

It is easier to hide some kinds of income than others. If you are the employee of a large firm and your salary is your entire income, what you report to the IRS is probably very close to what you actually make. If you are self-employed, the opportunities for converting consumption into business expenses for tax purposes—or even concealing income entirely— are much greater. If your income is from capital, you may not be able to conceal it; but you can, at some cost, convert it into capital gains, which were until very recently taxed at a lower rate. Or you can convert your capital into state and municipal securities—which pay a lower interest rate than other investments but are tax exempt.

These complications, and others both legal and economic, imply that the actual tax system redistributes in many different directions. While there is some tendency for richer people to pay more than poorer, thus making the income distribution more equal, there is also a tendency for people with identical incomes to pay very different amounts of tax, thus making the after-tax distribution less equal. Determining what really happens is difficult. The main source of statistics on incomes and taxes is the IRS, and what one is interested in is, in large part, the income that is not reported to the IRS.

Conclusions

Even if the system did, on net, make the income distribution more equal, that would not necessarily mean that the poor would be better off. A more equal distribution would mean a larger share of the pie for the poor; but the allocational costs discussed earlier imply that under a progressive system the pie as a whole is smaller. It is hard to know what the net effect actually is.

The fundamental mistake in popular discussions of this issue and many others is the assumption that what is good for the rich is *necessarily* bad for the poor, and vice versa. That way of looking at it is an example of the noneconomist's tendency to assume that all issues are distributional. To take a simple counterexample, consider a rich man who is in a 50 percent bracket, earns $200,000/year, and (legally or illegally) conceals most of it—at a cost (to himself) of 45 cents on the dollar. He is behaving rationally—it is worth paying 45 percent to avoid paying 50 percent. If the tax rate falls to 40 percent, he finds it is no longer worth the cost of concealing his income; the rich man is better off, and the IRS collects more money.

The classic example of this phenomenon is due not to Arthur Laffer—who recently popularized it under the name of the "Laffer Curve"—but to Adam Smith. His example was an import duty—a tariff—so high that everything that came in was smuggled. If the duty were lowered to the point where it was no longer worth the cost of smuggling, both consumers and tax collectors would be better off.

PROBLEMS

1. In my final discussion of price control, I listed a series of alternatives starting with simple price control, going on to price control plus rationing, going on to price control plus rationing plus transferable ration tickets, and ending with all that plus uncontrolled prices for additional output. The examples I used involved oil and gasoline. In the case of rent control, what would correspond to each of those arrangements?

2. Suppose a town has rent control without legal subletting. From time to time an apartment becomes vacant and the landlord decides who he will rent it to. Laws forbidding landlords to accept bribes from prospective tenants are strictly enforced.

   How do you think landlords will decide which tenants to rent to? What will the effect be over time on what sort of people rent apartments in that town?

3. The chapter suggests reasons why rent control is more common than most other forms of price control. Give examples of other goods or services that it might be politically profitable to price control for similar reasons. Give examples of goods or services for which price control is very unlikely. Discuss.

4. Regulation Q prohibited banks from paying interest on checking accounts. Banks argued that since this lowered the amount they had to pay to get money, it lowered the amount at which they could lend it out, hence made mortgages less expensive. Discuss.

5. In Chapter 10, I said that Disneyland should charge a per-ride price just high enough to reduce the line at each ride to about zero. Explain why this is true. You will want to combine the analysis of Chapter 10 with the analysis of this chapter. (This is a hard problem.)

6. I demonstrated that in a world of identical individuals, a flat-rate tax was superior to a progressive tax. Is the flat-rate tax the most efficient

way of collecting a given amount of revenue in such a world, or is there another alternative that is even better? Discuss.

7. I claimed that the increased income as a result of lowering the marginal tax rate represented a net improvement. Suppose one could somehow impose a negative tax rate: On the margin, for every dollar you earn, the government gives you $0.20. Assuming that the government can get the money in some way that imposes no excess burden, would the resulting increase in the number of hours people worked represent an improvement or a worsening? Explain your answer.

8. Figure 17-5 reproduces only part of the preceding verbal argument; it does not show the result of reducing the tax rate to a level that brings in the same amount of tax ($4,000/year) as the progressive system. Draw a new figure showing the budget line for that rate and the resulting equilibrium point, along with points A and B and indifference curves U_1 and U_2. Draw in additional indifference curves if necessary.

chapter 18

MARKET FAILURES

TRANSACTION COSTS: BARTER, MARRIAGE, AND MONEY

So far, I have generally assumed that if there is a possibility for a trade—if I am willing to sell something at a price at which you are willing to buy it—the trade occurs. I have ignored both the problems of finding a trading partner and negotiating a trade and the associated transaction costs.

Barter vs Money

The simplest form of trade is barter; I trade goods that I have and you want for goods that you have and I want. This raises a problem. I must find a trading partner who has what I want and wants what I have: what economists call a **double coincidence of wants**. In a simple society in which there are only a few goods being traded, this may not be a serious problem; but in a complicated society such as ours, it is. If I want to buy a car, I first look in the classified ads to find someone who is selling the kind of car I want, then call him up and ask him if he wants to be taught economics in exchange for his car. This drastically reduces the number of potential trading partners.

The solution is the development of money—some good that almost everyone is willing to accept in exchange. Money usually starts out as some good (gold, cloth, cattle—the word "pecuniary" comes from the Latin word for cattle) valued for its own uses; people are willing to accept it even if they do not intend to consume it, because they know they can later exchange it for something else. In a money economy, I find one person who wants what I have, sell it to him, and then use the money to buy what I want from someone else.

The advantage of money is obvious; the disadvantage is that you cannot eat it or wear it (exception: *wadmal*, wool cloth used as money in medieval Iceland). If markets are **thin**—if there are few people buying

504

or selling—the individual who chooses to hold a stock of money may find that he cannot easily exchange it for what he needs when he needs it.

Thin markets cause two different problems for someone who wants to buy or sell. The first is that there may be nobody who wants what he is selling today or is selling what he wants to buy; the mere process of locating a trading partner may be expensive and time consuming. The second is that if he does find a trading partner, he becomes part of a bilateral monopoly—one buyer, one seller. Bilateral monopoly, for reasons discussed in an earlier chapter, can lead to substantial **transaction costs**: time and energy spent haggling over the price, and deals that do not get made because of a breakdown in bargaining.

In a society in which markets are thin and the number of traded commodities is small enough so that the double coincidence problem is not too serious, individuals may find it more convenient to hold wealth in the form of goods rather than money. This was probably the situation in early medieval Europe. Coins existed and were used in exchange; but barter was, for several centuries, more common.

A Market We All Know and Love

In order to understand the difficulties of barter, it is useful to consider the large-scale barter market of which you are all part—the marriage/dating/sex market. The reason this is a barter market is that if I am going out with or married to you, you are necessarily going out with or married to me. I must find a woman whom I want and who wants me—the double coincidence of wants.

We observe, in this market, large search costs, long search times, lots of frustrated and/or lonely people of both sexes—in other words, a market where traders have a hard time getting together, due largely to the high transaction costs of barter.

PUBLIC GOODS AND EXTERNALITIES

In Chapter 1, I pointed out that even if every individual in a group behaves rationally, the result may be undesirable—for every individual. This happens when one person's actions impose costs or benefits on others. The examples I gave in Chapter 1 involved students cutting across the lawn and fighters running away in battle, shooting their weapons without aiming them, or not shooting at all. In such situations, the rationality of the individual does not imply that the group acts as if it were rational.

The rest of this chapter will be devoted to a discussion of situations of this sort. I will start with a number of specific examples and then go on to explain the two general categories under which many such problems are usually classed in economics: public goods and externalities. I will end by discussing the special problems associated with imperfect information.

I will give three examples of conflicts between the individual rationality of the members of a group and their welfare. Two—the first and the last—are situations that should be familiar to every reader over the age of 17. The other is a widely discussed public policy issue with which I hope most of you have had no personal experience.

To Vote or Not to Vote? In deciding whether to vote in the next election, one should consider both costs and benefits. The costs are fairly obvious: a certain amount of time standing in line and additional time spent studying issues and candidates in order to decide how to vote. The benefits are of two sorts: those that do not depend on the effect of your vote on the election, and those that do. An example of the first sort might be your feeling of having done your civic duty or your pleasure at voting against a candidate you particularly dislike.

The second sort of benefit comes from the effect of your vote on the outcome of the election. In evaluating such benefits, you should consider two questions: how important it is that the right candidate win and how likely it is that your vote will affect the outcome. In most large elections, the probability that your vote will affect the outcome is very small; in a presidential election, it is well under one in a million. Unless getting the right person elected is immensely valuable to you—so valuable that you are willing to bear the costs of voting in exchange for one chance in a million of influencing the outcome—the effect of your vote on the election is not a good reason for voting unless you expect the election to be extraordinarily close. If you vote anyway—because you enjoy voting or because you believe that good citizens vote or because you like being part of a history-making event reported on nationwide television—the effect of your vote on the election is not likely to be enough of an incentive to make you go to much trouble to be sure you are voting for the best candidate.

The usual response to arguments of this sort is either "You are saying people should be selfish" or "What if everyone did that?" The answer to the first is that I have not assumed that you are selfish in any conventional sense of the word. I assume you are concerned with costs and benefits, but I include as a benefit the achieving of whatever objectives you happen to have. Obviously individuals have objectives that are not selfish in any narrow sense—they value the welfare of their children, their friends, and (to a lesser degree) people they do not even know. One reason you might put a high value on electing the right candidate is the belief that doing so will benefit not only yourself but hundreds of millions of other people. If you were so altruistic as to give the same weight to the welfare of every other person as to your own, then the benefit of electing the right candidate would be hundreds of millions of times as great as the direct benefit to you. That might be a sufficient reason to spend an hour or two voting, even if you realized that all you were buying was one chance in a million of influencing the outcome of the election. Casual observation suggests that few people are that altruistic.

The question "What if everybody acted like that?" can be answered in two ways. The first is to point out that if enough people refrained from voting, the remaining voters would each have a substantial chance of influencing the outcome of the election, and it would then pay them to vote. The equilibrium would be a situation in which the (say) 10,000 most concerned citizens voted.

The second answer to the question "What if everybody acted like that?" is to point out that the question implicitly assumes that true beliefs must have desirable consequences—and therefore that beliefs with undesirable consequences must be false. There is no reason why this must always be so. Perhaps it is true both that sensible people will not vote and that if everyone acts on that principle the consequences will be bad. If so, it might be wise for me not to tell you that sensible people do not vote, but that does not make it untrue. A statement may be both true and dangerous. The previous sentence is such a statement—since it provides ammunition for those who wish to argue against free speech.

The apparent paradox—that if everyone correctly perceives how to act in his own interest and does so, everyone may be worse off as a result—comes from the fact that different people have different objectives. Suppose there are a hundred of us, each of whom can individually choose action A or action B. My taking action A gives me $10 and costs the rest of you a total of $20. Your taking action A gives you $10 and costs the rest of us, including me, a total of $20. As long as we act separately, it is in the interest of each of us to take action A—making us all worse off than if we had all taken action B. The problem is that I only control my action—and I am better off taking A than B. This, of course, is the problem we encountered long ago in the discussion of why soldiers run away.

A simple and striking example of such a situation is the prisoner's dilemma discussed back in Chapter 11. Joe and Mike, the two accused criminals, would both be better off if they both kept silent. But if Mike confesses, the D.A. will have the evidence needed to convict Joe—and will punish him for his silence with a stiff sentence. So if Mike is going to confess, Joe had better confess too. If Mike stays silent and Joe confesses, the D.A. will express his gratitude by letting Joe off with a token sentence. So if Mike is not going to confess, Joe is better off confessing. Whatever Mike does, Joe is better off confessing, and similarly for Mike. They both confess, and both get worse sentences than if they had both kept silent.

Plea Bargaining: A Real-World Prisoner's Dilemma. A plea bargain is an arrangement by which a prosecutor, instead of trying a defendant on a charge of, say, first-degree murder, allows the defendant to plead guilty to a lesser charge, such as second-degree murder or manslaughter. It is widely criticized as a way of letting criminals off lightly. In fact, it seems likely that the existence of plea bargaining results in criminals being punished, on average, more severely rather than less. If plea bargaining were abolished—as some people suggest it should be—the result might well be to reduce the sentence received by the average criminal.

How can this be? Surely a criminal will only plead guilty to the lesser charge if doing so is in his interest—which means that a certain conviction on the less serious charge is preferable, for him, to whatever he believes the chance is of being convicted on the more serious charge. True. But the chance of a conviction depends on what resources, of money and time, the prosecution spends on that particular case—which in turn depends on how many other cases had to go to trial and how many were settled by plea bargaining.

Suppose there are 100 cases per year, and the district attorney has a budget of $100,000. He can only spend $1,000 on each case, with the result that 50 percent of the criminals are acquitted. With plea bargaining, the D.A. concentrates his resources on the ten criminals who refuse to accept the bargain he offers. He spends $10,000 prosecuting each of them and gets a conviction rate of 90 percent. Each criminal deciding whether to accept the D.A.'s offer knows that, if he refuses, he has about a 90 percent chance of being convicted—so he accepts any offer that he prefers to a 90 percent chance of conviction. On average, all the criminals, both the ones who accept the bargain and the ones who do not, are worse off—more severely punished—than if the D. A. prosecuted all of them on the more severe charge and convicted half. Each individual criminal benefits by accepting the D.A.'s offer—but by doing so, he frees resources that the D.A. can then use against another criminal, raising the average conviction rate. The higher conviction rate makes criminals willing to accept worse bargains (i.e., ones implying more severe punishment). All of the criminals would be better off if none of them accepted the D.A.'s offer, but each is better off accepting. This is the prisoner's dilemma in real life.

Why Traffic Jams.   This is a situation in which each individual takes the action that is in his individual interest; they are all, as a result, worse off than if they had acted differently. A more familiar example of such a situation occurs twice a day, five days a week, about two blocks from where I used to live. The time is rush hour; the scene is the intersection of Wilshire Boulevard and Westwood Avenue in Los Angeles, said to be the busiest intersection in the world. As the light on Wilshire goes green, ten lanes of traffic surge forward. As it turns yellow, a last few cars try to make it across. Since Wilshire is packed with cars, they fail and end up in the intersection, blocking the cars on Westwood, which now have a green light. Gradually the cars in the intersection make it across, allowing the traffic on Westwood to surge forward—just as the light changes, trapping another batch of cars in the intersection.

If drivers on both streets refrained from entering the intersection until there was clearly enough room for them on the far side, the jam would not occur. Traffic would flow faster, and they would all get where they are going sooner. Yet each individual driver is behaving rationally. My aggressive driving on Wilshire benefits me (I may make it across before the light changes, and at worst I will get far enough into the intersection not to be blocked by cars going the other way at the next stage of the jam) and harms drivers on Westwood. Your aggressive driving on Westwood benefits you and harms drivers (possibly including me) on Wilshire. The harm is much larger than the benefit, so on net we are all worse off. But I receive all of the benefit and none of the harm from the particular decision that I control. I am correctly choosing the action that best achieves my objectives—but if we each made a mistake and drove less aggressively, we would all be better off.

My point, in this and the previous examples, is not that rationality implies selfishness. That is a parody of economics. Drivers may value other people's time as well as (although probably not as much as) their own. In Chapter 21, we will discuss the economics of **altruism**—the behavior of people who value the happiness of other people. If drivers value the welfare of other drivers, rationality may prevent the jam instead of causing it.

The point—which to some readers may seem paradoxical—is that rational behavior by every individual in a group may sometimes lead to an outcome that is undesirable in terms of precisely the same objectives (getting home earlier in this case or getting a light sentence or surviving a battle in some of the other cases we have discussed) that each individual's rational behavior is correctly calculated to achieve. Such situations often involve what economists call public goods or externalities, two concepts that we will now discuss.

Public Goods

There are a number of different, closely related definitions of a **public good**. I prefer to define it as *"a good such that, if it is produced at all, the producer cannot control who gets it."* The public-good *problem* arises because the producer of a public good cannot, like the producer of an ordinary (private) good, tell the consumer that he can only have it if he pays for it; the consumer knows that if it is produced at all, the producer has no control over who gets it.

One example of a public good is a radio broadcast; if it is made at all, anyone who owns a radio and lives in the right area can receive it. This example demonstrates several important things about public goods. The first is that whether or not a good is public depends on the nature of the good. It is not that the producer *should* not control who gets it but that he *cannot*; or, at least, he can control who gets it, if at all, only at a prohibitively high cost (hiring detectives to creep around people's houses and arrest them if they are listening to the broadcast without having paid for it). While the publicness of a good may be affected by the legal system (whether it is legal to listen to a broadcast without the broadcaster's permission), it is mostly just a fact of nature; even if it were legal to forbid unauthorized listening, the law would be prohibitively expensive to enforce.

A second important thing to note about a public good is that it is *not* defined as a good produced by the government. In this country, radio broadcasts are mostly private; they are still public goods. Many of the things government does produce, such as mail delivery, are private goods; the government can and does refuse to deliver your letter if it does not have a stamp on it. The fact that a good is public presents a problem to a private producer—the problem of how to get paid for producing it— but the problem is not necessarily an insoluble one, as the example of a radio broadcast illustrates.

Private Production of Public Goods.   There are a number of ways in which the problem of producing public goods privately may be solved. One, which works best if the size of the public (the group of people who will receive the good if it is produced) is small, is a unanimous contract. The producer gets all the members of the public together, tells them how much he wants each to pay toward the cost of producing the good, and announces that unless each agrees to chip in if everyone else does, the good will not be produced.

Assume that they believe him. Consider the logic of the situation from the standpoint of a single member of the group deciding whether he should agree to chip in. He reasons as follows:

> Either someone else is going to refuse, in which case the deal falls through, I get my money back, and my agreement costs me nothing, or else everyone else is going to agree. If everyone else agrees and I refuse, I do not have to pay for the public good, but I also do not get it. So as long as the good is worth more to me than my share of the cost, I ought to agree.

The same argument applies to everyone, so if the public good is worth more to the consumers than it costs to produce, the entrepreneur should be able to divide up the cost in such a way that each individual finds it in his interest to agree.

One difficulty with this is that if the public is large, it may be hard to organize a unanimous contract. One solution is to find a **privileged minority**: a subgroup of the public that is small enough so that its members can form their own unanimous contract and that receives enough benefit from the public good so that its members can be persuaded to bear the whole cost. When I mow my front lawn, I am acting as a privileged minority (of one); the mowed lawn makes the neighborhood more attractive, benefiting everyone, but I receive enough of the benefit to be willing to pay the whole cost.

Consider how this might work in the case of one of the largest public goods in our society and one of the most difficult to produce privately: national defense. Suppose the inhabitants of Hawaii believe that there is a 10 percent chance of a nuclear strike against their island next year. If the strike occurs, the island will be wiped out. The inhabitants can flee the island before the attack, so the cost will be distributed roughly in proportion to the value of the land they own. Table 18-1 is an (entirely imaginary) listing of how land ownership is divided on the island and how much each owner would pay, if necessary, to prevent the attack.

Suppose an entrepreneur comes up with a system for defending Hawaii from nuclear attack at a cost of $100 million. He goes to Dole, Hilton, United Fruit, and Maxwell House and tells them that if they pay him $110 million, he will defend the island. Since the value to them of the defense is more than that and since there are only a few firms that have to agree, they raise the money.

In this case, the story has a happy ending. Suppose, however, that the total cost of the defense is $149 million. It is still worth having—the top five landowners alone value it at more than its cost—but it will be very hard to get. If the entrepreneur asks the Big 5 to each put up the same proportion of the value of their land (just under 10 percent), Howard Johnson will refuse. Unfortunately for Hawaii, the Howard Johnson firm is run by an optimist who believes the chance of an attack is only 5 percent and therefore is willing to pay only 5 percent of his land value to protect against the attack.

If the information on Table 18-1 were a matter of public knowledge, agreement could still be reached, with Howard Johnson contributing at half the rate of the other four. The problem is that the other contributors are likely to view Howard Johnson's optimism as a bargaining ploy, a way to get them to pay more than their share of the cost. If there is no simple rule for dividing up the cost of defense, agreement on who pays what may well be impossible.

The larger the number of people whose agreement is needed and the less obvious it is how much each values what he is getting, the harder it will be to get agreement. If the public good is cheap—if defense costs only $40 million—the problem is soluble; the entrepreneur can either leave Howard Johnson out of the contract or else charge everyone 5 percent

Table 18-1

Landowner	Value of Land	Value of Defense
Dole Pineapple	$500,000,000	$50,000,000
Hilton Hotels	$400,000,000	$40,000,000
United Fruit Co.	$300,000,000	$30,000,000
Maxwell House Coffee	$250,000,000	$25,000,000
Howard Johnson's	$200,000,000	$10,000,000
Everyone Else	$900,000,000	$90,000,000

of land value and still raise enough money. But if the cost of the public good is a large fraction of the benefit it produces and if the benefit is spread among many people, raising the money is a serious and perhaps insoluble problem.

In the example discussed, the concentration of land ownership in Hawaii greatly simplified the situation. The Big 5 were a privileged minority; they received a large fraction of the total benefit, so the entrepreneur could, with luck, raise the money he needed from them while ignoring the large number of small holders. The term "privileged minority," which is commonly used in this way, has always struck me as somewhat strange, since the minority has the "privilege" of paying for what all the other members of the public get for free.

Unanimous contracts are one solution to the problem of producing a public good. Another solution is to convert the public good temporarily into a private good. Suppose the public good is flood control; building a dam will reduce floods in the valley below, increasing the value of farm land there. One way to pay for the dam is for the entrepreneur to buy up as much as possible of the land in the valley (or buy options on the land at its current price), build the dam, then sell the land back (or sell the options back to the owners). Since the new flood protection makes the land worth more than when he bought it, he should be able to get a higher price than he paid, for either the land or the options.

Another ingenious solution, which would never have occurred to me if I had not seen it in operation, is to combine two public goods and give away the package. The first public good has a positive cost of production and a positive value to the customer; the second has a negative cost of production and a negative value to the customer. The package has zero or negative cost of production and positive value to the consumer.

This is how radio and television broadcasts are produced; the first good is the program and the second the commercial. Commercials have a negative cost of production from the standpoint of the broadcaster; he gets paid by the sponsor to broadcast them. Since there is usually no convenient way to listen to the program without hearing the commercials, the listener must choose to accept or reject a package deal—program plus commercial. If the net value of the package is positive to him, he will accept it. If the net cost (cost of operating the station minus payment from the sponsor) is negative, if advertising revenues more than cover operating expenses, the broadcaster can and will stay in business.

An interesting example of the public-good problem, and several interesting solutions, occur in the computer industry. A $300 computer program can be copied onto a $3 floppy disk. Programs can be protected against copying, but this is inconvenient for the user, who would like at least one backup copy in case his original gets damaged and who may also find it convenient to copy several of the programs he has purchased onto one disk. Even if programs are protected, someone with a reasonable amount of expertise can frequently "break" the protection—figure out how to copy them. There are even programs on the market designed to copy copy-protected programs. In one case, a program capable of copying other copy-protected programs was copy-protected against itself; a second company sold a program to copy it!

If you cannot effectively copy-protect a program, selling it to one person means, in effect, giving it to everyone. The program is then a public good and figuring out how to make money producing it is a public-good problem. Firms that produce and sell software have come up with a number of ingenious solutions. One of them is *bundling*. You sell a computer along with a bundle of programs designed to run on that particular computer; in effect you charge for the programs in the price of the computer. Anyone can copy the programs—but to use them, he has to buy the computer. Another kind of bundling is to sell a package consisting of a program plus service: a voice on the other end of a telephone to answer questions about how to make the program work. The seller keeps track of who bought the program and only gives help to registered owners. A third kind of bundling is exemplified by the way in which I "sell" the computer programs that go with this book. A professor who adopts the book is given a free copy of the programs and permission to make copies for his students. I get paid for my work writing the programs in increased sales of the book. I hope.

As these examples suggest, there are a variety of ways in which public goods can be privately produced. Each of these may succeed, under some circumstances, in producing some quantity of a public good. None of them can be relied on to lead to an efficient level of production in the strong sense in which we have been using the term—an outcome so good that it could not be improved by a bureaucrat-god. Typically, the private producer of a public good succeeds in collecting only part of the additional value of each unit of the good produced. He produces up to the point where what he gets for an additional unit (an additional hour of broadcasting, or an additional dollar spent making the program better) is equal to what it costs him. That is a lower level of output than the efficient point where marginal cost to the producer equals marginal value to the consumer.

To see more clearly the sense in which private production of public goods is inefficient, consider some of our examples. In the Hawaiian defense case, Hawaii was worth defending as long as the cost was less than $245 million, since that was the total value of the defense to all the inhabitants put together. If the cost of the defense happened to be only $40 million, private arrangements might produce it, which is the efficient outcome. If the cost were $235 million, it is unlikely that the defense would be produced; since it still costs less than its value, a bureaucrat-god who ordered Hawaii defended would be producing a net benefit. So if the cost of defending Hawaii is $235 million, private production results in an inefficient outcome. Hawaii is worth defending—and is undefended. The private production of public goods is inefficient in the sense of sometimes leading to an inefficient outcome—failing to produce a good that is worth producing.

We have assumed that there are only two possible amounts of defense: none or enough. Whether or not that is plausible in the case of defense, the equivalent assumption is obviously wrong for radio broadcasts or computer programs; in each case, the manufacturer decides how much he will spend and what quality of product he will produce. The efficient outcome is one in which he makes all quality improvements that are worth more to the consumers than they cost him to make. But from his standpoint, improvements are worth making only if they increase his revenue by at least as much as they cost. Since he will be able to collect only part of the value he produces, there may be improvements worth making that he does not find it in his interest to make; so here again the outcome could be improved by a bureaucrat-god. The good may be produced, but it is generally underproduced: An increase in quality, number of hours of broadcasting, or some other dimension would result in net benefits. So private production of public goods is generally inefficient in the technical sense in which I have been using the word.

The Efficient Quantity of a Public Good. While we have talked about producing the efficient outcome, we have not yet discussed how, in principle, one would find out what it is. Figure 18-1 shows the answer to that question, for a very small public. D_1, D_2, D_3 are the demand curves for radio broadcasting of three listeners. Each shows how much broadcasting a listener would buy if it were an ordinary private good—how many hours per day he would pay for as a function of the price per hour. The figure assumes that number of hours per day of broadcasting is the only relevant quality variable, the only way in which the broadcaster can affect the value to his "customers" of what he produces. MC shows the marginal cost curve faced by the broadcaster—how much each additional hour per day of broadcasting costs him.

As usual, the efficient solution is to produce where $MV = MC$—to keep increasing the number of hours as long as the value of an additional hour to the listeners is at least as great as its cost of production. We know from Chapter 4 that each demand curve is also a marginal value curve. Each extra hour of broadcasting benefits all three customers; its marginal value is the sum of its marginal value to Customer 1, its marginal value to Customer 2, and its marginal value to Customer 3. So the total MV curve is the vertical sum of the MV curves for the customers, each of which equals the corresponding demand curve. The result is shown on the figure. Q^* is the efficient quantity.

Public Production of Public Goods. One obvious solution to the public-good problem is to have the government produce the good and pay for it out of taxes. This may or may not be an improvement on imperfect private production. The problem is that the mechanism by which we

Figure 18-1

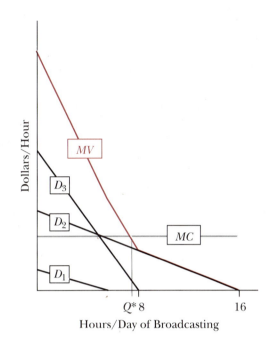

Calculating the efficient quantity of a public good. *MV* shows the total marginal value to the three customers, the vertical sum of their demand curves. The efficient quantity *Q** is where *MV = MC*.

try to make the government act in our interest—voting—itself involves the private production of a public good. As I pointed out earlier in this chapter, when you spend time and energy deciding which candidate best serves the general interest and then voting accordingly, most of the benefit of your expenditure goes to other people. You are producing a public good: a vote for the better candidate. That is a very hard public good to produce privately, since the public is a very large one: the whole population of the country. Hence it is underproduced—very much underproduced. The underproduction of that public good means that people do not find it in their interest to spend much effort deciding who is the best candidate—which in turn means that democracy does not work very well, so we cannot rely on the government to act in our interest.

If we cannot rely on the government to act in our interest, we cannot rely on it to produce the efficient quantity of public goods. Just as with a government agency regulating a natural monopoly, the administrators controlling the public production of a public good may find that their own private interest, or the political interest of the administration that appointed them, does not lead them to maximize economic welfare.

Even if the government wishes to produce the efficient amount of a public good, it faces problems similar to the problems of regulators trying to satisfy the second efficiency condition. In order to decide how much to produce, the government must know how much potential consumers value the good. In an ordinary market, the producer measures the demand curve by offering his product at some price and seeing how many he sells. The producer of a public good cannot do that, since he cannot control who gets the good, so the government must find some indirect way of estimating demand. Individuals who want the public good have an incentive, if asked, to overstate how much they want it—which means that a public opinion poll may produce a very poor estimate of demand.

In dealing with the public-good problem, just as in dealing with the closely related problem of natural monopoly, we are faced with a choice among different imperfect ways of solving the problem, some private and some governmental. None of the alternatives can be expected to generate an efficient result. As I pointed out earlier, the fact that something is inefficient means that it could be improved by a bureaucrat-god. That does not necessarily mean that it can be improved by us, since we do not have any bureaucrat-gods available.

As you may have realized by now, public-good problems of one sort or another are very common—indeed many common problems, both public and private, can be viewed as public-good problems. One example is the problem of getting anything accomplished in a meeting. Most of us like attention: When we are in a meeting and happen to have the floor, we take the opportunity not only to say what we have to say about the issue on hand but also to show how clever, witty, and wise we are. This imposes a cost on other people (unless we really are witty and wise); if there are 60 people in the room, every minute I speak costs a person-hour of listener time. Brevity, in this case, is a public good—and underproduced.

At the beginning of this section, I mentioned that different economists use slightly different definitions of a public good. The definition I have used emphasizes **non-excludability**: the inability of the producer to control which consumers get the good. The other characteristic usually associated with a public good is that one person's use does not reduce the amount available for someone else. A different way of stating this is to say that the marginal cost of producing the good is zero on the margin of how many people get it, although there may still be a cost to producing more on the margin of how much of it they get. Something that is a public good in only this sense (it has zero marginal cost, but the producer can control who gets it) is simply a natural monopoly with $MC = 0$. Since the problems associated with natural monopoly have already been discussed, I prefer to concentrate on the inability of the producer to control who consumes the good, which seems to me to be the essential characteristic of public goods responsible for the special problems associated with them.

Externalities

The long-winded speaker is underproducing the public good of brevity. Another, and equivalent, way of describing the situation is to say that he is overproducing his speech. The problem can be described either as underproduction due to the public-good problem or as overproduction due to the existence of an externality.

An **externality** is a net cost or benefit that my action imposes on you. Familiar examples—in addition to the cost of listening to me talk too long in a meeting—are pollution (a *negative* externality—a cost) and scientific progress as a result of theoretical research (a *positive* externality—a benefit). Externalities are all around us: when I paint my house or mow my lawn, I confer positive externalities on my neighbors; when you smoke in a restaurant or play loud music in the dorm at 1:00 a.m., you confer negative externalities on yours.

The problem with externalities is that since you, rationally enough, do not take them into account in deciding whether or not to smoke or play the music, you may do so even when the total cost (including the cost to your neighbors) is greater than the total benefit. Similarly, I may fail to mow my lawn this week because the benefit *to me* is less than the cost, even though the total benefit (including the benefit to my neighbors) is more.

As you can see by these examples, "externalities" and "public goods" are really different ways of describing the same problems. A positive externality is a public good; a negative externality is a "negative" public good and refraining from producing it is a positive public good. In some cases, it may be easier to look at the problem one way, in some cases the other—but it is the same problem.

Figure 18-2 is a graphical analysis of the inefficiency due to an externality. D is the demand curve for steel. S is the industry supply curve for the competitive industry that produces steel. The industry produces a quantity Q_s at a price P_s.

In addition to the costs that the industry pays for its inputs, there is another cost to producing steel: pollution. For every ton of steel it produces, the industry also produces a negative externality of $10. So the true marginal cost of a ton of steel is $10 above the marginal private cost, the cost to the industry, which is what determines the industry's supply curve. S' is what the supply curve would be if the industry included in its calculations the cost of the pollution it produced. The efficient level of output is where marginal cost equals marginal value—where S' intersects D at a quantity of Q_s'. From the standpoint of efficiency, the situation is exactly as if the supply curve were S' but the industry, for some reason, produced Q_s. The resulting inefficiency is the colored area A on the figure. The society as a whole—producers, consumers, and victims of pollution—is that much worse off than if the firms produced the efficient quantity Q_s'.

Figure 18-2

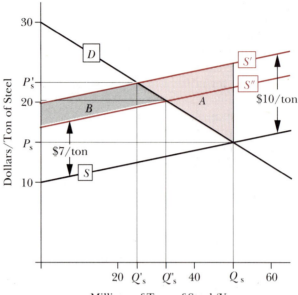

Supply and demand for steel. (Q_s, P_s) is the uncontrolled equilibrium. S' is what the supply curve would be if the steel firms included in their cost calculations the cost ($10/ton) that their pollution imposes on others. S'' is what it would be if the firms included pollution cost, but reduced it by purchasing the efficient level of pollution control, as shown on Figure 18-3.

So far we have assumed that the only way of reducing pollution is to reduce the amount of steel produced. There may be other alternatives. By filtering its smokestacks or using low-sulfur coal, the firm may be able to eliminate a dollar's worth of pollution at a cost of less than a dollar.

Figure 18-3 shows that possibility. For simplicity, I assume that the cost for a given reduction of pollution per ton is proportional to the amount of steel the firm is producing. TC is the total cost function for producing pollution control. It shows how many dollars must be spent on pollution control per ton of steel produced in order to reduce pollution per ton to any particular level. MC is the corresponding marginal cost function, showing the cost of the additional pollution control required to eliminate an additional dollar's worth of pollution.

As we already know, the efficient quantity of output occurs where marginal cost equals marginal value. The value of eliminating $5 worth of pollution is $5; marginal value is $1 per dollar. The steel firm should keep increasing its expenditure on pollution control until the last dollar buys exactly a dollar's worth of pollution control. The efficient amount of pollution per ton is at Q_p, where MC crosses MV.

Section IV Judging Outcomes

Figure 18-3

Cost curves for controlling pollution. *TC* shows total cost/ton of steel for reducing pollution as a function of the amount of pollution produced. *MC* is the corresponding marginal cost, *MV* the marginal value of pollution control.

If steel firms install the efficient level of pollution control, they will spend $2.50/ton on pollution control and produce $4.50/ton worth of pollution. The cost of producing steel, including the cost to the producers of controlling pollution and the cost to everyone else of the pollution they do not control, is $7/ton higher than the cost to the firms of producing steel with no pollution control. The corresponding supply curve is S'' on Figure 18-2. The efficient quantity of steel is Q_s''.

What is the efficiency loss from producing Q_s without pollution control instead of Q_s'' with pollution control? Producing Q_s without pollution control instead of Q_s' without pollution control costs area *A*. Producing Q_s' without pollution control instead of Q_s'' with pollution control raises the supply curve from S'' to S' and moves quantity from Q_s'' to Q_s', so it costs the shaded area *B*, the resulting change in total surplus. Going from S' and Q_s to S' and Q_s' saves area *A*, going from there to S' and Q_s'' saves an additional area *B*; so the net savings in moving from the initial inefficient outcome to the final efficient one is $A + B$. That is the inefficiency of the uncontrolled outcome, compared to the outcome that would be chosen by a bureaucrat-god.

Efficient Pollution and How to Get It: The Public Solution.   The text-book solution to externalities is to impose the cost on, or give the benefit to, the producer. If I am benefiting others by scientific research, subsidize me; if I am polluting the air, charge me an **effluent fee** of so many dollars per cubic foot of pollution emitted, corresponding to the costs that my pollution imposes on others. I will continue to pollute only if the net value of what I am doing is more than the damage done—in which case, pollution is efficient. If each steel firm must pay an effluent fee of $1 for each dollar's worth of pollution it produces, the supply curve for steel will shift to S'' and the quantity produced will be Q_s''. The industry will produce an efficient amount of steel—and an efficient amount of pollution.

"Pollution" is a loaded word. To be in favor of pollution sounds like being in favor of evil; the phrase "an efficient level of pollution," lifted from a book like this one, would be fine ammunition for a speech on the inhumanity of economics—and economists.

If you find the idea that some amount of pollution is desirable a shocking one, consider that carbon dioxide is commonly regarded as a pollutant, and the only way you can stop producing it is to stop breathing. This is an extreme case, but it makes an important point—that the real issue is whether, in any particular case, the costs of pollution are greater than the costs of not polluting.

While there is, in this sense, an efficient level of pollution, it is not clear how to get that level. The problem with using effluent fees to control externalities is the same as the problem with government provision of public goods; it depends on the government finding it in its interest to act in the interest of the public and knowing how to do so. Just as in previous cases, "knowing how" includes somehow estimating the value of something to people by some method other than offering it at a price and seeing whether they take it. The result of the governmental solution may be better or worse than the alternatives of either accepting the over-production of negative externalities and the underproduction of positive ones, or dealing with the problem in some imperfect private way.

Private Solutions.   How might one control externalities privately? One (real-world) solution is a proprietary community. A developer builds a housing development and sells the houses with the requirement that the buyer must join the neighborhood association. The neighborhood association either takes care of lawns, painting, and other things that affect the general appearance of the community or requires the owners to do so. A friend of mine who lived in such a community could not change the color of his front door without his neighbors' permission.

This sounds rather like government regulation masquerading as a private contract, but there are two important differences. It is in the private interest of the developer to set up the best possible rules, in order to maximize the price for which he can sell the houses. And nobody is forced to purchase a house and membership from that developer; if the package is not at least as attractive as any alternative, the customer can and will go elsewhere.

There is another private solution that applies to the case where "You" and "I" are not two people but two firms—**merger**. If a factory and a resort are both on the same lake and the factory's pollution is ruining the resort's business, one solution is for the two firms to join. After the resort buys out the factory, or vice versa, the combined firm will be trying to maximize the combined income. If controlling the factory's effluent increases the resort's income by more than it costs the factory, it will pay the merged firm to control the effluent. The externality is no longer external.

One way of looking at firms is precisely as ways of controlling such problems. As I pointed out back in Chapter 7, one could imagine an economy of tiny firms, perhaps with only one person in each, coordinating their activities through the market. One reason we do not do things that way is that, when many firms are jointly producing a single product, decisions by each one affect all the others. If I am doing a crucial part of the job and make a mistake that delays it for six months, I am imposing large costs on the other firms—which I may not be able to compensate them for. By combining all of us into one firm, that sort of externality is internalized.

The disadvantage of doing it that way is that we introduce a new kind of externality. Now that I am an employee instead of an independent business, the cost of my sleeping on the job is borne by everyone else. So a firm must monitor its employees in ways in which it does not have to monitor other firms. The efficient size of firm is then determined by the balance between problems associated with coordinating a lot of small firms and problems associated with running one large firm.

Another solution to externality problems is the definition and enforcement of property rights in whatever is affected by the externality. It is in one sense a governmental solution, since property rights are defined by courts and legislatures, and in another sense a private solution, since once property rights are defined it is the market and not the government that decides what happens. An example is the case of British trout streams. Trout streams in Britain are private property. Each stream is owned by someone—frequently the local fishing club. An industrial polluter dumping effluent into such a stream is guilty of trespass, just as if he dumped it on someone's lawn. If he believes the stream is more valuable as a place to dump his effluent than as a trout stream, it is up to him to buy it. If he believes (and the fishing club does not) that his effluent will not hurt the trout, he can buy the stream and then—if he is right—rent the fishing rights back to the previous owners.

As this example suggests, what is or is not an externality depends in part on how property rights are defined. When I produce an automobile, I am producing something of value to you. It is not an externality because

I can control whether you get it and will refuse to give it to you unless you pay me for it. Some externality problems arise because property rights are not defined when they should be: If land were not property, my fertilizing it or planting a crop would confer positive externalities on whoever later came by and harvested my crop. Under those circumstances, crops would not be planted. Other problems arise because there is no way of defining property rights that does not lead to externalities in one direction or another. If I have to get your permission to play my stereo when you want to sleep, I can no longer impose an externality on you—but your decision to go to sleep when I want to play my stereo imposes an externality on me! If only two people are involved, they may be able to work out an efficient arrangement by mutual negotiation—but air pollution in Los Angeles affects several million people. Just as in the case of producing a public good, the problems of negotiating a unanimous contract become larger the larger the number of people involved.

One way of looking at this is to say that all public-good/externality problems are really transaction-cost problems. If bargaining were costless, then the problems leading to inefficiency could always be solved. As long as there was some change that would produce net benefits, someone could put together a deal that would divide up the gain in such a way as to benefit all concerned. This argument has a name—it is called the **Coase Theorem** (after economist Ronald Coase). Looked at in this way, the interesting question is always "What are the transaction costs that prevent the efficient outcome from being reached?"

Joint Causation, or Why Not Evacuate Los Angeles?

Half of Coase's contribution to understanding externalities was the observation that the problem would vanish if bargaining between the affected parties were costless; the problem could thus be seen as the result not of externalities but of transaction costs. The other half was the observation that the traditional analysis of externalities contained a fundamental error.

So far we have followed the pre-Coasian analysis in treating an externality as a cost imposed by one person on another. That is not quite right. As Coase pointed out, the typical externality is a cost jointly produced by the actions of both parties. There would be no pollution problem in Los Angeles if there were no pollution, but there would also be no problem, even if there were lots of pollution, if nobody tried to live and breath in Los Angeles.

If evacuating Los Angeles does not strike you as a very satisfactory solution to the problem of smog, consider some more plausible examples. The military owns bomb ranges: pieces of land used to test bombs, artillery shells, and the like. If you happen to be camping in one, the dropping of a 300-pound bomb next to your tent imposes serious externalities. It seems more natural to solve the problem by removing the campers than by removing the bombs.

Another example is airplane noise, which can be a considerable problem for people who live near large airports. One approach to the problem is to modify planes to make them quieter, close the airport when people are asleep, and instruct pilots to begin their descent as near the airport as possible. An alternative is to soundproof the houses near the airport. Another alternative is not to have anyone living near the airport: Keep the land empty, use it for a water reservoir, or fill it with noisy factories where no one will notice the minor disturbance produced by a 747 two hundred feet over the roof.

It is not immediately obvious which of these alternatives provides the most efficient way of dealing with airport noise. If we try to solve the problem by the equivalent of an effluent fee (more generally described as a **Pigouvian tax**, after A.C. Pigou, the inventor of the traditional analysis of externalities), we may never find out. Charging the airlines for the cost of the noise they produce gives them an incentive to reduce noise, but that may be the wrong solution—it might be less costly to soundproof the houses or pay their occupants to move out.

The problem is that the cost is jointly produced by the actions of both parties. If we do nothing, the cost is entirely borne by one party (the homeowners in our example) so the other has no incentive to reduce it— even if he can do so at the lower cost. If we impose a Pigouvian tax on the "polluter," the "victim" may find that his best tactic is to do nothing— even if he is the one who can solve the problem at the lower cost. If, as a third alternative, we let the victim sue the polluter, the victim has no incentive at all to avoid (or reduce) the cost—whatever he loses he gets back in damage payments. Any of the alternatives might or might not give the efficient outcome, depending on whether it happens to impose the externality on the party who can avoid it at the lowest cost. If the efficient solution requires actions by both parties—soundproofing plus some noise reduction, for example—none of the alternatives may be able to produce it.

What lessons can we learn from this depressing tangle? The first is that the traditional analysis of externalities, and the associated solution of Pigouvian taxes, applies only to the special case where we already know which party is the least cost avoider of the problem—that emission controls for automobiles in southern California cost less than evacuating that end of the state. The second is that in the more general situation, where we do not know who can solve the problem at lowest cost, the best solution may be to fall back on Coase's other idea: negotiations between the parties. If the airlines are liable for damage produced by noise pollution, they may choose to pay people living near the airport to soundproof their houses. They may even choose to buy the houses, tear them down, and rent out the land to people who want to build noisy factories. If the airlines are not liable for damages, it may be in the interest of the local homeowners to offer to pay the cost of noise reduction if that is cheaper than soundproofing. So the best solution to such problems may be for the legal system to clearly define who has the right to do what and then permit the affected individuals to bargain among themselves.

In defining the initial rights—in deciding, for instance, whether the airlines have the right to make noise or must buy that right from the homeowners—one should consider the transaction costs of getting from each possible definition to each possible solution. If there are 10,000 homeowners living near the airport, raising money to pay the airlines to keep down their noise will be a public good for a public of 10,000; so it will almost certainly not be produced, even if it is worth producing. If the airlines have the right to make noise and not pay damages, they will continue producing noise whether or not it is efficient—homeowners will put up with the sound, soundproof, or sell out. If the airline is permitted to make the noise but must pay damages to affected homeowners, the airline can negotiate separately with each homeowner, buying or sound-proofing some houses and paying damages on the rest if that is cheaper than modifying the planes—which should ultimately lead to the efficient solution.

Suppose, as another alternative, that each homeowner has an absolute right to be free from noise. In that case it does the airline no good to soundproof houses or buy them unless all 10,000 are included. The result is a **holdout problem**. Any one homeowner can try to get the airline to pay him the entire savings from soundproofing the houses instead of the planes, by threatening to withhold his consent. With 10,000 homeowners, every one of whom must agree, the deal is unlikely to go through—even if it is the lowest cost solution to the problem.

In this particular case, the best solution may be a legal rule permitting homeowners to collect damages but not to forbid the noise. That allows whichever of the three solutions turns out to be most efficient to occur with either no transaction (the airline reduces its noise) or a relatively simple and inexpensive one (the airline deals separately with the home-owners who are willing, and pays damages to the holdouts). This solution depends, however, on the damage done by the noise being something a court can measure. One can imagine many cases where that would not be the case, and where a different rule might be more likely to lead to an efficient outcome.

Voluntary Externalities: Sharecropping

Externalities can be eliminated by a contractual arrangement, as when two firms merge or when I agree, in exchange for a payment, not to do something that injures you. Externalities can also be created by contract. One example that I will discuss a little later is the case of insurance. By purchasing fire insurance, I create an externality: If I am careless with matches, part of the cost will be borne by the insurance company instead of by me. A second example is the case of **sharecropping**.

Sharecropping means that a farmer pays, instead of rent, a fixed percentage of his crop to the owner of the land he farms. It seems an odd and inefficient arrangement. If I must pay half of my crop to my landlord, it only pays me to make investments of labor or capital if the payoff is at least twice the cost. I have, by contract, created an externality of 50 percent.

This raises an obvious puzzle. Sharecropping is a common arrangement, appearing in many different societies at different times in history. If it is inefficient, why does it exist?

One way of answering the question is to consider the alternatives. There are two obvious ones. The landlord could hire the farmer to work his land, paying him a fixed wage, or the farmer could pay a fixed rent to the landlord and keep all of the crop.

Converting the sharecropper into an employee is hardly a solution; instead of collecting half the return from additional inputs of labor he collects none of it. Switching from sharecropping to renting may be a solution, but it has some problems. For one thing, farm output may vary unpredictably from year to year. If the farmer has agreed to pay a fixed rent, he does very well in good years but may starve to death in bad ones—the rent may be more than the full value of his crop.

Seen from this standpoint, sharecropping is, like insurance, a device for spreading risk. The landlord and the farmer divide the risk, instead of the farmer taking all of it. If the random factors affect different pieces of land differently, a landlord who owns several pieces of land can expect random effects to average out, just as they do for an insurance company. When there is lots of rain he gets very little from tenants farming low-lying areas, which flood, but lots from tenants farming hilltops that are usually too dry to grow much. Just as with insurance, the two parties pay a price in inefficiency due to externalities in order to get a benefit in risk spreading.

One way of reducing that price is for the landlord to monitor the farmer—just as he would do if the farmer were an employee. If he concludes that the farmer is not working hard enough there is nothing the landlord can do this year, but he can find another share-cropper next year. Sharecroppers require more monitoring than tenants but less than employees, since they get at least part of the output they produce.

Another explanation for sharecropping, at least in some societies, may be that the landlord is also contributing inputs: experience, administration, perhaps capital. If so, giving him a fraction of the output reduces the farmer's incentive but increases the landlord's. In this case, as in many others, there may be no efficient contract—no contract that does as well as rule by a bureaucrat-god. Just as in choosing firm size, or controlling externalities that are jointly caused, or picking a rule for product liability, choosing the optimal contract involves trade-offs among different imperfect ways of coordinating individuals whose actions are interdependent.

Pecuniary Externalities

Suppose something I do imposes both positive and negative externalities, and by some coincidence they are exactly equal. I will, as always, treat the external costs and benefits as if they were zero—and in this case, I will be right. Since on net all of the costs and benefits caused by my action are borne by me, I will make the efficient decision as to whether or not to do it.

One would think it an unlikely coincidence for positive and negative externalities to precisely cancel; but there is an important situation, called a **pecuniary externality**, in which that is exactly what happens. Whenever I decide to produce more or less of some good, to enter or leave some profession, to change my consumption pattern, or in almost any other way to alter my market behavior, one result is to shift slightly some supply or demand curve and so to change some price; this affects all other buyers and sellers of the good whose price has changed. In a competitive market, the change in price due to one person's actions is tiny—but in calculating the size of the effect, one must multiply the small change in price by the large quantity of goods for which the price has changed—the entire market. When, for example, I decide to become the million and first physician, the effect of my decision in driving down the wages of each existing physician is tiny, but it must be multiplied by a million physicians. The product is not necessarily negligible.

It appears that there can be no economic action without important externalities. But these are precisely the sort of externality that can be ignored. When price falls by a penny, what is lost by a seller is gained by a buyer; the loss to the physicians is a gain to their patients. The result is a pecuniary externality. My decision to enter a profession, to buy or to sell goods, may have more than a negligible effect on others through its effect on the price of goods or services they buy or sell, but that effect imposes neither net costs nor net benefits, so I can ignore it in deciding what to do without producing an inefficient outcome as a result.

Religious Radio: An Application of Public Good Theory

Whenever I spend much time listening to a variety of stations on the radio, I am struck by how many of them are religious. One could take this as evidence that America is a very religious country—except that the popularity of religion on the airwaves does not seem to be matched elsewhere. If I go to a newsstand or a bookstore, I see relatively few religious newspapers, magazines, or books—far fewer, as a percentage of the total, than radio programs.

There is a simple explanation for this discrepancy. Publishers can control who gets their publications; broadcasters cannot control who listens to their broadcasts. Broadcasters, unlike publishers, are producing a public good and depend on some solution to the problem of producing a public good privately in order to stay in business.

Commercials are one solution to that problem; religion is another. The people who listen to religious broadcasters presumably believe in the religion. For most of them, that means that they believe in the existence of a god who rewards virtue and punishes vice. If, as many radio preachers claim, donating money to their programs is a virtuous act, then the program is no longer a pure public good. The preacher may not know which listeners help pay for the show and which do not, but God knows. One of the benefits produced by the program is an increased chance of a heavenly reward; you are more likely to get that benefit if you pay for it. Thus religion provides a solution to the public-good problem.

Nothing in the analysis depends on whether the particular religion is or is not true; what matters is only that the listeners believe it is true and act accordingly. The result is that religious broadcasters have an advantage over secular broadcasters. Both produce programs that their listeners value, but the religious broadcaster is better able to get the listener to pay for them. The religious publisher has no corresponding advantage over the secular publisher. So religion is more common on the air than in print.

INFORMATION PROBLEMS

Long ago and far away—in Chapter 1, to be precise—I pointed out an ambiguity in the definition of "rational." In some contexts a rational individual was one who made the right decision, the decision he would have made if he knew all of the relevant facts; in other contexts a rational individual was one who made the right decision about what facts to learn and then the best possible decision in the context of what he knew. I suggested that the latter definition is appropriate in situations where an essential part of the problem is the cost of getting and using information.

It is tempting to argue that information costs are simply one of the costs of producing and consuming goods, and so can be included in our analysis just like any other costs. In some situations that argument is correct. But, as we will see in this part of the chapter, information costs are frequently associated with problems that lead to market failure.

Information as a Public Good

One cost of buying goods is the cost of acquiring information about what to buy. This may be one reason firms are as large as they are; brand names represent a sort of informational capital. There may be a better deal available from an unknown producer, but the cost of determining that it is a better deal may be greater than the savings. Not only do you know that the brand-name product has been of good quality in the past, you also believe that the producer has an incentive to maintain the quality so as not to destroy the value of his brand name.

Why do we rely on brand names instead of buying information about the quality of goods from someone who specializes in producing such information? To some extent, we do buy information: by reading *Consumer Reports*, *Car and Driver*, or *Handgun Tests* and by taking economics courses. Yet much of the information we use we produce for ourselves—probably a much larger fraction than of most other things we consume. Since we do not have the time to become experts on everything we buy, we end up depending on brand names and other indirect (and very imperfect) ways of evaluating quality.

Why do we produce so much information for ourselves? Why is information a particularly hard good to produce and sell on the market?

The problem is that it is hard to protect the property rights of a producer of information. If I sell you a car, you can resell it only by giving up its use yourself. If I sell you a fact, you can both use that fact and make it available to all your friends and neighbors. This makes it difficult for those who produce facts to sell them for their full value. It is the same problem that I earlier discussed in the case of computer programs—which can be thought of as a kind of information. Information is in large part a public good; because it is a public good, it is underproduced.

One solution to this problem is provided by large brand-name retailers such as Sears. Sears does not produce what it sells, but it does select it. You may buy any particular product only once every year or two, which makes it hard to judge which producer is best. But you buy something from Sears much more often, so it is easier for you to judge that Sears (or one of its competitors) "on average" gives you good value for your money. Sears is in the business of learning which brands of the products it buys represent good value for the money and selling them to you under its brand name, thus implicitly selling you the information. By not telling you who really makes the product, it prevents you from reselling the information—to a friend who would then buy the same brand at a discount store. All you can tell your friend is to buy from Sears—which is fine with Sears.

Information Asymmetry—The Market for Lemons

Consider a situation where information is not merely imperfect but asymmetrical. The market for used cars may be a good example. The best way of finding out whether a car is a lemon is to drive it for a year or two. The seller of a used car has done so; potential buyers have not. While they can, at some cost, have the car examined by a mechanic, that may or may not be sufficient.

Suppose, to simplify our analysis, that there are only two kinds of cars: good cars and lemons. There are also two kinds of people: sellers and buyers. Each seller has a car, which he is interested in selling if he can get a reasonable price. Half have good cars; half have lemons. Each buyer would like to buy a car—if he can get it for a reasonable price. Sellers know what kind of car they have; buyers do not.

Both buyers and sellers prefer good cars to lemons. Sellers value lemons at $2,000 and good cars at $4,000—at any price above that they are willing to sell. Buyers value lemons at $2,500 and good cars at $5000—at any lower price they are willing to buy. It appears that all of the cars should sell—lemons for between $2,000 and $2,500, good cars between $4,000 and $5,000.

There is a problem. Buyers cannot, at a reasonable cost, tell whether a car is a lemon. The sellers know, but have no way of conveying the information, since it is obviously in the interest of every seller to claim that his car is a good one. So each buyer is buying a gamble—some probability of getting a good car and some probability of getting a lemon.

It looks as though the probabilities are 50-50, since half the cars are lemons. If so, and if the buyers are risk-neutral, they will offer no more than the average of the values of the two kinds of cars, which is $3,750. At that price, owners of lemons will be glad to sell, but owners of good cars will not.

The buyers can work out the logic of the preceding paragraph for themselves. While a car offered for sale has a 50 percent chance of being good, a car that is actually sold is certain to be a lemon, since owners of good cars will refuse the best offer buyers are willing to make. Buyers take that fact into account, and reduce their offers accordingly. All of the cars are worth more to the buyers than the sellers, but only the lemons get sold. That is an inefficient outcome. In more complicated situations, with a range of qualities of cars, the result may be even worse; in some cases only the single worst car gets sold.

One obvious solution is for sellers with good cars to offer a guarantee—perhaps a guarantee to buy it back a year later for purchase price minus a year's rental if the buyer decides the car is a lemon. One problem with this solution is that the condition of the car a year hence depends on a lot of things other than its condition today, including how it is treated by its new owner.

Adverse Selection

The problem I have just been describing is known, in the context of insurance markets, as **adverse selection.** Consider health or life insurance. The customer has information about himself that the insurance company cannot easily obtain: how carefully he drives, what medical problems he has had in the past, whether he is planning to take up hang gliding, skydiving, or motorcycle racing in the near future. The more likely a potential customer is to collect on his insurance the greater its value to him—and its cost to the insurance company. If the customer knows he is a bad risk and the insurance company does not, insurance is a good deal—for the customer.

The good risk would be happy to buy insurance at a price reflecting the low probability that he will get sick or die next year, but the insurance company will not offer it to him at that price, since the insurance company does not know he is a good risk. The result is that bad risks are more likely to buy insurance than good risks. Insurance companies, knowing that, must adjust their rates accordingly—the very fact that someone buys insurance is evidence that he is a bad risk and should therefore be charged a high price. The higher price results in even fewer good risks buying insurance—resulting in an even higher price. The equilibrium result may well be that many good risks are priced out of the market, even though there is a price at which they would be willing to buy insurance and the insurance companies would gain by selling it to them. Just as with automobiles, one can even construct a situation where only the worst risks end up insured, everyone else having been driven out of the market. Again we have an inefficient outcome.

Insurance companies try to control this problem in a variety of ways, including medical checkups for new customers and provisions in insurance contracts denying payment to people who say they have no dangerous hobbies and then die when their parachutes fail to open two miles up. A less obvious solution is selling insurance to groups. If all employees of a factory are covered by the same insurance, the insurance company is getting a random assortment of good and bad risks. The good risks get a worse deal than the bad, but since they still get insured the insurance rates reflect the risk of insuring an average employee rather than an average bad risk. If insuring everyone is the efficient outcome, the group policy produces an efficient allocation of insurance, plus a redistribution of income from the good risks, who are paying more than their insurance costs to produce, to the bad risks, who are paying less.

One argument in favor of universal, governmentally provided health insurance is that it is a group policy carried to its ultimate extreme—everyone is in the group. It thus eliminates the problem of adverse selection (except, perhaps, for people with health problems who decide to immigrate in order to take advantage of the program). Whether the net effect is an improvement depends on how well the government can and does deal with other problems of providing insurance.

Moral Hazard

It may have occurred to you that there is another potential inefficiency associated with insurance. Most of the things we insure against are at least partly under our own control. That is true not only of my health and the chance of my house burning down, but even of losses from "acts of God" such as floods or tornadoes. I cannot control the flood, but I can control the loss—by deciding where to live and what precautions to take.

Whether or not I am insured, I take those precautions, and only those precautions, that save me more than they cost me. Once I have bought fire insurance, part of the cost of being careless with matches and part of the benefit of installing a sprinkler system have been transferred to the insurance company; the cost to me is no longer the entire cost, so the result is no longer efficient. If a sprinkler system costs $1000 and produces a benefit of $800 to me in reduced risk of being burned alive and another $600 to the insurance company in reduced probability of having to replace my house, it is worth buying—but not to me.

So people who are insured will take less than the efficient level of precaution. This problem is known as **moral hazard**. It is an inefficiency resulting from an externality; once I am insured someone else bears some of the cost of my actions.

Insurance companies try to control moral hazard just as they try to control adverse selection. One way is by specifying, so far as possible, the precautions that the insured will take—requiring a factory to install and maintain a sprinkler system as a condition of providing fire insurance. Another is **co-insurance**—insuring for only part of the value, in order to make sure that the customer has at least a substantial stake in preventing the risk that is insured against. If, in my previous example, the house was insured for only half its value, the sprinkler system would be worth more to me than it cost, so I would buy it. If, at the opposite extreme, the insurance company makes the mistake of insuring a building for more than it is worth, the probability of a fire may become very high indeed.

WARNING

In thinking about market failure, it is often tempting to interpret the problem in terms of fairness rather than efficiency. Externalities are then seen as wrong because they are unfair, because one person is suffering and another gaining, and public goods as a problem because some consumers get what others pay for.

That is a mistake. Consider the situation of 100 identical individuals polluting and breathing the same air. On net there is no unfairness—everyone gains by being able to pollute and loses by being polluted. Yet because each person bears only 1 percent of his pollution, each pollutes at far above the efficient level and all are, as a result, worse off. This is precisely analogous to the effect of the potato subsidy discussed in Chapter 3; everyone gets back in subsidy as much as he pays in taxes yet ends up worse off, not because he is poorer but because he is buying too many potatoes.

The same is true for the other kinds of market failure. The ultimate problem with public goods is not that one person pays for what someone else gets but that nobody pays and nobody gets, even though the good is worth more than it would cost to produce. The major cost of adverse selection is not that some people buy lemons or write life insurance policies on skydivers. The major cost is that cars are not sold, even though they are worth selling, and people do not get insured, even though they are worth insuring.

PROBLEMS

1. Describe two public-good problems that you have yourself observed in the past year and discuss how they might be dealt with; you should not use any that are discussed in the chapter.

2. In ordinary markets, supply and demand are balanced by price. Given that our customs prohibit, in most social contexts, cash payments as part of a date (or a marriage), what sorts of "prices" balance those markets in the U.S. at present? If supply and demand on the dating/sex/marriage market are not balanced (quantity supplied is not equal to quantity demanded—more men want to go out or have sex or get married than women, or vice versa), what mechanisms ration out the insufficient supply (decide which men get women, or vice versa)? What prices balance supply and demand for similar markets in other countries or have done so at other times?

3. How would the style of dating and marriage change if a war substantially reduced the ratio of men to women? How would it change if a lot of men migrated to the United States, substantially raising the ratio of men to women?

4. "Heterosexual men are traditionally hostile to homosexual men. If they correctly considered their own interests, their attitude would be just the opposite." Discuss.

5. "The public-good problem is both an argument *for* government intervention in the market and an argument *against* government intervention in the market." Explain.

6. Students frequently argue that grades should be deemphasized or abolished. The same students start the first class of the quarter by asking me about my grading policy—and continue throughout the course to exhibit a keen interest in what will or will not be on the final exam. Is their behavior inconsistent?

7. A tape recorder can copy a recording of a concert onto a cassette just as a computer can copy a program onto a disk. Why is the problem of pirating (making copies without paying royalties) less serious in the case of tapes than in the case of programs?

8. In my experience, FM radio is less religious than AM; you may wish to check that conclusion for yourself. Can you suggest any reasons why? (I am not sure I know the answer to this one.)

9. Last year Bryan and Brian occupied separate apartments; each consumed 400 gallons per month of hot water. This year they are sharing a larger apartment. To their surprise, they find they are consuming 1,000 gallons per month. Explain.

10. One of my students cannot possibly take the midterm at the scheduled time. I am afraid that if I give it to him early, he might talk about it to other students, giving them an unfair advantage, and that if I give

it to him late, other students might talk to him about it, giving him an unfair advantage. Given the problems associated with property in information, which problem do you think is more likely to arise? Discuss. Does it depend on whether the students believe that I grade on a curve?

11. The following table shows, for three different goods (produced by three different firms), total cost of production (as a function of quantity produced), total external cost imposed by producing the goods, and their total value to the consumer. Assume the manufacturer can sell the goods at their value, which is the same for all three goods ($10/unit). He must pay the cost of production but does not have to pay for the external cost. Fractional units cannot be produced; output can be 0,1,2,3, ... but not 2½.
    a. How much does each firm choose to produce?
    b. In which, if any, cases is the outcome efficient?
    c. In the inefficient cases, how large would the net gain be if the firm was forced to produce the efficient level of output instead of the profit-maximizing level?

| | Lamps | | Books | | Pies | | |
# of Units	Production Cost	External Cost	Production Cost	External Cost	Production Cost	External Cost	Value
1	$ 6.00	$0.50	$ 9.00	$2.00	$ 8.00	$1.00	$10.00
2	$14.00	$1.00	$18.00	$3.00	$16.00	$2.00	$20.00
3	$25.00	$1.50	$27.00	$4.00	$25.50	$3.00	$30.00
4	$39.00	$2.00	$39.00	$5.00	$36.00	$4.00	$40.00

12. " . . . another reason to contribute to our fund-raising campaign is self-interest. The money you give us will improve the quality and reputation of the University, raising the value of your degree. If each alumnus gave $100 . . ." (extract from a fund-raising letter). What is wrong with this argument? Why is it unlikely to succeed?

13. While visiting one of the publishers that wanted to publish this book, I raised the question of whether the book should be published with or without color figures. Using color makes a book more attractive but more expensive to produce. I was told that they preferred to decide such matters at a later stage in the process of producing the book.
    a. Why do you think they do it that way?
    b. What conclusions do you think I drew about the publisher? Do you think they ended up publishing the book? Explain.
    Hint: An author's royalties are usually a fixed fraction of revenue; the publisher receives the rest, and pays all expenses of producing and selling the book.

14. Many of the efficiency problems discussed in previous chapters could be described in terms of externalities; give three examples, with brief explanations of each.

FOR FURTHER READING

Carlo M. Cipolla, *Money, Prices, and Civilization in the Mediterranean World* (Staten Island, NY: Gordian Press, 1967). This book contains a number of interesting essays on the economics of the past, including an interesting discussion of barter in the Middle Ages.

The Coase Theorem first appeared in Ronald Coase, "The Problem of Social Cost," *Journal of Law and Economics*, Vol. 3 (1960), pp. 1–44.

My discussion of information asymmetry is based on: G. Akerlof, "The Market for Lemons," *Quarterly Journal of Economics*, Vol. 336 (1970), pp. 488–500.

APPLICATIONS –
section V
CONVENTIONAL AND UN

chapter 19

THE POLITICAL MARKETPLACE

The purpose of this chapter is to use some of the ideas developed in previous chapters to understand the behavior of political institutions. It contains three parts. The first is an analysis of the effects of tariffs— in particular, the question of whether imposing a tariff is a Marshall improvement or a Marshall worsening. The second is a sketch of two variants of **public choice theory**—the economic analysis of government— intended in part to explain the inconsistency between the sorts of tariffs that economists can defend as efficient and the sorts that exist. The third part uses the concept of rent seeking, introduced in Chapter 16 in a different context, to analyze the cost of government activity.

TARIFFS

Chapter 5 introduced the principle of comparative advantage and showed why such standard arguments for tariffs as "The Japanese can produce everything cheaper than we can" or "Tariffs protect American jobs" are wrong. Showing that particular arguments for tariffs are wrong is not the same thing as showing that tariffs are undesirable. We saw why mutual gains from trade were possible, but we did not, at that point, have the tools necessary to determine whether those gains were maximized by free trade, or might be increased by appropriate tariffs or trade subsidies. Now we do. As you will shortly see, the answer to that question depends both on what we assume about international markets and on whose interests we take into account in judging one arrangement superior to another—only the interests of Americans or the interests of both Americans and the people we trade with.

In the first section of this part of the chapter, I will prove that *if America as a whole is a price taker in international markets*, then American tariffs are undesirable even if we take into account only the interests of Americans—or, in other words, that the abolition of American tariffs would produce net benefits for Americans. The result will be proved once graphically and once verbally, using a number of simplifying assumptions. In the next section, I will show several exceptions to the general rule that tariffs are undesirable; in each case, the exception depends on dropping one of the assumptions used in the proof. Some of the exceptions are cases where tariffs may be desirable if we consider only the interests of Americans but not if we include the effect on foreigners; others are cases where the imposition of a particular tariff is a Marshall improvement even when we count effects on everyone.

Having answered the question of what tariffs we *should* have, I will then, in the second part of the chapter, take up the question of what tariffs we *do* have and why.

Why Tariffs Are Undesirable

I will start by listing the assumptions that will be used in the proof. We assume only one good is imported (autos) and one good is exported (wheat). We assume that America is a price taker in international markets: Changes in our production of wheat and consumption of autos are not sufficient to change the rate at which autos exchange for wheat abroad. The wheat and auto industries in the United States are price-taking industries with no substantial net externalities. Transport costs are zero.

The Geometric Proof. Figure 19-1 shows the supply curve for American production of automobiles and the demand curve for American consumption of automobiles, both before and after the imposition of a tariff. P_A is the market price before the tariff, P'_A after the tariff. Q_A is the quantity of imported cars before the tariff, Q'_A after. Figure 19-2 shows the corresponding curves, prices, and quantities for wheat.

The first thing that should strike you about Figure 19-1 is that at neither P_A nor P'_A is quantity supplied equal to quantity demanded. This is because the price at which U.S. quantity supplied would equal U.S. quantity demanded is above the world market price; the United States therefore imports autos. Quantity demanded is equal to quantity supplied (by the U.S. auto industry) plus imports. Similarly, in Figure 19-2, the price at which quantity of wheat supplied and quantity demanded in the United States are equal is below the world price of wheat. The United States therefore exports wheat. Quantity produced (by U.S. farmers) equals quantity demanded (by U.S. consumers) plus exports.

The next question that might occur to you concerns Figure 19-2. The tariff is on autos; why should it affect the price of wheat? The answer is that wheat is what we are sending foreigners in exchange for the autos they are sending us. If, because of the tariff, fewer dollars go abroad to buy foreign cars, then foreigners will have fewer dollars with which to buy American wheat. Foreign demand for American wheat falls; the price of wheat in America drops. This effect is shown on Figure 19-2.

Figure 19-1

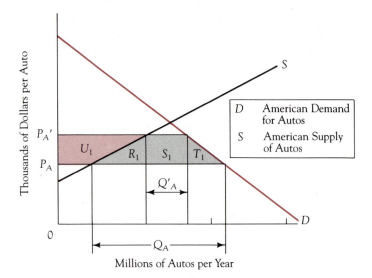

The effect on the domestic auto market of a tariff on autos. D and S are the domestic demand and supply curves for autos. Q_A is the rate at which autos are being imported before the tariff is imposed, Q'_A the rate after. P_A is the U.S. price of autos before, P'_A the price after.

The colored area U_1 on Figure 19-1 is the increase in (American) producer surplus as a result of the tariff; U_1 plus the shaded area $R_1 + S_1 + T_1$ is the reduction in (American) consumer surplus. The shaded area is the net loss (to Americans) of surplus on autos as a result of the tariff. Similarly, on Figure 19-2, U_2 is the gain in (American) consumer surplus as a result of the fall in the price of wheat produced by the tariff on automobiles, and $U_2 + R_2 + S_2 + T_2$ is the loss of (American) producer surplus. The shaded area $R_2 + S_2 + T_2$ is the net loss (to Americans) of surplus on wheat as an indirect result of the tariff on autos.

There is one more term to be considered in calculating the net effect of the tariff on Americans: the money actually collected by the tariff. If the tariff is $\$t$/auto, the government collects t dollars on each of Q'_A autos imported each year, so its revenue from the tariff is $t \times Q'_A$. If that is larger than the sum of the two shaded areas, then the tariff produces net gains and is a Marshall improvement; if it is smaller, then the tariff is a Marshall worsening and its abolition would be a Marshall improvement. What I am going to show is that $t \times Q'_A$, the revenue collected by the tariff, is equal to the area $S_1 + S_2$. Since $S_1 + S_2$ is only part of the cost of the tariff, that will imply that the total cost is larger than the revenue collected, and hence that the tariff produces net costs rather than net benefits.

Section V   Applications—Conventional and Un

Figure 19-2

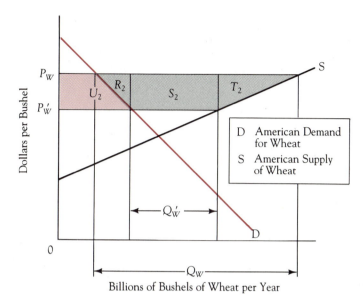

The effect on the domestic wheat market of a tariff on autos. *D* and *S* are the domestic demand and supply curves for wheat. Q_W is the rate at which wheat is being exported before the tariff is imposed, Q'_W the rate after. P_W is the U.S. price of wheat before, P'_W after.

I will use two relations implicit in the situation I have described. The first is that since America is assumed to be a price taker in international markets, the tariff does not affect the relative prices of autos and wheat outside the United States. Before the tariff, the price ratio is P_A/P_W. After the tariff, the price of wheat abroad (in dollars) is P'_A, the price of autos abroad is $P'_A - t$, so the price ratio is $(P'_A - t)/P'_W$.

How do I know that the world price of autos is $P'_A - t$? P'_A is the price of autos in the United States. In order to get foreign autos into the United States you must pay their world price plus the tariff t; the price in the United States is P'_A, so the world price must be $P'_A - t$.

Since the price ratio outside the United States is the same before and after the tariff, it follows that:

$$\frac{P_A}{P_W} = \frac{P'_A - t}{P'_W} \qquad \text{(Equation 1)}$$

Autos are, by assumption, our only import and wheat our only export, so the total number of dollars foreigners get for the cars they sell to us must equal the number of dollars they spend for the wheat they buy from us. Using prices and quantities after the tariff is imposed, this gives us:

$$P'_W \times Q'_W = \text{\$'s spent on wheat by foreigners}$$

$$= \text{\$'s received for cars by foreigners}$$

$$= (P'_A - t)Q'_A. \qquad \text{(Equation 2)}$$

(We spend P'_A on each car, but since t goes to the government to pay the tariff, only $P'_A - t$ goes to foreigners).

Finally, from Figures 19-1 and 19-2, we have:

$$S_1 + S_2 = (P'_A - P_A)Q'_A + (P_W - P'_W)Q'_W. \qquad \text{(Equation 3)}$$

Equations 1 and 2 imply that:

$$Q'_W = Q'_A\left(\frac{P'_A - t}{P'_W}\right) = Q'_A\left(\frac{P_A}{P_W}\right).$$

Substituting this into Equation 3 gives us:

$$S_1 + S_2 = Q'_A(P'_A - P_A) + Q'_A\left(\frac{P_A}{P_W}\right)(P_W - P'_W)$$

$$= Q'_A\left\{P'_A - P_A + \left(\frac{P_A}{P_W}\right)(P_W - P'_W)\right\}$$

$$= Q'_A\left\{P'_A - P_A + P_A - P'_W\left(\frac{P_A}{P_W}\right)\right\}.$$

If we cancel out $-P_A + P_A$ and use Equation 1 to replace P_A/P_W with $(P'_A - t)/P'_W$, we get:

$$S_1 + S_2 = Q'_A\left\{P'_A - P'_W\left(\frac{P'_A - t)}{P'_W}\right)\right\}$$

$$= Q'_A(P'_A - P'_A + t)$$

$$= Q'_A \times t \qquad \text{(Equation 4)}$$

Since $S_1 + S_2$ is only part of the net loss to American consumers and producers caused by the tariff and $Q'_A \times t$ is all of the revenue collected by the tariff, net loss is larger than revenue; the imposition of the tariff is a Marshall worsening and its abolition would be a Marshall improvement.

The Verbal Proof.   I have now proved my result—that if the United States is a price taker in international markets and American firms are price takers in domestic markets, American tariffs on net injure Americans—mathematically. Next I will prove it again in another language: English.

From the standpoint of the United States, foreign trade is a technology for turning wheat into autos at the rate P_A/P_W. We proved in Chapter 16 that a competitive industry (without externalities) is efficient. Hence the result of the competitive industry for turning wheat into autos is efficient. A tariff alters that result, taxing the conversion of wheat into autos and so reducing the quantity of wheat used and autos produced. That change could be made by a bureaucrat-god. A bureaucrat-god cannot improve an outcome that is already efficient—that is the definition of "efficient." So a tariff cannot be a Marshall improvement. Since it alters a situation that is already efficient, it is almost certain to be a Marshall worsening.

Capital in Action.   There are two things I would like you to notice about what we have done so far in this chapter. The first is that our proofs are themselves examples of the use of capital in production. We have spent the previous 18 chapters accumulating intellectual capital, learning a complicated set of ideas, many of which must, at times, have seemed entirely useless. Using that capital, we have now, with a few pages of high school geometry and algebra plus a paragraph of reasoning, proved one of the more important practical results of economic theory—twice.

The second thing I would like you to notice is the contrast between the two proofs, a contrast typical of the differences between the two languages we used. The advantage of the verbal proof is that it helps us to intuit why tariffs are undesirable—provided we have previously learned to intuit why a competitive industry is efficient. Trade is simply a technology for converting exports into imports; a competitive industry uses that technology up to the point where the benefit of one more unit of imports is balanced by the cost of producing the exports that must be exchanged for it. A tariff adds an additional cost of production; the industry reduces its output, depriving some consumers of imported goods that they valued at more than their cost but less than their cost plus the tariff. The tariff is simply a tax on a particular way of producing things; the net loss is the resulting excess burden, just as with any other tax. It is zero only if either the demand or supply curve is vertical.

Does this conclusion depend on assuming that the United States is a price taker in international markets? For the mathematical proof, the answer is yes; that is how we got Equation 1, which was used twice in the proof. In the verbal proof, however, I said nothing at all about whether the United States as a whole was a price taker; all I assumed was that the export and import industries were price takers within the United States (and therefore efficient). That is not at all the same thing. If United States agriculture consists of a million small farms, each farmer is a price taker; but if the United States produces 90 percent of the world's wheat, the United States as a whole is not—changes in how much wheat we export will affect world prices.

In fact, the verbal proof does depend on the United States being a price taker, but the reason is a somewhat subtle one. If the United States is not a price taker, then the quantity of wheat exported (and autos imported) affects the price ratio abroad, which means that it affects the rate at which we can convert wheat into autos. From the standpoint of the United States that is an externality; when I buy autos abroad, I drive up their price (and drive down the price of the wheat I use to pay for them), making it more expensive for you to buy autos abroad. If we think of trade as a way of converting wheat into autos, this is like a situation where my increased production of widgets somehow makes your widget factory less productive—which would be an externality. We know from Chapter 18 that a competitive industry with externalities does not generally produce an efficient outcome. So if the United States is a price searcher, the initial situation (without a tariff) is not efficient, and it is possible that a tariff may improve it.

From the standpoint of the world as a whole, the externality in question is a pecuniary externality, so it may be ignored; if my purchases of automobiles drive up the world price, that is a loss to the other buyers but a gain to the sellers. But if the buyers are Americans, the sellers are foreigners, and we consider only the interests of Americans, there is a net externality—we count the loss and ignore the gain. So if the United States is a price searcher in international markets, the outcome without tariffs is efficient if all interests are considered but inefficient if only American interests are.

The Exceptions—"Good" Tariffs

Three important assumptions went into the proof that tariffs were undesirable: that the United States was a price taker in international markets, that American import and export industries were price takers within the United States, and that they had no important externalities. We will discuss the results of dropping two of them.

America as a Monopolist.   Suppose the United States is not a price taker in international markets; suppose, for example, that we have a monopoly on wheat. Individual farmers are still price takers, so they produce up to the point where $MC = P$. All of the farmers taken together, however, would do better if they acted like a monopoly or a cartel, restricting their production and driving up price to the point where $MC = MR$. The government can produce that result by imposing an **export tax**—a sort of backwards tariff—on wheat. The export tax drives up the price of wheat abroad; Americans as a whole (including the government collecting the tax) gain just as they would if the farmers had gotten together and raised their price. The same result can also be produced by a tax on imports—an ordinary tariff. Importing and exporting are two sides of the same transaction—trading wheat for cars—so it does not matter at which point you impose the tax. It follows that if we are price searchers in international markets, a tariff may produce net benefits for us.

The same argument applies if we are price searchers as consumers of automobiles: monopsonists. In that case, a tariff on automobiles drives up their price in the United States, lowers U.S. consumption, and so drives down the price of automobiles abroad. Since the United States is a net importer, we benefit by the lower price.

What happens in both of these cases is that without a tariff, individual Americans function as price takers in international markets even though America as a whole has some monopoly power. The tariff, in effect, creates a monopoly (or monopsony) out of a multitude of small firms. The result is a net gain at the expense of our trading partners. When we drive the international price of autos down (by imposing a tariff that decreases our consumption) or the international price of wheat up (by imposing an export tax on wheat), we benefit, since we are sellers of wheat and buyers of autos. Our trading partners lose, since they are buyers of wheat and sellers of autos. Just as in the (single-price) monopolies discussed earlier, the result is a net loss but a gain for the monopolist. Such a tariff is a Marshall improvement if we consider only gains and costs to Americans; it is a Marshall worsening if we include gains and losses to foreigners. Just as with other cases of monopoly pricing, demand and supply curves are likely to be more elastic in the long run than in the short run, so our gains from the tariff may be only temporary. One other problem with such a tariff is that we may not be the only country with a monopoly or a monopsony. If we use a tariff to exploit our monopoly power against our trading partners, they may do the same thing to us.

Protecting Infant Industries.   A tariff designed to create monopoly profits for the nation that imposes it is one example of a tariff that may be efficient, provided that we ignore the effect on foreigners. A second example, and one often used by supporters of tariffs, is a tariff to protect an **infant industry.**   This can, under some assumptions, result in an improvement even if we include the effects on foreigners.

Assume the United States has the potential to produce and export tin but does not yet have a tin industry. A company that tries to start a tin foundry in the United States will have a hard time of it—American workers do not know how to work with tin, American railroads have no experience shipping tin and no special freight cars designed to carry it, and American coal mines have no experience producing the particular kinds of coal needed to refine tin from tin ore. Until all those problems are solved, American tin will be more costly than imported tin. If only the tin industry could get established, it would be profitable, but nobody wants to be first.

One problem with the argument as stated is that if the tin industry is going to be profitable in the long run, tin companies should be willing to accept losses in the first few years, treating them as an investment to be paid back out of later profits. If companies are not willing to do that, perhaps the profits are not large enough, or certain enough, to make the losses worth taking.

To get around this argument, one must assume that the process of development occurs within the industry but outside the firm. No firm can do it by itself, but if they all do it together, workers will become skilled in working tin, subsidiary industries will grow up to support tin manufacture, and so on. Another way of putting this is that there are large positive externalities produced by the first few firms in an industry; while they are losing money producing tin, they are also producing a body of skills and knowledge in their employees and suppliers that will lower the costs of future producers.

If this is true, then since the initial firms do not include the (external) benefits they produce for others in calculating the value of what they produce, they may never start production unless they are subsidized by a temporary tariff that raises the cost of imported tin. This is the argument for an infant industry tariff. We have dropped the assumption that the firms in the industry have no important externalities; the result is that a tariff may be desirable—imposing it may be a Marshall improvement. In this case, unlike the previous one, a tariff may be desirable even if we take into account the interests of everyone concerned. If the United States has the potential to produce tin less expensively than it can be imported, the gains to the U.S. producers and their customers may ultimately outweigh the losses to foreign producers.

Should vs Will.   So far, I have shown that tariffs are usually undesirable but that there are exceptions—situations where tariffs are desirable, at least from the standpoint of the countries that impose them. Is that why the United States, and most other countries, have tariffs? Apparently not. The tariffs we observe in the real world have little resemblance to the ones that can be defended as economically desirable. It is not infant industries that get protection but senile industries—American auto, shoe, and steel producers, for example. Why?

To answer that question, we need to understand not what laws *should* exist but what laws *will* exist. We need, in other words, an economic theory of politics. The branch of economics that deals with such questions is called public choice theory, presumably because it explains public choices, while ordinary economics deals with private choices. The name is somewhat deceptive, since what makes public choice theory part of economics is that it analyzes the behavior of political institutions as the outcome of the choices of rational individuals, each seeking his own objectives. It is a theory of the behavior of political institutions that results from private choices on the political marketplace.

In the next section, I will sketch one version of public choice theory; after doing so, we will see how that theory can be used to explain the observed pattern of tariffs. One of the questions we will be interested in is whether the political system can be expected, like the competitive market of Chapter 16, to generate efficient results. If so, we would expect the tariffs actually observed in the real world to correspond fairly closely to the "good" tariffs discussed above.

If, on the other hand, the political market—like the private market with monopoly, externalities, or public goods—produces inefficient outcomes, then there is little reason to expect the tariffs that economists observe to correspond to those they recommend. The problem is then to predict the outcomes of the political market—to show which particular industries will or will not get tariff protection. Having done so, we can compare the predictions of the theory with what we actually observe, in order to test the theory and perhaps, if its predictions turn out to be correct, understand the reasons for the outcomes we observe.

PUBLIC CHOICE: ECONOMIC ANALYSIS OF THE POLITICAL MARKET

Public choice theory is simply economics applied to a market with peculiar property rights. Just as in the economic analysis of an ordinary market, individuals are assumed to pursue their separate objectives rationally; just as in that analysis, one may first make and later drop simplifying assumptions such as perfect information or zero transaction costs. The property rights on the public market, however, are different from those on the private market; they include the right of individuals to vote for representatives, of representatives to make laws, of government officials to enforce the laws, of judges to interpret them, and so on.

Ordinary economics is greatly simplified if we treat firms as imaginary individuals trying to maximize their profits; in this way, we convert General Motors from several hundred thousand individuals into one. There is some cost to the simplification, since it ignores the conflicts of interest within the firm among managers, employees, and stockholders. So far, no alternative simplification seems to work as well. So economists continue to analyze an economy of profit-maximizing firms, except when the particular problem being considered hinges on intrafirm interactions—as it does, for instance, in the theory of the firm, of which the optional section of Chapter 9 and the discussion of mergers in Chapter 18 provide brief samples.

One of the ways in which different public choice theories differ from each other is in what they take to be the equivalent of the firm on the political market and what it is assumed to maximize. For the moment, I shall consider the entrepreneurs on the political market to be elected politicians and limit my discussion to the market for legislation.

This is a simplification of the political market and only one of several possible simplifications—two others will be discussed in later sections—but it provides a convenient way of sketching the theory.

The Market for Legislation

Consider, then, the market for legislation. Individuals perceive that they will be benefited or harmed by various laws. They offer payments to politicians for supporting some laws and opposing others. The payments may take the form of promises to vote for the politician, of cash payments to be used to finance future election campaigns, or of (concealed) contributions to the politician's income. The politician is seeking to maximize his long-run income (plus nonpecuniary benefits, one of which may be "national welfare"), subject to the constraint that he can only sell legislation for as long as he can keep getting elected.

Is It Efficient?   To see whether we can expect the outcome of this market to be efficient, let us consider a simple example. A legislator proposes a bill that inefficiently transfers income from one interest group to another; it imposes costs of $10 each on 1,000 individuals (total cost $10,000) and grants benefits of $500 each to 10 individuals (total benefit $5,000). What will be "bid" for and against the law?

The total cost to the losers is $10,000, but the maximum amount they will be willing to offer to a politician to oppose the law is very much less than that. Why? Because of the public-good problem. Any individual who contributes to a campaign fund to defeat the bill is providing a public good for all 1,000 members of the group. The same arguments used in Chapter 18 to show that public goods are underproduced apply here. The larger the public, the lower the fraction of the value of the good that can be raised to pay for it.

The benefit provided to the winners is also a public good, but it goes to a much smaller public—10 individuals instead of 1,000. A smaller public can more easily organize, perhaps through conditional contracts ("I will contribute if and only if you do"), to fund a public good. Even though the benefit to the small group is smaller than the cost to the large one, the amount the small group is able to offer politicians to support the bill will be more than the amount the large group will offer to oppose it.

The effect is reinforced by a second consideration—information costs. Assume that information about the effect of legislation on any individual can be obtained, but only at some cost in time and money. For the individual who suspects that the bill may injure him by $10, it is not worth obtaining the information unless it is very inexpensive. His possible loss is small and so is the effect of any actions he is likely to take on the probability that the bill will pass. The member of the **dispersed interest** chooses (rationally) to be worse informed than the member of the **concentrated interest**.

If we abandon the particular example and consider instead an American presidential election, the argument becomes even clearer. Suppose the election result is about equally likely to be a 5 million vote victory for one candidate, a 5 million vote victory for the other, or any point in between. The probability that the election will be a tie, hence that one additional vote can decide it, is then one in 10 million. So the return to an individual who figures out who is the "right" candidate and votes accordingly, instead of voting at random (or not voting at all), is an increase by one chance in 10 million of the probability that the right candidate will be elected. Unless the voter has an extraordinarily high value for electing the right candidate, it is not worth paying very much in order to increase the probability of that outcome by one in 10 million, so he does not pay the information costs necessary to decide for whom he should vote. This is an example of **rational ignorance**; it is rational to be ignorant if the cost of information is greater than its value.

Let us now return to the case of a proposed bill that injures 1,000 individuals by $10 each and benefits 10 by $500 each. We see that the interests of the smaller group are much more heavily weighted on the political market than those of the larger. This is true both because the smaller group can more easily overcome the public-good problem of raising money to buy legislation and because individuals in a small group with a large benefit per individual have more of an incentive to bear the information costs necessary to determine what political actions it is in their interest to take.

What Does Concentration Mean?   So far, I have discussed only one characteristic of a group—its size. It is useful to think of the terms "concentrated" and "dispersed" as useful shorthand for the whole set of characteristics that determine how easily a group can fund a public good; the number of individuals in the group is only one of those characteristics.

Consider, for example, a tariff on automobiles. It benefits hundreds of thousands of people—stockholders in auto companies, auto workers, property owners in Detroit, and so forth. But GM, Ford, Chrysler, and the UAW are organizations that already exist to serve the interests of large parts of that large group of people. For many purposes, one can consider all of the stockholders and most of the workers as being four individuals—a group small enough to organize effectively. The beneficiaries of auto tariffs are a much more concentrated interest than a mere count of their numbers would suggest. That may explain why such tariffs exist, even though the costs they impose on consumers of automobiles and American producers of export goods, both dispersed interests, are larger than the benefits to the producers of automobiles.

The reason the public-good problem leads to inefficiency in ordinary private markets is that the amount a group can raise to "buy" a public good benefiting that group is less than the total value of the good to the members of the group; hence some public goods that are worth more than it would cost to produce them fail to get produced, which is inefficient. The reason it leads to inefficiency in public markets is that both costs and benefits are only fractionally represented on the market, because of the public-good problem. If potential gainers and losers from proposed legislation raise different fractions of their gains and losses to bid for and against the laws, as will usually be the case, laws that impose net costs may be passed and laws that impose net benefits may not be. This again is inefficient.

Predictions. What predictions can we make on the basis of this simple model of individuals and interest groups bidding for legislation? One is that legislation will tend to benefit concentrated interest groups at the expense of dispersed interest groups—where "concentrated" and "dispersed" describe the bundle of characteristics that determine how large a fraction of the benefit that the members of the interest group would receive from legislation can be raised by the group to buy the legislation.

A second prediction is that although the system may frequently generate inefficient outcomes, nonetheless more efficient outcomes will be preferred to less efficient, all other things being equal. Consider, for instance, a politician choosing among different ways of subsidizing a particular concentrated interest at the expense of a particular dispersed interest. One scheme will provide the beneficiaries with $1 million and cost the victims $10 million; an alternative will provide $1 million and cost $5 million. The amount spent to oppose him will be less in the second case than in the first, so he prefers it; he is choosing a transfer with an overhead of 80 percent ($0.20 return for every dollar of cost) over one with an overhead of 90 percent. The same argument applies if both schemes cost the victims the same amount but one provides $1 million to the beneficiaries and one provides $2 million. The larger the benefit, the larger the amount he can get paid, in one form or another, by the beneficiaries.

So far, we have two predictions. Transfers go from dispersed interests to concentrated interests, and they are made as efficiently as possible, all other things being equal. This raises an obvious problem: Why do we ever observe inefficient transfers, such as tariffs? Why do not politicians always prefer to simply tax the proposed victims and turn the receipts over to the proposed beneficiaries, thus reducing transfer costs to the unavoidable minimum: the administrative cost of collecting the tax and paying out the benefits, and the associated excess burden?

One answer is that there is a third prediction implicit in our model. Politicians will prefer transfers for which the information cost of figuring out what is really happening is as high as possible for the victims and as low as possible for the beneficiaries; if the cost is the same for both victims and beneficiaries, high information costs will generally be preferred to low ones.

The first half of this is obvious: The harder it is for the victims to know they are victims, the less they will spend trying to prevent the legislation; and the easier it is for the beneficiaries to know they are beneficiaries, the more they will spend supporting it. The second half, the general preference for high information costs, follows from the fact that beneficiaries are generally more concentrated than victims. As I pointed out earlier, it is easier for a concentrated interest to overcome the problems associated with information costs. So if information costs are high, it is likely that the beneficiaries will still pay them—and support the legislation—while the victims will fail to pay them and so fail to oppose it.

The preference for high information costs helps to explain the existence of inefficient forms of transfer. Given the choice, the sponsors of legislation designed to benefit some people at the expense of others would prefer to disguise it as something else. A bill to tax consumers and give the money to GM, Ford, Chrysler, and the UAW is likely to encounter more opposition than an auto tariff designed to do the same thing—because the auto tariff can be (and is) defended as a way of "protecting American jobs from the Japanese."

We now have three predictions about the outcome of political markets: They favor concentrated interests, they prefer more efficient to less efficient transfers, and they prefer transfers disguised as something else. How do these fit what we observe?

Tariffs in the Real World. One common observation about real-world tariffs is that they tend to go, not to infant industries, but to senile ones. In part, this is what we would expect from our discussion of concentrated versus dispersed interests. The American steel industry is a powerful concentrated interest; potential infant industries that do not now exist but could be created by an appropriate tariff are not. So it is the old industries that get the protection.

This explains why infant industries do not get tariffs, but it does not explain which industries do get them. If tariffs tend to go to declining industries, a satisfactory theory should explain why. The discussion of sunk costs in Chapter 13, combined with the prediction that politicians will prefer transfers that give the highest possible ratio of benefit to cost, all other things being equal, can do so.

Suppose a tariff is imposed on imports that compete with a growing, competitive, domestic industry. Before the tariff, price was equal to average cost, so economic profit was zero. The tariff reduces the supply of imports, so prices and the industry's output rise. But once enough new firms have entered the industry to reestablish equilibrium, average cost is again equal to price—profit is again zero. There is no gain to the industry, hence no reason for it to reward the politicians who imposed the tariff, save during the adjustment period.

If some of the inputs used by the industry are in fixed supply, such as certain types of land, their value will be bid up; their owners may be willing to offer part of the increase to get the tariff passed and maintained. If the inputs instead have a highly elastic supply curve, or if their ownership is divided among many individuals, no one of whom finds it worth his while to work for a tariff (because of the public-good nature of lobbying), then only transitional profits are available to reward the supporters of the tariff.

Consider next the case of a tariff on a declining industry. In such an industry there is usually an important resource in fixed supply: factories that produce enough revenue to be worth keeping but not enough to be worth building. The ownership of that resource is as concentrated as the industry is. The tariff increases demand for domestically produced goods by raising the cost of the competing imported goods and so increases the present value of the factories. In this case, unlike that of a growing industry, a large part of what the consumers lose in higher prices the producers receive in increased wealth.

The cost of the tariff is still larger than the benefits—but the cost is spread among many consumers and the benefits are concentrated on a few producers. Since the benefits to the industry are much larger in the case of a declining industry than in the case of a growing one, declining industries will be willing to work much harder to get tariffs. It is not surprising that they are generally more successful. The result is a pattern of tariffs almost exactly opposite to the pattern that could be justified as efficient.

The same analysis explains why tariffs on agricultural products are common—not so much in the United States, which is a net exporter of farm products, as in Japan and the countries of the European Economic Community, which are net importers. In the case of a tariff on farm products, the relevant fixed resource is land; increased demand for domestic crops drives up its price. Just as in the case of a declining industry, the producers get a large fraction, although not all, of what the consumers lose. If the fraction is large enough, and if the producers are sufficiently concentrated and well organized in comparison to the consumers, the result may be a tariff.

Alternative Approaches

So far, my discussion of public choice theory has focused on the market for legislation in a way that appears to downplay the arrangements by which we are taught, in high school civics classes, that our society is run: democratic elections. My reasons for doing so are in large part implicit in the discussion. Information costs make it difficult for voters to know which politicians are really acting in their interest, and the public-good problem means that it is rarely in the interest of voters to pay the costs and buy the information necessary to recognize and support "good" politicians.

This is one approach to public choice theory, but not the only one. There are other approaches, some of which choose to ignore such problems and analyze a democratic government in terms of the outcome of a system of majority voting among voters who correctly perceive their own interests and the positions of the candidates. The following is an example, applied to a recent election.

Hotelling and Hayden.   You are planning to build a store on the block shown in Figure 19-3. After you build your store, your competitor will build his. The customers are evenly distributed along the block; each customer always goes to the nearer store. Where do you build?

One wrong answer is shown in Figure 19-3a; your store is A, and your competitor's store is B. By locating his store as shown, he gets all of the customers to his right. He maximizes the number of customers he gets by building next to you, on the side toward the center of the block. Your correct strategy is to build in the center, as shown on Figure 19-3c, forcing him to build on one side or the other. You each get about half the market.

A few years ago, while teaching one of the courses out of which this textbook developed, I was reminded of this simple but elegant argument (originated by Harold Hotelling, the economist whose analysis of depletable resources was discussed in Chapter 12) by the campaign advertisements of Tom Hayden and his Republican opponent. Hayden was running a very left-wing campaign for the California legislature from a district including the city of Santa Monica—sometimes referred to by those unhappy with its politics as the People's Republic of Santa Monica. His opponent appeared to be taking very left-wing stands for a Republican: support of rent control, opposition to offshore drilling, and the like. The obvious interpretation is shown in Figure 19-3b, which is merely 19-3a relabeled. With Hayden far to the left on the political spectrum, his opponent maximizes his votes by being almost equally far left. Voters to his right have nowhere to go.

The same analysis explains the tendency of the American political system to nominate two similar candidates, both near the political center. That corresponds quite nicely to the prediction shown on Figure 19-3c. The fact that presidential candidates are not always at the center, like the fact that Hayden ran (and won) on a noncentrist platform, may be a result of additional complexities in the system. For one thing, issues cannot be perfectly represented as a one-dimensional left-right spectrum. For another, political support is not limited to voting; a voter near one

Figure 19-3

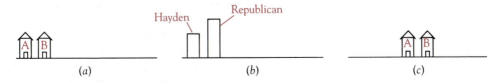

(a)   (b)   (c)

The Hotelling Theorem applied to stores and to politicians.

end of the spectrum may be willing to vote for a candidate he perceives as only a little less bad than his opponent, but be reluctant to donate time or money to his campaign. Finally, political parties are not infinitely flexible, at least in the short run; the Republican party of California may have been unable to field a candidate who could convince the voters that he was almost as far left as Tom Hayden.

Hotelling's argument, as applied to politics, is called the **median voter model.** The idea is that on any issue for which positions line up in a one-dimensional pattern, such as the issue of how large government spending should be, the outcome will always represent the desires of the median voter. Any position on one side of that favored by the median voter (such as a proposal to spend slightly more money than he wishes spent) will be defeated by a coalition consisting of the median voter and everyone on the other side of him (those who want to spend less than he does)—just over 50 percent of the votes. So will a position on the other side of him. So the median voter gets exactly what he wants.

Here again, the conclusion depends on issues having an unambiguous one-dimensional ordering and on the voters correctly perceiving their own interests and voting accordingly. In a more realistic model, the results become much more ambiguous. If, for example, the issue is income redistribution, the voter with the median income might be defeated by a coalition of the two extremes—rich and poor voting to tax the middle class for their joint benefit. That coalition could in turn be defeated by a coalition between the middle and the poor (or the rich), that by still another coalition, and so on without end. This is the same endless cycle that we saw in Chapter 11 when we analyzed the game of three-person majority vote.

The Revenue-Maximizing Bureau. As a final example of the diversity of public choice theories, consider William Niskanen's theory of bureaucracy. In his analysis, the essential actor is the government bureau: the U.S. Department of Defense, the Water and Sewer Department of the City of New Orleans, or any other organized body of bureaucrats with a common interest. The objective of each bureau is to maximize its budget in order to maximize the power and income of its members.

Since bureaus usually cannot impose their own taxes, they must get money from a legislature—which can. They do so by offering the legislature a selection of price/output packages, each consisting of a certain amount of output (defense, water and sewers, schooling, or whatever) to be produced with a budget of a specified size. Since, in Niskanen's model, bureaus know their own cost functions but legislatures do not, the bureau can and does lie to the legislature about the cost of alternative levels of output. Its objective is to get the largest possible appropriation. To do that, it understates the amount it could produce with lower budgets, in order to make those packages less attractive in comparison to the (high-budget) package it is trying to sell the legislature. The strategy of the revenue-maximizing bureau turns out to be very similar to the strategy of the monopolist with perfect price discrimination. Each is trying to offer its customer a package that he will just barely accept, in order to transfer as much of the resulting gain as possible to itself.

This model too has its problems. For one thing, it is not clear that bureaucrats would want to maximize their budgets even if they could do so. If in order to get the maximum budget, the bureau must promise the legislature—and produce—a large output, it might be better off with a slightly smaller budget and a much smaller set of obligations. If less has to be produced, more money will be available to be spent on the salaries (and other perquisites) of the bureaucrats.

RENT SEEKING AND THE COST OF GOVERNMENT

In Chapter 16, I introduced the idea of rent seeking in order to explain why perfect discriminatory monopoly might, under some circumstances, be the worst rather than the best way of organizing an industry. The term "rent seeking" was actually introduced to economics in a context more appropriate to this chapter. The analysis goes as follows.

How Not to Give Things Away

A government has valuable favors to give out—import permits, licenses, or the like. They take the form of pieces of paper giving the recipient permission to do something. Each piece of paper is worth $1 million; a potential recipient would, if necessary, pay up to that amount to get it. A thousand such pieces of paper are to be given out.

If you are giving away something worth $1 million, there will be no shortage of claimants. Some way must be found to choose among them. Suppose, to begin with, that the permits are supposed to be given out to those firms that will use them "in the public interest." The society is a democratic one; government officials try to give the permits to the firms that the voting public prefers.

Firms can and do act to influence the public's perceptions. If your firm wants a permit and does not expect to get it, it may be worth spending some money on improving your public image—perhaps by advertisements telling the general public how important your product is to the national welfare, how many jobs depend on you, and how crucial it is that you get the permit.

How much will you be willing to spend on such advertising? If it makes the difference between getting and not getting the permit, anything up to the value of the permit—$1 million. Initially, perhaps, you can get away with less. But when other firms observe that your $100,000 ad campaign is going to result in your getting one of the permits and their not getting one, they start their own ad campaigns—budgeted at $200,000. You reevaluate the situation and increase your budget. They do the same.

As long as, on average, an expenditure of less than $1 million on advertising gets a government favor worth $1 million, there will always be more firms willing to enter the game. By doing so, they either raise the amount that must be spent or lower the probability of success. Equilibrium is reached when each firm, on average, spends as much to get the permit as the permit is worth. If the firms that spend more are certain to get the permits, the result is that 1,000 firms spend $1 million each. If the situation is more uncertain, there may be 2,000 firms spending $500,000 each and each ending up with a 50 percent chance of success.

From one standpoint, the result is unsurprising; in equilibrium, marginal cost (as usual) equals marginal value. From another, it is very surprising indeed. The government is giving out, for free, $1 billion worth of special favors, and the recipients are ending up with nothing—the full value of the favors is used up in getting them.

I have assumed that potential recipients of the permits can influence their chances by using advertising to improve their public image. The result does not depend on that particular assumption. One can imagine a variety of other ways in which potential recipients might influence the result, including political donations to the party in power and bribery of the officials allocating the permits. The logic of the situation remains the same—the firms spend as much getting the favors as the favors are worth.

The term "rent seeking" was introduced to economics in an article by Anne Krueger. The principal example she considered involved countries that maintain an official exchange rate for their currency higher than the market rate and use import permits to ration the resulting shortage of foreign currency. If a native of (say) India earns dollars by selling goods abroad, he is supposed to turn them over to the government at the official rate—which means that he gets fewer rupees for his dollars than they are worth on the market. Indians who are given import permits by the government can then buy those dollars with rupees at the official rate, and use the dollars to buy goods abroad and import them into the country. Such permits are worth a great deal of money. Krueger concluded that a conservative estimate of the market value of the permits and other favors given out by the governments of Turkey and India, and hence the amount wasted on rent-seeking activity, was about 7 percent of national income for India and 15 percent for Turkey.

Rent seeking is not limited to poor countries with exchange controls. In analyzing the market for legislation, I concentrated on the outcome of that market without discussing its costs. If special interests buy legislation from politicians, that increases the value of being a successful politician, which in turn increases the amount spent on getting and keeping political office. This brings us to an interesting puzzle.

The Cost of Elections

It is common, especially around election time, to read articles lamenting how much is spent on campaigning. What surprises me is how little is spent on political campaigns, considering the stakes. In a presidential year, total expenditure by both parties on the presidential race and all congressional races is on the order of a few hundred million dollars. The prize is control of the federal government for several years, during which that government will spend several trillion dollars—or about ten thousand times total campaign expenditures.

One explanation for the disproportion between the prize and what is spent to get it is the public-good problem faced by even a relatively concentrated interest group. If a group can only raise, for political contributions, 10 percent of the value to its members of what it is buying, then the ability to deliver a dollar's worth of benefits is worth only $0.10 to the politician delivering it. A second explanation is the inefficiency of even relatively efficient transfers; a government expenditure of $10 million on behalf of some interest group may provide them with only $1 million worth of benefits. The difference between cost and benefit represents, in effect, the cost of hiding the transfer; a more direct and less inefficient arrangement would also be more obvious to the victims, hence less politically attractive. Combining the two effects would mean that a politician controlling $10 million in expenditure would end up with only $100,000 in campaign contributions.

A final explanation is that much of the cost of buying a political office never appears in records of campaign expenditure, not even the politician's private records. It consists of promises of a share of the loot— or, to use less loaded language, political commitments given to individuals and groups in exchange for their support.

PROBLEMS

1. Suppose the United States, with a monopoly of wheat production, imposes an export tax on wheat in order to raise the world price and exploit its monopoly position. The revenue from the tax is used for general government expenditure. Are American wheat farmers better or worse off as a result of the tax? You may assume that they are a very small fraction of the population and so get a negligible fraction of the benefit from the money collected.

2. It is easy to prove, for the wheat-auto case analyzed in this chapter, that a tariff and an export tax have the same effect; they tax the same transaction (trading wheat for autos) at different points. Similarly, an export subsidy and an import subsidy have the same effect. Yet we observe that tariffs and export subsidies are reasonably common, while export taxes and import subsidies are rare. Why?

3. In proving the inefficiency of tariffs, we used ideas from many parts of the book. Draw a diagram showing the relevant ideas and how they connect. Each box should be labeled by a chapter and an idea in that chapter. While I do not expect a complete diagram, you should show the major items; I would expect at least ten boxes, and probably more.

4. We have proved that tariffs—taxes on imports—are typically a Marshall worsening. Does that imply that subsidies to imports would typically be a Marshall improvement? Discuss.

5. It is commonly said that we need auto tariffs to protect the jobs of American auto workers. Where in our calculations did we include the value to the workers of the jobs they will lose if tariffs are abolished? Explain.

6. Is the fact that so many people bother to vote evidence against the analysis of voting in this chapter? Discuss.

7. Plumbers were for many years successful in getting city building codes to prohibit new technology, such as plastic pipe, which reduced the demand for their services. The analysis of this chapter suggests that a declining industry with lots of capital in the form of sunk costs, such as obsolete factories, would be relatively successful in obtaining favorable legislation. What form do you think the sunk costs of the plumbers took?

8. When a tariff is imposed on some particular import good, the beneficiaries are the domestic producers that the imported good competes with. The victims include not only consumers of that good but also producers of the export goods that would have been exported in exchange for the imports. There is no particular reason to expect the typical export industry to be any less concentrated than the typical import-competing industry. Nonetheless, exporters, like consumers, are a dispersed interest. Explain.

9. When auto tariffs are debated in Congress, the principal opponents tend to be distributors and retailers of foreign autos—even though the cost to them must be a small fraction of the cost to consumers. Explain.

10. Discuss the rickshaw surplus of Chapter 7 in terms of rent seeking.

FOR FURTHER READING

The article that first used the term "rent seeking" is: Anne Krueger, "The Political Economy of the Rent-seeking Society," *American Economic Review*, Vol. 64 (June, 1974), pp. 291–303.

Other forms of essentially the same idea appeared earlier in:

Gordon Tullock, "The Welfare Costs of Tariffs, Monopolies and Theft," *Western Economic Journal*, Vol. 5 (June, 1967), pp. 224–232.

David Friedman, *The Machinery of Freedom: Guide to a Radical Capitalism* (New York: Harper & Row, 1973; Arlington House, 1978; Open Court, 1989), Chapter 38.

Other sources for public choice theory include: James Buchanan and Gordon Tullock, *The Calculus of Consent* (Ann Arbor, MI: University of Michigan Press, 1962); Anthony Downs, *An Economic Theory of Democracy* (New York: Harper & Row, 1957); William Niskanen, *Bureaucracy and Representative Government* (Chicago: Aldine-Atherton, 1971); and Mancur Olson, *The Logic of Collective Action* (Cambridge, MA: Harvard University Press, 1965).

A discussion of the market for legislation similar to that in this chapter appears in Gary Becker, "A Theory of Competition Among Pressure Groups for Political Influence," *Quarterly Journal of Economics*, Vol. 98 (1983), pp. 371–400.

Hotelling's original contribution is in Harold Hotelling, "Stability in Competition," *Economic Journal*, Vol. 39, No. 1 (March, 1929), pp. 41–57.

chapter 20

THE ECONOMICS OF LAW
AND LAW BREAKING

This chapter consists of five parts. The first two take the existing legal structure as given, using economics first to understand criminal activity and suggest ways of defending against it and then to analyze the net costs of crime and in the process to suggest why certain things should be illegal.

The remaining parts of the chapter take the existing system of laws and law enforcement as an object of study rather than a framework within which to study crime. The third part sketches the analysis of what the punishment for crimes ought to be and how hard we should try to apprehend criminals: how much we should spend and what fraction of the criminals we should catch. The fourth part discusses the advantages and disadvantages of two alternative systems for catching and convicting offenders—public, as in our present criminal law, and private, as in our present civil law. The final part of the chapter works through, in some detail, the economic analysis of the civil law of accidents.

PART 1—THE ECONOMICS OF CRIME

By the economics of crime, I do not mean the effect of crime on the GNP or why poverty causes crime. Economics means the same thing here that it meant in Chapter 1 and has meant throughout the text—a particular way of understanding human behavior. The economic approach to analyzing crime starts from the assumption that a burglar burgles for the same reason I teach economics—because he finds it a more attractive profession than any other. It draws the obvious conclusion that if one wishes to reduce burglary—whether one is a legislator or a homeowner—one does so by raising the costs of the burglar's profession or reducing its benefits.

Many years ago, I had a disagreement with a friend concerning a practical element of life in New York City; our argument illustrates in a small way the difference between the economic and the noneconomic approach to crime and criminals. I was at the time living in a somewhat hazardous part of Manhattan. When I found it necessary to go out at night, I was in the habit of carrying with me a four-foot walking stick. My friend argued that I was making a dangerous mistake; potential muggers would feel challenged and swarm all over me. I felt, on the contrary, that muggers, like other profit-maximizing businessmen, would prefer to obtain their income at the lowest possible cost. By carrying a stick, I was not only raising the cost I could inflict on them if I chose to resist, I was also announcing my intention of resisting; they would rationally choose easier prey.

I never got mugged, which is some evidence that my view of the matter was correct. More evidence comes from observing who the people are who do get mugged. If muggers are out to prove their machismo, they ought to pick on football players; there is not much glory in mugging little old ladies. If muggers are rational businessmen seeking to obtain revenue at the lowest possible cost, on the other hand, mugging little old ladies makes a lot of sense. Little old ladies—and other relatively defenseless people—get mugged. Football players do not. It is said that someone once asked Willie Sutton why he robbed banks. "That's where the money is" was his (rational) reply.

The same analysis that helped me decide what to take with me on my evening strolls around Manhattan's Upper West Side can also be used in analyzing a question that often comes up in discussions of gun control. Opponents argue that gun control, by disarming potential victims, makes it more difficult for them to protect themselves from criminals. Supporters reply that since criminals are more likely to know how to use guns than victims, the odds in any armed confrontation are with the criminal. This is probably true, but it is almost entirely irrelevant to the argument.

Suppose one little old lady in ten carries a gun. Suppose that one in ten of those, if attacked by a mugger, will succeed in killing the mugger instead of being killed by him—or shooting herself in the foot. On average, the mugger is much more likely to win the encounter than the little old lady. But—also on average—every 100 muggings produce one dead mugger. At those odds, mugging is a very unattractive profession—not many little old ladies carry enough money in their purses to justify 1 chance in 100 of being killed getting it. The number of muggers—and muggings—declines drastically, not because all of the muggers have been killed but because they have, rationally, sought safer professions.

When, as children, we first learn about the different sorts of animals, we are likely to imagine them arranged in a strict hierarchy, with the stronger and more ferocious ones preying on everything below them. That is not how it works. A lion could, no doubt, be fairly confident of defeating a leopard, or a wolf of killing a fox. But a lion that made a habit of preying on leopards would not survive very long. While any particular leopard would probably lose the fight, there would be some small chance of the lion getting killed in the process and a larger chance of his getting injured. That is too high a price for one dinner. That is why lions prey on zebras instead. In just the same way, a potential victim does not have to be more deadly than the criminal, just deadly enough so that the cost to the criminal is a little greater than the benefit.

This does not, of course, prove that gun control is a bad thing; while I have rebutted one argument, there are many others, both pro and con. It does illustrate an important general principle. In analyzing conflict, whether between two animals, criminal and victim, competing firms, or warring nations, our natural tendency is to imagine an all-out battle in which all that matters is victory or defeat. That is rarely if ever the case. In the conflict between the mugger and the little old lady, the mugger, on average, wins. But the cost of the conflict—1 chance in 100 of being killed—is high enough so that the mugger prefers to avoid it. In this case, as in many others, the problem faced by the potential victim is not how to defeat the aggressor but only how to make aggression unprofitable.

> Economics Joke #3: *An economist and a businessman were walking in the woods when they encountered a hungry bear. The economist turned to run. "That just goes to show how ridiculous you economists are with your assumptions," said the businessman. "You're assuming you can outrun the bear." "Wrong!" replied the economist. "I'm only assuming that I can outrun you."*

Economics of the Spaceways

There is a nice fictional illustration of this point in a science fiction story by Poul Anderson. The setting is a far future in which interstellar travel and trade are common. There is a potentially profitable trade route connecting two groups of stars. Unfortunately the route runs through the territory of a nasty little interstellar empire. The nasty little empire (Borthu) has the unpleasant habit of seizing passing starships, confiscating their cargo, and brainwashing their crews; the crew is then added to Borthu's fleet, which is critically short of trained manpower.

Borthu is a nasty *little* empire; the trading corporations could, if they chose, get together, build warships, and defeat it. But doing so would cost more than all of the profits to be made on the trade route. They could also arm their trading ships—but the cost of building and manning an armed ship would more than wipe out the profit the ship would generate. They can win—but, being rational profit maximizers, they won't.

The problem is solved by Nicholas Van Rijn, the head of one of the trading corporations—after he has first persuaded his competitors to agree to pay a fraction of their profits on the route to whoever solves the problem. The solution is to arm one ship in four, reducing the profit but not eliminating it. Warships carry larger crews than merchant ships. Three times out of four, the empire attacks a trading ship, capturing it and its four-man crew. One time out of four, the trading ship is armed; the empire loses a warship and its twenty-man crew. Every four attacks cost the empire, on net, eight crewmen. Piracy is no longer profitable, so it stops.

The logic of the problem, and the solution, is nicely summed up in Van Rijn's reply to one of his colleagues, who suggests that they should fight even if it costs more than the trade is worth to them.

> *Revenge and destruction are un-Christian thoughts. Also, they will not pay very well, since it is hard to sell anything to a corpse. The problem is to find some means within our resources to make it unprofitable for Borthu to raid us. Not being stupid heads, they will then stop raiding and we can maybe later do business.*

—"Margin of Profit," in *Un-man and Other Novellas* by Poul Anderson

Superthief

I recently came across another discussion of the economics of crime and crime prevention in a book on the subject written from the inside—in several senses. The title was *Secrets of a Superthief* (by Jack Maclean). The author, according to both his own account and the journalist who wrote the introduction, was a spectacularly successful burglar, specializing in high-income neighborhoods. As he tells it, he ran a class act—when a house contained nothing he thought worth stealing, he would pile up the rejected booty on the kitchen table and steal the control panel from the burglar alarm. His general policy was to reset burglar alarms on his way out, to make sure no less discriminating thief broke in and messed up the house.

Eventually Superthief made a small professional error and found himself taking an unplanned vacation, courtesy of the State of Florida. Being an energetic fellow, he spent his time behind bars polling fellow inmates on their techniques and opinions and writing a book on how not to get burgled. One of Superthief's principal insights is the same as Van Rijn's—the essential objective in any conflict is neither to defeat your enemy nor to make it impossible for him to defeat you but merely to make it no longer in his interest to do whatever it is that you object to.

In giving advice to potential victims, Superthief argues that making it impossible for a burglar to get into your house is usually not an option; few doors will stand up to a determined burglar properly equipped. The function of strong doors and locks is not to make burglary impossible but to make it more expensive, by increasing the skill and equipment needed by the burglar as well as the chance that he will be detected before finishing the job.

A less expensive approach is to use what Superthief calls "mind games." Figure 20-1a shows my version of one of his suggested tricks— in the form of a note taped to my back door. Both Mrs. Jones and Rommel are wholly imaginary. A potential burglar may suspect that, but he has no way of being sure. Exterminators are common enough in this part of the country, the reference to the back rooms is vague enough to make it uncertain just where he can go without breathing insecticide, and

Figure 20-1

Mrs. Jones—

The exterminators came and we
have not aired the house yet,
so stay out of the back rooms.
                                        Mr. Friedman

P.S. Rommel is in the bedroom.

Dangerous Chemicals
Keep Out
This means you, Patri

Low-cost burglar repellents. Fictitious notes to a fictitious cleaning lady and a real son.

Rommel, presumably a German shepherd or Doberman pinscher (can you imagine a poodle named Rommel?), is in the room that, according to Superthief, burglars consider most worth robbing. Superthief's version of the note referred to pet rattlesnakes loose in the house—a better story than mine but less likely to be believed. Superthief gives many other examples of simple and inexpensive mind games—such as leaving a large dog-feeding dish or a jumbo-sized rubber bone lying around the backyard.

Figure 20-1*b* shows another of my precautions—a solution to a problem that Superthief does not discuss. One of the rooms in the back part of my house contains some things that a thief might well find worth stealing; for that reason, I have equipped it with its own deadbolt lock. This raises a problem. A rational thief will assume I am a rational victim and deduce that if I have a lock on that door, it is probably because I have things worth stealing behind it. My solution is the sign shown in Figure 20-1*b*. It is intended to suggest an alternative explanation for the lock—dangerous chemicals in the room and a curious child in the house. The solution is original with me, but I believe Superthief would approve.

Illegal Markets

> *"(On earth they) even have laws for private matters such as contracts. Really. If a man's word isn't any good, who would contract with him? Doesn't he have reputation?"*
>
> —Manny in *The Moon is a Harsh Mistress* by Robert Heinlein

So far, we have been using the economic analysis of crime to figure out how, on an individual level, to deal with it; the discussion is in that sense practical as well as theoretical. Before ending the section and going on to analyze questions of law and law enforcement, we will first use economic analysis to explore an equally interesting but less immediately useful question—the structure of illegal markets.

We are used to thinking of markets as public, socially accepted institutions such as the stock market, the wheat market, or a supermarket; one important feature of such markets is that the agreements to buy and sell made in them can usually be enforced, if necessary, in the courts. But the concept of a market is much broader than that. There are markets for political influence in the Soviet Union—and in Washington. There are markets for illegal drugs and stolen goods. There are markets for sex, both legal (see Chapter 21) and illegal. The enforceability of contracts by public courts may be useful for the working of markets, but it is certainly not essential.

Economics applies to illegal markets as well as to legal ones. When one input to production is eliminated, substitutes become more valuable; if contracts cannot be enforced in the courts, alternative ways of getting people to abide by their contracts become more important. We would expect substitutes for the service provided by the court system to be important elements of illegal markets. One substitute is reputation. The traditional definition of an honest politician is one who stays bought. Another and more violent substitute for the courts will be discussed a little later.

Another characteristic of illegal markets is that the handling of information is more costly than in legal markets; the same information about your employees that you want in order to decide on your future dealings with them is also useful to a prosecutor deciding on his future dealings with you. This is one of the reasons that I (and others) regard "organized crime" or the "Mafia" as largely mythical, at least as they are commonly portrayed. A "General Motors of Crime" makes little sense. For such a firm to work, someone at the top has to know what people at the bottom are doing, in order to (among other things) decide whether they are earning their pay. Passing such information up many levels of hierarchy would be hazardous in the extreme. It seems more likely that most crimes are committed by individuals or small firms and that organized crime is analogous, not to a giant corporation, but to something more like a chamber of commerce or better business bureau for the criminal market.

Such an interpretation flies in the face of what we are usually told, in newspapers and congressional hearings alike. Before you reject it on that basis, it is worth considering how credible the sources of information for the newspapers and the committees are and whether their incentives are geared to generating accurate research or exciting stories. Newspapers want to sell copies and politicians want to get reelected; announcing that organized crime is not a major threat seems a poor way of doing either. The sources of information are either law enforcement officials, who want to prove that they need more money and power to fight organized crime, or criminals testifying in exchange for immunity—with an obvious incentive to say whatever their captors wish to hear. It is interesting, in reading such accounts, to compare descriptions of the power and importance of the Mafia with descriptions of how the witnesses actually ran their criminal enterprises; the latter generally portray the witnesses as independent entrepreneurs, not employees of some criminal superfirm.

Academic studies of the criminal market involve certain difficulties not present in most other fields of research. Nonetheless, such studies have occasionally been done, and there is at least some scholarly evidence that seems to support my conclusions. For example, a study of illegal gambling in New York, based on records produced by police wiretapping, found that bookies were small independent operators and that numbers operators were somewhat larger but also competitive. Neither bookies nor numbers operators seemed to have much ability to use violence against their competitors; they even had difficulty enforcing profit-sharing agreements with the subcontractors who brought in their customers.

A more entertaining (but possibly less reliable) way of learning about organized crime is by reading what claim to be inside accounts. *The Last Testament of Lucky Luciano* contains a revealing incident. After a gangland war over who was to be *Capo di Tutti Capi*—boss of the Mafia—the winner called together gangland leaders from all over the country. He announced that:

> *everything would now be combined into a single organization under one rule—his. . . . The key was discipline, Maranzano emphasized repeatedly, rigid discipline, with Maranzano himself the supreme arbiter of all disputes, as he would be supreme in everything. That discipline . . . would be strictly enforced.*

In less than five months he was dead.

My own conjecture is that what the Mafia really is, at least in part, is a substitute for the court system; its function is to legitimize the use of force. To see how that might work, imagine that you are engaged in some criminal enterprise and one of your associates pockets your share of the take. Your obvious response is to have him killed—murder is one of the products sold on the market you are operating in. The problem with that is that if people who work with you get killed and it becomes known that you are responsible, other participants in the illegal marketplace will become reluctant to do business with you.

The solution is to go to some organization with a reputation, within the criminal market, for fairness. You present the evidence of your partner's guilt, invite him to defend himself, and then ask the "court" to rule that he is the guilty party. If it does so—and he refuses to pay you appropriate damages—you hire someone to kill him; since everyone now knows that he was in the wrong, the only people afraid to do business with you will be those planning to swindle you.

That, I suspect, is one of the functions that the Mafia and similar organizations serve on the criminal market. This is a conjecture about organized crime, not something I can prove; but it is not, so far as I know, an implausible one.

PART 2—THE COST OF CRIME

So far, I have taken the legal structure as given and used economics to analyze the behavior of criminals. The next step is to use economics to analyze the cost imposed by crime. The objective in doing so is in part to show why, from the perspective of economics, certain things should be illegal, and in part to show how the analysis of the market for crime can be fitted into the general framework of economics. Here and in the remaining parts of this chapter, we will continue to assume that the participants in the criminal marketplace—criminals, victims, and law enforcers—are rational, correctly choosing the means to achieve their differing objectives.

What Is Wrong with Robbery Anyway?

We take it for granted that certain activities, such as robbery, theft, and murder, are bad things that ought to be prevented. From the standpoint of economic efficiency, it is not immediately obvious why. Theft appears to be merely a transfer; I lose $100 and the thief gains $100. From the standpoint of efficiency, that appears to be a wash—costs measured in dollars just balance benefits in dollars. If so, what is wrong with theft?

If that were all that happened, theft would indeed be neutral from the standpoint of efficiency, neither an improvement nor a worsening. It is not. Theft is not costless; the thief must spend money, time, and effort buying tools, casing the house, breaking in, and so forth. How much time and effort? To answer that question, we do not have to find any actual thieves and interrogate them. Economic theory tells us what the cost will be—at least for the marginal thief. In equilibrium, on the thieves' market just as on other competitive markets, marginal cost equals average cost equals price. The marginal thief has no gain to balance the cost he imposes on his victim. The analysis goes as follows.

Suppose that anyone who wished to become a thief could steal $100 at a net cost, including operating expenses, value of time, and risk of being caught, of only $50. Revenue is greater than cost, so economic profit is positive; firms enter the industry. If stealing pays better than alternative occupations, people will leave those occupations to become thieves.

As more people become thieves, the marginal return from theft falls. Many of the most valuable and easily stolen objects have already been stolen. Every diamond necklace has three jewel thieves pursuing it. A thief breaks into a house only to discover that Superthief has stolen all the more valuable jewelry—and reset the alarm. Just as in other industries, increased output drives down the return, although not for quite the same reason. The "price" that a thief gets for his work, the amount he can steal for each hour of his own time that he spends stealing, falls.

How far does it fall? As long as stealing yields a higher return than alternative occupations, people will leave those occupations to become thieves. Equilibrium is reached when, for the marginal thief, his new profession is only infinitesimally better than his old—and for the next person who considers becoming a thief and decides not to, it is infinitesimally worse. In equilibrium, the marginal thief is giving up a job that paid him, say, $6/hour in order to make, after subtracting expenses of his new profession such as lawyer's fees and occasional unpaid vacations, $6.01/hour.

So in equilibrium, theft is not a transfer at all. The marginal thief who steals $100 spends about $100 in time and money to do so. His costs and his return almost exactly cancel, leaving the cost to the victim as a net loss. The transaction is not a wash but a Marshall worsening of about $100.

So far, I have discussed only the marginal thief. What about the individual who is exceptionally talented at stealing or exceptionally bad at alternative professions, so that being a thief is more attractive to him, relative to other professions, than to the individual who just barely decided to become a thief? His situation is like that of the firm with a particularly good production function, discussed in Chapter 9; at a price at which marginal firms just cover their cost, the inframarginal firm, or thief, makes a profit. When he steals $100, he does so at a cost of only $50, leaving him $50 ahead. Since the victim ends up $100 behind, the result is still a Marshall worsening, although not by as much as in the case of the marginal thief.

So far, we have the following result. If all thieves are marginal thieves—if, in other words, there is not much variation among potential thieves in their comparative advantage for thievery—the net cost of theft, including costs and benefits to both thieves and victims, is about equal to the amount stolen. If thieves vary widely, the net cost is still positive, but less than the amount stolen.

There are two directions we can go from here in analyzing the cost of theft. One is to make the analysis more realistic by including some costs that so far have been omitted—the costs of defense against theft. These would include both private costs—locks, burglar alarms, security guards, and the like—and the public costs of police, courts, and prisons. While I have not actually done such calculations, my guess is that such costs are much larger than the net gains of theft to the inframarginal thieves, making the total cost of theft more, not less, than the total value of all goods stolen.

The other thing we can do at this point is to see how the analysis of theft fits into the general structure of economic theory. We will start by converting the verbal analysis of marginal and inframarginal thieves into something very similar to a conventional supply and demand diagram. We will go on to show that the undesirability of theft can be seen as merely a special case of something we already know—indeed of two different things we already know.

Figure 20-2 is a supply and average revenue diagram for theft. The horizontal axis shows hours of theft per year. The vertical axis shows dollars stolen per hour—the "wage" that thieves receive. The supply curve S, like any other supply curve, shows how much labor will be supplied at any wage—how the number of hours spent stealing depends on the number of dollars per hour that can be stolen. The average revenue curve AR shows how the revenue from an hour spent stealing varies with the amount of theft. As the number of thieves stealing increases, the return per hour falls, so AR slopes down, just like a demand curve.

By using the number of hours as my measure of quantity, I have implicitly assumed that the difference among thieves is in how much it costs them to spend an hour stealing, not in how much they can steal in an hour. Such differing costs reflect differences among the thieves in their taste for leisure, their earning opportunities in alternative employments, and their estimate of how likely they are to be caught. I could, if I preferred, take account of differing abilities to steal by defining my unit as some kind of standard hour—where an hour spent by an incompetent thief counts as half a standard hour, and an hour spent by Superthief counts as ten. Doing this would make the analysis a little more complicated without changing anything essential.

The curve labeled S is a supply curve, but AR is not a demand curve, although it serves much the same function in our analysis. If, in an hour, you can bake 20 cookies and sell them to me at $0.25/cookie, that tells us

Figure 20-2

The market for theft.   The shaded area L shows the net loss resulting from theft—the loss to the victims minus the producer surplus (colored) received by the thieves.

not only something about your opportunities but also something about my tastes. The fact that in ten hours you can steal $50 from me tells us something about your opportunities to steal but does not imply that I like being stolen from, since the transaction is not a voluntary one. *AR* is not, like a real demand curve, equal to a marginal value curve. The area above *S* and below *P* is producer surplus, just as with an ordinary supply and demand diagram, but the area below *AR* and above *P* is not consumer surplus.

The total amount stolen per year is average revenue—the amount stolen per hour—times the number of hours of theft per year. On the figure, that is the shaded area plus the colored area. The thieves receive that as income, bear costs equal to the shaded area, and receive a producer surplus equal to the colored area. The victims lose the amount stolen and receive nothing. The net loss *L*, the shaded area under the supply curve, is equal to the loss to the victims minus the gain to the thieves. If *S* were nearly horizontal, corresponding to a highly elastic supply of thieves, net loss would be almost the entire amount stolen. That is the case described earlier, where all thieves are marginal thieves.

Supply and revenue curves are one way of looking at the market for theft and analyzing its costs. Another is as an example of the inefficiency of rent seeking. Both thieves and victims are competing for possession of the same objects—all of which, initially, belong to the victims. Expenditures by a thief either result in his getting the loot instead of some other thief or in his getting the loot instead of its owner keeping it. Defensive expenditures by the victims are also rent seeking—the function of a burglar alarm is to make sure that the property remains in the hands of its original owner.

What we have really been doing is showing the advantage of a system of secure property rights. If property rights are insecure, some individuals have an incentive to spend resources trying to get property transferred to them, while some have an incentive to spend resources keeping property from being transferred away from them. That is true whether the transfer is done by private theft or government taxation. Some of the inefficiencies we have just been discussing for the former case are known as excess burden in the latter; they were discussed at some length in Chapter 7. Not earning taxable income or not buying taxed goods are (costly) ways of defending yourself against taxation, just as installing a burglar alarm is a (costly) way of protecting against theft. Other inefficiencies on the political marketplace are classified as costs of lobbying. Making campaign donations to a candidate who promises to provide special benefits to you and your friends is an expenditure on transferring property in your direction almost precisely analogous to a burglar's expenditure on tools.

Yet another way of looking at theft—or rent seeking in general—is as a special case of the inefficiency of markets with externalities. Suppose auto firms spend $10,000 producing a car and in the process produce some air pollution. The result is inefficient—not because air pollution is evil but because it is not, like other costs, included in the firm's calculation of whether and at what price to produce. If the industry is competitive, everyone to whom a car is worth at least $10,000 gets one. If the air pollution does $5,000 worth of damage, then the real production cost is $15,000; anyone who values the car at more than $10,000 but less than $15,000 is getting something that is worth less to him than it costs to produce.

Theft is an extreme case of this: The external cost, imposed on the victim, is the entire value of what is stolen. The thief steals up to the point where the (marginal) value to him of what he steals is equal to the (marginal) cost to him of stealing it; since he ignores the cost to the victim, equilibrium occurs at a point where marginal cost to all concerned is much larger than marginal benefit.

We have now used economics to analyze the market for theft. In doing so, we took the system for preventing theft—police and punishments—as a given, one of the elements determining the cost to the thief of stealing. The next step is to use our analysis to say something about how that system should work: what should be illegal, what the nature and amount of the penalty should be, and how much we should be willing to spend on catching and convicting thieves. All of those can be viewed simply as issues of economic efficiency. While you may not believe that that is all they are, you should find the attempt to analyze them from that standpoint an instructive exercise.

PART 3—EFFICIENT CRIMES AND THE EFFICIENT LEVEL OF CRIME

In discussing the market for theft, I used the word "value" to describe both the value of what was stolen to the victim and its value to the criminal, without distinguishing between them. If what is stolen is money, gold, bearer bonds, or other **liquid** commodities—things that can be easily bought and sold at about the same price—that is a reasonable way of using the word. In other cases, it is not.

I have spent 20 hours searching art galleries to find a painting I particularly like and then bought it for $100. Replacing it will require a similar effort and a similar expenditure, so a thief who steals it injures me by considerably more than $100. The thief himself will be lucky to get $50 for it; even if he finds the right gallery and the right buyer—one who does not recognize the painting and does recognize its quality—he will get what the gallery pays for paintings, not what it gets for them.

In such a situation, the value to the thief of what he steals is much less than its value to the victim. That is why in many societies, including our own, there are well-established procedures by which thieves sell things back to their owners. Kidnappers are an extreme example of this. They steal something—a person—whose only value to them is what they can get by selling it back to (representatives of) its "owner."

This divergence between value to victim and value to thief suggests another way of looking at the inefficiency of theft. If you have something that is worth more to me than to you, I have no need to steal it; I can buy it from you. Goods that a thief is willing to steal but would not be willing to buy must be worth more to their present owner than to the potential thief. So the additional transfers that become possible as a result of theft are inefficient ones—transfers of a good to someone who values it less than its present owner. That is why I asserted, earlier, that the efficient level of theft was zero.

There are exceptions—what we may call "efficient crimes." Suppose, for example, that you are lost in the woods and starving. You come upon an empty, locked cabin. You break in, feed yourself, and use the telephone to summon help. Almost certainly, the value to you of using the cabin was greater than the cost you imposed on its owner; you will probably be glad to replace both his food and his lock. Your "crime" transferred a resource—temporary control of the cabin—to someone to whom it was worth more than its value to the initial owner. You could only do it by a crime, not by purchase, because the owner was not there to sell it to you.

This is one example of an efficient crime, a crime that is a net Marshall improvement. A less exotic example is speeding when you are in a hurry. We have speed limits, at least in part, because driving fast increases the chance of an accident. That is a cost but not an infinite one; there are times when getting somewhere quickly is sufficiently important to justify doing so at 80 miles per hour. One way of dealing with such situations is for the law to make it illegal to drive faster than 70 miles per hour except when there is an important reason to do so. The problem with such a law is that it may be difficult or impossible for a court to judge whether your reason was really good enough to justify an exception. An alternative solution is for the law to impose a penalty large enough so that only those who really have a good reason to drive faster will find it worth breaking the law and paying the penalty. Speeding is then always a crime—but if the punishment is correctly calculated, it is a crime that occurs when, and only when, it is efficient.

Seen in this way, a speeding law is a Pigouvian tax, like the emission fee discussed in Chapter 18. If air polluters must pay an emission fee equal to the damage done by the pollution, they will choose to pollute—and pay—only when the value of what is being produced is greater than the cost, including the cost of the pollution. Similarly, if driving fast imposes costs on other drivers, we can use speeding tickets to force motorists to take account of those costs in deciding how fast to drive.

The analysis so far suggests a simple rule for setting punishments: "The amount of the punishment should equal the damage done by the crime." That way, only efficient crimes will be committed—crimes for which the value to the criminal is greater than the amount of damage done.

There are two things wrong with that rule. The first is that criminals are not always caught. If a criminal faces only one chance in ten of being caught and convicted, he will discount the punishment accordingly in calculating the cost to himself of committing the crime. Roughly speaking, the punishment should then be ten times the damage done by the crime in order to assure that only efficient crimes, crimes for which the gain to the criminal is greater than the cost to the victim, occur. A more precise rule would have to allow for the criminal's attitude toward risk, as discussed in the optional section of Chapter 13; if the criminal is risk averse, one chance in ten of losing $100 may from his standpoint be more than equivalent to a certainty of losing $10.

This raises an interesting problem. The enforcement system can choose among many different combinations of probability and punishment; the same deterrence may be provided by a certainty of a $1,000 fine, a 50 percent probability of a $2,000 fine, a 10 percent chance of a $10,000 fine, or any of a variety of other alternatives, including some in which the punishment is not a fine but imprisonment or execution. How should it decide which to use?

The answer is the same as the answer to a similar problem many chapters back: the problem of choosing the mix of inputs for producing an output. Just as in Chapter 9, the first step is to pick a level of output and find the least costly way of producing it. In our present situation, the output is deterrence; it is produced by imposing a cost on the criminal. Pick a punishment—a fine of, say, $100 imposed with certainty on anyone who commits the crime. Consider all the combinations of (lower) probabilities and (higher) punishments that the criminal considers equivalent to a certainty of paying $100—and that will therefore have the same effect in discouraging him from committing the crime. For each combination, calculate the cost of catching that fraction of the criminals and imposing that punishment on each. Find the combination for which that cost is lowest. You now know the cost of the least cost way of imposing an expected punishment equivalent to a $100 fine. Now pick another punishment—say a fine of $200 imposed with certainty— and repeat the calculation. When you are finished, you will have a total cost curve for deterrence and you will know, for any level of deterrence, what combination of probability and punishment should be used to produce it.

Two sorts of costs go into the calculations I have just described: enforcement costs and punishment costs. The nature of enforcement costs is fairly clear; they represent the expense of paying police, running the courts, and the like. But what are punishment costs?

Consider a fine. The convicted criminal pays $1,000, the court system collects $1,000. The money may be used to pay the expenses of operating the court system, given to victims of crime, or in some other way transferred, directly or indirectly, to someone other than the criminal. What the criminal loses someone else gains, so the net cost is about zero.

Suppose that instead of fining the criminal we execute him. The cost to him is his life; there is no corresponding gain to the rest of us. Suppose that, instead of fining or executing the criminal, we simply lock him up. The cost to him is his freedom. We get nothing—worse still, we must pay the cost of running the prison. The cost of the punishment—the cost to him plus the cost to us—is greater than the amount of the punishment.

As a rule, it is easier to collect small fines than large ones, since criminals are more likely to be able to pay them. So, as a general rule, punishment cost increases with the size of punishment. Enforcement cost, on the other hand, is larger the larger the percentage of criminals you are trying to catch. As we move from small punishments imposed with high probability to large punishments imposed with small probability, we are trading off a decrease in enforcement cost against an increase in punishment cost; somewhere between one extreme (catching 100 percent of the criminals and making them give back what they stole) and the other (catching only one criminal and boiling him in oil), there is likely to be an optimal combination.

Figure 20-3 shows the logic of the situation graphically. We are varying the probability of punishment from 0 to 1, while maintaining a constant level of *expected* punishment (equal to probability times punishment: $p \times F$) and hence of deterrence; the lower the probability (p), the higher the punishment (F). The horizontal axis shows both probability and punishment; the vertical axis shows cost. The curve EC is enforcement cost. The larger the fraction of criminals we want to catch the more we must spend on police and courts, so EC rises as probability increases. The curve PC is punishment cost. The more severe the punishment the higher the

Figure 20-3

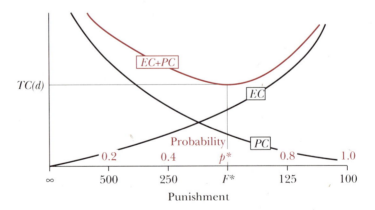

Calculating the least-cost combination of probability and punishment to produce a given level of deterrence. $p \times F = 100$.

cost of imposing it, so *PC* increases with amount of punishment (and thus decreases with probability of punishment). *EC* + *PC* is the total cost of catching and punishing criminals. Its minimum is at p^*, so p^* (and the corresponding punishment F^*) represent the lowest cost combination of probability and punishment to produce a given expected punishment and hence a given level of deterrence. By repeating the calculation for every level of deterrence we could generate a total cost curve $TC(d)$, showing the cost of producing any level of deterrence, d.

Our analysis has still not fully taken account of the costs of catching and punishing criminals. Consider a crime that does $10 worth of damage each time it is committed. If there is no punishment at all, 100 crimes per year will be committed, so the total damage will be $1,000/year; the net cost, including the benefits to the criminals and assuming the victims spend nothing on protecting themselves, will be between zero and $1,000.

The police force would like to impose an expected punishment of $10 on the criminals, as suggested by our previous discussion. The least expensive way to do this turns out to be catching one tenth of the criminals and fining them $100 each. Unfortunately, the cost of doing so is $2,000/year. The "efficient" level of punishment involves spending $2,000 to eliminate less than $1,000 of net damage! Obviously, that is the wrong answer; in the situation as described, the least bad solution may be to put up with 100 crimes a year.

As this suggests, the full analysis of what should be a crime, what percentage of the criminals should be caught, and what should be done to them is moderately complicated. The answer depends on the supply curve for offenses, on the damage done by the crime, and on the cost functions for producing apprehensions, convictions, and punishment. In principle, we now know how to solve the problem—just as, in principle, we know how to calculate how much a firm should and will produce, or what prices and quantities will be in a competitive equilibrium.

How do you calculate the efficient solution for the problem of preventing crime? Start by writing a cost function that includes costs and benefits to everyone affected. Next assume criminals and victims will choose values for the variables they control—amount of crime and amount of private defense against crime—that maximize their own welfare. Finally, find values for the remaining variables—percentage of criminals convicted, nature and amount of punishment—that maximize net benefits.

PART 4—PRIVATE OR PUBLIC ENFORCEMENT OF LAW?

When we talk about law enforcement, we usually mean law enforcement by police officers. In fact, much of law enforcement is private. If someone breaks your arm, you call the police; but if he breaks a window or a contract, you call a lawyer. In the one case, law is enforced by government employees who gather evidence, present it to the court, collect the fine, and run the prison or close the switch on the electric chair. In the other case, law is enforced by a private individual, working for pay or a share of the settlement; he is responsible for gathering evidence and presenting it to the court, and he and his employer, the injured party, receive the "fine" paid by the convicted offender.

In our system, the division between public and private enforcement roughly corresponds to the division between criminal and civil law. Criminal law involves police, district attorneys, and sentences for criminals; civil law involves private detectives, private attorneys, and damages paid by defendants to plaintiffs. The form is in many ways different, but the substance is similar. In both cases it is alleged that someone has done something he should not have, and in both something unpleasant happens to the convicted defendant—whether we call it punishment or paying damages.

This raises some interesting questions about our system. Is there something natural about the present division into public and private enforcement? What are the advantages and disadvantages of the two systems? Could we have a system in which all law enforcement was public, so that a businessman who failed to deliver goods on time would be arrested, indicted, and jailed? Could we have a system in which all enforcement was private, so that a murderer would be sued for damages by the heirs of his victim?

Whether our present system is in some sense natural or efficient is a subject of dispute among economists involved in the economic analysis of law; my own belief is that it is not. Different divisions between private and public enforcement are possible and have existed in other societies and at other times. They include some in which enforcement was entirely private; killing someone resulted in a lawsuit instead of an arrest. Whether or not we have the correct mix of private and public enforcement, it is clear that both systems have advantages and disadvantages. One of the inherent disadvantages of public enforcement is illustrated by the following immoral tale.

You are a police officer. You have got the goods on me. You have collected sufficient evidence to arrest and convict me; the resulting punishment would be equivalent, to me, to a $20,000 fine. Perhaps the punishment is a $20,000 fine; perhaps it is a period of imprisonment that I would pay $20,000 to avoid. For the purposes of the story, we will assume the former.

Arresting me will improve your professional reputation, slightly increasing your chances of future promotion. That is worth $5,000 to you in increased future income. Seen from the viewpoint of *Dragnet*, the rest of the story is clear; you arrest me and I am convicted. Seen from the viewpoint of this book, the result is equally clear. You have something—the collected evidence against me—that is worth $5,000 to you and $20,000 to me. Somewhere between $5,000 and $20,000, there ought to exist a transaction in our mutual benefit. I pay you $10,000, and you burn the evidence.

So far as you and I are concerned, that is an eminently satisfactory outcome, but it is not a very effective way of enforcing the law. In this respect, the public enforcement system is not **incentive compatible**. The system requires you to do something—arrest me—in order for it to work, and the system makes it in your interest to do something else. The system, of course, can and will try to control the problem—for example, by punishing police officers who are caught accepting bribes. But the fact that it must devote some of its limited resources to catching police officers instead of catching criminals is itself a defect.

Another way to solve the problem is to pay you, not a wage, but the value of the fines collected from the criminals you convict. Under such a system, you lose $20,000 when you burn the evidence, so $20,000 is the lowest bribe you will accept. Since $20,000 is also the cost to me of being convicted, there is little point in my offering you that much to let me off— save perhaps as a way of saving the time and expense of standing trial. If I do bribe you, no damage has been done; I have still paid $20,000 and you have still received it. We have merely eliminated the middleman.

This may sound like an odd and corrupt system, but it is the way in which civil law is presently enforced. The enforcing is done by a lawyer, acting as the agent of the victim; the fine is paid by the defendant to the victim. What we call bribery in criminal law is called an out-of-court settlement in civil law. The only addition to my scheme needed in order to make it correspond exactly to ordinary civil law is to make the claim against the criminal start out being the property of his victim; the police officer—who in this system is a private entrepreneur rather than a government employee—buys the claim from the victim before hunting down the criminal.

Elements of such a system for enforcing criminal law existed in the United States in the last century, as shown by the "Wanted Dead or Alive: $200 Reward" posters familiar in films and books about the Wild West. The policemen of that system were called bounty hunters. A complete system of private enforcement existed in Iceland in the early Middle Ages. Not only was killing treated as a civil offense, but the enforcement of court verdicts, including the job of hunting down convicted defendants who refused to pay and were consequently declared outlaws, was left to the plaintiffs and their friends. Odd as it may seem, the system appears to have worked fairly well; the society of which it was a part was one of the most interesting and in some ways one of the most attractive then existing. It was the source of the original *sagas*—historical novels and histories written in the thirteenth and fourteenth centuries and in many cases still in print today, in English translations.

Private enforcement has some advantages over public enforcement. It also has some problems. One is that many criminals are **judgment-proof**: they lack the assets necessary to pay any large fine. A public enforcement system can punish such criminals by imprisoning (or, in extreme cases, executing) them, but it is not immediately obvious how a private enforcer can make a profit that way. One cannot get blood from a turnip, and while a pound of flesh may add drama to a Shakespearean play, its market value is near zero. If a private enforcer cannot make money out of catching criminals, he has no incentive to do so, just as there is little incentive in our civil system to sue someone, however guilty, if he obviously cannot pay.

In analyzing the choice between private and public enforcement, as in discussing the problem of optimal punishment earlier, we get into complications that cannot be adequately dealt with in this book; so I will leave unresolved the question of whether our system of enforcement should be more private or less so. Some further discussions, including two of my articles, are listed at the end of the chapter.

> Economics Joke #4: Incentive Incompatibility.
> *José robbed a bank and fled south across the Rio Grande, with the Texas Rangers in hot pursuit. They caught up with him in a small Mexican town; since José knew no English and none of them spoke Spanish, they found a local resident willing to act as translator, and began their questioning.*
> *"Where did you hide the money?"*
> *"The Gringos want to know where you hid the money."*
> *"Tell the Gringos I will never tell them."*
> *"José says he will never tell you."*
> *The rangers all cock their pistols and point them at José.*
> *"Tell him that if he does not tell us, we will shoot him."*
> *"The Gringos say that if you do not tell them, they will shoot you."*
> *José begins to shake with fear.*
> *"Tell the Gringos that I hid the money by the bridge over the river."*
> *"José says that he is not afraid to die."*

PART 5—ACCIDENT LAW

The economic analysis of accidents starts with the observation that they are not entirely accidental. I do not choose to run my automobile into a pedestrian, but I do choose what kind of a car I drive, how often and at what speed I drive it, and how often to have my brakes checked. These decisions and many more affect the probability that I will be in an accident and thus the cost my driving imposes on other people. It then seems natural to ask what set of legal rules will lead me to make such decisions in the most nearly efficient manner.

The simplest approach to generating efficient behavior is direct regulation. Let the law state how cars must be built, how many miles people may drive and at what speed, how often their brakes must be checked. This solution runs into problems that we have already discussed, in the context of monopolies, public goods, and externalities. In order to set efficient values for all of the variables, the legislature would require detailed information about individual tastes and abilities that it has no way of getting; if it had the information, using it to calculate optimal behavior would involve daunting mathematical problems. Even if the legislature could calculate and enforce optimal behavior, there is no obvious reason why it would be in the interest of the legislators to do so.

Similar problems arise if we try to control accidents by Pigouvian taxes on the behavior that causes them. The probability that I will be involved in an accident depends on many choices, only some of which are observable. If by driving an extra mile I impose an expected cost of five cents on potential accident victims, then a tax of five cents a mile will induce me to do the efficient amount of driving. But what tax will prevent me from paying a more than optimal amount of attention to the radio and a less than optimal amount to the road?

The solution to this problem is to charge by results: If I cause an accident I must pay the cost. Externalities are then internalized; I have an incentive to engage in an efficient level of accident provision on every margin. In our legal system, such costs are imposed mainly through civil suits for damages.

This produces new problems. Driving becomes a lottery with large negative prizes. If drivers are risk averse they have an incentive to insure themselves—and, by doing so, reduce their incentive to take precautions. Many drivers will be judgment-proof, unable to pay the cost of a major accident. That can be solved by requiring drivers to be insured, but again with negative effects on incentives.

There is another and deeper problem. As Coase pointed out, the Pigouvian approach contains a fundamental error; it treats external costs as if they were the result of only one party's action. The probability that I will run you down depends on your decisions as well as mine, on how carefully you cross the street as well as on how fast I drive. Ideally, both of us should take all cost-justified precautions. But if the driver is responsible for all costs of the accident, the pedestrian has no incentive to take precautions.

There are at least three solutions to this problem. One is a rule of negligence. The driver is liable if and only if he is negligent, with negligence defined as failure to take all cost-justified precautions. Under that rule, drivers find it in their interest to take the efficient level of precautions; pedestrians, knowing that drivers will not be negligent and thus not be liable, find it in their interest to take an efficient level of precautions as well.

A second solution is a rule of strict liability with a defense of contributory negligence. A pedestrian who has taken less than the efficient level of precautions cannot collect damages from the driver. This rule again leads to an efficient level of precaution by both parties.

Both of these suffer from the same problem as direct regulation. In order to apply either negligence or contributory negligence, the court must be able to calculate the efficient level of precaution and observe whether it is taken. They are an improvement only in restricting the problem to cases where an accident actually occurs.

Even if the court can judge whether the driver was negligent in how he drove, it can hardly judge whether he was negligent in how much he drove—whether his marginal trip was worth taking, given the expected accident costs it produced. Under a negligence rule, drivers drive too much since, having taken the efficient level of precaution, they are no longer liable for damages. Under a rule of strict liability, with or without contributory negligence, there is an efficient amount of driving but an inefficiently large amount of walking, since pedestrians are reimbursed by drivers for the cost of accidents.

The solution to this problem carries us outside of the context of civil damages. If the driver pays damages but the pedestrian does not receive them—more generally, if each party to the accident must separately pay its full cost—then each has the efficient incentive to avoid the accident. The damage award has been converted into a fine.

This solution generates new problems. If the injured party receives no damages he has no incentive to sue, so the accident never gets reported. In converting damages into fines we have gone from a private to a public system of law, and must provide some public mechanism to report damages and institute cases. In doing so, we encounter precisely the same problems that I discussed earlier as arguments for converting public enforcement into private enforcement.

The essential problem in accident law, as in more direct forms of government regulation, is that we have no bureaucrat-gods. If only there were an institution, whether regulatory agency or court, that knew everything and wished only the general good, the production of efficient outcomes would be fairly simple. As it is, we must choose among a bewildering variety of imperfect solutions, private and public, criminal and civil. The economic analysis of law helps us to understand the problem but it does not, at least so far, give us any clear answer.

In fact, I have not given final answers to many questions in this chapter, nor have I solved many problems. What I hope I have done is to convince you that economic analysis can be used to evaluate such fundamental issues as what the laws should be, what the penalties should be for breaking them, and how those penalties should be enforced. The economic analysis of law is an important part of what some of us like to call **economic imperialism**—the use of economics to analyze what have traditionally been considered "noneconomic" questions—and, as you may have guessed, one that I have found particularly interesting.

PROBLEMS

1. Suppose Nicholas Van Rijn applied his talents to the problem of preventing airplane hijacking. What might he suggest?

2. There is a way to make theft forever impossible—perhaps by adding a "guilt drug" to the water supply that would make anyone who steals anything feel intolerably guilty. Would all, some, or none of those who are presently thieves be in favor of doing this? Discuss.

3. In Chapter 18, I discussed problems associated with software piracy—the unauthorized copying of computer programs. As the name suggests, this can be regarded as a form of theft; indeed, I once shocked one of my colleagues by suggesting that his possession of disks full of pirated software made him the moral equivalent of a burglar. Suppose there is some way of making such software piracy impossible. Should none, some, or all of those who presently use pirated software be in favor of the change? Discuss.

4. In this chapter, I have argued that certain things should be illegal on grounds of economic efficiency. If this is our criterion, what things that are presently illegal should not be? Should they be illegal on other grounds? If so, why? Discuss.

5. Throughout the chapter, I have ignored the possibility that some people might abstain from stealing because they thought it was immoral. How could we include that possibility in the analysis? Would it change any of the results? Discuss.

6. a. You see a highway sign that says "$500 Fine for Littering." What is the economic rationale for having a fine on littering and why is it so high?

   b. On the same road, the fine for speeding is only $100. Does that mean that the government is more concerned about littering than about speeding? What is the economic rationale for a fine on speeding? Discuss.

   c. In what senses might a fine for speeding be too high? Discuss.

7. "We can always lower the cost of our criminal justice system by catching half as many criminals as before and punishing them twice as harshly; the system will be just as effective as before at deterring crime and we will not need to hire as many police officers." Discuss.

8. Some legal scholars object to the economic analysis of law on the grounds that laws should be just, not efficient. This may be seen either as the claim that consequences do not matter (*Fiat justitia, ruat caelum*—let there be justice though the sky fall) or that consequences do matter, but economic efficiency is the wrong way of judging them. Discuss.

FOR FURTHER READING

My analysis of private enforcement is in "Efficient Institutions for the Private Enforcement of Law," *Journal of Legal Studies* (June, 1984), which also contains references to earlier work on the subject by others, not all of whom agree with me. *The Machinery of Freedom*, cited in the previous chapter, contains a nontechnical discussion of how a fully private system of courts, police, and laws might work.

My earlier article, "Private Creation and Enforcement of Law—A Historical Case," *Journal of Legal Studies* (March, 1979), describes the working of the Icelandic system, as does *Feud in the Icelandic Saga* (Berkeley: University of California Press, 1982) by Jesse Byock (a historian, not an economist). My "Reflections on Optimal Punishment Or: Should the Rich Pay Higher Fines?" in Richard Zerbe (ed.), *Research in Law and Economics*, Vol. 3 (1981) contains a detailed analysis of optimal punishment. My essay "Economic Analysis of Law" in *The New Palgrave: A Dictionary of Economic Theory and Doctrine*, John Eatwell, Murray Milgate, and Peter Newman, eds. (Macmillan, 1987) gives a general overview of the subject and an extensive list of references.

Other works of interest include: Norval Morris and Gordon Hawkins, *The Honest Politician's Guide to Crime Control* (Boston: Little, Brown & Co., 1977); Gordon Tullock, *The Logic of the Law* (New York: Basic Books, 1971) and Richard Posner, *Economic Analysis of Law* 3rd Ed. (Boston: Little, Brown, 1986). Posner, who is one of the leading writers on the economic analysis of law (and a federal judge), argues that the common law tends, for a variety of reasons, to be economically efficient. If he is right, then efficiency may be useful for explaining what the law is, whether or not it is useful for deciding what it ought to be.

The Last Testament of Lucky Luciano, by Martin A. Gosch and Richard Hammer (Boston: Little, Brown: 1974), claims to be based on information given to Gosch by Luciano on condition that it not be used until ten years after his death. It is an interesting, and on the whole plausible, account of the workings of organized crime from the viewpoint of one of its leading members.

"Fact, fancy, and organized crime," by Peter Reuter and Jonathan B. Rubinstein, *The Public Interest* 53 (Fall, 1978) pp. 45–67. This article provides evidence and arguments that support my view of organized crime, including the results of the study of bookmaking and numbers mentioned in this chapter.

chapter 21

THE ECONOMICS OF LOVE
AND MARRIAGE

This chapter consists of two parts. The first discusses the economics of marriage; it starts with an analysis of the marriage market and goes on to consider what marriage is and why it exists. The second part of the chapter is devoted to the **economics of altruism**: the analysis of rational behavior by an individual who values the welfare of another. It demonstrates that altruism, which one might think of as outside of economics, actually fits neatly into economic theory. The result is not merely to accommodate the theory to an important feature of the real world but also to use economics to derive some surprising results about the consequences of altruism.

THE ECONOMICS OF MARRIAGE

We start our discussion of marriage by taking marriage itself as a given. We assume that some people want to marry other people and that they prefer some potential partners to others. We also assume that although marriage partners, potential and actual, may put considerable value on each other's welfare (a phenomenon to be analyzed in the second part of the chapter) there is still room for some conflict of interest between them. There is therefore also room for some bargaining over the terms, implicit or explicit, of the marriage.

To add interest to the discussion, I will focus on a particular policy issue. In our society, only *monogamous* marriages are permitted—one husband, one wife. In various other societies, *polygynous* marriages (one husband, two or more wives) and *polyandrous* marriages (one wife, two or more husbands) have also been legal. What would the effect of legalizing polygyny or polyandry be on the welfare of men? On the welfare of women? On the net welfare of all concerned?

In order to answer this question, we require a formal model of the marriage market. I will work out the implications of two different ones. The first is designed to make the marriage market appear very similar to the markets with which we are by now familiar; the second is designed to emphasize two of the respects in which it differs from such markets.

One element common to both models is the assumption that women and men belong to themselves: The marriage partners are the only ones whose consent is required in order for the marriage to take place. This is appropriate if we are considering marriage in the United States or some similar society, since adults in such societies do, in that sense, belong to themselves. But in many past societies (and some present ones), unmarried women were to some degree the property of the male head of their household; his consent was required in order for them to be married. Economic analysis is as applicable to such a society as it is to ours, but the results must be modified to take account of the different property rights; gains that in our society would go to the bride may in such a society go to her father instead. Similar modifications would apply in the less common case where sons, as well as or instead of daughters, were the property of their families.

Model 1: A Market with Prices

In many societies, marriage is commonly accompanied by payments— bride price paid by the groom or his family to the family of the bride, dowry provided by the bride's family to the new couple, and so on. While explicit payments of this sort are not a part of our marriage institutions (unless you count expenditures on the wedding and the wedding gifts), one may argue that a marriage still contains an implicit price. When two people get married, they do so with some general understanding of the terms they are committing themselves to: how free a hand each will have with the common funds, what duties each is expected to perform, and so on. One may think of the terms of this understanding as corresponding to a price and serving the same function as an explicit price in other markets.

Imagine, for example, that a plague kills off many young women of marriageable age. After the plague is over, young women find it easy and young men difficult to get married. One result we would expect is a shifting of the "price" associated with marriage. Men will find that they are implicitly bidding against each other for wives; the terms of the bidding may include the willingness of the men to accept marriage terms pleasing to the women. This is particularly likely in a society in which divorce is relatively easy, so that either partner can enforce the terms of the contract by threatening to dissolve it and find someone else. If, in a society where women are scarce, the man who promised before the wedding to do everything his wife wanted proves less accommodating afterward, some other man will be willing to take his place. Similarly, if a war greatly reduced the population of marriageable men, we would expect to find the terms of the marriage contract swinging toward the men's side.

For our first model, then, we will think of the marriage market as an ordinary market with a price. The price is defined relative to an arbitrary "standard" marriage contract. Any other contract can be viewed as a standard contract plus or minus a certain number of dollars paid by the husband to the wife; plus represents a contract more favorable to the wife than the standard, while minus represents one less favorable. Supply and demand behave just as they do on any other market. The quantity supplied of wives—the number of women willing to marry— will be higher, and the quantity demanded lower, the higher the price. The model is entirely symmetrical, as we will see on Figures 21-1a and 21-1b; we can just as easily speak of the quantity demanded and quantity supplied of husbands. As long as all marriages are monogamous, the number of husbands supplied and the number of wives demanded are the same, since a man seeking to become a husband is a man seeking to obtain a wife, just as, on a barter market, someone who offers to trade wine for beer is both supplying wine and demanding beer.

Omissions. Before using this model to analyze the consequences of polygyny and polyandry, several additional points should be made. We have so far ignored quality differences in potential husbands and wives— the fact that some people are more desirable marriage partners than others. We can, if we wish, include this in our model by including quality in our definition of the standard contract. Marrying an unusually desirable woman at a price of zero would correspond to a marriage contract in which the woman received specially favorable terms to balance the advantages the husband received from having a particularly desirable wife. Perhaps the husband would have to agree to wash all of the dishes.

Seen from this standpoint, attractiveness is simply one element of the initial wealth of an individual. A man or a woman who has good looks or a pleasant disposition is wealthier, has a greater command over the desirable things of life, than someone who has not, just as someone who has inherited $1 million is wealthier than someone who has not.

We would still be failing to take account of another important feature of marriage: not everyone has the same tastes. The woman I recognized as a one in ten thousand catch was not even being pursued by anyone else, with the result that I married her on quite reasonable terms; I did not even have to agree to wash all of the dishes. Some of the women that my friends married, on the other hand, were of no interest to me. Yet my friends obviously preferred them, not only to remaining bachelors but to trying to lure my intended away from me.

This feature of the marriage market is not, of course, unique to it. We would observe the same thing in the market for houses or the market for jobs—indeed in most markets where both the good and the purchaser are very inhomogeneous, so that the problem is not merely the allocation of limited quantities but the proper matching of buyer

Figure 21-1

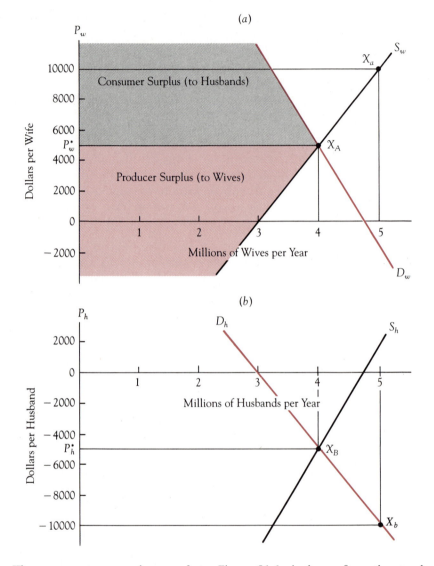

(a)

(b)

The monogamous marriage market. Figure 21-1a is drawn from the stand-point of a potential husband, who sees the market as a market for wives. Figure 21-1b is drawn from the standpoint of a potential wife, who sees it as a market for husbands. P_w is the price of a wife, defined as the terms of the actual marriage contract relative to the terms of some arbitrary standard contract. P_h is the price of a husband, defined similarly relative to the same standard contract. P_w is positive (and P_h negative) if the terms of the actual contract are more favorable to the wife than the terms of the standard contract.

Section V   Applications—Controversial and Un

and bought. One of the implications of such situations—high transaction costs—was mentioned in the discussion of barter in Chapter 18.

I think it would be possible to take account of this feature of the marriage market without substantially altering the results of our analysis, although I cannot be sure, since I have not actually tried. It would, however, make the model too complicated for our present purposes. We will therefore ignore complications associated with varying quality of potential mates until we come to the second model and ignore complications associated with differing tastes throughout this chapter.

The Effect of Legalizing Polygyny or Polyandry. Figures 21-1*a* and 21-1*b* show the same marriage market seen from two sides. In Figure 21-1*a*, S_w is the supply curve for wives, D_w the demand curve for wives; in Figure 21-1*b*, S_h is the supply curve for husbands, D_h the demand curve for husbands. In Figure 21-1*a*, P_w is a price (positive or negative) paid by husbands to wives—the price of a wife. Similarly, in Figure 21-1*b*, P_h is a price paid by wives to husbands—the price of a husband. Both figures convey the same information; S_w is identical to D_h except for the differing definitions of price. For $P_w = +\$10,000$/wife, quantity supplied = 5,000,000 wives per year (point X_a); for $P_h = -\$10,000$/husband, quantity demanded = 5,000,000 husbands per year (point X_b). A price of \$10,000 paid by a husband to a wife is the same thing as a price of $-\$10,000$ paid by a wife to a husband. Both prices represent the same contract, one that is equivalent to a standard contract plus a \$10,000 payment by the husband to the wife. At this price, the quantity of wives supplied is greater than the quantity of wives demanded (or, equivalently, the quantity of husbands demanded is greater than the quantity supplied).

P_w^* on Figure 21-1*a* is the equilibrium value of P_w, the value for which quantity of wives supplied equals quantity demanded. $P_h^* = -P_w^*$ is similarly the equilibrium value of P_h on Figure 21-1*b*. On the particular marriage market shown by the figures, the equilibrium price of a bride is \$5,000; in order to get married, a man must offer marriage terms that are \$5,000 more favorable to the wife than the standard marriage contract relative to which P_w is defined.

Figure 21-2*a* shows what happens if polygyny is legalized; Figure 21-2*b* shows what happens if polyandry is legalized (with polygyny still illegal). The essential thing to notice about the figures is that $P_w^{*\prime}$ is higher on Figure 21-2*a* than on Figure 21-1*a*, and $P_h^{*\prime}$ is higher on Figure 21-2*b* than on Figure 21-1*b*. Wives get better terms, more attractive marriage contracts, when polygyny is legal than when it is not; husbands get better terms when polyandry is legal than when it is not. The result is exactly the opposite of what one might expect; polygyny benefits women and polyandry benefits men!

Why? On Figure 21-2*a*, the supply curve for wives is the same as on Figure 21-1*a*. The legalization of polygyny does nothing to increase or reduce the number of wives willing to accept any particular marriage contract. Of course, a woman willing to accept a monogamous marriage may be unwilling to share the same husband with another wife, but that is already taken into account in the definition of P_w. P_w was defined relative to a standard contract, one of whose features was monogamy. A bigamist who offers a price $P_w = 0$ for a wife must be offering her terms sufficiently favorable to balance the cost to her of having to share

Figure 21-2

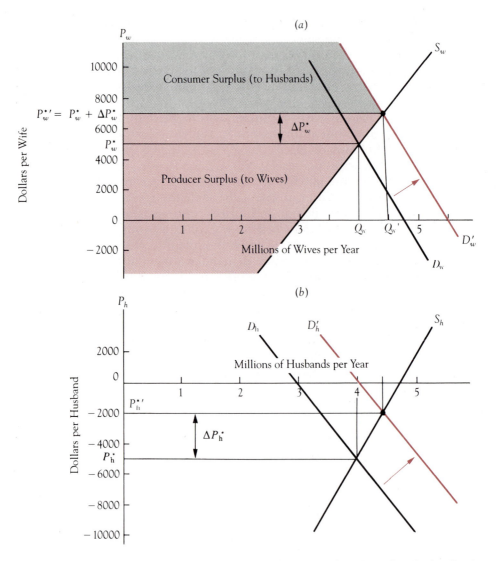

Polygamous marriage markets. Figure 21-2*a* shows the market for wives after the legalization of polygyny; Figure 21-2*b* shows the market for husbands after the legalization of polyandry.

him with another wife, making the marriage equivalent, for her, to a standard contract. The same applies at all other values of P_w; we define the price corresponding to any particular bigamous marriage contract as the price earlier assigned to that monogamous contract that potential wives consider equivalent to it.

We can now see why the equilibrium price in Figure 21-2a is higher than in Figure 21-1a. Suppose it were not; suppose the two prices were equal. Quantity supplied on Figure 21-2a would then be the same as on Figure 21-1a, but quantity demanded would be higher. Legalizing polygyny will hardly make a man who before wanted one wife decide that (at the same price) he now wants none, but it will allow some who before wanted one to marry two instead—even if they must offer terms at which potential wives are willing to accept half a husband apiece. So when polygyny becomes legal, quantity demanded at any price rises; the demand curve shifts out from D_w to D'_w. At the old equilibrium price (P_w^*), quantity demanded is now higher than quantity supplied. So the price must rise; the new equilibrium price ($P_w^{*'}$) must be higher than the old. Since price is defined in such a way that an increased price means a contract more favorable to the wife, this means that women are better off.

What about men? Those who end up with only one wife are worse off, since they must offer her more favorable terms than before. They are worse off by $\Delta P_w^* = P_w^{*'} - P_w^*$, the increase in the price they must pay for a wife. Those who end up with two (or more) wives may or may not be better off. The fact that someone chooses to marry two wives shows that at a price of $P_w^{*'}$ he prefers two wives to one; it does not tell us whether he prefers two at $P_w^{*'}$ to one at P_w^*.

Is the change a Marshall improvement or a Marshall worsening? It is a Marshall improvement. To see this, imagine that we go from Figure 21-1a to Figure 21-2a in two steps. The first consists of transferring ΔP_w^* from every husband to every wife. That is a pure transfer; wives gain what husbands lose. The next step is to allow husbands and wives to adjust to the new price; quantity of wives increases from Q_w to Q'_w. That is a Marshall improvement. Men who do not change the number of wives they have are unaffected; men who reduce the number of wives they have from one to zero in response to the higher price or increase the number above one to take advantage of the legalization of polygyny, and women who at the old price did not choose to marry but at the new price do, are better off. A pure transfer plus a Marshall improvement adds up to a Marshall improvement.

Figure 21-2b shows the effect of legalizing polyandry. The logic is exactly the same as for polygyny, with the roles of women and men reversed. Since some women now buy two (or more) husbands, the demand curve for husbands shifts out. At the old price for husbands, quantity demanded is greater than quantity supplied, so the price rises. Women marrying only one husband must compete against the polyandrous women to get him, hence must offer better terms than before. Men are better off, monogamous women are worse off, and polyandrous women may be better or worse off. The net effect is a Marshall improvement.

To many readers, the conclusion may seem extraordinary—how can women possibly be made better off by polygyny and men by polyandry? That reaction reflects what I described in Chapter 2 as naive price theory. Naive price theory is the theory that prices do not change. If polygyny were introduced and nothing else changed, then it seems likely that women would be worse off—except for those who prefer to share the burden of putting up with a husband. But when polygyny is introduced, something else does change; the demand curve for wives shifts up, and so does the price for wives implicit in the marriage contract. Those wives who end up with one husband get him on more favorable terms—he must bid more for a wife because of the competition of his polygynous rivals. Those who accept polygynous marriages do so because the price they are offered is sufficient to at least balance, for them, the disadvantage of sharing a husband.

Another reason why you may regard the result as implausible is that in many historical societies, including some of the polygynous ones, women did not belong to themselves. In such a situation, a woman's father, or whoever else was in a position to control whom she married, could have ended up receiving a large part of the price implicit in the marriage contract. If so, the demonstration that women are benefited by the legalization of polygyny no longer holds. That is why, at the beginning of the discussion, I explicitly assumed a society in which men and women belonged to themselves.

The result would seem less paradoxical if we substituted cars and car buyers for wives and husbands (or husbands and wives). Suppose there were a law forbidding anyone to own more than one car. It seems obvious enough that the abolition of that law would increase the demand for cars. Sellers of cars would be better off. Buyers who did not take advantage of the new opportunity—those who bought only one car—would be worse off, since they would have to pay a higher price. Buyers who bought more than one car would be better off than if they bought only one car at the new price (otherwise that is what they would have done) but not necessarily better off than if they bought one car at the old price, an option no longer open to them.

One thing you may find confusing in all this is the time sequence. Am I describing a situation in which, after polygyny becomes legal, some men divorce one wife to marry two others, and some women insist on renegotiating their marriage contracts? No. What I am doing is comparing two alternative futures, one with polygyny (or polyandry) and one without. The man who would have married one wife if polygyny had remained illegal either marries one wife on different terms if polygyny is legal, marries two (or more) wives, or is priced out of the market and remains a bachelor.

The Second Model

So far, we have modeled the marriage market in a way designed to make it seem as similar as possible to more conventional markets. The next step is to switch to an entirely different model—one that some of you may find more realistic.

We start by assuming that there is no way marriage partners can offer prices to each other, implicit or explicit. One reason might be the difficulty of enforcing such contracts, especially in a society where divorce is difficult. The obvious strategy in such a situation is "Promise anything but don't wash the dishes." Actual cash payments between the mates are impractical if, after the marriage, all property is held in common; there is little point in bribing someone with what will belong to him or her after the marriage anyway.

In such a society, the marriage market is a market without a price. The absence of a price does not eliminate the fundamental problem of scarcity; it just means that some other means of allocating the scarce supply of desirable mates (of both sexes) must be found.

We will now explicitly include one of the features that we earlier pushed into the background—the varying quality of mates. We suppose that all of the potential mates of each sex can be arranged in a hierarchy ranging from "most desirable" to "least desirable" and that everyone agrees on who belongs where in the hierarchy.

We now have a very simple rationing mechanism. The most desirable woman has her pick of mates, so she accepts the most desirable man; he, having his pick of mates, is only interested in her. The second most desirable woman would gladly accept the most desirable man, but he is already taken, so she settles for the second most desirable man. The process continues until all the members of whichever gender is less plentiful on the marriage market have been paired up, leaving the least desirable members of the other gender unmarried.

Suppose we now introduce polygyny. The most attractive woman can no longer be certain of marrying the most attractive man. He may prefer two less attractive women—and they may each prefer half of him to all of a less attractive man. If fewer men than women want to get married, some women may be choosing half of a husband over the alternative of no husband at all.

The result is no longer an unambiguous improvement from the standpoint of women, as it was in the first model. Some women at the top of the hierarchy find themselves with less attractive men than before. Neither is it an unambiguous worsening; some women who were previously unmarried may now have (half of) a husband, while others may get half of a man instead of all of a dolt.

It may or may not be an unambiguous improvement for the men. Some men benefit by getting two wives instead of one. In addition, every time a man near the top of the hierarchy settles for two (lower quality) women instead of one (high-quality) one, he opens up a rung on the ladder; the men below him move up a step and end up with more desirable wives than they could have before. Figure 21-3 shows such a change; *A, B, C,* . . . are the men, in order of desirability, while 1, 2, 3, . . . are the women. When *B* chooses 7 and 8 instead of 2, whom he would have married in a monogamous society, *C–G* all find themselves with more attractive wives as a result.

Figure 21-3

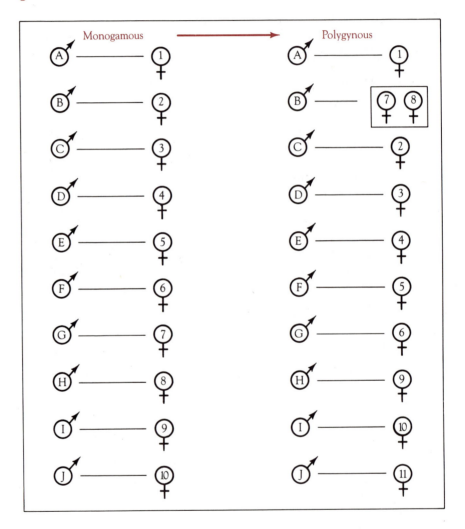

The effect of polygyny in a marriage market without prices. Both men and women are ranked (*A, B, C,* . . .; 1, 2, 3 . . .) according to their attractiveness as marriage partners. If polygyny is illegal, *A* marries 1, *B* marries 2, etc. If it is legal, *A* marries 1, *B* marries 7 and 8, *C* marries 2, etc.

How can the change injure men? A man is worse off if someone above him marries two wives, both higher in the women's hierarchy than the woman he was going to marry. That eliminates one step above him on the men's ladder and two steps on the women's, pushing his relative position down a step; he must be content with a woman one step below the one he could have gotten if monogamy were the rule. In Figure 21-3, that is what happens to H and everyone below him.

Just as in the first model, the argument can be repeated for the case of polyandry, with essentially the same results. When polyandry becomes legal, some men near the top of the hierarchy almost certainly lose; some near the bottom—in particular any who before could not find a wife— gain. Women may all gain, or those at the top may gain at the expense of those at the bottom.

Markets with and without Price— Some General Comments

Whenever it is suggested that something should be provided on the market instead of produced and allocated by government, one of the objections made is that such a proposal only benefits the rich, since if something is sold, "The rich get it all." The outcome of the marriage market I have just described—a market without price—is much more like that stereotype than is the outcome of an ordinary market with a price. On an ordinary market, differences in income are one of the factors determining who gets what, but not the only one. An individual who particularly values something—car, clothes, books—may end up with more of it than a competitor with higher income but different tastes. And the outcome is not all or nothing; the individual who spends more money gets, not all of the good, but an amount proportioned to what he is willing to spend.

On the monogamous marriage market without price, it does not matter how much a man wants an intelligent and beautiful wife and how many other things he is willing to give up to get her; if anyone above him on the hierarchy also wants her, he has no chance. Wealth—not in money but in whatever makes for an attractive mate—is the sole determinant of who gets what. And the competition, for any particular mate, is all-or-nothing; if you have half the attractiveness of your competitor, the result is not that you get a third of what you want and he gets two thirds but that he gets all of it.

In the Soviet Union some goods, such as meat and out-of-season vegetables, are sold at low prices but are frequently unavailable in ordinary stores. They can be found only in special stores to which ordinary citizens do not have access. In that respect, at least, inequality is greater under communism than under capitalism—precisely because goods are not allocated by the market. Similarly during World War II, when the United States had price control and rationing on food, what you ate often depended less on what you were willing to pay than on whom you knew.

Money, Beauty, and Folk Songs

The Brown Girl she has house and lands, fair Ellender she has none.

—No. 73 of *The English and Scottish Popular Ballads* collected by Francis James Child

At the end of this chapter, there is a brief discussion of the anti-money bias of our culture, the attitude that regards money transactions, especially in a social context, as somehow base or corrupt. Those who do not believe such a bias exists may find it instructive to reread the earlier parts of this chapter or explain them to their friends and then examine their own and their friends' reactions to describing marriage as buying a wife or husband.

One aspect of this that is particularly relevant to our two models of the marriage market—with and without price—is a motif frequently seen in folk songs. A young man must choose between two women, one beautiful and one rich. Almost invariably he chooses the rich one. The result is tragedy; at least two and often all three of the parties end up dead. The lesson is clear: Marry the beautiful woman.

It is clear in such songs that marrying a woman for her money is bad, but marrying her for her beauty is fine. It is less clear why. True, the Brown Girl (dark complexioned, hence less attractive than "Fair" Ellender) has done nothing to deserve her wealth; one could argue that she therefore does not deserve to get Lord Thomas. But no more does Fair Ellender deserve her beauty. All either of them has done is to pick the right parents, the one for wealth and the other for looks. Why then is it good and noble for Lord Thomas to reject wealth for beauty and base and wicked for him to reject beauty for wealth?

One answer may be that the plot depends on something that I earlier assumed away. In the world of folk songs—and in many, perhaps most, human societies—the bride and groom are not the only ones whose interests are involved in their marriage, nor are they the only ones with some control over it. Both sets of parents are involved as well. What may really be going on in "Lord Thomas and Fair Ellender" (and other songs with the same plot line) is a conflict of interest between the groom and his family. If Lord Thomas marries Fair Ellender, he will be the only one to benefit by her beauty; if he marries the Brown Girl, his parents may reasonably hope to get their hands on some of her wealth. Perhaps they are counting on it to support them in their old age. It is Lord Thomas's mother who persuades him to marry the Brown Girl.

If that is what is going on, it is clear enough which side of the generation gap the singer is on. Or, more precisely, which side he believes his audience is on.

What and Why Is Marriage?

> *(Miss Manners) also asks that you not bore her with explaining the comparative quality of marital and nonmarital relationships, especially when using the term "honesty" or asking the nonsensical question of what difference a piece of paper makes. Miss Manners has a safe-deposit box full of papers that make a difference.*
>
> —*Miss Manners' Guide to Excruciatingly Correct Behavior* by Judith Martin

So far in our discussion of the marriage market, we have taken the existence of marriage for granted. We will now turn from examining the market to examining the institution. Our first questions are "What is marriage" and "Why does it exist?"

Marriage as a Firm. One way of looking at marriage is as a rather odd sort of package deal, an exchange in which the two parties agree to share income, housing, sexual favors, and a collection of productive activities such as cooking meals, cleaning house, washing dishes, and rearing children. Seen from this standpoint, the motivation for marriage is, in part, the existence of economies of scale in production—it is easier to cook one meal for two people than two meals each for one person—and, in part, the advantage of division of labor. A marriage is simply a particular kind of two-person firm.

But a firm is not the only way of taking advantage of division of labor—there is the alternative of the market. Most of us take advantage of the comparative advantage of the butcher, the baker, and the brewer; but we do not have to marry them to get our dinner. The wife in a traditional marriage may have a comparative advantage over the husband in cooking, and the husband might have a comparative advantage over the wife in carpentry. But outside of the household, there are surely better cooks and better carpenters than either of them. Why does the couple limit itself to division of labor within the household?

The Reasons for Household Production. Few couples do; most of us obtain much of what we want by buying it on the open market. The typical family does, however, rely on household production for a considerable range of what it consumes—most meals, most domestic cleaning, much child care and education, and so on. Why are not these things too purchased on the market?

One reason is the existence of transaction costs. If you are going to build a house, it is worth hiring a carpenter. If you are simply fixing a few loose shingles, the time and trouble of finding a good carpenter, negotiating mutually satisfactory terms, and making sure he does the job may more than wipe out the carpenter's comparative advantage. The carpenter may be better at fixing the shingles than I am, but I am the one who gets wet if the roof leaks, so I have an incentive to do a good job even if nobody is watching me. And I have no incentive to waste time and energy haggling with myself over the price.

A second reason may be specialization—not in a particular product but in a particular set of customers. The cook at the restaurant my wife and I would go to if we spent less time cooking and more time earning money to pay for going to restaurants may be better at cooking than we are. But the restaurant cook is worse than we are at cooking *for us*. We, after all, are specialists in what we like. This may be still more true for some other forms of household production.

We now have at least a partial explanation for the existence of marriage. A second element worth investigating is the fact that marriage, in most societies, is a very long-term contract. Why?

Marriage and the Costs of Bilateral Monopoly.   The answer was given back in Chapter 9, in the discussion of bilateral monopoly as a reason for long-term contracts. Before I went to work at UCLA, both I and the economics department were participating in a large and moderately competitive market. Once I had accepted the job and spent a year or two learning to do it, we were both to some degree locked into a bilateral monopoly. Both they and I had borne substantial costs associated with training me for that particular job and equipping the department to deal with that particular professor.

Marriage is a more extreme version of the same situation. Individuals choose their mates on a large and competitive market, however much they may protest that there could never have been anyone else. But once they are married, they rapidly acquire what in other contexts is known as **firm-specific capital**. If they decide to end the contract and find other partners, they incur very large costs that they would have avoided if they had chosen the right partners to start with. Their specialized knowledge of how to live with each other becomes worthless. One, at least, must leave a familiar and accustomed home. Their circle of friends will probably be divided between them. Worst of all, the new mate, whatever his or her advantages, is not the other parent of their children.

As I explained in Chapter 6, one problem with acquiring firm-specific capital is that it creates a large bargaining range between the two parties. Each may be tempted, in trying to get things his way, to take advantage of the fact that the other is locked into the relation and will choose to leave it only if things get very much worse. There is no way to eliminate such problems entirely, in marriage or in other contexts, but long-term contracting, explicit or implicit, is a common way of reducing them.

Enforcement Problems.   The marriage contract involves two different elements, one a good deal more enforceable than the other. The agreement to remain married "till death do us part" is to a considerable degree enforceable; in many societies, although not ours at present, getting out of one marriage and into another is a difficult and expensive undertaking. Henry VIII, as you will remember, had to change the religion of an entire country in order to cancel his long-term contract with Catherine of Aragon.

But preventing the parties to a contract from backing out of it entirely does not solve the problem unless the contract specifies the precise obligations of each party—and does so in a way that can be enforced. Marriage without divorce can result in an even larger bargaining range than marriage with divorce, since one party can threaten to make the other's life so unpleasant that divorce would be an improvement. Whether the threat is a believable one may depend on the cost of carrying it out. If both parties know that when the argument is over they are still going to be married to each other, that may give them an incentive to avoid extreme strategies.

This suggests that the ideal solution would be a long-term contract that completely specified the obligations of both parties. Before the contract is signed, there is no marriage, no bilateral monopoly, and not much of a bargaining range. After the contract is signed, there is nothing left to bargain about.

To some extent, marriage is such a contract. It is, in principle, possible for a husband or wife to claim that the other is not living up to his or her responsibility—for a wife to sue a husband for failing to support her, for example. The problem is, first, that one can never write a contract detailed enough to specify all the relevant terms and, second, that even if one could, it would be almost impossible to enforce it. Here, as with price control, the individual who is legally obliged to provide a specified product at a specified price can generally evade the obligation by lowering quality. So far as I know, nobody has ever successfully sued his or her spouse for cooking—or making love—badly. So a considerable amount of bargaining room remains, and is used, even in marriages in traditional societies.

Love and Marriage. So far in this chapter I have said nothing about love, which is widely believed to have some connection with marriage. It may seem odd to ask why we marry someone we love, instead of marrying someone whose tastes agree with and whose skills complement our own and then conducting our respective love lives on the side, but it is a legitimate question.

There are two answers. The first is that love is associated with sex, for reasons that can be explained (by **sociobiology**—economics applied to genes instead of people) but will not be here, and sex with having children. Parents much prefer rearing their own children to rearing other people's, and much of child rearing is most conveniently done in the home of the rearer. So it is convenient, to say the least, if a child's parents are married—to each other.

The second answer is that love reduces, although it does not eliminate, the conflicts of interest that lead to costly bargaining. If I love my wife, her happiness is one of the main things determining mine; we therefore have a common interest in making her happy. If she also loves me, we also have a common interest in making me happy. Unless our love is so precisely calculated that our objectives are identical, there is still room for conflict, in either direction; if we love each other too much, my attempts to benefit her at my expense will clash with her attempts to benefit me at her expense.

A more precise discussion of the logic of such situations will have to wait for the second part of the chapter, where I work out in some detail the effect of altruism on the behavior of altruist and beneficiary.

The Decline and Fall of American Marriage.   Now that we have at least a sketch of an economic theory of marriage, we might as well do something with it. One obvious thing to do is to explain the decline of marriage in the United States (and some similar societies) over the course of this century. Why has marriage become less common and why has the effective term of the contract become so much shorter?

The simple answer is that the amount of time spent in household production has declined drastically, and with it the amount of firm-specific capital acquired by the partners, especially the wife. Earlier I remarked that it was not necessary, in order to get dinner, to marry one's butcher, baker, and brewer. In fact, a few hundred years ago, it was not uncommon for a man to be married to his baker and brewer and a woman to her butcher—all three of those professions were to a considerable extent carried out within the household, especially in rural areas. Dorothy Sayers, in one of her essays, suggests that men who complain about women stealing men's jobs should be asked whether they wish to return to women all the industries that used to be conducted by housewives and have now moved onto the market, such as brewing beer, preserving food, and making clothes.

One factor reducing the amount of household production has been the increase in specialization over the past few centuries. Bacon, clothing, jams, and many other things are now mass-produced instead of made at home. A second factor has been the mechanization of much of what remains. Clothes and dishes are still washed at home, but a good deal of the work is really done by the firms that make the washing machines. A third factor has been the enormous decrease in infant mortality. It used to be necessary for a woman to produce children practically nonstop in order to be fairly sure of having two or three survive to adulthood, with the result that bearing and rearing children was virtually a full-time job. In a modern society, a couple that wants two children produces two children.

The result of all three changes has been greatly to reduce the amount of work done by an average housewife. Housewife is no longer a full-time profession, save in certain unusual cases—families that want a lot of children, couples going "back to the land," and the like. But household production in general and child rearing in particular are responsible for a large part of the specialized capital associated with marriage. If husband and wife each spend 80 percent of the day working at a job and 20 percent taking care of the household and if they have no young children, the costs of divorce are not all that great. Even for a somewhat more traditional family, with the husband working full time and the wife dividing her time between work, housekeeping, and rearing one or two children, the costs of divorce are much lower than they were a few generations ago.

Divorce is not all costs. There are benefits too; otherwise nobody would ever get divorced. If the benefits remain unchanged and the costs are reduced, the number of cases in which at least one partner finds that benefits are greater than costs will increase. Judging by the divorce rate, it has. Seen from this standpoint, the increase is neither inherently good nor inherently bad, neither evidence of increased freedom nor a consequence of declining moral standards. It is merely a rational adjustment to a changing world.

It is good insofar as it reflects, and accommodates, an increase in the range of choice available to individuals. We could choose to live in eighteenth century households, tanning our own leather and brewing our own beer. Some people do—you can read about their lives in *Mother Earth News* every month. The fact that most do not is evidence that, for most of us, the costs of living that kind of life instead of our present one are larger than the benefits.

The increased divorce rate, and the general difficulties with modern marriage, are bad things only to the extent that they reflect the failure of our institutions and expectations to adjust completely to new circumstances. The terms on which two people can live a happy and productive life together are not so simple that each couple can invent them independently in a few hours. The division of labor has a place in building institutions as well as houses. In a relatively static society, we can observe successful arrangements, patterns that have worked in the past and will probably work in the future. In a rapidly changing society, it is more difficult to figure out what kind of a contract we should or should not agree to and what kind of a marriage—or alternative arrangement—we should or should not choose. Hence there are likely to be more mistakes. Here as in most other areas, economic theory is more useful for describing the equilibrium than for describing the process by which we move from one equilibrium to another.

THE ECONOMICS OF ALTRUISM

A common argument against economics is the claim that economists either assume or advocate selfishness, whereas people in the real world should and do care for others. There is some truth to this charge, but not very much. Economists assume that people have their own objectives and act to achieve them, but, as I have pointed out several times, there is no reason why those objectives must be selfish; economists can and do assume that one of the things some people value is the welfare of other people.

Geometric Version

Someone who values the welfare of someone else is called an **altruist**. It is possible to use economics to analyze the rational behavior of an altruist and of the person whose welfare he cares about, and in the process to derive some surprising results.

Figure 21-4a shows the indifference curves of an altruist A, who is concerned with his own consumption, C_A, shown on the vertical axis, and the consumption of a beneficiary B, C_B, shown on the horizontal axis. Both C_A and C_B are goods for A, so his indifference curves slope down and to the right; both exhibit declining marginal utility, so the curves are convex toward the origin. In drawing the figure, I have assumed that both C_A and C_B are normal goods; as his income rises, he buys more of both. That assumption will be retained throughout the discussion.

A has an income I_A and B an income I_B. If A gives nothing to B, each will consume his own income, putting them at point X ($C_A = I_A$, $C_B = I_B$). A can, if he wishes, transfer part of his income to B, reducing his own consumption and increasing B's. As he does so, he moves down the line L. The slope of L is -1; when A gives B a dollar, A's consumption goes down by a dollar and B's goes up by a dollar. A will continue to make transfers

Figure 21-4

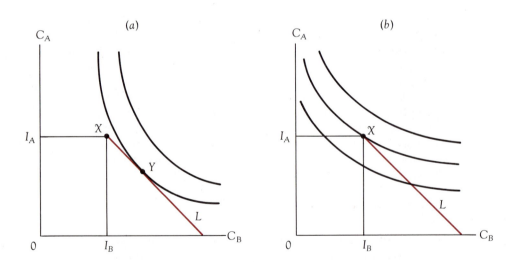

Budget line/indifference curve diagram for an altruist. By choosing how much of his income (I_A) to give to the beneficiary, the altruist is choosing a point on the budget line L. Figure 21-4a shows an interior solution at Y; Figure 21-4b shows a corner solution at X.

Section V   Applications—Controversial and Un

until he reaches point Y, where an indifference curve is tangent to L. This is his optimal point on L, just as the point where an ordinary budget line is tangent to an indifference curve was the optimal point for an ordinary consumer in Chapter 3—it is the most desirable bundle available to him.

Figure 21-4a shows a situation in which the altruist chooses to make transfers to the beneficiary. Figure 21-4b is similar, except that the altruist's preferred point is X, where he starts out. Any transfer will move him to a lower indifference curve. The altruist consumes his entire income (I_A), and the "beneficiary" consumes his entire income (I_B). A is still an altruist, since he still values B's utility, but he does not value it enough to buy any of it, given its cost.

Figures 21-4a and 21-4b are almost exactly like the budget line-indifference curve diagrams we constructed in Chapter 3. A is "buying" two goods, C_A and C_B, with a "total income" of $I_A + I_B$. The only difference is that since the altruist can make transfers to B but cannot force B to make transfers to him, the line stops at X; there is no way he can choose a bundle higher and further to the left than that. In effect, the altruist is deciding how to divide the total income $I_A + I_B$ between himself and the beneficiary, subject to the condition that the beneficiary has to end up with at least I_B.

Figure 21-5a shows the effect of two possible changes in the situation. The budget line df is the result of decreasing I_A by \$10 (Case 1);

Figure 21-5

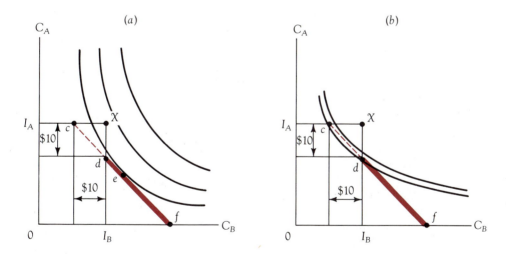

The effect on an altruist's situation of a change in the combined income of altruist and beneficiary. df is the budget line after a \$10 reduction in the altruist's income, cf the budget line after a \$10 reduction in the beneficiary's income. In Figure 21-5a, where the optimum is an interior solution, it is the same for both cases; in Figure 21-5b, one of the optima is a corner solution (no transfer) and is not the same as the other.

cf (*df* plus the dashed extension *cd*) is the result of instead decreasing I_B by \$10 (Case 2). The two lines are identical except that the dashed line goes a little farther up and to the left. The optimal point chosen by the altruist (*e*) is the same in both cases.

As you should be able to see from the figure, this is not an accident. The two lines, one representing the situation where the altruist loses \$10 and the other the situation where the beneficiary does, are the same except for the dashed section *cd*. So unless the altruist's optimal point is on *cd*, it must be the same for both cases. If the optimal point is on *cd*, as shown on Figure 21-5*b*, then in Case 1, where the altruist loses the money, his new optimum is at *d*. The altruist chooses not to transfer anything, so each ends up consuming all of his own income.

Verbal Version

The analysis can be put in words as well as in figures. The altruist, in deciding how much of his income to give to the beneficiary, is dividing the combined income of the two ($I_A + I_B$) between them, subject to the condition that he can only give, not take, so the beneficiary cannot end up with less than he starts with (I_B). A \$10 decrease in either the altruist's or the beneficiary's income means that there is now \$10 less to be divided between them. The only difference is that if the decrease is in the altruist's income, the least the beneficiary can end up with is I_B; if it is in the beneficiary's income, the least he can end up with is $I_B - \$10$—his new, lower, income. If the altruist's preferred division involves the beneficiary consuming more than I_B, as it does in Figure 21-5*a*, that difference does not matter; even if he could create a division in which the beneficiary consumed less than I_B, he would not choose to. So the outcomes of Case 1 and Case 2 are the same, as shown on Figure 21-5*a*.

This means that as long as we only consider situations in which the altruist chooses to make some transfer (unlike Figure 21-4*b* and Case 1 on Figure 21-5*b*, where he does not), changes in the combined income of altruist and beneficiary have the same effect on the consumption of both, whether they change the altruist's income or the beneficiary's income. The beneficiary, if he understands this analysis, will find it in his interest to pay as much attention to maintaining the income of the altruist as to maintaining his own. In this respect, the beneficiary ends up acting rather as though he too were an altruist—even though he is actually indifferent to the altruist's welfare.

It is in the interest of the beneficiary to take any action that produces net gains to himself plus the altruist, in exactly the same sense in which we discussed net gains in the context of Marshall efficiency. Any change that is a Marshall improvement will also be an improvement for the beneficiary once we include in our calculations the effect of the change on the amount that the altruist chooses to transfer. A change that benefits the altruist by \$5 and hurts the beneficiary by \$3 will also result in the altruist increasing his transfer to the beneficiary by at least \$3 and less than \$5; a change that injures the altruist by $5 and benefits the beneficiary by $3 will result in a reduction of the transfer by something between $3 and $5. I have proved this result graphically in the simple two-dimensional case where all changes are in money; the proof in the more general case (where the loss might be a broken arm, a broken window, or even a broken heart) is similar but more complicated.

Your response to this result may be that it is not surprising; if the beneficiary hurts the altruist, the altruist punishes him by reducing the transfer, so the beneficiary finds it in his interest not to offend his patron. That is not what is happening. Nothing in the argument I gave, or the more general argument whose results I described, depends on the altruist knowing that the beneficiary is responsible for the change. Exactly the same thing will happen in the case of a change produced by some third party, or by nature. If the change is a Marshall improvement, both beneficiary and altruist end up better off after the change—and the resulting change in the amount the altruist chooses to transfer. If it is a worsening, both end up worse off.

You can see that result in Figure 21-5a, where the equilibrium position depends only on the combined income $I_A + I_B$, not on the individual incomes. That remains true as long as, both before and after the change, the altruist chooses to make some transfer to the beneficiary. Figures 21-4b and 21-5b show situations where that is not true; two of the equilibria on those figures are corner solutions with zero transfer. Since in such situations, $C_A = I_A$ and $C_B = I_B$, the division of consumption depends on I_A and I_B, not just on their sum.

The Rotten Kid Theorem

Consider a situation with one altruist ("parent") and two beneficiaries ("kids"). One of them is a rotten kid who would enjoy kicking his little sister. The analysis I have just described implies that if the dollar value to the rotten kid of kicking his sister (the number of dollars worth of consumption he would, if necessary, give up in order to do so) is less than the dollar cost to the sister of being kicked, the rotten kid is better off not kicking her. After the parent has adjusted his expenditure on the kids in response to the increased utility of the kid and the decreased utility of the kicked sister, the rotten kid will have lost more than he has gained. Here again, the argument does not depend on the parent observing the kick but only on his observing how happy the two kids are.

This result—that a rotten kid, properly allowing for the effects of parental altruism, will find it in his self-interest to kick his sister only if it is efficient to do so—is known as the **Rotten Kid Theorem**. There is a sense in which the altruist in such a situation functions, unintentionally, as a stand-in for the bureaucrat-god, at least as far as the tiny society made up of altruist and beneficiaries is concerned. Because of the altruist's peculiar utility function—which contains the beneficiaries' utilities among its arguments—both altruist and beneficiaries find it in their private interest to maximize Marshall efficiency, to make decisions according to whether the net effect on altruist and beneficiaries is or is not a Marshall improvement.

Altruism and Evolution

What, if anything, is this analysis of altruism useful for, other than entertainment? Gary Becker, the economist whose ideas I have been describing, has used them to try to resolve one of the principal puzzles of sociobiology: the existence of altruism. If, as the theory of evolution seems to imply, animals (including ourselves) have been selected by evolution for our ability to serve our own reproductive interest (roughly speaking, to act in such a way as to have as many descendants as possible), those who sacrifice their interest for the interest of others should have been selected out. Yet altruism seems to occur among a variety of species, possibly including our own.

One explanation is that altruism toward kin (most obviously toward my children, but the argument turns out to apply to other relatives as well) is not really altruism from the point of view of evolution; I am serving my reproductive interest by keeping my children alive so that they can have children. This still leaves altruism toward non-kin as a puzzle to be explained. Becker's argument is that altruism generates cooperative behavior via the mechanism described above and so benefits the altruist as well as the recipient, by giving each recipient an incentive to behave efficiently vis-à-vis the entire group. A group containing an altruist will therefore be more successful than one that does not; it will have more surviving descendants, and its genes, including the genes for altruism, will become increasingly common.

At the same time the altruist is promoting the reproductive success of his group vis-à-vis other groups, he is also sacrificing his own reproductive success vis-à-vis other members of his group. He is, after all, transferring resources of some sort from himself to them. If Becker's analysis is correct, genes for altruism should be becoming less frequent over time within groups containing one or more altruists, but the genes of such groups should be becoming more frequent over time; only if the second process at least balances the first will altruism survive.

Fair Ellender and the Rotten Kid

In the first part of this chapter, I asked why marrying for beauty is generally considered better than marrying for money. We now have a possible answer. It is widely believed that beauty is, and wealth is not, one of the things that makes men fall in love with women. Our analysis of altruism suggests that people will work together much more easily if one of them is an altruist with regard to the other, since it is then in the interest of both altruist and beneficiary to maximize their joint welfare. Lord Thomas is in love with Fair Ellender and is not in love with the

Brown Girl, as he informs her immediately after the wedding—with the result that the Brown Girl stabs Fair Ellender, Lord Thomas kills the Brown Girl, and Lord Thomas then commits suicide, thus ending the song and presumably teaching his parents a lesson. If we are willing to identify "being in love" with altruism, perhaps the moral of the song is correct. If you marry the beautiful woman, you get not only beauty but also the advantage of being part of an efficient household—coordinated by your own altruism.

Of course, it only works in one direction; we have no reason to believe that Fair Ellender's beauty makes her any more likely to act altruistically toward Lord Thomas. But that is not an important objection to the argument; we know, from the Rotten Kid Theorem, that one altruist in a family is enough.

A more serious objection is that it is not clear how close the relationship is between "being in love" and altruism; Fair Ellender's response to being jilted by the man she was "in love" with was to dress up in her finest ("every village she came through, they thought she was some queen") and go spoil her ex-boyfriend's wedding. "Being in love" seems to describe a mix of emotions, some of them far from altruistic. To what extent the elements in the mix associated with physical beauty involve altruism, and, if they do, whether they are likely to survive the first six months of marriage, is at least an open question.

Gift vs Money

Why do people ever give gifts in any form other than money? If, as we normally assume, each individual knows his own interest, surely he is better off getting money and buying what he wants instead of getting what the donor decides to buy for him.

There are two obvious reasons to give gifts instead of cash. The first is that the donor may believe the recipient's objectives are different from his own. I may give you a scholarship not because I like you but because I want there to be more educated people in the society or more smart high school students going to my alma mater.

Another example is the food stamp program. The idea is not merely to help poor people, but to get them to buy more food. This leads to another question: Why do we care what the poor people spend the money on? If they feel clothing or shelter is more important than food, why not let them make that choice? One answer to that question is that the program is largely supported by politicians from food-producing states.

A second reason for giving restricted gifts is paternalism. If you believe that you know better than the recipient what is good for him, you will naturally want to control how he spends your money. The obvious example is the case of parents dealing with children. A second reason to give food stamps instead of money may be the belief that some of the poor should spend money on food but, if given a choice, will spend it on whiskey instead.

It is not entirely obvious that paternalism is a sensible policy even applied to children. When I was quite small, my family traveled by train from Chicago to Portland, Oregon, to visit grandparents. The trip took three days and two nights. My father offered me and my sister the choice of either having sleeping berths or sitting up and being given the money that the berths would cost. We took the money.

This brings us back to the question of why we give gifts instead of cash—to our friends and even our parents on Christmas, birthdays, and the like. Even if paternalism is appropriate toward one's children, it hardly seems an appropriate attitude toward one's parents. A possible answer is that, in this particular small matter, we do think we know their interest better than they do—we are giving, say, a book we have read and are sure they will like. I doubt that this is a sufficient explanation; we frequently give people gifts we have no special reason to think they will like. I suspect that the correct answer is somehow connected with the hostility to money, especially in personal interactions, which seems typical of our society. Consider, for example, the number of men who would think it entirely proper to take a woman to an expensive restaurant in the hope of return benefits later in the evening, but would never dream of offering her money for the same objective.

Many readers find this particular example a disturbing one, in part because it seems to imply that a good deal of conventional dating is simply a disguised form of prostitution. Much the same assertion has occasionally been made about marriage. In both cases, the argument seems plausible and yet the conclusion absurd. This raises a variety of interesting questions, starting with the question of why we have such strong negative feelings about prostitution—why, in a variety of societies, the sale of sex is regarded very differently from the sale of other services, and why our condemnation does not extend to situations in which sex is, implicitly and perhaps ambiguously, part of a much broader transaction. Students interested in exploring that question may find that the ideas of this chapter, the discussion of commitment strategies in Chapter 11, and the evolutionary explanations of behavior in books such as *The Selfish Gene*, provide at least a starting point for an economic explanation of such apparently uneconomic attitudes.

Suspension of Disbelief

Some of my more courageous readers may at this point be about ready to ask whether I expect them to take this chapter seriously. Do I really believe that love and marriage can be analyzed with the abstract logic of economics? Do I really believe that a 7-year-old boy, in deciding whether or not to kick his little sister, works out a cost-benefit calculation based on economic theory that is fully understood by almost no one without a Ph.D. in economics?

The answer is "yes, but." I do believe that the analysis of this chapter is useful in understanding love, marriage, and children as they exist in the real world. I do not believe that the analysis is sufficient to understand them, without also knowing a good deal about what it is like to be human, to love, to be a child, to be a parent. Nor do I believe that if theory clashes with what we observe in the real world, it is the real world that must back down; I am not willing to say, in the words of a famous German philosopher confronted with evidence contrary to his theories, "So much the worse for the facts."

Economics is one way of understanding the real world. It depends, in virtually all practical applications, on using an approximate picture of the real world, one that retains the essential features while eliminating inessential elements whose inclusion would make the analysis intolerably complicated. Making such approximations correctly is a matter of judgment; one way of finding out whether you have done so is by seeing how well the predictions of the theory fit what you actually observe. It is most unlikely that they will fit perfectly, since the world you observe is not identical to the simplified picture of it that you have analyzed. But an approximate theory may still be better than no theory at all.

All that being said, it is also true that for some of us the creation of economic theory, especially economic theory of things that everyone else regards as outside of economics, is an entertaining game and even, perhaps, a form of art. As long as that is all it is, the theory is properly judged by artistic criteria: elegance and consistency. It is only when we stop sketching out theories for fun and start testing them against the real world that economics becomes a science as well as an art and its analysis useful as well as entertaining.

PROBLEMS

1. In the first model of marriage, an increase in the price that potential husbands offered for wives resulted in an increased quantity of wives supplied, since improved marriage terms made more women willing to marry. Suppose we were considering a society in which the price went to the bride's parents instead of the bride. Discuss how and why the quantity of wives would depend on the price, in both the short and long run.

2. In analyzing the effects of polygyny, I claimed that the polygynists themselves—the men who ended up with more than one wife—might be worse off as a result of the legalization of polygyny. How can that be—if they are worse off, why do they not simply decide to marry only one wife?

3. It is said that there exists a traditional society in which every year there is a bride market. It takes the form of an auction, starting with the most desirable bride. The money paid by suitors for the desirable brides is collected. When the auctioneer gets to a bride nobody wants

to pay to marry, the price goes negative—he starts offering a payment to potential suitors, paid out of the money collected. As the brides get less desirable, the payments get larger. The auction continues until all of the young women of the appropriate age have been auctioned off.

Discuss the workability and the implications of this system. What would be the effect of legalizing polygyny? Polyandry? Who do potential brides "belong to" under this system?

4. Historically, most marriages have been monogamous, but many societies have also permitted legal polygyny. Polyandry seems to be much rarer. Can you suggest reasons?

5. Can you suggest economic reasons for the hostility to money, especially in social contexts, discussed in the chapter? Can you suggest noneconomic reasons? If so, can you translate your noneconomic reasons into economic language?

6. One interesting characteristic of gift-giving that should be explained by an adequate theory is the tendency to give gifts that are pleasurable but ephemeral, luxuries such as candy and flowers. What do you think the explanation is?

7. In discussing the nature of marriage, I presented reasons why both love and sex are normally part of the package, along with cooking, home repairs, child rearing, and a variety of other services. This does not seem to have been true of French upper-class society in the nineteenth century, at least as depicted by French novelists. One has the impression that every well-to-do husband had a mistress and every wife a lover.

Discuss why marriage may have taken the form it did in that society. In general, what relation would you expect to observe between income and the stability of marriage? Does this correspond to what actually happens, in that society and others?

8. Figure 21-6 is the indifference map for an altruist A. Draw his budget line and indicate the equilibrium if:
   a. His income is 30, the beneficiary's income is 10.
   b. His income is 20, the beneficiary's income is 20.
   c. His income is 10, the beneficiary's income is 30.

9. Do Problem 8 on the assumption that there is a gift tax of 33 percent: for every $3 the altruist gives, $2 goes to the beneficiary and $1 to the government. The government spends its tax money on people whose utility is not of value to the altruist.

10. Throughout the analysis of altruism, I assumed not only that the beneficiary's utility was a good for the altruist but that it was a normal good. Suppose it is instead an inferior good. How would the conclusions of the analysis be changed? How would the beneficiary find it in his interest to behave?

11. Suppose the utility of one person is a bad for another. How might one describe this situation? What results would you expect?

Figure 21-6

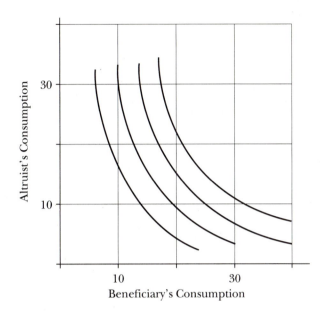

Indifference curves for an altruist. For Problems 8 and 9.

12. Suppose we concede that my sister and I correctly perceived our own interest when we chose money over berths for our train trip. What reasons can you suggest, in terms of the analysis of this book, why letting us make the choice might nonetheless not have led to the efficient outcome?

FOR FURTHER READING

An excellent introduction to sociobiology—the study of the behavior of animals, including humans, on the assumption that it has been "designed" by evolution to maximize the reproductive success of the individual's genes—is Richard Dawkins, *The Selfish Gene* (New York: Oxford University Press, 1976).

For a more advanced discussion of the economics of marriage (and other things), I recommend Gary Becker, *A Treatise on the Family* (Cambridge: Harvard University Press, 1981). An interesting article on the economics of marriage, and one that takes a somewhat pessimistic view of the move towards easier divorce, is: Lloyd Cohen, "Marriage, Divorce, and Quasi Rents; or, 'I Gave Him The Best Years of My Life'," *Journal of*

Legal Studies, Vol. XVI, No. 2, (June, 1987). An interesting discussion of altruism, arguing that Becker's theory does not explain observed behavior and suggesting an alternative, is: Howard Margolis, *Selfishness, Altruism, and Rationality* (Cambridge University Press, 1982). A less theoretical and more practical guide to (among other things) courtship and marriage is Judith Martin, *Miss Manners' Guide to Excruciatingly Correct Behavior* (New York: Atheneum Publishers, 1982). Finally, for a witty and intelligent discussion of the differences between men and women, written some 60 years ago and well designed to infuriate equally all parties to the issue, I recommend H. L. Mencken, *In Defense of Women* (New York: Octagon Books, 1976).

In a recent article, I combine some of the ideas of this chapter and of Chapter 15 to discuss, among other things, the economics of gift taxation. See David Friedman, "Does Altruism Produce Efficient Outcomes? Marshall vs Kaldor." *Journal of Legal Studies*, Vol. XVII (January, 1988).

WHY YOU SHOULD
section VI
BUY THIS BOOK

chapter 22

FINAL WORDS

One defect of many economics textbooks, especially at the elementary level, is that they teach you about economics instead of teaching you economics. The result is to produce students who may be equipped to talk about economics but certainly not to do any—a sort of academic equivalent of learning what names to drop at cocktail parties.

You have now spent 21 chapters learning to do economics. In this final chapter, I shall try to tell you something about economics: what it is good for, how it is done, and to what degree economists know anything.

WHAT IS ECONOMICS GOOD FOR ANYWAY?

Looking at the title of this section, it may occur to you that it belongs in the first chapter of the book, not the last. As a believer in rational behavior, I should perhaps have explained to you why economics was worth learning before expecting you to spend a lot of time and trouble learning it. Unfortunately, if I had told you what economics was good for before you read the book, you might reasonably enough have dismissed my claims as no more than deceptive advertising. You may still come to that conclusion, but at least you now have some evidence on which to base your conclusion.

There are at least four different reasons to learn economics. The first is that economists, in the process of developing a theory of human behavior based on rationality, have done quite a lot of useful thinking about how it is rational to behave. While we may know very little about what your objectives are or should be, we know quite a lot about how, given a set of objectives, they can best be attained. Once you understand concepts such as marginal cost, marginal value, sunk cost, and present value, you should find them to be useful tools in making decisions about how to organize your life. When you finally realize that you have invested six months of effort and heartache pursuing a member of the opposite sex who has no interest at all in you, you can sum up your situation—and reluctantly reach the correct conclusion concerning what to do about it—with the observation that sunk costs are sunk costs. When deciding whether to spend another few weeks looking for a better buy in a house or a car, you can put the issue more closely by asking, not whether you have found the best possible buy, but whether the expected return from additional search is greater or less than its marginal cost.

A second reason to learn economics is in order to understand and predict the behavior of other people, especially the effects of the behavior of large numbers of people, so that you can take account of it in planning your own life. This should be useful whether you are an investor trying to make money on the stock market, a general trying to keep his soldiers from running away, a homeowner trying to discourage burglars, or a student trying to predict future wages in different professions. In none of these cases will a knowledge of economics by itself be enough to answer your questions—you always need facts and judgment as well. But in all of those cases and many more, economics provides the essential framework within which knowledge and judgment can be combined to reach, perhaps, a correct conclusion—or at least a better conclusion that could be reached without economics.

A third reason to study economics may be that you expect to be a professional economist: someone employed to teach economics, to create economic theory, or to apply economic theory to questions that your employer wants answered. Obviously I believe that being an economist is an attractive profession; if I did not, I would be doing something else for a living. As a missionary, I hope some of you have come to the same conclusion. Of course, as an individual concerned with his rational self-interest, I hope that I have not persuaded enough of you to become economists to reduce my income significantly—or that if I have, you will have the consideration not to enter the field until after I have retired, or at least signed a long-term contract.

The fourth reason to learn economics is that it is fun. Once you understand the logic of economics, you can make sense out of elements of the world around you that you could not otherwise understand, which is entertaining as well as useful. You can also make the process of extracting a rational pattern from apparent chaos into a game played for its own sake—even in cases where it is likely enough there is no pattern there to be extracted.

It may occur to you that I have omitted a fifth reason to learn economics, one that many textbooks would put first: to make yourself a better citizen and a better informed voter. It is true that understanding economics makes you much more likely to perceive correctly the consequences of actual or proposed government policy. But while that may be a good reason for me to teach you economics, it is not, unless you are quite an extraordinary individual, a good reason for you to learn it. In a society as large as ours, your vote, as I have pointed out several times, has a very small chance of affecting anything. If you are extraordinarily altruistic, the large number of people benefited by an improvement in government policy may balance, for you, the tiny chance that your actions will produce such an improvement. If you expect to be unusually influential—perhaps because your name is Kennedy or Rockefeller—you may conclude that the public benefit of making yourself an informed citizen justifies the cost. If neither is the case, it is unlikely that the effect on you of the public benefits produced by your improved understanding of economics will be worth the private costs.

WHAT ECONOMISTS DO

So far as I can tell, economists employed in business or government have two functions. One is to use economic theory to answer questions their employees want answered—to tell Ford what the demand for autos will be next quarter or to estimate for the Treasury what effect a change in the tax laws will have on tax revenues. The other is to use economic language to construct plausible and professional-sounding arguments in favor of whatever their employers want.

Since I am myself an academic economist, I have a somewhat more detailed picture of what academic economists do. What academic economists do is to teach courses like the one you are taking, write books such as the one you are reading, and write articles and do research designed to use economics to explain, predict, and prescribe.

Of the three activities, research is the one with which you have had the least contact. I commented in an earlier chapter that doing economics involves a continual balance between unrealistic simplification and unworkable complication. I might have added that striking the balance—producing pictures of reality simple enough to be analyzed and understood and accurate enough, in their essential structure, to tell us something useful about the real world—is an art, not a mechanical process that can be learned from this book or any other. One discovers whether the attempt has been successful by seeing whether the theory generates predictions about the real world that are not obvious and are true.

This raises a problem: How can we distinguish between things a theory logically implies and things it "predicts" only because its author knew they were true before constructing the theory? There is a fine line between using knowledge of the real world to construct a correct theory and constructing a theory that is no more than a complicated restatement of things you already know.

One solution to this problem is to predict things you do not know—preferably things you cannot know because they have not happened yet. This is a very convincing way of demonstrating the usefulness of your theory, especially if other people with other theories are making different predictions, and theirs turn out to be wrong and yours right. Unfortunately, this way of testing a theory only works for theories whose implications can be tested over a fairly short period of time and under conditions that currently exist. The first article I ever published in an economics journal was entitled "An Economic Theory of the Size and Shape of Nations." Its predictions were tested against the changing political map of Europe, from the fall of the Roman Empire to the present. If I had restricted myself to testing my theory against future events, the first tentative results might have come in during the lifetime of my great-grandchildren.

One way to stay on the right side of the line dividing prediction from description is to only predict the future. Another way is to adopt what appears to be an unreasonably rigid insistence on following out the logic of complete rationality. Most of us believe that actual behavior is a mixture of rational and irrational elements. It is tempting, in constructing an economic theory, to start with a model based on rationality and then introduce elements of irrationality whenever they are needed to resolve a conflict between the predictions of the model and what is actually observed. The resulting "theory" looks more like a description of the real world than would a theory that assumed rationality everywhere, but it is very much less useful. If you feel free to assume irrationality wherever convenient, you can explain anything—and having done so, there is no easy way for either you or anyone else to know whether your theory works because it is right or because you knew the answers before you started and modified the theory accordingly.

If, instead, one insists on assuming rationality everywhere, even in the behavior of small children deciding whether or not to kick their siblings, one has much less freedom to alter the predictions to fit the facts. Once the basic assumptions have been set up, the model is driven by its own internal logic. It takes you wherever that logic needs, whether or not you want to go there. One advantage of this is that it may take you to conclusions that you know are false, providing evidence that the initial model was wrong. Another advantage is that it may take you to conclusions you thought you knew were false—thus showing you something you did not already know and would never have learned from a "theory" constructed to fit what you thought were the facts.

Seen in this way, the economist's assumption that individuals are rational is in part, as I argued in Chapter 1, a way of deducing the predictable element in human behavior and in part a way of keeping the economic theorist honest.

MODEL, MODEL, AND MODEL

The term "model" is used in economics to describe three quite different things. Explaining the different sorts of models prevents confusion among them: it is also a way of sketching out three quite different things that economists, especially but not exclusively academic economists, do.

One kind of model is a simplified picture designed to make it easier to analyze the logic of a situation while ignoring inessential complications. Models of this sort have been used repeatedly in the previous chapters.

One example is the discussion in Chapter 7 of the effect on landlords and tenants of legal restrictions on rental contracts. I assumed that all landlords were identical, that all tenants were identical, and that the restriction affected cost (to the landlord) and value (to the tenant) in a way similar to the effect of a tax or subsidy. I made these assumptions not because I believed they were true, but because they made the problem simple enough to be analyzed, without changing the essential logic of the situation. Once one has used this sort of model to figure out what is happening in the simple situation and why, one is prepared to analyze more realistic—and difficult—cases. Other examples in this book would be the barbershop problem in Chapter 11, the analysis of the effect of tariffs—in a world where wheat is the only export and autos the only import—in Chapter 19, and the two models of the marriage market in Chapter 21.

A second and different sort of model is used in mathematical economics. A typical example might start by assuming a world of N commodities and M consumers—where the numbers could be 10, 100, or 1 billion. Simplifying assumptions are then made, not about the number of goods or participants but about the mathematical characteristics of elements of the model such as utility functions and production functions. These assumptions are useful not to solve the model—nobody expects to solve that sort of model anyway, in the sense of plugging numbers in and getting numbers out—but to prove theorems about what the solution must be like. I have not done any of that sort of rigorous mathematical economics in this book, but I referred to it in Chapter 8, when I explained how, in principle, one would solve an economy, and again in Chapter 16, when I suggested that my proof of the efficiency of a competitive market could be translated into a more precise form. One of the things mathematical economists prove theorems about is under what circumstances an economy is efficient.

The third sort of model, which I have not used at all in this book, is a large-scale econometric model. Unlike the other two, this sort of model attempts to give a quantitatively accurate picture of a particular economy—say, the United States in January of 1991. It does this by first simplifying the real situation—rather as I simplified it in Chapter 14 when I reduced everything to three factors of production, although not quite that drastically—and then using real-world data and statistics to estimate actual numbers for the quantities and relationships of the model. It is thus a crude picture of a real economy. Its objective is not so much understanding as prediction.

As you probably realize by now, a real economy—say, the U.S. economy in January of 1991—is an enormously complicated interacting system. Econometric models generally take the form of computer programs run on very large and expensive computers. Even with the best computers available, any model simple enough to produce a prediction of what will happen next year and take less than a year to produce it has to ignore most of what is really happening in the economy being modeled. Econometric modeling is then the art of building models simple enough to be useful but with enough resemblance to the real economy being modeled to be of some use for predicting what will happen. Seen from the perspective of an economic theorist, it is an art made up in roughly equal parts of economics, statistics and witchcraft.

Econometric modeling survives and prospers, despite the difficulty of doing it and the unreliability of its predictions, because of the immense value of the information it is trying to generate. If you knew what was going to happen to interest rates for the next year, you could make a very large fortune playing the bond markets. Even if the predictions of such models are not very good, knowing a little bit, having a prediction that may well be wrong but has a slightly better than random chance of being right, is worth enough to pay the cost of many hours of computer time and the salaries of many econometricians and programmers.

IS ECONOMICS A SCIENCE?

One side effect of econometric modeling, unfortunately, is to encourage the idea that economists are people who spend their time trying to predict what the economy will do next and that economics is either a confidence game or a very primitive science, since "economists never agree with one another." It would make about as much sense to say similar things about physics and physicists and to cite as evidence the poor performance of weather forecasters. On questions of economics, economists often, perhaps even usually, agree with each other. They disagree about quantitative predictions of the outcomes of systems much too complicated to be solved in any other than a very approximate sense.

A second cause of the popular belief that economics is a highly unscientific endeavor is that economic theory often concerns issues of considerable real-world importance. An economist who says that we would be better off if tariffs were abolished is making a statement that several large and wealthy organizations—GM and the United Auto Workers, for example—would like to believe is false, or would at least like other people to believe is false. In such a situation, the publicity given to opposing views has very little relation to the percentage of the profession that supports them. If 99 percent of all economists agree that tariffs should be lowered (only a slight exaggeration of the real situation), the supporters of tariffs will surely be able to find at least one articulate member of the remaining 1 percent to represent their views. The public impression will then be that "some economists are for tariffs; some are against them."

The same thing happens in other fields. Physics is generally regarded as the hardest of the hard sciences. But when it comes to issues about which many people feel deeply it rapidly begins to seem as though physicists too "never agree with each other." Consider the controversies over whether nuclear reactors are safe, what the long-term effects are of nuclear war, or whether space-based defenses against a nuclear attack are practical. For all I (or, probably, you) know, there is a right answer to each of these questions, subscribed to by the great bulk of those competent to hold an opinion. But as long as there are at least a few people on the wrong side equipped with the right credentials, and as long as large and influential groups support both sides, the impression received by the general public will be that the profession is more or less evenly divided.

Several years ago, the *American Economic Review* published the results of an opinion poll sent to a large number of economists, some academic, some employed by business or government. The questions—and the results—divided fairly clearly into three categories. One consisted of reasonably straightforward issues of price theory: the effect of rent control, of minimum wage laws, of tariffs. On these questions, there was general agreement, often by more than 90 percent of those polled. The second category involved questions, mostly "macroeconomic," in areas where there is considerable professional controversy; as one would expect, opinion on those questions was divided. The third category consisted of questions where the answer depended in large part not on economics but on issues of moral philosophy—what one believes to be a good or just world. An example would be the question "Should the income distribution of the United States be made more equal?" In this category too, there was widespread disagreement. My conclusion from the results of the poll was that economists, like physicists, generally agreed about the solved questions of their science, disagreed about areas where work was still going on, and disagreed on issues where their conclusions depended largely on things other than economics.

PROBLEMS

1. In discussing reasons for learning economics, I asserted that making you a better informed voter was not a good reason for you to learn economics but might be a good reason for me to teach it. Explain. You may have to assume that I take a very optimistic view of how successful this book is going to be.

2. Apply economics in an original way to something that has not been analyzed in this book. Ideally, your analysis should use one or more of the ideas developed in this book to provide some nonobvious explanations of or predictions about real-world phenomena. Some possible subjects are: professional sports, college sports, intramural sports, sex, mental illness, dieting, the relation between students' GPAs and other characteristics, religion, landscaping of different campuses, attractiveness of female students with different majors at different campuses, attractiveness of male students with different majors at different campuses, dorm food, climates and the people who live in

them, pet ownership, the notorious inability of Americans to speak foreign languages, why drivers are more courteous in some cities than in others, relation between amounts of partying engaged in by students and other characteristics of themselves or their campuses, and differences between the attitudes and behavior of residents of small towns and those of inhabitants of big cities.

3. In the course of reading this book, you have been learning two things—a general approach to understanding behavior (economics) and a particular application of that approach (price theory). In many cases, an idea that was worked out as part of price theory can be applied more generally to understand what people do or what you should do. Examples include armies running away (an application of externalities), giving up on a romantic lost cause (sunk costs), and discouraging muggers by carrying a big stick (firms exit an industry when profit is negative).

    a. Briefly give two more examples from the book.

    b. Briefly give three examples of your own, not in the book.

    c. Take one of the three and work it out in some detail, showing how the economic ideas can be used to see things that would otherwise not be obvious.

4. Give a consistent and plausible-sounding economic explanation of something that you are sure cannot be explained economically.

5. Reread your answer to Problem 4. Are you still sure your explanation is wrong? Discuss.

FOR FURTHER READING

My first economics article, referred to in this chapter, is David Friedman, "An Economic Theory of the Size and Shape of Nations," *Journal of Political Economy,* Vol. 85, No. 1 (February, 1977), pp. 59–77. The poll of economists is reported in J. R. Kearl, et al., "A Confusion of Economists?" *American Economic Review: Papers and Proceedings,* Vol. 69, No. 2 (May, 1979), pp. 28–37.

Students who would like to learn economics from its inventors should read Adam Smith, *An Inquiry into the Nature and Causes of the Wealth of Nations* (New York: Oxford University Press, 1976); David Ricardo, *The Principles of Political Economy and Taxation* (Totowa, NJ: Biblio Distribution Centre, 1977); and Alfred Marshall, *The Principles of Economics* (8th ed., London: Macmillan, 1920).

The three books are very different. Smith's is the most far-ranging and entertaining. Ricardo's is the most difficult; in it he works out the essential logic of economics—what we would now call general equilibrium theory—without any of the mathematical tools that we would consider essential for doing so. The modern economist reading Ricardo's *Principles* feels rather as a member of one of the Mount Everest expeditions would feel if, arriving at the top of the mountain, he encountered a hiker clad in T-shirt and tennis shoes. Marshall's *Principles* is the book in which modern economics was first put together; it is the only one of the three that could, for a sufficiently ambitious reader, serve as an alternative to a modern textbook.

Students who would like the help of a modern discussion of the classics of economics should read Mark Blaug, *Economic Theory in Retrospect* (New York: Cambridge University Press, 1978). For a series of interesting essays on the economics of past societies, I recommend Carlo Cipolla, *Money, Prices, and Civilization in the Mediterranean World* (Staten Island, NY: Gordian Press, 1967). Two books that I recommend as alternatives or supplements to this one, covering much the same materials in a different and interesting way, are Milton Friedman, *Price Theory* (Hawthorne, NY: Aldine Publishing, 1976) and Armen Alchian and William Allen, *University Economics* (Belmont, CA: Wadsworth Publishing, 1964). A shorter version of the latter also exists as Armen Alchian and William Allen, *Exchange and Production: Competition, Coordination, and Control* (Belmont, CA: Wadsworth Publishing, 1983). A much simpler introduction to economics is *The Economic Way of Thinking* by Paul Heyne (Chicago: Science Research Associates, Inc., 1987).

INDEX

Condorcet, 448
Condorcet Voting Paradox, 448
Constant-cost industry, 229
Constant returns to scale, 240
Constraints, 146
Consumer:
    choice, indifference curves and, 38
    marginal value, marginal utility, consumer surplus and, 82
Consumer surplus, 82, 92–95, 107, 170
Consumption, 24
Consumption possibility frontier, 437
Consumption possibility set, 437
Contract curve, Edgeworth Box and, 148–149
Contracts, conditional, 464
Core, in game theory, 328–329
Corner solution, 11, 49
Cost(s):
    average, 215
    of crime, 565–569
    of elections, 555
    fixed, 213, 360
    of government, rent seeking and, 553–555
    long-run, 367–377
    marginal, 214
    nonpecuniary, 483
    non-sunk, 360
    opportunity, 42–43, 229
    price, value and, 38
    recoverable, 360, 369
    search, 396
    short-run, 367–377
    sunk, 359–367
    total, 368
    transaction, 187, 464, 504–505
    variable, 220, 368
Cost curves, 201, 213–218
    average, 215
    average variable, 369
    fixed, 213
    marginal, 214
    total, 203
Crime:
    cost of, 565–569
    economics of, 558–565
    efficient, 570
    efficient level of, 569–573

Cross-licensing of patents, 315
Cui bono, 378
Curves:
    demand, 57–59, 89, 90
    elastic, 254
    indifference, 38, 44, 45–46, 72–75, 123–126
    inelastic, 254
    reaction, 321–323
    shifting, 160–164
    unit elastic, 254

Declining marginal rate of substitution, principle of, 74
Declining marginal utility, 84–85
Declining marginal value, 87–88
Decreasing returns to scale, 240
Demand:
    changes in, 162
    marginal value and, 88–91
    supply and, 177–182
Demand curve, 57–59, 89
    Hicksian, 57, 90
    income-compensated, 57, 59, 90
    input, 211–212
    invisible, 178–179
    market, 156, 157
    Marshallian, 57
    ordinary, 57, 58
    residual, 319
Depletable resource, 341–347
    pure, 347
Diminishing returns, law of, 208
Discriminating monopoly, 248, 474–476
Discriminating pricing, 255–263
    market segmentation and, 261–263
    perfect, 257
Discriminatory solution, in game theory, 327
Disequilibrium, 427–428
Dispersed interest, 546
Distribution, 500–501
    allocation, effects of intervention in market and, 494–496
    allocation versus, 486
Dominant strategy, 292, 294
Double coincidence of wants, 504
Double coincidence problem, 186
Duopoly, 321